D1640707

FINANCIAL MARKETS IN EUROPE:
TOWARDS A SINGLE REGULATOR?

# Financial Markets in Europe: Towards a Single Regulator?

Editors

## MADS ANDENAS

*and*

## YANNIS AVGERINOS

KLUWER LAW INTERNATIONAL
LONDON / THE HAGUE / NEW YORK

Library of Congress Cataloging-in-Publication Data

Financial market supervision in Europe : towards a single regulator / Mads Andenas and
    Yannis Avgerinos (eds).
        p. cm.
    ISBN 90-411-2159-5 (cloth : alk. paper)
        1. Financial services industry—Law and legislation—European Union countries.
    2. Securities—European Union countries. I. Andenæs, Mads Tønnesson, 1957- II.
    Avgerinos, Yannis V., 1975-

    KJE2188.F557 2003
    341.7′522′094—dc21                                                         2003051699


ISBN 90-411-2159-5

---

Published by
Kluwer Law International,
P.O. Box 85889, 2508 CN The Hague, The Netherlands
sales@kluwerlaw.com
http://www.kluwerlaw.com

Sold and distributed in North, Central and South America by
Aspen Publishers, Inc.
7201 McKinney Circle, Frederick, MD 21704, USA

Sold and distributed in all other countries by
Turpin Distribution Services Limited
Blackhorse Road, Letchworth, Herts.,
SG6 1HN, United Kingdom


*Printed on acid-free paper*

# Contents

**Foreword** . . . . . . . . . . . . . . . . . . . . . . . . . . . . . . . . . . . . . . . . . . . . . . .  ix
*Charles A.E. Goodhart*

**Notes on Contributors**  . . . . . . . . . . . . . . . . . . . . . . . . . . . . . . . . . .  xi

Introduction: **Who is Going to Supervise Europe's**
**Financial Markets**  . . . . . . . . . . . . . . . . . . . . . . . . . . . . . . . . . . . . . . .  xv
*Mads Andenas*

### PART I: REGULATING AND SUPERVISING THE SINGLE
### FINANCIAL MARKET

1. **The Legal Integration of Financial Markets of the Euro Area**  . . . . .  3
   *Antonio Sáinz de Vicuña*

2. **Towards a Single European Capital Market and a Workable**
   **System of Regulation** . . . . . . . . . . . . . . . . . . . . . . . . . . . . . . . . . . .  35
   *Jan H. Dalhuisen*

3. **Fifteen Regulators for a Single Capital Market: The Project of**
   **Regulatory Harmonisation in Europe** . . . . . . . . . . . . . . . . . . . . . . . .  75
   *Stavros B. Thomadakis*

4. **Problems with Home Country Control and Investment Services**  . . .  83
   *Yannis V. Avgerinos*

5. **Private Law Approaches to Enhancing Financial Stability:**
   **The Hague Convention on Indirectly Held Securities and**
   **European Union Collateral Directive**  . . . . . . . . . . . . . . . . . . . . . . . .  121
   *Kern Alexander*

### PART II: CENTRALISATION OF SECURITIES
### MARKET SUPERVISION: TOWARDS A EUROPEAN
### SECURITIES REGULATOR?

6. **The Need and the Rationale for a European Securities Regulator**  . . .  145
   *Yannis V. Avgerinos*

7. After the *Lamfalussy* Report: The First Steps towards
   a European Securities Commission? . . . . . . . . . . . . . . . . . . . . . . . .   183
   *Gilles Thieffry*

8. Regulating European Securities Markets:
   Beyond the *Lamfalussy* Report . . . . . . . . . . . . . . . . . . . . . . . . . . .   211
   *Rosa M. Lastra*

9. Towards a European Securities Commission: A View from
   the Securities Markets Industry . . . . . . . . . . . . . . . . . . . . . . . . . . .   223
   *Gregor Pozniak*

10. The Case for a Single European Securities Regulator . . . . . . . . . . .   235
    *Eric J. Pan*

### PART III: HORIZONTAL CONSOLIDATION OF FINANCIAL SUPERVISION: THE NATIONAL, EU AND INTERNATIONAL PERSPECTIVES

11. International Capital Markets and the Future of Economic Policy:
    A Proposal for the Creation of a World Financial Authority . . . . . .   263
    *John Eatwell and Lance Taylor*

12. International Standards and Standards Implementation . . . . . . . .   283
    *George A. Walker*

13. FSA Revisited, and Some Issues for European Securities
    Markets Regulation . . . . . . . . . . . . . . . . . . . . . . . . . . . . . . . . . . . . .   323
    *Clive Briault*

14. Issues in Accountability of a Single Financial Services Regulator:
    The UK's Financial Services Authority (FSA) . . . . . . . . . . . . . . . . .   339
    *Vasiliki An. Galanopoulou*

15. Financial Market Regulation in Germany: The New Institutional
    Framework . . . . . . . . . . . . . . . . . . . . . . . . . . . . . . . . . . . . . . . . . . .   359
    *Mads Andenas and Jens-Hinrich Binder*

16. Twin Peaks *à la francaise*: Reforming Financial Services
    Regulation in France . . . . . . . . . . . . . . . . . . . . . . . . . . . . . . . . . . . .   381
    *Duncan Fairgrieve*

17. Financial Market Regulation: The Case of Italy and a Proposal
    for the Euro Area . . . . . . . . . . . . . . . . . . . . . . . . . . . . . . . . . . . . . . .   397
    *Giorgio di Giorgio, Carmine di Noia and Laura Piatti*

18. The Swedish Financial Market in a Legal Perspective –
    Some Aspects . . . . . . . . . . . . . . . . . . . . . . . . . . . . . . . . . . . . . . . . . .   421
    *Lars Gorton*

19. **A Path-dependent Route towards a Single Financial Regulator: The Experience of Denmark** ............................. 447
*Jesper Lau Hansen*

20. **Horizontal Consolidation of Financial Supervision: Impact on the Operations of the European Investment Bank** ................. 457
*Roderick Dunnett*

# Foreword

*Charles A.E. Goodhart*

There are three main sources of external funding for borrowers to tap. These are equity markets, bond markets and bank borrowing. Before becoming too depressed about the prospects for an efficient integration of European capital markets, perhaps in part as a result of reading the excellent contents of this book, it would be well to remember that one component of the European capital market, that is, the *Euro-bond* market, has been a dramatic success story in the last few years since the adoption of the Euro. The enhanced efficiency and growth of this market, to the point where it compares well with its US counterpart, has been well documented.

In some part the comparative success of the Euro-bond market has been due to the fact that, as a market dominated by professionals (rather than by retail, small investors), it has been lightly regulated. In turn the comparative failure to move forward to a more unified European equity market, and to lower the transactions costs in the continuing segmented member national equity markets, are due to the regulatory process in the EU itself. This was high-lighted by the Lamfalussy (Wise Men) Reports (initial and final), which formed the back-drop to this book.

There is a splendid American phrase, 'If it ain't broke, don't fix it'. Both the Lamfalussy Report and many of the chapters in this book reveal that the mechanism for operating equity markets in the EU is now 'broke', and in two main respects. First, EU equity markets remain segmented with relatively high (compared to the US) transactions costs. Second, this is, in some large part, due to the fact that the EU regulatory process is slow, and can be (and is) used to protect (inefficient and high cost) national institutions, rather than construct an EU (equity) capital market. As is described in detail in the Lamfalussy Report and in the chapters in this book, the process of agreeing (and transposing) Directives is grindingly slow (often over 5 years); the Directive procedures are inflexible, without any mechanisms for enabling secondary legislation, in a rapidly evolving financial system – where the regulators/supervisors really need to be able to adjust flexibly to such evolution; and sufficient loop-holes remain in the system (via host-country control over conduct of business issues and the 'general good' provision in particular and subsidiarity in general), to allow those who want to do so to slow down any harmonisation towards a centralised European equity market to a snail's pace.

What to do? Lamfalussy's response was to try to reform the governance procedures for financial regulation in the EU. While this was accepted in principle at the Stockholm Council meeting in 2001, it is too early yet to tell how this may work in practice. If it should fail to work satisfactorily (and how might a 'satisfactory' outcome be defined?), Lamfalussy has suggested that the next alternative might be a move towards a European SEC, or possibly more likely a European FSA.

Although I have not done an exact chapter count, my impression is that the majority of contributors to this book would prefer to move directly to the more radical alternative of a European SEC (or FSA). The real question is whether the political will to do so is yet present in a Union comprised of countries with differing legal systems, traditions and structures.

Legal issues are central to this discussion. The editors of this book, (who are also primary contributors), are to be congratulated on having brought together an excellent collection of legal and practitioner experts (and some count as both) to comment on this topic. The chapters provide the best available snapshot of current capital market regulatory conditions both in the main member countries and in the European Union as a whole, and a wide range of arguments about future prospective developments. While most of the contributors are lawyers, it will also be of great interest to practitioners, regulators and all those concerned with the current and future development of European financial markets.

Again, the book is primarily about regulation in European securities (equity) markets. But many, probably most, of the problems that arise in the European context with the regulation of securities will arise with banking regulation also; indeed the advent of the Basel Capital Adequacy proposals (Mark II) makes this imminent. Moreover, the blurring of dividing lines between financial intermediaries operating in capital markets (or insurance) and those operating in commercial banking makes it doubtful whether one can, or should, aim to divorce institutional reform in securities markets from similar reforms in banking. This too is a theme in several of the chapters in this book. Whether supervision should be undertaken in a single body (both at the European or member state level), or in separate bodies, and if a single FSA is adopted, what should be the relation of the Central Bank (ECB or NCB) to it, is a secondary theme in this far-ranging book.

Both themes are 'hot' topics in Europe, and are likely to remain so over the foreseeable future. This book throws much light on them. You will enjoy it.

# Notes on Contributors

## EDITORS

**Mads Andenas**, MA (Oxon), PhD (Cantab) is Director of the British Institute of International & Comparative Law, Supernumerary Fellow at Harris Manchester College, University of Oxford and Senior Fellow at the Institute of European and Comparative Law, University of Oxford.

**Yannis V. Avgerinos**, LLM (Warwick), PhD cand. (London) is a Research Fellow at the British Institute of Internatio,.al & Comparative Law, and Emile Noël Fellow at the European Union Center, Harvard University.

## CONTRIBUTORS

**Kern Alexander**, MPhil (Oxon), MPhil (Cantab), PhD (London) is the Newton Trust Senior Research Fellow in International Financial Law at the University of Cambridge, Attorney-at Law at the States of Florida, Minnesota and the District of Columbia and Solicitor of the Supreme Court of England and Wales.

**Clive Briault**, MPhil (Oxon) is Director of the Prudential Standards Division of the Financial Services Authority (FSA), former Director of Central Policy at the FSA, former Head of Capital and Wholesale Markets Division of the Bank of England and former Head of the Monetary Assessment and Strategy of the Bank of England.

**Jens-Hinrich Binder** is a PhD candidate at the Albert-Ludwigs-University of Freiburg; and holds an LLM at the London School of Economics.

**Jan H. Dalhuisen**, LLM, Dr. Juris, is Professor of Law at King's College, London, Visiting Professor at UC Berkley, Corresponding Member of the Netherlands Academy of Arts & Sciences, Freehills Visiting Fellow UNSW Sydney 2001, FCIArb., Member of the New York Bar, Member of the SFA Consumer Arbitration Panel, former Secretary General of IPMA and Executive Director of IBJ International Plc.

**Giorgio di Giorgio** is Associate Professor of Monetary Economics at LUISS University, in Rome. He holds a PhD from Columbia University and has previously taught at the University of Rome La Sapienza. He was a visiting professor at the Universitat Pompeu Fabra in Barcelona and at Columbia University. He has also served as a member of the Technical Secretary of the Economic Policy Evaluation Unit at the Italian Ministry of the Treasury.

**Carmine di Noia** is Senior Economist at Assonime (the Association of Italian Companies). He was previously an economist in the Research Department and then Head of the Market Information Office at Consob. He received a PhD in Economics at the University of Pennsylvania and a doctorate in Economic Theory and Institutions at the University of Rome.

**Roderick Dunnett** is Assistant General Counsel at the Legal Affairs Directorate of the European Investment Bank (EIB).

**John Eatwell** is the President of Queens' College, University of Cambridge.

**Duncan Fairgrieve** is Laming Junior Fellow, The Queen's College Oxford and Maitre de Conférences invité, L'Université de Paris II Panthéon-Assas.

**Vasiliki An. Galanopoulou**, LLM (Edinburgh), PhD cand. (London) is a lawyer, Member of the Athens Bar.

**Charles A.E. Goodhart** is Deputy Director of the Financial Markets Group and Norman Sosnow Professor of Banking and Finance at the London School of Economics.

**Lars Gorton**, LLM (Lund) is Professor of Banking Law at the University of Lund and Professor Adjunct of International Business Law at the Stockholm School of Economics.

**Jesper Lau Hansen**, LLM (Cantab), Dr.Jur. (Cantab) is Professor at the Department of Legal Science A of the University of Copenhagen Law Faculty.

**Rosa Maria Lastra**, MA, LLM (Harvard), PhD (Madrid) is Senior Lecturer in International Financial and Monetary Law at the Centre for Commercial Law Studies, Queen Mary & Westfield College, University of London.

**Eric J. Pan**, J.D. (Harvard), MSc (Edinburgh) is a lawyer at Covington & Burling, Washington DC, and former Lecturer in Law at the University of Warwick.

**Laura Piatti** is Senior Executive at Reale Mutua Insurance Corp., and Head of the Research and Financial Studies Unit. She also teaches Financial Market Regulation at the Politechnics in Turin. In the past, after spending a period as a visiting scholar at Harvard University, she served as an economist at Consob, the Italian Securities and Exchange Commission and at the Competition Authority.

**Gregor Pozniak**, MSc (Vienna), PhD (Vienna) is Deputy Secretary General of the Federation of European Securities Markets, former Head of Listings and Membership at Vienna Stock Exchange and former Deputy Head of Investment Research at Creditanstalt Vienna.

**Antonio Sàinz de Vicuña** is the General Counsel of the European Central Bank (ECB). He has held numerous high level legal positions in the Spanish Government and the European Community and he has been an Adjunct Professor at several Spanish Universities.

**Lance Taylor** is Director of the Center for Economic Policy Analysis at the New School for Social Research, New York.

**Gilles Thieffry** is Partner and Head of Capital Markets at Andersen Legal, Solicitor of the Supreme Court of England and Wales, Member of the New York Bar and the Paris Bar.

**Stavros B. Thomadakis**, BA (Yale), MSc (MIT), PhD (MIT) is Chairman of the Capital Market Commission of Greece. He has been Professor for many years at different U.S. Universities and at the University of Athens, former member of the Monetary Committee of the European Community and of the BOD of the European Investment Bank and the Commercial Bank of Greece, member of the Greek Council of Economic Advisers, Economic Counsellor of the Hellenic Banks Association and Chairman of the Greek Centre of Planning and Economic Research.

**George A. Walker**, DipLP (Glasgow), DAES (Bruges), LLM (London), PhD (London) is a Fellow and Lecturer in Banking and Finance Law with the International Financial Law Unit at the Centre for Commercial Law Studies, Queen Mary & Westfield, University of London. He is a Legal Consultant with Farrer & Co, and the International Monetary Fund.

# Who is Going to Supervise Europe's Financial Markets

*Mads Andenas*

## 1 SEPARATING MONEY AND SUPERVISION

Monetary policy and supervision of financial institutions or markets were until recently an unchallenged competence of the nation state; some would regard it as being at the very core of the modern state. All the European Community could offer was a low level of coordination of economic and monetary policy and a severely restricted free movement of financial services with a limited harmonisation of supervisory rules. European Economic and Monetary Union has introduced a geographical separation between money and supervision of financial institutions and markets. In the euro area, with a single currency, it is still the many different national authorities that are regulating or supervising banks and other financial institutions. The European Central Bank defines and implements the single monetary policy as one of its basic tasks. But within a harmonised legislative framework in the directives, national authorities (in some countries there are more than one) remain responsible for banking supervision. The European Central Bank's complementary supervision role in relation to banks and payment systems adds to the complication.[1]

One of the major obstacles to the development of an Internal Financial Market was the economic policies pursued by Member States. The old quantitative regime regulated the supply of credit. It did this through the fixing of interest rates, loan terms and quotas for credit, both on the total lending by different financial institutions and on what sectors of the economy they could lend to. It restricted the access to the bond market. There were numerous other regulatory techniques applied. This kind of credit policy as well as monetary policy was a matter for Member States. And it could not be effective unless capital flows between Member States were kept to a minimum. Responsibility for policies concerning money and banking supervision had to be united in the Member States. This has changed, partly as a consequence of the new economic and monetary policies that have taken over. In the following section, I will look further into this background.

There are a number of issues that need to be resolved when money and supervision is separated. There is first the question of the lender of last resort (LOLR) and the wider handling of banking crises. The central bank acts as the banks' LOLR, providing liquidity when the market does not do so. This will often extend to a more extensive responsibility for the handling of banking crises, and crises of other financial institutions or markets.

This leads to the issues of regulation and supervision of institutions and markets generally. Are there problems in separating the handling of crises and the preventative

---

[1] See the discussion in M Andenas and C Hadjiemmanuil, 'Banking Supervision, The Internal Market and European Monetary Union' in M Andenas (ed.) *European Economic and Monetary Union: the institutional framework* (Kluwer Law International, London, Doordrecht 1997) 373.

*Mads Andenas and Yannis Avgerinos (eds), Financial Markets in Europe: Towards a Single Regulator?* xv–xxvi.
© 2003 *Kluwer Law International. Printed in Great Britain.*

regulation and supervision? Does separation result in any distortions or perverse incentives on the side of regulators or the regulated?

There are also the questions of efficiency and of transparency and democratic control. It is not clear that the present uncertain and complex situation scores highly on either of these boards.

What is then the optimal institutional outcome? What should remain at a national level, and how would the tasks at a European level best be organised? One major problem here is that financial market regulation has rarely come about as a consequence of rational deliberation. Historically, regulatory reform has taken the form of panic stricken short-term responses to the crisis that has just passed.

One also has the situation that authorities in this field are generally not too concerned with acquiring any formal responsibility. Although increasingly formalised through detailed rulemaking, the regulatory competences remain broad and widely discretionary. Sanctions and enforcement remain uncertain. Certain central bank or regulatory functions, such as the LOLR, are traditionally left open ended in order not to affect market behaviour. It is assumed that clear rules could lead to distortions and perverse incentives. A situation where responsibility is not clearly allocated can have its further advantages for a regulator. Financial market crises will continue to occur and not having the formal responsibility (the European Central Bank) or not having the tools (national regulators) for handling them, may disperse the institutional repercussions of flawed supervision.


## 2    KEEPING MONEY AND SUPERVISION TOGETHER – THE OLD MODEL UNDER THE QUANTITATIVE REGIME

The relationship between financial market regulation and economic policy is a complex one. Major changes in the established policies and the abolition of capital controls have been necessary for the development of the Internal Financial Market. The Euro will bring it further and will also entail further challenges.

Let us go back to the Commission's 1985 White Paper *Completing the Internal Market*.[2] The White Paper set out the legislative programme for the creation of a single market by the end of 1992. Free movement of capital and financial services stood out as an area where little had been achieved and as to which the Commission proposed many ambitious measures. One reason for the slow progress of the internal market in financial services was that it depended on capital liberalisation, that is, on the abolition of restrictions and administrative controls on cross-border financial transactions. Capital liberalisation would, in fact, inevitably have two consequences. First, deregulation of financial markets, and, second, the abolition or easing of rules with respect to the participation in domestic financial markets of foreign institutions.

Capital restrictions were a necessary precondition for the effectiveness of the direct instruments of monetary and credit control. Credit control imposed limitations

---

[2] COM (85) 310 final.

on the growth of clearing banks' assets (in some cases also their liabilities). It usually extended to other financial institutions' assets and to markets such as those in corporate bonds. With the help of such instruments, monetary objectives could be achieved at a lower interest rate than would otherwise be possible.

Capital restrictions made it possible to pursue relatively autonomous monetary and credit policies. Such policies depended on the possibility of maintaining an interest rate different from that of neighbouring countries. Capital restrictions were instruments to limit capital inflows and outflows. Their importance would depend on the trends in other financial markets. Restrictions on capital outflows – so that savers and investors could not go abroad – allowed, in the short term, the preservation of low interest rates. It impeded downward pressures on the currency's exchange rate. In the long term, they protected domestic savings and domestic capital markets. Particularly strict restrictions on pension funds and life-assurance companies, affecting their ability to diversify their investments by investing abroad, could have both such short- and long-term effects.

Restrictions on capital inflows – for instance, so that lenders could not go to banks or securities markets abroad to raise capital – preserved, in the short term, price stability and avoided upward pressure on the exchange rate. In the long term, restrictions on foreign investors contributed to the protection of the domestic control of key industries, which in several countries was considered to be an important matter of national sovereignty. The national interest in domestic control of business enterprises was thought to be particularly strong in the area of financial institutions, such as banks, pension funds and insurance companies. Strong partnerships would be established between the authorities in charge of banking supervision and the quantitative restrictions, providing an effective shield against foreign establishment or direct competition. Similar intensity partnerships were established in the other financial industry sectors.

Capital controls have been applied by all countries, in different ways and to different degrees. There is a tidal quality to capital controls, which rise and subside with some regularity. In the late eighties and early nineties they had subsided to a lower ebb than ever before in modern history. Economic policy in the 1980s became increasingly based on a doctrine of greater market orientation. Indirect instruments, seeking to influence credit expansion through price mechanisms, gradually replaced the direct instruments of monetary control. This is what is usually described as liberalisation in domestic economic policy and in domestic financial markets.

The final conversion to liberalisation came after the experiences of the late 1970s and early 1980s. Skeptics had to accept that the existing controls were characterised by a low degree of effectiveness and high costs. There were costs of an administrative nature. More importantly there was a macroeconomic cost in that distortions in asset prices and interest rates could lead to a sub optimal allocation of capital resources. Financial markets became less effective. There were also problems following from shielding financial markets from foreign competition. Temporary advantages could be outweighed by the cost of postponing the economic policy and private sector adaptation to changes in international economic circumstances.

The direct instruments of monetary and credit control had created a close relationship between the major players. They were the financial institutions, in particular large clearing banks, and the monetary authorities, ministries of finance and central banks. Banking supervision became subordinated to this relationship, and played a limited role. Prudential rules – for instance, liquidity requirements – were turned into instruments of monetary policy, with a view to influencing interest rates. Competition polices were not developed, or at least not enforced with any rigour. In many countries the banking supervisory authorities managed to keep their sector out of the remit of the general competition authorities. All the parties to those close relationships had a strong interest in retaining them.

Eventually, the gradual deregulation in domestic credit and monetary policy, with the abolition of direct controls, spurred a strengthening of prudential requirements and supervision and of competition policies.

Some degree of internationalisation of financial markets and institutions took place under the capital controls in spite of the restrictions of national monetary and credit policies. This clearly undermined the effectiveness of these quantitative policies. There was no immediate link between, on the one hand, domestic deregulation and, on the other hand, the opening-up of domestic markets for financial institutions from other Member States or the development of an internal financial market in other ways. The financial services industry continued to enjoy a close relationship to the authorities. In some countries, the state would even directly own the major clearing banks. For most Member States, retaining domestic control over the financial services industry was considered to be of vital importance; financial institutions and markets should remain in the hands of their own nationals. The prospect of clearing banks, pension-fund managers or life-assurance companies being bought up by nationals of other countries appeared distant. Any other direct access to markets for foreign institutions was seriously curtailed.

Gradually, however, deregulation in domestic monetary and credit policy did lead to the implementation of free movement of capital from 1990, on the basis of the Capital Liberalisation Directive,[3] which was adopted in 1988. This was the first time that all Member States agreed that the escape clause in Art. 67 of the Treaty (abolishing capital-movement restrictions 'necessary to ensure the proper functioning of the common market') implied a full liberalisation.

With the lifting of capital controls, an internal financial market was now possible – and even necessary for ensuring that financial business would not drift to the Member State that would offer the least intensive regulatory environment and the best financial and tax incentives. The economic policies of Member States did not any longer depend on domestic markets. Most of the other obstacles just mentioned were still in place. The attempt to resolve them, guaranteeing unrestricted market access, was made in a series of financial market directives, the most important of which has been the Second Banking Directive of 1989.[4] Abolishing capital controls was an easy step in terms of execution, when the economic polices allowed it. It was

---

[3] Council Directive 88/361/EEC of 24.6.88 for the implementation of Art. 67 of the Treaty.

[4] Second Council Directive 89/646/EEC of 15.12.89 on the co-ordination of laws, regulations and administrative provisions relating to the taking up and pursuit of the business of credit institutions and amending Directive 77/780/EEC.

mainly a question of abolishing some rather simple regulation. Making free movement work was much more complicated.

Before the 1992 deadline of the Commission's 1985 White Paper, the major directives in this area of financial services and financial institutions were either adopted or going through the late stages of the legislative process, with a common position having been reached, guaranteeing their adoption.[5] The 1992 deadline was extremely tight in an area where so little had been achieved, placing considerable pressure on both the Member States and on the Commission. This was bound to have some impact of the form of the solutions that were found, and certain issues could not be explicitly resolved in the directives.

Making free movement work required more than abolishing capital controls and the supervision of financial institutions and the regulation of financial services. A large number of further issues have had to be addressed. The cost of cross-border payments have become a concern. The euro contributes to making the right to free movement of capital more effective; it could even be seen as the ultimate harmonisation measure! The introduction of the euro harmonises the currency or capital itself and takes care of mutual recognition in a way one could not in practical terms have done if the different national currencies were to be maintained.

### 3 CAPITAL, SERVICES AND ESTABLISHMENT IN THE EC TREATY

The original provisions of the free movement of capital in the Treaty of Rome (Arts 67–73) were more conditional than those concerning the other Treaty freedoms, such as those on the right to provide services and the right of establishment which have provided the basis for review of national financial market regulation. The obligation to progressively abolish restrictions on capital applied only to the extent necessary to ensure the proper functioning of the common market.

One consequence of this was that the European Court held that the Treaty freedom was not directly effective. With the revisions of the Maastricht Treaty the free movement of capital was formulated in a broader and less conditional way than any other Treaty freedom. But even before those amendments entered into force, the European Court held in *Sanz de Lera* [1995] ECR I-4821 that the Treaty freedom was directly

---

[5] In addition to the Second Banking Directive, one must refer here to the following instruments: First Council Directive 77/780/EEC of 12.12.77 on the co-ordination of laws, regulations and administrative provisions relating to the taking up and pursuit of the business of credit institutions (the 'First Banking Directive'); Council Directive 89/299/EEC of 17.4.89 on the own funds of credit institutions (the 'Own Funds Directive'); Council Directive 89/647/EEC of 18.12.89 on a solvency ratio for credit institutions (the 'Solvency Ratio Directive'); Council Directive 92/30/EEC of 6.4.92 on the supervision of credit institutions on a consolidated basis (the 'Second Consolidated Supervision Directive'); Council Directive 92/121/EEC of 21.12.92 on the monitoring and control of large exposures of credit institutions (the 'Large Exposures Directive'); Council Directive 93/6/EEC of 15.3.93 on the capital adequacy of investment firms and credit institutions (the 'Capital Adequacy Directive'); and Directive 94/19/EC of the European Parliament and of the Council of 30.5.94 on deposit-guarantee schemes (the 'Deposit-Guarantee Directive').

effective. The Court argued that the Treaty provisions had to be read in the context of secondary Community legislation giving effect to the freedom, in particular the Directive abolishing the Member States' right to restrict capital movements.

The free movement of capital has been further strengthened by the unconditional and wide formulation in the Treaty. One issue which has been discussed in the legal literature is that of horizontal direct effect. In *Sanz de Lera* the action was against the state and the Court only had to address vertical direct effect. Horizontal direct effect, where a private party invokes the Treaty freedom against another private party, has not yet been addressed by the Court. Treaty provisions are normally capable of both horizontal and vertical direct effect. *Sanz de Lera* does not in any way indicate the contrary in relation to Art. 56. Art. 56 itself does not depend on implementing measures and is widely formulated. Argument to the contrary may be derived from Art. 28 (ex Art. 30) on the free movement of goods which is limited to actions against the State, and there are certain parallels between the provisions.

The Treaty freedoms do provide a powerful tool for review of national regulation. Most of the field is now also based on EC directives, and harmonisation should reduce the restrictive nature of traditional financial market regulation.

But there remain several issues in relation to the institutional solutions, in particular concerning the level of regulation at European Union and national level, and beyond harmonisation which is based on national legislation and actual supervision. The most pressing is to what extent a European supervisor has to be established, and what should be the relationship with the supervisory functions that remain at the Member State level.

## 4  'REGULATION' AND 'FINANCIAL MARKETS' – WHAT DO WE MEAN?

Much of the discussion about financial markets and institutions would focus on one kind of institution or market. Traditionally regulation and supervision has developed in very different ways. Banking supervision has focused on banks and their solidity or their supporting role in the traditional credit policies described above. Life insurance and pension fund regulation has had its focus on securing the interests of the insured, and the contractual terms have been regulated often in great detail. Securities markets have been regulated with investor protection as the focus, and fraud legislation an integral part of the regulatory model. The regulators have been based in different ministries and they have championed 'their' industry against the others. Not only the content or character regulation but also the intensity of regulation have varied between these three main sectors.

Similar products are now offered by institutions that are primarily based in any of these three main sectors. Cross ownership requires new consolidated supervision. And there is an increasing interdependency between financial markets going beyond what can be explained by these features of the development. If sectoral supervision is to be maintained it must be heavily coordinated. In many countries new models of a universal regulator have been developed. In the Scandinavian countries this took place in the 1980s, in the United Kingdom in the late 1990s.

Banking supervision is increasingly influential as the emerging paradigm of financial market regulation. The basic regulation relates to capital adequacy and in matching the financial exposures. Risk is priced correctly and the systemic risks of a meltdown of a financial sector or the whole financial market is reduced.

## 5   FINANCIAL MARKET REGULATION REMAIN NATIONAL LAW

Basically, banking supervision was created to provide solutions for domestic markets. That remains as a limitation even in its modern form. If anything this applies with even greater force to other sectors of financial market regulation. To some extent regulation and the actual supervisory functions undertaken have developed to restrict capital flows from other countries or protect against competition from foreign institutions or markets. Globalisation creates a new role for financial market regulation which has had to become increasingly European and international.

The process of internationalisation of domestic financial market regulation has created problems both for national authorities and for institutions and markets that have an international dimension in their activities.

Other important surrounding areas of law with important impact in this field, such as contract law and company law, remain even more traditionally national. This leads to problems that are becoming increasingly more pressing. Banks and other financial institutions are authorised in one jurisdiction and it remains very difficult to move that authorisation to another Member State. In practice one can establish a branch in the other country which will remain supervised primarily by the authorities of the first country of authorisation. Establishment through a subsidiary is not covered by the authorisation by the home country supervisor. Moving to another jurisdiction is also still impossible as a matter of company law. One cannot move a company from one jurisdiction to another: it remains a foreign company in the new jurisdiction. There are of course techniques that alleviate this. Establishing a subsidiary in the new jurisdiction, and then transferring assets and activities. But a full recognition of a foreign company, so that it can reincorporate or register in the new jurisdiction (acquire a new nationality or citizenship so to speak) is still not possible in the national company laws of Europe. The *Centros* decision[6] of the European Court of Justice has limited, as a matter of EU company law, the possibility to withhold the recognition of foreign companies or their branches. For the purposes of financial market regulation, financial institutions had already achieved this. Authorities cannot discriminate on the grounds that the authorisation has been granted in another Member State. But the company law restrictions remained as for all other companies. The European Commission has drafted a proposal for a new directive on the ultimate free movement issue: how can a company register (or re-register) in a new jurisdiction. But this proposal still has a long way to go.

---

[6] Case C-212/97 *Centros Ltd v Erhvervs- og Selskabsstyrelsen* [1999] ECR I-1459.

## 6   The Internal Market Issues

The separation of money and financial market supervision provides an opportunity to revisit the obstacles to the development of the Internal Financial Market. The old model under the quantitative regime did more than keeping money and supervision together. It created regulatory systems which had, as one of their primary aims, to limit capital flows. The present level of harmonisation through the directives in the sector has not done away with this.

Even a very high degree of harmonisation will still lead to the double burden of having to follow more than one set of national rules. The proposed mechanism to limit double regulation in the directives – home country control – is not sufficiently effective. Its extent is not clear enough, there are too many and too wide exceptions, and the reporting even when it applies has proven too burdensome.

The recent proposals from the European Commission are still based on the home country control principle.[7] The otherwise very timely proposals deal with the programme of developing and modernising the harmonised regulatory rules. The new model for the adoption of these rules comes from the proposals from the Lamfalussy Committee. The Lamfalussy proposals included the adoption of a new legislative procedure and the use of regulations instead of directives. This has a huge potential when it comes to making the regulatory procedures more rapid and the adopted rules more effective.

It does however not resolve the basic problem of double burden that remains if there are all these different national regulators that remain in charge of the actual supervision. The intensity and extent of regulation of financial institutions is such that this burden is higher than in most other sectors.

## 7   The Market Regulatory Issues

The Lamfalussy proposals included as mentioned the adoption of a new legislative procedure and the use of regulations instead of directives. This is now adopted for both investment services and (from 2002) for banking. The regulatory procedures become quicker and the adopted rules more effective. But can national regulators deliver a sufficient level of efficiency? They may not only provide restrictions on the free movement which is necessary to get the internal market to function. It is questionable whether they provide the level of effective regulation that is required for the market to function. The European Commission has continued its adherence to home country control. The remedy is seen to be in an elaborate structure of bodies to promote cooperation and coordination between the national regulators.

There is no doubt that coordination is necessary and that much can be achieved this way. But it is very uncertain if it can achieve the sufficient level of efficiency. Where there are different national interests of some strength, one would expect the

---

[7] Financial Services: Implementing the framework for financial markets: Action Plan. Communication of the Commission. COM (1999) 232, 11.05.99.

agreement to be less lasting. It may not take that much of divergence for cooperation to break down.

## 8  THE SYSTEMIC STABILITY ISSUES

The aim of systemic stability is now at the core of modern financial market regulation. Financial stability cannot be achieved at a national level with the present level of market integration, not even when it is supported by an extensive body of harmonised EU legalisation in directives and regulations. Here, there will often be strongly diverging national views, and the different fora for cooperation and coordination cannot mediate effectively between these interests.

## 9  HANDLING OF CRISES

The handling of financial crises is one area where the lack of a European institutional solution seems particularly critical. The lender of last resort (LOLR) function depends on arrangements at member state level.

The existing LOLR arrangements are not adequate to deal with liquidity issues in the context of a European banking system. This is the case for both systemic and individual liquidity crises. In case of a systemic problem, the ECB lacks the supervisory information needed to judge on the systemic effect of liquidity problems and decide quickly on the collateral issues. In case of liquidity problems at individual financial institutions, the national central banks along with the national supervisory authorities will act and take on the LOLR costs only when the liquidity crisis poses systemic risks for their own banking system. Even if they are concerned with the implications for the European market, they might lack both the necessary resources and the ability to assess the severity of the liquidity problems. Neither is it clear whether authorization by the ECB is also required.[8] Finally, cooperation on the basis of Memoranda of Understanding (MOU) does not secure the necessary real-time information sharing and action, and the availability of resources is questionable.

A centralized LOLR competence at the ECB level will deal more effectively with most of the inadequacies of the current decentralized framework. The ECB will be able to intervene effectively and timely when the emerging pan-European financial institutions face liquidity problems. It will avoid coordination problems – present in a decentralized system involving discussions between the interested central banks and consultations at the ECB level – and it will be able to decide quickly. It will have the capital resources required and will ensure a proper allocation of the LOLR costs across the Community. It will also reduce the anti-competitive effect of national central bank policies and decisions on eligible collateral, and of interventions in support of insolvent institutions.[9] Still, the precondition for a successful LOLR role by

---

[8] The ECB may prohibit or restrict LOLR functions by the national central banks. ESCB Statute Art. 14(4).

[9] It should be mentioned that the ECB can already affect these policies as under 14(4) it may restrict national policies that interfere with the ECB's objectives and tasks.

the ECB will be the establishment of information-sharing arrangements. Such information-sharing arrangements are needed to provide the real-time information necessary for an accurate assessment of the systemic effect of liquidity problems, a decision on the adequate collateral, and a real-time intervention.

Two major arguments can be added in favour of the ECB's handling the LOLR situations. First is that national authorities may act counter to the requirements of monetary policy. It may be to prefer that the balancing of financial stability and monetary policy is undertaken by one institution. This runs counter to some of the arguments brought up by others on this point that seems to build on an ordo liberal division of functions to secure the uncorrupted exercise of monetary policy powers.

Second is that national authorities would easily act against the rules on state aid. ECB could not be restricted under these rules. Time pressures and other factors in this kind of financial crisis will make it less realistic that a solution may be achieved at the national level.

## 10   REGULATORS SHOULD FOLLOW MARKETS

At this stage it may be useful to sum up some points relating to regulatory jurisdiction. Regulators should follow markets. This seems as an obvious starting point when one deals with regulation aiming at increasing market efficiency or counteracting market failure. Regulators do not follow markets. They follow national jurisdictions and state organisation that less and less often coincide with markets. New economic policies and market conditions should have removed obstacles so that regulators now could follow markets. The way they presently divide them up apply also within domestic markets and not only in relation to foreign markets and institutions.

National jurisdictions divide markets up. National regulation tends to obstruct market integration. It also makes regulation less effective. Any form of cooperation between regulators will provide less than optimal efficiency, both in terms of costs to business (in the European Union, one still has to submit to 12 different regulatory regimes) and in achieving the primary goals of financial market regulation (increased financial stability, effective competition, market surveillance and sanctions against transgressors).

In the financial markets regulators have traditionally divided markets up, making borders between countries effective barriers, such as protecting their 'own' financial institutions against competition and also making economic policies effective. Today the European Union and also broader forms of international cooperation, WTO/GATS, limit the power of regulators to achieve this. Most will be critical to this at a wholesale level: there are good reasons also to challenge it in relation to consumer or investor protection.

A discussion of national regulation as a barrier leads to the following question. How can so many obstacles remain which are that much against the interests of the financial services industry that wishes to establish itself or sell its products in other Member States. Partly the answer must be that there are other interests that are served by most of the regulatory regimes. There are client relationships where the regulators protect 'their industry' against foreign competition. The other is the inertia that is displayed by many of the main players. It is not so that the interests are carefully balanced and the best solutions automatically chosen. The story of the Merger Regulation and the 'one stop shop' is indicative. Only when the EU regulation was a fact that could not be avoided did business involve itself, in spite of the obvious benefits of EU level regulation. Business did not move to make merger control an EU competence. Only when this had come about did business take steps to avoid having authorities at both the European Union and the national level dealing with the individual cases at the same time.

## 11   THE INDEPENDENT REGULATOR

Conversely, for the international financial institution, the independence of the regulator can be of importance. There is a problem with the lack of independence in a national context. Regulators are too closely involved with the political process. National business interests form too close relationships with the regulator (regulatory caption).

These problems are still there at EU level but there is less scope for caption than in the more limited national political and business environment. There is a case for saying that financial market regulation and supervision cannot be effectively developed and exercised at a national level: it is too vulnerable to pressure and the formation of too many and too close client relationships. National lobbying at EU level is also a problem, but not as great a problem as at the national level.

## 12   REGULATORY CHANGE

What can lead to regulatory change in Europe? The needs of the Internal Financial Market, spurred on by the introduction of the euro, seem to be a realistic platform. However, reform of financial market regulation has rarely come about as a consequence of rational deliberation. Historically regulatory reform has taken the form of panic stricken short-term responses to the crisis that has just passed. Furthermore, authorities in this field are generally not too concerned with extending their formal responsibility. The consequences at a national and a European level are these: formal competences remain at national level where there is little actual competence to deal with the next systemic crisis.

There is a European trend towards a universal regulator. Are there any lessons to be learnt from the last decade? One may discern an emerging European model: a *domestic* universal financial market regulator in a rather tight European framework responding quickly to international developments. The most recent developments include the establishment of the British Financial Services Authority, and the German reforms. Their consequences for Europe are still not clear.

There is also a global financial policy challenge. The major issue here is that there is no viable political structure to support an international regulator, universal or sectoral. International financial liberalisation results in a major increase in risk in both national and international real economy. An effective policy towards financial markets must be international in character. Recent financial instabilities, such as the

Asian crisis, as well as collapses of financial institutions such as BCCI and Barings call for more efficient regulation and for an effective LOLR. Demand for international financial regulation cannot be coped with by traditional forms of international cooperation between regulators. We need a tighter organisation; an IMF for financial market supervision, not only one that deals with such questions as a sideline to currency issues. The IMF, OECD and World Bank have been concerned with financial systems in the developing countries. There are legitimacy concerns with the present international standard setting. They cannot be remedied by civil society participation through consultation. The need is for a political institutionalisation – but that seems to be unrealistic in the medium term perspective.

## 13  THE FINANCIAL REGULATORY POLICY CHALLENGE IN EUROPE

Here we return to the question of whether home country control does achieve the primary internal market aims? The answer must be that very limited financial integration has been achieved. This limitation does, on the other hand, not exclude the increased interdependence and systemic risk.

The introduction of the euro has changed the situation. Here are two perspectives. It shows the costs and inefficiencies of existing market divisions. It also leads to increased integration which in turn increases systemic risk.

Even in more integrated financial markets, such as that of the European Union, cooperation between national authorities is not enough to handle crises. Although certain steps have been made in the field of capital adequacy, arrangements for regulation and monitoring is inadequate in today's markets.

Consolidation of financial services calls for consolidation of supervision at EU level. It is not easy today to distinguish between market risk and the risk of financial institutions. A single supervisor could better function as coordinator of national regulatory authorities and LOLR.

A single regulator with LOLR responsibilities could also respond better to a financial crisis, which would need immediate and resolute action. Negotiations and compromise between national regulators may not provide the optimal process. A constant challenge of other EU policies, for example, on state aid will remain.

The role of the European Central Bank in this: is it the most realistic prospect that it will gradually be filling the void? Its present role is limited but is increasing.

There is a need for analysis and further sorting out of the issues to provide basis for rational policy discourse. The ECB must be discussed as a model in relation to the sectoral regulators or the European super regulator. In itself the ECB and the European System of central Banks (ESCB) may provide an organisational model for the development of a European super regulator.

*Part I*

Regulating and Supervising the Single Financial Market

*Chapter 1*

# The Legal Integration of Financial Markets of the Euro Area[1]

*Antonio Sáinz de Vicuña*[2]

## A    Introduction

The motto 'one market, one currency', which justified the initial plans leading eventually to the single currency, has been achieved with the introduction of the euro. This paper addresses the legal consequences of the monetary union, and its conclusion may be summarized in the motto 'one market, one currency, one law'. A new light on the old topic of harmonization of laws arises out of the introduction of the single currency: the emergence of new harmonized or even uniform legal environment and contractual practices that will result from an enhanced pan-European economic intercourse arising from the common use of a single currency. The Delors Report stated that 'economic and monetary union implies far more than the single market programme'. The euro is a 'quantum jump' giving a new dimension to the internal market, it brings economic agents closer together and has the effect of increasing and intensifying legal relationships across the euro area. This chapter submits that the legal consequences of monetary unification will be no less than fostering a high degree of legal harmonization and, in some areas, uniform commercial practices.

## B    Monetary Union: Effects in the Internal Market and in the Legal Sphere 'One Market, One Currency, One Law'

Monetary unification in Europe comes at a moment where the world economy is being governed by the following universal trends, currently named as 'New Economy':

(a) spread of modern technologies permitting real-time access to markets and instant economic intercourse between market participants;
(b) globalization of markets, in goods and services;
(c) de-regulation, privatization, liberalization and free competition.

---

[1]  This contribution is based on the General Report presented by the author to the Millenium Congress of the Fédération Internationale de Droit Européen (FIDE) held in Helsinki in the summer of 2000.
[2]  The author is the General Counsel of the European Central Bank (ECB). The opinions expressed in this chapter are purely personal and do not engage the ECB.

*Mads Andenas and Yannis Avgerinos (eds), Financial Markets in Europe: Towards a Single Regulator?* 3–34.
© 2003 *Kluwer Law International. Printed in Great Britain.*

The economic consequences of such trends are a drive towards (i) market integration, meaning a reduction of the impact of protectionist and administrative distortions, (ii) increased international diversification, and (iii) economies of scale, meaning market consolidation ('bigger' dimension of market participants, by way of mergers, acquisitions, groupings or associations) and conglomeration ('wider' scope of activities for market players).

Monetary union in Europe comes after the abolition of exchange restrictions in July 1992 and the completion of the program leading to a single internal market fostered by the Single European Act, and in this context the single currency entails:

> (i) the abolition of exchange risks;
> (ii) an enhanced transparency and comparability in the formation of prices;
> (iii) an increased facility to make cross-border payments, because of elimination of currency exchanges, consequent availability of technical systems for real-time payments, and reduction of intermediary costs;
> (iv) a general environment of macroeconomic convergence and stability within the whole euro area, and synchronized budgetary policies of the participating Member States.

Monetary union operates as a catalyst of the trends summarized above entailing a geometric progression, within the euro area, of market integration and consolidation.

In the financial markets of Europe the trend towards market integration and consolidation is shown by, *inter alia*, the following events.

(a) In the money markets, by the success of the new euro-wide reference interest rates, the Euribor and the Eonia, and the disappearance of the national reference rates (FIBOR, PIBOR, MIBOR, etc.); such success means that interbank money market intercourse is done European-wide with no frontiers, by intensive use of the TARGET payment system and other payment systems. However, whilst the above holds true for the un-collateralized money market, the cross-border collateralized or repo market is still limited, one of the reasons being, as will be developed below, the lack of legal harmonization in the securities 'leg' of that market.

(b) In the equity markets, following the huge re-denomination into the euro of the stock of all major euro-area listed corporations, and the switch into euro of market price quotations in all euro-area stock exchanges, market integration and consolidation is shown by the initial 1999 project to integrate eight major European Stock Exchanges, subsequently superseded by alternative projects: the Euronext arrangement (functional merger between the Stock Exchanges of Paris, Brussels, and Amsterdam), the failed iX project (merger between the London Stock Exchange and the Deutsche Börse of Frankfurt), the pooling of the trading on certain kind of equities (the NEWEX arrangement between the Frankfurt and Vienna Stock Exchanges), and the surge of other London-based pan-European exchanges (i.e. Tradepoint, E-Crossnet, Jiway, Virt-x) or transatlantic (i.e. BrokerTec; in the reciprocal direction, NASDAQ has applied to the FSA to expand its trading to Europe). This is not, still, the final picture of the consolidation process in the equity markets: the situation is not static and conversations are taking place between the several players for further possible multi-jurisdictional combinations.

(c) In the public debt market, where the whole public debt of the 11 participating Member States was re-denominated into euro on January 1999, integration is shown by the creation and development of a common trading platform called EuroMTS, a screen-based electronic system based in Milan organized jointly by the primary dealers of the seven major euro-area public debt issuers (Belgium, Spain, Germany, France, Italy, the Netherlands, and Austria); and by the works[3] of the so-called 'Brouhns Group' which tries to establish synchronization mechanisms between sovereign issuers, leading perhaps to the creation of a Single Public Debt Issuing Agency.

(d) In the bond market the International Securities Market Association (ISMA) launched in May 2000 a FSA-recognized exchange called COREDEAL[4] with central electronic price-making replacing the still predominant direct OTC trades, and with a central clearing house (TradeGO, pertaining to Euroclear).

(e) Four initiatives are underway to have central clearing houses for organized markets (single counterpart for market participants instead of them having to find *ad hoc* counterparts, with the combined advantage of anonymity of trades and of netting): The London Clearing House (LCH), launched Repoclear in August 1999 as central counterpart for euro-denominated repos; LCH is since February 2001 providing central counterpart services to the electronic order book of the London Stock Exchange, and that service is being extended to the Irish Stock Exchange and to Virt-x (the functional merger of the Swiss Stock Exchange and UK's Tradepoint); Clearnet (Paris-based central counterpart) is the French–Belgo–Dutch central counterpart for Euronext, and also for other exchanges (i.e. BrokerTec, LCH); the German–Luxembourg merged security settlement system named Clearstream (see below) is launching the European Clearing House based on the German Eurex. Another initiative underway is the creation of a pan-European exchange for mortgage bonds based on the 'Pfandbriefe' legal structure, under the name of EuroCreditMTS. Central clearing houses in a multi-jurisdictional scenario entails the use of a single set of standard contracts and terms and conditions throughout the several jurisdictions involved.

(f) Some European cross-border consolidation also took place in the derivatives markets: Eurex is the result of a functional merger between the Zurich and the Frankfurt options and future exchanges (keeping, though, the two legal structures in place).

(e) The security settlement systems (SSS), numbering more than 30 in Europe when the euro was introduced, are also under a process of cross-border integration and consolidation. On the one hand, the European Central Depositories Association (ECSDA) has organized a network of bilateral links between pairs of SSS that permit the transfer of securities' electronic registers from one SSS to the other by way of sub-accounts. A total of 65 of these links have been examined by the ECB and admitted for the taking of collateral on a cross-border basis by the Eurosystem.

---

[3] Available in the website of the European Commission: <http//:www.europa.eu.int/comm/economy_finance/efc/index_en.htm>.

[4] Available in the website of ISMA: <http//:www.isma.org>.

On the other hand, the SSSs of Germany (Deutsche Börse Clearing) and of Luxembourg (Cedel) merged on January 2000 and created Clearstream as a functionally-single SSS (legally, the two pre-existing structures remain); and the SSSs of Belgium (Euroclear) and of France (Sicovam) merged on January 2001 (also here the merger was functional and not legal, since the two pre-existing structures remain). Both Clearstream and Euroclear are parties to the network of SSS links organized by ECSDA. Thus, dematerialised securities may move from one SSS to another in real-time.

(f) Finally, in the credit market since the start of monetary union an on-going process of consolidation of the banking sector is taking place, still basically within the domestic markets and with relatively few cross-border mergers and acquisitions[5]; however, one can see the prospect for pan-European banks within the immediate future.

The above provides evidence of the fact that national boundaries are becoming more and more irrelevant for the financial markets. Intensified trends of integration and consolidation of financial markets in Europe means that subsistence of differing underlying laws is rather more a nuisance than a benefit; that more and more market participants will avoid abiding by old-fashioned national codes, which may only become relevant in cases of litigation or bankruptcy. And at the end of this process one can see a higher degree of legal harmonization and of unification of market rules and practices. The aim between 1957 and 1990 was the motto: 'one market'. The aim of the 1990s was 'one market, one currency'. The aim of this early XXIst century is: 'one market, one currency, one law'.

What has been described above for the financial markets applies also to other markets. For any entrepreneur, avoidance of exchange risks, macroeconomic convergence, and technological developments entail that the purchase of supplies may be widened to the whole currency area. He will compare offers and decide without the uncertainties that the pre-EMU situation entailed. He will be able to outsource – with no currency risks – outside its normal national market those parts of his productive activity in need of external provision. He will advertise and sell his products throughout the euro area. The whole net of legal relationships of that entrepreneur will start to become more multinational: its supplies, its outsourced services, its marketing and sales, will be a combination of contractual relationships with other agents located in the several jurisdictions of the euro area. It is sub-optimal that such a range of private relationships needs to be different because the laws governing them are different. Sooner rather than later, as economic agents intensify their cross-border relationships, it will be found out that there is general advantage in playing under the same rules.

---

[5] The Dutch ING acquired the German BHF Bank; the Belgian banking group Fortis took control of the French Société Génerale; Dexia group integrated Crédit Communal de Belgique and Crédit Local de France; the Finnish Merita Bank, the Swedish Nordbanken and the Danish Unibank merged into the Nordic Holding group; the German HypoVereinsbank acquired BankAustria and the Spanish Banco Inversión; the Luxembourg's Kredietbank acquired Spain's Banco Urquijo. This list is only indicative and does not pretend to be exhaustive.

C   SOME HISTORICAL AND COMPARATIVE EXAMPLES OF THE DRIVE OF UNIFIED
MARKETS TOWARDS UNIFORM RULES

The law of contract is seen in today's Europe as a basic domain of national law. The Treaty of Rome was signed by six countries that had civil and commercial codes that were, and still are, roughly comparable in the domain of contract law. They moreover shared a similar construction of administrative law. Perhaps because of these underlying legal similarities, the Treaty did not vest in the Communities powers in the area of contract law, its provisions were exclusively public in inspiration and scope, and there was no evident need for private law harmonization. Below we will see how this philosophy did not sustain itself in the long run, and practical considerations led to a – certainly limited – Community competence in the area of contract law.

However, what needs to be said here is that in the domain of contract law, even if it basically remains a national affair in the Europe of this early XXIst century, all of its component Member States share a basic common ground.

Codification[6] started in Europe in the second half of the eighteenth century, with the Codex Maximilianeus Bavaricus (Bavaria, 1756) and the Prussian Allgemeines Landrechts (1794), but it really expanded in the nineteenth century following the enactment of the Code Napoléon in 1804 and the Code de Commerce of 1807. The French codes applied in, or influenced the codification of, Belgium, Luxembourg, the Netherlands, Italy, Spain, and Portugal. The Prussian and Bavarian codes influenced codification in Austria (1811).

The All-German Civil Code (BGB), adopted in 1896, substantially influenced the Greek Civil Code (1946). What matters here is that all these codes did not invent the wheel but merely systematized existing law; and such existing law was none other than Roman and Canon law. All legal teaching in Europe at the time of European codification focused on the Corpus Iuris Civilis[7] of Justinian, as commented by Italian scholars in the twelfth and thirteenth centuries, and on the Corpus Iuris Canonici as compiled and enacted in the Decretum Gratiani in medieval times. Canon law was not strange to, but rather an extension of, Roman law. Both Roman and Canon law formed the *ius commune* (i.e. the common law) of Europe before codification. The whole of educated Europe shared a single and undifferentiated knowledge of law, and all legal doctrine and university textbooks of the times before codification commented on the same legal sources. Codes were framed on similar codes, precisely due to the common underlying shared tradition.

Therefore, 10 continental Member States of the European Union do indeed have a common legal background that inspired their national codes on which contract law is framed.

---

[6] This paragraph is based on the articles by Reinhard Zimmermann, 'Roman Law and European Legal Unity', and Bollen and De Groot, 'Sources and Backgrounds of European Legal Systems', both published in AS Hartkampt (ed.), *Towards a European Civil Code* (M Nijhoff Publishers, 1994).

[7] Itself a casuistic compilation of rules, legal opinions and commentary, doctrine, case law, and fragments of pre-existing compilations (from the XII Tables to the Digest).

What about the five remaining EU jurisdictions? England/Wales and Ireland[8] did not embark upon the process of codification that swept over continental Europe in the eighteenth and nineteenth centuries, and today it is generally thought that these countries are distant from the so-called 'civil-law' countries.

This is not a correct perspective. A system similar to common law is what might have been the case for the whole of Europe without the process of codification and without the surge of administrative law as a new and different area of the law. But common law cannot be considered as an autochthonous national achievement, in isolation from the rest of Europe. Right up to the nineteenth century, Cambridge and Oxford remained the only English universities, and in both cases Roman law was the very core of legal studies, with Latin as the normal vehicle for its teaching. Until the Reformation, Canon law was also influential, both in university legal teaching and in the decisions adopted by courts, in particular in courts judging on equity and in ecclesiastical courts.

Persons coming from Oxford or Cambridge would typically be appointed to all senior legal positions in the United Kingdom, and therefore Roman law was ultimately a basis for their actions. Legal literature and case law showed explicitly its Roman law foundation and the continental tradition. Scholars were hired from the continent to teach in Cambridge and Oxford, and British scholars translated continental books and visited European universities. English trade was mainly with the continent, and the Law Merchant that emerged from that trade did not differ from the *lex mercatoria* (customary law) applied by its counterparts, itself inspired by Roman law. Scotland is considered to pertain to the family of 'civil-law' countries, because of the persisting influence of Roman law in the private domain.

One may even argue that the United Kingdom did not follow the continental codification approach of the nineteenth century because of its wars against Napoleon and political hostility towards the thinking of French revolutionaries. Should it have embraced the idea of codification, the resulting code would not have differed substantially from continental codes. Interestingly enough, the Law Commissions of England and of Scotland of the British Parliament decided in 1965 to embark on a project to codify the contract law of England/Wales and of Scotland, integrating the two traditions into a single code. The two commissions did not achieve such a demanding task, but a draft code, mainly prepared by the Oxonian Professor Harvey McGregor, saw the light in 1972;[9] the lack of official follow-up is no detriment to the conceptual merit of uniting in one single code the two traditions, which, as explained above, are based on common root.

The Nordic group of EU Member States was less influenced by Roman law. However, a collection of civil laws ('Danske Lov') was adopted by the Kingdom of Denmark in 1683, prepared by academics from Bologna and reflecting both Roman and Canon Law. Most of their current private law statutes, all dating from the second half of the nineteenth century and the twentieth century, have been framed

---

[8]   Prior to Irish independence in 1922 Ireland and Northern Ireland formed a common jurisdiction; even as differentiated jurisdictions, they both share common law.

[9]   *'Contract Code'* (Ed Giuffré, 1993) in Italy; and (Ed Bosch, 1997) in Spain.

on comparative law, and therefore reflect the general concepts and doctrine of continental Europe. Such statutes were, moreover, adopted within a framework of Nordic co-operation that lead to highly harmonious rules.

National codification processes were in many instances a response to the political surge of nation states.

Following the defeat of Napoleon, the Netherlands in 1838 enacted the civil and commercial codes that replaced the Napoleonic codes that had hitherto applied, and from which differences were rather minimal. When Germany unified in 1870, the Napoleonic code applied in some of its territories, whilst Bavaria and Prussia had their own codes, and Roman law applied elsewhere; achieving a single code was a national aspiration,[10] even though in substance there was already a similar *substratum* evidenced by its daily application in the internal trade of the common economic area (the 'Zollverein').

The same could be said about Italy, some of the territorial components of which had codes copied from the Napoleonic codes: following Italian unification in 1861, civil and commercial codes, both framed on the Code Napoléon, were enacted in 1865.

Thus, one may conclude that all basic elements of the law of contract were shared throughout Europe, and merchants could rely on a single set of rules wherever they traded. The nationalization of private law in the nineteenth century has not de-naturalized its European-wide common substance and roots, namely in the realm of contract. National 'particularisms' have been more of a technical or formal nature, rather than in the *substratum* of contract law. Therefore, endeavours to re-Europeanize substantive[11] contract law should not lead to any unacceptable revolutionary changes, but rather to a rediscovery and appreciation of the common legal roots of Europe in this domain.

Curiously enough, there is a certain parallelism between monetary integration and codification.

Following political unification of Germany in 1871, a new national monetary unit based on the gold standard, the Reichsmark, was introduced in 1875, replacing seven different monetary systems and treasury notes of 22 different former states and territories, and banknotes of 33 banks authorized to issue banknotes. An internal market with free movement of goods already existed because of the customs union (Zollverein) dating from 1833. In spite of such internal market and of the introduction of a common currency, several private-law regimes subsisted (the Prussian and Bavarian codes, the Napoleonic code, Roman and Canon law, etc.) for a lengthy period of almost 30 years. Codification discussions started soon after the Second Empire, and the unified Civil Code (BGB) finally entered into force in 1900.

---

[10] With debates about whether such unification should come 'top-down' (Thibault) or 'bottom-up' (Savigny).

[11] As pointed out by Prof. Juan C Fernández Rozas, Europeanization of 'conflict of laws' has been much easier than that of substantive private law ('Los procesos de unificación internacional del Derecho privado: técnicas jurídicas y valoración de resultados'), in H. McGregor *et al.* (eds), *La unificación jurídica Europea* (Ed Civitas, 1999).

In Switzerland, the Constitution of 1848 provided for a single market, uniform customs and a single currency, but not for a unified private law system; this was kept within the domain of the cantons. This state of affairs was unsatisfactory enough to end with a revision, in 1874, of the Constitution, allowing for codification. The 'Code des Obligations' was adopted in 1883.

The case of the United States of America is also of interest. One of the aims of the integration of European markets is to create an area that compares itself with the economic might of the United States of America. Whilst in terms of population the European Union beats the United States of America, in macro-economic terms Europe lags well behind America. The United States of America is a federal union of 50 states, each with its own legislative and political powers, but it is, however, a single market. Of course sharing not only a currency, but also a common language and a federal central government and legislature is of the essence for such single-ness. Europe has just started with one of these three: a single currency. The Community is no more than an embryo of a federal authority, with limited powers that are moreover subject to the principle of subsidiarity.

Civil and contract law belongs, in the United States of America, not to the federal level but to the state level. And in this a certain comparison with Europe might be made: how has it been that the United States of America shows a single market in spite of the 50 state laws on contract?

One first answer is the general predominance of common law. Except in the state of Louisiana where the Napoleonic influence still persists, all remaining states adhere to the common law system, according to which judicial precedents may be authority to local courts even when coming from different jurisdictions. Thus, for instance, a decision of a New York court dealing with a sophisticated financial dispute would have legal authority for local courts throughout the United States of America.[12] This is far from the situation in Europe, where private law disputes are adjudicated at national level with no cross-border authority.

In common law systems many courts create case law on a daily basis. In order to enhance the legal certainty that such situation entails, the American Law Institute in 1923 adopted the technique of *Restatements*. By way of Restatements the existing jurisprudence in certain fields of the law is organized in a systematic manner, so as to formulate legal rules in a comprehensive fashion. It is a permanent effort of systematization of case law. Nine fields of private law have been the subject of Restatements: the law of contract, the law of property, of security, on tort, on agency, on restitution, on trusts, on conflict of laws, and on judgments.

In addition, since the beginning of this century the United States of America embarked on process leading to the uniformity of the laws of commerce. Before the turn of the nineteenth century a National Conference of Commissioners on Uniform

---

[12] Some common law jurisdictions (i.e. Australia, New Zealand, Canada, Ireland, India, etc.) are very receptive to the precedential value of decisions adopted in other common law jurisdictions; in the United States of America, this has been the case in the past century, but today it is very rare to see references to English court decisions.

State Laws was put in place, which adopted in 1896 its first act: the Uniform Negotiable Instruments Law. In 1906 two more uniform laws were adopted, on Sales and on Warehouse Receipts, respectively, and half a dozen more uniform laws were promulgated thereafter until 1940. At that point in time, the Commissioners decided to embark on the project of a Uniform Commercial Code (UCC) that would update and replace the existing set of uniform laws. In 1952 a first draft of the UCC saw light, but after a round of discussions with state legislators the first official text was adopted only in 1957. The text was revised and updated on several occasions.[13] It currently covers general contract principles, transactions in goods, negotiable instruments, bank deposits and bank collections, documents of title (bills of lading, warrants), secured transactions, letters of credit, leases of goods, and issuance of securities and collateral.

The UCC is a relatively flexible tool. It is not mandatory *per se*, but requires endorsement by state legislators, who can select parts of the code and not all its provisions, and who can modify or supplement its content. It is conceived as an on-going project, and not as a finalized immutable code; it will add articles as the need will demand; it is subject to the revisions that time may require. A Permanent Editorial Board is entrusted with the out-of-court interpretation of its provisions, and may submit *amicus curiae* briefs to judicial courts where interpretative questions are to be solved. Fifty state legislators have endorsed the UCC; the state of Louisiana has endorsed most but not all provisions of the UCC; the UCC has also been adopted in Washington, DC, and the US territories of Guam and the Virgin Islands.

The historical example of the Nordic countries (Sweden, Denmark, and Norway) may be also added to the list of countries where common laws came after monetary unification. The three states agreed in 1871 on a Scandinavian monetary union that lasted until 1914 (and from which the three kingdoms retain a common name for their respective, now separate, currencies, the 'krone'). These Nordic countries did harmonize legislation, inclusive of legislation on real property, on commercial topics and on contract law. A common law on contracts, on debt recognition and on shipping exist for the three countries. A proper common codification has been, however, always outside the scope of Nordic ambition and tradition.

One may be tempted to conclude that the historical examples shown above may support the idea that the combination of internal market with a single currency in territories with different laws lead inevitably, in the shorter or longer run, to the unification of the rules applying within that market ('one market, one currency, one law'). Germany, Switzerland, the United States of America, and to a lesser extent the Nordic countries, are evidence in this respect.

However, there is one case where such evidence fails: the United Kingdom. The monetary union between England/Wales and Scotland in the early eighteenth century did not lead to a systematic harmonization of civil and commercial law; furthermore, Art. 18 of the Act of Union stated that 'no alteration may be made in

---

[13] 1958, 1962, 1972, 1978, 1987, 1989, 1990, and 1994.

laws which concern private right'. In the domain of the law of contract differences subsist between English law and Scottish law. However, this needs to be put in contrast with the overwhelming economic pre-eminence of London in the world of trade and finance, namely *vis-à-vis* Scotland, with the consequence of a *de facto* unification and general application – within not only the United Kingdom but also in the British Empire and in the Commonwealth – of the rules being applied by the City of London.


### D    HARMONIZATION BY LEGISLATIVE MEANS: TOP-DOWN APPROACH

The enhanced integration of the markets that arises out of monetary union has lead the public authorities in Europe to share a genuine concern for removing the existing legal barriers to such integration. The introduction of the euro has made evident the inadequacies of the Community internal market legislation as it exists at the start of monetary union, most of which pre-date not only the Third Stage of Economic and Monetary Union but even the start of the Second Stage in January 1994. Such legislation, the product of lengthy negotiations and procedures, already constituted only the lowest common denominator on which EU Member States could compromise, whilst preserving their own views and, to the maximum extent, their legislative capacity. The diversity in the national implementation of Community directives appears now, in many cases, as a non-quantitative barrier to a single-currency financial market.

The European Council at its meeting in Cardiff in 1998, a few months before the introduction of the euro, already recognized these existing inadequacies and instructed the Commission to table a 'framework for action' to improve the single market for financial services, and, in particular, to 'identify the weaknesses which may require amending legislation'. The Commission took this mandate on board, made a wide-ranging consultation of European-level representative bodies of financial services users, market practitioners, financial entities, and national administrations, and submitted to the Council later that same year a comprehensive plan called a 'Financial Services Action Plan'[14] which was endorsed by the European Council of Cologne in 1999.

This European Commission plan contains a full legislative program targeted at removing existing regulatory barriers in the financial markets area. It builds on the existing framework, but stresses the need to streamline the Community legislative procedure and legislative technique, so as to enhance flexibility for the legislator in order to accommodate the changing needs of the immediate future. The Commission's Action Plan will not be the final end to the changes that monetary union will bring to the regulatory and supervisory framework for financial services,

---

[14] 'Implementing the framework for financial markets: Action Plan'. Commission Communication of 11 May 1999, COM(1999)232. Available on the Commission's website: <http//:www.europa.eu.int/comm/dgs/economy>.

but rather the commencement. Additional changes have been announced as necessary in the European supervisory framework[15] and even a European Securities Commission been advocated for.[16]

The ECOFIN Council decided on 17 July 2000 the establishment and terms of reference of a Committee of Wise Men,[17] with the objective of analysing the shortcomings of the current European regulatory framework of the securities markets, evaluate the priorities of the measures contained in the Commission's Action Plan, assess further the needs 'to ensure greater convergence' of markets, and recommend the way ahead to satisfy those needs.

The Wise Men organized an open consultation to all kind of financial organizations, evaluated responses, produced an interim report in November 2000, endorsed by the ECOFIN and by the European Council on 27 November and on 10 December 2000 respectively, and a final report[18] in February 2001, endorsed by the ECOFIN and subsequently submitted to the European Council on the 23rd March 2001, which endorsed it.

Such Report contains an analysis of the benefits that a better-harmonized legal framework would entail for the euro capital markets, the shortcomings of the current situation, and the recommendations to achieve such harmonisation. In a nutshell, the Report recommends the creation of a Securities Committee and of a Regulators' Committee; the first with a legislative role[19] together with the European Commission,[20] and the second with an advisory function. It recommends the priorities and deadlines for the finalization of the measures foreseen in the Commission's Action Plan. It recommends the 'networking' of regulators, and an active role of the Commission in the enforcement of the new legal framework.

The assessment of the Wise Men Report will have to be made after some few years. Its success requires, as the Report itself recognizes, 'the ability and willingness of the principal actors, the Commission, Council of Ministers, European Parliament, and national regulators to play a co-operative game'. In one word: political will. The Wise Men have set aside alternative proposals like recommending an independent European Securities Commission in the American SEC style, or allowing for supervised self-regulation (as has been the case for the City of London and

---

[15] T. Padoa-Schioppa, 'EMU and Banking Supervision', Lecture at the London School of Economics, 24 February 1999, available in the ECB website <http//:www.ecb.int>.

[16] G. Thieffry, 'Towards a European Securities Commission', *International Financial Law Review*, October 1999. Several presentations made by financial industry practitioners and representatives at the Conference organized by the British Institute of International and Comparative Law on 26 January 2001 under the title 'EU Financial Supervision: Towards a Single Regulator?' favoured openly the establishment of a European Securities Commission.

[17] A. Lamfalussy (Chairman), C. Herkströter, L.A. Rojo, B. Ryden, L. Spaventa, N. Walter, and N. Wicks.

[18] <http://www.europa.eu.int/comm/internal_market/en/finances/general/lamfalussy/htm>.

[19] Under the so-called 'comitology' procedure, as established by the Council Decision 1999/468/EC of 28 June 1999 (OJ L184/23-26, 1999).

[20] Under 'comitology' procedures, the Commission exercises delegated legislative powers when acting in accordance with the Committee.

for the Eurobond market), or streamlining the comitology legislative procedure by having only one, less political and more professional committee, or simply by asking for the use of regulations instead of directives. The Wise Men have inclined themselves to the more prudent institutional approach reflected in the Report in the hope that may succeed when there is political will among all players. But they have inserted the need to have 'a full and open review of the 4 level process in 2004', and assess then whether such hope was correct.

It needs to be noted that the Financial Services Action Plan contains some initiatives in the domains of Company law and of Contract Law which may merit some comment.

### a    Company law

Perhaps the most important novelty of the projects in the domain of Company Law is the resuscitation of the 30-years old project for a European Company Statute, the last legislative effort for which was made in 1991. The Commission's plan timidly labels it 'Political agreement on the European Company Statute', and confirms its purpose of achieving a 'legal template for pan-European operations'. Consolidation of financial market participants, such as creation of pan-European stock exchanges, the appearance of pan-European credit institutions, of multinational SSSs, of central counterparties for repo clearing houses, etc., would indeed benefit from a legal construction that is single and valid throughout the European Union, whereby raising capital, corporate governance, etc. would have a unified regime operational on a EU-wide basis. Some initiatives by economic agents in 1997 and 1998 suggested adding a European Closed Corporation Statute, not targeted to large pan-European corporations seeking (or already having) public listings in European Stock Exchanges but rather to medium-sized non-listed companies with a pan-European operation; such initiative has regretfully not been retaken by the Commission's Plan. The principle of subsidiarity should be correctly interpreted and not construed to impede the quantum-leap forward required in this domain. Reluctance by Member States to go forward with those plans may be a serious hindrance for the development of the cross-border consolidation process required for the new dimension of the euro-wide financial market.

Consolidation processes of financial markets players to match the new dimension of euro area requires completion of the projected 10th Company Law Directive on Cross-border Mergers, the 13th Company Law Directive on Take-over bids and of the 14th Company Law Directive on Cross-border transfer of corporate seats. All are included in the Commission's Plan. Pending issues are the automatic recognition of foreign companies, where a convention of 1968 never entered into force, and the harmonization of the criteria for determining the nationality of corporations.

A certain degree of harmonization of insolvency proceedings was recently achieved by way of a Regulation based on Arts 61 and 67 EC Treaty,[21] which together

---

[21] Council Regulation (EC) 1346/2000 of 29 May 2000 on Insolvency proceedings.

with the harmonization by way of directives of insolvency provisions regarding credit institutions and insurance undertakings,[22] politically agreed but not yet adopted, are positive steps towards the integration of financial markets. At a wider level UNCITRAL is advancing at a good rhythm in the finalization of a model law for international insolvencies. If account is taken that there are also rules that apply in the cases of insolvencies within other legislative acts, such, as for instance, the protection of collateral under the Settlement Finality Directive[23] or in the prospective Directive on Collateral, the only matter of concern is due consistency between all these texts.

Accounting and financial reporting. This item of the Financial Services Action Plan has lead to a proposal for a Regulation on the Application of International Accounting Standards, which will align accounting and reporting of listed corporations to the International Accounting Standards (IAS); non-listed companies will continue being subject to the provisions of the 4th and 7th Company Law Directives. A comitology procedure is envisaged to determine which of the IAS and under what rules is to apply. In addition, the Commission will recommend the application of the International Standards of Auditing. It is intended to achieve a uniform accounting and reporting system, facilitating raising capital on an EU-wide basis if not on a global basis.

Corporate governance. The Financial Services Action Plan foresees a review of the EU corporate governance practices. There is a tendency by all Member States to follow the UK's Code of Best Practice ('Cadbury Code'), but with national variations. This is an area where a certain uniformity would be warranted throughout the euro-area, if not singleness of rules. A single European Code of Best Practice in this new era of unified and international stock exchanges and investment services is warranted. The work by the Commission in this respect should contribute to that end.

### b  Contract law

The Financial Services Action Plan includes a proposal for a Directive on Cross-border Use of Collateral,[24] in order to ensure 'validity and enforceability of collateral provided to back cross-border operations'.

Practice shows that in the financial markets two classes of collateral techniques are used: pledge and temporary transfer of title ('repo'). Although both kinds of transactions have roots in Roman law (*'pignus'*, *'fiducia cum creditore'*), the process of codification has lead to particularisms in the rules applying to these operations in the Member States. The differences in such rules have been identified by financial market organizations and groupings as hindering the integration of the securities markets. For instance, the so-called 'Giovannini Group' composed of senior representatives of major banks, SSSs, market organizations (i.e. ISMA, ECSDA, ISDA, etc.), and financial law firms, issued an authoritative report to the Commission in

---

[22] COM (1988) 004 final and COM (1989) 394 final.
[23] OJ L 166/45 of 11.6.1998.
[24] A preliminary text of which was first produced by the Commission on 17.10.2000.

October 1999 under the title 'EU repo markets: opportunities for change'[25] where it is forcefully argued that national legal differences are indeed 'obstacles' to the integration of the repo market, and where the need for Community legislation is shown. Other examples are the works of the ISDA's Collateral Law Reform Committee, and of the European Financial Market Lawyers Group organized by the ECB.

Pledge is submitted in many jurisdictions to onerous formalities and limitations: formalities for the perfection of the pledge contract, identification of pledged securities, permission or not for substitutions, top-ups and negative pledges, conditions for enforcement, and procedures or rules on enforcement. In addition, differences exist as regards the ranking or priority of the pledge in cases of insolvency, the rules about 'stay' or 'freeze' on enforcement and the effects of 'suspect period' rules and retroactive effect of insolvencies. Although Art. 9(2) of the Settlement Finality Directive establishes a rule about which law governs the pledge of dematerialized securities, implementation of that directive by Member States differ and solutions are not homogeneous. All in all, the costs of having pledge of securities on a multi-jurisdictional basis is high, in particular by legal expenses, timing and legal uncertainties, which add to the functional costs (custodial fees, system and delivery insufficiencies, etc.). And what matters more, a collateral taker cannot have a multinational portfolio of securities held as collateral subject to a single legal regime. The Settlement Finality Directive has only partially given a solution, but its implementation raises the issue as to what extent directives are the appropriate legal instrument to achieve the necessary uniformity.

In spite of the above, the substance of pledge is identical in all jurisdictions, with roots in Roman law. Differences are of secondary ontological importance, and it would not be revolutionary to eliminate them. Moreover, today's financial world requires some additional features that could not exist in Roman times: pooling of dematerialized securities, mark-to-market valuation schemes, top-ups, and the capacity to re-use the pledged securities because of their full dematerialization and the possibility to have a kind of *'possesio longa manu'* through custodians keeping the computer registers, instead of a physical possession of the pledged assets. Finally, some specific forms of taking collateral have been organized by individual jurisdictions that may be expanded to the whole European Union if legislation at that level was enacted: one example would be the French *Loi Dailly*[26] allowing for pledge of non-tradable private claims (i.e. bank credits to individual borrowers) in book-entry form and without need to notify the debtor for its perfection. Thus, it is possible and convenient today to dismantle national differences for the pledge of securities, on the one hand, and to organize a single regime for such pledge that may enhance the economic efficiency of available collateral taking stake of the state-of-the-art in the national jurisdictions and choosing the most modern and efficient features or elements for the new system.

With regard to the temporary transfer of title, called reverse repurchase agreement or more simply repo, national laws differ as regards the risk for re-characterization

---

[25] Available in the website of the European Commission: <http//:www.europa.eu.int/comm/economy_finance/document/europap/eup35en.htm>.

[26] Law 81-1 of 2 January 1981 on Easing the Granting of Credit to Enterprises (Journal Officiel du 3 Janvier 1981).

(i.e. to be considered as a creation of a security interest or as a charge on the securities), the criteria to identify the law applying to the transaction, the finality of the transfer, the capacity to re-use the repoed securities, the validity and enforceability of margins, of top-ups, of close-out provisions, and of multilateral netting. The sheer concept of a repo operation is not identical in all Member States. All the above may warrant unifying legislation if the repo market is to be fully integrated in Europe.

The proposed new Directive on Cross-border Collateral should address all these items and provide a common regime for collateral. Both pledge and repo of securities require urgent harmonization.

The Community has been hampered in its effort to harmonize contract law by the need to respect the principle of subsidiarity, and the need to have sufficient legal basis. It has been said that harmonization of private law is beyond the scope of powers attributed to the Community; however, when there is a need to approximate national laws, whether these belong to public or private law is irrelevant. Such distinction is not even the same throughout the Community, and what is public in one Member State may not be qualified as such in other Member State. As a matter of fact, the legislation of the Communities has addressed the domain of the law of contract from several perspectives:[27]

- the protection of consumers,
- the law of agency,
- liability for damages,
- industrial and commercial property,
- labour relationships,
- commercial registry publicity,
- (contractual aspects of) company law (i.e. mergers, divisions, etc.),
- advertising (i.e. misleading advertising),
- securities (i.e. UCITS directive, Listing directive, Prospectus directive, etc.),
- the law of collateral (Settlement Finality directive).

This list shows that there is no systematic approach to contractual issues, but rather an *ad hoc* legislative response to specific problems, and legislative action by the Community may have had different legal basis. The result, in a horizontal analysis of the 'Community Contract Law', may be qualified as 'patchwork'. Monetary unification may have set the ground to advance in contract law unification in a more consistent manner.

E    HARMONIZATION FROM MARKET PARTICIPANTS: BOTTOM-UP APPROACH

There have been some initiatives to prepare a draft European Code of Contracts. The Commission on European Contract Law, established in 1980 under the chairmanship of Professor Ole Lando of Copenhagen and composed of academics, partially funded

---

[27] See the full list of 'private law' directives in Peter-C Müller-Graff, 'Private Law Unification by Means other than Codification' in *Towards a European Civil Code* (M Nijhoff Publishers, 1994).

by the Commission, began the preparation of common principles for contract. By 1995 it produced Part 1 of the 'Principles', dealing with performance, non-performance, and remedies. In 1998 Part 2 of the 'Principles' was finalized: formation (inclusive of contracts through agents), validity, and interpretation. The Lando Commission keeps working at present on a Part 3 of the 'Principles': set-off, assignment, subrogation, and statute of limitations.

Another grouping of civil law academics around two Italian professors, Antonio Trabucchi and Giuseppe Gandolfi,[28] has been gathering since the early 1990s in the Academy of European Private Law of Pavía (Italy), to prepare a European Code of Contracts, the results of which are still preliminary.[29] Perhaps it is noticeable that this projects aims at a comparative approach between the German and French civil codes, since both of which influenced the Italian Code of 1942, and the contract code draft by Prof. H. McGregor at the behest of the English and Scottish Law Commissions.

Other initiatives might be mentioned, as evidence of a *substratum* of academic concern about the subsistence of different national contract rules where the spirit of the times require more unity, and where the roots of contract law would permit a return to the lost times of legal uniformity. The Italian professors Mattei, Bussani and Graziadei did launch the so-called 'Trent Project', purported to identify the 'common core of private law in Europe'. Three periodicals have been created to foster integration of private law in Europe: 'Zeitschrift fur Europaisches Privatrecht' (since 1993), European Review of Private Law (since, also, 1993), and 'Europa e Diritto Privato' (since 1999).

The European Parliament has twice adopted a resolution[30] asking the Commission and the Council to organize the preparation of a European Civil Code. Following the second of such recommendations the Dutch Presidency organized a wide conference that gathered in Scheveningen near The Hague in February 1997, where the several routes towards achieving harmonization of private law were discussed, however inconclusively.

In the meantime, the Rome-based Institut International pour l'Unification du Droit Privé, founded in 1926 by the League of Nations and better known by its tradename UNIDROIT, in 1995 issued its 'Principles of international commercial contracts', with 119 articles dealing with formation, validity, interpretation, content, performance, termination, and damages in cases of non-performance.[31] In 1998, it announced a second round to revise, translate, and further advance the scope of harmonization. UNIDROIT's membership of 56 states includes most of the EU members, its work has to a great extent inspired the principles enacted by the Commission of European Contract Law chaired by Professor Ole Lando, referred to above, and the approaches of the two organizations are therefore not identical but basically consistent.

---

[28] *See* description of this project in J.L. de los Mozos, 'El anteproyecto de Código Europeo de Contratos de la Academia de Pavía' [1999] *La unificación jurídica europea*.

[29] Sergio Cámara, 'Hacia un Codigo Civil Europeo: ¿realidad o quimera?', [1999] *La Ley* 4748.

[30] 26 May 1989 [1989] OJ C158/400; 6 May 1994 [1994] OJ C205/518.

[31] Available in the website of Unidroit: <http//:www.unidroit.org/english/principles/contents.htm>.

However, in spite of the interest that a European Contract Code would entail for 'an ever closer union among the peoples of Europe' and for the integration of European markets, it is submitted that it is an ambitious project, the achievement of which may take a lengthy period of time unless the public authorities assume primary responsibility for it and provide the means and the political will to achieve it.[32]

Monetary union imposes more urgent approaches, tailored to the needs of facilitating the integration of financial markets in the euro area within a relatively short period of time.

The market has not remained inactive in harmonizing some of the contractual framework. Euro-denominated payments have flowed since January 1999 throughout the banking system of the whole Community. Inter-bank payments are the subject of either explicit contractual agreements or established practices; the new multi-jurisdictional dimension of such flows has encouraged a group of banks spontaneously to harmonize some of the rules. This initiative emerged from a forum of some 50 leading banks from Europe, New York and Japan, known as the 'Heathrow Group' (so named in consideration of the normal place of the group's gatherings). A series of conventions and guidelines were agreed in this informal forum, which subsists as a meeting place for issues related to interbank euro payments.[33] National conventions, criteria and practices were replaced by single rules. In addition to this, the European Banking Federation adopted and published in December 1998 a set of 'Guidelines on liquidity management within the framework of TARGET', to be complied with by the participants of the euro inter-bank money market.[34]

In the course of 1998, fostered by several market organizations, there was agreement regarding some of the techniques and concepts used by credit institutions: the so-called 'market conventions'[35] referring to, for instance, the manner of computing interest rates, the periodicity of paying interest coupons, treatment of bank holidays, time differences, the method of making and describing rates between currencies, and the settlement periods (i.e. same day, 2 days, etc.). In the retail sector, by contrast, no such conventions were adopted (and this despite the enactment by the Commission of recommendations in fields such as dual price displays and charges for intra-Euro conversions).

In the course of 1999, sponsored by the European Banking Federation and other credit market organizations, a standard agreement for repo and other transactions involving netting clauses was approved ('European Master Agreement' or 'EMA'),[36] to replace the several models used in the domestic markets. In spite of having been seen as an alternative to the PSA/ISMA global master repurchase agreement ('GMRA'),[37]

---

[32] *See* in this regard the opinion of the President of the European Parliament, Mr José M. Gil-Robles, 'La unificación jurídica como aspiración desde una óptica europeísta' in *La unificación jurídica europea* (Ed. Civitas, 1999).

[33] Available in the website of the European Banking Federation: <http//:www.fbe.be/e_pages/heathrow.htm>.

[34] <http//:www.fbe.be>.

[35] Available in the website of the European Central Bank: <http//:www.ecb.int>.

[36] Available in the website of the European Banking Federation: <http//:www.fbe.be>.

[37] Available in the website of ISMA: <http//:www.isma.org>.

the EMA serves the purpose of unification, since domestic markets did not normally use the Anglo-Saxon-styled GMRA, used mainly in New York, London and in the international market. In the domestic markets of the Euro zone, the use of such standard documentation, prepared under either a New York or English legal perspective, is limited, and even inadequate.

Other international organizations have established standard contracts for trades in securities; thus, the increasing desire to collateralize derivatives business has led ISDA to develop credit support documents;[38] there are specialist texts for securities lending (developed by ISLA and OSLA). However, in all these cases the sponsoring organizations need periodically to carry out legal investigations into whether such standard contracts are valid and enforceable in all the relevant jurisdictions, and qualifications are sometimes raised in the corresponding legal opinions. In particular, enforceability of netting and close-out provisions, of margining and substitution, the avoidance of re-characterization risk, and other technical aspects, is not ensured in all jurisdictions. Uniformity in the applicable substantive laws would avoid such concerns.

Unification of rules governing the use of euro-denominated securities as collateral has been the subject of several groupings of market participants. The work by ISDA's Collateral Law Reform Group and by the 'Giovannini Group' have been influential and authoritative. The European Financial Markets Lawyers Group (EFMLG), assembling legal experts from major European banks, may also be referred to: the topics analyzed have so far been the differences of the legal concept of 'dematerialization' of securities, the parameters for uniformity of rules for the pledge of securities, the concept of 'force majeure', and the elements for a legal definition of 'debt securities'. The EFMLG was organized by the ECB because of the impact of national law divergences in the achievement of a single monetary policy, and thus the need to see to what extent market participants would support efforts to reduce such divergences.

That such divergences do matter for the level playing field is shown by the fact that the techniques used by the national central banks (NCBs) to obtain collateral for monetary policy operations differ, and approximately half of the 11 euro-area NCBs use pledge, whilst the other half use the repo. Moreover, it has been forcefully argued[39] that legal systems condition the structure of financial markets, and such structure affects the transmission of monetary impulses, with the conclusion that legal differences may have an impact on the single monetary policy of the ESCB.[40]

### F    AREAS OF HARMONIZATION

Harmonization of European 'Company Law' is a must, and it is feasible. There is already a collection of 11 Company Law Directives that have launched a first

---

[38] Available in the website of ISDA: <httpl/:www.isda.org>.

[39] Stephen Cecchetti, 'Legal structure, financial structure and the monetary policy transmission mechanism', contribution to the conference held in the Deutsche Bundesbank in Frankfurt on 26–27 March 1999, on 'Monetary transmission process: recent developments and lessons for Europe'.

[40] Where capital markets are the predominant way of getting finance, such impulses tend to be more stable and slow than when financing is obtained mainly in the credit market.

generation of common rules, two more are within the Commission's Financial Services Action Plan, and, as mentioned above, the project for a European Company Status has gained a new momentum. A common and shared substratum therefore exists to undertake the task of elaborating a single set of rules for the establishment of companies, and such single set of rules may take the name of 'European Code of Company Law'. Such Code would be prepared on existing directives but would give a single and uniform 'implementation' of such directives, and this single framework be made legally available for every entrepreneur in Europe. National law may provide additional rules for other kinds of companies, but should at least permit the choice for those creating a company to opt for a single set of rules identical and effective in all EU jurisdictions. Existing divergences in the national implementation of EC Directives are, to say the least, a nuisance for establishing a single market. These have, in general, little to do with political choices or with national interest, and are rather technical. However, it is difficult to have an integrated equity market if some countries do permit, for instance, the existence of 'non-par value shares' (i.e. shares without a nominal amount, representing a quota of the capital), whilst in other Member States this is not permitted. It is difficult to have an integrated capital market if accounting rules differ, and unification of accounting rules is, in any event and *per se* a top priority. Examples of issues where such divergences are an underlying obstacle to market integration abound. Now that stock markets are under a consolidation process that will create one or two exchanges in the whole of Europe, it is paramount that the equities there traded, issued by companies located in different jurisdictions, respond to the same company rules. This approach would mirror somehow the American system, where company law is based on 'model laws' integrated into the legislation of the states.

The same might be said with respect to the rules of best practice or 'Corporate Governance' rules, where already there is a common approach to the substantive issues in the several national examples. There is no convincing explanation of why what seems sound practice in one country should not be seen as equally sound in the others, and thus divergences seem illogical and difficult to sustain. Moreover, such common sharing of substantive principles is shown by the approval by the OECD in April 1999 of a set of non-binding corporate governance standards: the 'OECD Principles for Corporate Governance'.[41] The surge of a single euro-denominated equity market would demand single governance rules; since this needs not being binding, a 'European Code of Corporate Governance' might be achieved relatively easy.[42]

The introduction of the single currency and the integration of the financial markets will diversify the location of parties concerned in the event of insolvency of an issuer of securities or, more generally, of any multinational debtor. Insolvency situations may be more complex than normal if there is not a clear and harmonized conflicts-of-jurisdiction system and substantive insolvency rules which are common in the various Member States. In particular, the ranking of claims and formalities needed therefore, the validity of pacts on ranking, statutory privileges, rights *in rem*

---

[41] Document SG/CG(99)5.

[42] *See* in this respect: Karel Landoo: 'A European perspective on corporate governance' (1999) *Journal of Common Market Studies* 269–94.

(i.e. the seller against the chattel sold and unpaid), liens of specific assets in favour of specific creditors (i.e. the builder over the construction work), etc. There is already a substantive sharing of principles in the insolvency laws of the Member States, from which to build a single set of rules that would regard the above issues and not only conflicts-of-jurisdiction. It may even be said that there is at global level more similarity in insolvency laws than disparities, as shown, for instance, in a well-researched booklet produced by the Legal Department of the International Monetary Fund, building on some other pre-existing reports, and which serves as a basis for the technical assistance missions of the IMF.[43] There are no conceptual obstacles for such single rules, and much has been done already in the European Union, as mentioned above, as well as in fora such as UNCITRAL. The common European rules may establish the parameters which should be common, and of which some have already European positive law behind: that is, the insulation of securities deposited with a custodian from the insolvency of that custodian, the protection of collateral securities from the insolvency of the debtor, etc. It could moreover include minimal harmonization of credit ranking in cases of insolvency: mortgage, credit of the constructor over the assets constructed for the debtor, tax priorities, employees' salaries, etc. A single 'European Insolvency Code' might be a quantum-leap forward in the necessary progress towards integration of the euro-markets.

In contemplation of the unifying effects of the euro in the capital markets, participants achieved some uniform rules in contractual domains of the capital markets: methods for interest rate calculation, periodicity for interest payments, etc. (so-called 'market conventions', above described). What the market participants cannot undertake is the wider unification of basic rules regarding securities. The measures foreseen in the Financial Services Action Plan in this regard are welcome, and the fast-track securities legislation proposed by the Wise Men Report as well. However, this may not be final picture. The scenario to be addressed is a single market, meaning a drive towards a single European-wide or even cross-Atlantic stock exchanges and trading platforms, single multi-jurisdictional central counterparties, real-time mobility of book-entry securities between inter-connected or merged SSSs, etc. An 'upgrade' of the Listing Particulars Directive or of the Investment Services Directive might not be enough, namely because the use of directives means diversity of national rules in the detail,[44] whereby one single and clear set of rules is what the market would wish.[45] All directives concerning the capital markets have been a compromise between Member States having differing views.[46] The creation of a European capital market is not a new idea, but goes far back to the 80's, where several market organizations had some initiatives[47] and the Commission prepared a

---

[43] 'Orderly and Effective Insolvency Procedures: key issues'. IMF, 1999.

[44] *See* Ferrarini 'Towards a European Law of Investment Services and Institutions' (1994) CMLRev 1283 *et seq.*

[45] The plan to merge the stock exchanges of London and Frankfurt include the drafting of unified listing rules and market conventions.

[46] *See* Ferrarini 'The European regulation of stock exchanges: new perspectives' (1999) CMLRev 569 *et seq.*

[47] 'Euroquote' initiative; the 'Eurolist' initiative.

'White Paper' on completion of the internal market in 1985. The introduction of the euro permits finally the creation of such European capital market, as shown by the trends towards consolidation and integration described above. What remains is a single set of rules.

A single set of rules for the capital markets, which could take the brand name of 'European Securities Code', is a desirable target. Following the huge re-denomination of securities into euro, of the quotation in euro of all organized cash and derivative securities markets in the euro area, of the consolidation process of trading systems (Euronext, EuroMTS, CoreDeal, etc.), of SSSs (Clearstream, Euroclear), the creation of European-wide central counterparts for those trades that used to be done over-the-counter, and the spread of modern technologies that permit instant remote access to markets and operators by the wide public, the maintenance of national rules on securities is an enormous hindrance to the integration of the capital markets.

A European Securities Code should deal with the following.

(a) A European-wide definition of, at least, certain kinds of securities. National laws define what 'securities' are in several Member States, and such legal definitions, of course, differ. Under the name of 'security' many kinds of legal concepts may be included. Registered or bearer, fully dematerialized or in paper form (and these either in global immobilized manner, or in definitive individualized titles), individualized or fungible, gross or net paying securities, uncollateralized or asset-backed securities, nominal equity or expressed as a percentage ('no-par value'), subordinated or non-subordinated, convertible or non-convertible, securitized portfolio of assets, UCITs securities (fixed or variable shares, participations, etc.), and other. However, as explained above, monetary union and new technologies permit the trading and use of securities as indistinguishable assets, frequently traded 'in bulk' by wholesale market participants, with no attention whatsoever as to the national legal particularisms regarding what a 'security' legally is. However, defining a certain number of most widely traded 'securities' is perhaps the basis for building a uniform regime for such instruments. In this respect EC law does not give an appropriate answer. In the 1930s some negotiable securities which are widely used internationally have been the subject of uniform or model law or customized practice: bills of exchange, promissory notes, cheques (Geneva Uniform Laws), and, to a certain extent, bills of lading and letters of credit (namely, by the International Chamber of Commerce). Today, some uniform legal regulation is warranted by the electronic age and the singleness of the euro market.

Securities can be defined neither by a system of 'lists', which will never be complete and are a drawback for market innovation, nor by descriptions, as this is done by the Investment Services Directive ('transferable securities means those classes of securities which are normally dealt in on the capital market', providing thereafter a list). The starting point for a legal definition needs to be the economic function they perform: to raise funds from the investing public or institutions. The First Banking Co-ordination Directive defined 'credit institutions' in a functional manner, and such definition has served all Member States and has survived until this day. A simple definitory example might be: 'All electronic or paper instruments issued in series for the collection of funds, independently of its legal form or denomination'.

(b) Issuance of securities. It is imperative to have single rules about the process of issuing securities. All legal systems should permit the issuance of fully demateri-alized securities. The Code should establish a single European-wide legal regime for such fully dematerialized titles (issuance formalities, authorized registers, legal value of book-entries, role and duties of custodians in transfers, charges and pledges of securities, enforcement, etc.). The question of collective representation of future and actual investors (trustees, bondholders representation, etc.) should also have some common parameters throughout Europe. Transparency and information at issuance may be also referred to in a common regime for securities issuances. The power for scrutiny and registration of prospectuses and periodic disclosure obligations in cases of securities issued on a multijurisdictional basis and above certain thresholds might be vested on a European authority (for instance, the European Commission), and use state-of-the art techniques (i.e. Internet) in this respect. The basic parameters for this may be usefully contained in the suggested European Securities Code.

(c) Trading of securities: transfers, pledges, repos, charges. What is foreseen to pertain to the projected new Directive on Cross-border Collateral of the Commission's Financial Services Action Plan may usefully be included in a single code of securities having direct applicability and effect, and the same might be said about the rules on collateral introduced by the Settlement Finality Directive, which have regretfully been so differently implemented by the Member States. Once more, the question that is raised is the use of 'directives' for these purposes, since these lead to differing national laws in a market that has gone beyond the boundaries of any single Member State.

(d) Time-limits. The diversity of time-limits creates a hidden potential discrimi-nation between issuers: no logical reason supports the maintenance of such diversity of prescription periods like 30 years for principal and 4 years for interests in Germany as against 10 years for principal and 5 years for interests as in Italy.

(e) Rules about issuer's notices to and communication with investors, where a diversity of national rules is also striking, should be in today's world a unified regime.

(f) A potential European Securities Code may usefully contain a single 'imple-mentation' of the up-graded Investment Services Directive and of the Listing Particulars Directive. A certain degree of harmonization was achieved by way of the Listing Particulars and Prospectus Directives of 1989.[48] However, cumulative appli-cation of 'home' and 'host' rules makes multi-jurisdictional listings cumbersome and impractical. The new dimension of the euro market, the mergers between exchanges and the new electronic trading platforms, may demand a uniform set of rules, so that securities which are to be issued and traded throughout the whole area are subject to identical rules wherever the place of the issuer is, and whichever the targeted markets are. The EU Investment Services Directive (ISD) of 1993 (93/22/EEC)[49] made the repartition between the home and the host jurisdictions of the rules and competences applying to the cross-border provision of investment services. The question arises whether such repartition achieves the goals of clarity and

---

[48] [1994] OJ L135/00 and [1989] OJ L124.
[49] [1993] OJ L141/00.

homogeneity that the new multi-jurisdictional dimension of the Euro securities markets demand, or whether uniform rules would here be a benefit, namely by establishing a European-wide Code of Business Conduct. The Commission's Financial Services Action Plan contemplates an 'upgrade' of those directives, which perhaps may satisfy the above concerns. Being, however, a 'directive', it will entail diversity of laws at national level; the suggested European Securities Code would have, on the contrary, direct applicability and effect, and thus achieve the singleness of rules that a single and integrated market requires.

(g) Asset-backed securities receive normally high ratings because of their soundness, are a very popular investment and qualify as the second-preferred choice for investments after public debt in the euro markets. Currently, asset-backed securities are only addressed at Community level by one article[50] of the UCITS Directive. One of the most sound and secure kind of securities is the mortgage-backed securities that finance the real estate market, and some of the most heavily traded euro securities are this kind of asset-backed security (e.g. the German *Pfandbriefe*). However, there are wide national legal differences in both the underlying mortgages, and in the configuration of these securities and of the mortgage market. Following the success of the *Pfandbriefe* other Member States[51] are introducing legislation copying the German model. Integration of markets may benefit from a European-wide legal regime for such kind of popular assets, rather than by keeping a series of similar (but always different) national laws. The possibility of regulating a 'Eurohypothèque', so that the mortgage-backed market would expand cross-border, has been suggested by some authors.[52] This is not a new topic in the history of the European Community. Already in 1966 the Commission prepared a report (the 'Segré Report') which advocated for the harmonisation of the national laws regarding mortgages and mortgage securities. In 1984 the Commission had a proposal for a directive on mortgage securities and mortgage credit, discussed by the European Parliament, but which could not see finally the light.[53] In 1987 draft uniform legislation concerning 'euro-mortgages' prepared by the 'Latin Public Notaries International Union' was submitted to the EC Council without noticeable follow-up. The introduction of the euro and the integration of capital markets may warrant a renewed effort in this respect. A comprehensive European Code of Securities should include a chapter on mortgage securities giving a single regulation to this popular market.

Other areas of the financial market where legal uniformity might be warranted are the following.

(a) The legal regime for 'bills of exchange, cheques and promissory notes'.[54] These tradable instruments were already unified in the 1930s through model laws

---

[50] Art. 22(4).

[51] France, Spain, Italy, and Ireland.

[52] Hans G. Wehrens, 'Reflections on a Euro-mortgage', in A.H. Hartkampf *et al.* (eds), *Towards a European Civil Code* (M. Nijhoff, 1994). Otmar Stöcker 'L'eurohypothéque', Banque et Droit 1996, note 49.

[53] COM(84) 730 final, OJ C42 14.2.1985.

[54] Updating in a uniform manner the old Uniform Laws of the 1930s (which were moreover not uniformly enacted in every Member State), to take into account modern technologies.

adopted by way of conventions that sovereign states were free to adhere to. It harmonized to a great extent the laws of continental Europe, but to which neither the United Kingdom nor the United States of America adhered and aligned their laws on these instruments to the model laws. Subsequent to that period, in recent times modern technologies have permitted new ways for banks to refinance and clear these instruments without having to resort to their physical handling. This has entailed new laws in many Member States. Appearance of pan-European banks, increase in the cross-border use of these instruments, and the relatively recent electronic treatment of these instruments might suggest that a renewed effort at achieving a European-wide modern 'uniform law' on cheques, bills of exchange and promissory notes is undertaken.

(b) 'Cash collateral'. It is one of the topics under current consideration by the Commission for its projected Directive on Cross-border Collateral, as it relates to one element of the legal regime under which repo transactions are documented: cash collateral may be one of the items comprised in the calculation of the Final Settlement Amount at Early Termination of the GMRA standard repo agreement. Formalities and limitations on this kind of collateral differ from one country to another, and an integrated market would also require some common rules that are beyond the contractual domain of market participants. Cash not being a 'security', this kind of collateral would fall outside the suggested European Securities Code.

(c) Liberatory effect of 'scriptural payments'. The euro was introduced on 1 January 1999 without monetary signs (banknotes and coins), and is thus being operated as a 'scriptural' currency. In view of the increasing importance of scriptural payments as compared with the stabilized if not decreasing use of cash payments, the Dutch Civil Code in 1992 already contemplated the liberatory effect of such scriptural payments;[55] that provision of the Dutch inspired Art. 8.3 of the Council Regulation 974/1998 of 3 May 1998 introducing the euro, which permitted scriptural payments in euro to discharge debts denominated in national units. Some Member States introducing legislation for the adoption of the euro have followed suit[56] and provided the possibility to discharge debt obligations by scriptural payments in euro (i.e. credit transfers by book-entries) when scriptural discharge was permitted for debts denominated in national units. Scriptural payments are today the most important way of discharging monetary debts, not only in the wholesale market but also in the retail sector (credit/debit cards, electronic purses, cheques, transfer orders) and therefore the legal principle employed by the Community for the transitional period of the introduction of the euro in the participating Member States should become a permanent principle of civil law applicable, why not, in all Member States.

This paper has mainly referred to the domains where the impact of monetary unification will be more intense. But there is a plethora of other areas where the process of market integration and market consolidation will demand uniformity

---

[55] Section 6:114 of the Dutch Civil Code.
[56] *See* for instance Art. 14(2) of the Spanish Law.

of rules. Sale of goods, public procurement, distribution contracts, advertising, publishing, licensing, franchising, transport, insurance, etc. Achievement of the work initiated by several groupings of academics purported to have a 'European Code of Contracts' that would deal with the general theory of contract, should be a must. Europe shares a common ground, shown not only by history as summarized above, but by present-time judgements given by the European Court of Justice where use of principles 'common to Member States' abound, and where judges of different national background are able to discuss and agree on difficult legal cases. This *ius commune* is also shown by the current trend among law-firms to expand beyond their national boundaries, and establish themselves in foreign capitals; the success of such trend proves that lawyers are able to work in foreign legal environments giving legal support to cross-border activities of their clients. New problems have arisen that are common to all EU Member States (i.e. is a computer breakdown *'force majeure'*?; this is a question *majeure* in the computerized world of today's markets, and one which still depends on the different jurisprudence of Member States – not codes because being from of the pre-computer age they could not deal with this; however, multi-jurisdictional intercourse would require a common approach to this issue). Preparatory work for a European-wide codification of contractual rules is very much advanced, as reflected above. Other fora such as UNIDROIT have invested enormous time and there is altogether a mature material on which to base further efforts and finalize the unfinished work. Forceful argumentation has been placed on the possibility and need to achieve that project.[57] What remains after the introduction of the single currency is only the political will to support that project.

## G   Means of Harmonization

The first question that comes to mind is whether the use of directives as legal means to achieve the necessary singleness of some parts of the Law is the proper approach. An extensive use of directives by the Community for achieving the internal market and for the harmonization of laws, based on the principle of subsidiarity,[58] has not solved the divergences between national laws. Now that the euro has swept away the last barriers, this legal diversity appears as an obstacle to the full integration of markets.

Community directives are the result of compromise and political negotiation between law-making entities (Member States and Community), are dependent on political events and priorities, usually ends up being the lowest common denominator between Member States' positions, and they are rarely a perfect, comprehensive, and consistent piece of legislative art.

---

[57] *See* for instance Jürgen Basedow 'A common contract law for the common market' (1996) CMLRev 1169 *et seq.*, and authors quoted in that article. Also, M. Elmer and L. Skovby 'Vers un droit européen des biens et des obligations' (Mélanges Schockweiler, Baden-Baden, Nomos Vertrag 1999).

[58] *See* Protocol on Subsidiarity annexed to the Treaty, in particular para. 6: 'Directives should be preferred to regulations and framework directives to detailed measures'.

The use of directives faces a dilemma: they either miss the objective of harmonization by granting Member States leeway to implement them, or otherwise they restrict such leeway by being so detailed that the use of such instruments is de-naturalized. The ability to harmonize depends also on the kind of directive used: directives normally purport a *de minimis* harmonization, whereby Member States may add to the content of the directives, or more rarely a *de maximis* rule, whereby Member States may deviate within certain limits. An example of the above-mentioned dilemma is the Settlement Finality directive of 19 May 1998 (98/26/EC),[59] whose Art. 9(2) aims at harmonizing the conflict-of-laws rules applying to rights on securities placed and traded in a multi-jurisdictional market. It had to be implemented by Member States by 11 December 1999. As shown by Richard Potok,[60] its national law implementation has left a situation of non-harmonization, which will possibly merit a further legislative initiative for the revision of the directive by the Commission. An example of the problems faced by *de minimis* directives is the Prospectus directive, which gives leeway to Member States to add items for the prospectuses of new securities, ending with the need for issuers to ascertain national prospectus requirements before placing securities on a multi-jurisdictional basis.

Legislative reforms takes an awful amount of time, especially if the 'implementation time' at Member State level is added to the usually long periods that the Community legislative process entails. The speed of changes in the financial markets and in the economy in general requires a legislative system 'plus agile'.

All this was recognized by the Financial Services Policy Group[61] when suggesting in October 1999 to the Commission to obtain from the Council the use of fast-track and more flexible 'comitology procedures' for legislation purported to implement the Financial Services Action Plan. It has been the core of the recommendations contained in the Wise Men Report, whereby two committees are suggested, one advisory (the Regulators' Committee) and one regulatory (the Securities' Committee), and where detailed Community legislation should be done through 'fast-track' comitology procedures.

The above reasons seem to have given the ground for the inclination of the Wise Men Committee towards a more general use of regulations in the task of achieving an integrated financial market following the monetary unification, instead of directives. The Wise Men Report recommends that 'more use should be made of Regulations, rather than Directives. Regulations can speed up the implementation process because they are directly applicable in the Member States. The Committee considers that Regulations should be used whenever possible, along with fast track procedures, although these techniques will not be able to resolve all the problems'. The Wise Men Report has been endorsed by the ECOFIN and by the European Council.[62]

---

[59] [1998] OJ L166/00.

[60] Richard Potok, 'Legal Certainty for Securities Held as Collateral' (December 1999) *International Financial Law Review*.

[61] The senior group advising the Commission on the Financial Services Action Plan.

[62] Stockholm European Council of 23 March 2001.

However, the scope of the Wise Men Report is limited to the capital markets. It only addresses 'securities regulation'. Such Report, moreover, does not seem to recommend achieving a single, consistent and comprehensive legal regime for euro securities, but rather the more pragmatic approach of addressing specific areas in need of further harmonization. A good legislator, and the Commission may qualify for that, would make some planning with a strategic overall target before starting the submission of legislative initiatives. Such planning requires caring for consistency and for comprehensiveness. Even if the legislative proposals follow a non-systemic path, because of priorities and needs, the Commission should draw an internal plan that would, piece by piece, add consistently and progressively to the achievement of the material objective of a European Securities Code, whatever the name may be given at the end to a codification of those several pieces.

What about other domains of the law?

'Company law' has been addressed normally by way of Community Directives, with a total of 11 directives enacted until this year 2000. Regulations have been rather the exception and been used in areas related to Competition Law (control of concentrations), and for the European Economic Interest Groups. Two projects are currently under the format of regulations: The European Company Statute and Accounting Principles. Whilst Member States should keep their capacity to legislate on company law and permit different types of corporations, integration of euro markets would require the possibility for national companies to align themselves into a single set of pan-European rules.

An ideal European Company Code should:

(a) contain the European Company Statute allowing for truly 'pan-European' companies, and
(b) provide to Member States a detailed and complete set of rules implementing in uniform manner the collection of Company Law directives, whilst allowing for
   (i) the maintenance of the 'nationality' of those companies subject to such uniform rules and
   (ii) for the maintenance of 'national company codes' containing national variations and models for companies, as an option.

A European Company Code would thus permit entrepreneurs freely to submit their companies to a single set of European rules (either to the European Company Statute or to the European uniform rules for national companies) or to the national company laws adopted by Member States, in some aspects framed by the Community Directives.

This scheme would require the use of a Regulation.

To establish a uniform European Code on 'Corporate Governance' there is no need for a legally binding act. The Commission may use a Recommendation.

What are the legal means to achieve greater and more consistent harmonization of 'contract law'?

The Community is handicapped by the need to base its contractual legislation on Treaty provisions where private law does not seem to exist. Private law is fiercely defended by some Member States as a national domain where subsidiarity may be invoked.[63] This is what leads to lack of internal consistency and to the current situation of 'patchwork' described above when addressing this topic. There is no specific legal base to harmonize private law as an end in itself; it has to be based on other and specific legal basis.

Most frequently-used basis are Arts 43–55 regarding right of establishment and free provision of services, which require for harmonization to be seen as necessary in order to establish the internal market. It has been used for harmonization of Company Law, but are hardly a sound legal basis for contractual unification.

Art. 65 is a suitable legal base to adopt legislation regarding civil and commercial proceedings and on conflicts of law and of jurisdiction. It has served as legal basis for the EU Regulation on Insolvency Proceedings adopted in 2000. However, this article hardly serves for substantive contract law unification.

Arts 94–97 provide a legal basis when the objective is to achieve or maintain the internal market (Art. 14 sets the Community aim of establishing an internal market). Art. 123(4) is a legal basis to adopt 'the other measures necessary for the rapid introduction of the [euro] as the single currency of those [participating] Member States'. It seems difficult to argue that this provision enables the Community to legislate on contract.

Finally, Art. 308 is a subsidiary legal base not linked to the internal market, but merely requiring that a Community action be necessary in order to attain a Community objective. Since contract law unification does not specifically appear in the list of Community objectives of Arts 2 and 3, and since Art. 308 requires unanimity, it may be difficult to use it for contractual codification purposes. The ECJ's Opinion 2/94 [1996][64] has established the 'constitutional limitations' to the use of Art. 308 as legal basis for legislation: it cannot serve for widening the scope of Community powers, nor to implicitly amend the Treaty. Enacting a European Code of Contract might be seen as going beyond the authorized boundary of Art. 308. The main problem to face is that 'establishing an internal market' has been conceived as the dismantling of barriers to free movements of goods, services, capital and persons, and the harmonization of access rules. It consisted of elimination of market compartmentalization. The surge of a unified body of rules for the already existing internal market seems to be one step beyond. Differences between national legal systems may entail more costs in cross-border transactions, but costs are not an obstacle to the internal market and thus reduction of legal costs in cross-border activities is not a Community objective. A better functioning of the financial market may not be seen as justification for Community legislation.

With regard to obtaining a general set of substantive rules (i.e. not only procedural, where Art. 65 seems to provide sufficient legal basis) on 'Insolvency'

---

[63] *See* in that respect D Caruso, 'The Missing View of the Cathedral: the Private Law Paradigm of European Legal Integration' (1997) 3 *European Law Journal*. Also worth reading is: C. Joerges, 'The Impact of European Integration in Private Law: A New Constitutionalist Perspective' (1997) 3 *European Law Journal*.

[64] ECR I-1763.

(a European Insolvency Code) that would apply to the multi-jurisdictional but integrated market that the introduction of the euro should achieve, the same problems exist: lack of proper Treaty legal basis. However, as mentioned above, basic concepts on insolvency are similar throughout Europe, and to provide for some common basic substantive rules does not seem an impossible task.

What to do? For Insolvency and Contract Law the American UCC experience provides a useful reference. The 'American model' shows:

- The possibility for non-politicians to embark on the technically-demanding task of unifying some parts of private law; in Europe, the uniformity suggested on Insolvency and Contract Law should not create in itself political problems: some background exists already in the current *'acquis communautaire'*, there is a *communis opinio* on many topics in addition to common historical roots, and also a non-negligible number of market conventions, contractual standards and practices (i.e. *lex mercatoria*), whereby no revolutionary changes are to be thus expected in these areas of Insolvency and Contract Law. It could be left to non-politician jurists (practitioners, academics, judges, expert national civil servants) to provide for the appropriate drafts.
- The possibility to rely on moral authority for national legislators to find advantageous the adoption of unified rules; the UCC was not imposed on the federal states, but offered to them and freely adopted (not by all, not in its entirety).
- The possibility to avoid the main criticism that codification has, namely, that codified law is frozen law, incapable of matching the needs of the times; in America, the UCC has been amended as many times as it has been felt necessary to accommodate the law to the market needs.

In Europe, instead of the US 'National Conference of Commissioners on Uniform Law', a Council of Justice Ministers exists and might be the superior body organizing the proper forum along the American lines: a grouping of national legal experts, market practitioners, academics, and perhaps lawyers of selected European financial market organizations, with a mandate to prepare and produce the drafts of the suggested European codes on Insolvency and Contract Law.

Private law has been traditionally, in continental Europe at least, an area of competence of the Departments of Justice, and it should be for them to launch, monitor and assess the project of unification of the Law of Insolvency and of the Law of Contract. The mandate to such a grouping could establish the principle of building upon (i) existing *acquis*, so that continuity and consistency with the existing positive European law is kept, (ii) the work done by the informal groupings (i.e. the Commission on European Contract Law, the Academy of Pavía, etc.) so as to profit from endeavours of the recent past, (iii) the work of international organizations (UNCITRAL, UNIDROIT, IMF, Hague Conference of International Private Law), and (iv) the principles common to the Member States. The Commission should have the chairmanship and leadership of that (or those) groups of experts, as well as the financing of costs, but under the monitoring of Justice Ministers. The draft codes should be submitted to the Council of Justice Ministers, which would examine disagreements, and would not adopt any binding act but simply a non-binding Recommendation to the Member States to adopt the codes.

Another possibility would be to 'amend the Treaty'.

Following the treaties of Maastricht and Amsterdam the so-called Third Pillar may have the adequate architectural political balance between the European and the national spheres, based on an intergovernmental rather than a supranational conception. However, such architecture may provide the necessary legal tools to achieve in a quick manner the necessary law unification for Contract and for Insolvency as described above. The Third Pillar currently provides for 'Cooperation in the Fields of Justice and Home Affairs', and addresses the harmonization of penal laws and the co-ordination of judicial procedures. There is hardly any ontological reason for accepting European harmonization in these two domains, criminal law and judicial procedure, which are much more than Private Law a *sancta sanctorum* of national competence, and not to admit the same Treaty architecture to embark on the process of selective contract law and insolvency unification. It would require an amendment to the Treaty so as to include unification of private law within the scope of the Third Pillar.

As an alternative, the Treaty amendment could simply slightly re-draft Arts 65 and/or 95 so as to cover contract law harmonization *per se*, and substantive insolvency harmonization, without the doubts that currently exist.

## H   Conclusions and Recommendations

The thesis that is hereby submitted is that the introduction of the single currency is a catalyst of trends that already existed beforehand towards closer integration of European markets, because of (i) internal market Community legislation, (ii) technological developments, (iii) globalization of markets, and (iv) consolidation of market participants. It is submitted that the outcome of this trend will be enhanced harmonization or even unification of the rules and practices under which financial markets operate, in addition to the process of further regulatory harmonization that Community institutions have already started. Such private law harmonization would be based on the sharing of a common legal background and history, and would follow a drive similar to what other comparable historical cases underwent. This paper suggests that such prospect for increased harmonization may benefit from an active role of the European legislators and political authorities, so as to facilitate a trend that has initiated bottom-up from concerned parties.

The prospect of Community enlargement, with a scenario of 27 national laws and rules applying to a market that is based on a single currency, makes the business case for prompt legal harmonization/unification much more strong.

'One market, one currency, one law'. The achievement of a single market has been one of the goals of the Communities since their inception in the IGC of Messina in 1956, when the media spoke of the 'Common Market'. The introduction of the single currency is a qualitative step forward in that direction, which follows years of legislative efforts by the Community targeted at achieving what was later termed as an 'internal market'. Now, what the singleness of a currency demands is that market participants play with single market rules. A multiplicity of national laws is finally an obstacle to the singleness of the market. A quote from the Heidelberg professor and well-known nineteenth century legal writer Anton FJ Thibaut is relevant here: '[i]f there is no unity of laws the terrible and odious practice of the conflict of laws will arise so that in their intercourse the poor subjects will be stuck and suffocated in such a constant maze of uncertainty and chock that their worst enemies could not advise them worse. Unity of laws would, however, make smooth and safe the road of the citizen from one state to the other, and wicked lawyers would not longer have the opportunity to sell their legal secrets and thereby to extort and maltreat the poor foreigners'.[65]

The introduction of the euro has set the momentum for fostering a higher degree of uniformity in selected areas of private law. There is a public law side of the harmonization required by monetary union, namely the regulatory framework on which markets operate. The Community institutions have begun preparations for this and it is likely that further harmonization will be in place sooner rather than later. But there remains a world of differences in the national legal systems that govern private relations. This side-effect of monetary union thus consists of the necessity to enter into the area of private-law harmonization. The Europe of monetary union needs, at least, a uniform set of rules governing selected areas of financial activity, and these will later have to expand to cover other non-financial contractual domains.

This chapter makes a summary review of the legal history of Europe, and concludes that the differences in the private law systems of Member States are not substantive, and date from codification times; it moreover argues that codification did not disrupt the basic common European-wide understanding of contract law, which therefore, below the formalities, remains common. It considers the case of the United States of America, where the singleness of the market has been achieved, *inter alia*, by way of *Restatements* of the law, which somehow resemble the codification exercises of the last century, and by the enactment, more recently, of the Uniform Commercial Code. It is finally submitted that the American example gives a sound direction towards which Europe should drive.

Whilst a European Company Code might be achieved by existing Treaty provisions, and whilst the implementation of the Wise Men Report may set the ground for a desirable European codification of Securities rules, the Treaty does not contemplate private law-harmonization as a stand-alone Community competence.

If harmonization of contract law and of basic rules of insolvency is to be achieved, this may be done under two models:

– the 'American' model, based on an expert codification plus a voluntary acceptance at national level of such codification, or
– new competence at European level by way of amendment to the Treaty.

This chapter suggests addressing four main areas of law unification:

(a) *Securities:* this is an area where the impact of monetary unification has been greater, on top of the new technologies and general trend towards globalization of

---

[65] Quoted from Prof. Ole Lando: 'European Contract Law after 2000' (1998) CMLRev 35.

capital markets. Building on existing '*acquis*', upgrading it and aligning it to state-of-the-art modern capital markets, using intensively the 'comitology procedure' suggested by the Wise Men Report, and using Regulations rather than Directives as recommended by the Wise Men, the prospect of obtaining a collection of single set of rules for the euro-area capital markets seems feasible. Such collection of legal acts should try to achieve not only internal consistency but also comprehensiveness, and may one day be codified in a systematic manner so as to take the format of a 'European Securities Code'.

(b) *Company law:* building on existing 'acquis' in this domain, it is now advisable to have a single 'European Code of Company Law' with single rules effective throughout, at least, the euro area, in addition to the possibility of allowing for a continuation of national company laws as optional vehicles. A common European Code of Corporate Governance seems also feasible, because of the similarities between the national codes, and the possibility to use non-binding legal acts, such as a Recommendation, to encompass such single code.

(c) *Insolvency:* again building here on some existing 'acquis', on principles common to the Member States, and on work done by international organizations (IMF, UNCITRAL), a single set of some basic rules for cases of insolvency seems warranted. Ideally, a 'European Insolvency Code' should be the vehicle containing those substantive rules, and may encompass (and complete) the procedural rules so far embedded in the Council regulation on insolvency proceedings adopted in 2000.

(d) *Contract law:* building on the work done by the several groupings of academics that have worked on European contract law unification, on the work done by UNIDROIT, and on the rediscovery of the common roots of contract law throughout Europe, the arrival of the euro gives a new momentum to give official backing to those initiatives so as to achieve a common set of basic rules for contracts, which may take the format of a 'European Contract Code'.

This paper also identifies some other areas where unification might be desirable in order to further the integration of the banking market: bills of exchange, cheques, promissory notes, cash collateral.

*Chapter 2*

# Towards a Single European Capital Market and a Workable System of Regulation

*Jan H. Dalhuisen*

## 1 INTRODUCTION

Whilst dealing with financial regulation, it is absolutely necessary to draw some lines. The key is to determine what exactly is the financial activity exactly we want to regulate, how and why. Even amongst legislators and regulators there appears to be confusion on this point. Is the true concern in commercial banking is for example, systemic risk or is it the protection of depositors, or perhaps the proper functioning, access and cost of payment systems, or concern with the integrity of the financial system as a whole? Another issue may be the access of especially consumers and smaller businesses to banking (loan) facilities at competitive prices.

In modern (commercial) banking regulation, all seem to play a role, but it is less clear what the true aim is or what relative weight must be given to any of them when they are not compatible. Thus concern for depositors may easily conflict with the requirements of the smooth operation of the financial system as a whole and with the minimising of systemic risk.[1]

---

[1] This was an issue in the BCCI case, *cf.* the *House of Lords in Three Rivers District Council and Others v. Governor and Company of the Bank of England* [2000] 2 WLR 1220 which seemed in this case less concerned with depositors but accepted – absent bad faith – the prevailing statutory restrictions on liability for banking supervisors as an adequate defence, even if in the UK more extensively interpreted than elsewhere, like in France, where administrative courts now accept in this connection *faute simple* as sufficient ground for liability, therefore leaving more room for depositors protection, *see Cour Administrative d'Appel de Paris*, 30 March 1999. In Three Rivers, reasonable policy objectives and considerations connected with systemic risk or the smooth operation of the financial system did not seem to figure and were in any event not weighed against the statutory requirements of depositors' protection as laid down in Sec. 3 of the UKL Banking Act 1987. It is assumed in England that the First Banking Directive of 1977 (77/780/EEC), now superseded by the Credit Institution Directive of 2000 (2000/12/EC), even though clearly concerned with depositors, did not give depositors extra rights in this connection either. Whatever the objective of that Directive, there was not considered to be any direct effect as the relevant provisions were not deemed sufficiently clear, precise and unconditional. No guidance from the European Court was sought, *see* also M. Andenas, 'Liability for Supervision' (2000) *Euredia*, 379. Protection of regulators appeared here as an objective in itself although not everywhere as widely interpreted as in the United Kingdom.

At least in the United Kingdom, the tensions that exist here may be further increased, now that systemic risk is becoming an issue in banking regulation as well, see for the concept, Ross Cranston, Principles of Banking Law (1997), p. 71. Even without a statutory change, the re-focussing of the banking supervision objectives in this direction has become clear from the annual reports of the Bank of England on banking supervision

*Mads Andenas and Yannis Avgerinos (eds), Financial Markets in Europe: Towards a Single Regulator?* 35–73.
© 2003 *Kluwer Law International. Printed in Great Britain.*

On the other hand, one may ask whether in the regulation of investment services systemic risk is a true issue.[2] Or is its objective rather the protection of investors or only of the smaller of them, or is it the integrity of the financial system as a whole or of the capital markets more in particular? The access to the various market support functions at reasonable prices is another important public or competition concern in this area. Is there as a consequence also in the regulation of investment services a mix of all of these objectives?

Indeed it would appear that in both commercial banking and investment services there is some such a mix with the result that it is often unclear what the true regulatory perspective is.[3] We may have to live with this but must realise that it leads to instability at the very core of the regulatory system. It is in any event clear that whatever this mix, the dominant regulatory objective is not the same for commercial banks and investment services and may in the latter case in any event vary per service. In fact, although in academic writing on the subject, financial services tend to be treated as all the same and the main cue is taken from commercial banking, investment services and their regulation are very different from commercial banking services and their regulation. This difference is especially in Europe so far too little understood and explored.

In the former, concern for systemic risk now seems to prevail even over depositors' protection (which is primarily deemed achieved through deposit guarantee schemes). Liquidity and insolvency risk is then considered mainly from this perspective and so are the authorisation, prudential supervision and capital adequacy regime. Yet, it has become abundantly clear that modern regulation and the limited capital requirements it can impose have not reduced the bankruptcy risks in the banking system. One could even say that modern regulation has proved irrelevant in this aspect, whilst the insolvency problem continues to be effectively left to lenders of last resort or governmental intervention. Systemic risk would not appear therefore capable of being managed by regulation with its authorisation, prudential supervision and capital adequacy requirements.

---

before this activity was handed over to the Financial Services Authority (FSA) as from 1997. If managing systemic risk becomes a valid regulatory objective, it may easily be at the expense of depositors' protection. It is in any event clear that this protection objective is less overriding than it once was. It seems that in a modern banking regulation system, they are primarily left to whatever protection depositor guarantee schemes may give them and whatever protection capital adequacy requirements may yield them in a macro sense.

[2] It has led to a difference of opinion within the European Central Bank (ECB), with Germany wanting to consolidate the regulatory functions at national levels in a single regulator, whilst the ECB, invoking systemic risk concerns also in investment services (and hedge fund activity), sees here a special role for the national Central Banks within its European System of Central Banks (ESCB), *see* Financial Times 7 March 2001.

[3] *See* also Dalhuisen *International Commercial, Financial and Trade Law* (2000), 720. The EU Directives do not throw much further light. This is understandable as they are in this area co-ordination directives concerning the relative competence of the domestic (Member State) regulators involved and do not have as their main objective to provide for a regulatory regime. In dealing primarily with the EU's overriding concern for the free movement of these financial services, which could conflict with (some of) the tenets of (domestic) financial regulation, this vagueness is all the more understandable. Yet, in Preamble 5 of the Credit Institutions Directive, reference is made to the protection of savings and in Preamble 66 to depositors and the stability of the financial system, whilst the Preamble of the Investment Services Directive refers to investors' protection as one of its objectives, not spelling out any others.

On the other hand, it must be admitted that systemic risk is not truly the major issue in investment services (even if Central Banks are trying to use this argument to become more involved in investment services regulation).[4] Here investors' protection, at least the protection of the smaller ones, seems to have remained the major issue, although the integrity of the financial system as a whole and of the market function more in particular is also an often cited preoccupation. It could conceivably override the protection of individual investors, just as concern for systemic risk might that of depositors in commercial banks.

The regulatory preoccupation with the operation of the markets and its functioning in investments services is itself much more contentious. It can hardly be meant as intervention in the market mechanism and its operation. In essence, it must be seen as limited to combating market abuse, chiefly in terms of manipulation, monopolisation or insider dealing. Authorisation and prudential supervision were here never much of an answer. Consequently, this type of functional regulation was never a major issue in the Euro-markets that evolved freely into the largest capital market in the world, is efficient and trusted, whilst its integrity is not in doubt and guarded by the industry itself.

Given these perplexities, it could perhaps be concluded that the only true objective of financial regulation is much more abstract. It may simply be the creation of greater confidence, particularly in an ageing population increasingly concerned about its savings. As such it is a much vaguer and intangible objective that has much to do with perceptions. It requires a minimum degree of regulatory sophistication and a proper bite, but it may be that the details matter less than one might think, except, in investment services (which are in this chapter our main concern), a more precise protection of retail investors and the products that are sold to them.

In the EU, there is another concern and a special overriding preoccupation with the free flow of capital and financial services. As we shall see, this concern may not always square with the regulatory objectives pursued at national levels as financial regulation remains in essence a Member State matter. More severe regulation, in other Member States, could easily motivate those states to impose them on incoming financial services. The result is a double regulatory regime that would handicap the flow of financial services, like the sale of investment securities in other Member States.

The balancing of the EU overarching policy of free movement of these services with national regulatory requirements in commercial banking, investment services

---

[4] Another concern often expressed in this connection is the one with *asymmetric* markets. Naturally, in investment securities, the small investor in particular lacks sufficient information but he has his broker to guard his interests in this respect and in any event only deals more incidentally. In doing so he will be guided by prices obtained by the best informed players who make the market discounting all their information thus protecting the others. Whether the financial markets themselves suffer from basic asymmetry in information must also be doubted. There is in any event little proof that financial markets incline towards lower quality trading as a consequence. They have their own *decentralised* ways of information gathering and it is not at all certain whether regulatory insistence on transparency for example, can add a great deal in this connection. Asymmetric information concerns would at any rate not appear to justify or provide a proper argument for the centralisation and regulation of the market function as such, which is sometimes suggested as an additional remedy. Regulatory concern should be couched here in terms of market manipulation, for example, through insider dealing (and its true effects), not in terms of asymmetric markets.

and insurance, was the major subject of the EU liberalisation Directives. They came into force pursuant to the 1987 Single European Act meant to complete the common market also in financial services. The result was the Second Banking Directive (effective from 1 January 1993) now consolidated in the Credit Institution Directive of 2000, the Investment Services Directive (effective from 31 December 1995) and the Third Generation of Insurance Directives (effective from 1 July 1996).

Leaving insurance to one side, from the EU perspective there are here two distinct areas: the single market for banking services and the single market for investment services. Sustained by the free movement of capital, this translates in a EU-wide facility to recycle money through a single commercial banking market and a single capital market system. They should be well distinguished and in this chapter we shall be concerned mainly with the single capital market or the 'Single European Capital Market' and the investment services rendered therein. In this connection, the more precise issues to be discussed are the regulatory obstacles in the way of this single capital market, the proper role of regulation in this market and how it should be structured.

To get some better grip on this subject of a Single European Capital Market, I should first like to discuss the liberalisation of the capital flows and of the financial services themselves in the EU and note their interaction but also their fundamentally different nature. Then I should like to say something about what we do or should regulate in this connection in the European Union or not (even if only at Member State level) and, if we do, why and how, and to what extent it might be effective. Thirdly, I should like to mention the vital own market contribution to the creation of a Single European Capital Market, the own support functions and safeguards competition creates, and the resulting lesser needs for all-out re-regulation. Finally, I come to the EU Action Plan[5] and the February 2001 Report of the Committee of Wise Men under the chairmanship of Mr. Lamfalussy.[6]

On the whole it is not difficult to support the Wise Men's quest for an activist co-ordination Committee at EU level (the European Securities Committee or ESC), even without rule making powers (unless delegated to it), through which the Commission's role in the regulatory process is to be strengthened.[7] The hope must be that in this manner a better implementation of the EU Directives and a regular review and updating of them can be achieved to underpin this Single European Capital Market.

---

[5] The Action Plan was first requested by the June 1998 Cardiff European Council and was presented to the Vienna European Council in December 1998 in a text of 28 October 1998. It was adopted by the Commission on 11 May 1999 COM (1999) 232 and has a 2005 deadline. Shorter term priorities are set from time to time, *see* lastly Financial Services Priorities and Progress Sixth Report 3 June 2002, COM (2002) 267. Earlier Reports were presented in November 1999, June 2000, November 2000, June 2001 and November 2001. There are very regular updates.

[6] An Initial Report was published on 9 November 2000. The Final Report dates from 15 February 2001; *see* <www.europa.eu.int/comm/internal_market>.

[7] The March 2001 Stockholm Summit wanted, however, 'dominant views' in the EU Council to be taken into account which may in practices well amount to some veto of the larger countries over the ESC, *see* also the critical Leader in the Financial Times of 27 March 2001. *See* further Section 5.2 below.

Mainly for practical and efficiency reasons, I share their doubts, however, on the centralisation of the regulatory function itself, especially in investment services. I see no urgent need or even great feasibility in the *retail* area where, as I shall argue, financial regulation is the most important. It requires for its effectiveness an important domestic component. If confidence is the key factor, a regulator that is farther removed from retail is unlikely to carry sufficient credibility. In the professional area, in as far as regulation is necessary, it will also require a strong domestic component as the regulator in this area must be close to the markets of which there are many centres within the European Union. Centralisation is here likely to work only at the level of regulatory structure but its effectiveness will continue to depend on domestic components and supervision activities as long as there are financial centres in virtually each EU Member State. It would make such centralisation only a bureaucratic exercise, which, according to the type of activity and interest to be protected, would, for its effectiveness, still depend on local regulators and rules. It could therefore hardly be more than some façade in which infighting and demarcation wars with local regulators (and pass the parcel when anything went wrong) would be *de rigeur*. The term 'bureaucratic nightmare' has been used in this connection.

As was already mentioned, the domestic component may, however, be an important obstacle to the free movement of financial services and therefore also to the Single European Capital Market, but as I shall argue, this impediment can be exaggerated. To begin with, retail services do not have much of a trans-border element. They remain largely domestic or are otherwise predominantly solicited by the customer and rendered at the place of the (foreign) service provider (where the client's accounts are usually held), unless the latter established a branch in the country of its clients. That is rare in the investment industry where in such cases a foreign subsidiary, subject to full host regulation, is mostly preferred. (This is different for commercial banks, which operate internationally mainly on the basis of an international *branch* network.)

In the professional area, deregulation is or should be the natural starting point, so that regulation is not a large issue. Consequently, neither would be the question whether it is exercised at domestic or EU level and whether it is as such a major impediment to the free flow. At least in investment services, we can and should be much more relaxed about professional or experienced investors and accept for them further liberalisation of the regulatory regime.

This further liberalisation of investment services regulation is in my view much more important for the development of a true Single European Capital Market than the focus on regulation which unavoidably presents and impediment to the free flow of financial services and shifts the attention to home and host competencies, the question of mutual recognition, and the issue of harmonisation of the domestic regulatory regimes, important as they are. Instead, attention should be focussed on the true impulse of market forces in the creation of this Single Market, on the way it operates, and on the type of products it offers and the way it trades. It was only modestly done at the time the present EU regime of mutual recognition of regulatory regimes was agreed. It should be done more now it is being overhauled and the idea of the Single Capital Market is put at the centre of the EU Action Plan.

Indeed, from a Single European Capital Market perspective, it may be necessary to obtain a much better feel for the proper level of liberalisation before applying present (largely domestic) regulatory accommodations in this market or engaging in re-regulation. This is also relevant when we ask ourselves whether this type of regulation should be exerted at local or European level. It concerns here in particular the issuing and underwriting activity, disclosures in that context, the authorisation to trade, the listing and reporting requirements for trading on regular and informal exchanges, the related services used in clearing, settlement and custody, and the advisory functions in brokerage and investment management.

In fact, one of the major arguments of this chapter will be that the Single European Capital Market has no substance or meaning if contemplated in isolation, therefore separately from the substantially unregulated Euro-market which is much larger and mature. Of course, an attempt could be made at bringing this Euro-market itself within the EU regulatory frame work – and this is being tried over and again –, but it would largely be futile unless done at a level of regulation that this market would accept. Indeed there is no good reason to do otherwise as this market will ultimately operate from any centre that is more efficient and cheaper and that need not be in the European Union. It was imperceptibly created and moves imperceptibly about. It means that any stricter regime for a Single European Capital Market would be unlikely to work. Building a Single European Capital Market in this manner would largely be an irrational effort. It would be drowned in the competition with the freer off-shore markets. Most importantly, there is no good reason why it should be otherwise.

In practice, it will be argued that the concept of a Single European Capital Market has at the micro level only a meaning in protecting smaller investors and in providing better access to smaller issuers. Here domestic exchanges and regulation will remain important (although it is doubtful whether these domestic exchanges can survive on the basis of these needs only). At the macro level, the Single European Capital Market has a meaning only if it can show that it can better safeguard the integrity of the markets as a whole. Here the issue is not regulation of intermediaries (whether or not necessary or appropriate) at domestic or EU level, but proper rules against abuse. To the extent these rules must be enforced by regulators, they will have to work in each market centre, therefore again largely at domestic levels.

As a consequence, the issue of a (consolidated) Single Regulator at EU level is hardly a realistic alternative and therefore no life issue, at least not in the context of a Single European Capital Market and its operation.

2   THE LIBERALISATION OF THE FLOW OF CAPITAL AND OF THE FLOW OF FINANCIAL
    SERVICES AS MAIN SUPPORTS FOR THE SINGLE EUROPEAN CAPITAL MARKET

*2.1   The distinction between the free flow of capital and of
financial services*

In the context of the Single European Capital Market, there is a significant distinction to be made between the free flow of capital (and payments) and the free flow of financial services (complimented by the freedom of establishment). These differences are well known and were also noted in the important Reinhard Gebhard case.[8] It is the distinction between the 1988 Directive[9] on the one hand and the liberalisation Directives culminating in the Second Banking Directive, now replaced by the Credit Institution Directive, and the Investment Services Directives on the other.[10]

When we talk of a Single Capital Market, we mostly talk about both. In fact, the liberalisation of the capital flows was an important pre-condition for the liberalisation of the financial services and is itself reinforced by it as was also noted in Parodi v. De Bary.[11] It is certainly true that a single financial services market is not conceivable without a free flow of capital. However, it is not the same thing and there are here two different components of the Single European Capital Market at work with very different dynamics and impediments.

The freeing of the capital flows was in essence a *true* liberalisation measure which left only a few limitations in Arts 57–60 of the EC Treaty,[12] although it makes allowance for and is without prejudice to the supervision of financial institutions (Art. 58). It still presents problems, especially in respect of the movement of investments and the taxation of savings. It appeared that the freedom to move capital was in the mind of some, especially in France and Denmark, not to imply the freedom to move investments. This concerned especially pension funds, which remain subject to many domestic restrictions that may also affect their investments in other Member States. Both the Commission's Action Plan and the Lamfalussy Report ask to deal with this issue as a matter of urgency. It is all the more appropriate now that for investments in other countries adopting the Euro at least the argument of a currency mismatch between assets and liabilities of pension funds is gone. The intention is in this connection also to extend the coverage of the UCITS Directive in order to allow a better flow of investment fund products.[13]

As far as the tax aspects are concerned, one may refer to the commotion created in London around the EU withholding tax proposals of December 1998[14] and to the

---

[8] *Reinhard Gebhard* v. *Consiglio dell' Ordine degli Avvocati e Procuratori di Milano*, European Court Case C-55/94, [1995] ECR 4165.

[9] Council Directive 88/361 EEC [1988] OJ L 178.

[10] *See* for the Second Banking Directive the Council Directive 89/646 EEC [1989] OJ L386, for the Credit Institution the Directive 2000/12/EC [2000] OJ L126 and for the Investment Services Directive the Council Directive 93/22 EEC [1993] OJ L141.

[11] Case 222/95. *Cf.* also Art. 51(2) of the EC Treaty.

[12] *See* for these limitations N. Horn, 'The Monetary Union and the Internal Market for Banking and Investment Services' (1999), EBLR 150.

[13] *See* for the UCITS Directive expansion, COM (1998) 449 final and COM (1998) 451 final, further amended by the Commission in May 2000 and finalised on December 4 2001, *see* Directive 2001/107/EC and 2001/108/EC of 21 January 2002. In the case of pension funds it is the home regulator that is the problem; in the case of the free flow of collective investment funds under UCITS it is rather the host regulator. UCITS, with its marketing limitations in other EU countries, may well have outlived its usefulness as for collective investment schemes not under it there is now a freer cross-border regime. It is essentially subject to home regulation, although for host governments there remains the general good notion to guard against clearly undesirable products in retail.

[14] Community Preparatory Act 598PC0295.

settlement for the time being of the ensuing controversies late in the year 2000. It revolves around the alternative of disclosure of investments in bonds, but depends on the co-operation that in this connection must be sought from Non-Member States to prevent capital flight. It remains uncertain whether such a co-operation can be obtained from countries like Switzerland, which do not consider foreign tax evasion a matter of their concern, nor a criminal offence. The US seems at present to incline to a similar position. This issue is in the meantime increasingly connected with money laundering which itself risks to become in this manner a tax gathering preoccupation. It is undesirable because the moral high ground will be lost which will make the necessary international co-operation in this area increasingly elusive.

The direction is, however, clear and the point seems to be increasingly accepted that the capital, investment or saving flows should not themselves be burdened by regulation or taxation but should indeed be fully free beyond monetary and liquidity considerations.[15] This is indeed crucial and regulation or withholding tax or other imposts or impediments on these flows, whether of an European Union or domestic nature, should be deleted. If not, flows will be diverted. In regulatory terms, the location of the issue and perhaps its currency might then also become a focus. In taxation terms, by taxing the flows, the non-resident investors are punished and subjected to the complicated rules and extra cost of reclaiming these taxes. This is all undesirable. Participants, be they issuers, intermediaries or even investors should bear the burdens of regulatory, tax or disclosure concerns, but not these flows themselves. Consequently, these are matters of the competent jurisdictions concerning these participants. Thus if a country does not want its citizens to invest in foreign bonds or shares, such a rule should affect them only and not the trading of these bonds or shares (in that country) in respect of citizens of other countries or professional dealers who are not end investors.

This is not to say that these flows themselves cannot at times be motivated by irrational forces, hubris, overexcitement, overconfidence, sentiment, market 'noise' and gossip, lack of skills or incompetence, or by whatever its 'invisible' hand will do. Bubbles appear as do implosions, but it is not a matter of regulation, even if rational tools existed to even out these flows. If any of these traits must be countered it should be done through the regulation of intermediaries (like traders and their analysts or accountants).

So far the freeing of the capital flows. The freeing of the financial services is on the other hand a matter *not* merely of liberalisation but also of at least some *re-regulation*. Financial services need to be regulated to some extent. One may ask which ones exactly and in how far and for what – in the investment service industry it concerns here foremost the advisory business of placement agents, brokers and asset managers – and I shall come back to this in the next part of this chapter (and

---

[15] *See* for these considerations, which were at first left to host regulator control, Art. 14 of the Second Banking Directive, superseded by Art. 27 of the Credit Institutions Directive, and Section 2.8 below. In the EU, they are now subject to the measures necessary for the reinforcement of the European Monetary System, relevant especially for the countries that joined the EURO and accepted monetary policy to be determined by the ECB within the SECB.

argue that little is needed), but the principle is generally accepted and understood. Like the (smaller) depositors in banking, investors, especially the smaller ones, need some form of protection, particularly against their brokers or advisors as well as an uncomplicated and cheap complaints facility. But also the access of smaller issuers to this market and integrity of the financial services industry as a whole are legitimate consideration.

That means trustworthiness, efficiency and openness, not only in the advisory brokerage and investment management functions but also in the market support functions, like underwriting and trading activity, clearing and settlement and custody. Regulation may, depending on the activity, lead here to an authorisation requirement and to prudential supervision of the service provider, to conduct of business rules and to a concern for the suitability of the services and products sold to investors and their nature. It may also lead to emphasis on proper segregation of client assets and to adequate complaint procedures and redress. In the market support functions, there will be further concern about price transparency, information supply, market manipulation, insider dealing, perhaps also money laundering, and especially access and monopolisation. Again, regulation should concern the service providers or perhaps the investors, never the services and their free flow themselves.[16] It should not go any further than necessary and than can be efficiently and effectively enforced.

### 2.2　The early EU response to the movement of regulated financial services and the creation of the European Passport

The regulation of investment service providers, if exercised at national levels, is an unavoidable burden on the rendering of cross-border services. I do not need to relate the early problems with it in the Community. There resulted in essence no freedom to render financial services across border on a regular basis at all, exactly because of the host regulator's imposition of its own regulatory regime which stifled the free flow in the resulting system of *dual* financial regulation (by home and host country).

*De facto*, only irregular telephone transactions with foreign clients or a relationship with those who held an account with the broker in the latter's country or in a third country were free.[17] More substantial free movement of these services (including the right of establishment in other Member States) requires in essence regulation by the *home* regulator alone and recognition of that regulation (with its authorisation and supervision if deemed necessary by the home regulator) by all host regulators. Without it, the free movement will not work short of a full unification of the regulatory system with a centralised supervisor.

This full harmonisation of regulation proved impossible to achieve in the European Union. The creation of a single regulator was therefore also improbable and never seriously considered. As was already mentioned above, it is at the practical level in any event

---

[16] In the professional Euro-market these activities have in essence always been unregulated without much inconvenience. It is necessary to encourage the fullest participation in these flows and markets, to avoid any distortions, and to achieve the best distribution of investments and savings.

[17] *See* also Art. 50 last sentence EC Treaty putting emphasis on the temporary nature of this activity.

hindered by the typical requirements of retail investor protection. In the professional market supporting functions to the extent they need to be regulated, it requires a regulatory presence close to the providers of these services.

In the European Union in the end, the solution adopted in the freeing of the flow of regulated *goods* was largely followed in the freeing of the flow of regulated financial services and became the approach in the Single European Act. It led in the area of free movement of investment services (as well as in banking and insurance) indeed to mutual recognition and acceptance of domestic authorisation and prudential supervision elsewhere in the European Union. Thus *home* regulation became the essence, subject to some minimum (although very important) harmonisation requirements mainly in the area of authorisation and capital adequacy. For the rest, regulatory competition was accepted. In this way, the *general good* exception was harnessed and effectively limited. It had earlier supported host country rule at least for the protection of smaller investors. The result was the idea of the European Passport for these services under the control of the *home* regulator of the service provider.

It still left some (unspecified) room, however, for host regulation on the basis of this general good notion. It mainly concerns host regulators' powers , especially in the areas of conduct of business and suitability of products for retail investor. This was confirmed in Art. 11(2) of the Investment Services Directive. In practice, home regulators were generally happy to accept here a host country role as they were apprehensive to supervise their own authorised firms abroad in these aspects of their activities.

The result of this system is that *branches* (not subsidiaries) of foreign financial institutions for example, in London, are subject to different authorisation and prudential regimes depending on their home regulation. As already mentioned, in practice that is more relevant for banks than investment firms, who do not normally operate abroad through branches (but rather through subsidiaries fully subject to the regulatory regime of the country of incorporation), but for them the new regime remains relevant for direct foreign services.

The regulatory competition this engendered proved healthy, allowed for diversity of ideas and an evening out of rules. Although at first it was feared that it would induce home regulators to drive requirements down to the minimum, such a race to the bottom proved an unfounded concern. Theoretically, it could have lured regulators into lowering standards in order to attract more foreign financial service providers. However, as these regulators were at the same time protecting their investors, they were little tempted.

In any event, even service providers soon learnt that they could benefit abroad from a home regulatory regime that forced greater integrity upon them. The safest under them could thus attract the greatest foreign following especially amongst the large international professional investors and pension funds. Regulatory competition could even lead to higher standards. We shall see that such an upgrading of standards occurred under competitive pressures also in the issuing activities in the unregulated Euro-markets and especially in the modern International Style Offerings where it is particularly important.

There are certainly problems with the details. The system of prior host country notification by the home regulator of services to be rendered directly by foreign service providers has been identified as an unnecessary complication.[18] The frequent subsequent charging of these foreign service providers by host regulators upon such notification even though they were no longer the prudential supervisors was the undesirable consequence, and there are problems more generally with the general good being expanded by host regulators to broaden their jurisdiction. It tends to continue a dual regulatory regime, although probably unavoidable in the retail area. Important are in this connection, the limitations imposed by European case law[19] and the Commission's Communications on the general good for the banking and insurance sectors.[20] The latter proved more an expression of concern than a set of solutions, however.

### 2.3    The reason for host regulation in the retail area and its limited adverse effect on cross-border services in the European Union

I should like to make three observations in connection with the residual host regulator function. *First*, it is not in principle unreasonable that there remain residual host country powers for financial services especially in the retail area, just as there are in the free movement of goods, in that case on the basis of public health and safety.[21] However, in order not to unduly obstruct the free movement of services, it must remain a limited concept and should only be so applied. The limitations the European Court has imposed to avoid duplication in supervision, to eliminate discrimination especially on the basis of nationality, and to impose proportionality are well known,[22] but special concern for retail investors remains here in order. Even though the *retail* investor as a group is difficult to define – another primary concern of the Lamfalussy Report[23] – it seems unavoidable that they should have some host regulator protection. This is so not so much on the basis of different cultures and

---

[18] *See* also the Commission's General Goods Communication of 1997, OJ C 209 (1997).

[19] Summarised in Dalhuisen, *op. cit. supra* note 3, 791ff and 823ff.

[20] OJ C 209 (1997) and OJ C 365 (1997).

[21] It should be noted in this connection that the general good is not itself a concept used in the EC Treaty but was thought to operate in a similar manner in respect of services, as did the reference to public policy, public security and public health and similar considerations in respect of the free movement of goods under Art. 30 and the right of establishment under Art. 46, although even in these areas it served to amplify the existing exceptions. It could become, and indeed became, relevant especially to protect smaller local savers or depositors and could thus cover whole classes of activities especially to protect against conduct of business of intermediaries and enforce transparency in the type of products offered.

[22] *See* note 19 *supra*.

[23] The Forum of European Securities Commissions (FESCO, now the Committee of European Securities Regulators (CESR)) attempted a definition in its Report of March 2000 on Categorisation of Investors for the purpose of conduct of business rules, referred to also in the Communication from the Commission on the Application of Conduct of Business Rules under Art. 11 of the Investment Services Directive of 16 November 2000, COM (2000) provisional. FESCO's basic distinction is between automatic professionals and those who are professionals upon request. Individuals may only request this status if they have 1 year professional experience in the sector, a portfolio greater than 500,000 Euro and have done 10 significant transaction per quarter for a year. The Commission still has not been able to produce its long promised Communication on the Sophisticated Investor and the ISD.

practices, which in the financial area will soon enough align, but much more on the basis of different languages and the need for local complaint procedures, enforcement action and protection of client assets. My own long experience on the SFA consumer arbitration panel in London bears this out.

These practicalities suggest a *second* point: cross-border traffic of this nature into retail has many natural limitations that have nothing to do with regulation. Regulation, although especially relevant in this retail segment of the market, is here not truly or by no means always the main impediment of the free movement of investment services across border. There are many others that are often much more prominent. It is quite obvious for example, that insuring home contents against fire and theft with an insurance company in another country is unfeasible and that insurance companies will not go out and encourage this because they are unlikely to be able to evaluate the risk. It might be different for life insurance and main industrial risks (the latter concern professional dealings, however). It also seems to be so for car insurance.

Similarly, foreign banks might not be willing to deliver specialised mortgage products in other Member States, even if common there, as they may not sufficiently know the property market in that country. In the case of complicated mortgage products, like endowment mortgages, perhaps they should not be allowed to push their own products abroad anyway and the host regulator under the general good might then quite legitimately wish to intervene. Only in that case is there a true regulatory issue, but the key point here is that the regulatory issue may never arise because foreign service providers are unlikely to be interested in that business.

For similar reasons, host regulators might not wish foreign service providers to sell derivative products into retail in their country, but again service providers themselves may not be keen to do so either, because they cannot be sure of the insolvency risk of their foreign clients. Much more interesting for them is the advisory business for larger private investors in investment management and the cross-border investment funds business. Here the home country supervision of these operators and their more regular products could be quite sufficient as the UCITS experiences also show even though in that case advertising and marketing still remain host country regulatory affairs.[24]

Online trading may overtake it all. It may not always be a good thing for retail investors as it can be addictive, but perhaps little can or should be done about it. The *'caveat emptor'* notion was never dead. Indeed it must remain the basic rule. Regulation can only protect against a limited number of risks. Investor protection, however desirable, is always a limited affair. Some protection is nevertheless afforded in the European Union under the E-commerce Directive, as we shall see shortly.

Whatever the protections or regulatory concerns and their limitation of cross border services in the European Union, the conclusion must be that as least in retail the nature of the business itself often makes cross-border selling unlikely so that the truly inhibiting factor may not be regulation at all, whether of the home or host variety, but rather

---

[24] *See* also the observations in note 13 *supra*.

practicalities. Cross-border financial services remain in fact a facility of importance especially for the professional investor or the larger private investor. Retail trans-border business is by itself marginal and I doubt whether it deserves in this connection the attention it often gets.

A *third* point of interest is in this connection the *jurisdiction issue* in respect of cross-border services rendered by telephone or electronic communication either at the initiative of the investor or service provider. If the *location of the service* is in those cases considered to be at the place of the service provider, there is strictly speaking no question of cross-border services and the home regulator would be solely competent. The question is of immediate importance for the notification requirement for cross border services which under the applicable Directives[25] must be given by the home regulator to the host regulator when one of its authorised financial service firms wants to render services abroad. It is also important for the protections investors may subsequently expect from either the competent host or home regulator.

In this connection, the EU Commission has proposed the concept of the place where the *most characteristic obligation* must be performed to determine the issue, at least for banking. It suggests largely regulation by the home regulator of the service provider but has as such not found universal support.[26] In my view, the proper and by far most simple approach in investment services and banking is to see where the customer chooses to keep his account. Is that with the service provider in the latter's country, then the relationship must be considered to be in the home country of the service provider and there is no cross-border service. Such accounts will normally be opened at the request of the customer. Naturally, the opening of this relationship itself may be due to distance selling which may be made subject to some cooling-off period as far as the original client agreement is concerned but since it can normally be terminated at will this would seem hardly relevant.[27]

An entirely different matter is how such an account is subsequently handled especially in foreign investments, which raises the spectre of double fees etc., but this will be a matter foremost of the home regulator, also the complaint procedures. That is in that case the client's choice. Does the service provider on the other hand service his client in the host country and keeps the accounts there, then there would be a cross-border service and the ISD comes into play. As already mentioned several times, it will be rare in retail unless the service provider establishes a fuller branch organisation in the host country. In that case in investment services, normally a subsidiary is the preferred vehicle (subject to full host regulation). If the account is

---

[25] *See* Arts 20 and 21 Credit Institutions Directive and Arts 17(4) and 18(3) Investment Services Directive, *see* for this requirement also text at note 18 *supra*.

[26] *See* the Commission's Communication referred to in note 20 *supra*, *see* for alternatives Dalhuisen, *op. cit. supra* note 2, 821. The concept of the characteristic performance has left some observers unconvinced, mostly because of its drift towards full home regulation by rendering many transactions with international contacts purely domestic in nature. It would at least reduce the need for notification considerably and thus limit paper work for notification purposes, *see* for the usefulness of this notification and the doubts in this respect text at note 18.

[27] *See* also note 30 *infra* and accompanying text.

handled in a third country (through an agent or otherwise), it could be argued that the protections of that country should prevail.

## *2.4   Electronic trading and distance selling*

There are many ways in which electronic trading can be achieved.[28] In the primary market, in the US a difference is made between the bulletin and crossing method. In the first one, the issuers allow trading in their shares or bonds on their home page and they will look after settlement. For companies to do this, they need SEC approval. Foreign companies if accessed by US investors fall outside this supervision. The other method is the crossing method where an intermediary operates a matching system, which is normally connected to the established exchanges for settlement.

A simpler way of electronic dealing is on-line contact with a (discount) broker who will execute the trades and take care of settlement and custody in the required manner, whilst accessing himself to (either electronically or in other ways) the primary or secondary markets and its participants.

Cross-border contact is much facilitated in this manner. As just mentioned, American investors could access the home page of foreign companies in the bulletin method of electronic trading. Foreign investors may access American crossing systems. Discount brokers everywhere may be accessed on-line by foreign clients. From a regulatory point of view, the applicable regime will be foremost that of the *accessed party*. That party is likely to also make clear the conditions for payment and settlement. It leads to home regulation of the issuers, if directly accessed, or of the intermediaries or service providers, except if the notion of regulation at the place of the characteristic performance is accepted which is, as we saw, likely to lead to a similar result. In truth, no cross-border service results and in the European Union the home–host country regulatory framework would not come into play.

Within the European Union, this is indeed the approach sanctioned by the 2000 E-commerce Directive,[29] which deals with information society services. It also covers security trading on the Internet, although it was clearly not the main focus, which was to give legitimacy to all types of contracts concluded by electronic means (Recital 38). In this connection, e-commerce and internet trading are synonymous. Under Art. 3, the supervision of the (home) country of the accessed service provider applies to these services. There is an exception only if consumer protection is the issue whilst there is a great risk of impairment. Any host regulator measures taken in that connection

---

[28] *See* Dalhuisen, *op. cit. supra* note 3, 750.

[29] Directive On Certain Legal Aspects of Electronic Commerce in the Internal Market, 2000/31/EC, [2000] OJ L 178, adopted on 8 June 2000 to be incorporated in domestic laws not later than 17 June 2002. *See* also Guido Alpa, 'Trading On-line and the Protection of the Consumer' (2001) 12 *European Business Law review*, 244. Earlier IOSCO had formulated Principles of Regulation in Securities Activity on the Internet, Report by the Technical Committee (September 1998). The Directive whilst opting in essence for home country supervision does not go into this. It is intended to be completed by two further Directives: one on marketing of financial services on line (working document 6 October 2000 CONSOM/00/14) and one on liability of service providers.

must remain proportionate, however, after the home regulator has been asked to take the adequate measures first but fails to do so. The EU Commission must be informed.

It is another expression of the general good notion, which for financial services through e-commerce now falls outside the home/host regulator system of the ISD. The approach is therefore different from that of Art. 11 ISD in favour of a more unitary regime of the e-commerce service provider, also in respect of his financial products and their suitability.

As just mentioned, the reason is that the European Union does not truly see here cross-border service activity. Notification to the home regulator followed by the latter's notification to the host regulator is therefore also not necessary. There is no passport either which means that *branches* of Non-EU service providers in the European Union could also be accessed in this manner through e-commerce under home country rule. In this system, the host regulator's powers may remain relevant only in respect of active marketing of the service to retail on its territory, in which area a further E-commerce Directive is contemplated.

The emphasis is again different in the proposal for a EU Directive on Distance Selling of Consumer Financial Services, which is especially directed at consumer investors.[30] It is limited to the opening of the relationship and does not cover (follow-up) transactions. It has some basic requirements for the client agreement and notably limits the choice of law of a Non-Member country. The main protection is here the right of reflection and withdrawal during a short period. It would seem implied in the nature of a brokerage or investment management relationship that can be terminated at will. It is different for loan agreements and insurance policies. Transactions entered into in the mean time are not affected.

### 2.5   Investors protection in the EU

This may be the appropriate place to consider investment protection as a concept within the European Union. As we already saw, it may give rise to particular issues of regulatory protection, especially of the smaller retail investor. In that case it concerns the protection by the own (host) regulator under the notion of the general good whether or not elaborated (and thereby mostly curtailed) in the relevant directives like ISD, UCITS, the E-commerce Directive, and the Distance Selling Directive.

Investors protection is a more *general* subject when it concerns the providing of basic facilities and the integrity of the market. It is a more *specific* subject when it comes to the protection of individual investors, especially the smaller ones against their brokers in terms of conduct of business, suitability of product and proper segregation of client assets. In this connection, sometimes a distinction is made between *macro* and *micro* investors protection. There is clearly a regulatory task in respect of both. This task is in either instance quite different. In the macro approach, the supervision and punishment may be the focus whilst broader policy motives (like

---

[30] COM (1998) 468 final, amended in July 1999, COM (1999) 385 final.

systemic risk and market integrity) may dominate.[31] In the micro approach, it is a question of direct recourse against any perpetrators and damages for the injured party.[32]

Especially at the micro level, the regulation is for retail mainly of a domestic nature, therefore host regulation in respect of a foreign service provider as we saw. It is s such an expression of the general good notion and a likely impediment to the free flow of financial services, within the EU subject to the overriding notion of free movement. It should in this respect be noted that small investors' protection as such never found expression in EU treaties. This is quite different from the concept of consumer protection, which is now enshrined in Arts 3(t) and 153(3)(b) of the EC Treaty. There is as yet no equivalent for (small) investors' or even depositors' protection. It would therefore not seem that the consumer protection ethos extends to them.[33] Their special needs can only become recognised on the basis of the public or general good within host regulation. Without a stronger base in the Treaty, it must remain a limited concept in order not to obstruct the free movement of services altogether. Consequently, it is largely restricted to retail protections and even then depends on the complexities of the product and the sophistication of the individual investor.[34]

This concern for the free movement of financial services may easily be seen as the reason for the Commission's nervousness about the impact of the general good notion,[35] the emphasis on the place of the characteristic performance in order to determine the location of the service favouring home regulation, and the emphasis on the regulation at the place of the service provider in the E-commerce Directive. This is a concern, perhaps to a lesser extent, shared by the European Court but the Court is in charge of testing general good notions and has limited them, if not themselves already restrained by the texts of the various EU Directives in the field, in which connection it cannot be stressed enough that the general good exception cannot be used to circumvent the free movement rules specifically laid down at EU level.[36]

Although the emphasis on the free flows implies a liberalisation ethos, technically, the basic freedoms are compatible with regulation as long as the flows are not affected. That would be the case if regulation were centralised at EU level. As already

---

[31] *See* also the Prudential Supervision Directive, 95/26/EC, OJ l 84/22 (1997).

[32] Except for the modest effort in Art. 11 ISD, Art. 3 of the E-commerce Directive, the references to marketing and advertising in the UCITS Directive, and some further rules in the forthcoming Distance Selling Directive, there are no particular EU rules concerning investors' protection at the micro level.

[33] The Commission rejected the use of the overriding consumer protection in support of the Distance Market Proposal in its reply to the European Parliament, COM (1999) 385, 1.

[34] *See* the fundamental case of *Commission v. Germany*, European Court Case C-205/84, [1986] ECR 3755, which strictly speaking did not define the retail class but concerned itself rather with the type of products.

[35] *See* note 18 and accompanying text.

[36] *See* also C. Cruikshank, 'Co-operation and Convergence: The View from Brussels' in F. Oditah (ed.), *The Future for the Global Securities Market – legal and Regulatory Aspects* (1996) p. 268 noting also that so far the EU has mainly focussed on issuers and intermediaries, not therefore on investors.

mentioned, such regulation has so far never been attempted. There has only been harmonisation of domestic approaches in certain areas (like authorisation and prudential supervision requirements and sometimes in the area of conduct of business and product control) in order to safeguard the mutual recognition process concerning domestic regulation.

As such, it found a natural basis in Art. 47(2) of the EC Treaty. Any more, it will be argued, is unlikely to be successful for retail and is hardly justified for professionals. There is also much less of a basis for it in the Treaty, although Arts 55, 94 and 95 could be used in support, as was done for the E-commerce Directive and the Distance Marketing Directive, in which connection the subsidiarity doctrine of Art. 5 was, however, also considered (as is now being done in Recital 6 of the E-commerce Directive and in Recital 11 of the Distance Marketing proposal).

It is right to note in this connection that the division between home and host regulation – therefore the notion that financial regulation remains a domestic matter – at the same time functions as a *barrier* against over-regulation. This by itself could be an argument to retain this system. In other words, regulation at EU level would not be free flow intrusive and as such be subject to fewer limitations. There is constant tension here as, in the mindset of many, regulation is a good thing *per se* and therefore better handled at EU level even to the point of full re-regulation. Most importantly, it also provides a framework for *regulatory competition* and therefore for the dissemination of ideas and practices ion the view of different needs.

### 2.6 Special risks in international securities dealings. Regulatory response

In international transactions, the more limited and justified concerns for retail investors are the increase of their risk through the increase of their investment options in international transactions, their difficulties to protect themselves in view of the diversification of protection rules in foreign operations, and their problems in accessing the available complaint facilities. Core standards for conduct of business or their progressive full harmonisation may not truly or at least not fully address these issues even if the Commission appears to think so at the moment.[37] Neither would regulation centralised at EU level.

The extra risk inherent in trans-border financial activities is seldom separately analysed in legal writings and solicits equally seldom a special regulatory response, but are very important if we mean to promote these flows also in respect of smaller investors. The problems centre mainly around an assessment by investors who want to invest in other countries of:

(a) market access and liquidity,
(b) market transparency especially as to its functioning (including clearing and settlement) and prices, and
(c) extra costs of dealing,

---

[37] 1999 Communication on Implementing the Framework for Financial markets: Action Plan COM (1999) 232, 8.

(d)  the nature of the foreign financial product,

(e)  the nature of the relationship with the foreign intermediaries, and

(f)  the type of regulatory and private law protection elsewhere.

Thus there may be *extra country*, *legal* and *operational* risks.

These problems are from a regulatory point of view normally dealt with as a matter of domestic regulation of the service provider, therefore within his concept of 'suitability' and 'know your customer'. The service provider operates either in the country of the investor using corresponding brokers in the country of investment, or the service provider operates in the country of the investment being directly accessed by the investor. In the latter case it is unlikely that host country rule applies. Even if it does, a foreign broker can hardly know what his client's perspective and perceptions are. In other words, if a foreign intermediary operates in his own market and buys products alien to his retail client but totally normal for the intermediary, it may be that even under applicable host regulation (therefore under the rules of the investor) there is no special protection. It remains therefore the task of the investor to assess how, under the rules concerning his intermediary (in the other country or even in his own) or the market he accesses, he is likely to be extra exposed.

It shows the limit of host regulator protection or general good notions of the host country covering retail investors in the case of foreign investments. Naturally the extra risk and costs are for the investor but in terms of risk and cost warnings he may not be able to expect a lot. Domestic protections thus become much less relevant in dealing with an investor who seeks the services of a foreign broker to deal in foreign securities. Above in Section 2.3, it was already said that for practical reasons the foreign service provider is not so likely to want to serve this client in his own country anyway. Indeed he may want that client to keep an account with him so that in practice there is no host protection at all whilst the extra risks for the investor are not considered under the home regulation at all.

A broker in the investor's country who deals with foreign corresponding brokers to acquire foreign securities for his domestic client might be in a different position and have to assess extra risk and cost for his (retail) client, not the least in terms of extra fees. The cost may be higher than accessing a foreign broker, as there will be extra fees for correspondent brokers, but there may also be more protection in terms of suitability.

### 2.7   *Administrative and private law issues in financial regulation. Internationalisation of private law*

There is another important point that needs to be raised. The proper implementation of the EU Directives, in particular of the Investment Services Directive in the area of conduct of business and to a lesser extent of the prudential rules has created particular challenges in terms of reshaping local agency (seen as a conduct of business or host country concern in Art. 11 ISD) and segregation rules (seen as a prudential or home country issue in Art. 10 ISD). The problems are here to a large extent in the adjustment of *private* law in Member States which adjustment has not really taken place.

I emphasise here the peculiar and vital aspect of the necessity of *private* law harmonisation, particularly important in investment services. It is commonly overlooked in this connection. We think of regulation normally as an *administrative* law matter as indeed it is in the aspect of authorisation and mostly of prudential supervision, but not or not necessarily in the area of conduct of business and segregation or in the nature and legal characterisation of the investment products. As for the brokerage function is concerned, which operates under the law of agency, I only need to refer to the uncertainties in Civil Law as to the fiduciary and postponement duties in indirect agency and, as far as segregation is concerned, to the problems with tracing and constructive trust.

This being said, it should be realised that the re-enforcement of these concepts within the context of financial regulation lends some public law flavour to private law concepts. They may become mandatory as a consequence, could not then easily be set aside by the parties or be made subject to the election of a particular private law, especially of a Non-Member States, if it detracts from them, at least not in respect of retail investors located in the European Union. Normal choice of law or private international law rules are then also unlikely to apply. Nonetheless, the further evolution and harmonisation of these private law concepts would remain a matter of private law and recovery on the basis of them would in principle be through private actions (before the courts, compulsory arbitrators or ombudsmen) in terms of damages and not through administrative remedies.

These private law aspects thus remain of great importance and also arise in a most important manner in the types of investment products on offer and in their nature and transferability. To take an important example: company shares may be of very different types and are in any event products of national company laws and could differ greatly, especially in the aspect of negotiability or transferability and the way they are transferred.

The application of private law presents here a special opportunity. In the private law sphere, there is an innate unifying dynamic force at work inspired by internationalisation and globalisation. In the case of modern book-entry systems and entitlements for example, it presents an innate opportunity for equalisation, even though the law applicable to these book-entry systems is often still perceived to be a domestic one depending on where the registry is located, even though this location is often entirely fortuitous as for example, the location of Euroclear in Brussels. Indeed Art. 9(2) of the Finality Directive[38] still subscribes to this domestic solution.

However, earlier the traditional Eurobond as a bearer instrument was considered a trans-national instrument subject to the rules of the market in which it was traded.[39] It was also subject to the collateral rights and *bona fide* purchaser protections that obtained in that market. There is no reason why the same should not be true in principle also for these newer book-entry system entitlements. That should certainly be so in the Eurobond market and preferably also for all securities that may trade

---

[38] 98/26/EC [1998] OJ L166.
[39] *See* also Dalhuisen, *op. cit. supra* note 3, 107.

internationally. We should not forego the opportunity of *market induced* uniformity when it presents itself.[40]

Here are autonomous market forces at work resulting in important harmonisation on the basis of industry practices and needs. They have become the true initiators and motivators in this connection and allow the law to accommodate the legitimate requirements of the industry. They are likely at the same time to protect the investor better, as they always did in the case of bearer Eurobonds. That protection is in the very best interest of that market itself. There is no virtue here in the continuation of the dominance of national laws. They only serve to divide the market.

### 2.8    *Monetary restrictions on the movement of financial services*

In Section 2.1 above, other aspects of the re-regulation of the financial service providers were mentioned, like capital market considerations and monetary policy. Monetary policy and liquidity issues remain matters for home regulators under the Second Banking Directive now replaced by Art. 27 Credit Institutions Directive, always without prejudice to the new system of monetary policy created for the Euro.[41] They are closely connected with monetary policy, which remains also national to the extent not transferred to the ECB in those countries that take part in the Euro.

Monetary policy considerations have always been used by host regulators to keep an eye on bond issuing activity in their own currency. At least in part this was done in order not to allow this activity to move to other markets (notably not to the Eurobond market), in fact often to protect the own investment banks involved in this business even after the liberalisation directives. With the ascent of the Euro that should be less of a problem in respect of underwriting activity in other countries that adopted the Euro, but it could still play a role in respect of underwriting in Euro denominated issues in London. It was a major abuse, in this case induced by national Central Banks who wanted to keep the underwriting activity in their own currency bonds at home.

### 2.9    *The impact of the Euro-market and the relationship between this market and a Single European Capital Market. International Style Offerings*

In the above, the Euro-market has already been mentioned several times and it needs further consideration in the context of the discussion of a Single European Capital Market. The Euro-market (not related to the Euro currency which is only one of the currencies that can be used in the bond issuing activity in the Euro-market) is all around us and forms a true international capital market that almost imperceptibly became the largest in the world.

---

[40] *See* Dalhuisen, *op. cit. supra* note 3, 558 ff.
[41] *See* note 15 *supra*.

It developed autonomously since 1963, has its own issuing, underwriting and trading activity and market practices and functions subject to its own rules or recommendations in IPMA and ISMA, its own clearing and settlement in Euroclear and Clearstream, and has its own type of instrument: the trans-national Eurobond already referred to. Swap and repo activities in this market are supported by industry swap master agreements.[42]

This market is and remains in principle unregulated, even if pursuant to the ISD intermediaries located in EU countries can no longer escape an authorisation and supervision requirement if involved in underwriting or trading of whatever kind. Generally, the freedom from regulation in this market never caused great problems, not even when the Belgian Dentist as retail investor was the main investor. Retail is now marginalised in this market, which has become mainly a market for professional investors. It was always limited to the better credits as issuers. It does not often suffer major defaults and remains the foremost example of the own creative and liberalising forces in capital markets. It has shown that this type of deregulation is not investor protection adverse.

It also suggests that regulation itself is not instrumental *per se* in maintaining market integrity and is not indispensable in terms of investment protection, at least not in important segments of the financial markets, especially if targeted at professional investors. There is no reason to assume this to be any different in a Single European Capital Market. In fact, it is unlikely that the wholesale or professional sector of this market can be wholly distinguished from the Euro-markets. It is not necessary either. Only in the retail segment or in respect of smaller issuers might it be different, even though the Euro-market, in its infancy depending on them, did not disappoint. To put it another way, the Single European Capital Market may at most have a separate existence and regulatory need in respect of smaller investors and issuers and re-regulation would then mainly be relevant in that segment of the market only.

International (Style) Offerings[43] represent a special part of this international market (although they may have trenches in domestic markets) and mainly concern the placement of new share (not normally bond) issues across Europe or even into Asia and, to the extent permissible there, into the United States. Outside the home country of the issuer, these issues conform to *market standards* and tend not to be subject to any kind of domestic regulation.[44] On the other hand, there may be a regulatory choice if the issuer wants to issue in a particular domestic market (in whole or in part). In the International Style Offering, there is, in American terms, much similarity with

---

[42] *See* for the Swap Master, Dalhuisen, *op. cit supra* note 3, 773 and for the Repo Master, Dalhuisen, *op. cit. supra* note 1, 694. *See* for the international legal status of these underwriting and trading rules, Dalhuisen, *op. cit. supra* note 3, 111.

[43] *See* E. Greene, A. Beller, G. Cohen, M. Hudson, Jr., and E. Rosen, *US Regulation of the International Securities Markets*, 6.01, 6.02.

[44] H.E. Jackson and E.J. Pan, 'Regulatory Competition in International Securities Markets: Evidence from Europe in 1999 – Part I' (2001) *The Business Lawyer*, 653; *cf.* also S. Woolcock, 'Competition among Rules in the Single European Market' in W. Bratton *et al.* (eds), *International Regulatory Competition and Coordination* (1996), p. 292.

a private (share) placement targeted at professional investors. If a true Euro-market offering, there need not be a proper prospectus in the format as required under the EU Public Offer Prospectus Directive. Listing on domestic stock exchanges may still follow, however, and is common in order to reach retail or investment funds that may only invest in publicly quoted stock. In that case, the rules concerning domestic listing requirements with their need for a prospectus and the facility of reciprocal recognition of this prospectus will apply. This recognition may also cover the initial Public Offer Prospectus if the issue is subsequently listed on a regular domestic exchange. Below in Section 3.3, I shall come back to the existing European Directives in this area, which are now largely out of date, to be replaced by a new Prospectus Directive.

### 3   REGULATION IN THE SINGLE EUROPEAN CAPITAL MARKET

#### 3.1   What is the role of regulation in a Single European Capital Market? Investors protection and market integrity

I now turn to the second part of my topic. What do or should we regulate in a Single European Capital Market and how? If we look at the different financial functions in the area of investment services in a *functional* manner we have:

1. In the *primary* market:
   (a) issuers and issuing activity, questions of transparency of their operations, the financial products they offer, and their access to the capital markets,
   (b) underwriters and underwriting activity,
   (c) market integrity and especially the role of stabilisation (in grey markets), and
   (d) placement with investors, the role of placement agents (often the underwriters), and the protection of investors (especially in retail) in respect of conduct of business and suitable products (much like in the secondary market, see below)
2. In the *secondary* market
   (a) sale and purchase of securities, the role of brokers and investment managers (advisory services) and investors' protection (again especially in retail) against poor advice, conflicts of interest like competition with the broker for the best investments, proper segregation of investors' assets, realistic charges for the services rendered, and especially against churning or unnecessary charges for investments in other countries or untransparent foreign exchange costs
3. In *all* markets (whether official or non-official) we have to consider also:
   (a) efficiency of the market systems in official or unofficial markets, questions of transferability of securities or book-entry entitlements,
   (b) price transparency and information supply
   (c) role of, need for, and details of admission/listing and reporting requirements in official or perhaps also unofficial exchanges

(d) clearing, settlement and custody, proper protection of investors money and assets, speedy settlement, and safe custody of securities

(e) issues of efficiency and costs

(f) issues of market power, monopolies and access, and

(g) market integrity (no market manipulation, insider dealings or money laundering)

Some of these areas overlap and there may be more functions and concerns but these are the major ones. What are we or should we be doing about them?

I revert to a basic remark made in Section 2.1 in connection with the free flow of capital and increasingly of investments. In respect of the flow of financial services, especially in brokerage and advice, and in respect of the market support functions, especially in formal or informal exchanges, clearing and settlement and custody, we should not try to regulate these processes themselves, therefore not these flows and the services themselves, therefore not the markets and market systems, information supply, clearing and custodial services as such. At most, we should regulate *participants*, therefore issuers, service providers or intermediaries where it matters and sometimes also investors, the latter especially for taxation and, if necessary, investment restrictions, always subject to proper regulatory or tax jurisdiction having been exercised.

In doing so we should foremost try to eliminate or minimise the effect of some externalities, like market manipulation, insider dealing and anti-competitive behaviour *without* regulation of the market processes themselves, although, as for market integrity, proper price reporting and information supply could also be legitimate regulatory issues.

For the rest, we habitually concentrate only on certain participants for certain activities. We should only fully regulate certain intermediaries like the placement agents in the primary market, or brokers and investment managers in the secondary markets in respect of services to small investors. It means prior authorisation and prudential supervision, much like for commercial banks. The difference is that in investment services there is more in particular concern for conduct of business, suitability of products, segregation and complaint procedures, therefore for investment protection at the *micro level* and then more especially for retail investors. Thus prior authorisation and prudential supervision need here be considered *per function* and according to demonstrated need.

A most important question is in this connection whether, how or to what extent the issuers, underwriters and dealers should be fully more fully regulated also. Another question is in how far the market support functions, like clearing, settlement and custody, should be affected by such regulation as well and to what extent. This concerns not merely concern small investors but could be also a matter of market integrity or investors protection at the *macro level*. It should be recalled in this connection that, in the Alpine Investment case, the notion of the general good was used to widen the home regulators discretion in the regulation of intermediaries operating from its territory in respect of cold calling of prospective clients generally, therefore also those in other Member States, because of its reputational effect on the (domestic) market. This became not merely a question of authorisation and prudential supervision but of an outright prohibition of certain activities. In this connection reference was made to market integrity in view of the speculative nature of the product even in respect of calls to foreign professional investors, regardless therefore of the effect on the free flow of financial services.[45]

In its generality, this is obviously an important issue, but the Alpine Investment case may not entirely convince. As was already mentioned in connection with the operations of the Euro-market, markets have always been able to police themselves assuming they are open and subject to competition. They are and have proven in a major way to be able to provide adequate safeguards in this connection for their trading members and professional investors without regulation of issuers, under-writes and market makers, the providers of other support functions, including clearers, or even brokers. That is an important fact. On the coattails of the professionals and their choices of intermediaries, the investing public at large may also find some important protection.

Regulatory restraint is here possible and desirable unless specific needs can be identified. In a EU context it is all the more necessary in order to avoid any dual regulation or other regulatory complications resulting in an effect on the free flow of financial services. Hence the preference, or indeed the need within the Single European Capital Market for a minimalist or at least a clearly focussed approach to regulation in order for this market to acquire any real meaning at all.

### 3.2   Retail protection and the regulation of the underwriting, trading and market support functions in a Single European Capital Market

It is clear that the advisory services and brokerage functions need a minimum of regulation to protect in particular the smaller investor against their brokers and advisors in order to avoid conflicts of interests and to safeguard client assets and money, even if in the Euro-market this was never a problem when it was still mainly a small investors' market. Seen from this perspective, regulation is mainly a smaller investor protection issue and a limited concept, although that may be different for the segregation function, which, however, requires, as we saw in Section 2.7, a solution in private law rather than through regulation.

It was already asked in the previous section whether we should in this connection not only regulate the primary and secondary advisory and brokerage functions (through authorisation and prudential supervision), but also the underwriters, market makers or matching agents, information providers, clearers and custodians, even if we assume (as we should) that underwriting activity and markets (official, informal or over the counter), information supply, clearing and custody itself are allowed to develop according to market forces in a competitive environment. Yet, should the intermediaries or participants in these activities still be supervised, and if so to what extent and how?

---

[45] *Alpine Investments BV v. Minister van Financien*, European Court Case C-384/93 [1995] ECR 1-1141.

In underwriting and trading there would not appear much reason for regulatory concern. Of course, if these activities were done in commercial banks there would have to be some extra capital since there would be increased (position rather than counter-party) risk and therefore a greater chance of systemic risk (if one believes that regulatory capital as we have it ever prevents bank insolvencies and reduces systemic risk as a consequence). On a stand-alone basis, that risk would hardly seem to exist in investment banks. It was the basic philosophy at the time behind the Glass Steagall Act's separation between banking and underwriting business. The Baring's and Drexel insolvencies, which never gave rise to public support, bear this point out. In any event, the insolvency of underwriters and market makers hardly affects the investor. Trades on the day may be lost but this seldom spells disaster as underwriters and market makers do not handle client assets or moneys or, if they do, should have segregated them properly (provided the applicable private law supports it), so that these are not in danger. Reputational risk seems also limited, especially where only professional investors are targeted.

Where the market system is computerised matching, it is even more difficult to see why there needs to be regulation *per se*. Again, in the Euro-market, there never was any regulation of these functions or their operators and this has not led to serious problems. If we now think it must be different in a Single European Capital Market because it always was different in the official domestic exchanges, that is hardly a conclusive argument.

Nevertheless, the Investment Services Directive (Art. 3 ISD and Annex 1) still requires intermediaries in both in dealing and underwriting to be authorised and supervised and that now also concerns Euro-market underwriters and dealers to the extent they operate from a Member State. The benefit is that their underwriting and dealing activities into other countries will be covered by the European Passport. On the other hand, even *de minimis* foreign telephone dealings now would seem to require that Passport. It would therefore apply to any promotion of these services elsewhere in the European Union which for market making may mean no more than occasional contact with other market makers or brokers in other Member States, even if the initiative may make here a difference.[46]

On the other hand, the system of the ISD is that any one who is authorised as a dealer may do so and thus create an *unofficial* market. These markets are themselves *not* regulated; only the intermediaries are. That is indeed the right approach as far as market activity is concerned and the Directive follows here the British example. The only material obligation is for them the requirement under Art. 20 to report prices in their home state. That is also the requirement in the United Kingdom where recognised exchanges may have here a delegated function and act as price reporters for such informal trades.

The ISD approach to *official* or regulated markets is, on the other hand, very different and still based on the idea of regulation of markets as such in the context of national stock exchanges with some kind of national monopoly. In this connection,

---

[46] *See* note 27 and accompanying text.

Arts 14, 15, 16 and 21 ISD are of special interest. Art. 21 sets common standards for trade reporting and price transparency in these *regulated* markets which are so broad, however, that they are unlikely to promote much uniformity. Otherwise there are no substantive rules concerning the operation of the official markets, except that all investment firms with a Passport have the right to access them and to clearing and settlement systems if separate (Art. 15(1)). Indirectly, it may be concluded from Art. 15(4)[47] that these exchanges benefit themselves also from a European Passport as authorised investment firms elsewhere may access them whilst these markets may in turn provide the appropriate facilities in the home states of these firms (assuming that they operate without any requirement for a physical presence in their own state). It allows members located in other EU countries to trade on these regulated exchanges. This would not appear to be possible on the informal ones.

A move to give these regulated markets an official monopoly in respect of trading of their listed securities in respect of clients resident in the country of these exchanges (the concentration principle) was even accepted in principle in Art. 14(3), subject, however, to investors being able to opt out of this in Art. 14(4). It is an issue that raises its head, however, over and again.

So far the system for regulated or informal markets under the ISD. *Clearing and settlement* are not covered by this Directive as core activity (Annex C and Art. 14(1), see for access to these facilities Preamble 35 and Art. 15(1)) and have also never thrown up problems of a nature to suggest that regulation *per se* is advisable, not even where they operate on a stand alone basis, therefore separate from formal stock exchanges in competition with others, like Euroclear and Clearstream. In modern clearing, we have netting and margining and sometimes the guarantee of a central counter-party to guard against insolvency risk, all private arrangements in these organisations. Should insolvency ever be a problem, clearing members will be called upon to organise a lifeboat.[48]

It is true that there are important issues concerning the way forward: a European-wide central counter-party perhaps?[49] It might make all exchanges as we know them today redundant. Should there be competition or one public utility open to all? At present, the cost of clearing and settlement remains exorbitant in Europe, seven times that in the United States it is sometimes claimed. Perhaps someone should give here more direction and a push, and that could be the European Union as facilitator, but it is unlikely that modern regulators have here much of an inspiring view of their own

---

[47] *See* B. Steil, 'Equity Trading IV: The ISD and the Regulation of European Market Structure' in B. Steil (ed.), *The European Equity Markets. The State of the Union and an Agenda for the Millennium* (1996), p. 129. *See* also K.J. Hopt, 'Zum Begriff des geregelten Marktes nach dem Wertpapierdienstleistungsrichtlinie' in N. Horn *et al.* (eds), *Bankrecht – Schwerpunkte und Perspectiven, Festschrift Schimanski* (1999), p. 638.

[48] *See* for how this works, Dalhuisen, *op. cit. supra* note 3, 769 ff.

[49] *See* for an interesting discussion of the development of this notion of a central counter-party, R.S. Krozner, 'Can the Financial Markets Privately Regulate Risk? The Development of Derivatives Clearing Houses and Recent Over-the-Counter Innovations' (November 1999) *Journal of Money, Credit and Banking.*

or the power to enforce change. Rightly, the Lamfalussy Report accepts here market forces. More competition is the key.

The regular information supply is another important function and now also often offered by private companies well separated from existing exchanges. Again, there is no suggesting that this does not work without regulation.[50]

### 3.3 The issuing activity and the European Prospectus, Admission, Listing and Regular Reporting Directives

Whatever the ISD approach to underwriting and trading, there is no need *per se* for regulation in these areas. Personally, I cannot see why the *issuing* activity remains so strongly controlled either. In the United States, the SEC remains wedded to the registration requirement (including the need to present a prospectus) which is there holy writ. Any questioning of it is soon equated with favouring fraud, but, especially in the school of 'law and economics', this questioning has become common and not without good reason. The SEC is much set in its ways[51] probably because it has to face strong interest groups.

Yet, regulatory competition and a free choice of issuing regime could be a more sensible approach even in the United States.[52] Depending on that choice, it could mean virtually deregulation, if a more relaxed issuing regime can be chosen. In any event, whether the registration practice in the United States has really made all the difference and whether therefore regulation is here a better way than relying in essence on the sophistication of the professional investor and on market forces (signalling through the price mechanism acceptance or rejection of issuer and issue) has never been established beyond doubt. Most certainly many attach too much value to it and also overlook the delays and costs. As a result, even in the United States private placement exceptions cover ever more ground.

---

[50] The Financial Times of 19 January 2001 reported that Regulatory News Service (RNS) of the London Stock Exchange would be subjected by the FSA to competition of two American information providers: PR Newswire and Business Wire, to make regulatory company announcements subject to FSA standards. Companies would be required to pay for using their services.

[51] *See* for criticism of the patchwork approach and the reluctance of fundamental rethinking, M.H. Wallman, 'Competition, Innovation, and Regulation in the Securities' Markets' (1998) 53 *The Business Lawyer*, 341.

[52] There is an increasing literature on this subject, *see* H.E. Jackson and E.J. Pan, *op. cit. supra* note 43. Their research in Europe points to free markets and competition leading to *higher* voluntary disclosure (and increased cost) with the prospect of a greater proceeds. Regulatory competition and issuers choice of regulatory alternatives is another approach, *see* R. Romano, 'Empowering Investors: A Market Approach to Securities Regulation (1998) 107 Yale LJ 2359 and S. Choi and A. Guzman, 'Portable Reciprocity: Rethinking the International Reach of Securities Regulation' (1998) 71 S. Cal L Rev 903. *See* earlier, for serious doubts on the fairness and efficiency of mandatory disclosure systems, F. Easterbrook and O. Fischel, 'Mandatory Disclosure and the Protection of Investors' (1984) 70 Va LR 669 with a response from John C. Coffee, 'Market Failure and the Economic Case for a Mandatory Disclosure System' (1984) 70 Va LR 717. The true questioning of the traditional regulatory attitudes in the US goes back to Stigler, 'Public Regulation of the Securities Markets' (1964) 37 J Bus 117.

A prospectus requirement remains of course reasonable for public issues and is also in the issuers' interest to get their issues going and make them a success. Due diligence is in this connection of no less importance, nor is regular reporting of market sensitive issuer information thereafter, but at least for the professional investor the world has moved on from the 1930s in terms of financial reporting, communication speed, rating agencies and security analysts. Professionals have their own ways of evaluating issues and will evaluate new issues accordingly and are not primarily or at least not only moved by the official prospectus. They make the markets; retail will take its prices from them. It is an enormous implicit protection for the smaller investor. Of course, investors, even professionals, are subject to fashions and psychological hype. They like to sue on the basis of the prospectus when something goes wrong, whether or not as a result of their own misjudgement, and will vet them at that moment for clues, but one may well wonder how to the point this really still is.

Surely in the modern world, professionals must have some investigation duties themselves at the time the issue is brought or indeed ask for proper information if they are not certain. They also have their own analysts or can pay for analyst assessments. If they are no good, they have only got themselves to blame. They also can rely on rating agencies. As published accounts can only too easily be the subject of creative accounting, as the Enron disaster helps to remind us, here again own or independent research must be the answer, short of nationalising the rating agencies and the creation of an independent investigating office within the regulator that publicises its own ratings.

In the European Union, we have in connection with issuing activity the already mentioned Public Offer Prospectus Directive for all public issues whether or not listed, from which requirement Euro-market issues remain exempt. For them, the market still decides what is required in terms of information supply. This is often preciously little as the regular issuers in that market are very well known. They are usually states or state agencies, major banks or large corporations. More important is regular reporting of market sensitive developments in the issuer, especially if a corporate body. The requirement remains in the European Union wedded to listing on the official stock exchanges. For the official admission and listing on those exchanges, there is in the European Union yet another prospectus requirement.[53]

Here one may well ask whether in view of the many informal trading possibilities these uniform admission and listing requirements remain relevant at all. Why not leave them to each official market and its own conditions for listing or admission including a facility to recognise other listings and admit on the basis of it? The tendency is indeed in the direction of a passport as we saw bit only within a limited

---

[53] *See* for the details also G. Thieffrey and R. Brooks, 'The Law Applicable to Public Offerings in the UK' and G. Wegen and C. Lindemann, 'The Law Applicable to Public Offerings in Continental Europe', in H. van Houtte (ed.), *The Law of Cross-Border Securities Transactions* (1999), 103ff and 153ff. A consolidation took place in May 2001 in the area of listing through the Directive 2001/34/EC, OJ L 184/1 (2001).

time span after admission to the first exchange. It should be noted, however, that the United Kingdom (as in many other countries), the listing supervision has in the meantime shifted from the Stock Exchange to the FSA. It may be less logical. Whatever the correct answer, regular reporting would seem much more important and should be connected to the public offer, not to a listing on an official exchange.

In any event, whatever the merits of official listing in a system of ever more informal markets, the present EU rules act in a way that divides even the official markets and cause numerous problems when dual listings are sought on official exchanges, no matter the EU Reciprocal Recognition Directive. This is only to say that the Admission, Listing, Regular Reporting and Mutual Recognition Directives, which 20 years ago were the first concern of the European Union in this area and focussed largely on official exchanges and their operations, which each had a kind of monopoly within their own jurisdiction, are now out of date.

To repeat, neither public offer nor listing prospectuses nor even regular reporting were ever key in the Euro-market. It does not seem to have been detrimental to these markets or the investors in them. We need to rethink this area more fundamentally and should not hesitate to do away with a uniform system of listing requirements if its effects appear to be adverse in the operation of a Single European Capital Market in which both formal and informal markets have a place.

Certainly these regulatory requirements have proven their destructive impact in the attempt to merge the Frankfurt and London Exchanges, regardless of the uniformity they were meant to induce.[54] In the meantime, the Lamfalussy Report suggests an issuer passport.[55] It means that once a public offer prospectus has been properly published and a commitment to regular reporting under objective and uniform standards is in place, the relevant securities would be able to trade on any official or unofficial exchange within the European Union without further formalities, unless these exchanges themselves impose them. It is a good idea provided that the form and substance of such further requirements should be left to these exchanges in a competitive environment. It concerns here a cluster of issues that is now being re-considered in the proposals for a new EU Prospectus Directive.

---

[54] *See* for more details, text in Section 4.3 below. German stocks, the trading in which was to move to London, would have required new listings as the time for mutual recognition of listings is short under the present EU Directives. This proved a great barrier. Moreover, even though the administrative and operational sides of the exchanges were to be merged, it was considered that a full merger of the trading activity was not possible for regulatory reasons, each exchange having its own supervisor depending on location. Hence London would be earmarked for blue chip trading only and Frankfurt for growth companies. As is happened, by the middle of 2002 the Franfurt Neuer Markt had collapsed and was suspended.

[55] FESCO, (now CESR) was the first to come up with the idea of an Issuers' Passport in this connection, *see* Consultation Paper, *A 'European Passport' for Issuers* (10 May 2000). It would allow issuers to extend their offers of securities or to apply for a listing on a regular exchange to other Member States without having to produce duplicative sets of documentation or respond to numerous additional national requirements. The solution would be home country approval and host country recognition perhaps upon some form of notification between home and host regulator or upon the issuing of a certificate by the former. No attention was given here to the informal trading facilities.

### *3.4   Public policy concerns in the issuing, underwriting and market support functions. Attitude of FESCO*

In the issuing, underwriting and market support functions there may nevertheless be certain externalities that still raise some legitimate public policy concerns. The most important will be integrity in the operations, solvency, efficiency, proper management and systems, transparency at least of prices in trading, the fee structure and other charges, the need for lower cost and certainly also for competition and access. An essential point is certainly that whatever market, information, clearing, settlement and custody functions there are, they should be *open to all* who are willing to pay normal fees and these functions should develop in the most advanced manner. But how they develop should in essence be left to free market forces and to competition which will ultimately produce the most efficient facilities and also put a bonus on the most solid structures. That is also the view expressed in the Lamfalussy Report.[56]

Thus public concerns in these areas should be the subject of special rules and not result in full regulation of these activities. Naturally, there should be no market manipulation, no insider dealing, no money laundering, but also those concerns are hardly sufficient causes in themselves to fully regulate all participants in their various market functions, let alone these functions themselves.

In the meantime, (FESCO (now the CESR)) has tried to formulate in 1999 some standards for regulated markets only.[57] It wants more explicit regulatory standards for these markets. They concern the conditions for the operations of those markets and their transparency (but not settlement systems), conditions for access to these markets which concerns especially the investment firms from outside the European Union and professional investors who want direct access, and the conditions concerning listing or trading. Again rules like these are likely to divide markets and there seems altogether little need for them. It would only further impede the operations of the Single European Capital Market.

### 4   MARKET FORCES AND AN EFFECTIVE SINGLE EUROPEAN CAPITAL MARKET

### *4.1   The importance of market forces in shaping the infrastructure of a Single European Capital Market*

The third part of this chapter concerns more in particular the question what markets can or must do themselves to achieve a better capital market regime in Europe and in that way contribute to an effective Single European Capital Market. I have already mentioned the self-propelling forces in the Euro-market and those in a Single European Capital Market would not be very different. The latter could never be much more than a segment of the former, and there are no good reasons why that should not be

---

[56] *Ibid.*, pp. 16, 17.
[57] Standards for regulated markets under the ISD, 99-FESCO-C.

so or would be objectionable. There is no room for it as a less efficient and less liquid separate market.

There are a number of special problems. As mentioned before, one aspect of a Single European Capital Market may be the concern about access of smaller issuers to this market. The major difficulty may, however, be in the concern for smaller investors. For the smaller investor, it concerns here particularly the advice they receive and their protection against their brokers in respect of conflicting interests and their insolvency. In other words, on both: the access of issuer and investor, this market may have to be more all-inclusive and cannot be left to the professionals alone.

Investors guarantee funds help the small investors. It is not unreasonable to expect, however, that where depositor guarantee funds have allowed the regulatory interest in commercial banking to shift to broader issues like systemic risk and effective operation of payment systems, investors guarantee funds could similarly shift the regulatory focus. It could move into the direction of market integrity. Yet, insolvency risk is here not the only problem (in any event mitigated by segregation of client assets). There is also conduct of business and product concern for these smaller investors. Beyond this concern and the integrity issue – which are both narrower regulatory aspects – liberalisation would be the more likely competing force when investors are increasingly protected through investor's guarantee funds.

It would indeed leave ample room for market forces.[58] In Europe, the disturbing aspect is that market forces so far seem to have had much greater problems in achieving a Single European Capital Market than they had in achieving a single Euro-market when regulation of and restrictions on capital flows and services were much more severe. Why is this so? The answer is partly in the impact of *local regulated* markets and operators who still believe they have, or should have, something of a monopoly and will not let go. This is really as primitive as each country wanting to have its own airline and protecting it. It is urgent that these organised markets and clearing systems merge, if necessary a cross border. Yet, they do so hesitatingly and in the confusion it must probably be said that operators, especially clearing members, take advantage in the absence of open competition. In this situation only strong users, that is to say professional investors, can force change. But regulation itself has more generally also been a severe impediment, which the European Passport and home/host solution has not removed because the issue of deregulation and re-regulation was never been authoritatively addressed in that context.

Lack of internationalisation (or Europeanisation) and inefficiency is the unavoidable result, even if the overriding concerns with the free flow of many and services keep the lid on regulation to some extent within the European Union (see Section 2.5

---

[58] *See* also R.S. Krozner, *op. cit. supra* note 49; Jonas Niemeyer, 'An Economic Analysis of Securities Market Regulation and Supervision: Where to Go after the Lamfalussy Report?' *SSE/EFI Working Paper Series in Economics and Finance,* No. 482, 14 December 2001; Donald C. Langevoort, Taming the Animal Spirits of the Stock Markets: A Behavioral Approach to Securities Regulation, Law and Economics Seminar (Boalt Hall UC, California 15 April 2002); James D. Fox, The Death of the Securities Regulkator – Globalisation, Law and Economics Seminar (Boalt Hall UC, California 1 April 2002).

above *in fine*). It is no wonder that in this climate, clearing in Europe is believed to be at least seven times more expensive than in the United States. It benefits the clearing members in clearing houses, often still of a national character. They have no obvious interest in changing this situation as long as they are not challenged in a system of open competition, which must start with competition in the markets themselves.

Brokers should guide their clients to the most efficient markets whether official or not. They also should guide their clients through the most efficient and securest clearing and settlement systems. As brokers they have that duty and are paid exactly for their expertise in this area. There should not be major regulatory impediments for them to do so. It is as simple as that. The European Union should open up this process or at least expose the flaws in the present situation whilst national governments should be so brave as to require consolidation regardless of local cabals in formal stock exchanges. Eventually it will come anyway; clients will demand it, but it should not be forgotten that many investment managers and brokers have close corporate connections to market operators and clearing members and often have an interest in the *status quo*. The impact of these connections and *connected services* and the cost charged by brokers for them (like correspondent brokers, foreign exchange and clearing) are aspects that requires much more investigation in this connection. This form of monopolisation does not only concern the smaller investors who cannot easily fend for themselves, but is also a problem for the larger investor.

It remains indeed very common on the European Continent for in-house brokerage departments in large commercial banks to only guide their clients to their own trading desk, whilst charging a commission on top of what these other departments already make. When foreign securities are bought, they may even charge an extra commission although the foreign broker is only another part of the same bank. Exchange rates may be used that may be hardly competitive on the day. It is not only the law of agency that is here defective and underdeveloped, but there is also a competition element with banks taking advantage of the lack of immediate alternatives.

### 4.2   Recent market driven modernisation of EU securities and derivatives trading

Recently, several efforts have been made to consolidate at European level the present structure of stock markets, clearing and settlement. So far, the result has been modest. As suggested above, the reason is largely the misplaced nationalism that still drives many local interest groups, regulators and governments. Another reason is the effect of domestic regulatory differences. Also there are still many vested interests of intermediaries in leaving the situation as it is.

It is clear, however, that the position of the traditional stock exchanges that took also care of information supply, clearing and settlement, has been fundamentally challenged. In the bond market that challenge long existed because of the presence of the Euro-market, but they remained indeed largely confined to bonds although share offerings in it, often with domestic trenches, have become much more frequent in the International Style Offerings.

The present challenge to the existing exchanges goes to their traditional business and threatens to take away from them ever more of the dealings in their listed shares to informal markets. International investment banks as clients but also market intermediaries have often been instrumental in this development probably more so than the large international institutional or professional investors.

Over the last few years, formal alliances between stock exchanges started to emerge. In July 1998, the London Stock Exchange and the Deutsche Börse announced the formation of an alliance to establish a European exchange in the major European shares. In May 1999, it was announced that other European Stock Exchanges would join to make a group of eight with a single market platform. The idea was to connect the present trading systems but eventually to create a new integrated network. But true determination was lacking whilst investment banks started to move in through Tradepoint in London led by Instinet, which provided an electronic trading platform. The idea was to create a trading facility in this manner for the shares in 300–400 of the largest European companies. At the beginning of 2000, Morgan Stanley and the Swedish OM Gruppen formed a company in London called 2000 Jiway with the intention to create an electronic trading platform for the shares of 6000 European and American companies. The special feature was that Jiway would become the central counter-party and integrate in this manner clearing and settlement as is done in modern derivative exchanges. It would seem the way of the future and highlights the vital role of clearing and settlement at the expense of security markets and systems, even of the informal type.

Under these pressures, the existing stock exchange alliances fell apart. First, the Paris, Brussels and Amsterdam Stock Exchanges formed Euronext. It envisaged a merger of the trading networks, although not of the exchanges themselves, which remain subject to different regulation. Clearing and netting is, however, done by Clearnet, which is a French subsidiary of Euronext and operates under French law, whilst settlement is through Euroclear in Brussels.

Subsequently, the London and Frankfurt Exchanges (LSE and Deutsche Boerse) announced a kind of merger in May 2000 in the iX project. Two subsidiaries (an English and German one) of a London based holding company were to be set up which would take over both exchanges. They would not merge but split the business between blue chips (for London) and growth companies (for Frankfurt). The holding was to take care of the administrative and operational tasks. The German Xetra trading system was to be used in both exchanges. Clearing and settlement were not discussed at the early stages. The project was upstaged by the bid by OM Gruppen for the LSE in August 2000. It failed but led nevertheless to the collapse of the iX project. Third, in July 2000, the Swiss Stock Exchange and Tradepoint announced a plan for a new exchange Virt-x with cross-border facilities with a unified system of clearing and settlement with a single counter-party. London Clearing House, Crest and Euroclear also participated in this project.

The true issues are besides regulation (and its minimalisation), advance technology and the will to do things alone and broaden out internationally or do them together and try to reach all kind of compromises between the existing trading, clearing, settlement systems, and regulation of the traditional exchanges. Frankfurt now takes the go- it- alone approach. London is left with it. Important side issues remain in this connection the position of the small private investors and the fate of smaller companies and the trading in their shares.

The smaller investor not willing or able to go abroad remains dependent on formal markets closer to home with protection of the own regulator. But local formal exchanges can hardly survive on that business alone. Here international alliances are necessary that reduce at least some of the cost. It does not necessarily mean a unified market, as Euronext has shown or cheaper facilities to invest in foreign shares. In the absence of competition, it may also not bring down the cost of clearing and settlement.

The issuing and trading of the shares of smaller companies, on the other hand, may require a specialised market targeted at domestic investors who have some knowledge of these companies and follow them. It is not sure whether that service can remain on offer through regular domestic exchanges. Informal local dealing may become the only way for them whilst they may become more reliant on bank funding unless they are hot IPO material.

In all, there is only a proper trans-border financial servicing for professional dealings, involving therefore the larger issuer and larger investor. This is likely to be always so. They make in fact what we call the Single European Capital Market (in combination with the Euro-market as we saw). Because of this professional nature, protection in that market should be a limited affair, as it has always been in the Euro-market, and require only a minimum of regulation. It would in any event require a form of regulation far less pervasive than the Investment Services Directive still presumes. Wholesale and retail requirements should be fundamentally disentangled. Perhaps not properly studying the difference created a bias in favour of over-regulation for all at the time the ISD was drafted. From that perspective, the ISD is also out of date and may well be considered an impediment itself to the proper further development of a Single European Capital Market.

## 5   THE EU ACTION PLAN AND THE LAMFALUSSY REPORT

### 5.1   *Will centralisation of regulation and of the regulatory function help?*

The EU Action Plan,[59] although very much desirous of promoting a Single European Capital Market did not present a convincing road map. It motivated the creation of Wise Men who in March 2001 presented the Lamfalussy Report. A central issue in that Report became the question of whether a single regulatory regime and single regulator at EU level might help to bring about this Single European Capital Market. The true need is first to determine the case for such *uniform* regulation. In the professional area it would be difficult to establish except from the macro protection perspective of market integrity (like market abuse and inside information) but that

---

[59] *See* note 5 *supra.*

needs to be fought by other than the traditional regulatory means of authorisation, prudential supervision, conduct of business and product transparency and suitability. To the extent it relies on the protection needs of retail, it can only be repeated that the sum total of true cross-border retail business remains so small that from that perspective alone no special EU regulatory attention would be warranted in the context of building one Single European Capital Market, important as it is domestically.

In any event, because of the domestic nature of their investment business and their protection, a single regulatory regime and a single regulator would for them not be useful but become too remote. Thus such a system could not do without a substantial domestic layer, which only gives rise to duplication and extra cost and would hardly be effective.

If, as earlier suggested, liberalisation is the greater issue for the creation of a Single European Capital Market, it follows that there would be little to do for a single regulator. It could be different for commercial banks. Banking regulation is in fact simple and revolves around capital measurement, which is done at regular intervals subject to proper reporting. The essence of investment business is, on the other hand, the market, its operation from minute to minute and the creation of new products therein. This requires regulatory presence, to the extent needed, wherever a market operates and a single regulator is here hardly the answer in an area as large as the European Union with many financial centres.

Much more important than minute regulation at whatever level is that in this market access is given to all exchanges, formal or informal, subject to the own standards of these exchanges in a competitive environment. It may easily improve these standards if the more regular exchanges offer the better service and especially greater liquidity. It is in principle for the market, that is for the Single European Capital Market itself, to sort out and brokers would acquire here a key role in guiding their clients. Most desirable is that in this market most of the market activity is taken over by (a number of) central counter-party clearing and settlement systems as is already the case for marketable derivatives.

There may be more of a case for uniform regulation in the aspects of market integrity and perhaps in the standards and supervision of the issuing activity. As earlier suggested, common standards and a separation of prospectus and regular reporting from admission and listing on *regular* exchanges would solve many problems. It is not dependent on a single regulator either.

If there should nevertheless be a single European regulator, should banking, investment services and insurance regulation come together at the same time? In view of the very different regulatory perspectives and objectives and the resulting very different nature and ways of regulation, prudential supervision, and conduct of business and product control, I would hardly have thought so. Of course there is a strong intellectual argument to be made for financial regulation to be horizontally integrated in view of the problems with consolidated supervision in universal banks, which are the European model. The United Kingdom, Germany, Sweden and Japan have accepted the idea domestically but the set up of a single regulator in those countries remains untested for moments of stress. As was already discussed in Section 2.5 above, a large bureaucracy would become unavoidable at European level with unavoidable infighting with local regulators within the system, who especially in investment services would remain key in retail and probably also in wholesale because of the required closeness to the markets. For these reasons alone, it would be a premature development.

## 5.2   The Lamfalussy Report

Instead of a single regulator, the Committee of Wise Men proposed in the Lamfalussy Report that there should be a regulatory steering and policy group at EU level. It could be very useful. The problem here is how it could be empowered to give direct instructions or lay down rules directly for local regulators within the present EU framework of decision taking. It is a problem of comitology and may well require Treaty changes to ever become truly effective alternative in this area.

The European Council in its meeting in Stockholm in March 2001 whilst considering the Lamfalussy Report only contemplated a set-up within the existing Treaty provisions and, following the Committee of Wise Men, accepted a four level approach, the split between the first two to be decided on a case by case basis by the EU Council and the European Parliament. Subsequently, the European Commission set up two Committees: the ESC and the CESR.[60]

At the first level of *framework principles* it agreed the operation of a new committee, the ESC chaired by the EU Commission. Within the present set-up it cannot be more than an advisory committee without own powers, but at the second or *implementing* level, this Committee may receive delegated authority within new Directives. More importantly, in accordance with the 28 June 1999 Decision on Comitology,[61] it could also function as a Regulatory Committee but only in order to *assist* the Commission in the implementation pursuant to Arts 202 and 211 of the EC Treaty under which the Council has implementation powers and the facility to delegate these to the Commission.

In this connection it may be observed that the powers to lay down rules in the financial area itself belong to the EU Council and the European Parliament and not to the Commission (which only proposes, see Arts 47(2), 95 and 153(3)(b) EC Treaty). However, the Commission has original powers under Art. 226 EC Treaty in the area of enforcement of the obligations arising under the Treaty (and the rules issued there under). At Stockholm, it was specifically said in this connection that the Commission in its implementation activities in the financial area must not go against 'predominant views' which might emerge in the Council and which as such could derive from national considerations.[62]

---

[60] European Commission Decisions 6 June 2001, 2001/527/EC and 2001/528/EC, OJ L 191, 43 (2001). The legal basis for these decisions is unclear not withstanding the fact that Art. 7(4) of the Comitology Decision, *see* note 59 *infra*, requires it to be indicated. It is justified as a response to the Stockholm Conference resolution.

[61] Decision 1999/468/EC, OJ L 184/23 (1999).

[62] *See* also note 5 *supra*.

To further assist the implementation, there was also created an advisory CESR chaired by a representative of a national supervisory authority. This became the role of FESCO.[63] The ESC may give mandates to it. Together with national regulators, the CESR should also be instrumental in the transposition process (level 3). Here it has an independent task to ensure more consistent implementation of Community law. It must in this connection also consult market participants, consumers and end-users.

Enforcement (level 4) is left to national regulators but may be further strengthened at EU level. Under Art. 211 EC Treaty the Commission has own enforcement powers in the implementation of EU Directives. The idea here is that market participants will be encouraged to submit reasoned complaints to the Commission.

This new set up was put in place in 2002, to be reviewed in 2004.[64] The new Prospectus Directive and Market Abuse Directive are the first examples of the new approach and are drafted accordingly.

At the Lamfalussy Report's suggestion, the EU Commission is also to consider the more frequent use of Regulations to avoid the implementation process, which invariably gives rise to differences between Member States. Whether in practice this route will be chosen remains to be seen. Member States might not like as they will be deprived of the flexibility that was intended to be left them through the implementation of Directives. It seems that first the comitology route is being explored.

### 5.3    Lack of market-oriented direction

The overhaul of the present EU approach to financial services is characterised by a complete insensitivity to the proper place of regulation and its true objectives. It has

---

[63] The ECB may become involved under Art. 105(4) of the EC Treaty since it needs to be consulted 'on any proposed Community Act in its field of competence'. Under Council Decision 98/415/EC, OJ L 189/42 (1998) this role is interpreted to include all measures materially influencing the stability of financial institutions and markets. This Decision applies also to national legislation in the field in EMU countries and to Member States with a derogation under Art. 122(3) EC Treaty but not to the UK (Art. 5 UK Protocol). Thus the ECB was consulted on the latest UCITS proposals, see OJ L 285/9 (1999). Under Art. 105(4) the ECB may also give opinions in the field of its competence. Under Art. 105(6) it may even be given special tasks in this connection. There is therefore some basis in the treaty for a supervisory role of the ECB in banking or even more generally where the stability of financial institutions and markets is concerned, see also M. Andenas, 'Banking Supervision, the Internal Market and European Economic and Monetary Union' in M. Andenas *et al.* (eds), *European Economic and Monetary Union: The Institutional Framework* (1997), p. 402. It would seem to be geared, however, to prudential supervision and the operation of the financial system as a whole rather than individual investors protection and therefore plays a role largely in the area of systemic risk.

There is no equivalent for securities regulators or for an EU committee operating in their stead. The unstable relationship between domestic financial regulators who remain basically in charge and the EU institutions, particularly in the area of investment services has earlier been noted by W. Bratton, *op. cit. supra* note 37, 38. If the thesis of this contribution that liberalisation in this area is to precede re-regulation at EU level at least for professional dealings and that retail protection is better exercised at local levels is correct, this state of affairs cannot be considered immediately disturbing or in need of reform. It means, however, that there is little room at present for any real powers for the ESC.

[64] *See* also Yannis V. Avgerinos, 'Essential and Non-essential Measures: Delegation of Powers in EU Securities Regulation' (2002), 8 *European Law Journal* 269.

no concept of the role of market forces either. It is borne out by the Lamfalussy Report[65] and is particularly clear in the proposals for the new Prospectus Directive. The result is a considerable muddle and lack of direction.

Although the objectives changed during the progress of the EU Action Plan and have moved into the direction of (a) a single EU whole sale market, (b) open and secure retail markets and (c) state of the art prudential rules and supervision, it is clear that no fundamental evaluation is taking place of these objectives and what they entail from a regulatory point of view and that the approach is patchy and incidental. There is no clear view, rather some vague political aspirations.

## 6    CONCLUSIONS

In the discussion of a Single European Capital Market and its regulation we give too little attention to the risks involved in the various capital market functions, and we do not separate them adequately or ask ourselves properly what is needed as regulatory response in respect of them, both for professional and small investors, or from a point of view of market integrity. It should also be better considered what went before and the close connection of this Single European Capital Market with the Euro-market should be recognised. The Euro-market and its development provide a useful example and may be indicative of the level of regulation that could usefully apply in the Single European Capital Market. It concerns here wholesale or professional markets. A proper analysis of the regulatory needs in these markets would suggest that in investment services there is much room for deregulation.

The main regulatory concern in investment services is rather for adequate protection of the retail investor in the conduct of business, product transparency and suitability, and for proper complaint procedures under his own law. This is in any even logical to the extent an investor invests in his own domestic (regular) markets. On the other hand, foreign retail investment services are normally obtained through an account with a foreign broker, which must imply pure home regulation, or through an account with a subsidiary of a foreign service provider in the host country, which implies pure host regulation. In retail, there would not appear to be a sufficient market for direct cross-border retail investment services involving a foreign service provider with client accounts in the country of the client to be greatly concerned about. Double regulation and the consequential division of markets is therefore hardly an issue in that area.

This being the case, and also taken into account that retail investors have special protection through investor compensation schemes which have been harmonised at EU level, there is no good reason why retail regulatory protection issues should substantially enter the discussion concerning the evolution of a Single European Capital Market and the appropriate level of regulation therein. This is proper wholesale or professional territory where investors have the necessary support functions and ready information to look mostly after themselves.

---

[65] *See* also Jonas Niemeyer, *op. cit. supra* note 58, 61ff.

This suggests indeed a high level of liberalisation whilst much room should be left for market needs and practices, also as to the type of products traded. Forms of private law harmonisation are here important, however. In the Single European Capital Market, trans-national, market-practice related, book-entry entitlement structures in investment securities and similar contractual arrangements with single counter-party clearers should find a legal basis in harmonised or trans-nationalised private laws and as such be favoured. This harmonisation is also important in the segregation issue, even if the larger investor is less likely to allow brokers to handle his assets at all.

In this Single European Capital Market, the position of regulated markets must also be reviewed and as a minimum the prospectus and regular reporting requirements split from listing on regular or other markets. They should be attached to all publicly traded issues, whether or not quoted. Only prices should be centrally reported. The present EU approach is wrongly focussed on official exchanges and is even there out of date. In fact, over-regulation remains its ethos, even in the ISD, and now certainly also in the proposals for the Prospectus Directive.

In a Single European Capital Market, in essence the market should set its own standards for admission of securities in a competitive climate. The further development of market support functions like those in underwriting, market making, matching systems, clearing, settlement and custody should in principle also be left to market forces. For what ever may be left to regulators in that market, a single regulatory regime with a single regulator would not be opportune. In view of the large number of European financial centres it is unlikely to work efficiently and it would not work for retail protection either.

For market integrity issues like market manipulation, insider dealing, money laundering, access to the market support functions and anti-competitive behaviour, common EU regulatory standards should be set if they have not been already. They are and should remain incidental, do not require a full regulatory regime, but should as such be vigorously enforced. The proposals for a Market Abuse Directive should be directed along these lines.

A new Committee like the ESC may be useful to provide the necessary direction and push to guide the Single European Capital Market, but to be effective, it needs to be enlightened, deregulation-minded and minimalist until such time that practical needs suggest otherwise.

# Chapter 3

# Fifteen Regulators for a Single Capital Market: The Project of Regulatory Harmonisation in Europe

*Stavros B. Thomadakis*

## INTRODUCTION

Capital market regulation in the European Union has achieved a reasonable degree of uniformity through the national application of European directives. More important among these are the directives regarding conditions for the admission of securities to official stock exchange listing, prospectuses for new issues of securities, insider dealing in regulated markets, and the Investment Services Directive (ISD). The latter is a complex piece of legislation, which sets up the rules for prudential regulation as well as standards for behavioural regulation of authorised investment firms. Uniformity at the level of legislation is naturally an important prerequisite for a single European capital market, and it has been reasonably achieved through the directives. As we move, however, from the high level of directives and legislation to the lower and more practical level of regulations and their implementation uniformity gives way to significant variation.

## REGULATORY TRENDS AND HOME COUNTRY CONTROL

Before giving examples of these variations, and drawing out their implications, I should point out the more important regulatory trends in world capital markets, which inform the behaviour of regulators in Europe as elsewhere. Two fundamental trends are evident over the last 10 years. First, regulators have been consistently requiring and enforcing higher levels of disclosure on the part of issuers of securities and associated entities, such as underwriters, market makers, and financial advisers. This has led to better functioning markets but has also sharpened the need for uniformity not only of disclosure practices but also of the material which is being disclosed. For example, the necessity for comparable accounting standards is self-evident in that context. Second, the goal of investor protection has gained ground as a major objective of regulation, as more retail investors enter massively into equity markets, and as this entry exposes large numbers of the saving population to market risks. In response to this awareness, market authorities design and implement a variety of measures: investor compensation schemes, know-your-customer rules, codes of conduct for equal treatment, disclosure rules again.

*Mads Andenas and Yannis Avgerinos (eds), Financial Markets in Europe: Towards a Single Regulator?* 75–81.
© 2003 *Kluwer Law International. Printed in Great Britain.*

Both trends have brought forward a complex new set of regulatory requirements, and these have in turn created new ground for variation and national specificities among regulatory jurisdictions. I would venture the view that early in the process of financial deregulation, perhaps 20 years ago, pre-existing national variations were eliminated as public intervention in markets was removed. With new regulatory trends national variations have reasserted themselves, albeit not in terms of public intervention in pricing or allocation of finance, but in the features and behaviour of regulated entities and processes. These trends have taken hold in Europe as in the rest of the world. As market regulation evolved, European directives have created pressure for uniformity. Growing market needs for practical rules, which would govern disclosure and ensure higher levels of investor protection, pushed in the opposite direction, that is, towards national variation in regulatory practice. The project of a single European capital market must deal with this variation if barriers to market unification are to be overcome.

The principle of home country control has been a major conduit for the natural development of variation in regulatory practice, since it defines the powers and the limits of national jurisdictions in the European Union. I should discuss briefly here the case of the passport for providing investment services, as an example where variation arises naturally. The ISD has chosen to describe a list of primary and secondary services. Licensing of investment firms involves a specification of the services, which each firm is authorised to provide. Regulators have to make judgements about qualitative matters such as fitness and propriety of individuals who own or manage these firms, adequacy of internal organisation, and quantitative matters such as the adequacy of capital, and so forth. It is neither natural nor self-evident that national regulators will make similar choices with regard to these matters, especially the qualitative ones, if left on their own, and if based only on the culture and the context of their national market environment. On the other hand, it is neither feasible nor desirable that European directives reach down to the ground of market practice to ensure that national regulators, in spite of national market cultures, will make uniform choices.

It should of course be pointed out that the market itself acts as a force towards uniformity. This formed part of the theory behind the imposition of home country control and the mutual recognition of passports for offering investment services. Cross-border use of the European passport itself enhances a gradual convergence of market cultures, and this will in turn strengthen uniformity in regulatory thinking and practice. Yet, this process can be slow and uneven, as use of the European passport is quite uneven across the countries of the Union. The evidence seems to suggest, for example, that cross-border passport use is much more intense among large markets than among smaller peripheral markets, or between large and peripheral ones. The patterns of cross-border use of a passport do not provide for the smooth and evenly distributed effect, which is desirable for a single market strategy, although the use of the passport itself ultimately promotes uniformity. The market process must be supplemented by purposive political or administrative action, in my opinion. So much is evident from European realities until now.

## STRONG REGULATORY COORDINATION

The whole debate on diversity versus uniformity, and on whether uniformity is promoted by home country control and the principle of mutual recognition, would be vacuous if we could begin thinking of a single European regulator, of a European version of the Securities and Exchange Commission of the United States. Are political decision-makers willing and are markets ready for a single European regulator? The common answer to both these questions is no. The common reasoning used to arrive at the negative answer is that markets are not ready, because there is still considerable diversity in legal structures, in market structure, in modus operandi and in market culture. Consequently the task of a single regulator would be too complex and would prove almost impossible. I agree with the negative answer but disagree with the reasoning. The chief reason why a single regulator is not feasible is to be found in politics and not in markets.[1] A single regulator must draw legal authority from a sound political mandate and be accountable to well-defined democratic structures. This may be a political dream within present day European institutions, but I very much doubt whether it can soon be turned into reality. Europe must prepare for this, but the step must only come when political conditions are mature for it. Otherwise, if prematurely formulated, the single regulator will lack legitimacy and may damage rather than strengthen market integrity. The Committee of Wise Men's Report implicitly puts aside the creation of a single EU regulatory authority for financial services in the Community and describes a new medium term regulatory structure within the current boundaries of the Treaty. However, according to the Report, if the full review of the proposed new regulatory structure were to confirm in 2004 or even earlier that the approach did not have any prospects of success, such a Treaty change might indeed be appropriate to be considered. But this solution does not take into account the risk of premature political conditions I just stressed.

It is clear from the series of my previous arguments that there arises a gap which needs to be filled in Europe. If directives cannot enforce uniformity in regulatory detail; if markets do not push for convergence in an even fashion across the European financial space; if a single European regulator is a long prospect; if finally home country control makes the regulators, the regulated, and the customers aware of cross-border differences which can give rise to regulatory arbitrage, then there is only one possible response: regulatory coordination.[2] The national regulators of the European Union have taken up this challenge and have formed the Forum of European Securities Commissions (FESCO) 3 years ago. The driving force for the formation of FESCO has been the need to harmonise rules, which derive mostly from home country control. Mutual recognition obliges national regulators to seek this

---

[1] Political barriers are mentioned in the Wise Men's Final Report on the Regulation of European Securities Markets but from a different perspective: that of techniques to protect national markets or products in favor of local suppliers.

[2] According to the Wise Men's Final Report, the lack of coordination by an effective network of European regulators is a basic reason why there exists ambiguous implementation of EU directives and this is one of the major shortcomings of the current regulatory system.

route of action. How one licenses, how one implements qualitative criteria, how one supervises the correct application of directives and rules, how one enforces behavioural regulation, these are all matters requiring harmonised action. Regulatory practice, if undertaken under a cooperative scheme can become a source of uniform impulses upon markets, rather than a mechanism of diversity.

The formation and activity of FESCO have not been an official action of the European Union, but rather an initiative of the national regulators who have voluntarily created and entered the scheme. Accordingly, FESCO cannot issue official and binding decisions; nor can it impose rules, which will have universal application within Europe. It can do the next best thing: FESCO plays a leading role in addressing the regulatory issues raised by the Single Market with a triple purpose.

(i) The purpose of exchanging experiences and working together to facilitate the efficient realisation of the Single Market for financial services. FESCO has particularly endeavoured to overcome the prevailing regulatory diversity and national specificities in key areas of the legislative framework established by EU Directives, by creating specific experts groups. Their task is precisely to examine issues for which either great diversity and ambiguity in implementation prevail or it is believed that are not sufficiently covered by the latter. Currently, experts groups are working on European Public Offers, Investor Protection, Market Abuse, Primary market practices, and Alternative Trading Systems. As expected, all these issues derive from the two major regulatory trends to which I referred previously, namely disclosure and investor protection.

(ii) The purpose to develop common regulatory standards in areas of supervision that are not harmonised by the Directives. So far, FESCO has issued common standards on fitness and propriety of those who own and manage investment firms, standards for regulated markets, the definition of professional investor and rules for participants in offerings. FESCO is consulting on a paper designed to improve the existing framework of mutual recognition of prospectuses, certain rules relating to the primary markets as well as on standards for harmonising core conduct of business rules for investor protection.[3] In addition, with the aim of supporting the legislative programme set out in the EU's Financial Services Action Plan, FESCO has concentrated on mutual recognition/listing particulars, market abuse, alternative trading systems, and accounting.[4]

(iii) The purpose of providing broad mutual assistance between FESCO members for effective market surveillance and enforcement against market abuse. To this aim,

---

[3] European Standards on Fitness and Propriety to Provide Investment Services (April 1999). Market Conduct Standards for Participants in an Offering (December 1999). Standards for Regulated Markets under the ISD (December 1999). Implementation of Art. 11 of the ISD: Categorisation of investors for the purpose of Conduct of Business Rules (March 2000). A 'European passport' for issuers (Consultation paper, May 2000). Stabilisation and Allotment: A European Supervisory approach (Consultation paper, September 2000). Standards and rules for harmonizing core conduct of business rules for investor protection (Consultative paper 2001).

[4] A 'European passport for issuers' (Consultation paper, May 2000). A European Regime against Market Abuse (September 2000). The regulation of Alternative Trading Systems in Europe. A paper for the EU Commission (September 2000).

FESCO is already trying to facilitate the sharing of information and to improve the efficiency and effectiveness of enforcement by bringing together frontline enforcement staff within FESCOPOL, set up more than a year ago. FESCOPOL is responsible for ensuring that this process functions smoothly.

Naturally, in the area of actual regulations FESCO can work for the formulation of regulatory desiderata and have its members undertake the obligation that they will exercise their best efforts to achieve the desired goals. Those of you who have seen the FESCO papers will immediately realise that they reveal a great deal of work for the harmonisation of regulatory standards, but also that they include an aspirational element. Regulators not being legislators or initiators of legal change state their goals for achievement of uniformity in regulatory practice.

## THE NEED TO MAKE COOPERATION ON INSTITUTIONAL FEATURE

It seems to me that the process of regulatory cooperation among the 15 national regulators must be elevated to an institutional goal of the European Union and must become an official function. This is precisely what is put forward in the Wise Men's Final Report on the Regulation of European Securities Markets. Indeed, an indispensable element in the latter's proposed regulatory reform is the setting up of a politically endorsed high level EU securities regulators committee (ERSC) built on the structure already established by FESCO but with an enlarged official responsibility: not only that of ensuring consistent transposition and implementation of European Law (level 3 of the four level regulatory structure) but also that of being an independent expert advisor to the Commission (level 2 of the four level approach). Both of these roles have been successfully assumed unofficially by FESCO as of today.

In fact, this Committee should act in dual capacity. On one hand, ERSC is the essence of level 3. The national regulators will continue working in a cooperative network on joint interpretation, recommendations, guidelines, and common standards, even in areas not covered by EU legislation and in review and comparison of regulatory practice. Since FESCO's tasks must be enlarged in line with the Report's recommendations, a political resolution will be needed to mandate regulators to carry out all of this essential work. On the other hand, within the context of level 2, European regulators together with their experts, by advising the European Commission on the necessary implementing details of each subject, will play a central role in EU decision making. So far the European directives in the area of financial markets have occupied themselves with the substance of regulatory requirements, such as disclosure, investor protection, accounting standards, licensing requirements and so forth. As I explained, directives nevertheless allowed the creation of considerable diversity on the regulatory ground. More importantly, there is also substantial institutional diversity. Each national government has responded differently to the requirements of market regulation, even within the exercise of authority for the implementation of European directives. As a result, regulatory powers are currently vested in a variety of regulators that differ from each other in significant ways.

Let me offer briefly a description of the modalities of regulatory power distribution within national jurisdictions in Europe. First of all in some countries regulators are enforcers but not makers of regulations. The latter power is vested in Ministries of Finance, or other government organisations. Second, in some countries there is a common regulator for different financial services, for example, banking and security markets, in others there are separate regulators. Third, in some countries the regulator of the securities markets has broader powers than in other, a notable example being the supervision and enforcement of accounting standards. Fourth, in some countries security regulators divide their powers with stock exchanges, as for example, listing authority, supervision of listed firms, or on line surveillance of market operation. This great variety in regulatory architecture within national jurisdictions in the European Union must be eliminated because it creates significant problems in regulatory cooperation, harmonisation, and uniform enforcement. The importance of supervisory and regulatory convergence is of course stressed in the Wise Men's Report as an immediate condition for the EU securities regulators committee to successfully fulfil its role.

The time has come for one or more European directives that will seek a common regulatory architecture in member countries and this is a wider scope than that of the regulatory structure proposed in the Wise Men's Report. If national regulators are to work as a network, which will smooth the function of the Single Market and open the way for a future single regulator this harmonisation of architecture is a necessity.

In line with this aim but particularly with regard to market abuse, FESCO has already emphasised the necessity of having a single independent and accountable regulator in each country. The latter will have a duty to cooperate with its European counterparts and will be authorised to issue implementing rules and guidance on the detail of what constitutes market abuse, including the establishment of appropriate preventative measures as well as in order to accommodate any special technical characteristics of national markets. This innovative approach, which sees as a precondition for harmonised regulation the equality of investigative and enforcement powers granted to national regulators, could be addressed through an EU Directive. It must be noted that this original FESCO work on market abuse was the first paper to develop and put forward the concept of an enhanced network of national regulators. This network approach developed for market abuse but extended to all other areas of regulation is also a core element in the Final Report of the Committee of Wise Men.

Having touched on the need to work towards uniformity in the powers and jurisdiction of national regulators, we should also be cognizant of two other important features that must also be harmonised in the Union: the *independence* and the *accountability* of national regulators. Both these features have a double aspect. Independence is of course understood as the autonomy from political constraints and impositions. It is also understood as an element that sets apart the regulator from the regulated. The regulator should be able to pursue its goals and activities to ensure market integrity without dependencies and links to either political or specific market interests. Accountability is also understood as the specific way in which regulators will respond to democratic control of their actions and will seek legitimacy for their activities within the political structure. Accountability has an additional facet too.

The sensitivity of the regulator toward market needs must be enshrined in regulatory obligations to enter consultative processes with market representatives, without thereby sacrificing the objectivity of their actions. These two complementary features will indeed exist both at national and European level as soon as EU securities regulators committee acquires formal status within the Union.

## CONCLUDING REMARK

Regulatory coordination taking on a formal status, must seek to harmonise regulatory practice and enforcement, must be built upon sufficient independence and accountability, as well as on reasonable similarity of powers of regulators who form the constituent parts of the new regulatory architecture in Europe. Indeed, this formal status of regulatory coordination has been a major achievement of the agreement at European Council in Stockholm in 2000. Since the EU securities regulators committee falls outside the existing EU comitology procedure the next priority should be a political decision to set it up as an independent network of national regulators.

*Chapter 4*

# Problems with Home Country Control and Investment Services

*Yannis V. Avgerinos*

## 1 INTRODUCTION

The 1992 Single Market Programme has brought a new dynamic impetus to the morphology of European financial market regulation and supervision. The centrepiece of the 'new approach' has been the home country control principle, which has replaced previous full harmonisation strategies. Liberalisation has long been the desire of financial industries, regulators and consumers. However, it is often alleged that the effects of the new regime on the European Union (EU) financial markets could not have been straightforward. Almost eight years after its imposition, home country control may not have produced the results needed for a real single market. Besides a few brief reports of the European Commission on the progress of the free provision of financial services, there appears to be no overall assessment of the role of the home country control. But, what has been the impact of the current supervisory regime on the flow of capital and the provision of financial services within the Community? Has home country supervision been proven to be the tool for cross-border liberalisation of financial services, or is it time for EU leaders and regulators to consider other more efficient structural approaches?

In areas where competence is not exclusively held by the European Union, the test of 'comparative efficiency' should be applied. EU action should always be proportional to the dimension of the issue at hand. In case the disadvantages and costs of a regulatory and supervisory regime outweigh its benefits, the issues of regulatory approaches and institutional structures should be readdressed. In an area, such as financial services, where market developments move at extremely high speeds, regulatory responses should be prompt and efficient.

The current EU investment services supervisory regime constitutes a division of powers between the home and the host Member State and supports a predominant power of the former although the latter preserves important tasks especially in the area of conduct of business rules. The 'new' regime has offered the European passport to financial undertakings, which has made possible for them to move freely across their home country's borders. At the same time, however, it has failed to overcome certain hurdles to the free provision of investment services, or has even created new grey areas of uncertainty, which hinder intra-Community trade. In this paper I will endeavour to assess and critically analyse the impediments of home country control to the truly free provision of investment services. To assist my

*Mads Andenas and Yannis Avgerinos (eds), Financial Markets in Europe: Towards a
Single Regulator?* 83–120.
© 2003 *Kluwer Law International. Printed in Great Britain.*

discussion, I shall make a distinction between problems of structure and problems of substance.

## 2   PROBLEMS OF STRUCTURE

### 2.1   *Protectionism and regulatory arbitrage*

The philosophy underlined in the EC Treaty and the Single Market Programme is that of economic liberalisation; Member States' supervisory authorities are obliged to accept unduly provision of financial services within their territory originated from undertakings authorised by their home country. However, despite their agreements in drafting the investment services directives and taking advantage of the Achilles' heel of the present regime of home country control, national supervisory authorities may still attempt to protect their national financial markets, given their inherent strategic importance. The most problematic issue in this context is that EU law, which was designed primarily to promote competition, may be misused by a Member State to justify a protective national policy as a priority, which can have a negative effect on foreign financial undertakings.

It has been suggested that the EU regulatory and supervisory framework suffers from regulatory arbitrage,[1] which is not considered by the Community to be inherently desirable. Hence, the investment services directives lay down only minimum standards, which means that Member States can, if they so choose, impose stricter or additional conditions of authorisation or capital to those set out in the directives. However, the picture is not the same in fields which the EU harmonisation programme has left untouched. One such field is conduct of business rules. The trend towards consolidation of European stock exchanges may leave a bulk of EU peripheral countries out of the race. Hence, it would be not irrational to assume that these countries may endeavour to find other ways of attracting trading volume, without necessarily being interested in raising investor protection standards. Consequently, the hypothesis that some investment entities might be interested in the possibility of regulatory forum shopping and of becoming incorporated in the Member State, where conditions in general are perceived to be more favourable to them, becomes more realistic.

The same conclusion would be drawn if recent market developments were viewed from an economic and political analysis point of view. The theory of 'public choice' or the 'economic theory of regulation' use economic analyses to explain the outcome of collective or non-market decision-making.[2] Financial groups, which operate on a

---

[1] Usually the word 'arbitrage' or the 'Law of One Price' is used to define the non-speculative transfer of funds from one market to another to take advantage of differences in interest rates, exchange rates or commodity prices between the two markets; see Oxford Dictionary of Business (2nd edn, Oxford, 1996). However, here with 'regulatory arbitrage' we mean the establishment of an investment firm in the jurisdiction, which has the more favourable regulatory and supervisory standards, with the intention to commence business in another Member State with stricter rules, by use of the European passport.

[2] Buchanan, James, *Liberty, Market and State: Political Economy in the 1980s* (Brighton, Wheatsheaf, 1986) 19.

for-profit basis, may lobby Member States' governments and solicit their intervention in order to achieve maximum benefit. Accordingly, politicians and regulators might provide rules that serve particular financial institutions in order to further their own interest.[3] Consequently, it would not be immoderate to allege that the ability of host country's regulators to negotiate with market intermediaries and to enact rules under their responsibility is seriously prejudiced by the increased influence of financial institutions over national regulators' rule-making, and not by the public good.

### 2.2 Differences in legal systems and cultures

Differences between Member States' legal orders and cultures have always been one of the main obstacles to European integration. One could begin with the fundamental distinction between common law countries and civil law countries. Based on Roman Law, codification started in Europe in the second half of the eighteenth century, but it really expanded in the nineteenth century. However, a number of European Anglo-Saxon countries have pursued a different legal route, while others were less influenced by Roman Law.[4]

Variations between investment services and cultural differences between Member States may be illustrated by a number of paradigms. Characteristic is the paradigm of investment services marketing. Member States, where cold-calling[5] is a useful technique, are likely to regulate such activities in more detail than Member States where the phenomenon is unknown. It was a matter of time that a case with reference to cold-calling would reach the European Court. In *Alpine Investments*,[6] the Court has recognised the right to prohibit this marketing practice in financial services after examining a provision of Dutch law, which was designed to protect the reputation and reliability of the financial market in the Netherlands. Nevertheless, pending harmonisation in this area, we should avoid trying to establish a general rule for the compatibility of cold-calling and each case should be assessed individually.[7]

Another field where different cultures and lack of consensus have prevented the emergence of a Single Market is pension funds. Many Member States still impose portfolio restrictions that limit foreign investments. Consequently, pension funds

---

[3] For instance, electoral campaign contributions by the regulated or avoidance of industry financed opposition; *See* George Stigler, 'The Theory of Economic Regulation' (1971) 2 *Bell Journal of Economics* 3, 10–13; H. Siebert, and M.J. Koop, 'Institutional Competition *versus* Centralisation: Quo Vadis Europe?' (1993) *Oxford Review of Economic Policy* 15, 18.

[4] For some historical and comparative examples of the drive of unified markets towards uniform rules, *see* Sàinz de Vicuña, Antonio, 'The Legal Integration of Financial Markets of the Euro Area', *supra* in this volume, at Chapter 1.

[5] With the term 'cold-calling' we refer to the provision of financial services without prior solicitation.

[6] *See* Case C-384/93 *Alpine Investments BV* v. *Minister van Financien* [1995] ECR I-1141. For an analysis of the case, *see* Mads Andenas, 'Cross Border Cold-calling and the Right to Provide Services' (1995) 8 *Company Lawyer* 249.

[7] *See* Commission of the European Communities, *Amended Proposal for a Directive Concerning the Distance Marketing of Consumer Financial Services*, COM (1999) 375 final of 23 July 1999. Art. 10(2) provides for special arrangements concerning communications not solicited by consumers.

have little incentive to commence cross-border financial business.[8] The liberalisation of this field would surely give a great boost to cross-border financial services trade.

Divergences do remain between Member States' private laws, as the EU legislature does not have general competence to create harmonised or uniform private law. The multiplication of legal orders and variations in the level and methods of protection in the regulation of the same transaction leads to increased costs of compliance and raises the possibility of conflicts of rules.[9] Here, we can recall the paradigm of the German Stock Exchange Act, which protects investors against the risk of futures contract.[10] This provision has initiated the *Koestler* case, which involved a conflict between German and French rules.[11]

In addition, many Member States' cultural barriers are playing a significant role in slowing market integration. Two types of cultural barriers can be identified. *First*, those that can be dealt with by public policy, such as different approaches to corporate governance, market consultation, and, more importantly, to practical implementation of EU directives on the mutual recognition of prospectuses and listings.[12] In relation to the later, the discretion of Member States in the implementation of EU law also constitutes a part of the problem.[13] *Second*, others that hopefully will converge as markets integrate, such as different entrepreneurial cultures, which in many cases are slowing the supply of new high growth companies for the equity markets.[14]

Finally, differences may occur in interpreting certain conditions and provisions in the field of financial services. In electronic trading, for example, reaching consensus on a pan-European approach to the question of when a Web site communication will be considered to be an offer of financial services taking place within a particular

---

[8] *See* Gerard Hertig, 'Regulatory Competition for EU Financial Services' (2000) 2 *Journal of International Economic Law* 349, 357.

[9] Naturally, this paper is interested in 'real' rather than 'superficial' differences between national legal principles. Market participants may be indifferent to divergent legal formulations provided they lead to outcomes, which match their preferences. For example, it matters not whether a tort claim for pure economic loss will be rejected because there is 'no duty of care' (English law) or because it is *'dommage indirecte'* (French law). The result is the same. *See* Anthony Ogus, 'Competition between National Legal Systems: a Contribution of Economic Analysis to Comparative Law' (1999) 48 ICLQ 405, 409.

[10] Such contracts are only binding for private investors if they have previously been informed about the risks of such transactions through a written communication accompanied by oral explanations if necessary. *See* Norbert Horn, 'The Monetary Union and the Internal Market for Banking and Investment Services' in Joseph Norton (ed.), *Yearbook of International Financial and Economic Law 1998*, (London, Kluwer Law International, 1999), p.4 141.

[11] Case 15/78, *Societe Generale Alsacienne de Banque* v. *Koestler* [1978] ECR 1971. Koestler concerned the application of the German Stock Exchange Act, which perceived futures contracts as wagering agreements, to a series of stock exchanges speculative agreements, entered to France by a German national. Although French law regarded futures contracts as legal investment activity, the ECJ decided that the contract was void because the German rules applied in a non-discriminatory way.

[12] On these divergences *see* Horn, Norbert, *op. cit*, note 10.

[13] *See* Steil, Ben, 'Equity Trading IV: The ISD and the Regulation of European Market Structure', in B. Steil (ed.), *The European Equity Markets, the State of the Union and an Agenda for the Millennium* (London, Royal Institute of International Affairs, 1996),pp. 131–134.

[14] *See* Committee of Wise Men, *Final Report on the Regulation of European Securities Markets* (15 February 2001) 11 (hereinafter 'Final Wise Men Report').

jurisdiction is unlikely, because that determination must be based on the particular circumstances and the laws of each jurisdiction.[15]

It may be alleged that all these divergences pre-existed in the home country control regime. However, the regulatory competition fostered by the home country control principle has merely improved the situation. Instead, in many cases, it has created more gaps and less uniformity. Integration has been incremental, rather than dramatic. Many of these gaps and deficiencies are now being tackled by new legislation. But results will take far too long at the present rate of progress. Therefore, truly free intra-Community trade of investment services and a level playing field for financial operators require increased market integration and a different regulatory response by EU institutions and Member States' supervisory authorities.

### 2.3   Competence of competent authorities

The success of the home country control within the Single Market programme in investment services depends to a great extent on an assumption by each Member State that the supervisory authorities of the other Member States will be competent[16] to ensure that the investment undertakings, which they authorise and prudentially supervise, abide by the minimum standards prescribed in the relevant Directives and the soft law. However, there is no legal act or established body at EU level that specifies and ensures such a competence. Instead, Member States' competent authorities rely on their mutual trust and mutual agreements as well as established Community law and harmonised minimum standards.

Naturally one may wonder: who ensures the propriety of the national supervisory houses and how competent are the 'competent authorities'? Because of institutional, historical, legal and other factors, and besides a certain harmonisation in specific rules, different supervisory authorities tend to practise their supervision by different methods, and consequently there is no single methodology, which can be used as a 'standard' within the EU. The problem may acquire a more serious dimension, when their tasks comprise the consolidated supervision of multi-national financial groupings. Relationships created especially in the last three years within FECSO may have altered the situation. Nevertheless, although there is no mechanism to ensure the incompetence of a national supervisor, certain examples of behaviour may imply its lack of propriety.

*First*, one could mention the extent and quality of the prudential reports, which the home country supervisor receives. Do these adequately measure capital adequacy,

---

[15] Indeed, there is no relevant provision in the amended Proposal for a Distance Marketing Directive, *op. cit.*, note 7.

[16] With the word 'competent' we mean the extent to which the relevant supervisor will be capable of undertaking adequate regulation, rather than to the question whether it has been appointed appropriate legal power to undertake such a task. *See* Ruben Lee, 'Supervising EU Capital Markets: Do we need a European SEC?', in Richard Buxbaum, Hertig Gerard, Hirsch Alain and Hopt Klaus (eds), *European Economic and Business Law: Legal and Economic Analysis on Integration and Harmonisation* (Berlin, Walter de Gruyter, 1991) p. 4196.

market risks, asset quality and provisioning requirements? *Second*, the methods employed by or available to the competent authority to verify the accuracy of prudential reports. *Third*, the willingness and capability of home Member States' competent authorities to visit and examine entities in other countries, as well as the willingness of the host authorities to provide the requested information. It is essential that both authorities establish information links in order to overcome legal impediments, as bank secrecy rules. *Fourth*, the track record of the home supervisor in the taking of remedial action and the enforcement of rules, when problems arise in the home investment undertakings or financial conglomerates. *Last* but not least, the misunderstanding and misuse of certain concepts and principles. A characteristic and merely theoretic paradigm is the misuse of the 'general good' concept. In the area of financial services, there is evidence, in some cases, of the inappropriate use of the concept of 'general interest' or 'general good' to justify exemptions to the application of home country control and to prevent the marketing of financial products, which are sold validly in the home Member State. The European Commission has found that this misuse of the concept of 'general good' stems from differences in interpretation and application by the competent authorities of the Member States.[17] According to the analysis carried out by the Commission, there is a need to improve and reinforce the knowledge of the competent authorities of the Member States regarding the principles of home country control and mutual recognition.

Nevertheless, the most convincing and visible way of assessing the incompetence of a Member State supervisor is when one of the investment firms, which lie under its supervision, fails to meet the minimum standards when commencing business beyond its national borders. In this way, the incompetence of the home supervisor will become evident and may cause anomalies not only in the home market, but also in the host market, where the firm provides cross-border services. Consequently, the host competent authorities may become reluctant to welcome investment firms authorised by the supervisory authority in question, without first checking its competence, and thus an unpleasant situation would be created, which could undermine the free provision of services and the function of the 'European passport' itself.

On the other hand, it is a fact that the supervision over the behaviour of any institution, which conducts its investment business on a cross-border basis, is not the simplest task. A potential violation of its behaviour may test the competence of the host regulatory authority as well, since a request made directly to the investment firm may not be sufficient and the assistance of the host supervisor may be vital.

---

[17] *See* Commission of the European Communities, *Communication on the Mutual Recognition in the Context of the Follow-up to the Action Plan for the Single Market*, 16 June 1999, 6. For banking services, see Commission of the European Communities, *Freedom to Provide Services and the Interest of the General Good in the Second Banking Directive* (Interpretative Communication, SEC(97) 1193 final, 20 June 1997) (hereinafter '1997 Banking Communication') 17. For insurance services, *see* Commission of the European Communities, *Freedom to provide Services and the General Good in the Insurance Sector* (Interpretative Communication, C(1999)5046, 2 February 2000) (hereinafter '1999 Insurance Communication') 1. The Commission has also found differences in the core concept 'fit and proper'; *see* Commission of the European Communities, *Financial Services: Building a Framework for Action* (COM (1998) 625, 28 October 1998) 11.

Competence of the competent authorities is vital, for the credibility of the home country control approach requires mutual trust between the national supervisors. Welby writes that 'the law cannot and should not hope to cover every wrinkle of business practice. Poor ethics in the long term destroys business'.[18] If a national supervisory body does not trust the competent authorities of other Member States to keep the providers of financial services up to the minimum EU requirements, there will be a reluctance to recognise the services supplied from the country concerned. In such a case, pressure for the reintroduction or maintenance of national control on the host Member State basis could be increased, which could endanger returning to fragmented EU financial markets. At the very least, lack of mutual trust between the competent authorities would mean that the home country control regime does not work and could undermine the Single Market itself. Taken the above, it becomes evident that, if all Member States applied the same basic criteria to investor protection, they would be more likely to allow investment undertakings, which have been authorised in their home State, to deal with national clients under the right of establishment or the right to provide services, and to offer them financial products marketed in other Member States without imposing any further requirements on them.[19]

## 2.4   Complexity

Although financial services regulation at EU level may have simplified the work of the national regulators and politicians, it may also have increased the complexity of EU law as well as supervisory arrangements between Member States. Harmonisation of minimum standards has not been transformed directly to national law. Instead, regulation by directives presupposes a complex and time-consuming process, which may cause disparities between national laws. Despite the improving co-ordination role of the European Commission, in many cases it finds itself ill-equipped to monitor implementation and enforcement of Community measures.

The problem of complexity was highlighted in the Report of a high-level group appointed by the Commission,[20] which pointed out that by abandoning the imposition of uniformity, the new home country control approach had created intricate arrangements lacking transparency and requiring improved coordination.[21]

---

[18] J. Welby, 'Do Business Ethics Matter' (1992) 3 *International Company and Commercial Law Review* 46.

[19] The Commission has announced in its Action Plan of 1999 that it will draw up, in co-operation with the Member States, a list of obstacles to cross-border transactions between businesses and consumers for the financial services concerned and that it will analyse the conditions, in which the rules for protecting the consumers of the host Member State should be applied. *See* Commission of the European Communities, *Financial Services: Implementing the Framework for Financial Markets: Action Plan* (COM(1999) 232, 11 May 1999) 17 (hereinafter 'Action Plan').

[20] *See* P. Sutherland *et al.*, *Internal Market after 1992 – Meeting the Challenge: Report to the EEC Commission* (Brussels 1992).

[21] Although the Report accepted that in most areas enforcement must continue to be centralised, for some matters a more centralised regime has been found necessary.

The blurred supervisory responsibilities between the home and the host Member State in the field of financial services justify that approach.

Over-complex or ill-conceived legislation imposes additional costs and burdens on business, *inter alia* reducing competitiveness. The Commission has already made considerable efforts in this field[22] including the implementation of the SLIM initiative and the Business Test Panel scheme. The results, however, in terms of impact on existing or planned legislation, continue to fall short of the expectations of financial intermediaries, issuers and investors.

### 3   PROBLEMS OF SUBSTANCE

#### 3.1   What is the 'home country'?

For reasons of identifying the principal supervisor of a credit institution or an investment firm, it is essential to know where exactly a firm is incorporated. According to the ISD, the allocation of the home country is a simple task. It provides that 'home Member State' shall mean:

(a) where the investment firm is a natural person, the Member State in which his head office is situated and (b) where the investment firm is a legal person, the Member State in which its registered office is situated or, if under its national law it has no registered office, the Member State in which its head office is situated.[23]

Unsurprisingly, the Directive does not specify the definition of the 'head office'. It would be convenient to suggest that 'head office' is the establishment of the headquarters and the management of the firm. However, this solution would merely serve the scope of the Directive in the case, where a firm had its headquarters in a Member State, but it solely commenced investment business in another Member State.[24] Would it be rational for the first Member State to supervise a firm, which is not acting business within its borders? Apparently not for the drafters of the ISD.[25]

The interest is presumably less in the administration than where the business is done, where the records are kept, or where the contract notes are issued from.[26]

---

[22] *See* the 'Better Lawmaking' Annual Report, the most recent of which is COM(2000) 772 final of 30 November 2000; also, *see* the Annual Report on the Functioning of Community Product and Capital Markets, the most recent of which is COM(2000) of 24 January 2000.

[23] ISD, Art. 1(6).

[24] The Commission states in its Explanatory Memorandum that this reflects provisions of the UCITS Directive (Art. 3) and that it is designed to prevent the use of 'letter box' companies.

[25] It is stated in the Preamble that 'Member States must require that an investment firm's head office must always be situated in its home Member State and that it actually operates there'; *See* ISD, Recital 4.

[26] This interpretation offers a solution to the Commission's worry that firms would choose to set up a head office in a Member State, which is considered to have the least stringent regulatory requirements, but would then do most of their business in another Member State, thus encouraging 'regulatory arbitrage'. The ECJ has acknowledged that a host Member State is entitled to take steps to prevent a service

The ISD provides that not only has a firm to actually carry on its business to be granted authorisation by its home State, but it also has to deal at least with the 'core' investment services, specified in Section A of the Annex.[27] Nowadays, of course, the inquiry of where securities business actually takes place is not one without complexities. But, it would be appropriate to assume that the 'head office' is the location of the central administration and decision-making management of the firm *and* where the main or principal investment business is established.[28]

The abovementioned solution is valid whenever the competent authorities have to deal with a financial institution, which is dressed with a clearly domestic costume. But would it also apply to case, if financial firms were to be established solely under European law? As financial firms consolidate and reorganise themselves on a cross-border basis, their nationality and the identification of their responsible principal supervisory authority is becoming more difficult. In December 2000, the Council of Ministers has reached agreement on the Regulation to establish a European Company Statute. If the European Parliament endorses the texts, the European Company will become a reality some 30 years after it was first proposed. As a result, financial firms and their subsidiaries will have the option of being established as a single company under Community law and so be able to operate throughout the European Union with one set of rules and a unified management system. It is obvious that placing European financial companies under the home country supervision is extremely difficult, if not impossible. Although European companies will still have to be registered in the Member State where they have their head office, it is doubtful whether their supervisors will be able to efficiently keep under surveillance their whole pan-European business. In the light of this, the solution proposed by the European Commission, namely the appointment of a coordinating supervisor for large financial groups by national authorities,[29] is not one without problematic parameters.

A further problematic approach has been adopted by the E-commerce Directive and the adoption of the 'country of origin' principle. I will discuss this, however, later.[30]

### 3.2 Grey responsibilities between the home and the host Member State

The primary considerations and objectives of financial services supervision are market integrity and the protection of investors. To this end, home and host competent

---

provider whose activity is entirely or mainly directed towards its territory from improperly exercising the freedom to provide services of Art. 49 EC (formerly Art. 59) in order to circumvent the rules of professional conduct which would be applicable to him if he were established in the territory of that host State.

[27] ISD, Art. 3(1).

[28] It is interesting to note that if the investment firm has a registered office, it must have its head office in the same Member State as its registered office; *See* ISD, Art. 3(2).

[29] *See* Commission of the European Communities, *Progress on Financial Services*, 2nd Report, COM(2000) 336, 31 May 2000, at 10; Commission of the European Communities, *Proposal for a Directive on Financial Collateral Arrangements*, COM (2001) 168 final, 27 March 2001.

[30] *See infra* Section 4.

authorities are responsible for the prudential supervision and the business activities supervision[31] of financial undertakings respectively. However, the separation between prudential and transactions supervision implies two levels of regulation applying, which have the same focus and objectives. From the very moment the ISD was passed, it has been criticised for its failure to achieve this separation,[32] which has given rise to a great deal of rules overlapping and ambiguity. This problematic approach is more acute in the SBD, where no explicit division is made between authorisation and transactions, nor is there an Art. 11-style provision with regard to conduct of business rules.[33]

Although a certain harmonisation has already taken place in the area of consumer protection and in advertising,[34] one could identify various differences from Member State to Member State. *Generally speaking*, difficulties arise in the application of home country control and mutual recognition to investment services when host Member States take steps to protect the 'general good', as with investor protection. By this means, the principal Treaty freedom of services within the Single Market can be hindered. *Second*, variations could occur because of different interpretations of authorisation and prudential rules on one hand and transactional rules on the other and their assignment to the supervisory power of the home or the host Member State, respectively. The vague drafting of the relevant articles ISD intensifies the grey areas of responsibility. *Third*, rules of conduct between investment undertakings and their clients vary substantially from Member State to Member State. Consequently, a financial firm wishing to establish itself or to provide cross-border services can merely avoid complying to more than one set of rules of conduct, which constitutes a significant obstacle to the free provision of financial services. *Fourth*, problems could arise because of different priorities given to the needs of investors and depositors. Indeed, the ISD itself states that, when applying rules of conduct between the financial institutions and their clients, Member States shall take into account the professional experience of the person, to whom the service is provided. However, the Directive does not offer any further guidance regarding the shape of application of rules of conduct and the construe of 'professional' investors. It is, therefore, very probable that Member States, in which consumerism is more developed, will devise more stringent rules of conduct *vis-à-vis* inexperienced persons than other Member States.[35] *Finally*, rules relating to advertising and marketing of investment services

---

[31] When we refer to 'activities supervision', we mean the drawing up of rules of conduct and the supervision of the financial firms' transactions.

[32] *See* for example, Peter Haines, 'The Investment Services Directive: Progress to Date' (1995) 2 EFSL 30, 31; Dassesse Marc, Stuart Isaacs and Graham Penn, *EC Banking Law* (2nd edn, London, Lloyds Commercial Law Library, 1994), p. 61; Charles Abrams 'The Investment Services Directive – Who Should be the Principal Regulator of Cross-border Services?' (1995) 11 EFSL 317.

[33] *See* Dassesse Marc *et al., ibid.*, Paras 4.6 *et seq* and 7.5.

[34] These could be described as 'indirect' rules of conduct. *See* for example. Directive 97/7/EC of 20 May 1997 on the protection of consumers in respect of distance contracts, OJ L144/19 of 4 June 1997 and Directive 97/55/EC concerning misleading advertising so as to include comparative advertising of 6 October 1997, OJ L290/18 of 23 October 1997.

[35] Gerard Hertig, *op. cit.*, note 8, 224.

are not clearly allocated to the home or the host Member State, which could create a great deal of confusion. The letter of Art. 13 ISD lets us understand that advertising rules are subject to the host State power in the interest of the general good, but nothing hinders the home competent authorities from imposing their own rules on financial undertakings as well.

In an effort to assess the magnitude of problems in the provision of investment services one could follow potential complaints originated from businesses or individuals. In its Communication of 1999,[36] the Commission states that it has received many complaints for services including business communications, construction, patent agents and security services. However, if we attempted to apply this test on investment services, we could possibly come to the conclusion that the criterion for receiving complaints is not very appropriate in that providers of investment services, for example, do not tend to submit complaints to the Commission. Instead, in most cases, such complaints should be directed to the host Member State's competent authorities, with which the investment undertaking is required to develop a long-term relationship.

### 3.2.1 The general good

The main purpose of the main financial services directive is to enable authorised financial institutions in a Member State to supply, throughout the European Union, cross-border financial services either by the establishment of a branch or under the freedom to provide services. EU law has not, however, harmonised in full the content of financial activity. It is likely, therefore, that a financial firm wishing to provide services in another Member State will be confronted with different rules applicable both to the service itself and to the conditions, in which it may be offered and marketed.

As seen before, the home country control regime includes a mixture of responsibilities between the home and the host Member State. The struggle of the home and the host country to keep for themselves more and more regulatory and supervisory tasks, interferes with the 'general good' concept, which blurs even more this division. It is, thus, crucial in our assessment of the efficiency of the home country control regime to examine where lies the power of the host State to impose its own rules – namely rules of conduct and marketing rules – on foreign financial undertakings. The greater the competence of the host authorities, the greater the possibility for differences and conflicts, and the greater the disadvantage for firms, which provide intra-Community financial services. On the other hand, if the host country's supervisory responsibility is limited by the general good concept, the burden on foreign firms is lighter and the European passport acquires a more pragmatic dimension.

EU secondary legislation considers that a financial firm operating in the context of home country control could be forced to bring its services into line with the rules of the host country only if the measures relied on against it are in the interest of the

---

[36] Commission of the European Communities, *Communication on the Mutual Recognition, op. cit.,* note 17, 2.

general good, whether it is acting via a branch or under the freedom to provide services.[37] This approach is, moreover, confirmed by the European Court of Justice (E C J). In our analysis, I will examine the drafting of the ISD as well as the relevant case law of the European Court.

The financial services directives do not contain any definition of the general good concept.[38] The reason for this, according to the Commission, is that, in non-harmonised areas, the level of general good involved depends on the assessment of the Member States and can vary substantially from one country to another according to national traditions and the objectives of each Member State.[39] Similarly, the directives do not specify within what limits and under what conditions the host State may impose its general-good rules upon a European financial undertaking. It is, thus, necessary to refer to the relevant provisions, before exploring the case law of the ECJ. In investment services, a careful examination of the ISD reveals that, in general, various limitation on an *ad infinitum* applicability of the host country's rules of conduct already flow from its provisions. Therefore:

(i) Art. 28 ISD prohibits rules of discrimination,[40]

(ii) Art. 11(1) ISD requires that rules of conduct be '*applied in such a way as to take account of the professional nature of the person for whom the service is provided*',[41]

(iii) Certain conduct of business rules may fall under the provision of Art. 14(2) ISD, which prevents host Member States from applying on foreign investment firms' measures that have an equivalent effect to the provision of endowment capital,[42]

(iv) With regard to the establishment of a branch or the provision of cross-border services, Arts 17(4) and 18(2) ISD empower the host Member State to indicate the conditions of business of the foreign investment firms in the interest of the general good,[43] and

---

[37] *See* ISD, Recital 33, SBD, Recital 16, Third Insurance Directives (92/49/EC and 92/96/EC), Recitals 19 and 20, respectively.

[38] Preferring to maintain its progressive nature, the ECJ has never given a definition too.

[39] *See* 1997 Banking Communication, *op. cit.*, note 17.

[40] According to the Art. 'Member States shall Ensure that this Directive is Implemented without Discrimination'.

[41] This requirement constitutes an echo of the ECJ judgement C-205/84 *Commission* v. *Germany* [1986] ECR 3755, Para. 27. Also *cf.* Art. 11(3) ISD, 'Where an investment firm executes an order (...) the professional nature of the investor shall be assessed with respect to the investor from whom the order originates', which implies that the host State's conduct of business rules should take account of the position of wholesale investors.

[42] Pursuant to this article, 'Member States may not make the establishment of a branch or the provision of services (...) subject to any authorisation requirement, to any requirement to provide endowment capital or to any other measure having equivalent effect'.

[43] The two articles are similarly drafted. Art. 17(4) for example, provides that 'the competent authorities of the host Member State shall (...) prepare for the supervision of the investment firm (...) and, if necessary, indicate the conditions, including the rules of conduct, under which, in the interest of the general good, that business must be carried on in the host Member State'.

(v) In addition to the indication of conditions, Art. 19(6) empowers the host Member State '*to take appropriate measures to prevent or to penalize irregularities committed within their territories which are contrary to the rules of conduct introduced pursuant to Article 11 as well as to other legal or regulatory provisions adopted in the interest of the general good'.*[44]

As it becomes obvious, the wording of these provisions merely removes the ambiguity of the broad drafting of Art. 11. The latter provision of Article 19(6)[45] is less clear with respect to the dilemma in issue. If rules of conduct are considered to be part of the 'other legal or regulatory provisions adopted in the interest of the general good', then the host Member State can only impose conduct of business rules subject to the principle of 'general good'. On the other hand, it is argued that the word 'other' comes to distinct rules of conduct from the rules adopted in the interest of the general good.[46]

I cannot support the latter view. The formulation of the aforementioned provisions as well as the general background and objective of the ISD imply a different approach. The wording 'including the rules of conduct' of Arts 17(4) and 18(2) indicates that business of conduct rules constitute a part of the conditions, which lie under the scrutiny of the general good concept. In addition, when one observes the background of the ISD, one clearly realises that the aim is to secure freedom of establishment and freedom to provide services, through the principles of mutual recognition and home country control.[47] To this end, host Member States must ensure that there are no obstacles to prevent activities that receive the 'European passport' from being carried on in the same manner as in the home Member State, as long as they do not conflict with laws and regulations protecting the general good in force.[48] Although the ISD merely endeavours to completely eliminate the differences between the Member States' national regulatory and supervisory regimes, the broader the power of the host State, the greater the risk of dominant differences.[49] Limiting the host State's regulatory and supervisory power to the concept of the general good suits better with the main objectives mentioned above. At the end of the day, the concept of general good is an exemption to the fundamental principles

---

[44] A similar statement is provided in ISD, Recital 41. Thorkildsen contends that Art. 13 ISD, which states that host Member States may take measures governing the form and content of advertising subject to the interest of the general good, should also be taken into consideration; *see* Tarjei Thorkildsen, 'Power to draw up Conduct of Business Rules after the ISD' (1995) 15 *Company Lawyer* 102, 104.

[45] In particular the use of the word 'other' in the provision.

[46] *See* Jan Wouters, 'Rules of Conduct, Foreign Investment Firms and the ECJ's Case Law on Services' (1993) 13 *Company Lawyer* 194, 195, arguing that the '*formulation of Article 19(6) seems to indicate that a host Member State can enforce any rule of conduct, as long as it has been introduced pursuant to (the very broadly formulated) art 11*'.

[47] *See* Preamble to the ISD, Recitals 1–4, 28.

[48] *See ibid.*, Recital 33. This is similar with Recital 16 of the SBD. As to the controversy regarding the latter *see* Jan Wouters, 'Conflict of Laws and the Single Market for Financial Services (Part I)' (1997) 2 *Maastricht Journal of European and Comparative Law* 161, 185.

[49] *Ibid.*

of the Treaty with regard to free movement and must, therefore, be interpreted in a *stricto sensu* fashion.

Given the ambiguity of the ISD outlined before, one should read and interpret the host State's power to draw up and supervise rules of conduct in conformity with the ECJ case law. Although the Court has traditionally confirmed that only the general good rules can restrict the home country control and hinder the exercise of the two fundamental freedoms, namely the freedom to provide services[50] and the freedom of establishment,[51] *in praesenti* an uncertainty prevails with regard to the case law concerning the Treaty freedoms. Especially the *Keck* judgement has reopened the issue and initiated a new series of discussion.

Going back to *Cassis de Dijon*,[52] the ECJ tried to control the host (importing) State's power in light of Art. 28 EC Treaty (former Art. 30) by laying down two principles. *First*, it recognised a derogation from the free movement of goods in so far as the measures of the importing country are necessary to satisfy mandatory requirements.[53] *Second*, the Court accepted that the unilateral requirements imposed by the rules of the importing Member State are incompatible with the provisions of Art. 28 of the Treaty, if the goods have been lawfully produced and marketed in the home Member State.[54]

With regard to services, the Court made clear in *Sager* v. *Dennemeyer* that Art. 49 EC Treaty (former Art. 59) applies to host country's rules and requires the abolition of any restriction, even if it applies without distinction to national providers of services and to those from other Member States, when it may impede the activities of a provider of services established in another Member State. The only requirement is that host Member States may impose measures on a non-discriminatory basis justified by 'imperative requirements of public interest', if that interest is not subject to the rules of the home State, and that they are objectively necessary to attain the interest involved.[55] Applying the general good concept, the 'no overlapping controls' and 'proportionality' tests in a number of judgements,[56] the ECJ limited the power of the host State.

However, the ECJ in *Keck* found it necessary to re-examine its case law and widen the scope of application of the '*Cassis de Dijon*' doctrine arising from Art. 30 EC Treaty regarding free movement of goods. The Court made a distinction between provisions relating to 'marketing, selling arrangements and methods of sales

---

[50] *See* Case C-76/90 *Sager* v. *Dennemeyer* [1991] ECR I-4221, Para. 15. *See* also the analysis contained in the Commission Interpretative Communication concerning the free movement of services across frontiers (OJ C334 of 9 December 1993) 3.

[51] *See* Case C-71/76 *Thieffry* v. *Conseil de l'Ordre des Avocats à la Cour de Paris* [1977] ECR 765, Para. 12; Case C-55/94 *Gebhard* v *Consilio dell'Ordine degli Avvocati e Procuratori* [1995] ECR I-4165, Para. 35.

[52] Case 120/78 *Rewe-Zentral AG* v. *Bundesmonopolverwaltung für Branntwein* [1979] ECR 649.

[53] *Ibid.*, Para. 8(2). This is the so-called 'rule of reason'.

[54] *Ibid.*, Para. 14(3).

[55] Case C-76/90 *op. cit*, note 50, Para. 12.

[56] *See* Case 279/80 *Webb* [1981] ECR 3305, Para. 16; Case C-205/84 *Commission* v. *Germany, op. cit.*, note 42, Para. 39.

promotion' on the one hand, and rules laying down product requirements on the other.[57] The latter falls within the scope of Treaty provisions.[58] By contrast to what has previously been decided, the application to products from other Member States of the host State's former measures is not as such as to hinder directly or indirectly intra-Community trade, as long as the rules 'apply to all relevant traders' and affect them 'in the same manner, in law and in fact'.[59]

The Court clearly departs from its earlier practice relating to goods. In assessing the consequences for services, the difficulty lies in the application of the aforementioned distinction in the provision of financial services and especially in conduct of business rules.[60] Although the ECJ merely provides clear support for limiting the host State's power to draw up and supervise conduct of business rules, one should not immediately conclude in favour of its *in toto* authority. In addition, the case law does not achieve to remove the *in dubio status* of the ISD and clarify the dilemma. In any case, even if we accept that rules of conduct are not limited by the concept of general good, the general principle of EU law still remains, that national measures used to achieve a given end must not go beyond what is appropriate and necessary to achieve that end, *alias dictus* the proportionality test.[61]

At least in banking, however, the Commission's guidance[62] does emphasise that rules, whose objective is to protect clients, are more likely to be regarded as satisfying the general good test, except perhaps where the client has on his own initiative chosen to use a European institution established only outside his own Member State. Much will depend on individual cases, where the need for protection of the client will be examined, as well as his level of sophistication and the nature of the service.[63] In *Commission v. Germany*, the European Court held that 'there may be cases where, because of the nature of the risk insured and of the party seeking insurance, there is no need to protect the latter by the application of the mandatory rules of his national law'.[64] The scope of this ruling naturally goes beyond the field of insurance.

The ambiguity of the extend of the host Member State power interests our analysis in that it makes difficult to assess the hindrance to the cross-border provision of investment services and to the operation of investment firms in general. Moreover,

---

[57] *See* Joined Cases C-267/91 and C-268/91 *Criminal Proceedings against Bernand Keck and Daniel Mithouard* [1993] ECR I-6097, Para. 13–17.

[58] *Ibid.*, Para. 15.

[59] *Ibid.*, Para. 16.

[60] Thorkildsen argues that conduct of business rules seem to be more equivalent to the former 'rules for the sale' and, therefore, fall outside the Treaty provisions. *See* Thorkildsen, *op. cit*, note 44, 107.

[61] *Ibid*, 107–108.

[62] *See*, 1997 Banking Communication, *op. cit.*, note 17, 19. For these rules to be enforceable, however, some additional conditions may need to be met.

[63] The ECJ has recognised the difference in the service by imposing a less restrictive and more 'lightweight' legal framework for provision of services than for establishment. In *Säger* it held that a Member State *'may not make the provision of services in its territory subject to compliance with all the conditions required for establishment and thereby deprive of all practical effectiveness the provisions of the Treaty whose object is, precisely, to guarantee the freedom to provide services'. See* also Case C-198/89 *Commission v. Greece* [1991] ECR I-727, Para. 16.

[64] Case 205/84 *Commission v. Germany, op. cit.*, note 41.

the efficiency of the present system of allocation of supervisory responsibilities lies also *in dubio*. The lesser the supervisory rules are harmonised, the greater the power of the host State to impose its rules under the general good. And, the greater the power of the host State, the bigger the disadvantage for investment firms, which wish to commence investment business out of their home country, and the less the competition and the burden on national investment firm of the host State.

The Commission's guidance on banking and insurance does merely provide the final answer to everything. It may require radical changes to be made to domestic law, which, due to various legal and cultural differences, may be refused by Member States.[65] Consequently, ambiguity surrounding the interpretation and application of the general good concept makes financial firms face legal uncertainty, both as regards the arrangements applicable to them in the different Member States and as regards their supervisory authorities. This unsatisfactory situation may seriously undermine the workings of the machinery set up by the Single Market Programme and is thus likely to deter certain financial undertakings from exercising the freedoms created by the Treaty.

### 3.2.2   Authorisation

The responsibility to authorise investment undertakings lies in the hands of the competent authorities of the home Member State. However, it may be disputed whether sole competency is vested in the home country or whether the host competent authorities are allowed to carry out checks to determine if the financial firm, intending to operate in its territory under the freedom to provide services or through a branch, meets the standard conditions, under which it was granted the European passport in its home State.

It is obvious that such checks may be carried out by the home Member State alone. When the home competent authorities grant a licence to a financial firm to commence cross-border business, the host Member State should not be allowed to question the granting of such authorisation. Both the ECJ and the Commission[66] seem to support this view. In *Commission v Belgium*,[67] a case involving broadcasting services, the Court held that the receiving (host) Member State was not authorised to monitor

---

[65] The Commission's guidance is actually only that; although based on ECJ case law, it constitutes only an interpretative tool and neither a law in itself nor a Directive requiring Member States to comply with it.

[66] For credit institutions, *see* '1997 Banking Communication', *op. cit.*, note 17, 14. For insurance undertakings, *see* 1999 Insurance Communication, *op. cit.*, note 17. The Commission has been very sensitive with host Member States' measures derogating from the principles of home country control and mutual recognition. It has insisted, therefore, for the transparency of national measures, which would make it easier to deal quickly and at the appropriate level with problems, which may jeopardise the free movement of goods and services. *See* European Parliament and Council of the European Union, *Decision No. 3052/95/EC Establishing a Procedure for the Exchange of Information on National Measures Derogating From the Principle of the Free Movement of Goods within the Community* (OJ L 321/1 of 30 December 1995). Art. 1 of the decision states that 'where a Member State takes steps to prevent the free movement or placing on the market of a particular model or type of product lawfully produced or marketed in another Member State, it shall notify the Commission accordingly (...)'.

[67] Case C-11/95 *Commission* v. *Belgium* [1996] ECR I-4115, Para. 34.

the application of the law of the originating Member State applying to television broadcasts and to ensure compliance with the 'Television without Frontiers' Directive.[68]

If the host Member State has reasons to believe that the financial undertakings, which was granted authorisation, does not comply with the standard conditions, shall find other ways to satisfy itself. It may have recourse to Art. 227 EC Treaty (former Article 170)[69] or request the Commission to take action against the home Member State for failing to meet its obligations pursuant to Art. 226 EC (former Article 169).[70] In no circumstances shall it take action by itself and monitor compliance with the minimum requirements, which may well constitute an infringement of the Treaty freedoms of establishment and provision of services.

### 3.2.3 Prudential versus transaction rules

Articles 11 and 10 ISD contain respectively the rules of conduct an investment undertaking has to comply with and some rules about prudential measures that investment firms have to introduce with respect to their organisation in order to be able to comply with the code of conduct best possible. The distinction between prudential–organisational and transactional rules is significant for the application to non-core investment services and for the appointment of the principal country-supervisor. *Prudential rules* cover the authorisation and effective supervision of financial institutions to trade in securities. They control the conditions for the initial and continuing permission to offer securities to the public or to deal in securities on behalf of the investors.[71] On the other hand, *transactional rules* control the transactions between issuers, dealers and investors and impose the rules of conduct between the financial undertakings and their clients.

Regarding the former, I shall make the following distinction and observation. Arts 10 and 11 rules apply to all investment services listed in Section A of the Annex to the ISD.[72] In addition, however, the rules of conduct contained in Art. 11 may also apply 'where appropriate' to the non-core services listed in Section C of the Annex.[73] Consequently, although not explicitly drafted in the Directive, it is very probable that

---

[68] Council Directive 89/552/EEC of 3 October 1989 on the coordination of certain provisions laid down by Law, Regulation or Administrative Action in Member States concerning the pursuit of television broadcasting activities (OJ L 298/23 of 17 October 1989).

[69] According to Art. 227, 'a Member State which considers that another Member State has failed to fulfil an obligation under this Treaty may bring the matter before the Court of Justice. Before a Member State brings an action against another Member State for an alleged infringement of an obligation under this Treaty, it shall bring the matter before the Commission (...)'.

[70] Pursuant to Art. 226, 'If the Commission considers that a Member State has failed to fulfil an obligation under this Treaty, it shall deliver a reasoned opinion on the matter after giving the State concerned the opportunity to submit its observations (...)'. For national measures relating to goods, environment or working environment, *cf* Art. 95(4–5) EC (former Art. 100a).

[71] Phillipe Lambrecht and Haljan David, 'Investor Protection and the European Directives concerning Securities', in Hans van Houtte (ed.), *The Law of Cross-Border Securities Transactions*, (London, Sweet and Maxwell, 1999), p. 259.

[72] ISD, Art. 1(1) and 2(1).

[73] *Ibid.*, Art. 11(1).

a Member State imposes additional rules relating to underwriters, safe custody services, capital structure consulting or credit granting.

With regard to the latter, the clear distinction between prudential and transactional rules will automatically reveal the specific responsibilities of the home and the host regulators. Here, the drafters of the ISD have failed throughoutly. One could presumably imply that anything that is not specifically stated in the Directive as being a home country responsibility will fall to the host State and *vice versa*. However, the drafting of Arts 10 and 11 ISD do merely allow such a simple solution. Instead, they raise major questions and confusion, as the applicable rules may well cross the separation of competence for prudential and transactional supervision.

There is a considerable overlap, both conceptually and in practice, between prudential and conduct of business regulations. Both, for example, have a close and legitimate interest in the senior management of any financial undertaking subject to both these types of regulation, in particular because of the crucial roles of senior management in setting the 'compliance culture' of the firm.[74] On the other hand, the organisation and 'internal control mechanisms' of the financial undertaking[75] are directly related to the nature of the transaction from the investor protection perspective. The host competent authorities may have the reasonable interest on behalf of the general good in having some control on matters, which fall under the home country's prudential supervision. For instance, prudential rules for personal transactions by the firm's employees may well conflict with the host country's rules of conduct relating to conflicts of interest.[76]

In addition, the requirement that home Member States shall 'arrange for records to be kept of transactions executed' appears to imply that the host State would not have any power in that area. But is it not included in the host country's tasks – the ability to control its own markets and monitor the transactions taking place within them, for the interest of market confidence and investor protection? Rules on record keeping are closely interrelated with rules of conduct. If a host Member State is to be able to ensure that the participants in the markets, for which it is responsible, abide by host rules of conduct, it will be important for that host authority to have the ability to establish an 'audit trail' of transactions which have been undertaken by a particular firm in particular securities or on particular market within its jurisdiction. This significant tool of supervision may provide evidence of possible breaches of rules, not only those covered by the ISD, but also of breaches of national rules, as an example on insider dealing. It is, therefore, more than necessary for the host competent authorities to have the power to impose particular record keeping requirements, based on the nature of their markets in order to monitor their own rules of conduct.

The ISD has only taken account of the problem of conflicting rules with regard to conflicts of interest, at least in the case of a branch establishment.[77] Yet, the unhelpful

---

[74] *See* Clive Briault, *The Rationale for a Single National Financial Services Regulator* (FSA Occasional Paper No. 2, May 1999) 24.

[75] ISD, Art. 10, first indent.

[76] *Ibid.*, Art. 11(1), sixth indent.

[77] *See* ISD, Art. 10, fifth indent. Although it is pursuant to this provision that each home Member State shall draw up prudential rules to be observed 'at all times', as to the structure and organisation of the firm.

drafting of the directives' provision has not managed to overcome specific doubts. The host State may draw up a code of conduct to avoid conflicts of interest, or to ensure fair treatment, when such conflict cannot be avoided.[78] At the same time, the home country is vested with the power to require a certain structure and organisation by the financial firm, so that the client's risk of being prejudiced by conflict of interest is minimised.[79] Doubts need to be removed as to the ability of the host Member State to impose rules of conduct relating to the management and disclosure of conflicts of interest. This is not something that can be left exclusively to the home competent authorities. *A fortiori* doubts need to be removed as to the magnitude of the host country's power; it might be said that a power for the host State to draw up rules of conduct that is not limited by the 'general good' will make the risk of overlap even greater.[80] In any case, overlap might still occur, which could result in the host State's interference in the organisational structure of foreign investment firms.

Correspondingly, a major question arises from the last phrase of Art. 10: Does it establish a hierarchy between prudential and transactional rules, that is, between Art. 10, fifth indent and Art. 11, sixth indent?[81] The drafting design of that phrase leaves open the possibility that, at least in the case of a branch establishment, home State prudential rules may retreat in favour of the host State's rules of conduct, when they are controversial. However, if we accept that host country's rules prevail, we can easily be led to the unpleasant situation, where the structure of an investment firm depends on and is continuously adjusted according to the conflict of interest rules of every Member State, in which it provides cross-border services. It is self-evident that such a hierarchy and wider application of host country's rules cannot be accepted. In any case, it is necessary for any regulatory structure to address these issues because of the potential trade-off between rules of conduct and prudential objectives. Likewise, the need for a clear allocation of responsibility between the home and the host Member State is intensified.

### 3.2.4 *Rules of conduct*

The first Community initiative in the field of rules of conduct was the 1977 Commission Recommendation for a European Code of Conduct.[82] The Recommendation provided

---

'in such a way as to minimise the risk of clients' interests being prejudiced by conflicts of interest', it is added that where a branch is set up, 'the organisational arrangements may not conflict with the rules of conduct laid down by the host Member State to cover conflicts of interest'.

[78] *Ibid.*, Art. 11(1), sixth indent.

[79] *Ibid.*, Art. 10, fifth indent.

[80] *See* Thorkildsen, *op. cit.*, note 44, 105. Thorkildsen argues that there might be a lesser degree of overlap if the host State could only draw rules of conduct when justified by the general good. Therefore, the narrower interpretation of a host State's power should prevail.

[81] For an allegation that there is a clear hierarchy between these two articles, *see* Stefan Grundman and Wolfgang Kerber, Information Intermediaires and Extending the Area of Informed Party Autonomy – Securities and Insurance Markets, Paper submitted at the Conference 'Party Autonomy for the Internal Market' (King's College, London, 11–13 May 2000).

[82] Commission of the European Communities, *Recommendation 77/534/EEC of 25 July 1977 Concerning a European Code of Conduct Relating to Transactions in Transferable Securities* (OJ L 212/37 of 20 August 1977).

several principles and model rules with regard to market conduct and conduct of business in EEC financial markets. However, it is not surprising that Member States never implemented these rules, since the Single Market Programme came as late as fifteen years later. Instead, the Community's main harmonisation focus has been on listing and disclosure requirements.

Rules of conduct (Table 1) continue to differ significantly throughout the EU, wherever they exist of course.[83] Consequently, even if the European legislator was to achieve the clear differentiation between prudential and transactional rules and allocate the home and host country responsibilities in a functional manner, there will always be rules of conduct, which will play the role of the *apple of discord* between the jurisdictions.

The magnitude of the difficulties potentially created by the provisions of the financial services directives will be full appreciated when it is borne in mind that a single investment firm may have to obey fifteen different rules of conduct in order to commence cross-border investment business. The ECJ's jurisprudence regarding the scope of 'general good' restrictions provides guidance about the legal scope of national rules of conduct drawn under Arts 11 ISD and 16(4) and 21(5) of the SBD.[84] Thus, the functions of Arts 11(1)[85] and 11(2) directly or indirectly confirm that the host State's rules apply in addition to those of the home State. The ISD does not prohibit a home Member State from continuing to subject financial firms authorised by it to its rules of conduct even though the services are provided in other Member States.[86] As a consequence, a financial firm, which exercises its freedom to provide services, cannot only be hindered by rules of conduct of its home country, which its competitors in the host State do not have to comply with,[87] but it also runs the risk of being subjected to several overlapping or conflicting rules.[88] Un-harmonised rules of conduct, therefore, constitute an inevitable – often acute – hurdle to the Single Market race of free flow of investment and free provision of financial trade.

---

[83] In many countries, rules of conduct have been introduced with the implementation of the ISD; *see* Table 5.1.

[84] Eva Lomnicka, 'The Single European Passport in Financial Services', in Barry Rider and Mads Andenas (eds), *Developments in European Community Law Vol. 1/1996* (London, Kluwer Law International, 1997), pp. 198–199.

[85] It follows, *per contra*, from Art. 11(1), that, unlike its regime on prudential rules, which pursuant to Art. 10 have to be drawn up by each home Member State, the ISD assigns the task of drawing up rules of conduct to 'Member States' generally.

[86] On the contrary, the addition that these rules must be observed by the firms 'at all times' seems to lend support to such continuing application; *see* Art. 11(1) ISD.

[87] *See* in particular Adams, 'The Single Market in Financial Services – an Orwellian Approach', (1996) 3 EFSL 149, who recounts the following experience of an English bank: 'for our Swedish branch we asked the SFA if we could follow local rules and practice for [client money and customer asset rules]. SFA determined (accurately) that the Swedish requirements did not match the UK ones. So we were left with the option of exporting more onerous client money and customer asset rules to a country where our competition did not have to bear this regulatory and cost burden'.

[88] *See* Carol L'Heveder, 'The Investment Services Directive and Its Implications for Participants in Europe's Financial Markets' (1996) 1 JIBFL 5, 8. According to the author, the SIB has adopted an alternative and more pragmatic approach, *inter alia*, by encouraging a wider application of the professional's exemption of Art. 11(1) ISD.

*Table 1.* Rules of conduct in the EU Member States and competent authorities

| | Date of rules of conduct | Law | Supervisory authority | Year of establishment | Personnel (end 2000) |
|---|---|---|---|---|---|
| Austria | 30.12.1996 | Arts 11–18 Securities Supervision Act | Bundes-Wertpapieraufsicht | 1997 | 30 |
| Belgium | 6.4.1995 | Art. 36 Law on Secondary Markets | Commission Bancaire et Financiere | 1990 | 250 (all divisions) |
| Denmark | 22.5.1996 | Secs 5–6 Securities Trading Act 376 | Finanstilsynet | 1981 | 168 (all divisions) |
| Finland | 1989 | Ch.4 Securities Markets Act 495/89 | Rahoitustarkastus | 1993 | 120 |
| France | 2.7.1996 | Art. 32 Law 96–597 | Commission des Opérations de Bourse | 1967 | 300 |
| Germany | 26.7.1994 | Secs, 31–32 WpHG | Bundesaufsichtsamt für den Wertpapierhandel | 1995 | 140 |
| Greece | 30.4.1996 | Art. 7 Law 2396/96 | Capital Market Commission | 1995 | 80 |
| Ireland | 1.8.1995 | Sec. 37 Investment Intermediaries Act | Central Bank of Ireland | 1943 | 700 (all divisions) |
| Italy | 24.2.1998 | Art. 21 Legisl. Decree 58/1998 | Commissione Nazionale per le Societa e la Bors | 1974 | 450 |
| Luxembourg | 5.4.1993 | Art. 37 Circular 2000/15 | Commission de Surveillance du Secteur Financier | 1998 | 156 (all divisions) |
| Netherlands | 16.11.1995 | Art. 24 Besluit Toezicht Effectenverkeer | Stichting Toezicht Effectenverkeer | 1989 | 170 |
| Portugal | 10.4.1991 13.11.1999 | Law 142-A/91, Arts 304–317 New Securities Code 486/99 | Comissao do Mercado de Valores Mobiliarios | 1991 | 147 |
| Spain | 1993 | Royal Decree 629/1993 | Comision Nacional del Mercado de Valores | 1988 | 200 |
| Sweden | 18.12.1997 | FFFS 1997: 36 FFFS 1998: 21 | Finansinspektionen | 1991 | 160 |
| UK | 1985 | Financial Services Act | Financial Services Authority (ex Securities & Investments Board) | 1985 (SIB) 1997 (FSA) | 2000 (all divisions) |

© Avgerinos 2001.

The risk of rules overlap may also have a direct and diversifying effect on the protection of investors and the enforcement competence of each supervisory authority. Since each Member State has the task of regulating transactions and imposing rules of conduct within its own territory, the scope of investor protection and enforcement will inevitably vary between Member States. The minimum common base-line set by the directives does not necessarily reduce or soften the territorial divisions between national securities systems.[89] However, one may argue that the scope of investor protection extends beyond the express provisions of the financial services directives and the national securities legislation. It may include general matters of civil and commercial law, company law, competition law and consumer protection law.[90] On the other hand, investors will be mostly concerned with the reliability of their brokers and the reliability of their investment. Thus, the core concern is the transaction itself, which is regulated by the rules of conduct and supervised by the host country's competent authorities. When rules of conduct are not harmonised across the European Union, then diversities between investor protection standards can merely be avoided.

It is acknowledged by the Commission itself that there may ultimately be a need to reconsider the extend, to which host country application of rules of conduct is in keeping with the needs of an integrated market.[91] Verifiability under a justification and proportionality test does not only appear desirable with regard to rules of conduct, which increase cost for foreign investment and credit institutions, but also when impediments to market access originate from overlapping or conflicting national rules of conduct.

### 3.2.4.1.   *Wholesale market. Who is 'professional investor'?*
Whether or not investment undertakings could choose to obey one set of rules of conduct depends mainly on the relative size of the wholesale and retail markets. Art. 11(1) requires that Member States shall apply rules of conduct 'in such a way as to take account of the professional nature of the person for whom the service is provided'.[92] However, it may possible for Member States to draw up rules of conduct in violation either of the standards codified by the ISD Art. 11(1) or of primary

---

[89] Phillipe Lambrecht and Haljan David, *op. cit.*, note 71, at 260. Lambrecht and Haljan use the paradigm of differentiated investor/consumer standards across the European Union and of diverse treatment of the notions of 'investors' and 'consumers'. Indeed, not all safeguards and presumptions applying to consumers do necessarily apply to investors as well. In addition, they allege that the definition of 'consumer' for the purposes of the Brussels and Rome Conventions, having an autonomous EU interpretation, apply only for the purposes of these Conventions. There is no single EU definition of 'consumer' in the securities directives, except in the proposed Directive on distance marketing of financial services; *see* Directive, Art. 2(d), which simply defines 'consumer' as 'any natural person who, in contracts covered by this Directive, is acting for purposes which are outside his trade, business or profession'.

[90] Here is where the difference and similarities between consumer and investor standards become critical.

[91] *See* Action Plan, *op. cit.*, note 19, 5.

[92] *See* also ISD, Recital 32, which states that 'whereas one of the objectives of this Directive is to protect investors; whereas it is therefore appropriate to take account of the different requirements for protection of various categories of investors and of their level of professional expertise'.

EU law.[93] While other investors will require a level of protection that reflects their lesser expertise, professional investors for the purposes of conduct of business rules need fewer externally imposed intervention and protection.[94] To proceed even further, it is often alleged that sophisticated investors do not require protection at all, for it is in their own as well as in their clients' interest to assess the risks related to investment services and build a risk-efficient portfolio.[95]

Given the fact that wholesale investors need less protection than retail individuals, host competent authorities will logically be less concerned to offer them more protection with the imposition of their own rules of conduct. They will be more willing to waive such detailed requirements in order to win the confidence and give incentives to large investment houses.[96] In this way, they will achieve on one hand the opening-up of their borders and markets to foreign capital flows and cross-border services, without on the other hand placing under risk their primary objectives of investor protection and market integrity.[97] However, a number of key issues need to be addressed in this context: how should 'professional' market users be defined and with which criteria should market participants be differentiated according to their relative expertise? How should requirements for inter-professional business be structured in a manner consistent with regulatory and supervisory objectives?

The ISD is mute regarding the criteria and standards that distinguish between wholesale and retail markets and constitute an investor 'professional' or 'sophisticated'. To fill the gap, the members of Forum of European Securities Commission (FESCO) have issued a paper,[98] in which they adopt a set of criteria for defining professional

---

[93] In Belgium, for instance, rules of conduct are considerably extended applying for both retail and wholesale transactions, contrary to the spirit of Art. 11(1); *See* Eddy Wymeersch, 'The Implementation of the ISD and CAD in National Legal Systems', in Guido Ferrarini (ed.), *European Securities Markets, The Investment Services Directive and Beyond*, (London, Kluwer Law International, 1998), 36.

[94] This does not mean that professional investors should not be subject to any rules of conduct at all, but that there is no need in such situations for the full range of detailed rules. This can also be deducted from the wording of Art. 11(1), which makes no such comprehensive exemption even with respect to the most sophisticated institutional investors. Even though the 'principles' call for differentiation, they are still mandatory law; see Kondgen, Johannes, 'Rules of Conduct: Further Harmonisation?', in Guido Ferrarini (ed.), *op. cit.*, note 93, 128.

[95] *See*, for example, Christopher Cruickshank, 'The Investment Services Directive', in Wymeersch, Eddy (ed.), *Further Perspectives in Financial Integration in Europe* (Berlin, Walter de Gruyter, 1994), p. 76, who alleges that 'existing wholesale business should therefore be free to operate at present without the imposition of unnecessary and administratively burdensome conduct of business rules'.

[96] In contrast to investment services, in banking the most substantial increase in cross-border activity and market integration has taken place in wholesale activities. For example, the currency-based segmentation of the markets for unsecured interbank deposits disappeared very rapidly after the introduction of the euro; *see* Duisenberg Wim, The Future of Banking Supervision and the Integration of Financial Markets, speech delivered at the Conference 'Improving Integration of Financial Markets in Europe' (Turin, 22 May 2000).

[97] The broadening of the market size and increasing share of cross-border wholesale transactions has a positive impact on financial stability. If there were only a few market participants, the likelihood of a financial firm failure having stronger repercussions on the viability of other institutions would be greater. *See Ibid.*

[98] FESCO, *Implementation of Art. 11 of the ISD: Categorisation of Investors for the purpose of Conduct of Business Rules*, 15 March 2000. FESCO has also recently fulfilled its commitment to draft standards defining the rules of conduct regime that will apply to inter-professional relationships; See FESCO Consultative Paper, *Standards and Rules for Harmonising Core Conduct of Business Rules for Investor Protection* (February 2001).

investors and they bind themselves to implement these standards in their regulatory objectives and, when possible, in their respective rules. FESCO stresses in its paper that the conduct of business regime for professionals is an exceptional regime, that is, it should be considered as an exemption to the application of the standard rules of conduct, which aim to ensure adequate protection for less sophisticated investors.

Between the extremes of market professionals and retail customers lies a full spectrum of expertise. In this context, FESCO seems to have chosen a three-way classification as more appropriate than a two-way split.[99] As a result, its members have purported not only to waive the burdened rules of conduct for *de facto* professional investors, but also for *de jure* professional investors, taken that the latter obey a prescribed set of standards and preconditions. In any case, however, the latter should not be presumed to possess market knowledge and experience comparable to that of the authorised and regulated financial institutions.

Even though Member States have agreed on the content of the FESCO paper and have accepted the three-tier classification of investors, the constitutional and legal status of that agreement becomes critical. Yet, the paper remains a consultative document, without any legal binding effect. It still needs be implemented by Member States' legislation or be incorporated into EU secondary law. In either case, the intervention of the Commission is required in relation to its binding statement in its 1999 Action Plan on Financial Services. However, even if implemented, FESCO paper will reveal its weakness. Regretfully, it fails to address the crucial issue of which rules will apply in cross-border trades. Will it be those of the home Member State or those of the host? Will we have an enhanced home country control principle, or will the host country increase its supervisory power? Until it does, the paper will have little influence.

### 3.2.5   Marketing rules

As discussed above, rules of conduct govern in general the transaction of financial products and their delivery from the financial firm to its client. In this context they are closely related to rules controlling the marketing of these products and especially their advertising.[100] While authorisation and prudential supervision are requirements relating to the responsibility of the home Member State, Art. 13 ISD implies that marketing and advertising rules are a matter of the host State.

This division of competences is similar to the one established by the ECJ with respect to the free movement of products. In *Alpine Investments*, the Court has

---

[99] Generally speaking, a three-tier classification would distinguish between *de facto* professionals, *de jure* or semi-professionals and non-professionals. This approach offers a better tailoring of requirements and minimises the cost of transitional arrangements for firms.

[100] By advertising is meant 'the making of a representation in any form in connection with a trade, business, craft or profession in order to promote the supply of goods or services, including immovable property, rights and obligations'; *see* Council Directive 84/450/EEC of 10 September 1984 relating to the approximation of the laws, regulations and administrative provisions of the Member States concerning misleading advertising (OJ L 250/17 of 19 September 1984). *See* also Art. 2(f) of Council Directive 2000/31/EC on certain legal aspects of information society services, in particular electronic commerce, in the Internal Market (OJ L178/1 of 17 July 2000), which defines the notion of 'commercial communication'.

distinguished between marketing rules and product rules.[101] To avoid double burden, the Court's case law has divided regulatory capacities between Member States. In particular, the home country controls the product rules while the host country deals with selling arrangements.[102] However, if the home Member State endeavours to apply its own rules to selling arrangements, a double burden cannot be avoided. The justification for the measures has to be examined.[103]

One certain conclusion that can be drawn from the *Alpine Investments* decision is that national standards regarding the marketing of investment services vary significantly between Member States.[104] Moreover, the same case reveals the major difficulties that national regulators are facing to do something about these egregious practices.[105] Indeed, even compared to rules of conduct, marketing rules are lagged behind as far as their harmonisation process is concerned.[106] Without any particular explanation, the European legislator has chosen to provide investment firms with one more hurdle, when entering into cross-border financial business. Investment firms wishing to establish pan-European practices have to obey fragmented national marketing rules.

As with rules of conduct, the adoption by Member States of conflicting or different financial services marketing rules would impede the functioning of competition between firms and of common consumer protection standards within the Community.[107] To this end, a major step towards the completion of the Single Market will be achieved with the adoption of the proposed Directive on distance marketing. Because of their intangible nature, financial services are particularly suited to distance selling. It is, thus, in the interest of the consumers to have access without discrimination to the widest possible range of financial services available in the EU. This can only be safeguarded with the adoption of common marketing rules, which can accordingly ensure high degree of consumer protection and confidence, especially in the use of new techniques such as electronic commerce.

---

[101] *See* Case C-384/93, *op. cit.*, note 6; Opinion of Advocate General Jacobs, Para. 55.

[102] *See* Jukka Snell and Mads Andenas, 'Exploring the Outer Limits – Restrictions on the Free Movement of Goods and Services' (1999) EBLR 252, 265; also D. Chalmers and E. Szyszczak, *European Union Law. Volume II. Towards a European Policy?* (Ashgate, Aldershot, 1998), p. 304. The host country may experience difficulties in enforcing its rules as regards services moving, for example, by telecommunications or by post. For the notion of 'selling arrangements', *see* Stephen Weatherill, 'After Keck: Some Thoughts on how to Clarify the Clarification' (1996) 33 CML Rev 885, 894.

[103] *See* Snell and Andenas, *ibid.*

[104] Beyond marketing rules, traditionally there are different legal practices relating to them. A single financial services contract, for example, may be subject to different legal treatment in different Member States.

[105] *See* Kondgen, *op. cit.*, note 94, 127.

[106] To date, EU marketing law covers misleading advertising with Directive 97/55/EC, *op. cit.*, note 34, and doorstep selling with Council Directive 85/577/EEC of 20 December 1985, OJ L372/31 of 31 December 1985. The solicitation of customers at a distance by means of technology and telecommunications will be regulated by the proposed Directive on distance marketing of consumer financial services, *op. cit.*, note 7.

[107] *See ibid.*, Recital 8.

However, even if the difficulties encountered by regulators were overcome and marketing rules were harmonised to a minimum extend, there would still be doubts and ambiguities with regard to the country, which constitutes the *fons et origo* of remaining non-harmonised marketing rules. Similarly to free movement of goods, Art. 13 ISD does not establish that cross-border transactions falling within the ambit of the ISD are regulated exclusively under the host Member State marketing or advertising rules.[108] The feeling arousing from the wording of this provision is that, it is the rules of the *host* State that have to be adopted and examined in the interest of the general good. Again, the principle of general good will define the exact form and content of the rules to be applied and supervised by the host competent, without leaving it completely free to impose its own financial services marketing laws. This blurred division of responsibilities cannot be cleared out even with the final adoption of the Directive, which will harmonise minimum standards of marketing rules, but will also leave more specific responsibilities that have to be divided between the home and the host Member State. Certainly, as in the case of prudential and transactional rules, this dichotomy will not be without problems and bilateral conflicts.

### 3.3   What is the host country in cross-border services?

#### 3.3.1   The host Member State

According to the ISD, the European passport is only available when investment services are provided 'within' the host Member State, either through the establishment of a branch or through the provision cross-border services.[109] Sometimes issues are raised relating to the definition of a branch, or to the Member State where the cross-border services take place. If the recipient of financial services comes to the home country of the provider, a case can be made that *no* cross-border services are being rendered at all.[110] It is, thus, vital that the place of supply of financial services of a financial undertaking is 'located' in order to determine whether prior notification is required. Moreover, the question whether at the present stage we should return to the subject to the conduct of business rules and explore the possibility of harmonising them, so that the home Member State approach could cover cross-border investment business, depends on the correct interpretation of the definition of the host Member State.

The difficulty in locating the source and destination of financial services lies in the fact that, unlike other services (legal, medical, construction etc.), they are almost impossible to pin down and be connected to a specific location. They also differ

---

[108] The same applies for the proposed distance marketing Directive, which refers to 'Member States' in general.

[109] ISD, Art. 14(1). *Cf.* SBD, Art. 20.

[110] Jan Dalhuisen, 'Liberalisation and Re-Regulation of Cross-border Financial Services: Part III' (1999) 9–10 EBLR 358, 365.

significantly from one another and are increasingly provided in intangible form. The growth of distance services and use of electronic means of telecommunication make them even more untraceable.

Occasionally, questions may be raised with regard to the definition of a branch. In an attempt to provide solutions, the ECJ has made fairly clear that a permanent establishment, from which financial services are provided, will constitute a branch and will be covered by the Treaty provisions on the right of establishment. In *Gebhard*,[111] the Court held that:

> a national of a Member State who pursues activity on a stable and continuous basis in another Member State where he holds himself out from an established professional base to, amongst others, nationals of that State comes under the chapter relating to the right of establishment and not the chapter relating to services.

However, the permanent establishment can be extended beyond the form of a branch. In *Commission v Germany*,[112] a case relating to insurance services, the Court held that:

> (…) an undertaking of another Member State which maintains a permanent presence in the Member State in question comes within the scope of the provisions of the Treaty on the right of establishment, even if that presence does not take the form of a branch or agency, but consists merely of an office managed by the undertaking's own staff or by a person who is independent but authorised to act on a permanent basis for the undertaking, as will be the case with an agency.

The issue of provision of services can be more problematic,[113] especially where financial undertakings have to follow the notification procedure before they commence cross-border financial business. This issue is detailed below.

### 3.3.2 Prior notification

In an attempt to clear out and interpret the definition of the place of supply of financial services, the European Commission has examined certain possibilities for locating the service – originator of the initiative, customer's place of residence (*lex dominilii*), supplier's place of establishment (*lex sedis*), place where contracts are signed (*lex contractus*), etc. – and has considered that none could satisfactorily apply to all the activities listed in the Annexes of the ISD and the CBD. Rather, its guidance provides that the determinant is the place of 'characteristic performance'

---

[111] Case C-55/94, *Gebhard* v. *Consiglio Avvocati e Procuratori di Milano* [1995] ECR I-4165, Para. 27; *see also* Case C-221/89 *Factortame* [1991] ECR I-3905, Para. 20: '*the concept of establishment within the meaning of Art. 52 [now Art. 43] et seq. of the Treaty involves the actual pursuit of an economic activity through a fixed establishment in another Member State for an indefinite period*'.

[112] Case 205/84, *op. cit.*, note 41.

[113] *See* O'Neill, Nicholas, 'The Investment Services Directive', in Cranston (ed.), *The Single Market and the Law of Banking* (London, Lloyds of London Press, 1995b), p. 215.

of the service with a few implications, that is, the essential supply for which payment is due must be determined.[114]

In my view, the notion of 'characteristic performance' leaves unanswered questions and needs to be construed too.[115] It is worth noting that not all EEA Member States subscribe to the Commission interpretation.[116] The solution to the case of legal uncertainty of the notification procedure could be for financial institutions to make use of the notification procedures even if it appears that notification may not be necessary. It seems that such a possibility is open. However, it is doubtful whether blanket notification (i.e. notifying all activities in respect of all EEA Member States) regardless of any genuine intention to carry out the activity is encouraged. The reasons could be practical and financial.

The major problem seems to be the provision of distance financial services through the Internet. In the Commission's view – as indicated in the 1997 Banking Communication – the provision of services through the Internet does not require prior notification, since the supplier cannot be deemed to be pursuing its activities in the customer's territory.[117] Moreover, the Commission leaves it open for the financial institutions to choose, 'for reasons of legal certainty' to make use of the notification procedures provided even if, according to the criteria proposed above, notification may not be necessary.[118] But with such a freedom given to the undertakings, from where does legal certainty originate? If a financial undertaking chooses not to notify its intentions, how shall the host competent authorities be informed of the nature of the financial undertaking, of its programme of operation and the financial services that intends to provide? I will discuss the issue of electronic provision of financial services below.[119]

---

[114] *See* 1997 Banking Communication, *op. cit.*, note 17, 6. The Commission's Communication is not a ruling or soft law to be legally binding. However, it is supposed to play a persuasive role in the interpretation of the SBD. Although not directly applicable, the Communication may offer guidance for the interpretation of the ISD and the insurance Directives as well. Regarding the former, although the work of the drafters of the 1997 Communication was intended to cover only the SBD and not the ISD, it would be not unreasonable to approach the ISD using similar arguments; *see* Cruickshank, Cristopher, 'Is there a Need to Harmonise Conduct of Business Rules?', in Guido Ferrarini (ed.), *op. cit.*, note 93, 132. Regarding the latter, *see* 1999 Insurance Communication, *op. cit.*, note 17.

[115] The notion of 'characteristic performance' seems to owe its origin to Art. 4(1) and (2) of the Contracts Convention of Rome (OJ L266/1, of 19 June 1980); *see* Jan Wouters, *op. cit.*, note 48, 178; Dalhuisen, Jan, *op. cit.*, note 111, 355. However, its analysis is not within the scope of this paper. For this purpose, *see* Kondgen, *op. cit.*, note 94, 126; Cruicksank, Cristopher, *op. cit.*, note 114. Eventually, the case law of the ECJ will have to interpret this approach and determine whether it is the right one in the context of provision of services.

[116] *A fortiori*, the interpretation given by the Communication does not necessarily represent the often very divergent views put forward by the Member States and should not, in themselves, impose any new obligation on them. *See* 1997 Banking Communication, *op. cit.*, note 17, 3. Regarding civil-law sanctions, for instance, the Commission takes the view that the notification procedure should not affect the validity of a banking contract. Indeed, such a view can be supported only by Member States, the law of which upholds the principle that a simple agreement of the parties is sufficient to establish a contract (e.g. Greece, Germany, France). However, this may not be the case in other countries.

[117] *Ibid.*, 7. The Commission acknowledges that this solution will require a case-by-case analysis, which could prove difficult.

[118] *Ibid.*

[119] *See infra* Section 4.

Another question to be asked is: How shall the financial firm be informed of the host State's rules of conduct and the general good rules, with which it has to comply, if no notification has taken place? This approach makes evident the link between the notification procedure and the application of conduct of business and general good rules. A financial firm that moves 'out of its home' and provides services 'within' another Member State needs to notify its intentions, so that the host State's rules of conduct apply. This is a delicate matter for the host Member State, which involves sovereignty and its power to protect its own consumers and investors.

Furthermore, uncertainty may be also originated from the obligation incumbent on the host competent authorities. In its 1997 Banking Communication, the Commission argues that the wording of Art. 19(4) of the SBD does not justify the inference that the host country has an obligation to notify a credit institution wishing to set up a branch in its territory of its general good rules. Moreover, any un-notified rules would still be binding on it (*sic*).[120] I believe that a similar argument could be applied to investment services, given the wording of Art. 18(2) ISD. However, the Commission's stance could create competitive distortions between financial services providers operating in the same territory. Uncertainty as to whether the information supplied is complete can be a handicap for foreign undertakings, which may feel obliged to undertake their own research in order to avoid the risk of their transactions being invalidated.[121]

The complication of the issue of notification and the 'incapability' of the Commission to deal with it also becomes evident in the 1999 Communication regarding the insurance sector. Here, the Commission makes a 180-degree bend[122] and takes the view that insurance activities carried on via electronic commerce (e.g. the Internet) and covering a risk located in a Member State other than that, in which the insurer covering the risk is established, *are subject* to the provisions of the Insurance Directives relating to the freedom to provide services.[123] In plain English, under the latter view, insurance undertakings, wishing to conclude via the Internet insurance policies covering risks or commitments situated in other Member States, *should* therefore follow the notification procedure.

Although the two Communications do merely constitute binding legal documents for the Member States' competent authorities to follow, they do create inevitable confusion to supervisors, financial undertakings and to investors. It may be alleged that whether notification procedure is required or not, it does not mean that the financial activities under question are not the subject of mutual recognition and home country

---

[120] *See* 1997 Banking Communication, *op. cit.*, note 17, 16.

[121] It may be suggested that the supply of information to service providers be compulsory for the host competent authorities, at least with regard to references to the national legislation which applies to financial activities. However, taken that certain supervisory houses may face difficulties in compiling exhaustive lists of all the general-good-type rules and in keeping such lists up to date, it seems important that there should be a continued effort to harmonise these rules at EU level.

[122] 1999 Insurance Communication, *op. cit.*, note 17, 15.

[123] *See* Council Directive 88/357/EEC, Arts 14, 16 and 17, as amended by Council Directive 92/49/EEC, Arts 34, 35 and 36 (non-life insurance), and Council Directive 90/619/EEC, Arts 11, 14 and 17, as amended by Council Directive 92/96 EEC, Arts 34, 35 and 36 (life insurance).

control. Whilst the Commission considers the notification necessary for insurance undertakings, it points out that it merely is a consumer protection measure. Rather, the measure pursues a simple objective of exchange of information between supervisory authorities.[124] Therefore, and in accordance with the third phase of the SLIM project, the Commission has welcomed a recommendation to make adjustments and ease the burden for European insurers, without however evading the notification procedure.[125]

In my view, the above Communications reveal an artificial dealing of the issue, as they treat notification as a procedural issue of residual scope, without really considering its importance for consumer protection sensitivities of the host country supervisory authorities. In addition, they reveal the weakness of the present home country control system and the lack of programme at Community level regarding the future of the procedure. On the one hand, in 1997 the Commission was envisaging the abolition of this disproportionate restriction in the context of the freedom to provide services in order to bring it in line with the Treaty.[126] On the other hand, in 1999 it was proposing the adjustment of the procedure, without abolishing it completely. As the Commission has not yet issued a similar guidance regarding the provision of investment services, any speculations as to the interpretation of the term 'within' in Art 14 of the ISD are dangerous to be made.[127]

Whatever the future of the notification procedure may be, it will threaten the prosperity of the home country control regime. Even if abolished, the host supervisory authorities would still need a way to check compliance with the interest of the general good and with consumer protection rules. Even if adjusted, the notification procedure would still remain an administrative formality, a restriction to intra-Community provision of financial services. In any case, the existence of the current uncertainty could easily lead to the imposition of more than one set of rules of conduct, if more than one Member State considers the service to have been provided in its jurisdiction. The burden on financial firms will be retained and the Single Market Programme will be devalued.

## 3.4    E-trading

### 3.4.1    Developments and benefits

Trends such as globalisation, technological innovation and consolidation of financial services have an impact on how market services are being provided as well as on market structures themselves. Technology is perhaps the most powerful force. It has allowed intra-day trading, on-line provision of financial services, electronic broking, elimination of trading floors, on-line IPOs, dematerialisation of securities and creation of virtual exchanges. In Europe only, over 25 Alternative Trading

---

[124] 1999 Insurance Communication, *op. cit.*, note 17, 17.

[125] *See* COM(1999) 88 final, of 25 February 1999.

[126] 1997 Banking Communication, *op. cit.*, note 17, 8.

[127] For a different view, see Avgouleas, Emilios, 'The Harmonisation of Rules of Conduct in EU Financial Markets: Economic Analysis, Subsidiarity and Investor Protection' (2000) 1 ELJ 72, 79.

Systems (ATS)[128] are having a considerable impact on wholesale investment services. The number of online European trading accounts is expected to increase by ten times or more in the next four years.[129]

Stock exchanges are not just places where securities are traded; in fact, stock exchanges are hardly 'places' at all nowadays. Trading, clearance and settlement are in most of the world screen-based and electronic. It is, thus, not surprising that the emergence of new electronic trading systems raises new challenges not only for financial undertakings and investors, but also for regulators and supervisors.

The move towards electronic trading has brought many benefits to brokers and investors, but also has raised new issues of concern for supervisory authorities. The benefits can be easily figured out and will be outlined briefly. The first is *information*. Technology has the ability to produce huge quantities of information, which can be easily accessed by anyone, even the simplest retail investor. As a result, every investor can theoretically control his own order instructions. The second is *remote access*. A physical trading floor is no more necessary. Electronic markets can offer participation to far more people – and potentially a much wider range of people – than you could ever squeeze into a pit or on to a floor.[130] The final benefit is *speed, automation and cost*. Electronic markets have the capacity to perform these functions at mind-numbing cost-efficient speeds and. The boundaries of automation of trading are extended by the electronic nature of the system, without human intervention. Old market process has given way to accuracy, efficiency and low cost, which has opened up new business opportunities.

### 3.4.2 Challenges and obstacles

It is common belief that the unique cross-border characteristics that have emerged in financial markets due to the 'information universe'[131] constitute a regulatory and supervisory challenge for the supervisory authorities. Within the EU financial services arena, an electronic network not only challenges the system of home country

---

[128] Also known as proprietary trading systems (PTSs), electronic communication networks (ECNs), market services providers (MSPs) or simply electronic trading platforms, these quasi-exchanges are screen-based automated systems, run by broker/dealers as for-profit businesses, which produce in-house matching of buying and selling orders in either exchange-listed or OTC securities. *See* London Stock Exchange Consultative Paper, *Competing Market Mechanisms – Their Effect on the Rules of the London Stock Exchange* (September 1995).

[129] Although online securities trading is widely used in the United States (the number of households engaged jumped 30% between May 1999 and January 2000, from 2.7 million to 3.5 million), online EU brokerages are only recent entrants to e-financial commerce; 65% of them started business less than two years ago and only 20% have more than two years' experience. *See* 2nd *Report on Financial Services, op. cit.*, note 29, 6.

[130] *See* Wisbey, Gay, The Challenge of Technology – Regulation of Electronic Financial Markets, speech delivered at the conference 'The Challenges Facing Financial Regulation' (Cambridge, 6–7 July 2000).

[131] The term 'information universe' means the changing landscape of financial markets globally in the face of rapidly evolving information technology. *See* Tanzer, Greg, 'Developing Uniform Standards to Allow a Global Passport for Mutual Funds – IOSCO's Role' (2000) 5 *International Business Lawyer* 229, 234.

control, but it also questions its capability to follow market structures and even threatens its existence. Characteristic is the approach of the European Commission, which makes more evident the obstacles to cross-border sales of retail financial products as the new technologies bring retail financial services to the reach of any Internet user.[132]

The first obstacle is one of substance. The offer of investment services through electronic networks from an institution's home State, which can be used by Community investors based in different Member States, seems to fall outside the ambit of the financial services directives' 'Euro-passports'.[133] Art. 14 of the ISD and Art. 20 of the SBD require the financial services be offered 'within' the host Member State. The two contradicting Communications introduced by the European Commission do merely clear out the confusion. If the *locus* of the provision of services cannot be identified, then financial undertakings conducting electronic trading will not have to comply with the prudential and conduct of business rules of the Directives. Instead, primary Community law will apply and more specifically Art. 49 EC (former Art. 59 EC Treaty). Consequently, such activities face the realistic danger of being subject to the rules of conduct of not only the home country, but also of all the host Member States, which constitute the destination of the services and which can uphold their rules on the basis of the general good principle.

To solve the supervisory problem, the 2000 e-commerce Directive[134] has adopted a similar – but not alike – to 'home country' approach for information society services. Its cornerstone is the 'internal market clause',[135] which enables online providers to supply services throughout the EU on the rules of the Member State where they are established (country of origin). Although, however, the Directive was designed to ensure that online services can be freely provided throughout the Community, there are at least two issues that undermine such an optimistic proposition. The *first* is that the Directive itself provides for a number of significant *derogations* from the internal market clause, by means of 'host' country measures may hamper or, at least, make less attractive the provision of electronic investment services from other Member States and, thus, hinder intra-Community trade.[136] This, in turn, creates a distinct regime in respect of electronic cross-border trade from that using other distance selling modes. Where investment services are provided in part offline and in part online different legal regimes will be applied to each part, since offline activities are not within the Directive's scope even if connected with an online service. The *second* problem is one of definition. Differences in the competence and power of national supervisors still hinder the consistent application of EU legislation. The undefined country of 'establishment' or 'origin' in the e-commerce Directive might not be the same Member State as the 'home country' within the meaning of the ISD.

---

[132] *See 2nd Report on Financial Services, op. cit.*, note 29, 5.

[133] Avgouleas, Emilios, *op. cit.*, note 127, 79.

[134] *See* Directive 2000/31/EC *on e-commerce, op. cit,* note 100.

[135] *Ibid.*, Art. 3(1).

[136] These derogations fall into two categories: general and specific case-by-case derogations. *See ibid.*, Annex and Art. 3(4-6), respectively. Importantly, the Directive does not apply to insurance services, the advertising of UCITS and it does not affect the party autonomy to chose their law applicable to their contract. In the latter case, the Rome Convention will determine the law.

This may easily lead to confusion with regard to the country responsible for the prudential supervision of the information society or investment firm.

A similar problem seems to exist in the case of the ATS. It is a fact that the ISD does not contain any explicit reference to ATSs.[137] ATS do merely constitute regulated markets with the meaning of Art. 1(13) of the ISD. Most of them are authorised as broker/dealers and have differences with regulated markets in the area of access, transparency and market abuse. Here lies the difficulty with their surveillance.[138] In the case of regulated exchanges, the regulatory focus is on the supervision of the market, on its fair and efficient operation. In the case of brokers, supervision does not concern with the market *per se* but with the firm's conduct of business in relation to its customers and with investor protection. Given the above, the question arises, whether ATS should comply with the prudential and conduct of business rules of the ISD. Should they be treated as markets or as brokers? Will ATS cause the potential ending of broker intermediation as gatekeepers to the market? The current home country supervisory regime fails to address the issue of the dichotomy of supervisory responsibilities between the home and the host competent authorities, where electronic trading platforms conduct intra-Community trading.

In connection to the above, an issue faced by EU regulators may be that of risks inherent in the asymmetry of regulation and supervision of ATSs across Europe. Today, most EU jurisdictions regulate ATSs as investment firms rather than as regulated markets. Although ATSs usually fulfil at least some of the core functions of regulated markets, the question arises whether the current regulatory and supervisory approach on them is adequate to address the risks that their operations might pose to meeting the regulatory objectives. According to FESCO, a number of risks can be identified that ATSs might pose for *investor protection*: access to trading, best execution, and conflicts of interest. On the other hand, these risks are closely linked to those potentially created by ATSs in relation to *market integrity*: fragmentation, transparency, monitoring, enforcement, and operation risk.[139] Consequently, regulating ATSs as investment undertakings may not address the risks related with regulated markets and *vice versa*.

Especially the issue of monitoring and enforcement of ATSs with cross-border elements can constitute an extremely problematic issue. Electronic remote access, besides beneficial, can also prove a nightmare for supervisory authorities. How does an exchange with remote cross-border members enforce its rules, when each member-financial firm is subject to the regulators of its home country? Above all,

---

[137] The only reference to the type of activity carried out by ATS (in-house matching) is made in Recital 13: '(...) *the business of the reception and transmission of orders also includes bringing together two or more investors thereby bringing about a transaction between those investors*'.

[138] The differences between Member States approach to ATSs are significant. In Italy, for instance, ATSs are not subject to licence requirements at all. In Spain, an ATS has to be approved by the government in a procedure similar to that of an exchange. In Portugal, the legal and regulatory framework only distinguishes between regulated and non-regulated markets. Finally, if an ATS were to apply to Greece, the regulatory authorities would address the application on a tailor-made basis. *See* FESCO, *The Regulation of Alternative Trading Systems in Europe: A Paper for the EU Commission* (September 2000, 8).

[139] *Ibid.*, 12–14.

how does a market, a competent authority or a criminal prosecution authority enforce provisions against market abuse and fraud at a cross-border level?[140] Is the mixture of cooperation, exchange of information and the division of responsibilities between the home and the host State enough to address these issues? The present communication network facilities can be widely used in such a way that a criminal plan can be devised and put in practice so rapidly that the authorities are hampered in reacting promptly to it or in taking *ex ante* measures.[141] More than that, the 'de-localised' and 'non-territorial' character of electronic criminal activities makes it impossible to identify in proper time which competent authority is responsible for taking *ex ante* or *ex post* action.[142]

US securities regulators are leading the way. The SEC and the self-regulated National Association of Securities Dealers (NASD) have already taken countermeasures against electronic investment fraud. At the international level, IOSCO has discovered the sign of times and has established the Internet Task Force (ITF) to meet the challenges of electronic trading.[143] However, it is doubtful whether IOSCO's proposal for greater cooperation and coordination among regulators in different jurisdictions is feasible.[144] In any Internet investigation, huge amounts of information may need to be obtained from different countries, while illicit activity may implicate the investment services laws of several jurisdictions. It is evident in this context, that even an enhanced supervisory agreement as the 'traditional' EU home country control system will be ill-equipped to meet the new demands. New principles reconciled in a more liberal attitude need, therefore, to be taken into consideration.

A final fundamental issue is whether advertising and subsequent provision of financial services in an electronic network platform, such as on the Internet, fall within the scope of the financial services Directives. Are electronic financial services being provided at a cross-border basis, where a client is resident in a Member State different than that of the provider? Speaking in an electronic context, some may allege that there is no cross-border activity since the client visits the web site of the service provider and thereafter purchases the financial product in such a way, that the client 'virtually' visited the home State of the provider.[145] This is especially significant for the notification procedure. Logically the financial undertaking will argue that there was no requirement for notification, since the client has taken the initiative and has 'visited' the undertaking in its own home State. In any case, a link between advertising and notification would be artificial, for it is not the prior offer of a

---

[140] Electronic criminal activity or 'cybercrime' may include activities such as money laundering, market manipulation, or price manipulation, where operations are frequently on the borderline of lawfulness.

[141] *See* Conti, Corrado, 'The Impact of new technologies on the financial services industry' (1997) 11 EFSL 284.

[142] Especially when using the Internet, perpetrators of investment fraud can easily move both the *sites* location and the *target* location of their operations from one jurisdiction to another, or send the same message to multiple jurisdictions simultaneously.

[143] *See* IOSCO, *Report on Enforcement Issues Raised by the increasing Use of Electronic Networks in the Securities and Futures Field* (September 1997).

[144] *Ibid. See* also IOSCO, *Securities Activity on the Internet* (Part IV, September 1998).

[145] *See* Woolfson, Philip, 'Electronic commerce and the Single Market in financial services in Europe: What changes for success?' (1997) 4 *Journal of Financial Regulation and Compliance* 306, 312.

service but merely the intention to carry on activities within the territory of another Member State that the financial services Directives make conditional on notification.[146]

On the other hand, others may argue that the fact that financial services are advertised and provided in electronic form does not mean that they should be legally treated in a way different than traditional media, such as mail, telephone, fax or personal contact. Consequently, financial undertakings should follow the notification procedure before commencing electronic financial activities with clients of other Member States. In such a case, financial undertakings will be, practically, obliged to provide registration formalities, in order to identify the personal details of their potential clients, as well as disclaimers warning them that their services may not be available in specific jurisdictions, where the notification procedure has not been followed. Moreover, the blanket notification should be avoided for the reasons mentioned before.[147] However, the unduly legalistic and impractical character of such a solution should be examined. How could the accuracy of the registration procedure be monitored by the competent authorities?[148] And which country's competent authorities should pursue such an *ex ante* investigation, since at that early stage the nationality of the potential client of the financial undertaking cannot be known? These are enquires, which the principle of home country control leaves unanswered.

## 3.5  Third countries

Overlaps or conflicts cannot only arise between the rules of the home Member State and the country where the service is provided within the meaning of Art. 11(1) ISD, but also between these rules and the rules of the Member State where the service is actually carried out, if this )ccurs in a *third* Member State. One could give the paradigm of a French branch of a British investment firm, which carries out orders for its French clients on the Athens Derivatives Exchange (ADEX). By virtue of the ISD, the branch will be obliged to comply with the rules of the regulated market in question.[149] However, the case would be different if the abovementioned branch was commencing transactions on the Belgian futures and options market of EURONEXT,[150] where the rules of French and Belgian markets are harmonised.

---

[146] That is the view of the European Commission. See 1997 Banking Communication, *op. cit.*, note 17, 7, and 1999 Insurance Communication, *op. cit.*, note 17, 18. The Commission believes that such a link could lead to the anomalous situation where a banking or insurance undertaking could find itself invited to notify the authorities of all the Member States, in which its advertising could in theory be received, although the undertaking may not be planning to pursue its activities in these Member States.

[147] *See supra* Subsection 2.3.

[148] A potential client of a financial undertaking may easily declare false identification, residence or nationality on an Internet web site, since, in most cases, this is the only prerequisite for registration. In this way, the client could prevent the potential refusal of the undertaking to provide its services, in case he resides in a Member State, with which the undertaking has not established a notification link.

[149] Either as a member thereof or as a financial firm, which has been given access to this market; *see* ISD, Art. 15(2) and 15(4).

[150] EURONEXT is the new European Exchange created by the merger of Paris Bourse SA, Amsterdam Exchanges (AEX) and Brussels Exchanges (BXS).

In addition, does the ISD (or the SBD) allow a EU financial institution to provide cross-border services from a branch outside the EU or even the EEA? The Commission's guidance on the freedom to provide services[151] merely refers to that difficult question. As Art. 49 EC (former Art. 59), on which the Europassport is based, refers to a Single Market 'within' the Community, this is perhaps unlikely.

There is no sign that access to EU financial markets has been made easier for non-EU financial undertakings with the home country control regime.[152] At the moment, there is clearly a market difference in the treatment of investment firms, whose home country is outside the EU, by each Member State acting as host State. This is particularly evident in the field of capital flows and payments. The Treaty itself still makes a distinction between the relationships between Member States on the one hand and the relationships to third countries on the other, despite the seemingly clear wording of Art. 56 EC (former Article 73b).[153] Art. 57, 59 and 60 EC (former Arts 73c, 73f, and 73g, respectively) allow the continued application of restrictions that exist under national or EU law with respect to the movement of capital to or from third countries involving direct investment, provision of financial services or the admission of securities to capital markets. In most cases, the imposition of further restrictions to third countries becomes a matter of the Community and especially the Council. Nevertheless, the wording of Art. 58(1)b (former Art. 73d) may prove problematic. This provision entitles even Member States to take unilateral measures against third countries, particularly, *inter alia*, in the field of the prudential supervision of financial services, as long as they constitute infringements of their national law. However, despite the prohibiting wording of Art. 58(3), it may be difficult to distinguish between measures taken on the grounds of public policy or public security and measures which constitute arbitrary discrimination or disguised restrictions.

It becomes obvious that, with respect to relationships to third countries, EU law not only is ill-equipped to abolish existing restrictions, but also tries to freeze these restrictions or even impose new. If the aim of the Treaty, the ISD and the other financial services directives is not to close Community's financial markets, but rather to keep them liberal and open to the rest of the world,[154] an alignment of conditions for establishment and cross-border provision of services by investment firms of third countries should be promoted, at least in relation to countries, which meet the

---

[151] *See* 1997 Banking Communication, *op. cit.*, note 17.

[152] Major non-EU banks and investment firms were already established in the EU before the launch of the home country control programme. *See* T. Hoschka, *Cross-Border Entry in European Retail Financial Services: Determinants, Regulation and the Impact on Competition* (New York, St Martin's Press, 1993) pp. 19–24. In addition, efforts for further harmonisation outside the EU have merely been initiated by the EU. For example, the requirements for the ownership of capital by banks, which have set standards for the capitalisation of banks observed in many countries outside the EU, have been worked out by the Basle Committee.

[153] *See* Horn, Norbert, *op. cit.*, note 10, 152; Thieffry, Gilles and Jonathan Walsh, 'Securitisation: The New Opportunities Offered by Economic and Monetary Union' (1997) 12 JIBL 463.

[154] ISD, Recital 31.

requirement of reciprocity of treatment. It is obvious that such an agreement becomes almost impossible for non-EU financial undertakings, which wish to commence financial business within the Community, but have to face the rules of fifteen supervisory authorities.[155] On the other hand, the potential benefits of EU economic and regulatory reform will be considerably greater if they take place in a global environment of market opening and supervisory reform.

## CONCLUSIONS

Home country control does *not* work. This is being indicated by a bulk of substantive and structural problems in the current EU regulatory and supervisory regime of investment services. Indeed, the pan-European provision of financial services remains limited to specific areas and is difficult to evaluate in those areas where it does take place.[156] In any case, it does not seem to owe much to the home country control regime and the European passport. On the contrary, the new regime has been the source for the creation of more hurdles and grey areas of uncertainty, which freeze the development of intra-Community financial services trade.

Besides investment services, most banking activities, which have traditionally dominated the European financial arena, remain local. There are few banks that truly operate beside their home country borders, especially those of the commercial banking sector.[157] Similarly, banking credit markets still retain their local character,[158] and mergers and acquisitions in the EU are largely domestic affairs.[159] However, this may change in the medium or the long term, as the single currency is within reach and electronic financial trading becomes more common.[160] To this end, a regulatory and supervisory response to new developments constitutes an inevitable necessity.

Whilst part of the problem concerns the incomplete regulatory coverage at EU level, the greater part of the responsibility lies in the way in which EU legislation has been decided (or left undecided) and implemented (or not implemented) and in which financial institutions and markets have been supervised (or not supervised). The problem is the *system itself*. In areas where home country control could have

---

[155] Here is where the role and work of international organisation, such as IOSCO, Basle and IASC, becomes extremely useful and important.

[156] *See* J. Danthine *et al.*, *The Future of European Banking* (London, Centre for Economic Policy Research, 1999), pp. 46–47.

[157] In the Euroland, for example, entry into foreign markets in 1999 was still less than 10% on average in terms of banking assets. *See* Danthine *et al.*, *ibid.*, 33; Padoa-Schioppa, T., 'EMU and Banking Supervision (1999) 2 *International Finance* 295, 298.

[158] *See* M. Centeno, and A. Mello, 'How Integrated are the Money Market and the Bank Loans Market within the European Union?' (1999) 18 *Journal of International Money & Finance* 75.

[159] During the first half of 1999, only 24 of the 190 M&A's that occurred in the EU banking sector involved a foreign bank. 19 of these involved third country banks. *See* *2nd Report on Financial Services, op. cit.*, note 34, 5.

[160] *See* European Central Bank, *Possible Effects of EMU on the EU Banking Systems in the Medium to Long Term* (1999), pp. 18–20.

made a difference, the failure to omit obstacles and adopt EU minimum standards has prevented the emergence of a truly single financial market. Notions, like the 'general good' or the 'characteristic performance' do merely provide the European lawyer, the financial provider or the investor the legal certainty which is required when dealing with such a vague but dynamically changing business environment, as financial services. Instead, they create a legal risk, which naturally hinders the free flow of cross-border capital and the free provision of cross-border financial services. Efficient markets require a predictable and transparent legal environment, as well as clear allocation of supervisory responsibilities.

These problems require a regulatory response, which can have two solutions. The first would be the preservation of the present supervisory *status quo*, with the addition of significant changes in key issues, which are necessary to enhance the provision of cross-border investment services within the European Union and to facilitate their regulation, supervision and implementation by the Member States supervisory authorities. This route seems to be followed by the European Commission and the Council.[161] The second position would argue that the aforementioned problems of the current regime are so significant and hinder the evolution and development of intra-Community investment services in such a way, that they urge a major institutional and regulatory reform. Generally speaking, the first approach suggests an updated home country control and mutual recognition principle with a consolidated supervisory jurisdiction, while the second argues for the harmonisation of existing rules and the potential development of a pan-European Securities Regulator. Both are discussed in the following chapters of this book.

---

[161] *See* the Final Wise Men Report, *op. cit.*, note 14.

*Chapter 5*

# Private Law Approaches to Enhancing Financial Stability: The Hague Convention on Indirectly Held Securities and European Union Collateral Directive

*Kern Alexander*

## I INTRODUCTION

The globalisation of financial markets and the dramatic increase in cross-border capital flows have exposed financial systems to increased credit and market risk in part because of legal uncertainty concerning how to determine the law applicable to the taking of securities as collateral in cross-border transactions. One way parties seek to limit credit risk in financial transactions is through the provision of securities and cash as collateral. Today, most publicly-traded securities are held in multi-tiered structures composed of financial intermediaries and central securities depositories in which ownership interests in securities are recorded through electronic bookkeeping in what is known as 'intermediated book-entry securities'.[1] The flexibility and efficient functioning of financial markets has necessitated that securities clearance and settlement systems move away from the use of *direct holding* systems that hold securities in non-fungible custody accounts to *multi-tiered indirect holding systems* that hold securities in fungible custody accounts.[2] Traditional conflict of laws approaches that have been applied to determine the law applicable to transfers of interests in securities held in direct holding systems have proved complex and impractical when applied to securities traded in indirect holding systems, often resulting in uncertainty regarding the effectiveness of collateral as protection in cross-border transactions. Many experts have recognised, therefore, that a uniform legal framework is needed to determine which law should apply to the disposition of collateral interests in securities held in fungible custody accounts and traded in indirect holding systems.

---

[1] *See* R. Potok and M. Moshinsky, 'Cross-Border Collateral: A Conceptual Framework For Choice of Law Situations' (September 1998) *The Oxford Colloquium and Conflict of Laws* JIBL.

[2] Multi-tiered indirect holding systems are composed of various financial intermediaries, such as custodians and depositories, who operate pooled or 'omnibus' customer accounts who use electronic bookkeeping to amalgamate and record the securities holdings of all their clients, such as brokers, investment managers and other investors. *See* Bank for International Settlements (BIS), *Cross-Border Securities Settlements*, Report prepared by the Committee on Payment and Settlement Systems of the central banks of the Group of Ten countries, Basel, March 1995, pp. 40–42.

*Mads Andenas and Yannis Avgerinos (eds), Financial Markets in Europe: Towards a Single Regulator?* 121–141.
© 2003 *Kluwer Law International. Printed in Great Britain.*

This chapter discusses how certain private law approaches in the conflict of laws may reduce credit and liquidity risk in the cross-border trading of securities, and thereby promote a more efficient international securities market. Special emphasis is placed on the need to adopt a uniform conflict of laws rule that would determine which national legal system's secured transaction law should apply to the disposition of interests in securities held in indirect holding systems. This chapter will review recent efforts by the European Community and the United States to adopt such an approach with particular focus on the EU Collateral Directive. The chapter then discusses and analyses the relevant provisions of the recently adopted Hague Convention on Indirectly Held Securities. The Convention requires all signatories to adopt a uniform conflict of laws rule to all dispositions of interests in securities held electronically with a financial intermediary. The Convention would apply the law of the place of the financial intermediary to all transfers of interests in securities accounts that are maintained by that intermediary. This regime grew out of the Hague Conference Report on 'The Law Applicable to Dispositions of Securities Held Through Indirect Holding Systems'[3] ('The Hague Report').[4] The Convention's adoption of the basic principles of the Hague Report is viewed by proponents as an important step in reducing legal risk in international securities markets.

Although the Hague Convention's proposal for a uniform conflict of laws rule to be applied to all proprietary interests in securities is an important step in providing increased legal certainty for securities transactions, the chapter will discuss the various criticisms of the Convention that include those who call for more uniformity across national legal systems in adopting common principles and rules for the creation, perfection, and protection of collateral interests in securities. For instance, the Convention's proposals would be difficult to implement because of important differences across national legal systems in defining juridical concepts such as ownership and property and how certain ownership interests can be recharacterised as security interests under national bankruptcy regimes. The chapter will analyse other arguments that hold that the Convention's PRIMA approach will undermine financial stability and legal certainty by imposing a choice of law rule that will create additional interpretative problems in many jurisdictions and possibly conflict with European Union law.

## II   BACKGROUND

The taking of collateral interests in securities has become a major part of the international securities markets. Businesses face many different legal regimes for the

---

[3] This Report was prepared by Christophe Bernasconi, First Secretary of the Permanent Bureau of the Hague Conference on Private International Law. The Bernasconi Report was a response to a call by the Secretary General of the Hague Conference to assemble a group of experts to examine the need for a uniform rule of the conflict of laws to determine which jurisdictions law will govern the proprietary elements of collateral interests in securities.

[4] The Hague Report recommended either a uniform national conflicts of law rule for the taking of collateral interests in securities or a multilateral convention that would define an international property interest that collateral takers could obtain in securities held in indirect holding systems.

provision of collateral, with the potential for complicated conflicts between jurisdictions and uncertainties surrounding the law applicable to cross-border transfers of securities. Structural changes in financial markets have necessitated the move away from holding physical securities certificates in direct holding systems to the more flexible system of holding securities through multi-tiered structures of financial intermediaries.[5] These indirect holding systems usually involve financial intermediaries and central securities depositories located in different jurisdictions who register interests in securities through electronic bookkeeping. Legal uncertainty arises, and thus increased systemic risk, because traditional conflict of laws approaches (e.g. *lex rei sitae*) do not provide creditors with clear answers as to which legal system's rules for disposing of collateral interests in securities will be applied in any one transaction.

Many experts agree that the legal uncertainty surrounding the law applicable to the disposition of interest in securities in indirect holding systems has played a substantial role in causing past liquidity crises in financial markets.[6] The significant increase in the volume of cross-border securities transactions in recent years and the trend towards dematerialisation, immobilisation, and the use of indirect holding systems has necessitated the development of legal rules to keep pace with changes in the marketplace. As discussed above, the Convention on the Law Applicable to Certain Rights in Respect of Securities Held with an Intermediary seeks to remedy this problem by requiring signatory states to adopt a uniform conflict of laws rule that would apply the law of the place of the intermediary with whom the investor records its ownership interests in securities as the law applicable to the disposition, perfection, and the realisation of ownership interests in securities. This is known as the PRIMA approach and it seeks to reduce legal uncertainty in determining which jurisdiction's law should apply to proprietary interests in securities.

This chapter examines the Hague Convention and the PRIMA approach and draws some conclusions as to its efficacy *vis-a-vis* European Community law, especially in respect of the Settlement Finality Directive and the Collateral Directive. Before discussing the Hague Convention, it is necessary to analyse how the European Union and United States regulate the disposition of proprietary interests in indirectly held securities. Specifically, the European Union's Collateral Directive (2002) and Settlement Finality Directive (1998) provide a legal regime that seeks to assure post-settlement finality in financial transactions. The US Uniform Commercial Code's Revised Art. 8 (1994) regulating investment securities adopts a similar, but not identical, version of the PRIMA approach that applies a uniform choice of law rule to determine the law applicable to the disposition of interests in securities.

### III   COLLATERAL IN SECURITIES TRANSACTIONS

Generally, there are two essential components in collateral transactions or transfers of property: (1) the contractual element describing the parties' obligations; and

---

[5] The Report, p. 2.

[6] *See* generally, F. Oditah (ed.), *The Future for the Global Securities Market: Legal and Regulatory Aspects* (OUP, 1996). *See* also, James S. Rogers (1996) UCLA Law Rev 43: 1431–1545.

(2) the proprietary element dealing with rights and interests in property.[7] Regarding the proprietary elements of transfers in securities, there are three main issue areas: (1) the creation, perfection and enforcement of pledges over such interests; (2) the completion of a title of transfer or outright sale of such interests; and (3) the issue of priority between competing dispositions of interests in securities.[8] This chapter focuses only on the proprietary aspects (property interests) of a transfer of interests in securities and suggests that such interests should be governed by the law of the place of the intermediary which had maintained and recorded the securities account of the investor.

Before reviewing some of the conflict of laws issues and the various efforts at reform, it is necessary to review the legal concepts and terms that define collateral. Collateral is the property, such as securities or cash, provided by a borrower to a lender to minimise the lender's risk of financial loss in the event of the borrower's failure to repay in full its financial obligation to the lender. In sophisticated financial systems, collateral is used to support financial transactions and to assist companies in managing and reducing their credit risks arising from all kinds of financial transactions, from derivatives to general bank lending. Banks also use financial instruments as collateral on the money markets where the participants balance the overall amount of liquidity provided by central banks against transactions amongst themselves that match individual surpluses to shortages of liquidity.

At a basic level, the two main types of collateral arrangements are: (1) the 'pledge', and (2) 'title transfer'. A pledge involves the debtor providing the creditor with collateral, such as securities. The ownership of the collateral remains with the collateral giver (the debtor) but usually certain uses of the collateral are 'blocked' in favour of the creditor (the collateral taker). If the debtor fails to repay the debt, the creditor has the right to liquidate the collateral and thereby redeem a portion or all of the debt.

Title transfer ordinarily involves the debtor selling the collateral to the creditor in exchange for the loan. When the collateral is securities, the creditor (collateral taker) has a contractual obligation to redeliver equivalent securities to the debtor once the debt is repaid. A type of title transfer arrangement is the repurchase agreement, otherwise known as the 'repo' agreement. In the 'repo' agreement, the debtor agrees to sell the collateral to the creditor in exchange for the loan, and simultaneously the parties agree that the creditor will sell the collateral back to the debtor at a future date for an agreed price (the repurchase price), which typically includes the interest on the loan. If the debtor files bankruptcy, the creditor simply cancels the obligation to sell back the collateral and then sets off the value of the defaulted debt against the remaining debt owed ('netting'). In some countries, the repo agreement serves as a rational market response to the cumbersome procedures and uncertainties posed by

---

[7] *See* discussion in Richard Fentiman, 'Cross-Border Securities Collateral: Redefining Rechacterisation Risk' (September 1998) *Oxford Colloquium on Collateral and Conflict of Laws* 38–39.

[8] *See* R.D. Guynn and N.J. Marchand, 'Transfer of Pledge of Securities held Through Depositories', in Hans van Houtte (ed.), *The Law of Cross-Border Securities Transactions* (London, 1999) pp. 49, 51–52.

various national bankruptcy laws that have made it difficult for creditors to obtain the full value of pledged assets after debtors had defaulted and filed bankruptcy.

There are other forms of title transfer arrangements involving securities as collateral that include: 'buy/sell back transactions', 'securities loans', and swap transactions using a title transfer structure. Although these title transfer arrangements do not create a 'pledge' over collateral in the technical sense, they do provide an effective security function for creditors, and should therefore be regarded as collateral transactions. In regard to cross-border securities trading, the term 'collateral transaction' should be understood in a broad sense so as to encompass every transaction intended to secure outstanding credit, whether or not it creates a pledge over the property to which it applies.[9]

In addition, most legal systems adopt a broad definition of the term 'pledge' that includes both possessory and non-possessory security interests, while recognising that some common law systems define the term more narrowly to mean only possessory security interests.[10] Similarly, the term 'collateral' should be understood to apply to any property which is the subject of a collateral transaction. Moreover, the term 'perfection' should refer to the conditions necessary to protect a 'security interest' in order to make it valid against third parties. It is also important to note the different categories and classifications of securities in different contexts. In this regard, securities can be classified as 'certificated' or 'uncertificated', 'bearer' or 'registered', 'physical' or 'dematerialised', and even as 'immobilised securities'. Similarly, the term 'collateral' should be understood to apply to any property, which is the subject of a collateral transaction. As discussed below, the main focus will be on collateral transactions involving both 'pledges' and 'title transfers' because it is under these arrangements that the most significant conflict of laws issues arise with respect to the question of which legal system should govern the taking of collateral interests in securities.

IV   CONFLICT OF LAWS AND INDIRECT HOLDING SYSTEMS

Traditionally, most investors in securities had a direct ownership interest in the issuers of those securities, regardless of whether or not those ownership interests were recorded on the issuer's register or in the investor's physical possession as bearer securities. Securities were usually held in non-fungible custody accounts with an intermediary who had direct access to the physical certificates evidencing ownership of the security.[11] There was no commingling of interests in securities held in non-fungible accounts, and therefore it was possible to preserve the direct property right held by investors in securities traded in direct holding systems. The usual approach for determining the law applicable to collateral interests in securities held in such direct holding systems was the *lex rei sitae* or *lex situs*, which was the law

---

[9] The Report, p. 9.
[10] *Ibid.*, pp. 6–7.
[11] See Guynn, *supra*, P. C.

of the place where the security was located at the time of the relevant transfer or disposition.[12] This rule was based on the practical necessity that the *lex situs* of a security should be that jurisdiction where an interest in a security could be enforced.[13]

Although this rule posed few complications in the case of bearer securities, the attribution of a *situs* to registered securities involves a greater degree of artificiality that is reflected in a somewhat greater variety of approaches. For example, some jurisdictions regard the *situs* of securities to be the law of the place where the issuer is incorporated. Other jurisdictions regard registered securities as located at the place where the register of registered owners of the securities is maintained, while others use a combination of both approaches.[14] Although many jurisdictions have experienced satisfactory results in attributing a *situs* to registered securities held in *non-fungible* custody accounts in *direct holding systems*, the transformation of financial markets, and in particular the computerisation of clearance and settlement systems, have radically altered the way in which ownership interests are recorded and maintained by intermediaries and central security depositories.

In contrast, where securities are held through one or more intermediaries or depositories, many jurisdictions apply the so-called 'look-through' approach to locate the *situs* of indirectly-held securities by looking through the tiers of intermediaries and depositories to find one or more of the following: the jurisdiction of the issuer, the register, or the place of the registrar or of registered securities. Applying the 'look-through' approaches to ascertain the *situs* of securities in indirect holding systems produces significant conceptual and practical difficulties.[15] The major difficulty is the practical one of attempting to apply one of the above traditional approaches to determine the *situs* of securities by looking-through the tiers of intermediaries to the jurisdiction or level of the issuer, the register and/or the actual location of certificates.[16]

## Indirect holding systems

Advances in computer technology have altered the structure of securities markets and the way in which cross-border trading is processed in clearance and settlement systems. Indeed, the dramatic increase in cross-border securities trading and the large volume of collateralised arrangements involving securities has necessitated that clearance and settlement systems accommodate the need for rapid execution of

---

[12] Dicey and Morris, in L. Collins (ed.), *Conflict of Laws* (12th edn, 1993) Rule 120.

[13] If dealing with *bearer* securities, the applicable law would be that of the jurisdiction where the collateral taker takes possession of the securities certificate at the time of the transfer.

[14] This approach provides that a party's name on the register, rather than possession of a certificate, conveys legal rights to the securities. *See* Report, p. 27, note 107.

[15] The Report notes that the different approaches for determining the situs of securities by looking through multiple tiers of intermediaries to determine the law of the issuer, the register or the registrar, and/or the location of registered securities or the place of bearer securities can pose difficult conceptual and practical problems. The Report, pp. 26–27.

[16] The Report, p. 27.

trades and the transfer of interests in securities without reference to the physical possession of certificates. This has caused much complexity concerning the application of the *lex situs* rule to electronically recorded interests in securities.

Today, most publicly-traded securities are held in dematerialised form[17] in which the security is evidenced by computerised or electronic entries in a system maintained by the issuer or by a record holder acting for the issuer. These indirect holding systems often involve multiple tiers of intermediaries between issuer and investor, thus precluding physical possession and delivery of securities in certificated form.[18] Other important features are that interests in securities are reflected on the books of various intermediaries and depositories, transfers are effected by electronic book entry, and the need to transfer the instruments in which participating interests are held rarely arises. For example, Euroclear is an indirect holding system, based in Belgium, involving a network of 2,400 participating financial institutions and intermediaries throughout Europe that engage in cross-border securities transactions.[19]

When dealing with *registered securities*, many jurisdictions continue to apply the look-through approaches to ascertain the *situs* of securities held in indirect holding systems. Depending on the jurisdiction, this requires an examination of the various factors, including the law of the issuer's jurisdiction or the law of the jurisdiction where the securities records of the issuer (the 'register') or its official record holder (the 'registrar') are located at the time of transfer. This task becomes especially difficult when one must examine the electronic records and entries of multiple intermediaries and depositories located in different jurisdictions in order to ascertain where an investor's securities account is maintained and recorded. This legal uncertainty regarding the applicable law for the disposition of interests in securities held in indirect holding systems increases systemic risk in financial markets. It is therefore necessary to establish another connecting legal factor that provides certainty and stability regarding the applicable substantive law for ascertaining and enforcing collateral interests in securities held in indirect holding systems.

Traditional conflict of laws approaches relying on the 'look-through' approaches to determine the *lex rei sitae* of securities held in indirect settlement systems pose major conceptual difficulties in a legal and practical sense. For example, where a diversified portfolio of securities is provided as collateral, the collateral taker must satisfy the laws of one or more of the following jurisdictions: the laws of each issuer, the law of the place of the register, and/or the law of the place of the custodian with physical custody of the securities. Moreover, many jurisdictions do not provide a clear rule for determining which 'look-through' approach to apply; for example, is it the law of the issuer, the place of the register, or the place of the underlying securities.

---

[17] A security in dematerialised form is a security the issue and holding of which are evidenced solely by computerised or electronic entries in a system maintained by the issuer or by a record holder acting for the issuer. By contrast, the phrase 'physical securities' is generally used to refer to certificated securities.

[18] The great majority of these securities are held in omnibus customer accounts in which no information about the individual is recorded in the financial intermediaries and securities depositories that occupy the upper tier of these indirect holding systems.

[19] See more about Euroclear in chapter 7, *infra*.

Even if the collateral taker knows which test to apply, it may not have been possible to obtain the necessary information to determine how to apply the test. For example, the multiple tier structure of a particular securities holding may preclude a collateral taker from discovering where a national securities depository actually stores its certificates. In some cases, it may be impossible to designate a single jurisdiction as the *situs* where the certificates of a single issue are located in more than one jurisdiction.

A consensus view has emerged amongst a number of legal experts that the proprietary effects of a disposition of securities held in a fungible custody account should be determined by the law of the place where the account is maintained, and *not* the law of any other jurisdiction that might have applied had the underlying securities been held directly by the collateral provider.[20] Indeed, Professor Goode has argued that this analysis conforms with traditional English trust law concepts, such as the concept of equitable co-ownership of a pool of fungible securities, in which case a court would apply the law of the place of the trustee.[21] This view rejects traditional conflict of laws approaches, such as the *lex rei sitae* or *lex sitae*, or the law of the place of the issuer or registrar, as artificial. Rather, a new approach is necessary that embodies a conflict of laws rule that applies the law of the place of the intermediary with whom the investor directly holds an account. This is known as the place of the relevant intermediary approach, the essential elements of which appear in the European Union's Settlement Finality Directive and the proposed EU Collateral Directive.

V   THE EUROPEAN UNION'S LEGAL FRAMEWORK FOR REGULATING
COLLATERAL INTERESTS IN SECURITIES: THE EU SETTLEMENT
FINALITY DIRECTIVE AND THE COLLATERAL DIRECTIVE

The European Commission's Financial Services Action Plan recognises the importance of reducing legal uncertainty for payment and securities settlement systems, Central Banks, and participants in financial markets as part of a broader plan to further integrate EU financial markets and to support the smooth functioning of the single monetary policy in the Economic and Monetary Union. To this end, two Directives – Settlement Finality Directive and Collateral Directive – seek to support the EU Treaty objectives of free movement of capital under Arts 56–60 and free movement of services under Art. 49.

The European Union adopted the *Directive on Settlement Finality* in 1998 (Settlement Finality Directive) that provided a legal framework for regulating payment and securities settlement systems. The Settlement Finality Directive applies to the taking of cross-border collateral in financial transactions within the European Union where such transactions involve a designated securities settlement or payment

---

[20] *See* 'Oxford Colloquium on Collateral and Conflict of Laws' (1998) *JIBFL*.
[21] R. Goode, 'Security Entitlements As Collateral and the Conflict of Laws' (1998) *JIBFL*.

system, the European Central Bank, or the European System of Central Banks. The Settlement Finality Directive provides limited protection against the effects of EU Member State bankruptcy laws by insulating collateral given to the system operators, certain system participants, and EU central banks, but not to other financial market participants.

Art. 9, para. 2 of the Directive is important because it permits netting in settlement systems and clarifies the applicable law to dispositions of collateral interests in book-entry securities.[22] The Report notes that the original purpose of Art. 9, para. 2, was to benefit only EU central banks, the European Central Bank, and certain participants (i.e. central securities depositories) in designated payment and settlement systems who act as collateral takers. But a number of Member States have extended these protections further to include financial market participants, as defined in a more general sense. For example, the United Kingdom has adopted regulations to implement the EU Settlement Finality Directive entitled the *Financial Markets and Insolvency ('Settlement Finality') Regulations 1999*.[23] The 1999 Settlement Finality Regulations were amended in April 2001 by the *Financial Markets and Insolvency ('Settlement Finality Amendment')*. The UK Settlement Finality Regulations applies the protections of the Settlement Finality Directive to a broader range of financial intermediaries and defines broadly the type of securities covered by the Directive. UK implementation of Art. 9(2) of the Finality Directive has clarified some of the issues related to the legal location of interests in securities in electronic clearing systems.

## *The Collateral Directive*[24]

More recently, the European Council and Parliament adopted on 7 June 2002 a Collateral Directive, as part of its EU Financial Services Action Plan, that builds upon the Settlement Finality Directive. The Collateral Directive is intended to limit credit risk in financial transactions by creating a more uniform EU legal framework to govern the disposition of securities and cash as collateral under both pledge and title transfer structures. The Collateral Directive provides more certainty to the law

---

[22] The Report cites Art. 9, para. 2 as follows:

'Where securities (including rights in securities) are provided as collateral security to participants and/or central banks of the Member States or the future European central bank as described in paragraph 1, and their right (or that of any nominee, agent or third party acting on their behalf) with respect to securities is legally recorded on a register, account or centralised deposit system located in a Member State, the determination of the rights of such entities as holders of collateral security in relation to those securities shall be governed by the law of that Member State.'

[23] S.I. 1999 No. 2979, as amended with effect from 5 April 2001, by S.I. 2001 No. 997.

[24] 2002/47/EC on financial collateral arrangements, OJ 168, 27/06/2002 Art. 13 of the Directive requires Member States to implement the laws, regulations and administrative provisions to comply with the Directive by 31 December 2004.

applicable to ownership interests in securities recorded in intermediated book-entry form and traded in indirect holding systems. The Directive applies to securities traded on *both* a cross-border basis with parties located in different jurisdictions *and* between parties in the same EU Member State jurisdiction. It would do so by expanding the scope of coverage of the Settlement Finality Directive to 'any book-entry securities collateral [or cash collateral]' and the law for enforcing rights to such collateral 'shall be governed by the law of the country or, where appropriate, the law of the part of the country in which the relevant account is maintained, whether or not that country is a Member State'.[25] The Directive would essentially adopt the law of the place of the relevant intermediary account to determine all rights and interests in collateral interests in securities held in intermediated book-entry systems.[26]

Art. 1 sets forth the general purpose of the Directive as protecting the provision of financial collateral on a bi-lateral basis between two parties to a collateral agreement. Art. 2 defines the scope of the Directive's application to collateral that must be actually delivered or held in a specified cash or securities account. Art. 2(3) makes it clear that these specified 'cash' or 'securities' accounts makes it unnecessary for a new document to be executed in respect of each sum or delivery of securities credited to an account. Art. 2(6) expressly covers most future and contingent liabilities that may include liabilities under a swap or other derivative contract and liabilities of third parties.[27] This provision also applies to 'all monies' arrangements where the collateral is provided for any debt owed now or in the future to a collateral taker.[28]

The Directive applies to all 'financial collateral arrangement[s]', which are defined in two broad categories: (1) 'title transfer financial collateral arrangement' (repos and title transfer arrangements, for example, ISDA Credit Support Annex'); and (2) 'security financial collateral arrangement' (the traditional pledge or charge structure).

Art. 3 defines 'financial collateral' as

> ...shares in companies and other securities equivalent to shares in companies and bonds and other forms of debt instruments if these are negotiable on the capital market, and any other securities which are normally dealt in and which give the right to acquire any such shares, bonds or other securities by subscription, purchase or exchange or which give rise to a cash settlement (excluding instrument of settlement).[29]

The Directive provides two specific measures that seek to enhance liquidity in the collateral market. Art. 6 provides a clear statutory regime regarding agreements

---

[25] See proposed Collateral Directive, Art. 11, para. 2.

[26] European Commissioner for the internal market, Fritz Bolkestein, endorsed the proposed Directive by stating that '[t]his proposal would determine which law governs cross-border collateral arrangements and make it possible for market participants to conclude such arrangements in the same manner throughout the EU'. <http://europa.eu.int/comm/internal>

[27] Collateral Directive, Art. 2(6).

[28] *Ibid.*

[29] Art. 3(1)(h).

permitting the collateral taker to re-use the collateral for their own purposes under pledge structures.[30] Art. 6(2) allows 'collateral substitution', whereby the collateral provider can withdraw particular securities and replace them with other securities of equivalent value if the collateral agreement so provides.

Art. 7 recognises financial collateral arrangements regarding title transfer (e.g. repos). Member States are required to recognise that ownership of financial collateral passes to the collateral taker in accordance with the collateral agreement, if the collateral arrangement provides that ownership of financial collateral is to pass to the collateral taker on delivery or payment, subject to an obligation to deliver equivalent collateral.

Art. 8 addresses the issue of close-out netting, which forms a key part of the enforcement mechanism for repo and other title transfer collateral arrangements. The validity of close-out netting in cross-border transactions is undermined by the insolvency laws of some jurisdictions on the basis that it conflicts with mandatory rules prohibiting or restricting insolvency set-off. Art. 8(1) recognises the validity of close-out netting provisions in a financial collateral arrangement, whilst Art. 8(2) protects close-out netting provisions from third parties (e.g. assignees or judgment creditors) seeking to attach their interests.

Art. 9 precludes winding-up proceedings or reorganisations from having retroactive effects in regard to financial collateral arrangements, such as 'zero-hour rules', which give retroactive effect to the commencement of insolvency events, deeming them to have begun at midnight ('zero-hour'). Art. 9 protects financial collateral which has been delivered on the date, but prior to the time, that proceedings were initiated against automatic invalidation. Art. 9 also addresses the interaction in standard agreements between provisions dealing with 'top-up' and 'substitution' of collateral.[31]

The Collateral Directive regime has extraterritorial effect in so far as it applies to collateral takers and collateral providers from third countries, but only applies to the extent that the collateral taker or collateral provider is subject to the laws of a Member State, including its insolvency laws. Generally, a firm is subject to the insolvency laws of the jurisdiction where it is incorporated, organised, or has its principal place of business. The Directive's requirement therefore that Member States modify their insolvency laws applies to a Community collateral provider whether or not the collateral taker is from a Member State. For example, a French liquidator that seeks to wind up a Member State counter-party should not distinguish whether the collateral taker is from another Member State or from a third country. The regime will make it less burdensome for a collateral taker from a third country to make the necessary legal determinations to show that the collateral agreement is enforceable in the European Union in case of bankruptcy. The Directive seeks to reduce obstacles for Community collateral providers to seek credit or loans from collateral takers in third countries.

---

[30] Art. 6(1)–(3).
[31] Art. 9(1)–(3).

The Collateral Directive is intended to lead to more efficient price determination, and the expected reduction in market volatility could allow companies to buy or sell securities more easily and at a fairer price.

### The United States' Approach – Art. 8 of the Uniform Commercial Code

The 1987 stock market crisis led US authorities to undertake reform of Art. 8 of the Uniform Commercial Code (UCC), which deals with investment securities. The 1978 version UCC Art. 8 was designed exclusively to apply to investment securities traded in direct holding systems. The liquidity crisis of the October 1987 stock market collapse exposed the legal uncertainty surrounding the application of the 1978 version of Art. 8 to the modern market reality of indirect holding systems.[32]

Efforts to revise Art. 8 culminated in 1994 with the adoption of what has become known as 'revised Art. 8'. Revised Art. 8 makes a number of important changes that include an express definition of key terms such as 'securities intermediary', 'security'[33] and 'securities account',[34] and also provides the various duties of a securities intermediary to its security account holders. An important provision is the introduction of the concept of 'securities entitlement'. This new concept effectively means that an investor does not have a traceable property right to a specific security located somewhere in the vault of a depository or intermediary, but instead 'has a package of rights and interests against the securities intermediary' with whom the investor has a direct contractual relationship.[35] As one expert observed, a security entitlement is a form 'property interest, combined with a package of in personam rights against the intermediary'.[36]

Under this approach, a securities entitlement holder can only assert its rights or interests in securities against its own intermediary, that is, the intermediary who maintains the record of its interests. An essential feature of the security entitlement structure is that an entitlement holder's property interest is a bundle of rights that can be asserted directly only against the entitlement holder's own intermediary. The search for the location of a pledged interest in securities therefore ends at the intermediary where the interest is located at the place where the account in which it is recorded is maintained. The entitlement holder cannot assert rights directly against other persons, such as other intermediaries through whom the intermediary holds the position.[37] It is an efficient approach because the investor (entitlement holder) does not take the credit risk of the intermediary's other business activities; and if the intermediary files bankruptcy, its securities holdings corresponding to customer

---

[32] *See* James S. Rogers, 'Policy Perspectives on Revised U.C.C. Article 8' (1996) 43 UCLA L Rev 1431.

[33] Sec. 8-102(a)(15).

[34] Sec. 8-501(a).

[35] The Report, p. 25.

[36] *See* Rogers, 'Policy Perspectives on Revised U.C.C. Article 8' at pp. 1456–1457.

[37] *Ibid.*

claims will satisfy these claims before any are available to satisfy the claims of general creditors.

Art. 8 dramatically improves upon the 1978 version of Art. 8 by clarifying the fact that 'uncertificated securities' are not necessarily the same as securities held electronically through intermediaries. Art. 8 uses different terms to describe 'direct' and 'indirect' holding systems in order to make it clear that the commercial law rules for securities held through intermediaries differ from those of securities held directly. In this context, it should be noted that 'uncertificated securities' can be held in direct holding systems where ownership interests in securities are recorded on the books of the issuer's transfer agent. As discussed in Part 1, however, uncertificated securities are increasingly recorded electronically in book-entry form with intermediaries who in turn are registered as owning interests in the securities.

## VI  THE HAGUE CONVENTION

The Hague Convention was signed on 13 December 2002 and is open to ratification by its signatory states.

Under the Convention, 'securities' is defined broadly to include all financial instruments whether directly or indirectly held and 'other financial instruments or assets (other than cash)'. Art. 1(1) states in relevant part:

> 'securities' means any shares, bonds or other financial instruments or assets (other than cash), or any interest therein

The definition covers non-negotiable instruments and registered bonds. The term 'other financial instruments' appears to be a catchall that can be construed widely, which might undermine legal certainty by allowing certain unintended transactions to fall under the Convention's jurisdiction.

It is necessary to define 'securities' because parties to a disposition in securities would need to consider whether the financial instrument in question qualifies as a security in order to determine whether the Convention applies. This raises conflict of laws issues concerning how to determine whether an instrument qualifies as a security or not. The broad definition of 'securities' in the Convention leaves scope for market innovation and evolution. Another important issue arises regarding whether an issuer might decide, for legal or regulatory reasons, to issue instruments which do not qualify as securities. A conflict may develop where a financial instrument might not qualify as a security under the law of the issuer or the law governing the instrument, whilst it may qualify as a security under the Convention's broad definition. The negotiators felt however that the benefits of defining 'securities' exceeded the disadvantages. It should be noted that the definition of 'securities' covers only those securities that may be entered into an account and transferred by way of book entries; this would cover all securities held with an intermediary.

By contrast, the EU collateral directive tends to define securities by insisting on their intrinsic characteristics, in particular the market negotiability. Moreover, *instruments of payment* as such are excluded from the scope of the Directive rather than simply 'cash'. A view has emerged that a more detailed definition of securities is needed that is similar to the definition of the Collateral directive. Also, the Convention should indicate a list of securities that would qualify as covered securities under Art. 1(1) that takes into consideration the criterion whether an instrument may be credited to an account.

Art. 2 defines the scope of the treaty and its applicable law as applying to all proprietary interests in indirectly held securities. It states in relevant part:

> 2(1) This Convention determines the law applicable to the following issues in respect of securities held with an intermediary
>
> > (a) whether the right resulting from the credit of securities to a securities account are property, contract or other rights;
> >
> > (b) the legal nature and effects against third parties of a disposition of securities held with an intermediary;
> >
> > (c) the requirements, if any, for perfection of a disposition of securities held with an intermediary;
> >
> > (d) whether a person's interest in securities held with an intermediary
> >
> > (e) the duties, if any, of an intermediary to a person who asserts a competing interest in securities held with that intermediary;
> >
> > (f) the requirements, if any, for the realisation of an interest in securities held with an intermediary; and
> >
> > (g) whether a security interest in securities held with an intermediary extends to entitlements to dividends, income, other distributions or redemption, sale or other proceeds.

Art. 2(1) focuses on the proprietary aspects of indirect holdings of securities that involve transfers of interests in, and pledging, book-entry interests in securities. It does not address the assignment of contractual claims governed by different conflict of laws rules. Nevertheless, the scope of the Convention's applicability is drafted in broad terms, as it covers the character, nature, priority, perfection requirements, duties of an intermediary and requirements for realisation and entitlements *vis-á-vis* interests in indirectly held securities.

Art. 2(2), in contrast recognises at the same time that contractual aspects of the relationship between an intermediary and holders of securities accounts may be governed by a different law than the one selected pursuant to PRIMA. Art. 2(2) states in relevant part that the PRIMA approach will not apply to 'contractual rights and duties of parties to a transaction in securities', and the 'contractual rights and duties arising from relations between an intermediary and an account holder', or the rights and duties of an issuer of securities, its registrar or transfer agent, in relation to the holder of the securities or any other person:

As discussed above, the *lex situs (or lex rei sitae)* provided no certain *ex ante* objective criteria which could determine the applicable law to proprietary rights in securities held with an intermediary. Art. 4(1) seeks to define the place of the relevant intermediary by modernising the *lex situs* rule so that it applies the national law agreed by the intermediary and the account holder to govern proprietary aspects of a securities account held through an indirect holding system. This requirement is conditioned on the relevant intermediary to which the securities account is accredited maintaining an office that monitors the account in question in the jurisdiction so selected. Art. 4(1) is the central provision of the treaty, as it provides the criteria for determining which jurisdiction's law applies to proprietary interests in indirectly held securities. Art. 4 states in relevant part:

Determination of the applicable law – Primary rule

(1)  The law applicable to the issues specified in Article 2(1) is the law of the State agreed by the account holder and the relevant intermediary as the State whose law governs those issues provided that the relevant intermediary has, at the time of the agreement, an office in that State, and

 (a)  entries to securities accounts are effected and monitored at such office;

 (b)  the administration of payments or corporate actions relating to securities held with the intermediary is performing at such office;

 (c)  an account number, bank code, or other specific means of identification identifies securities accounts as being maintained at such office; or

 (d)  that office is otherwise engaged in a business or other regular activity of maintaining securities accounts.

During the *travaux preparatoires*, three options emerged for interpreting the PRIMA approach of Art. 4(1). Option A used the choice of law agreed to by the intermediary and the account holder without reference to the place where the securities account is maintained. Option B required that this choice of law must also designate the place where the account in question is maintained. Option A was criticised because it made no reference to the place where the office maintaining the securities is located and therefore did not take account of the PRIMA principle. Option B takes the location where the securities account is maintained as the decisive factor in determining the applicable law. This option was criticised as essentially changing the PRIMA rule to the 'Place Where the Relevant Intermediary Maintains the Account'.[38] Rather than use a look through approach to the underlying securities, Option B would have required collateral takers to look through to the intermediary's account maintenance practices. In the negotiations, it became clear that it would be difficult for purposes of the Convention to determine the place where the account is actually maintained, and that this would undermine the necessary legal certainty and predictability sought in the Convention.

Options A and B both permitted a certain degree of autonomy for the parties to choose the law applicable to proprietary interests in securities, but it became clear during the negotiations that it was necessary to have an objective and real connection between the chosen law and the securities in question. Therefore, a third option emerged as a sort of compromise between Options A and B that required the

---

[38]  *See* Summary of Comments of Canada (12 November 2002) p. 32.

intermediary to have an office in the state whose law the parties to the custody agreement have chosen. This became known as Option A+, which eliminates the requirement that the parties choose the law of the place where the securities in question are maintained. Instead, A+ requires that there is an office in the state whose law is selected and that the office in question fulfils tasks relating to maintaining the securities accounts. Option A+ would therefore allow an intermediary that operates in many states to provide securities accounts maintenance (i.e. transfers of interests, perfection, and enforcing rights in respect of securities) by any of its offices and by applying a law that is in force in one of the states where the intermediary has offices. Although this has been praised as a practical approach that accords with the PRIMA principle, there is a risk that the *relevant office* of the jurisdiction whose law has been chosen might be a sham, or merely a technology or mailing call centre.

Art. 4(2) seeks to address this issue by providing criteria for a legitimate relevant office. It does so by stating that an office is *not engaged* in a business or other regular activity of maintaining securities accounts merely because it is a place where '(a) the technology supporting the bookkeeping or data processing for securities accounts is located; (b) call centres for communication with account holders are located or operated; or (c) the mailing relating to securities accounts is organised and file rooms are located'.[39]

The A+ approach avoids the so-called magic words requirement of designating a particular jurisdiction as the choice of law without the intermediary also having a legitimate presence in that jurisdiction through the maintenance of like accounts. The A+ option has been criticised as resulting in uncertainty because it will result in different judicial interpretation in different legal systems. A+ also raises questions about the interpretation of pre-convention contracts (and thus to some extent the retroactivity of the Convention). Art. 20 (1)(b) needs to be clear on whether a pre-convention contractual choice of law in an account agreement should have the effect that the proprietary issues in Art. 2(1) would be governed by that law chosen after entry into force of the Convention.

Art. 4 also contains language that many observers interpret as extending the scope of the Convention to existing collateral arrangements that have been in effect preceding the adoption of the Convention. Moreover Art. 20 contains language that effectively guarantees the retroactive application of the Convention to collateral arrangements in effect at the time of the Convention. Significantly, the Convention's uniform choice of law approach will not apply to insolvency law issues, which will prove a significant issue as signatory states begin adopting legislation to incorporate the treaty into domestic law.

Art. 5 provides a fall-back rule in the case where Art. 4 cannot determine the applicable law to the proprietary interest in question. In such a case, Art. 5 would determine the applicable law based on either the law of incorporation or principal place of business of the intermediary to whom the securities account is accredited.

---

[39] The Convention, Art. 4(2).

Art. 5 would depart from the PRIMA principal because it places no importance on the actual location of the securities account or the office where the account is maintained. For example, the law of a foreign state would be applicable to a securities account maintained in the United States, if the domestic dependent office of a foreign legal person (i.e. incorporated in Germany) were acting as the intermediary.

Art. 10(1) and (2) provides the public policy exception for applying the obligations of the Convention. It stipulates that the provisions of any law determined by the Convention could only be disregarded if such provisions are 'manifestly contrary' to public policy. Art. 10(3) however appears to restrict the application of the public policy exception by disallowing any application of the 'laws of the forum' *vis-à-vis* perfection or priorities between competing interests unless it reflects the law of the PRIMA, which would be determined by Art(s) 4 or 5. Under this provision, a court would be able to apply its own laws to the extent that these are to be regarded as an expression of fundamental values which are so important that, as a matter of policy, local law should be applied even though the issues are otherwise governed by foreign law. This Article's scope of application is not clear. An important issue arises concerning the definition of the term 'forum'. Art. 11 addresses the complicated issue of multi-unit states, in which it allows the law of sub-states to be applied in cases where the nation in question has made a declaration that Art. 4 shall apply to the laws of sub-states within a multi-unit federation.

The European Central Bank criticised earlier drafts of the Convention because it failed to make a clear distinction between contractual and property rights. The ECB further argued that if a clear distinction is made in many jurisdictions with less sophisticated financial laws and regulations it will fail in its objective to enhance legal certainty and reduce systemic risk. In these jurisdictions, the mere adoption of a uniform choice of law rule to determine the applicable law for certain interests in property cannot be accomplished without adopting a uniform substantive law as well. In supporting this view, the ECB has observed that the UCC's Art. 8 'forms only one small part of a far larger code of law' intended to provide a comprehensive legal framework to reduce legal uncertainties for current securities holdings practices. Indeed, jurisdictions that have not adopted a complementary substantive law framework to accommodate the implementation of conflict of laws rules for determining ownership interests in property may suffer competitive disadvantages *vis-à-vis* jurisdictions like the United States that already have a comprehensive framework of substantive and choice of law rules to regulate securities holdings practices. This is because without a complementary substantive law framework the draft Hague Convention might result in some countries continuing to transfer ownership interests in securities directly and exclusively between the two parties in the transaction, whilst intermediaries in those jurisdictions would be capable only of transferring possession over the securities or transact simple bookings.[40] The ECB has therefore suggested that the PRIMA approach could only be efficiently and beneficially implemented in most EU Member States with parallel substantive law

---

[40] *Ibid.*

reforms, as was the case in the United States with the implementation of revised Art. 8. The ECB further observes that very little is known about the likely costs, benefit and impact of a measure 'in which the private international law of an overarching reform is passed into law without substantive reforms that have accompanied it in the past'.[41]

## VII    MOVING BEYOND PRIMA

The overriding purpose of the Hague Convention on Indirectly Held Securities is to reduce the uncertainty for creditors in determining which law applies to the disposition, perfection, and realisation of property interests in indirectly held securities. Although the Convention has a certain logical appeal, some observers have argued that it does not go far enough in addressing existing differences in national legal systems regarding the creation, perfection and protection in bankruptcy of collateral interests in securities. There are significant differences in how national legal systems protect collateral interests in securities that derive from history and from the economic and social structure of nations. The diversity of practices today in national legal systems poses an obstacle to the efficient operation of global securities markets. It would appear that the increasingly seamless nature of financial markets would require certain international or uniform rules and regulatory procedures to ensure that credit and liquidity risk is managed in an efficient manner. Moreover, the efficient regulation of risk in financial markets necessitates effective international legal standards that apply uniformly in all relevant markets. The PRIMA proposal should be taken further so that there are international legal standards that would encourage convergence and/or a substantial degree of uniformity in the way collateral interests are created, perfected and preserved in bankruptcy in all jurisdictions.

The problem posed by differences in national legal systems is that firms must adjust to a different set of rules for each country in which they operate. This has proved to be complex and costly and has distorted the efficient flow of cross-border capital to its most valued use. Moreover, even where PRIMA seeks to apply the law of the country of the immediate intermediary, this does not guarantee recognition and enforcement of interests created and perfected in conformity with that country's laws, because transfers may still violate the perfection requirements of the laws of other countries. For example, securities registered and perfected as a non-possessory pledge in conformity with the laws of the country of the intermediary which maintains the securities account will not necessarily be recognised as a perfected interest under the laws of the country where the company issuing the securities was incorporated. This is an example of a mandatory requirement of a foreign jurisdiction that operates irrespective of the *situs* of the asset and may therefore not be displaced by the *lex situs*.

These national differences in legal systems are particularly problematic with regard to bankruptcy law. Bankruptcy law generally aims to ensure that all creditors

---

[41] *Ibid.*

are treated equitably. These laws often invalidate certain transfers or transactions entered into by a debtor in favour of a particular creditor a short time before the debtor files bankruptcy because such transactions often favour that creditor at the expense of other creditors in violation of legal principles. For example, a bankruptcy trustee or liquidator normally has the power to declare invalid a debtor's transfer of an interest in collateral if such transfer occurs a short time before the debtor files for bankruptcy relief. There are important differences between national legal systems concerning the definition of whether a transaction favours a creditor and whether it should therefore be invalidated. Such variations may deter a creditor bank from accepting a pledge of securities from a borrower in a foreign jurisdiction because foreign bankruptcy laws could have an impact on the validity of an agreement with a foreign counter party. Thus, especially in regard to dispositions of interests in securities in cross-border transactions, firms must be aware of the whole range of bankruptcy laws in economies where securities transactions take place.

Moreover, recharacterisation risk arises where a collateral taker's pledged interests in securities located in the collateral taker's jurisdiction are recharacterised as unsecured claims by a bankruptcy trustee or liquidator acting for the collateral provider in a foreign jurisdiction. This type of recharacterisation risk could happen in a number of ways in the cross-border context. For example, where pledged securities are located in the collateral provider's jurisdiction and the contract creating the pledge is governed by the law of the collateral taker's jurisdiction, and the collateral taker registers or perfects its pledged interest in both jurisdictions, the collateral provider's bankruptcy trustee or liquidator would likely have the power to recharacterise the collateral taker's pledged interests to that of an unsecured claim in order to benefit other creditors.

In addition, there are rules regarding the procedures, which creditors must follow to ensure that they can enforce rights to collateral and to ensure priority over other creditors in accordance with the collateral agreement. These procedures are called perfection requirements and exist to ensure that the creditors do not illegally benefit from the collateral and prohibit further use of the collateral by the debtor. But many legal systems have complicated and impractical publicity requirements, whose origins are centuries old, to ensure that third parties are aware that the assets being provided as collateral would not generally be available in an insolvency situation. In some jurisdictions, collateral can be liquidated immediately, and in others the exercise of rights in collateral can take several months or even longer.

It is therefore extremely important to adopt a legal regime that can minimise counter-party insolvency law risk, or recharacterisation risk,[42] and provide more certainty as to which jurisdiction's perfection requirements will be applied and enforced, regardless of whether the intermediary or any other party files bankruptcy. Adopting such a regime at the international level would be very difficult to adopt and implement not least because national authorities are reluctant to change their legal

---

[42] *See* discussion in Fentiman, 'Cross-Border Securities Collateral: Redefining Recharacterisation Risk' in *Oxford Colloquium on Collateral and Conflict of Laws* JIBFL pp. 38–39.

systems in fundamental ways that affect the very notion of ownership in property and the delicate balance that exist between creditors and debtors which has evolved over the years according to a country's unique political, economic and social development. This is why the proposed draft Hague Convention on indirectly held securities, along with the European Union, the United States, and some other jurisdictions, has sought to address this difficult and complex problem by seeking only to regulate choice of law rule that would determine the law applicable to ownership interests in securities.

## VIII   CONCLUSION

This chapter examined how structural changes in financial markets have necessitated the move away from holding physical securities certificates in direct holding systems to the more flexible system of holding securities through multi-tiered structures of financial intermediaries.[43] Cross-border trading in securities is increasingly relying not on the physical exchange of securities certificates or the registering of interests in a company registrar but on electronic book-entries recorded with custodians and depositories in various jurisdictions. The lack of legal certainty regarding which law applies to the disposition of proprietary interests in indirectly held securities has increased systemic risk in the international financial system.

To facilitate the taking of collateral interests in securities traded on a cross-border basis, the European Union and the United States have adopted variations on the place on the relevant intermediary approach to determine the law applicable to transfers in interests in financial collateral or securities. In particular, the Collateral Directive aims to provide certainty and predictability to a narrow, but essential, area of securities transactions and provides the basis for further proposals to apply a uniform choice of law approach to determine the law applicable to proprietary interests in securities on an international basis. Similarly, Art. 8 of the UCC's definition of 'securities entitlement' and other key terms reflects an accurate description of the unique form of property interest that is a central element to the indirect holding system. Also, the search for the location of a pledged interest in securities requires the entitlement holder to look only to that intermediary where the account is maintained for performance of the obligations.

The Hague Convention adopts an international choice of law rule that would apply to proprietary interests in indirectly held securities. Under Art. 2, the Convention's broad scope covers the proprietary aspects of indirectly held securities, including transferring and pledging of book entry securities, the nature and priority of perfection requirements, duties of an intermediary, and requirements for realisation and entitlements *vis-à-vis* indirectly held securities, but it will not cover the contractual aspects of holdings in indirect securities. Art. 4 provides that the law chosen by the intermediary and investor will apply to the proprietary aspects of a securities account

---

[43] The Report, p. 2.

recorded with that intermediary so long as the intermediary maintains a legitimate office in the jurisdiction of the law chosen. Although the Convention does not incorporate a jurisdiction's insolvency law into the PRIMA rule, it is important step to providing more legal certainty to international securities markets. The insolvency issue and recharacterisation risk and its overlap with perfection and priority orders are likely to prove a contentious area in litigation for the courts of many countries. Also, there is bound to be conflict with the requirements of the Collateral Directive and how the Directive is implemented into the legal systems of EU Member States. Despite the uncertainties and ambiguities, the Convention will raise interesting interpretative issues for lawyers and have an impact on systemic stability in financial markets.

ABSTRACT

At present, businesses face many different legal regimes for the provision of collateral, with the potential for complicated conflicts between jurisdictions and uncertainties surrounding the law applicable to cross-border transfers of securities. Many experts agree that the legal uncertainty surrounding the law applicable to the disposition of interest in securities in indirect holding systems has played a substantial role in causing past liquidity crises in financial markets.[44] The significant increase in the volume of cross-border securities transactions in recent years and the trend towards dematerialisation and the use of indirect holding systems has necessitated the development of legal rules to keep pace with changes in the marketplace. In pursuit of this aim, the Hague Convention proposes the creation of a uniform conflict of laws rule that would apply the law of the place where the intermediary is located for determining the law applicable to taking and disposing of proprietary interests in securities. The Convention increases legal certainty for many types of international securities transactions, but it also fails to address some important issues that affect certainty and security in international financial transactions.

---

[44] *See* generally, F. Oditah (ed.), *The Future for the Global Securities Market: Legal and Regulatory Aspects* (OUP, 1996).

# Centralisation of Securities Market Supervision: Towards a European Securities Regulator?

*Chapter 6*

# The Need and the Rationale for a
# European Securities Regulator

*Yannis V. Avgerinos*

## A INTRODUCTION

A criterion that justifies action at EU level is the production of clear benefits by reason of its scale or effects compared with action at the level of the Member States. Does Europe need a pan-European securities regulator? If yes, is the creation of such a body feasible within the legal, political and economic context of Europe? These questions have recently gone beyond the purely academic domain to form the subject of specific political debate between regulators, practitioners and market participants. Although the results of these debates usually end up to give a negative dimension to such a suggestion,[1] the very fact that this question is raised up in this particular period of time reveals that something is wrong with the present regulatory and supervisory financial architecture.

It is important to stress that issues surrounding a pan-European supervisor go wider than the investment services sector. However, this analysis will limit itself to the securities sector. It is argued that, in order to prevent institutional structure from being a purely arbitrary and *ad hoc* process, several key issues need to be considered: the objectives of regulation, the clarity of regulatory agencies' remit, the costs of a particular institutional structure, the accountability of regulatory agencies, questions relating to the efficiency of the regulatory process, the merits of a degree of competition in regulation and issues relating to the concentration of power.[2] In addition to these, this chapter suggests that two more issues need to be examined: issues relating to administrative efficiency and externalities.

For the purposes of my discussion and because law on its own may not provide sufficiently accurate and reliable standards for evaluating the effects of legal rules and institutional structures, economic theory will also be incorporated into

---

[1] *See*, for instance, the Reports originated from discussions among the FESE and the Wise Men Group, chaired by Alexandre Lamfalussy: FESE, Report and Recommendations on European Regulatory Structures (September 2000) (hereinafter 'FESE Report'); Committee of Wise Men, Initial Report on Regulation of European Securities Markets, 9 November 2000 (hereinafter 'Initial Wise Men Report').

[2] *See* Charles Goodhart *et al.*, *Financial Regulation: Why, How and Where Now?* (Bank of England, London, 1998) 150.

*Mads Andenas and Yannis Avgerinos (eds), Financial Markets in Europe: Towards a Single Regulator?* 145–182.
© 2003 *Kluwer Law International. Printed in Great Britain.*

my legal analysis. In the light of this, by stressing the need to take the effects of the proposed action into account, the EC Treaty itself also rejects a pure legal formalistic approach.[3]

As far as systemic stability is concerned, the integration model of home country control has worked well so far.[4] It has failed, nonetheless, in delivering the full application of the principle of the free movement of financial services. *A fortiori*, the European supervisory and regulatory system, as it exists at present, cannot continue to be adequate for an increasingly integrated European financial market, given its evident weaknesses. Centralisation in supervision and more flexible regulation will be the only answer to the hurdles of inconsistencies and loopholes, systemic inflexibility, high-transaction cost, problematic cooperation and coordination and EU's failure to speak with one voice at international negotiations.

Whilst loopholes seem not to threaten systemic stability at the moment, they do diminish supervisory efficiency. When the regulatory and supervisory divergence of home country control and mutual recognition fails to deliver, centralisation appears to be the best solution for effective and free movement of financial services. When compared with the current regime of fragmented regulatory and supervisory structures, it is not unlikely that centralisation will facilitate cross-border financial activities and therefore regulatory competition. The following discussion will show that economics of scale and great power over individual regulated entities should make a EU securities supervisor more effective than national competent authorities. In turn, the reduction in the latter's responsibilities would permit more resources to be devoted to the more local areas that remain within their supervisory power, increasing their effectiveness.

Chapter 5 of this book has answered the question, whether there are any major problems with the existing legal and supervisory basis governing the financial and particularly the investment services in the EU. This chapter will endeavour to signal the ways – if any – in which the EU institutional structure might be changed in order to remedy such problems. To this end, this chapter will provide a cost–benefit analysis for centralisation and the potential establishment of a pan-European Securities Regulator by explaining its rationale and its legal, political and economic position within the Single Market for financial services. More specifically, it will focus on issues regarding transaction costs, independence and accountability, slow legislation and flexibility, consolidation and alliances of securities markets, the impact of the euro, crisis management, imperfect information and deficient cooperation of national authorities and access to and from third countries. Finally, the question will be raised,

---

[3] The wording of Art. 5 EC Treaty (former Art. 3b) invites such an economic analysis; to justify the exercise of powers by European Community institutions 'the scale or effects of the proposed action' must be taken into account.

[4] Padoa-Schioppa states that 'on the whole, (...) the legislative cum regulatory reform, although rather unusual and very diversified in comparison with those of most currency jurisdictions, does not seem to present loopholes or inconsistencies that may hamper the pursuit of systemic stability'. *See* Tommaso Padoa-Schioppa, EMU and Banking Supervision, lecture at the London School of Economics, Financial Markets Group, 24 February 1999.

whether at the end of the day the reasons for 'sabotaging' the establishment of the single regulator do not relate with its 'drawbacks' but with the political unwillingness of national regulators to lose their sovereignty.


## B    THE RATIONALE FOR A SINGLE REGULATOR

In an effort to explain the rationale for a single European securities market regulator, this analysis may borrow inspiration and arguments from the theory of neofunctionalism. Neofunctionalism originated as an optimistic analysis of the benefits of informal cooperation. The theory developed from the English political scientist David Mitrany's functional approach to world unification. However, its interpretation has evolved over time. Ernst Haas reformulated Mitrany's idealistic functionalism and applied it to European integration.[5] Haas questioned 'how and why nation-states cease to be wholly sovereign, [and] how and why they voluntarily mingle, merge, and mix with their neighbours so as to lose the factual attributes of sovereignty while acquiring new techniques for resolving conflicts between themselves'.[6]

Whatever the drawbacks and the criticisms levelled at neofunctionalism,[7] in a politicised environment, I believe that the theory has a role to play in explaining the emergence of the need for centralisation in the investment services field. Minimum harmonisation should be seen today as a transitory stage on the way towards European legal unity.[8] Even if it was initially designed to keep open competition between national legal orders, minimum harmonisation and home country control have failed their mission. On the other hand, competition among rules 'cannot be seen as an end in itself', but must be critically assessed against a range of possibilities, such as the desirability of transferring power to EU institutions. To this end, centralisation is important to avoid a reversion to regressive national tendencies.[9] The introduction of a EU supervisory authority with responsibilities in the investment

---

[5] Haas, Ernst (1958), 'The Uniting of Europe', in Brent Nelsen and Alexander Stubb (eds), *The European Union. Readings on the Theory and Practice of European Integration* (2nd edn, Macmillan, London, 1998) 139–144.

[6] *Ibid.*

[7] Some scholars conclude that neofunctionalism failed to provide an adequate explanation of the process of European integration. *See*, for instance, R. Keohane, and S. Hoffmann, 'Institutional Change in Europe in the 1980s', in Keohanne and Hoffman (eds), *The New European Community – Decisionmaking and Institutional Change* (Westview, Oxford, 1991); A. Moravcsik, 'Preferences and Power in the European Community: A Liberal Intergovernmentalist Approach' (1993) 4 JCMS 473; P. Taylor, *International Organization in the Modern World – The Regional and the Global Process* (Pinter, New York, 1993).

[8] For the opposite view see Johannes Kondgen, 'Rules of Conduct: Further Harmonisation?', in Guido Ferrarini (ed.), *European Securities Markets: The Investment Services Directive and Beyond* (Kluwer Law International, London, 1998) 129. Kondgen believes that minimum harmonisation was designed to safeguard national autonomy and to preserve competition among Member States rules.

[9] *See* William Bratton, Joseph McCahery, Sol Picciotto and Colin Scott (eds), *International Regulatory Competition and Coordination* (Clarendon Press, Oxford, 1996) 35.

services sphere would help to ensure that rules would be applied in the same way in all Member States.

Neo-functionalists were undoubtedly correct in assuming that the functional needs of an integrated European market would necessitate a considerable transfer of policy-making powers to the EU level.[10] With a single currency and a single market base, the lack of a single regulator is a dangerous absurdity.[11] Moreover, certain drawbacks, such as the cost of the investment services industry originating from the blurred home and host supervisory powers, slow and inefficient legislation, imperfect information exchange and deficient cooperation between Member States competent authorities, doubtful credibility and independence and lack of efficient crisis management in emergency situations, will support our analysis. Given this general approach, it is necessary to analyse the particular reasons that are relevant to the arguments for the establishment of a single regulator.

### *1   Transaction costs*

A simple reason why we need centralisation of investment services supervisory responsibilities is to exploit regulatory economies of scale and scope, especially for financial intermediaries, which already provide cross-border services in more than one Member States. If scale economies are important, central rule-making may be required.[12] As it would make little sense for water pollution standards to vary mile by mile along a river, so it would make no sense for regulatory and supervisory standards to vary from Member State to Member State. Multinationals and other export-oriented investment firms tend to prefer European to national supervision not only to avoid the costs of meeting different and often inconsistent national standards, but also to avoid the risk of progressively more stringent regulations in some of the Member States.[13] This section will make an effort to identify and prove the significant bearing of current supervisory structure on the costs of regulation and the benefits that may derive from a more centralised approach.

For the purposes of our discussion, it would be useful to examine all kinds of transaction costs after we endeavour to define them. In Coase's definition, transaction costs occur in order

> to discover who it is that one wishes to deal with, to inform people that one wishes to deal and on what terms, to conduct negotiations leading up to a bargain, to draw up the contract, to undertake the inspection needed to make sure that the terms of the contract are being observed, and so on.[14]

---

[10] Giandomenico Majone, *Regulating Europe* (Routledge, London, 1996) 66.

[11] Gilles Thieffry, 'Towards a European Securities Commission' (1999) 10 IFLR 14.

[12] Dieter Schmidtchen, and Robert Cooter (eds), *Constitutional Law and Economics of the European Union* (Edward Elgar, Cheltenham, 1997) 160.

[13] It could, thus, be also alleged that centralisation eliminates the negative effects of supervisory arbitrage; see Majone, Giandomenico, *op. cit.*, note 10.

[14] R.H. Coase, 'The problem of social cost' (1960) 3 *The Journal of Law and Economics* 1–44.

By adapting this definition and by moving a little further we could divide transaction cost into three categories: *institutional* or *direct* cost, *compliance* cost and *indirect* cost.[15]

## 1.1   Institutional or direct cost

First, with *institutional* or *direct* cost we mean the cost of operation of the regulatory and supervisory agencies themselves. The smaller the number of competent authorities, the lower should be the institutional cost. Albeit the institutional cost of competent authorities may be comparatively smaller than other kinds of cost, it may have a significant chain-effect on compliance and indirect cost. An ineffective institutional structure may raise overall cost on investment firms if it leads to inappropriate regulation and supervision.

Here is where the establishment of a single Securities Regulator would require particularly careful considerations and delicate actions. For example, a pan-European Securities Regulator may appear to reduce institutional cost, but unless it achieves to treat ATSs both as regulated markets and investment firms as well, then the overall cost of regulation may increase for the securities industry and investors. Moreover, to the extent that multiple regulators have overlapping competencies – as is the case with the home country control regime – so each regulator may impose costs on others. This lays the basis for what Scharpf has called the 'joint decision trap'.[16] The solution to avoid the overlapping 'trap' would be to provide a regime of clear allocation of responsibilities or to combine them in one body. In addition, given that the single Regulator would be responsible for a wider range of functions than national authorities, it would be more able to take advantage of economies of scale in their provision by allocating its resources in a more efficient way.

## 1.2   Compliance cost

Second, *compliance* cost is the cost imposed on financial firms. It seems to be the most significant drawback created by the present home country control regime. It refers to the incremental cost of compliance caused by regulation, but not to the total cost of activities that happen to contribute to regulatory compliance.[17] Although institutional structure may have an effect on compliance cost, the opposite (i.e. increase of the cost of the competent authority due to a specific regulatory measure) is unlikely to happen. Compliance cost may include information and research cost, legal cost and lobbying cost.

One of the main aims of financial services regulation should be the correction of *information asymmetries* between regulators and regulated institutions. Today,

---

[15] For similar or different categorisations of transaction cost, see Goodhart *et al.* (1998), *op. cit.*, note 2, 150; Giandomenico Majone, *op. cit.*, note 10, 69–70; Isaac Alfon and Peter Andrews, *Cost-Benefit Analysis in Financial Regulation* (FSA Occasional Paper Series No. 3, September 1999) 16–19.

[16] *See* F. Scharph, 'The Joint Decision Trap: Lessons from German Federalism and European Integration' (1988) 66 *Public Administration* 239.

[17] *See* Alfon and Andrews, *op. cit.*, note 15, 16.

European citizens and undertakings are confronted with a system of regulation that is difficult to comprehend. Given that keener competition in financial services could tempt some institutions to expose themselves to higher risks, the problem of asymmetric information becomes especially acute. Investors would not easily be able to identify a heightening of such a risk situation.

Under uniform pan-European regulation and supervision, national competent authorities and financial firms need not expend resources on information and research costs.[18] They do not have to inform themselves of differences in the substantive law of Member States and the way in which these rules are enforced. Centralisation in this manner tends also to produce more stable and predictable jurisprudence.[19] Nonetheless, the reduction of information and research cost constitutes only one part of our economic analysis; another part is the gains from legal certainty as an incentive for more efficient conduct.

*Legal certainty* is a very significant issue for lobby groups representing large industries. Large financial firms want to be informed as soon as possible about the legal validity of their cross-border transactions and the applicability of the supervisory regulation. One the other hand, smaller firms, which would traditionally provide services only at national level, would also welcome cuts in research and information cost as an incentive to enter intra-Community trade and expand their business.[20] To this end, supervisory fees of financial undertakings should decrease, insofar they no longer need to comply prudential rules or rules of conduct of both home and host Member States, and their overall lobbying costs may be reduced as they will have to deal with a single supervisory body. The assumed preference is for the minimisation of legal cost, consistent with ensuring the outcomes desired by those involved in the transaction.[21] A single Securities Supervisor could then operate a single database for the authorisation of financial firms, avoid unnecessary duplication or overlap across home and host country competent authorities and adopt a more effective and focused approach to areas of common interest to most regulated financial activities.

### 1.3    Indirect cost

Finally, *indirect* costs are those that are least obvious from a cash perspective. Although they are hard to measure they are not less important. Indirect costs include

---

[18] Information equilibrium may be also enhanced by the transparency that a centralised structure promises. *See infra* under 2.3 Transparency, accountability and legitimacy.

[19] Susan Rose-Ackerman, *Rethinking the Progressive Agenda: The Reform of the American Regulatory State* (Free Press, New York, 1993) 172.

[20] For a different view, see Roger Van den Bergh, 'The Subsidiarity Principle and the EC Competition Rules: The Costs and Benefits of Decentralisation', in Schmidtchen and Cooter, *op. cit.*, note 12, 168. Van den Bergh argues that 'the savings in search costs (thanks to legal certainty) accrue to export industry but are achieved at the expense of industries competing only in the home markets'.

[21] Although it would be wrong to assume that all market actors share the same preferences, it seems that the only ones that will not generate gains from decreased legal cost are those who gain from costly law, notably lawyers. *See* Anthony Ogus, 'Competition between National Legal Systems: A Contribution of Economic Analysis to Comparative Law' (1999) 48 ICLQ 405, 410.

those stemming from regulatory capture, regulatory escalation and moral hazard, costs of reduced competition and public choice theory problems.

The issues of regulatory capture, regulatory escalation and public choice theory will be discussed later in Sections 2.1 and 2.2. As far as moral hazard and competition is concerned, I shall make the following observations. The process of regulation and supervision is not simply one where the regulators command and the regulated obey. It involves a far more complex web of bureaucracy and bargaining, where regulated firms bargain for the rules that will be applied to them. Obviously such a practice is encouraged by supervisors, who are reluctant, for political reasons, to impose excessive cost on industry.

On the other hand, a single Securities Regulator may deliver benefits in the reduction of *moral hazard*, especially among retail investors. Investors, particularly non-professionals, always feel closer to their national watchdog. They tend to have a feeling of protection originating from the competent authority that regulates and monitors their national market and the financial firms that operate within that market. That feeling may more easily lead them to take risky decisions, which will increase moral hazard. However, a radical change in the regulatory structure of European securities market supervision would alter investors' psychological behaviour. Goodhart asks whether under a single regulator 'a potential moral hazard would result from a public perception that the risk spectrum among financial institutions had disappeared or become blurred'.[22] In practice, the public's understanding of the new regulatory system is – regrettably – likely to be so low that this type of moral hazard should not arise.[23] On the other hand, for those investors, who commence cross-border investment business, a single regulator would be a one-stop-shop for complaints handling, compensation schemes and information. This could facilitate the regulator's ability to enhance public awareness of the risks, costs and benefits of different investment services and to clarify the limitations of what regulation can deliver, thus reducing the potential moral hazard.

Finally, the cost from reduced or eliminated *competition* may have a severe impact on the free provision of financial services and on consumer protection. In a uniform market, different national regulators may have the effect of distorting competition, either because they interpret uniform regulations differently or because they react differently, or at different speeds, to new developments.[24] Domestic interests and protectionism also play a major role. When national authorities regulate and supervise in parallel in the Single Market, the principle of competitive neutrality[25] is at

---

[22] Goodhart *et al., op. cit.*, note 2, 154.

[23] *See* Clive Briault, *The Rationale for a Single National Financial Services Regulator* (FSA Occasional Paper Series No. 2, May 1999) 26.

[24] *See* Deutsche Bank Research, *Regulation and Banking Supervision: Caught between the Nation State and Global Financial Markets* (Frankfurt: EMU Watch No. 86, 29 June 2000) 4.

[25] 'Competitive neutrality' means designing a set of policies and legal arrangements ensuring that all individuals and organizations – public, for-profit, and non-profit – are treated in an equal manner in the bidding process. To the extent possible, all protections and special privileges that public units usually enjoy over private firms simply by virtue of public-sector ownership should be removed. The same should apply to the privileges that domestic firms usually enjoy over foreign ones.

risk. Imagine, for instance, a situation, where a financial firm wished to provide cross-border services in a host country and offered a financial product or service that was innovating for the domestic market and was not provided by domestic firms. In order to protect their institutions, host authorities could easily impede or prohibit the provision of that product or service on the grounds of the general good, so that domestic firms do not acquire an inherent disadvantage. It would take years for the foreign firm to bring the case to the ECJ, which would give enough time to domestic institutions to prepare and provide similar products or services. The home country control regime could give rise to several other similar impediments to competition, which could burden financial firms with additional and unjustified costs. Moreover, in contrast to the rhetoric associated with the launch of home country control,[26] investors are not benefited either. Investor choice is inhibited because investors are not able to buy or, in some cases, even be informed about what may be available from foreign suppliers.

In a perfect Europe without borders and a financial environment without transaction costs, there would be no reason for national authorities to transfer power to a centralised pan-European body. Instead, investment firms and markets could be managed by intergovernmental agreements or even by means of non-cooperative mechanisms. However, this is not the case we currently witness in Europe. To this end, there can be little doubt that a pan-European Securities Supervisor offers scope for significant efficiencies. At least in theory, a single supervisor ought to be able to generate a number of efficiency gains. Equally, however, it may be difficult to deliver these in practice, especially at the beginning of its function.

## 2   Independence and accountability

### 2.1   Public choice theory and independence

Any existence of multiple supervisory agencies and different regulatory regimes entails the possibility that powerful interest groups may impede any national or cooperative supranational developments. Public choice theory, which lies at the heart of the concern about regulatory failure, depicts the struggle over regulatory and supervisory action as a kind of competition between discrete groups and the general welfare, with information serving as the principal weapon. Financial firms, exchanges, issuers and investors have incentives to endeavour to influence the scope, content and enforcement of financial regulation in order to promote their private interests.[27] This, of course, might seriously undermine the independence of various Member States' supervisory authorities.

---

[26] *See*, for instance, ISD, Recital 2, which states: 'whereas firms that provide the investment services covered by this Directive must be subject to authorization by their home Member States in order to protect investors and the stability of the financial system'.

[27] Gerard Hertig, 'Regulatory Competition for EU Financial Services' (2000) 2 *Journal of International Economic Law* 349, 365. Generally speaking, the ability of pressure groups to influence decision-making differs across industries and subject matter. However, public choice teaches us that industrial groups will be more successful than investor groups. *See* Schmidtchen and Cooter, *op. cit.*, note 12, 165–166.

Regretfully, data regarding the role of interest groups in influencing regulation is not sufficient enough to comparatively assess the influence at national and EU level and thus to drive us to specific conclusions. Nevertheless, it may be possible to make certain speculations with regard to specific interest groups. Interest groups may be strong enough to prevent supervisory authorities. Firms, for example, established in jurisdictions with more costly legal structures and which have already invested resources in complying with such regimes will not wish to lose the competitive advantage, which they thereby acquire over newcomers.[28] On the contrary, financial firms, which yet face difficulties in penetrating markets beyond their home country, will have a more growing interest in centralisation.

Securities exchanges, for their part, have repeatedly lobbied for regulation at EU level to better incorporate tools allowing Member States to limit competition between them.[29] Although pan-European trading platforms consolidation plans have not been very successful in the past – with notable exceptions such as Euronext and Euro.NM – there is growing evidence that true pan-European exchanges will soon become common, chiefly owing to technological progress.[30] In this perspective, it is in the interest of major regulated markets to lobby to further diminish cross-border trading barriers and even campaign for a single European Securities Regulator.[31]

Finally, issuers and investors are unlikely to show much interest in the institutional supervisory structure, and, thus, have relatively less influencing power. They should be keener in harmonisation of Member States' laws with regard to accounting standards, disclosure, company law and consumer protection issues. It comes to no surprise that, for the very reason that these interest groups have limited powers in lobbying at EU level, harmonisation efforts of these issues have been blocked for decades. However, being in favour of a European passport and in order to reduce transaction costs and increase liquidity, they are more likely to support centralisation and consolidation of regulated markets as well as real freedom of cross-border trading. In this respect, a centralised body could be seen as the only means of making the single financial market a reality.

In short, heterogeneous interest groups have different powers in influencing the content, the scope and enforcement of financial regulation and supervision. Since the power of issuers, investors and smaller financial undertakings is limited to their home competent authority, it is more likely that a single Securities Regulator will be under less pressure. Diverse interest group pressure means diverse financial regulatory and supervisory standards. A centralised body should tackle this problem by establishing a level playing field as far as supervision is concerned and by keeping itself far from regulatory capture efforts. However, this issue is examined below.

---

[28]  Anthony Ogus, *op. cit.*, note 21, 411–412.

[29]  Ruben Lee, 'Regulation of Capital Markets in the European Union', in P. Newman (ed.), *The New Palgrave Dictionary of Economics and the Law Vol. 3* (Macmillan Reference Ltd, London, 1998) 230.

[30]  For the issue of securities exchanges' consolidation, *see infra* Section 4.

[31]  Werner Seifert, for instance, chief executive of Deutsche Börse, is frustrated by the lack of progress so far; *see* Anonymous, 'No SECs please, we're Europeans' (21 August 1999) *Economist* 62. However, the formal approach of the Federation of European Securities Exchanges hardly moves in the same line; *see* FESE Report, *op. cit.*, note 1.

## 2.2   *The problem of regulatory capture*

A response to the issue whether regulatory and supervisory decisions should be taken at national or EU level requires a comparison of the possibilities of decentralisation and centralisation to cope with the problem of regulatory capture. Keeping national supervisors' knowledge up to date may require structured training in cooperation with industry or a system of inward and outward secondments between supervisors and supervised. These steps would bring supervisors closer to the market, but carry the potential risk or perception of regulatory capture and conflict of interest.

Indeed, Ogus suggests that large areas of law are 'interventionist' in that they protect defined interests and/or supersede voluntary transactions.[32] Such 'interventionist' law creates winners (the beneficiaries of protection) and losers (the subject of legal obligation), who, in a decentralised regime, will both attempt to exert pressure on and capture lawmakers for more favourable law. National regulators, on the other hand, may also benefit from their close relationship with the market. They could, thus, allege that the closer a regulator physically is to the firm and the market that it regulates, the better and more efficient its supervision is. Nevertheless, any close relationship entails the risk of regulatory capture. But again one may ask: do not we always face the risk that market participants will try to capture their regulator in order to promote their own interests, irrespective of their distance with it? This chapter argues that the possibilities of regulatory capture have their limitations in the design of institutional structure. Although appropriate institutional architecture, such as a centralised supervisory body, will not prevent regulatory capture altogether, it may limit its scope. I elaborate below.

A centralised supervisory body should redress the imbalance. The risk of capture of a national regulator is higher compared to a supranational supervisor, which keeps itself at a safe distance from the financial institution it regulates. This may be depicted by the recent experience in many East Asian countries.[33] Also in Europe, incidents such as Credit Lyonnais and Banco di Napoli suggest that domestic supervisors have sometimes been too close to the institutions they regulate, thus risking being captured, particularly when those institutions are state owned and supported by powerful political lobbies.[34] The natural distance that a pan-European Securities Regulator should keep appears as a healthier solution. Being less sensitive to external influence, a single Regulator should respond with two different, but complementary characteristics: transparency and accountability.

## 2.3   *Transparency, accountability and legitimacy*

Under the current home country control regime, every competent authority is and should be independent and accountable at an appropriate national level and subject

---

[32] Anthony Ogus, *op. cit.*, note 21, 412.

[33] Before the crisis, 'lax prudential rules and financial oversight led to a sharp deterioration in the quality of banks' loan portfolios'. *See* Stanley Fischer, *The Asian Crisis: A View from the IMF*, Midwinter Conference of the Bankers' Association for Foreign Trade (Washington, mimeo, 22 January 1998).

[34] *See* Danthine Jean-Pierre, Francesco Giavazzi, Xavier Vives and Ernst-Ludwig von Thadden, *The Future of European Banking* (CEPR, London, 1999) 98.

to full judicial review of its implementing rules. It is certain that all Member States' legal systems contain rules, which try to promote and improve political accountability. Nonetheless, the, often, unclear distinction between national authorities' responsibilities may undermine such efforts. It is thus logical to assume that there is a great deal of accessibility asymmetry between market players that are close to the national regulator and other market participants – possibly from other Member States – that lack these advantageous contacts. Lack of clarity in the objectives of multiple regulators equals to lack of accountability, not only across themselves, but also across the institutions and markets they regulate. In addition, practical hurdles, such as language and distance foster the problem.[35] As a result, Member States' competent authorities are far away from producing an open, transparent and accountable regime.

On the other hand, if a single Regulator is given a clear set of responsibilities, then it ought to be possible to increase transparency and accountability,[36] not least in terms of its accountability for performance against its statutory objectives, for the regulatory regime, for the cost of regulation, for its disciplinary policies and for regulatory failures.[37] When the pan-European supervisory framework is clear, then it has the advantage of pinning appropriate accountability on the different actors in the system. Moreover, an open pan-European Regulator will be better accepted by individuals and undertakings. Edwards argues that Europeans need to have more than a minimum knowledge of the European institutions, procedures, norms and values in order to accept them.[38] This is the definition of legitimacy.[39] Transparency, thus, is an integral factor in the process of legitimisation and the single Regulator, as every other EU institution, must be seen as more efficient, democratic and effective, both in terms of policy-making and policy implementation. Sometimes, however, as a result of transfer of certain powers to a new organ some of the legitimacy may be lost. Legitimacy, for instance, may not automatically follow delegation of powers from the Commission or the Council to the ESR. On the other hand, it is also possible that transparency and legitimacy are enhanced. This is likely to be the case when powers are transferred from the less powerful national supervisory authorities to a centralised body. It is, thus, vital in this context that the new Securities Regulator creates and establishes its own legitimacy, which, as the establishment of the ECB has shown, may take a significant amount of time.

---

[35] Considerations of efficiency and cost have generally led national authorities to the usage of the home language only. It remains a fact that most competent authorities' Internet Web Sites do not yet provide all documents and legal resources in English.

[36] *See* Michael Taylor, *Twin Peaks: A Regulatory Structure for the New Century* (Centre for the Study of Financial Innovation, London, December 1995) 15.

[37] *See* Howard Davies, *Building the Financial Services Authority: What's New?* (Travers Lecture, London Guildhall University Business School, mimeo, 11 March 1999).

[38] Geoffrey Edwards, 'Legitimacy and Flexibility in Post-Amsterdam Europe', in den Boer, Guggenbühl and Vanhoonacker (eds), *Coping with Flexibility and Legitimacy after Amsterdam* (European Institute of Public Administration, Maastricht, 1998) 139.

[39] According to Snyder, legitimacy refers to the belief that a specific institution is widely recognised or at least accepted as being the appropriate institution to exercise specific powers; *see* Francis Snyder, 'EMU Revisited: Are we making a Constitution? What Constitution are we making?', in Paul Craig and Grainne de Burca (eds), *The Evolution of EU Law* (OUP, Oxford, 1999) 463.

This chapter recognises that the creation of a pan-European Securities Regulator will result in a significant increase in concentration of supervisory powers to a single body. There is always a concern that a single regulator 'could potentially become an over-mighty bully, a bureaucratic leviathan divorced from the industry it regulates'.[40] It is therefore vital that this body establishes a robust transparency and accountability framework, explicitly laid down in Art. 1 EC Treaty, so that firms, individuals and markets approve and accept its competence.

Transparency is improved if the influence of considerations is made visible.[41] Of particular importance hereby is the right of access of documents. It should be noted, however, that the new right of access, as introduced in Art. 255 EC, is limited to the documents of the three main institutions,[42] and hence does not seem to cover other bodies. Nonetheless, encouraged by recommendations of the European Ombudsman that agencies, too, should adopt rules on access to documents,[43] most institutions have adopted relevant decisions.[44] Irrelevantly to the responsibilities undertaken, the single Regulator should be obliged to undertake consultation on all harmonised rules and guidance that it adopts; it should publicise all responses received and explain the reasons that led to specific policy decisions; in making its proposals, it should include a cost-benefit analysis of potential measures adopted; also, it should submit reports to the European Parliament and the ECOFIN Council on its work and publicise the records of its meetings[45]; finally, all measures adopted should be subject to judicial review.[46] At the same time, the accountability and legitimacy of regulation of the Securities Supervisor can be fostered by its relationship with the network of Member States' authorities. The better the relationship and interaction with existing national regulators, the more open and accountable its decision-making process will be.

To conclude, it is obvious that an open and easily accessible single regulator is more likely to reduce the information asymmetries for market participants by facilitating public access to financial market information and, thus, by coping with

---

[40] Michael Taylor, *op. cit.*, note 36.

[41] Schmidtchen and Cooter, *op. cit.*, note 12, 173.

[42] Art. 255(1) states that 'any citizen of the Union, and any natural or legal person residing or having its registered office in a Member State, shall have a right of access to European Parliament, Council and Commission documents'.

[43] Special report from the European Ombudsman to the European Parliament following the own-initiative inquiry into public access to documents, OJ C44/9, 10 February 1998.

[44] For paradigms, *see* Ellen Vos, 'Reforming the European Commission: What Role to Play for EU Agencies?' (2000) 5 CMLRev 1113, 1125.

[45] In this way, the Securities Regulator should avoid the criticism of lack of transparency often targeted to the ECB.

[46] In relation to judicial review, recent developments indicate that the ECJ would be prepared to loosen the strict *Meroni* requirements. In *Les Verts*, the Court had already elucidated that EU is based on the rule of law, thus permitting the Court to review the legality of all acts adopted by the institutions. *See* Case 294/83, *Parti ecologiste 'Les Verts'* v. *European Parliament*, [1986] ECR 1339, para. 23. This decision should also apply to the Securities Regulator, irrespective of whether it would qualify as 'institution' or not. *See* Koen Lenaerts, 'Regulating the regulatory process: "delegation of powers" in the European Community' (1993) 18 ELRev 23, 46.

unequal costs of gathering information. On the other hand, it has by definition a significant advantage compared to a more fragmented supervisory structure: as soon as it keeps a clear distance with the industry it regulates, it will dramatically lessen the possibilities of being captured or pressured by private interest groupings. As long as it manages to incorporate an independent administrative structure and culture of open communication and clear lines of accountability, it will enhance decision-making and will maintain confidence in the European financial system.

### 3   Slow legislation and flexibility

In the European securities industry, there is no structure parallel to the legislative committees existing in the banking and insurance field.[47] This means that any technical adaptation of the core directives needs to take the form of a formal amendment, with the problems and delays this can imply. In this light, it is debatable whether the Securities Committee, proposed by the Lamfalussy Group, will be able to change the scenery.[48]

The current supervisory regime has practical implications on how legislation is passed. Here, we should pay special attention to the lock-in problem that the home country control regime presents. As admitted by the Commission and the Wise Men Committee, the present functioning of the European legislative system cannot meet the challenge of regulating modern financial markets.[49] It is beyond evidence that every attempt to regulate at EU level and to implement at Member State level is doomed to be lost in the vortex of severe delay and bureaucracy.[50] It takes time and effort to construct a pan-European regulatory regime, as each Member State negotiates both with its counterparts and with domestic lawmakers and interest groups. The current process for promulgating and amending Directives is inadequate to deal

---

[47] In banking, three committees are in place: the Banking Advisory Committee, the Groupe de Contact and the Banking Supervisory Committee of the ECB. In insurance, we have the Insurance Committee and the Groupe de Contact by the Conference of Insurance Supervisors. In securities, it should be noted that a High Level Securities Supervisors Committee is in place since 1992. However, most of its functions have been undertaken by FESCO. Also, two Contact Committees, one for the listing and prospectus rules and one for UCITS, exist to facilitate harmonised implementation. Nevertheless, these committees have no comitology powers, which partially explains their weak influence.

[48] For more on the Securities Committee proposed by the Wise Men Report, *see* Chapters 9 and 10 in this volume.

[49] *See* Commission of the European Communities, *Financial Services and Progress: 3rd Report*, COM (2000) 692/2 final, 8 November 2000, 4 (hereinafter 3rd Progress Report); The Commission admits that 'there are a number of serious concerns and the worry that without more effort in next few months the FSAP will fail to maintain sufficient momentum to achieve the ambitious 2005 deadline'; Commission of the European Communities, 'Working Together to Maintain Momentum': 2001 Review of the Internal Market Strategy, COM (2001) 198 final, 11 April 2001, at 4. Also Initial Wise Men Report, *op. cit.*, note 1, 23. The Committee is indeed concerned that the present system will not be able to deliver the FSAP on time.

[50] The delay suffered in the genesis of the ISD, for example, illustrates the difficulties surrounding the liberalisation of financial markets in several Member States. The first proposal was submitted by the Commission in February 1989 and the Council finally adopted the Directive in May 1993.

with fast moving financial markets so that 'even new provisions for setting standards, by the time they are enacted, may very well be out of date'.[51] Directives end up being rather inflexible and almost impossible to alter once adopted. It seems, thus, likely that EU regulation runs the risk of becoming outmoded and anachronistic.[52] A *fortiori*, it also runs the greater risk of being less qualitative and efficient, since it will constitute the product of controversies and compromises.

On the other hand, even if adopted, EU laws – mostly in the form of Directives – are delegated to Member States to be implemented. Since national securities markets regulation is often differently organised at Member States' level and national supervisors merely share the same powers, it is inevitable that the principles of EU law will be turned into workable day to day rules in a way that only as uniform could not be characterised.[53]

It has been suggested that the Council should adopt EU investment services rules using 'fast track' procedures, namely in the form of Regulations, in order to improve transparency, speed and accuracy of transposition and implementation.[54] In my view, however, it is debateable whether Regulations will achieve the so-desirable efficiency and uniformity. Since they do not need Member State transposition,[55] Regulations often constitute a mixture of controversial trends and require greater efforts and compromises by national governments to reach agreement; and like most compromises, they are likely to be unsatisfactory – from the outset, slow to draft and simultaneously difficult to amend in the light of changing circumstances. Normally 'every "t" must be crossed and every "i" must be dotted since Member States are not to tamper with them'.[56] In such a complex and technical area of law as financial services regulation, it is almost impossible to devise Regulations, which have the requisite specificity and are also suited to immediate impact into all of the Member States.

---

[51] Howard Davies, *Introductory Remarks* (Paris, Eurofi Conference, 15 September 2000).

[52] Directives' provisions can be divided in to two categories: (a) provisions that leave considerable discretion to Member States and supervisors to set out the detailed regulatory requirements and (b) provisions that allow less discretion. The disadvantage for the former is obvious; each Member State adopt its own standards and implementation methods. The problem with the latter is that, with the boom in securities market developments, the details of the Directives are often out-of-date and each Member State then needs to find its own legal solution.

[53] The recent 2001 Review of the Internal Market Strategy, *op. cit.*, note 49, 5, reveals that not only have key legislative proposals been delayed, but progress in implementing existing Internal Market rules has been disappointing.

[54] *See* Initial Wise Men Report, *op. cit.*, note 1, 24.

[55] The precise meaning of the term 'directly applicable' of Article 249 EC has been the subject of debate among commentators. *See*, for example J. Steiner, 'Direct Applicability in EEC Law – A Chameleon Comncept' (1982) 98 LQR 229; A. Dashwood, 'The Principle of Direct Effect in European Community Law' (1978) 16 JCMS 229. However, the ECJ has signified that Member States should not pass any measure which purports to transform a Community Regulation into national law and thus obstruct its direct applicability; *see* Case 34/73 *Variola* v. *Amministrazione delle Finanze* [1973] ECR 981, para. 10. Moreover, 'all methods of implementation, which would have the result of creating an obstacle to the direct effect of Community Regulations and of jeopardizing their simultaneous and uniform application in the whole of the Community, are contrary to Treaty'; *see* Case 39/72 *Commission* v. *Italy* [1973] ECR 101, para. 17.

[56] Craig Paul and Grainne de Burca, *EU Law* (OUP, Oxford, 1998) 108.

For this reason, they are by nature often less detailed and more vague than Directives, which explains their rare usage by the Community legislator.

Here lies the weakness of Regulations. Vagueness may easily upset the advantage of direct effect. According to Craig and de Burca, if a provision is vague, if it sets out only a very general aim which needs further implementing measures to be made concrete and clear, then it is difficult to accord direct effect to that provision and to allow its direct application by a national court.[57] Indeed, despite its general disapproval to Member States' transposition, the ECJ did accept in *Amsterdam Bulb* that Member States could provide in national legislation for appropriate sanctions, which were not provided for in the Regulation, to assist in its enforcement.[58] This opens the way for domestic legislation to continue to regulate various related matters, which – given its less detailed and inflexible structure – were not specifically covered in the Regulation.

The lock-in problem of inflexibility of the present regulatory system admits of two solutions. *First*, Member States may delegate substantial lawmaking to a pan-European body to permit flexible responses to changes in the regulatory environment of investment services. *Second*, Member States could explore alternatives to regulatory cooperation at EU level. With regard to the latter, however, it will be shown below[59] that current coordination efforts between national competent authorities have not been proved efficient enough. Nothing indicates that this situation is about change in the near future.

At this stage, it is vital that investment services lawmaking is delegated to a single Securities Regulator. Presumably, reversing an assignment of regulatory power through Member States' negotiations would be as difficult and cumbersome a process as extending the authority in the first place. However, the very belief that this will strongly contribute to the increase of the speed and efficiency of future legislation makes any such suggestion a minor issue. National regulators have to realise the significance of flexibility on the one hand and to abandon the principle that the current allocation of responsibilities between them is sacrosanct on the other. Bearing in mind that, even with a fair wind, a new Directive scarcely ever takes less than three years between inception and delivery, decisions originating from the pan-European Regulator would speed up the legislative process in Europe.

### 4  Securities exchanges consolidation and alliances

A further reason that demands the centralisation of securities regulation and supervision is the consolidation and the alliances between securities exchanges and trading platforms. Despite growing consolidation efforts between financial markets, a strong home bias persists in primary and secondary market activity in EU. Partly, this situation reflects inertia in investment patterns. However, it is also the case that

---

[57] *Ibid.*, 168.
[58] *See* Case 50/76 *Amsterdam Bulb BV* v. *Produktschap voor Siergewassen* [1977] ECR 137, para. 33.
[59] *See infra* Section 7.

cross-border issuance, trading and settlement are beset by 'numerous outstanding legal and technical obstacles'.[60] On the other hand, it becomes now evident in Europe that the investment horizons of funds and private investors are slowly becoming more European. Exchanges, traditionally organised and managed as national monopolies, are now competing for order flows between themselves and with new competitors that offer trading services, such as ATSs. As a consequence, many of them are seeking European reach through organic growth, while others are looking to far-reaching alliances or fully-fledged mergers. This paper will argue that this situation raises new consideration and challenges that are unlikely to be met by the existing financial institutional structure. Therefore, truly pan-European markets will soon require a real pan-European Regulator.

### 4.1   Exchanges

The higher the cost of transacting cross-border deals in Europe compared to the United States, means stock exchange consolidation is necessary and inevitable.[61] Once the traditional fragmentation of European markets has been resolved, the pan-European market will be able to respond in terms of cost, technological development, capacity to adapt and strategic vision. In the short to medium term, market developments' effects on the regulatory mechanisms for securities markets will gain substantial gravity.[62] But there is more. All this is happening at a time of unprecedented volatility in stock market indexes, driven in part by the behaviour of the 'new economy' and in part by the weak single currency and world financial situation.

New types of markets create new types of investors and new types of risks, which in turn require new types of solutions. Whatever the outcome of the market consolidation initiatives across Europe, there will be tough questions posed for national regulators. What will the role be for national regulators of undertakings operating as remote central exchanges? How can we ensure an adequate degree of harmonisation to allow an exchange to operate in a number of different Member States? Regulators will face a difficult task. A complex one. The challenge of progress. A challenge, which will imply overcoming the internal inefficiencies that stem directly from the desire to continue with local *status quo*.

The boom in telecommunications and the introduction of the euro have weakened the importance of the *locus* of financial centres and geographical mandates. What we experience today is a de-localised world, in which markets are no longer national organisations. Rather they have turned to a pan-European – or even international – phenomenon, which is interlinked and intertwined. *Vis-à-vis* this environment, regulators cannot remain still. Since present and future markets will soon have very

---

[60] *See* Initial Wise Men Report, *op. cit.*, note 1, 11.

[61] Pen Kent, Executive Chairman of the European Securities Forum, speech at a lunch of the IBA's capital markets committee; *see* <http://www.legalmediagroup.com/default.asp?Page=1&SID=4899>.

[62] For how market developments have influenced securities regulation and organisation in Member States, *see* Guido Ferrarini, 'Exchange Governance and Regulation: An Overview', in Guido Ferrarini (ed.), *European Securities Markets: The Investment Services Directive and Beyond* (Kluwer Law International, London, 1998) 245 *et seq.*

little in common with the 'regulated markets' envisaged in the ISD, it becomes blurred who will regulate and supervise them. Under the ISD, for instance, home competent authorities oblige 'regulated markets' to deal only in formally 'listed' stocks. As a result, it is completely unclear under the current regime whether a trading system operator designated as a 'regulated market' in one Member State will not be denied single passport rights in another jurisdiction on the basis that the particular operator does not itself 'list' the securities that it trades.[63] On the other hand, let us assume that an ATS, established in a home Member State, wishes to enter the market of another (host) Member State by use of its screen-based capacity. The ISD states that Art. 15 'shall not affect the Member State's right to authorise or prohibit the creation of new markets within their territories'.[64] It seems that the intent of this provision was to furnish the host State with another escape clause from the European passport for screen-based electronic trading systems. By declaring a foreign trading system to be a 'new market', any host Member State could deny it European passport rights. The potential for abuse is now considerable. And the question arises: will national supervisory authorities be more capable than a pan-European regulator to deliver the job and offer solutions? A centralised supervisory regime will offer solutions at least in three fields, namely single passport for markets, competition and transmission effects.

*First*, under a centralised supervisory regime, any physical or electronic market, wishing to offer cross-border listing or trading services, would not need to face any EU authority's denial of its single passport rights on the grounds that it is seeking to create a 'new market' in its territory. After a single authorisation for operation and with a fully operational single passport, markets will be free to place screen trading facilities in partner Member States, so as to serve 'remote members' in other Member States. This will tackle the problem of fragmentation[65] and will boost the potential for competition.

*Second*, closer integration of securities markets increases the possibility that regulatory or supervisory differences influence competition between exchanges for trading volume. Unless a pan-European Regulator eliminates these differences, there is a risk that competition between regimes will come at the expense of transparency and efficiency of European markets. With the notable exception of Euronext, most of the planned alliances have failed the last couple of years.

*Finally*, developments in one regulated market may well have immediate and potentially major repercussions on the trading environment in other Member States. A centralised body would serve as rapid response of upholding market integrity, confidence and stability. Regulatory or supervisory arrangements governing a large scale of European markets cannot be permitted to evolve on an *ad hoc* basis in response to the technical challenges presented by a particular merger or alliance.

---

[63]  *See* ISD, Art. 1(13).

[64]  *Ibid.*, Art. 15(5).

[65]  It is a fact that some exchanges, such as Madrid and Athens, have no remote members; *see* Commission of the European Communities, *Communication on upgrading the Investment Services Directive (93/22/EEC)* (16 November 2000) 7.

As it will be analysed *subsequently*,[66] building a mechanism of concentrated regulatory and supervisory power would offer legal certainty, stability and efficiency in a fast-evolving and so volatile European market.

### 4.2  Clearing and settlement

Relevant to the challenge of the ESR to ensure the proper function of the market is the need to eliminate undue and unnecessary risks and costs of inefficient and inadequate clearing and settlement systems within Europe. It has been calculated that as much as €1 billion a year of operating cost savings would be secured if equity settlement were conducted as efficiently as that in the United States. As part of this saving, economies of scale could be created and the larger part of the cross-border clearing and settlement in Europe could be eliminated, greatly reducing risk, if a single European central counterparty (EuroCCP) were introduced in displacement of the present fragmented netting arrangements that operate mainly on Member State basis.[67] This would have the advantage of allowing netting of all national and cross-border transactions concluded on the same day and, ideally, compress all transactions of a trading participant into a single cash flow or obligation.[68]

Although further restructure of clearing and settlement systems seems necessary in the European Union, we have to agree with Dalhuisen that the unproblematic history of these systems does not call for their regulation *per se*.[69] Rightly, the securities industry and the Final Wise Men Report accept that market forces should determine the contours of clearing and settlement in Europe.[70] However, this does not mean that there are and there will be no public policy issues that have to be addresses and coped with by a central public body. Albeit the establishment of a EuroCCP seems an early target for the short-to-medium term, the benefits that this achievement would deliver, such as risk reduction at a member and systemic level, cost savings, reliability, scalability and integrity of services, call for a move towards this direction in the long term.[71]

---

[66] *See infra* Section 6.

[67] Recent developments confirm the trend towards consolidation. At the beginning of 2000, Luxembourg-based Cedel and Deutsche Börse Clearing (DBC) merged to create Celarstream International, only to be followed next year by the Euroclear Clearance System, which emerged from the merger of Brussels-based Euroclear and Paris' SICOVAM. Both mergers, however, were functional and not legal, since the two pre-existing structures remain. *See* Antonio Sáinz de Vicuña, 'The Legal Integration of Financial Markets of the Euro Area', in this volume.

[68] The Depositary Trust and Clearing Corporation, the US umbrella organisation that brings together clearing and settlement for the US securities markets, shows that a single provider can work in the case of certain brokerage operations, such as trade confirmation, settlement and regulatory compliance; see Von Rosen, Rüdiger, 'Clearing up Europe's Exchanges' (9 February 2001) FT 19.

[69] Jan Dalhuisen, 'Towards a Single European Capital Market and a Workable System of Regulation', in this volume.

[70] *See* FESE, Second Report and Recommendations on European Regulatory Structures, January 2001, 6; Committee of Wise Men, Final Report on the Regulation of European Securities Markets (hereinafter 'Final Wise Men Report'), 15 February 2001, 16.

[71] *See* the Key Principles of the European Securities Forum, http://www.eurosf.com/key_principles.htm.

In the light of this, even if the EuroCCP were to be governed and regulated by private market forces, there will ultimately be a need for oversight by the ESR with regard to prudential and competition implications in order to avoid duplication of compliance and shield its members from systemic risk.[72] Central supervision should be sought given the pan-European character of an integrated financial market. When a central settlement counterparty is established, only a European regulator will have the proper resources to carry out its oversight functions, such as gathering information on the participants' systems, assessing the operation and design of the systems and taking action to promote systems' observance of European standards.

## 5   *The euro as a catalyst*

One of the most significant economic effects of EMU will be the achievement of an internal financial market as envisioned in Art. 14(2) EC. The motto of the Maastricht Treaty has been 'one market, one currency'. The introduction of the euro in 12 EU Member States constitutes a 'quantum jump' which gives a new dimension to the internal financial market, brings economic agents closer together and has the effect of increasing and intensifying legal relationships across the euro area.[73]

European financial markets, however, have not been automatically unified by the introduction of the euro. Nor has financial supervision. Local habits, regulations and vested interests will keep market segmented for some time.[74] But it is also certain that competitive pressures will become irresistible in the medium to long run. EMU has made evident the inadequacies of the Community internal market legislation as it exists at the start of the third stage.[75] Moreover, the geographical domain of monetary policy and prudential supervision do not coincide anymore; monetary policy is now conducted at the euro area level, whereas supervision of markets and individual financial institutions has remained the responsibility of national authorities.[76] By the same token, Monetary Union is triggering a broad debate on the adequacy of the supervisory framework for financial institutions and markets.

---

[72] As stated by the BIS, '... safe and reliable settlement systems are essential not only for the stability of securities markets they serve, but often also to payment systems, which may be used by an SSS or may themselves use an SSS to transfer collateral'; *see* BIS, *Recommendations for Securities Settlement Systems*, Consultative Report, January 2001, at 7. Especially for risks in cross-border settlement, *see* Guido Ferrarini, 'The European Regulation of Stock Exchanges: New Perspectives' (1999) 3 CMLRev 569, 592.

[73] *See* Antonio Sáinz de Vicuña, *Legal Consequences of the Single Currency* (General Report at the International Federation of European Law (FIDE) Congress, Helsinki, 1–3 June 2000).

[74] The divergences between technical market issues is not within the scope of this chapter. For such an assessment, see the first paper issued by the Giovannini Group, Commission of the European Communities, The Impact of the Introduction of the Euro on Capital Markets (Communication II/338/97, July 1997).

[75] The diversity, for instance, in the national implementation of Community Directives appears now as a non-quantitative barrier to a single currency market.

[76] Economic and Financial Committee, Report on Financial Stability (EFC/ECFIN/240/00 – Final, 8 April 2000) (hereinafter 'Brouwer Report').

This debate involves three concerns: *first*, strong interpenetration of financial markets as a result of EMU poses a challenge to the home country control principle in the supervision of financial firms and to the limited integration and cooperation in the supervision of financial markets. *Second*, the trend towards conglomeration in the financial services sector, party caused by the single currency, raises the question of whether the current institutional structure for the supervision of financial intermediaries is adequate for the task. *Finally*, the transfer of monetary policy to the ECB raises the question of what role it will play in the area of prudential supervision and financial stability, which yet remain Member State responsibilities. This section addresses the first two issues, the consequences of the introduction of the single currency in market developments and in the supervision of financial firms and markets. Its conclusions may be summarised in the motto 'one market, one currency, one regulator'.

### 5.1   Impact on financial markets

European financial markets have gone through a major structural change with the introduction of the euro. Twelve national markets have received a strong impetus to integrate into a single euro area capital market.[77] This means that divergences purely related to the locus of market participants within the euro area become less and less relevant over time. In particular: the reduction in government debt securities owing to fiscal consolidation under EMU, low inflation rates, elimination of exchange risk and the commitment of national governments towards improving the sustainability of public finances is expected to boost markets for securities issued by private entities.[78] This is also likely to be supported by the enhanced liquidity and less transactions cost of the private stock and bond markets resulting from the increase in the number of investors and issuers operating in the same currency.[79] A research conducted by Hardouvelis, Malliaropoulos and Priestley has shown that the average cumulative saving in the cost of capital from integration of stock exchanges over the period 1992–1998 is estimated at around 2% for the EU-12 countries.[80] It is also likely that a larger currency area, the 'Euroland', will attract new foreign investors and issuers to the European securities markets. In this context, the efforts already undertaken to set up alliances and mergers between stock exchanges will be facilitated.

Nevertheless, while joint ventures and mergers among exchanges are yet in planning process, there are numerous obstacles to their successful fruition. European markets still compete with each other with regard to liquidity, transparency

---

[77] Wim Duisenberg, Financing in the European Capital Markets (speech delivered at the Waarborgfonds Sociale Woningbouw, Utrecht, 14 June 1999).

[78] *See* European Central Bank, *Possible Effects of EMU on the EU Banking Systems in the Medium to Long Term*, February 1999, 12.

[79] Between 1999 and 2002 only a core of operations has to be carried out in euro. The private sector will be convinced on purely economic grounds when the euro is available in physical form. The marginal cost of using a particular currency depends on how much it is used. Hence, a widely used currency has usually lower transactions cost.

[80] *See* Gikas Hardouvelis, Dimitrios Malliaropoulos and Richard Priestley, *EMU and European Stock Market Integration* (CEPR Discussion Paper 2124, London, April 1999) 33.

and cost.[81] Within euro, they also compete for listings, including new products.[82] Stock exchanges have already been privatised and now are demutualising. Some have and others may become listed companies, while their corporate structure differs. Mutual companies are difficult to merger, while merger of a mutual company and a limited company is even more complex. Take, for example, the collapse of the iX project, the once promising alliance plans between London and Frankfurt exchanges: what disclosure and accounting standards would apply to their listed companies? Which regulator should monitor trading and enforce insider dealing and similar laws? These problems were partly set out in a report issued by Merrill Lynch, advisers to the London exchange: 'UK regulators believe that Anglo-German attempts to harmonise share trading rules will be a "nightmare" if the London Stock Exchange and the Deutsche Börse merge to create iX. The report says that senior staff at the FSA have said privately that it will be difficult to achieve "any practical level of harmonisation" of United Kingdom and German stock market regulations'.[83]

All these developments involve conflicts of interest between the commercial interests and regulatory responsibilities of exchanges that stand in the way of an integrated European regulatory system for a pan-European securities market. This conflict could be best addressed and eliminated by an independent central authority, which will have no such commercial interests and will guarantee efficiency and stability in the function of European markets. On the other hand, a single authority will be needed in the near future to independently scrutinise the various inter-exchange cooperation agreements for their effects on competition between exchanges. To the extent that cooperation leads to substituting a single trading platform to competition for trading in specific securities, the agreements may be considered to produce anticompetitive effects in the relevant market and may run contrary to Article 81 EC (former Art. 85).[84] Albeit current securities markets' agreements are framed in a context of 'competition', in which inter-exchange competition and cooperation are said to coexist, the issue will remain crucial for future European financial market supervision structures.

## 5.2   *Impact on financial institutions*

The impact of the euro on financial intermediaries providing financial services is not as direct as that on financial markets. Over the past few years a favourable climate has prevailed across the entire European capital market, in bonds as well as equities. Buoyant securities markets have stimulated new issues and helped to finance a wave of mergers and acquisitions (M&A). An ongoing wave of mergers is occurring within

---

[81] *See* Marco Onado, 'Competition Among Exchanges or Financial Systems?', in Guido Ferrarini, *op. cit.*, note 62, 228.

[82] *See* Doderick Dunnett, The Transition to Stage Three: Impact on the Financial Markets (lecture given at the Workshop on Institutional Aspects of the EMU at King's College London, 26–27 January 1996) 11.

[83] *See* Boland Vincent and Francesco Guerrera, 'FSA staff brand iX plan a "nightmare"' (8 September 2000) FT, 1.

[84] *See* Michel Tison, *The Investment Services Directive and its Implementation in the EU Member States* (Financial Law Institute WP 1999-17, Ghent, 1999) 32.

the EU banking and investment systems, which is expected to keep momentum at least in the short to the medium term. Although most M&A at EU level take place in the domestic area, with reference to cross-border M&A, two basic strategies are to be observed: *first*, expansion into market niche abroad and, *second*, entering into foreign retail markets. The latter involves a need for access to an adequate distribution network, which is easier to achieve via strategic alliances or mergers. The introduction of the single currency and developments in electronic remote provision of investment services facilitate the cross-border conduct of financial services. This is likely to outweigh traditional hurdles of cross-border M&A, such as legal, fiscal and cultural differences with regard to management style and strategic goals.

The single currency will also have a significant effect on the risk faced by financial firms when conducting cross-border business, which may give them an incentive for increasing their intra-Community trade. Overall, credit, market, liquidity and market liquidity risks are generally expected to decrease, whereas legal and operational risks are likely to increase at least in the short term.[85] The positive macroeconomic effects of EMU are expected to mitigate credit risk in European financial markets. In addition, market, liquidity and market liquidity risks will be positively affected by deeper and more liquid markets. On the other hand, while legal and operational risks are expected to increase in the short term owing to the major changes to the overall legal environment, they are likely to decrease in the long term.

The creation of mega pan-European financial institutions and holding companies of financial groups in EMU brings the question of the division of responsibilities for such businesses into sharp focus. The post-BCCI Directive provides for a measure of financial firms holding supervision by the home competent authority. However, the holding companies themselves are not subject to prudential control. They are supervised indirectly in the context of control of authorised financial institutions. The pan-European Securities Regulator may take an interest in the application of this Directive and study whether there is a need for further Community legislation to enable pan-European holding companies to be established and supervised on a European basis. Indeed, the emergence of large banking and financial groups seems to require an adequate legislative and supervisory response, which, in view of the size and the spread of the entities concerned, should come about at EU level, instead of being confined to national competent authorities.[86]

In the same line comes the resuscitation of the 30-years-old project for the European company, the last legislative effort for which was made in 1991. When the bulk of the business of the financial undertakings is conducted domestically, the home authority has the least difficulty in carrying out consolidated supervision. But, will the solution of home country consolidated supervision apply to the case, where financial firms are established solely under European law? In December 2000, the Council of Ministers has reached agreement on the Regulation to establish a European Company Statute. If the European Parliament endorses the texts, the European Company will become a reality some 30 years after it was first proposed.

---

[85] *See* European Central Bank, *op. cit.*, note 78, 26.

[86] On the supervision of financial conglomerates in a global context, see the documents released jointly by the Basle Committee, IOSCO and IAIS on 18 February 1999.

As a result, financial firms and their subsidiaries will have the option of being established as a single company under Community law and so able to operate throughout the European Union with one set of rules and a unified management and reporting system. Indeed, consolidation of financial market participants, such as pan-European stock exchanges, banks and investment firms, multinational SSSs and EuroCCP for repo clearing houses, would benefit from a legal construction that is single and valid throughout the European Union.

It is obvious, however, that placing European financial companies under the home country supervision system is extremely difficult, if not impossible. The European Company framework, when it will result in institutions having a substantial share or even the majority of their operations in other than their establishment countries, is bound to loosen the ties with their home supervisors.[87] Although European companies will still have to be registered in the Member State where they have their head office, it is doubtful whether their supervisors will be able to efficiently keep under surveillance their whole pan-European business. When this project becomes reality, it will radically change the concept of home country control, as we perceive it today. Just as national companies need national supervisors, European companies will need the supervision of a European Regulator. As European companies' activities will not be limited by Member States' borders and as the currency will be common in the whole Euroland, so should a centralised European Authority have surveillance powers beyond them.

In general, EU Member States have decided to abandon their national currencies and join a common money area in an attempt to integrate their financial markets. However, the main problem that financial services are not yet enjoying full free movement lies with national regulators themselves. Yet, governments remain answerable to their national electorates. Monetary union notwithstanding, Member States still defend their economic policies on the grounds of protection of the people within their jurisdiction. The road towards financial market integration is of an evolutionary nature, where each legal action is determined on a case-by-case basis.[88] In order for financial markets to take full advantage of the introduction of the euro, we need an institutional convergence to complete legal convergence and enhance operational convergence. 'One regulator' should be added to the 'one currency' in order to deliver the 'one market' that will contribute to the smooth and efficient functioning of financial services.

## 6   Externalities and crisis management

International securities swindles have undermined the global financial system from the time of the 1929 stock market crash to the 1998 collapse of the Russian and

---

[87] This means that, with growing cross-border exposures, failures in foreign activities constitute an increasing threat for the solvency of the entire financial firm and for the stability of the entire common market. *See* David Mayes and Jukka Vesala, On the Problems of Home Country Control (mimeo) 13.

[88] Wim Duisenberg, The Euro as a Catalyst for Legal Convergence in Europe (speech on the occasion of the Annual Conference of the International Bar Association, Amsterdam, 17 September 2000).

East Asian economies.[89] There is no need to assess the cost of such financial crises.[90] Albeit each crisis has a set of local explanatory factors, they share a common element. Their impact cannot be 'local'.

The purpose of this section is to explore the possibilities of effective crisis management by the current home country supervision regime and to examine whether a more centralised structure would execute a more successful rescue programme in the case of an emergency. In this regard, it is useful to consider the circumstances surrounding the bankruptcy of BCCI, once the fastest growing bank in the world, in 1991.

### 6.1    BCCI

The collapse of BCCI was the result of a massive fraud. It has posed particular supervisory problems because the two companies, through which it carried out its international banking business, were registered in Luxembourg and the Cayman Island, its principal shareholders were latterly based in Abu Dhabi and the group was largely managed from London.

The Bank of England had been aware of some of the problems facing BCCI, but had judged that, on the information then available to it and in the light of a commitment from its principal shareholders to recapitalise the bank and to oversee changes to its management, systems and groups structure, the interests of depositors would be best served by dealing with the weakness within the on-going business.[91] The formal enquiry, conducted by Lord Justice Bingham after the BCCI failure,[92] criticised the Bank of England's supervisory approach, although it did not call for any radical changes to the basic system.[93] *Per contra*, in the *Three Rivers* case, the House of Lords did not accept that the Bank of England failed to provide continuous and effective supervision according to the provisions of Community law and, thus, it refused to recognise enforceable rights for depositors on the basis of the FBD.[94]

From an EU international standpoint, the most important legacy of the Bingham Report was the attention, which it drew to the prevailing shortcomings in

---

[89] For a description of recent financial crises in Europe, *see* Harald Benink, The Future of Banking Regulation in Developed Countries: Lessons from and for Europe (mimeo) 6.

[90] For a comprehensive analysis, see Huw Evans, Plumbers and Architects: A Supervisory Perspective on International Financial Architecture (FSA Occasional Paper Series No. 4, January 2000) 6.

[91] Tony Latter, *Causes and Management of Banking Crises* (Centre for Central Banking Studies, Bank of England, London, Handbook No. 121997) 36.

[92] Lord Justice Bingham, *Inquiry into the supervision of Bank of Credit and Commerce International*, (HMSO London, 1992) (hereinafter 'Bingham Report').

[93] The Bank of England, however, accepted Bingham's recommendations and proceeded to the establishment of a legal unit and a special investigation unit within it.

[94] Namely, Arts 6–8, First Banking Directive; *see Three Rivers District Council and Others* v. *Governor and Company of the Bank of England* [2000] 2 WLR 1220, [2000] 3 CMLR 205, [136]–[140]. The Court not only failed to refer the issue to the ECJ under Article 234 (former Art. 177) EC Treaty, but it also failed to take sufficiently into account supervision developments in other jurisdictions. For an extensive and critical analysis of the comparative and community law aspects of the *Three Rivers* case, *see* Mads Andenas, *Liability for Supervisors and Depositors' Rights – the BCCI and the Bank of England in the House of Lords*, Euredia (2001).

the supervision of internationally-operating financial groups.[95] This has led to a tightening of international standards, as established by the Basle Committee, which have since given legislative backing in the EU. The post-BCCI Directive constitutes an emblematic paradigm. The Bingham Report did merely pose the major questions with regard to the appointment of BCCI – and generally of pan-European or international financial firms – to national or international regulators. Was the Bank of England or the Institut Monetaire Luxembourgeois (IML) the principal supervisor of the BCCI?

The fragmentation and the tensions in reconciling domestic and international policies encourage the regulatory process to be primarily state-centred. In the case of the BCCI, its trading activities had considerable impact on the United Kingdom; accordingly, the United Kingdom should be obliged to accept major responsibility for regulating the BCCI empire and to cooperate with other regulators in a cross-border context. Here, an intersection of domestic and global interest was extremely significant. However, 'each regulator tended to focus on its own domestic concerns rather than accepting full collegiate responsibility'.[96] The Bank of England, for instance, could have closed BCCI at any time since its arrival in the United Kingdom, especially as it lacked a LLR and an effective supervisor, or as it was involved in money laundering activities. But, in its interest to encourage foreign investment in the United Kingdom, the Bank permitted BCCI to trade.

Certainly Luxembourg had a problem, because BCCI was registered and licensed there and the IML was the lead supervisor under the Basle Concordat. But it was also the Bank of England's problem because BCCI's effective base was in the United Kingdom, it was widely perceived as a British bank and UK depositors stood to lose much more than those of Luxembourg had things gone wrong.[97] Both Member States, however, refused to accept the burden of consolidated supervision. Consequently, BCCI continued worldwide operation without being monitored on a concrete and consolidated basis.

Both the Bingham Report and the *Three Rivers* case raise questions about the adequacy of the decentralised framework based on minimum harmonised prudential standards and suggest a review of the effectiveness of the current EU supervisory arrangements. The House of Lords case is exactly what the FBD was to prevent: that regulators can claim non-responsibility because of the involvement of other Member States' regulators.[98]

Obviously, had a centralised pan-European supervisor existed at that time, it would have taken the aforementioned responsibility. The Treasury and Civil Service Committee, in its Report on BCCI,[99] noted that a number of parties involved

---

[95] *See* Bingham Report, para. 3.19 *et seq.*

[96] House of Commons, Banking Supervision and BCCI: International and National Regulation (Treasury and Civil Service Select Committee, London, 4th Report, 1992) ix.

[97] *See* Bingham Report, para. 2.70.

[98] *See* Laxaros Panourgias, and Mads Andenas, *Euro, EMU and the UK Law* (Report submitted for the Euro-Spectator Project, Brussels, April 2001).

[99] House of Commons, *op. cit.*, note 96, 177.

considered the College[100] a second best solution when compared to a single supervisory authority. Although it would not be safe to make assumptions of the likely course of events in that case, it is without doubt that the pan-European supervisor would be the best means of requiring a much more detailed independent examination of the group's worldwide business. What it might have discovered is speculative. But again, both the Bank of England and the IML failed to measure up the task.

### 6.2   Crisis management and pre-crisis analysis

The BCCI collapse represents without doubt a conflict between the domestic and international interest of supervisors. Both the United Kingdom and Luxembourg, Member States of a union that was supposed to guarantee close avenues of collaborative work, were reluctant to undertake their responsibilities. This leads us to five factors, which determine the appropriate structure and size of the supervisory domain and reveal the need for a single supervisory authority to protect investors and retain financial stability.

The *first* factor, which has attracted a great deal of debate, is the timing for intervention in the event of a crisis. EU regulators agree that the objective of regulation is 'not to pre-judge where all market developments are heading to, but to ensure that, in the face of massive change, investors do not lose the protection that they can rightly expect to receive from the regulatory system'.[101] I do not share this proposition. Of course, prevention and cure are related, since the way in which each crisis is managed sends out powerful signals for the future. Nonetheless, incidents of the past clearly indicate that today supervision must be forward looking. The lesson derived from failures of the past is that 'more important than crisis management is pre-crisis risk analysis and loss prevention'.[102] Almost all crises of the past – especially the latest Asian crisis, besides their weakness in the fundamentals, shared the element of panic. And panic cannot be an effective consultant is such circumstances. What was needed then was a stronger surveillance, which would be more focused on preventing policies that enabled a panic in financial markets. Similarly, European regulators must always be looking for trouble ahead instead of waiting for a crisis to occur. *Prolepsis* is the key in efficient crisis management and the European supervisor can be the key-holder.

The *second* factor is speed. When the principals of the hundred-billion-dollar hedge fund LTMC called the New York Fed in September 1998 and declared their

---

[100] The 'college' refers to working relationships between more than two sets of national supervisors with regard to a particular institution. With regard to the use of supervisory colleges, *see* George Walker, 'Conglomerate Law and International Financial Market Supervision' (1998) *Annual Review of Banking Law* 287, 302.

[101] *See* FESCO, *Report 1999–2000* (15 November 2000) 9. Also Kanda would be surprised if the EU were seriously considering the establishment of a European Securities Commission in the absence of preceding scandals; *See* Kanda, Hideki, 'Commentary 1 on Ruben Lee's Report No 1, Supervising EU Capital Markets: Do we need a European SEC?', in Richard Buxbaum, Hertig Gerard, Hirsch Alain and Hopt Klaus (eds), *European Economic and Business Law: Legal and Economic Analysis on Integration and Harmonisation* (Walter de Gruyter, Berlin, 1996) 205.

[102] George Walker, *op. cit.*, note 100, 327.

inability to meet margin calls on the huge positions accumulated in several markets, they knew they were calling an institution with unmatched clout. As a supervisor, the Fed had detailed information on the financial situation and relationship to LTMC of most major players on the worldwide financial scene. In a very short time, the Fed was able to congregate all the large creditors of LTMC and twist their arms into allotting US$3.6 billion in the recapitalisation of the failing hedge fund, thus reinstoring its ability to meet outstanding obligation and preserving the financial stability of the US market.

On the morning of 24 September, the Fed in New York took a few hours to guarantee LTCM positions. Would such a swift and effective response be possible within EMU if a similar situation were to arise? A similar intervention by the ECB would require agreement with each national authority. Every central bank would have an interest in not declaring the exposure of its own banks, hoping to limit its exposure to a rescue operation.[103] The same applies to the investment services field. In a major emergency situation, there may be time to make some phone calls or call a meeting, but not to get involved in complex bureaucratic procedures. It is certain that the less the supervisory bodies involved in an emergency crisis, the faster and the more focused response could they achieve. In this respect, the existence of a single supervisor appears ideal. Only a single body would be able to guarantee prompt and efficient crisis management without having to take into consideration micro-political issues of purely domestic Member State interest.

The *third* factor-query that arises is what kind of information supervisors will likely want to obtain during the course of an emergency situation and how feasible it is to obtain such information. In contrast to basic financial and operational information generally available to home supervisors, the information that a competent authority will likely want to obtain from a supervised entity during an emergency would not necessarily be available to the supervisor prior to the emergency situation.[104] It would be the particulars of the emergency – the nature and scope of the problem – that would indicate what information would be required by supervisors. Moreover, it is the very scope and nature of the crisis that will usually indicate to supervisors, which financial firms would likely be affected by the spillover of the emergency. The 'Europeanisation' of investment business makes it extremely hard for the home supervisor to keep track of risk exposures of individual financial firms continuously. Centralisation of supervision, on the other hand, could enhance supervision practise by putting some emphasis on public disclosure and internal control mechanisms.

The *fourth* factor has to do with incentives. Under the home country control regime, home and host countries do merely share the same incentives for effective supervision. While home countries would be more interested for protecting financial institutions established within their territory, host supervisors' incentives to monitor foreign firms and deliver their input to the supervisory process may be blunted by

---

[103] *See* World News, 'Europe's central banks hinder transfer of real power to ECB' (30 October 1998) FT.

[104] *See* Basle Committee, *Supervision of Financial Conglomerates*, Joint Forum on Financial Conglomerates (February 1999) 92.

the fact that they do not have the ultimate responsibility of overseeing the safety and soundness of these firms.[105] The differences between market sizes within the EU also play a role in incentives issues. It would be logical to assume that the provision of investment services by small financial firms in large financial centres may not receive so much attention from the host authorities. Per contra, a supranational supervisor will not have any particular reason for not being equally interested in the effective monitoring of all EU firms and markets that will fall under its competency, irrespectively of where they operate.

Finally, the *fifth* problematic issue is the potential conflict of interest between the various authorities involved in the case of emergency. The early stages of the BCCI incident demonstrate that supervisors trying to protect their own investors, depositors and creditors can actually work against each other rather than cooperatively, when the appropriate crisis management mechanisms do not exist.[106] In any crisis event, the home supervisor will be focused on the consequences in the home country. The problems caused in the host country will be of secondary importance. Whilst the United Kingdom, Luxembourg and other College authorities ultimately cooperated to close down BCCI in July 1991, they also remained sensitive to 'local' interests.[107] Such conflicts should be overcome by the creation of a single regulator, which would surely refrain from such sensitivities and would act on behalf of all interested parties in a more objective and non-discriminatory manner. The European Regulator could then be required to lay down a specific set of procedures, which it would follow in emergency circumstances, in advance so that its actions are predictable. It would also be easier for it to cooperate with the other non-EU supervisors involved in the case and avoid this 'tragedy of errors, misunderstandings and failures of communication',[108] which is often unavoidable in any network, which tries to coordinate.

In light of these factors, coordination among 15 or more supervisors runs two additional risks: *first*, it is unlikely that a rescue operation could be carried out without market participants being aware that such an operation is in progress. *Second*, national supervisory authorities have private information concerning the exposure of individual financial firms in their jurisdiction and they might be reluctant to reveal such information due to their interest to protect them. Coming to a decision for immediate action could thus involve a complex game: among the supervisors first and then between the supervisors and the financial firms. This may severely cause delays in the information exchange, which could undermine any rescue operation itself.

All these require the immediate action that only a pan-European centralised body could offer. This chapter suggests that the recurrence of financial failures calls for

---

[105] Mayes and Vesala, *op. cit.*, note 87, 18.

[106] *Ibid.*, 26.

[107] For example, government efforts to restructure, rather than close down BCCI branch banks, were more extensive in countries, such as Pakistan, where BCCI dominated the market and was well linked with the political and economic establishment. Also, it seems that the UK's concern to protect depositors was secondary to the concern to safeguard the interests of the City of London as a citadel of finance capital.

[108] Bingham Report, para. 2.480.

a combined preventive and remedial response.[109] Crises management may involve gathering and updating of information from more than one financial undertakings and groups in more than one jurisdictions in order to expedite the assessment of the emergency's impact. A pan-European securities regulator is compelled to act immediately when the signals of threat become traceable. Moreover, the host country's incentives problem could be overcome by placing the weight of the systemic and cross-border issues at EU fora, where host supervisors could base their contribution on their expertise of local market conditions. *Per contra* it is unlikely that a network of fragmented supervisors – irrespectively how well organised and communicative it is – will be able to deliver the job. However, this issue will be discussed in the following section.

## 7  Imperfect information and deficient cooperation

It is widely accepted that the key issues of regulation and supervision of financial institutions are exchange of information between supervisors and coordination of effectives mechanisms for their supervision and intervention when problems arise. However, problems of coordination will emerge in any structure of multiple agencies.[110] Beyond the doubtful competent and sufficient trust between national competent authorities other factors, such as lack of loyal cooperation and imperfect flow of information, may undermine the efficiency of cooperation between multiple players. This section will attempt to support the idea that, albeit current coordination structures have been improved at EU and international level, there are still not enough to prevent future crises and guarantee financial stability and consumer protection within the Single Market. This has been clearly the outcome of an assessment conducted by the Group of Wise Men.[111] To assist our argument, this paper will make use of the results and considerations that followed the collapse of Barings, the UK's oldest merchant bank, in February 1995.

### 7.1  Barings

Although the Barings incident exceeds the geographical borders of the European Union, the assessment of its causes may assist our discussion in assessing the weakness of national supervisory networks to supervise transnational investment business.

A general problem in financial regulation is that the jurisdiction of national regulators is smaller than the geographical business area of regulated financial

---

[109] The problem is that 'the use of crisis management instruments has traditionally been confined to banks, because *they are the most relevant from the viewpoint of financial stability*' (emphasis added); *see* Brouwer Report, *op. cit.*, note 76, 22.

[110] Charles Goodhart *et al.*, *op. cit.*, note 2, 155.

[111] Forty-five percent of the responses to the Wise Men questionnaire on the regulation of European securities markets stated that the current arrangements for cooperation and mutual assistance between national supervisors are not sufficient. The main perceived shortcomings are differences in supervisory powers and duties, duplication of supervisory control, deficient channels for cooperation, excessive cost and lack of expertise and transparency. *See* Initial Wise Men Report, *op. cit.*, note 1, 34.

institutions.[112] In contrast to the BCCI case, the Barings collapse was brought about by the trading activities of a member of its Singapore Futures branch combined with a failure of oversight and compliance at every level of organisation.[113] Responsible for the consolidated supervision of the Barings Group was the Bank of England, which acted as the 'lead supervisor'.[114] The Bank received and considered data on Barings' consolidated capital ratios and consolidated large exposures, but was not responsible for the individual supervision of its subsidiary, Barings Futures Singapore (BFS). However, the Bank of England Report found that the Bank did not review Barings' overseas subsidiaries. Instead, it relied on the auditors and reporting accountants' statements regarding the existence of the connected lending limits of Barings' exposure to the overseas securities subsidiaries. Moreover, the Bank of England also relied on the supervision of BFS by the relevant overseas regulators.[115] The Bank Report clearly criticised the inefficient way the Bank of England was cooperating with overseas supervisors and recommended that it should clearly define its relationship with other regulators and effectively coordinate with them.[116] Moving a step forward, the Singapore Report surpassed the Bank of England Report in criticising the Singapore Monetary Exchange (SIMEX) for having concerns about BFS' activities, not following up on them with urgency and not informing the central bank of Singapore and the Bank of England of these concerns.[117] In addition, the Report observed that the Singapore supervisors should diligently initiate enforcement actions against BFS rather than rely on the parent institution's reputation or on foreign authorities supervising the activities of the head office of such an institution.[118]

## 7.2   Is cooperation adequate?

The Barings collapse clearly represents a textbook example of the failure of respected national supervisory authorities to carry out their mission and to coordinate and exchange information on a cross-border basis to prevent the failure of a well-respected financial group.[119] Both Reports made clear that, just as in the BCCI incident, international coordination and cooperation were ineffective until true damage was complete.

---

[112] Charles Goodhart *et al.*, *op. cit.*, note 2, 173.

[113] See the *Report by Singapore Inspectors on Baring Futures Singapore*, Financial Regulation Report, October 1995 (hereinafter 'Singapore Report'). On the contrary, the findings of the Bank of England Report were that the collapse was chiefly due to ineffective risk management and inadequate internal control. See HMSO, *Report of the Board of Banking Supervision Inquiry into the Circumstances of the Collapse of Barings* (18 July 1995) Chapter 13, paras 13.10–13.11 (hereinafter 'Bank of England Report').

[114] Although the Barings case falls outside the ambit of the EU home country control system and the relevant Directives, similar elements of supervisory structures can be traced at the international context. The concept of 'lead supervisor', for instance, is recognised internationally in the Basle Concordat of 1983.

[115] *See* Bank of England Report, para. 13.58.

[116] *Ibid.*, para. 14.35.

[117] *See* Singapore Report, para. 15.41.

[118] *Ibid.*, para. 15.43.

[119] Joseph Norton and Christopher Olive, 'Globalization of Financial Risks and International Supervision of Banks and Securities Firms: Lessons from the Barrings Debacle' (1996) 2 *International Lawyer* 301, 341.

As with transaction costs, given complete information between Member States' competent authorities, there would be no need for sovereign states to delegate power to supranational bodies. Nevertheless, this is hardly the case in real life. The problem with national supervisory authorities is that they are working in the context of national laws and regulations, whereas the core institutions of the EU financial system are now mainly pan-European in coverage. Coordination, for instance, of reporting standards is no small difficulty. As new issues arise, each supervisor will adopt its own reporting requirements to deal with them.[120]

A second problematic issue, especially acute within the EU context, is the institutional structure of financial markets supervision. While some countries, such as the United Kingdom, Luxembourg and Denmark, have adopted the idea of a single regulator for their financial sector, different structures are in place elsewhere in Europe, some within finance ministries, some outside. These differences should have a practical impact on collaboration at cross-border level. Given the consolidation of financial services and their regulatory approaches, channels of cooperation may well require feedback from more than one supervisory institution in each Member State, which can easily jeopardise the reliability of communication.

A major issue in this debate is compliance, not in the sense of firms complying with the supervisors' standards, but in the sense of supervisors complying with their international and EU agreements and standards. 'Setting standards is the first step: maintaining them is the hard part', was an apt lecture title by Charles Goodhart.[121] For instance, IOSCO has issued a Report, which is hoped to serve as guidance on information sharing between national regulators during periods of crisis.[122] Nonetheless, even in the unlikely case that all these recommendations are followed to the letter, certain problems may be impossible to overcome. *First*, authorities may be sensitive on giving information with an inherent significance for their domestic financial markets.[123] *Second*, the requested information may be in the possession of more than one authorities, which may complicate the cooperative mechanisms. *Third*, there may be legal or practical reasons, which prevent the exchange of information in some jurisdictions,[124] confidentiality laws that accommodate access to and sharing of information or legal conditions that have first to be met.[125] Serious delays, therefore, are almost inevitable to occur.

In the EU context, FESCO members have agreed on a Multilateral Memorandum of Understanding,[126] which establishes a general framework for cooperation and

---

[120] Charles Goodhart *et al.*, *op. cit.*, note 2, 40.

[121] Centre for Financial Research, Cambridge, 20 February 1998.

[122] IOSCO, *Guidance on information sharing*, November 1997; *see* also IOSCO, *Report on Cooperation between Market Authorities and Default Procedures*, March 1996.

[123] On this issue, *see* Section 6.

[124] National authorities maintain the right to refuse provision of information in instances where that transmission could violate public policy, sovereignty, national security or other essential interests.

[125] In some jurisdictions, information that discloses the positions and funds of individual customers may not be available under relevant bank secrecy and similar laws.

[126] FESCO, *Multilateral Memorandum of Understanding on the Exchange of Information and Surveillance of Securities Activities* (February 1999).

consultation between supervisory authorities. Nevertheless, it is debatable whether the response to a potential emergency crisis will be facilitated by the time-consuming procedure described in this informal Memorandum (in as much as it is not legally binding) with regard to information exchange, investigations, compliance and enforcement assistance.[127] Albeit more information is available on MoUs between securities supervisors and regulated markets, cooperation through MoUs raises the questions of effective coordination of supervision, of supervisory methods[128] and of the content of information exchange.[129] According to Mayes, MoUs do merely provide for regular transfer of routine information among supervisors, but only in the case where possible supervisory problems arise, including suspected misconduct.[130]

The BCCI and Barings crises taken together mandate that cross-border coordination and cooperation in the supervision of financial groups are equally as important as national supervisory efforts.[131] However, their mandate is not equally powerful. In any given network, from IOSCO to Basle and FESCO, all members-supervisors seek to operate by consensus. None has formal powers to censure let alone impose sanctions on members. After all, all these groups are composed of national representatives, who – unlike, for example, members of the European Commission or ECB's Governing Council – do not have an explicit mandate to discard their national perspective in favour of a pan-European one.[132]

While these networks are mostly concerned with firms' ongoing business, it is doubtful whether their contacts and mutual trust built up are helpful if crises occur and information is sought at very short notice. If national authorities withhold information from each other and treat feedback as unwarranted criticism, conciliation to resolve conflicts is unlikely to be perceived as legitimate. Given that 'constituent organisations lack the capacities and incentives to overcome the obstacles to collective action posed by joint decision traps',[133] it may come to no surprise that networks, such as FESCO, are often undermanaged. Since reliance on hierarchical authority

---

[127] Art. 4(3), for instance, requires that any request addressed to a supervisory authority should specify, *inter alia*, the following: (a) a description of the subject matter, the purpose for which the information is sought and the reason why this information will be of assistance, (b) a description of the specific information requested and the relevant Community law pursuant to which the authority discharges its responsibilities, (c) in case the request results from investigations of violations of any laws or regulations, a description of them and a list of the persons and institutions involved, and (d) whether the requesting authority is in contact with any other authority or law enforcement agency in the country of the requested authority,

[128] According to Prati and Schinasi, supervisory practices vary considerably in the EU; *see* Alessandro Prati and Garry Schinasi, *Will the ECB be the LLR in EMU?* (Paper presented at the SUERF Conference, Frankfurt, October 1998).

[129] Karel Lannoo, *Challenges to the Structure of Financial Supervision in the EU* (CEPS, Brussels, July 2000) 14.

[130] Mayes and Vesala, *op. cit.*, note 87, 16.

[131] Norton and Olive, *op. cit.*, note 119, 342.

[132] *See* Rolf Breuer, *Convergence of Supervisory Practices – A Banker's View* (Conference of European Banking Supervisors, Copenhagen, 20 November 2000).

[133] Les Metcalpe, 'Reforming the Commission: Will Organizational Efficiency Produce Effective Governance?' (2000) 5 JCMS 817, 829.

is ruled out, capacity development depends on multilateral negotiations to define the terms of reliable regulatory and supervisory cooperation.

A centralised institution should not simply be a body that develops and imposes regulatory procedures. It should also be a forum, within which the objectives and rules of European financial cooperation are developed and implemented. Many of the goals of an efficient EU financial policy can be achieved by effective coordination of the activities of national authorities. The problem is that the means of achieving that coordination are, at the moment, quite limited. The European supervisor will fill that gap. Such a model should not preclude the establishment of an arrangement to assist or add value to the existing role of Member States' competent authorities and FESCO. In particular, the European supervisor could play a constructive role in making FESCO a viable and effective organisation for harmonising regulation and ensuring enforcement cooperation.

Of course, this chapter does not allege that a perfect institutional structure is attainable. Also within a single regulator structure, there will always be potential problems of communication, information sharing and persistency. But, it is difficult to see how these problems could be more acute within a single regulator with a unified management structure and an effective internal decision-making process than across multiple authorities, each with their own individual and largely independent cultures and decision-making structures.[134] What will the case be after the impending enlargement of the Union to CEECs, Cyprus and Malta? No matter how developed and enhanced cooperation is achieved, as a growing body of opinion now demands,[135] it will never substitute the timely access to information and the facilitation of coordination of a single regulator.

Speed is the 'A' and the 'Z' in responding to any fraudulent activity or default, especially when conducted within an electronic network.[136] A centralised regulator should seek out opportunities to leverage national supervisors' efforts to investigate transactions that they view as questionable. Acting as a neutral and independent coordinator, the single regulator will achieve better flow of information, exchange of supervisory mechanisms and equivalence of regulatory capacities between national bodies. This is required, if not demanded, when problems involved are EU area-wide – because of the institutions and markets involved – or there are concerns of systemic problems spreading across borders. Moreover, centralisation enhances the quality of supervision by examining common trends in the financial system that may not be revealed from the national perspective only.

---

[134] Clive Briault, *op. cit.*, note 23, 19.

[135] *See*, e.g. Wim Duisenberg, The Future of Banking Supervision and the Integration of Financial markets (speech delivered at the conference 'Improving integration of financial markets in Europe', Turin, 22 May 2000); ESFRC, 'The European Shadow Financial Regulatory Committee: a new initiative' (1999) 2 JIBR 137, 140; David Green, 'Enhanced Co-operation among Regulators and the Role of National Regulators in a Global Market' (2000) 2 JIFM 7, 12.

[136] Perpetrators of Internet securities fraud, for instance, can easily move both the location of their web sites and the target location of their fraudulent scheme from one jurisdiction to another, when they encounter difficulties in a particular jurisdiction; see IOSCO, Securities Activity on the Internet (September 1998) 37.

To conclude, despite existing enhanced cooperative efforts within the European supervisory regime, it is important that these be underpinned by a clear EU-wide coordinating authority, which will eliminate and substitute misunderstandings, institutional rivalry and excessive forbearance by national regulators. Managerial time is limited in the period before, and even more after a crisis, where response needs to be prompt and efficient. The gradually consolidating European markets cannot afford a crisis to emerge in order to realise that current regulatory and supervisory arrangements are ill-adapted to deliver the job.

## 8   Access to and from third countries

In this critical period of time, where the Community moves towards its objective of a fully integrated financial services market, it is essential that our trade concerns emerge beyond the EU internal market as well. European Union is not an island in financial markets. Financial transactions between EU markets and the rest of the world are as important as those within the European Union. It is, therefore, equally important that European financial institutions have unconditional access to the markets of EU's competitors, as foreign organisations have access to the Member States' markets. However, barriers do remain in many markets, including the large market of the United States. Many paradigms can be recalled here regarding investment services. Foreign financial firms do not 'benefit' from the 'European passport' and the home country control principle. On the other hand, EU securities markets cannot establish trading screen in countries such as the United States, even though the core principles protecting investors and market integrity are similar in both jurisdictions. Furthermore, even though US investment funds can be freely marketed in the European Union, EU funds are required to establish 'mirror funds' in the United States before they can market their products.[137]

With regard to supervision, today there are at least 15 governmental voices, besides the Commission, speaking on regulatory and supervisory issues on behalf of Europe. Even a regime for supervisory cooperation in external relations requires, at a minimum, that the EU 'speaks with one voice' and ensures that divergences of view among Member States are dealt with. Even this modest level of coordination will not work unless consultation and communication networks between the relevant national and EU actors are reliable.

This situation does not give Europe the effectiveness with respect to international issues that it would have if a single negotiator, a pan-European Commission existed. This could be better understood in bilateral relations with powerful counterparties. The need, for instance, to harmonise United States and European securities regulation[138]

---

[137] Similar concerns exist for banking and insurance services regulation and supervision; *see* Commission of the European Communities, 3rd Progress Report, *op. cit.*, note 49, 13.

[138] *See* Paul Arlman, 'European Equity Markets after the euro: Competition and Cooperation across new Frontiers' (1999) 2 *International Finance* 139, 146–147. FESE also points out that modernisation of regulation in Europe has to be accompanied by rapid agreement with the US authorities aiming at full and immediate reciprocity of securities market access; *see* FESE Second Report, *op. cit.*, note 70, 6.

could be accomplished more easily by a single European regulator working with the SEC than by 15 or later 27 different negotiators. When EU capital markets become integrated, the size and power of a pan-European market would make the single regulator an effective and reliable negotiator on issues of policy and law enforcement. Moreover, the ESR would be the perfect authority to maintain and foster these issues on the WTO agenda.

Given the fact that supervisory policies become increasingly important elements in international financial trade, developments in this field will become more rather than less important for international trade relation.[139] 'We must ensure that European markets are attractive to capital from outside the Union and that our regime is market-friendly'.[140] The establishment of a single supervisory authority in Europe constitutes an urgent need not only within the EU market, but also in the international context. With growing international economic interdependence, existing WTO principles of national treatment are reaching the limits of their effectiveness. Markets remain more integrated than their regulation and supervision. A pan-European authority, which could multiply existing integration efforts, could more easily export its work to the international multilateral system. Instead of importing standards and implementing them to fifteen different systems, the pan-European body could have the power and the impetus to find wider acceptance abroad.

## 9    Identifying the problem: real drawbacks or political unwillingness?

Given the necessity and feasibility of transfer of certain regulatory and supervisory tasks from regional to centralised level, one may logically but also naively wonder: why is there still such an opposition to a pan-European Securities Regulator? It may be alleged that the logic of functional effectiveness is unable to fully explain current Community competences. In the words of Majone,

> even in the case of economic regulation, where functional logic is most compelling, the timing and quality of many developments cannot be understood without taking into consideration other factors such as the policy entrepreneurship of the Commission or the activism of powerful actors who cannot wait for incremental task expansion to produce the policy outputs they want'.[141]

After assessing the pros and cons of the single Securities Regulator idea, the issue boils down to the political question, whether Member States would be ready and willing to give up their powers over the biggest, most sophisticated flagship. Therefore, one cannot really expect national supervisors to show a lot of enthusiasm for the prospect of being relegated to a local league and the role of junior partner to

---

[139] *See* Stephen Woolcock, 'Competition Among Rules in the Single European Market', in William Bratton *et al.*, *op. cit.*, note 9, 292.

[140] Howard Davies, Introductory Remarks (Eurofi Conference, Paris, 15 September 2000).

[141] Giandomenico Majone, *op. cit.*, note 10, 66.

some remote super-body.[142] This becomes evident when Professor Lamfalussy, the chairman of the Wise Men Committee, which concluded that a pan-European regulator is not yet feasible, explicitly admitted that he has given instructions by the Council to propose a solution only within the restrictions of the present Treaty.[143]

The principle of home country control has brought a negative effect on how Member States perceive 'home country' supervision. Member States, today, do hardly look beyond their national markets and have less interest in how supervision is done in other countries. This is best illustrated by the Chairman of the FSA himself: 'While we have no formal responsibility for the prudential supervision of Deutsche Bank, it would be curious if we did not take an interest in what it got up to in the London market, where its presence is very considerable and even profitable on occasion'.[144] The notion of the phrase 'take an interest' is debatable.

Although regulators acknowledge the deficiencies of the existing regime, they consider them relatively unimportant because they may not affect financial stability at the moment. A piece of the Brouwer Report deserves to be quoted in length:[145]

> The regulatory framework in Europe leaves some discretion to national authorities for interpretation and translation into national legislation. This could potentially result in regulatory arbitrage and an unlevel playing field. (...) However, this does not necessarily mean that the stability of the European financial system is negatively affected by remaining differences in national financial regulation. (emphasis added)

Albeit many believe that a single regulator in investment services is a necessity, steps cannot be implemented towards this end until the political patrons of the national authorities are persuaded that it is the right direction to take. Now is the time. European financial market integration cannot be jeopardised by unnecessary national disputes and misunderstandings, while the international community is moving towards a single body to monitor the global financial architecture.[146]

---

[142] Daniel Zuberbühler, The Financial Industry in the 21st Century (Speech at the Jubilee International Conference of Banking Supervisors, Basle, 21 September 2000).

[143] See Alexander Lamfalussy presentation on the Special Roundtable on the findings of the Committee of Wise Men on the Regulation of European Securities Markets (CEPS, Brussels 29 November 2000) (hereinafter 'CEPS Roundtable').

[144] Howard Davies, Convergence of Supervisory Practice (Speech at the Banking Supervision Conference, Copenhagen, 20 November 2000).

[145] Brouwer Report, op. cit., note 76, 14–15.

[146] This is evident in the March 2001 IMF's plans to establish an International Capital Markets Department to enhance its surveillance, crisis prevention and crisis management activities; see http://www.imf. org/external/np/sec/nb/2001/nb0124.htm. See, also, the proposal for a World Financial Authority (WFA) in Chapter 13 of this volume, John Eatwell and Lance Taylor, International Markets and the Future of Economic Policy.

## C CONCLUSIONS

Is what is being done or proposed enough? The answer of this chapter would be: no. To date, the availability of the European passport and home country control has not produced the so desirable freedom of pan-European provision of investment services. Home country control has its limits. As a result, both major financial undertakings and investors have an interest in further supervisory centralisation supplemented or not by further harmonisation.

The proposals of the Wise Men Committee to speed up the legislative process are welcome. However, Europe cannot stop here. A strong trend towards a single European Regulator is perceived. Albeit, as a first step, a pan-European Securities Supervisor could be solidly built on the current provisions of the Treaty, a more powerful body with decision-making and supervisory powers will need to become part of a new IGC.

Rephrasing the theory of neo-functionalism, the functional needs of a single market in investment services would necessitate a considerable transfer of policy-making powers to the EU level. Regulatory economies of scale and scope for financial undertakings and securities markets call for efficiency gains that only a central regulator can deliver. The potential integration of financial markets and 'Europeanisation' of investment and generally financial services, which will be boomed as the introduction of the euro breaks down the barriers in Europe, will pose serious problems to the current fragmented multiplayer regulatory and supervisory structure.

The current supervisory regime has implication on the slow legislation process that we all witness in Europe. Nobody argues against that but also nobody moves against it. Today comes the proposed regime by the Commission and the Wise Men, which, nevertheless, is doubtful whether it will speed up securities markets and investment services integration. In any case, supervision remains untouched, while developments cannot wait. Home supervisors will find their task more difficult to extend their supervisory power to financial business conducted abroad. Host supervisor, on the other hand, are likely to become less informed about the firms and the market as a whole, which means that their ability to take *ex ante* action and resolve a crisis situation is limited.

Thoroughgoing 'enhanced' cooperation between members of FESCO may ease the problem of information exchange but this is not adequate. The need to act promptly, decisively and away from national political and socio-economic interests in emergencies supports a wider role for a pan-European supervisor with clear crisis management tasks. The single regulator can be more flexible. Lawmaking in its hands will never follow market developments, while its flexibility will smooth national conflicts and provide an adequate forum for exchange of expertise and information, as a better shield to repulse or even prevent emergencies. In addition, the pan-European Regulator will constitute the powerful counterparty that will negotiate and foster the European interests in the global financial arena and the WTO.

In light of its functions, it is important that the European Regulator remains immune to political pressure and regulatory capture. Its tasks and operation should be designed in such a clear way as to promote transparency and accountability. In turn, transparency will reduce information asymmetries within European markets and accountability will foster confidence, democracy and legitimacy.

Albeit regulators acknowledge the deficiencies of the present regulatory and supervisory system, short-sighted perspectives and partial success of the past make them reluctant to move towards its radical reform. Nevertheless, the issue of a single EU regulator cannot be avoided by the markets and their participants. The new regime would have the advantage on the *status quo* of a bigger body of common regulations, lower costs and greater flexibility.

As put by Demarigny, the problem of European securities market regulation and supervision today is basically a lack of a 'bridge' between the upper level, the EU Directives written in stone, and the lower level, the day-to-day practical implementation at a national level.[147] The pan-European Securities Regulator could be seen as the 'constructor' of the 'bridge', as soon as micropolitical interests and national conflicts are left aside. The next chapter will endeavour to identify the structure, the competencies and the role that the proposed 'constructor' will be needed to play.

---

[147] Fabrice Demarigny, comment at the CEPS Roundtable, *op. cit.*, note 143.

Chapter 7

# After the *Lamfalussy* Report: The First Steps towards a European Securities Commission?

*Gilles Thieffry\**

## INTRODUCTION

Economic and Monetary Union (EMU), the cornerstone of European economic integration, was implemented by the Maastricht Treaty in 1992.[1] EMU is now a reality with the successful introduction of the euro as of 1 January 1999.[2] The effect of the introduction of the euro has been to create a massive market of euro-denominated securities (second only to the US$). For example, EMU resulted in the conversion of the international debt market into a 'dual currency' market. In 1999, there was US$1.4 trillion equivalent of new issues in the international bond market, of which 43.1% was denominated in the euro.[3]

The enormous impact thus far of EMU is undeniable. The focus now shifts towards greater harmonisation and integration of the European securities regulatory environment to capitalise on the effect of monetary union on the euro-zone securities markets. Initiatives towards the consolidation of European stock exchanges have developed rapidly and such acceleration, unprecedented in the history of Europe's capital markets, should be viewed in the context of the growing trend towards the globalisation of the world's financial markets. The formation of entities such as Euronext and the tumultuous attempted mergers and/or take overs of the London Stock Exchange (LSE) in 2000 have been well documented in the financial press[4] but no doubt there will be further news of another merger/potential take over of the LSE and/or of rival entities emerging to challenge for a greater market share in Europe (if not globally). The question now is not whether the regulatory regime in Europe can cope with these

---

\* The author wishes to thank his colleague Inès Balaÿ for her help in preparing this chapter. This chapter does not necessarily reflect the opinion of Andersen Legal and/or Arthur Andersen.

[1] Treaty establishing the EU, OJ C 224/1, 7 February 1992.

[2] This marked the third and final stage of EMU with 11 Member States ceding to the irrevocable fixing of the interest rates. Euro banknotes will begin to be issued in Member States as of 1 January 2002.

[3] IPMA, *The International Capital Markets* Report (March 2000). Based on current growth rates, the figures for 2000 will reach at least US$1.7 trillion equivalent. It was noted that the market share of euro-denominated securities was only marginally lower than that of US$ (45.5%).

[4] *See*, for example, 'Werner uber alles', The Economist, 6 May 2000; 'Deutsche Börse backs merger with London', The Financial Times, 23 May 2000; 'Euronext plans to compete with ix', Financial News, 29 May 2000; 'Euronext Stock Exchange Deal may be Sealed by October', WSJ Europe, 4 July 2000; 'Stock Markets Eye Nasdaq Deal', The Financial Times, 18 July 2000.

*Mads Andenas and Yannis Avgerinos (eds), Financial Markets in Europe: Towards a Single Regulator?* 183–210.
© 2003 *Kluwer Law International. Printed in Great Britain.*

market innovations (one might suggest 'no' for an answer) but instead when will the regime change in view of these market developments?

The author has advocated in earlier articles for a change in EU regulatory approach and indeed opinioned on a movement towards the formation of a European Securities Commission (ESC).[5] The purpose of this chapter is to reassess (and reassert) that position, especially in light of recent market developments, the growth of the euro-zone market and the release of the Report of the Committee of Wise Men chaired by Mr. Alexandre Lamfalussy under the aegis of the European Union (EU)[6] (the 'Lamfalussy Report'). A single currency deserves a single capital market but the present fragmented regulation is impeding progress towards the aim of a unified financial services market in Europe.

The chapter will be set out as follows: (1) a brief look at the motivations for pan-European harmonisation; (2) an assessment of the present (and unsatisfactory) EU position on securities regulation, including a discussion of the Lamfalussy Report; (3) setting out the case for an ESC, postulating the possible forms of such a body (by considering both European and US models); and finally (4) the author's concluding remarks.

PART I

*1    Why harmonise?*

The aim of integrating the European securities markets is enshrined in the Treaty of Rome 1957 as amended (the 'Treaty').[7] Under the Treaty, the principle of free movement of capital and services (as well as the free movement of goods and persons) was formulated. The reasons for harmonisation and integration are manifold. These have been espoused on numerous occasions and they may be briefly summarised as follows. First and foremost, harmonisation of securities laws aims to create a 'level playing field' for investors throughout the European Union. Second, a truly Community-harmonised policy will provide the safeguard for the proper functioning of markets and enhance the transparency which the newly unified markets lack. Improved efficiency of the capital markets through common high levels of disclosure and transparency would also optimise the allocation of capital and improve liquidity. Furthermore, it has been argued that if the securities markets are not uniformly regulated, it may give rise to regulatory arbitrage and 'forum shopping'. In such circumstances, regulators would be in direct competition and this would affect the

---

[5] Gilles Thieffry, 'Regulation of the Securities Markets and the Euro' European Single Financial Market, September 1998, pp. 6–9; Gilles Thieffry, 'Regulation and the Euro' The London Financial News, 23–29 June 1997, p. 7; Gilles Thieffry, 'Towards a European Securities Commission' (IFLR 1999) XV(iii)9, p. 14.

[6] *Final Report of the Committee of Wise Men on the Regulation of European Securities Markets*, Brussels, 15 February 2001.

[7] Treaty Establishing the European Economic Community, Rome (25 March 1957), as amended.

quality of the national stock exchanges since Member States, would adopt a relaxation of the rules in a 'race to the bottom' so as to attract market participants. In turn, market participants would be able to choose between Member States and inevitably opt for the regime which is the cheapest and least onerous. Finally, a harmonised co-ordination of the regulatory rules would remove obstacles for issuers, equalise conditions of competition and, more significantly, reduce the cost of cross-border capital raising. EMU has eliminated the exchange risk for issuers and investors alike. However, as it will become apparent from the discussion below, the sound economic reasons set out above have not led to the harmonisation of European securities regulation. It should be remembered that the 'Single Market' for financial services was due in 1993. It is fair to say that this deadline was, by and large, missed.

The call for a unified regulatory regime has become an obvious necessity to all those waiting to capitalise fully on the creation of a market denominated in euro and the advent of new placement media such as the Internet. It is presently virtually impossible to emulate the US market in Europe, which is an unacceptable situation for the financial industry and a loss of opportunity for the economy at large. As Stephen Kingsley suggests: 'Europe needs a cheap and efficient market for securities and their derivatives. Until it gets one, we will all continue to pay the price through unnecessarily high transaction costs and therefore reduced investment performance.'[8] In the Initial Report of the Committee of Wise Men on the Regulation of European Securities Markets (the 'Initial Lamfalussy Report'),[9] the Committee provides extremely telling data highlighting the cost paid by the European economy at large for such inefficiencies. For example, in 1999 in the euro-zone, the Bank loans to the Corporate sector represented the equivalent of 45.2% of GDP against 12.4% in the United States. Corporate fixed income securities accounted for a mere 7.4% of GDP against 29% in the United States and, perhaps more telling, the stock market capitalisation in the euro-zone was half of that of the United States.[10]

It is impossible to imagine an efficient euro-denominated securities market without, if not totally integrated regulations, a very high degree of harmonisation which does not exist yet. Any person who doubts the attractiveness of the US model of an integrated securities market, providing deep and liquid source of financings for issuers, and a wide array of financial products for investors, must have been deaf to large sections of the European financing community (corporate and sovereign issuers, investors and investment bankers alike).

For example, the inability of effecting pan-European retail IPOs limits the ability of many issuers to raise funds efficiently. Equally, the lack of common standards for the use of the Internet on a cross-border basis deprives the European securities industry of one of the most efficient cost-cutting tools used so efficiently by the US domestic market. This is caused solely by the incompatibility of the securities

---

[8] 'A Blueprint for the New Exchange – Stephen Kingsley Suggests the Principles Europe's Bourses Must Follow to Keep Up with Technological Innovation', *Financial Times*, 18 September 2000.
[9] *The Initial Report of the Committee of Wise Men on the Regulation on European Securities Markets*. Brussels, 9 November 2000.
[10] *Initial Report of the Committee of Wise Men on the Regulation of European Securities Markets*, p. 10.

regulatory regimes in the various Member States. As mentioned by Mr. Alexandre Lamfalussy in his opening comments on the release of the Lamfalussy Report:

> The basic legislation for an integrated financial market is not in place. The mosaic of European regulatory structures is well documented – over 40 of them – with different powers and competencies. The current regulatory system is simply too slow, too rigid and ill-adapted to the needs of modern financial markets. Even when it does work, which is rare, it often produces texts of legendary ambiguity – along with little or no common effort to transpose the agreed texts consistently – nor enforce their proper allocation.
>
> All the weaknesses are compounded by a plethora of other complexities, such as clearing and settlement systems that fragment liquidity, increase costs and present a real barrier to financial market development in the European Union. Add on top differences in legal systems, taxation, external trade barriers, different cultural approaches and a lack of identified regulatory priorities and you have a remarkable cocktail of Kafkaesque inefficiency that serves no-one – neither consumers, nor investors, nor SME's nor large companies, nor governments.

## 2   Why is this so important?

Because the Committee believes that the economic gains for the European Union of an integrated financial market will be very substantial. In macroeconomic terms, the productivity of capital and labour will increase – enhancing the potential for stronger GDP growth and job creation throughout the Union.

## Part II

### 1   Attempts at harmonisation

Presently, attempts at harmonisation of European financial markets have been achieved, in theory, by implementing EU Directives,[11] notably the Second Banking Directive (indirectly), the Admissions Directive, the Listing Particulars Directive, the Public Offers of Securities Directive and the Investment Services Directive (ISD).

- The Second Banking Directive imported the notion of the European banking 'passport' under home country rule in relation to the authorisation and supervision of certain financial institutions.
- The Admissions Directive established minimum conditions for the listing of both debt and equity securities on stock exchanges situated or operating in Member States.

---

[11] The Directives are based on Art. 54(3)(g) of the Treaty.

- The Listing Particulars Directive deals with the publication of sufficient information about the applicant for listing to satisfy and protect investors. This Directive was amended in 1987 to provide for a system of mutual recognition where listing was requested in more than one Member State.
- Likewise, the Public Offer of Securities Directive imposes an obligation on companies to provide a prospectus for all public offerings (on- or off-exchanges) that conforms to certain minimum requirements, in the interest of investor protection.
- The ISD, the most significant Directive thus far in achieving harmonisation of securities regulation, establishes the 'single passport' in investment services for specialised securities firms, that is, it enables investment firms authorised in one Member State to provide investment services in other Member States on the basis of their 'home' state authorisation.

The standards (defined in these Directives) establish a minimum regulatory foundation necessary for the correct operation of the markets and for the protection of investors. They leave it up the national regulatory authorities to apply these Directives and to co-operate with one another to ensure the best functioning of the whole market.

In theory, the concept of mutual recognition ought to mean that it is possible for securities offerings to be extended to other Member States. However, those familiar with market realities and legal practicalities know this is not the case.

Although access to 'regulated markets' and exchanges has been liberalised from a market perspective there are still too many regulatory and bureaucratic barriers which make it hard for issuers to make an effective use of this mutual recognition. Equally, the same situation can be assessed in the field of investment services where the seamless use of the single passport is far from having been achieved. An extensive and complete review of the Directives and in particular the ISD is required so as better to reflect the market change that is witnessed by exponential growth in equity volumes and the erosion of national financial frontiers.

For example, there is no harmonised definition of what constitutes a public offer in Europe, and conditions for admission to a regulated market are still very different across Member States. Continuing obligations of issuers have not been fully harmonised and in certain countries, the language in which the disclosure documents are written still remains an obstacle. In certain countries, consumer protection legislation is sometimes a bar to the use of a Directive. Finally, certain regulators are not necessarily displaying a great deal of enthusiasm in implementing the spirit of these Directives.

Directives are often the result of political compromises following protracted negotiations and bargaining. They end up being rather inflexible, almost impossible to alter once they are adopted and thus are rarely implemented into national laws uniformly and promptly. For example, the Public Offers of Securities Directive's stated objective of creating a level playing field in the information provided to investors throughout Europe has not been achieved.[12]

---

[12] Rubin Lee, 'Should there be a European Securities Commission? A Framework for Analysis' EBLR (1992).

Despite these efforts to regulate and harmonise EU capital markets, different rules and practices have developed in accordance with the history and the characteristics of each national market, in part due to national regulators' competition to develop the most attractive market environment and partly due to their unwillingness to assess the consequences of non-co-operation. The terms and conditions under which enterprises finance investment and the role of intermediaries still vary considerably from country to country in the European Union. This is due to deeply rooted structural differences in legal systems, development of markets and institutions, and the role of the State.[13] Each market's characteristics are the result of distinctive historical, political and cultural developments. The implementation of the Directives has not been consistent nor timely as these different philosophies continue to apply and influence political decisions. It is therefore not surprising that the Initial Lamfalussy Report indicated that the respondents to the Committee's survey quoted the inconsistent transposition of the directives as one of the main causes of the lack of harmonised securities regulation.

## 2   Movement towards integration of the European stock exchanges and clearing systems

The past couple of years have seen an increased awareness amongst European stock exchanges for the need to co-operate more closely and to consolidate. Yet it is only since 2000 that we have witnessed a flurry of 'demutualisation' and consolidation activities by the exchanges.[15] In spite of announcements last year of closer alliances between the leading eight European stock exchanges,[14] the reality is that most of the planned alliances have failed, with the notable exception of Euronext.

More interesting for the purpose of this chapter is the collapse of 'iX', which should have been the resulting entity following the merger of the LSE with Deutsche Börse. This 'merger of equals' was representing the coming together of the LSE and the Deutsche Börse (50% of share capital going to Deutsche Börse and 50% to LSE shareholders), creating what would have been the leading European exchange in terms of volume and value of equity trading.[16] Under the proposals, the 'blue chip' market would have been based in London whilst the European 'growth' technology and derivatives markets would have been located in Frankfurt.

The 'blue chip' market was supposed to be in London and subject to the UK's Financial Service Authority (FSA), while the Bundesaufsichtamt für den

---

[13] Karel Lannoo, 'The First Weeks in Euroland: A More Market-Based System to Emerge?' (1999) Journal of International Banking and Financial Law 14(3) 81.

[14] Amsterdam, Brussels, Madrid, Milan, Paris and Zurich stock exchanges signed a Memorandum of Understanding with London and Frankfurt to form the European Alliance.

[15] 'End of the Stock Exchange as a National Institution', Financial News, 29 May 2000.

[16] The exchanges accounted for over 50% of European equity traded volume in the 12 months up to 31 March 2000. In addition, 41% of Europe's top 300 companies have their primary listing on either the LSE or the Deutsche Börse.

Wertpapierhandel (BaWe) would have overseen the 'growth' and high technology stock markets. However, it is unclear as to how this dual regulation would have worked in practice (and indeed the role of the US NASDAQ *vis-à-vis* the growth market and whether a full merger would subsequently have meant a surrender of iX's dominant position in Europe for little return).[17]

The proposed merger collapsed as a result of a hostile take-over bid by OM of Sweden[18] and the scepticism of several important market players. One of the reasons for this scepticism was set out in a report issued by Merrill Lynch (advisers to the LSE). It was reported that:

> UK regulators believe Anglo-German *attempts to harmonise share trading rules will be 'a nightmare'* if the London Stock Exchange and Deutsche Börse merge to create iX. This emerged on Thursday as further details came to light from a report commissioned by Merrill Lynch, the investment bank advising the LSE. The report says senior staff at the Financial Services Authority have said privately that it will be difficult to achieve 'any practical level of harmonisation' of UK and German stock market regulations.[19]

In addition, the consolidation efforts of the national stock exchanges are forcing the various European settlement and clearing systems into pacts. At the start of 2000, Clearstream International ('Clearstream') was formed,[20] with currently €7 trillion worth of assets in custody and over 80 million transactions made each year, only to be followed by the Euroclear Clearance System ('Euroclear')[21] resulting in the world's largest settlement system for internationally traded securities. Its combined annual turnover value of transactions settled will exceed €80 trillion and its aggregate annual pre-netted transaction volumes will reach 100 million. Further consolidation is evidenced by the Settlement Alliance between London's CrestCo and the Swiss SIS (SegaInterSettle). CrestCo and Clearstream had also placed, as a top priority, discussions as to linking up their systems by virtue of the iX proposals.

Talk of big cost-savings to result from increased trading efficiency through combined exchanges would be futile unless we see a coming together of the different settlement and clearing systems in Europe. Whilst the issues surrounding the stock exchange mergers impinge on national sensibilities and therefore are overtly politically sensitive, the significance of unity among the clearing and settlement systems cannot be underestimated. Integration in this respect is the real prize and where the big cost-savings will be found.[22] At present, settlement costs in Europe can be as much as 10 times higher

---

[17] iX are in talks with NASDAQ 'To Explore the Possibility of a Complete Merger of the Markets'. The Financial Times, 18 July 2000.

[18] 'OM Posts Bid for London Stock Exchange', The Financial Times, 11 September 2000.

[19] 'FSA Staff Brand iX bourse a Regulation "Nightmare"' The, Financial Times, 7 September 2000.

[20] This represents the merger between Luxembourg-based Cedel International and Germany's Deutsche Börse Clearing (DBC) which was formalised on 10 January 2000.

[21] 'The Merger of Euroclear, Based in Brussels, and Paris' SICOVAM announced on 24 March 2000.

[22] 80% of potential savings will come from making the 'back office' process more efficient whilst only 20% will be attributable to trading efficiency.

than in the United States. Not only from a costs perspective, market players also want to see a real drive to create a centralised counterparty, enabling trades to be netted and thereby reducing counterparty risk. Influential market players, notably senior bankers at the US major investment banks, view this as an integral aspect of a flexible and liquid pan-European securities market.[23] More and more members of the securities industry agree that a Europe-wide central counterparty would be the solution which would enable a reduction of back office costs by avoiding duplicating technology investments.

Whatever the resistance of the clearing agencies could be, the financial community is aware of the necessity to examine and may change the clearing systems in Europe. The Commission itself declared on 20 February 2001 that it would have a serious look at the clearing system situation in Europe.[24] This position of the Commission follows the declaration made by the Committee of Wise Men having noticed that 'fragmented and high cost of processing trade in Europe [...], was a major factor holding back development of Europe's capital markets'. The Lamfalussy Report makes it clear that the EU executive should check if 'competition policy is being properly respected in this crucial sector' (i.e. clearing). Amelia Torres, spokeswoman for European Commissioner Mario Monti declared that although she was 'not aware that the Commission had received any formal complaints against existing clearers tying and exclusivity of clearing systems in Europe' were the sort of issue which would certainly pose competition concerns.

It is clear that the consolidation move within the clearing systems is necessary as such organisations lie at the very heart of an efficient and vibrant securities market.

### 3    The Lamfalussy Report – where to from here?

There is a certain degree of inevitability about the creation of some form of central regulator. The on going consolidation may be regarded as inevitable in the face of competition and indeed these mergers are sensible at least in principle, and will hopefully serve 'as a catalyst for new thinking',[25] one which ideally would lead to a consideration of a unified European regulator for a pan-European securities market. In light of the recent consolidation process of European stock exchanges, politicians are urgently pushing for the harmonisation of European securities regulations. For example, Laurent Fabius, the French Finance Minister, proposed a Working Group to take a comprehensive look at how to achieve a single market in financial services and the co-ordination of regulation at an EU level.[26] The work of the Committee of

---

[23] *See*, for example, the views of Pen Kent, Chairman of the European Securities Forum, and Sir David Walker, European Chairman of Morgan Stanley, the latter suggesting that if the big settlement organisations do not start to merge, then the big investment banks could break away and set up a NewCo running the system they want.

[24] Nick Antonovics, 'EU may Probe Clearing and Settlement in Europe', Reuters News, 20 February 2001.

[25] Editorial comment in The Financial Times, 18 July 2000.

[26] William Wright, 'Fabius in Push to Harmonise Rules', Financial News, 29 May 2000; 'Europe's Regulatory Muddles', The Economist, 10 June 2000.

the Wise Men as well as the Communication on Upgrading the Investment Services Directives[27] published by the European Commission in November 2000 form part of a concerted strategy to reinforce the EU's legislative framework for securities markets, following the Financial Services Action plan ('FSAP'). Essentially, the Committee of Wise Men's task was to determine and propose how to improve the process of rule-making, supervision and enforcement of EU rules in order for the EU to develop a coherent response to the fundamental changes sweeping through European financial markets.

The Interim Lamfalussy Report on 9 November 2000, reviewing the EU's current regulatory conditions and proposing tools to create a fully integrated financial market in the European Union.

The Interim Lamfalussy Report described the benefits of European financial integration, the trends in the European financial markets, and the shortcomings of the current European regulatory framework. The Committee stated that the current regulatory system is too slow and rigid, contains too much ambiguity resulting in inconsistent implementation, and relies heavily on European legislation to provide detailed rules.

With respect to European regulation, the Committee recommends in its interim report that one possible solution would be to introduce a four-level action plan to regulation, which involves:

- enacting an EU securities legislation that allows a framework of broad principles on various issues;
- creating (on the basis of the comitology procedure) an EU Securities Committee that would be responsible for the implementation of the broader EU legislation;
- having Member States responsible for implementing the community law in the context of enhanced and strengthened co-operation among the regulators; and
- strengthening enforcement of community rules through more vigorous action by the Commission and enhanced co-operation between the Member States and their regulators.

In the Lamfalussy Report, published on 15 February 2001, the Committee of Wise Men confirmed the approach put forward in its initial report and reiterated that the 'development of EU financial market development [is] hindered by a plethora of barriers' (e.g. the absence of clear Europe-wide regulation which prevents the mutual recognition system from working efficiently; the EU inefficient decision making system, the absence of common interpretations of rules, and the high cost of transactions due to the clearing and settlement system in place).

In the Lamfalussy Report the Committee has refined its approach, in particular in defining more precisely the content of the four levels of action set out above.

---

[27] Commission on line, 'Commission Urges Update of Current Rules to Spur Close Market Integration and Improve Investor Protection'; Securities markets, 16 November 2000.

As regards level 1, the Committee has defined its understanding of the framework principles. The Committee has declared that the purpose of level 1 is to fix the general regulatory principles and the nature and the extent of the technical implementation measures that should be taken at level 2 and the limits within which the resulting provisions can be adapted and updated and that the Commission should indicate the type of implementation details that could be covered at level 2.

Only the technical application of the essential elements defined at level 1 should be delegated to level 2.

According to the Committee the advantage of the new approach is that the legislative process would speed up because the key level 1 political co-decision negotiations between the Commission, the Council of Ministers and the European Parliament would focus only on the essential issues and not on technical implementation details. The process would also be democratic and flexible, the Committee having emphasised that it was of paramount importance to ensure that the Commission consult, in a very open, transparent and systematic way.

At level 2, the Committees would be set up by the end of 2001, that is, an EU securities committee with regulatory function and an EU Securities Regulators Committee with advisory functions.

The essence of level 3 would be to greatly improve the consistency of the day-to-day transposition and implementation of level 1 and 2 legislation. The national regulator would have the prime responsibility for this work, acting in a cooperative network.

Finally, level 4's aim is to guarantee the enforcement of community rule. To that end, the Committee has suggested that the Commission should be 'bolder in enforcing community law and checking the accurate transposition of agreed legislation.' The Committee of Wise Men has made clear in its final report that it disagreed with the current practice by which the opening of a case by the European Commission results in rapid solutions being agreed with the offending Member State.

The Committee has expressly proposed that a strong reporting and monitoring system is put in place at level 4 to identify the bottlenecks and responsibilities but has surprisingly remained silent on how to sanction any breach of community law.

A full review of the implementation of the Lamfalussy Report should take place in 2004, coinciding with the next Inter-Governmental Conference.

In addition, it is expected that one of the next steps is the upgrading of the ISD. Internal Market Commissioner Frits Bolkestein said:

We need to update the Union's securities markets legislation to reflect profound changes in securities trading infrastructure, exchanges, clearing, and settlement systems since the Investment Services Directive came into force five years ago. Under the influence of the euro and new technologies the pace of change can only accelerate. We want to ensure that the new rules protect investors, promote orderly, efficient and integrated markets, and preserve financial stability. We have launched this review of the legislation in order to encourage as wide a range of contributions as possible from all interested parties, including the European Parliament, national authorities, market players and regulators.

The European Commission has launched in particular via its Communication on Upgrading the ISD an extensive review on how this legislation, now in force for five years, could be best updated to reflect the profound changes in investment services and the securities trading infrastructure in the European Union. The Upgrading of the Financial Securities Directive has been identified by the Commission as one of its ten priorities under the Financial Services Action Plan (FSAP).

This report, as part of the level 1 actions recommended by the Lamfalussy Report and the transparency and democratic recommendation made by the Committee of Wise Men is currently circulated for consultation.

The Communication charts two broad areas of working and the consultation, which will run until 31 March 2001 and take into account the Lamfalussy Report, will focus on (i) how to create the legal environment in which the passport can become effective immediately for inter-professional business; (ii) be progressively extended to cover provision of services to retail investors; and (iii) what is the appropriate regulatory framework for the trading infrastructure.

The Commission has proceeded to a general assessment of whether or not national authorities are implementing conduct of business rules in conformity with the principles and requirements laid down in Article 11 of the ISD.

According to the Commission it might be useful ultimately, to amend the ISD to further clarify its application in some areas. The Communication is rather instructive in this respect as it offers the Commission's view on how national authorities could comply better with the stipulations of Article 11. For example, it suggests that Member States could all agree to use the FESCO (Forum of European Securities Commissions) definition of what constitutes a professional investor. It also suggests that Member States might choose to apply host country rules only to retail investors, rather than to professionals. The logic here is that retail investors, since they are not 'professional' need the additional protection of home country rules.

The Commission has also identified certain areas in which compliance by Member States with relatively clear and unconditional provisions of the ISD has been less than systematic. The Commission has made it clear that these areas will be scrutinised and closely controlled particularly now that the concept of 'professional investor' for the purposes of Article 11(1) has been clarified in the Communication.

The application of host country rules in the interest of investor protection is another area of concern for the Commission as it is an evident hurdle to the cross-border provision of investment services. This Commission is of the view that the upgrading of the ISD should also aim to clarify jurisdictional issues so as to better reconcile investor protection with the proper functioning of the 'single passport'. It should aim to allow inter-professional business to take place subject only to home-country rules.

New proposals to this effect should coincide with the entry into force of the E-commerce Directive (17 January 2002) under which investment firms should be able to provide investment services electronically, subject only to the rules of their country of origin (IP/00/442). The application of the country of origin principle could mean that the current role for host country authorities is heavily circumscribed (there are limited derogations to the internal market clause of the E-commerce

Directive, but they are strictly delineated). In upgrading the ISD the Commission will aim to identify and create the legal and practical conditions for smooth transition to country of origin for provision of investment services to retail investors.

As mentioned above, the Commission will be waiting for the results of the consultation process to help determine its future approach. No need to say that it can take quite a long time to conclude the co-decision process for formal adoption of legislation proposals (i.e. 2–3 years) followed by a 1–2 year period for national transposition which is probably far too long and could be reduced if the appropriate method is applied. The proposals of the Wise Men and the Commission, if they correspond to what is currently legally feasible, are probably not the best way to build an efficient legal framework in the EU securities market of tomorrow. Albeit theoretically faster (though the Comitology procedure has been seldom used and with very limited success), the Lamfalussy Report recommendations still rely largely on directives and the co-operation of the regulators. Whilst reinforced, this system is, in essence, the same as the system which has, so far, failed to deliver the necessary level of action. Mr Dirk Tirez, for instance, recently declared that in his view:

> they [the EU Wise Men] look at what is achievable at the level of the European Ministers of Finance [the Ecofin Council]. This is the right direction, but I think what is important is that the Lamfalussy report clearly made an economic and financial analysis of what is needed. They clearly understand the *need* for an integrated European market, and they have recommended action which it is feasible to achieve in the short term.

But this is not necessarily the best way to guarantee the success of a pan-European project, that is, a single set of rules, a single trading system, and single settlement system. A European 'Securities Exchange Commission' (SEC) would be, according to the author of the Chapter, the real answer allowing in particular truly pan-European transactions.

Another initiative drive in Europe comes from the FESCO, an organisation formed by the national supervisors of the European Economic Area (EEA),[28] which strives towards closer co-operation in regulatory work, information exchange and joint research in order to boost transparency, harmonisation and integrity of the European markets in the aftermath of the introduction of the euro. In December 2002 European regulators took a major step towards a more unified approach within the EEA when FESCO adopted common standards for regulated markets.[29] These standards are intended to supplement the requirements of the ISD and they will be

---

[28] It came into being when the 17 securities commissions of the EEA signed a Charter in December 1997. The European Commission attends FESCO meetings as an observer. FESCOPOL was established in January, 1999 to facilitate effective, efficient and pro-active sharing of information to enhance co-operation and co-ordination of surveillance between FESCO Members.

[29] 'Standards for Regulated Markets under the ISD', 99-FESCO-C, 22 December 1999. In finalising the paper, FESCO consulted the Federation of European Stock Exchanges (FESE) and the European Community Option and Futures Exchanges (ECOFEX).

introduced into each FESCO Member's regulatory objectives and ideally and where possible, in their respective rules. FESCO is also pushing for a 'European Passport' for issuers, enabling an EU-wide offering of securities by reducing regulatory hurdles without compromising investor protection. Whilst FESCO's work is commended as a major step in reducing cross-border inconsistencies and thereby improving investor protection, FESCO is still in its infancy and has yet to prove that informal cooperation will be adequate for proper and effective regulation of Europe's financial markets. Almost certainly, in the longer term, as markets become more integrated, there will be pressure for a more coordinated and formal approach to rule-making and enforcement in a common institutional framework for a truly integrated market.[30] We could wait until necessity forces some Community action, but it would be better to take anticipatory action to support the financial markets.

In essence, relying on the sum of the parts of the European regulatory jigsaw to create a unified European regulatory structure might overlook the fact that national regulators may have diverging, rather than converging interests and agendas. If EMU and the resulting creation of the European Central Bank ('ECB') and the European System of Central Banks ('ESCB') is anything to go by, it is clear that the impetus had to be, first and foremost, imposed by political will before being successfully implemented and supported by the national central banks (NCBs) and other relevant domestic regulators.

PART III

*1   The case for an ESC*

In its FSAP issued in 2002, the Commission acknowledged that the current *ad hoc* organisation cannot keep up with the rapid market integration and that more changes to the current system are needed before Europe has a single, homogenous, capital market. Furthermore, the paper called for 'any remaining capital market fragmentation [to be] eliminated'[31] and suggested that a 'more wide-ranging rethink of the way in which policy for financial markets is processed is required'.[32]

The fragmented regulatory structure is such that competition between national governments to satisfy their domestic constituents naturally encourages protection of their own interests. Indeed it is difficult to justify why market participants should deal with such varying complexities and the cost of compliance with several quite different national laws when they are dealing, or would want to deal, with only one euro-denominated securities market. It will be impossible to stimulate full cross-border competition in the financial services industry unless a single, expert, flexible

---

[30]   Michael Taylor, 'A European SEC?' (September 1998) FRR, p. 1.

[31]   The European Commission, '*Implementing the Framework for Financial Markets: Action Plan*' (May 1999) p. 1.

[32]   The European Commission, *ibid.*, at p. 14.

and forward-thinking regulatory body is established, one which is able to enforce its policies uniformly throughout the European Union. Otherwise with the (relatively) weak regulatory framework which applies in the euro-zone, we run the serious risk of undermining the entire EMU. One should note that the ECB, the only pan-European regulator for the euro-zone, does not have any jurisdiction over the securities markets[33] although its example might provide a starting point of a radical re-think.

There is consensus that the status quo needs improvement as evidenced by the various on-going initiatives across Europe. The question then becomes one which considers the need and scope for an ESC. Opponents of an ESC have doubted the viability of such a body on constitutional grounds and also fear the enormous costs required in setting up and operating it. ESC-sceptics have furthermore argued that the notion of a supra-national supervisor is not a pragmatic solution.[34] It is argued that given the fragmented nature of Europe's securities markets, it is untenable since such an idea presupposes that Member States are willing to make political concessions as well as complete harmonised regulations, technologies and infrastructure. There is an immediate need first for more harmonisation of securities market regulation. Thus, at this stage it is more important to strengthen co-operation between Member States through international movements like IOSCO and FESCO rather than opt for a 'wholesale' change.

Many have strongly doubted the feasibility of the single currency and, likewise have been negative about an ESC. However, often the same opponents see the benefits of a single national regulator for various market segments/products, as it offers 'one-stop shopping' for market participants with improved economies of scale as a result of pooled resources and management, lower supervisory costs and more transparent to consumers than with a fragmented system. Already this rationale has been entrenched in various European countries (e.g. United Kingdom, Germany, Sweden, Denmark, Norway, Iceland, Finland) as well as further afield as Japan and South Korea more recently.[35] If this reasoning is correct at a national level, it should logically apply at the European level, in the context of a single currency, a single market, free capital flows and an increasingly global market place. Debating the desirability of an ESC is putting off the inevitable. If the US precedent is anything to learn from (as discussed below) the initial reluctance to adopt federal regulation fell away in the face of the Wall Street Crash of 1929.

In response, the author would counter such arguments by submitting that an ESC is entirely plausible in the present institutional EU framework and that such a body

---

[33] The ECB role is limited to monetary matters. For further information on the ECB's jurisdiction, *see* the ECB's website: <http://www.ecb.int>. Also *see* Erwin Nierop, 'A New corpris iuris monetae for Europe' (2000) BJIB&FL 15(5), p. 157. Butterworths Journal of International Banking and Financial Law.

[34] See, for example, Karel Lannoo, 'A European SEC? (Part II)' (March 2000) FRR, p. 1; James W F Watson, 'International Co-operation in the Field of Financial Regulatory Enforcement, Part 2 – the EU approach' (2000) JIBFL 15(1), p. 13; Clive Briault, 'The Rationale for a Single National Financial Services Regulator' Financial Services Authority Occasional Paper Series No. 2, May 1999).

[35] Clive Briault, *ibid.*, at pp. 11–12. In addition, very recently, Luxembourg introduced its Financial Sector Surveillance Commission.

would assist in the furtherance of the harmonisation and integration of securities regulations. First, let us turn to constitutional matters.

*1.1  Constitutional Issues*

Some commentators have objected to the creation of the ESC on the grounds of a lack of a constitutional basis. Their objection rests on the theory that the European Community (EC) is based on the principle of limited or conferred powers, that is, Community institutions possess only those powers conferred on them. It has been suggested that creating such a body would involve amending the Treaty; that the Treaty is silent on how and by whom any centralised policies on financial services should be implemented;[36] and that the EU authorities have no power under present Treaty provisions to establish new organisations entrusted with rule or policy-making powers.[37]

A detailed analysis of these issues, the interpretation of relevant Treaty provisions and European precedent and practice has been outlined by the author in a previous articlei.[38] It suffices to say in summary that the practical significance of the concept of conferred powers is diminished mainly by Article 308 (better known under its old number of Article 235 used by many EC Regulations) of the Treaty, upon which the formation of a body such as the proposed ESC can be legitimately based. Article 308, in essence, grants power to the European Council to take any steps to take whatever measures are necessary to attain the objectives of the Community. Whilst the scope of Article 308 is not without limitations,[39] it is argued that the formation of an ESC falls within its scope on the basis that such a body is required to foster greater economic cohesion. A review of the practical application of Article 308 in EU jurisprudence will illustrate that this Article has been interpreted in such a wide and radical manner,[40]

---

[36] Howard Davies, Chairman of the FSA, in his speech on 'Euro-Regulation' at the European Financial Forum Lecture in Brussels (8 April 1999).

[37] Eddy Wymeersch, 'From Harmonisation to Integration in the European Securities Markets', *Journal of Comparative Corporate Law and Securities Regulation* (1981) 3, 1.

[38] Gilles Thieffry, 'Towards a European Securities Commission' *op. cit.*, note 7.

[39] For a judicial commentary on the limitations of Art. 308, *see Opinion 2/94 (Re the Accession of the Community to the ECHR [1996] ECR I-1759 2 Common Market Law Reports 265)* which concerned the legality of using Art. 308 (or Art. 235 as it then was) to accede to the 'ECHR'. The court stated that accession to the ECHR would result in a *substantial change in the present Community system* for the protection of human rights, as it would involve the Community entering into a distinct international institutional system as one of integration of all the provisions of the Convention into the Community legal order. As this was of constitutional significance, it would be such as to go beyond the scope of Art. 235. *See* also Paul Beaumont, 'The European Community Cannot Accede to the ECHR' Edinburgh Law Review pp. 235–249. It is submitted that the formation of an ESC is not a substantial change in the Community system; the single currency and single market already exist and it is simply contended that the securities markets be regulated at a European level, in order to protect the integrity of the single currency and the single market, or to adopt the wording of Art. 2 of the Treaty, to 'strengthen economic ... cohesion'.

[40] Art. 235 has been applied in the context of the European Monetary Co-operation Fund; harmonisation of certain aspects of company law; the granting of emergency food aid to developing countries; and the establishment of European Economic Interest Groupings (EEIGs). It was also used to implement certain regulatory provisions applicable to the introduction of the euro.

that 'it would become virtually impossible to find an activity which could not be brought within the objectives of the Treaty'.[41]

There are two schools of thought in the debate as to the institutional form the European supervisor should take. The first suggestion is closer cooperation between Member States' existing regulators at national and EU levels. We have already visited this point and we concluded that the measures being discussed and implemented remain crucial in the harmonisation exercise but also questioned the efficacy of such informal co-operation continuing in the long term. Thus, we turn to the alternative school of thought, which suggests the notion of a supranational body, akin to the ECB in the banking industry, but one with powers broadly similar to those of the US Securities Exchange Commission ('SEC').[42]

## 1.2    The US SEC Precedent

Proponents have often cited the American SEC as the only real precedent in this field.[43] The history behind the SEC will demonstrate the relevance of that parallel, and how much it might help us shape future European regulation. The SEC, created in July 1934 under the Securities Exchange Act 1934, is an independent, quasi-judicial body empowered to regulate and primarily supervise the US securities markets.

### 1.2.1    A Potted History

Its origins date back to an era that was ripe for reform at a time when the United States was in deep depression following the Crash of 1929. Prior to the 1929 Crash, there were problems of non-disclosure, questionable promotional practices and the marketing of fraudulently valued securities resulting in spiralling market speculation and the huge increase in trading on margin.

At that time also, politically, economically and between regulators, there was fragmentation, ineffective delegation and non-cooperation. It was a case of everybody 'cooperating', but without a unified market perspective and without the power to act swiftly before the crisis hit. Responsibility for market regulation fell to several different authorities. No one took action either because they simply did not want to assume responsibility for the crash or because another authority disagreed. For example, bodies such as the Investment Bankers Association (IBA) resisted 'undesired regulation' and advocated the application of generic fraud laws, which did not include the demand for full financial disclosure.[44] The lack of central regulation therefore gave rise to the opportunity for widespread market manipulation by market players and private organisations.

---

[41] J. Weiler, 'The Transformation of Europe' (1991) 100 Yale Law Journal 2403, at 2445–2446.

[42] Karel Lannoo, 'Financial Supervision in EMU' (1999) CEPS, Brussels, pp. 5–15.

[43] The SEC has long placed consumer protection in a level playing field as its primary goal. 'We are the investor's advocate' is the often cited motto of William O. Douglas, SEC Chairman (1937–39), which features prominently on the SEC website: <http://www.sec.gov>.

[44] Bealing, Dirsmith and Fogarty, 'Early Regulatory Actions by the SEC: An Institutional Theory Perspective on the Dramaturgy of Political Exchanges', Accounting Organisations and Society (1966), 21(4), 317–338.

Between 1910 and 1933, most States had enacted their 'blue sky laws'[45] to prevent the growing fraudulent securities dealing and trading on margin. Each State had a bureau and a commission to implement the laws and their administrative functions were mainly to investigate dealings and to require the disclosure of certain information (not unlike the powers of the SEC today, one might say!) before determining whether such securities could be sold within the State. Yet the inadequacy of State legislation soon became apparent. First, some State legislatures chose not to adopt the legislation. Others followed the precedent of those States with legislation in place, but they would 'tinker' here and there in trying to improve the legislation in places. In many cases, there was a reluctance of State legislatures to provide for effective enforcement. Consequently, similar to the varying regulatory levels between Member States in modern-day Europe, it quickly became apparent that 'there [was]… a lamentable lack of uniformity in [the State securities laws]'.[46] This enabled fraudulent dealers to 'forum shop', that is, choose the State with the least or no regulation to evade liability (once again, a concern outlined for today's European regulators). With increasing inter-state business in the 'boom years', it became extremely difficult for a State to attempt to protect its citizens against mail-order selling campaigns. The State could not prosecute the promoters because they were not committing their offences within the State borders, but their acts had the effect of nullifying the State laws. '[T]he most effective and widely used method for evading the provisions of State blue sky laws consists in operating across State lines' was the conclusion reached in a Department of Commerce Report in 1933.[47] Even at this stage a single regulatory system was called for, on the basis that 'unless the Federal Government takes action to control inter-state commerce in fraudulent securities the laws of the several States will in a large measure become ineffective'.[48]

### 1.2.2 The Case for Federal Regulation

The concept of federal regulation of exchanges was strongly resisted in the US before the 1930s, some doubting the constitutional ability of Congress to legislate for what were essentially voluntary organisations, just as in Europe today.[49] Yet, in 1923

---

[45] Kansas is credited for the first 'blue sky law' in 1911 when it introduced the first comprehensive licensing system. There are numerous explanations for the derivation of the term 'blue sky', the most common of which is that the purpose of the Kansas' statute was to protect Kansas farmers against the industrialists selling them to 'building lots in the blue sky in fee simple'; Thomas L Hazen, *Treatise on the Law of Securities* (3rd edn, 1995) Vol. 1.

[46] Statement of Hon. Edward E. Denison, Representative of Congress from the State of Illinois, Subcommittee of the Committee on Interstate Commerce (6 December 1922) 2.

[47] Department of Commerce, 'A study of the Economic and Legal Aspects of the Proposed Federal Securities Act' submitted for hearings before the House Committee on Interstate and Foreign Commerce, HR 4314, 73rd Cong., 1st Sess. 87, 100 (1933).

[48] *Op. cit.*, note 59 at p. 3.

[49] A series of cases in the early 1920s regarding federal legislation in various areas such as the federal taxing power and the Child Labor Tax for example in *The Bailey Case* 259 US 20 42 Sup Ct 449, had held that federal legislation that intended to do merely what State legislation could and should do was unconstitutional. The Future Trading Act of 1923 was held to be invalid in *Hill v Wallace* 259 US 44 42 Sup Ct 453. This was on the basis that it was a device to regulate the boards of trade, that Congress lacked the power to do so because when enacted they had not had the commerce power in mind.

a Supreme Court decision confirmed that the enactment by Congress of federal legislation (on any subject-matter including the regulation of securities) in reliance on the 'commerce power' would be held constitutional and perfectly acceptable.[50]

The case for federal regulation and an SEC-styled organisation was not without momentum in the late 1920s. For example, such a body was recommended as early as 1909 by Charles E Hughes in relation to insurance companies.[51] The Hughes Report of 1909 highlighted the need to 'adopt methods to compel the filing of the financial condition of the companies who are listed' and various other requirements similar to those eventually imposed in 1934. It recognised the need for some sort of a 'planned economy' in the monetary field, to prevent the excessive flow of credit into the New York money market from being destructive to legitimate business throughout the country. On another occasion, the Pujo Report in 1913 also recommended similar action.[52] In 1922, Congressman Denison proposed Bill 11. R. 10508, which sought to introduce federal regulation for securities.[53] It is clear then that the Americans 'recognised that this required federal legislation, that it was beyond the power of a single State'.[54] Following the enactment of these early State securities laws and the posturing over proposals for a SEC-type body, the straw that finally broke the camel's back came when the stock markets crashed in 1929.[55]

In 1932, while depression continued throughout the US economy, commentators realised that dismissing the concept of federal regulation was only possible if one were convinced that the numerous separate exchanges were enforcing the highest practicable standard of business ethics. If there was even the slight likelihood that central governmental intervention could better the situation, then this required action from Congress.[56]

In March 1932, Senate Resolution No. 84 was agreed to, which authorised the Committee on Banking and Currency to investigate the practices of buying and selling securities and devise some appropriate legislation. In particular, the Report of

---

[50] In 1923, the Future Trading Act 1923 was re-enacted as the Grain Futures Act. Essentially there are no real differences between the two Acts other than the fact that the latter was correctly based upon the commerce power and not described as a tax measure. This made it valid, as held in *Board of Trade of the City of Chicago* v *Olsen* 262 US 1, 37, 43 Sup Ct 470. This mere technicality of a proper legal basis mirrors the current debate concerning the suitability of Art. 235 as a foundation for the ESC.

[51] Congressional Records – House 1934 at p. 7927.

[52] Congressional Records, *ibid.*, at p. 7927.

[53] This was on the basis that 'the Federal Government alone can stop such commerce, and the Federal Government ought to co-operate with the several States'. It was felt that for the welfare of the Nation all powers to control or regulate interstate commerce ought to be surrendered to the Federal Government. Although the bill was approved by the executive committee of the National Association of State Securities Commissioners, the Investment Bankers' Association refused to accept the more stringent approach and due to their size and strength in the market the bill was not passed.

[54] Congressional Records, *op. cit.*, note 64 at p. 7927.

[55] The aggregate value of all stocks listed on the New York Stock Exchange fell from US$89 billion (in September 1929) to US$15 billion (in 1932). Bond losses increased the total depreciation to US$93 billion.

[56] John Hanna, 'The Federal Regulation of Stock Exchanges' (1931) Southern California Law Review, 32, Vol. V.

the Committee commented that attempts by individual State exchanges 'far from precluding the necessity for [federal] legislative action, emphasise its need'.[57] President Roosevelt, in 1934, spoke of how 'the unregulated speculation in securities and commodities was one of the most important contributing factors in the artificial and unwarranted boom which had so much to do with the terrible conditions of the years following 1929' and identified the need for 'legislation with teeth in it', under which the Government could itself correct future abuses should they arise.[58] The case for a federal regulator was clearly defined in the Fletcher Report of 1934:

> The contention of stock exchange authorities that internal regulation obviates the need for governmental control seems unsound for several reasons. In the first place, however zealously exchange authorities may supervise the business conduct of their members, the interests with which they are connected frequently conflict with the public interest. Secondly, the securities exchanges have broadened the scope of their activities to the point where they are no longer isolated institutions, but have become an important element in the credit structure of the country that regulation, to be effective, must be integrated with the protection of our entire financial system and the national economy. Thirdly, the control exercised by stock exchange authorities is admittedly limited to their own members, and they are unable to cope with those practices of those non-members which they deplore but cannot prevent. Fourthly, the attitude of exchange authorities toward the nature and scope of the regulation required appears to be sharply at variance with the modern conception of the extent to which the public welfare must be guarded in financial matters. Their adherence to the view that manipulation, pool activities, and the creation of illusory 'price mirages' are proper and legitimate, except where certain technical violations of their rules are involved, is inconsistent with the type of regulation the public interest demands.[59]

Today, the SEC has transformed into a highly successful 'super' federal agency, its framework much admired and modelled around the world. Its extensive legislative powers derived from various provisions of the federal securities laws (including the ability to issue interpretative rules) has resulted in a flexible regulatory environment that upholds Congress' primary objective in 1934 – investor confidence – whilst allowing the market to develop on its own and the SEC adapting its rules to accommodate any new developments. Crucial to the SEC's effectiveness as regulator is its Division of Enforcement, which investigates all potential violations of each act that the SEC administers, for example, insider dealing, accounting fraud, and false or misleading information about companies. Finally, through its Divisions and Offices, the

---

[57] Senate Report No. 792 of 73D Congress 2d Session on the Federal Securities Exchange Act of 1934. Senator Fletcher, at p. 4.

[58] Letter from President F.D. Roosevelt to the Chairman of the Committee on Banking and Currency, 26 March 1934.

[59] 'Federal Securities Act of 1934' in *Fletcher Report from Committee of Banking and Currency* (17 April 1934), 73D Congress, 2D session, p. 2.

SEC maintains close communication with other federal agencies, the self-regulatory organisations (e.g. stock exchanges) and the State securities regulators.

## 1.3　The ECB as a Model?[60]

If one is not persuaded by the American SEC precedent, then one could look closer to home to the ECB, 'guardian of the European currency constitution', as a plausible working model for a pan-European securities regulator. Clearly, the analogy between the ECB and ESC is only valid from an institution stand-point and not from a purely regulatory view point. The ECB is in charge of the monetary policy of the euro-zone and banking regulation has been left with the central banks. However, an analysis of the institutional structure of the ECB[61] will hopefully provide some clues as to how a proposed ESC might operate albeit with a very different jurisdiction.

The Treaty and the Statute of the ESCB and of the ECB (the 'Statute'), which is annexed to the Treaty as a Protocol,[62] establish the ESCB. The ESCB consists of the ECB and the NCBs of the 15 EU Member States. When the euro was finally introduced on 1 January 1999, these 11 NCBs submitted their competence with regard to monetary policy to the ECB. As there are (presently) four Member States not participating in the single currency,[63] the term 'Eurosystem' has been coined to refer to the ECB and the 11 NCBs who have adopted the euro, as distinguished from the ESCB.

The Eurosystem's primary objective is price stability and in keeping with this objective, the Treaty and the Statute impose certain tasks upon the Eurosystem, *inter alia*, to define and implement monetary policy of euro land; to conduct foreign exchange operations; to manage the official reserves of Member States; and to issue euro banknotes.[64]

The ECB, recognised as a legal personality[65] under public international law, is able to participate in matters relating to its field of competence (i.e. monetary policy). Although the ECB has overall responsibility for its mandate, it adheres to the principle of decentralisation (or 'subsidiary'), that is, 'to the extent deemed possible and appropriate [...], the ECB shall have recourse to the NCBs to carry out operations which form part of the tasks of the ESCB'.[66]

### 1.3.1　Policy-Making Ability

In order to carry out these tasks (those are clearly limited to the monetary field), the ECB has been given regulatory powers through which it may adopt a variety of

---

[60] For background reading, *see* the *ECB Monthly Bulletin*, July 1999, pp. 55–63, and the *ECB Annual Report* 1999. *See* also Erwin Nierop, *op. cit.*

[61] For a more detailed discussion, *see* J.A. Usher *The Law of Money and Financial Services in the European Community* (OUP, 2000).

[62] Protocol No.18 to the Treaty, OJC 191, 29 July 1992.

[63] The four Member States are Denmark, Greece, Sweden and the UK.

[64] Arts 2 and 3 of the Statute.

[65] Art. 9.1 of the Statute.

[66] Art. 12.1 of the Statute.

legal acts.[67] The types of legal acts range from Regulations to Guidelines. Regulations, in accordance with normal EU law principles, are directly applicable in all Member States although in the context of EMU, they are only binding on the Eurosystem. These have been effected in areas such as minimum reserves,[68] the collation of statistical data[69] and more importantly, sanctions.[70] At the other end of the scale, are Recommendations and Opinions, which are regarded as authoritative statements from the ECB *albeit* without binding effect. The ECB, more commonly, issue Guidelines addressed to the NCBs and these will normally require implementation through the adoption or adjustment of national legislation and regulatory rules. The ESCB and the Eurosystem are governed by the decisions made by the various ECB decision-making bodies: the Governing Council, the Executive Board (and for as long as there are Member States who have not yet adopted the euro, the General Council).[71] The Governing Council, which consists of members of the Executive Board and the Governors of the NCBs within the 'Eurosystem', is the supreme decision-making body. On the other hand, the Executive Board is there to implement monetary policy in accordance with the guidelines and decisions laid down by the Governing Council by instructing the NCBs accordingly.[72]

### 1.3.2 Independence and Accountability

Another important facet of the institutional framework of the ECB, which lends it creditability as a centralised European regulator, is its independence – both from a financial and an institutional perspective. The ECB has its own budget, independent from that of the European Union, thereby avoiding any interference from any Community institutions with its administration. In addition to having personal independence for members of the ECB's decision-making bodies and for the ECB's personnel, its accounts are audited by independent external auditors.[73] Countervailing this high degree of independence are the requirements of accountability on the part of the ECB (by way of weekly financial statements and Annual Reports and for the President of the ECB to appear before the European Parliament to report on various issues[74]) and judicial scrutiny of its 'acts and omissions', including those *vis-à-vis* NCBs, which are subject to review and interpretation by the ECJ.[75]

---

[67] Arts 34.1 and 34.2 of the Statute

[68] Regulation (EC) No. 2818/98 of the EBB, 1 December 1998.

[69] Regulation (EC) No. 2819/98 of the ECB, 1 December 1998.

[70] Regulation (EC) No. 2157/99 of the ECB, 23 September 1999.

[71] The General Council, comprising the members of the Executive Board and the Governors of all 15 NCBs, takes over the matters from the European Monetary Institute by virtue of the fact that some Member States have yet to adopt the euro and thus, the ECB is still charged with implementing the final stage of EMU. This primarily involves reporting on the progress made towards convergence by the non-participating Member States and advising on the necessary preparations for irrevocably fixing currency exchange rates of these Member States.

[72] Arts 10–12 of the Statute.

[73] Art. 27.1 of the Statute.

[74] Art. 15 of the Statute.

[75] Art. 35.1 of the Statute.

### 1.3.3    Powers of Enforcement

The ECB's role as a regulator is further strengthened by its ability to impose sanctions relating to 'infringements' (defined as any failure by an undertaking to fulfil an obligation arising from ECB regulations or decisions[76]). To this end, the ECB is entitled to impose fines or periodic payments after it, through the Executive Board or the 'competent NCB's'[77] investigation,[78] concludes with its decision which may be published in the Official Journal. These fines and periodic payments are subject to upper limits (€500,000 and €10,000 per day in respect of a maximum period of six months, respectively) and are arguably not sufficiently onerous.

It is clear that the ECB, an independent body entrusted with Community-wide monetary policy for EMU, could usefully provide lessons for a new ESC. In overseeing EMU, the ECB is able to issue legal acts which impact directly on Member States. Furthermore, the concession of sovereignty in respect of monetary matters by the 11 NCBs suggests that this political issue is not entirely insurmountable (but not without difficulties!). This is evidenced by the close cooperation of the NCBs in the Governing Council. Finally, its ability to impose sanctions for infringements lends great credence to the ECB as a pan-European regulator.

### 1.3.4    The ECB/ESCB Model for an ESC

It is certainly feasible to imagine the creation of an ESC, setting pan-European rules and principles which would then be implemented, under ESC supervision, by each existing national regulator. The first type of underlying objection to the creation of an ESC rests on the theory that the European Community (EC) is based on the principle of limited or conferred powers – that is, that EC institutions possess only those powers conferred on them. It has been suggested that creating such a body would involve amending the Treaty establishing the EC; that the Treaty is silent on how and by whom any centralised policies on financial services should be implemented; and that the EC authorities have no power under present Treaty provisions to establish new organisations entrusted with rule or policy-making powers.

These objections are ill-conceived and short-sighted. It is true, for example, that there is no express mention of an ESC within the Treaty. But at the time of drafting the Treaty the ultimate (and seemingly unattainable) goal was the introduction of the single currency – to prevent proper regulation of the securities market on the basis that the draftsmen had simply not thought this far ahead is irresponsible. I shall answer these objections by looking into the Treaty, its interpretation and European precedent and practice.

The second type of objection revolves around the actual need to create a pan-European regulator. The only relevant precedent in this field can be found in the United States and the creation of the SEC; and it will be clear that parallels can be

---

[76] Art. 1.4 of Council Regulation (EC) No. 2532/98 of 23 November 1998, OJ 1998 L318/4. In this context, 'undertakings' is widely defined in Art. 1.3.

[77] Defined as the NCB of the Member State in whose jurisdiction the alleged infringement has occurred: Art. 1 of the ECB Regulation (EC) No. 2157/1999, *op. cit.*, note 83.

[78] Here, the ECB also has relatively extensive investigatory powers in the conduct of its inquiry – *see* Arts 3–9 of the ECB Regulation, *ibid.*

drawn between the United States and Europe. Once more, history will prove the relevance of that parallel and how much it should help us in designing the future.

The practical significance of the concept of conferred powers is diminished mainly by the existence of Art. 235 (which has now become Art. 308) of the Treaty, upon which the formation of a body such as the proposed ESC can be properly based. This provides that:

> If action by the Community should prove necessary to attain, in the course of the operation of the Common Market, one of the objectives of the Community and this Treaty has not provided the necessary powers, the Council shall, acting unanimously on a proposal from the Commission and after consulting the European Parliament, take the appropriate measures.

Essentially therefore, this article grants power to take whatever measures are necessary to attain the objectives of the EC. To understand fully the ambit of the power it is necessary to consider the procedural and substantive requirements of the article.

In summary, to be beyond challenge by EC institutions at a later stage, legislation must be necessary to attain an objective of the Community. This must take place within the operation of the Common Market and the measure must be appropriate. Finally, there must be no specific powers provided for elsewhere in the Treaty. This final element can be disregarded as I agree with the opinion that the Treaties are silent on the formation of this body (although I disagree with the conclusion that this will prevent its establishment altogether).

The objective is contained in Article 2 of the Treaty:

> the Community shall have as its task, by establishing a common market and an EMU and by implementing common policies or activities referred to in Articles 3 and 4, to promote throughout the Community a harmonious, balanced and sustainable development of economic activities and economic and social cohesion and solidarity among Member States.

and Article 3.1(c) and (g) provide:

> 1. For the purposes set out in Article 2, the activities of the Community shall include, as provided in this Treaty and in accordance with the timetable set out therein:
>    (c) an internal market characterised by the abolition, as between Member States, of obstacles to the free movement of goods, persons, services and capital; and
>    (g) a system ensuring that competition in the internal market is not distorted.

It is safe to assume that this objective will be accepted by the European Court of Justice (ECJ). Opinion 2/94 (the key case law on the ambit of Article 235) stated that the limitation to Article 235 was that it cannot serve as the basis for widening the scope of EC powers beyond the framework created by the Treaty taken as a whole, and in particular by those provisions that define tasks and activities of the EC.

The reference to 'tasks' echoes the wording of Article 2 of the Treaty and the reference to 'activities' picks up the language of Articles 3 and 3a of the Treaty. So it is reasonable to assume that the Court considers that the objectives of the EC are principally set out in Articles 2, 3 and 4 of the Treaty (see, e.g., Paul Beaumont ELR Vol. 1 1975). Moreover, since Article 235 does not specifically refer to those objectives it might be possible to infer additional objectives from other provisions of the Treaty.

The next stage is to show that EC action is 'necessary' to attain it. This is not merely a decision of fact but involves a great deal of discretion on the part of the European institutions and will be made, at least in the first instance, by the Commission and the Council. This should provide some comfort when one considers the robust way in which the Commission has interpreted the powers given to it in other contexts (e.g. in the field of competition law).

Despite this, the case for the ESC must be set out strongly, as there is a difference between something that would promote an objective of the EC and one that is absolutely necessary to achieve it. This is a far harsher test but one that can be satisfied. The need to avoid arbitrage and forum shopping, the need for the uniform implementation of rules and policies, and the need to protect investors and to control the market are clearly of paramount importance. A single regulatory body is the only method of properly achieving this, but it may be argued (against all evidence) that the present system could achieve these goals and that these objectives, while desirable, are not necessities. More importantly though, we all know that events in the securities markets (and the related derivatives market) can totally and immediately undermine the economy – the 1929 crash was a dramatic example of such an occurrence, but the LTCM incident of 1998 proves beyond doubt the direct correlation between events taking place in the securities markets, monetary policy and the economy at large.

It is also necessary for the objective to be attained within the operation of the Common Market, the precise meaning of which is slightly unclear although it has been suggested that it means either establishing the Common Market (rather than simply carrying out common policies) or, a slightly less strict view, that it means no more than that the action must fall within the context of the Treaty (as discussed by Dashwood in The Limits of European Community Powers 1996). In either case this is satisfied. Finally, the act must be appropriate, and this encompasses the principle of proportionality. Clearly, given that one of the objectives of effective market regulation is the prevention of market failure and when one considers the social, political and economic consequences of major market disruptions, it cannot be said that the foundation of a regulatory body is disproportionate.

As well as the mere existence and usage of Article 235, there is evidence that the purposive attitude of the courts undermines the principle of limited powers. For example, there is increasing recognition that the EC recognises the implied powers doctrine which is a recognised international legal principle. This is subject to two interpretations. The narrow view is that the existence of a power within a Treaty article necessarily implies that all other powers necessary for the exercise of that former power be implied. This has largely been accepted by the courts. Alternatively, an EC institution might claim that a mere function or objective of a Treaty article implies powers to enable the institution to carry them out. This wider view could be said to be encapsulated within Article 235 itself.

Further, the phrase 'necessary Community action' has received rather lenient interpretation by the EC institutions. Opinion 2/94 actually referred to previous rulings of the European Court of Human Rights which has repeatedly equated necessity with a 'pressing social need' (as Paul Beaumont points out, as above). While there is no real evidence that the ECJ would adopt this approach it serves to re-emphasise the characteristically purposive stance the Community has taken when it decides that something must be done.

The author is not claiming that Article 308 is limitless. Its limitations were well set out in Opinion 2/94 which concerned the legality of using Article 308 (or Article 235 as it then was) to accede to the European Convention of Human Rights (ECHR). The court stated that accession to the ECHR would result in a 'substantial change in the present EC system' for the protection of human rights, as it would involve entering into a distinct international institutional system as one of integration of all the provisions of the Convention into the European legal order. As this was of constitutional significance it would go beyond the scope of Article 235. The formation of an ESC is not a substantial change in the European system; the single currency and single market already exist and I am merely recommending that the securities markets be regulated at European level to protect the integrity of the single currency or the single market. To use the words of Article 2 of the Treaty, to 'promote economic cohesion'.

The Opinion cited the main limitation to Article 235 – that it cannot serve as the basis for widening the scope of powers beyond the framework created by the Treaty, and in particular by those provisions that define tasks and activities of the EC. Neither can it be used as the foundation for the adoption of provisions which would, in substance, amend the Treaty without following the necessary amendment procedure. But for the reasons given earlier, these limitations are not relevant to the proposed creation of an ESC.

Instead it is more useful to focus on what, in practice, Article 235 (now Article 308) has been used to achieve. It has proven to be a useful residual legislative power for the EC, filling the gap where it did not possess more specific legislative authority in substantive areas at the relevant time. It has been used to legitimise legislation on the environment and has also been used in the conclusion of international agreements and the granting of emergency food aid.

Article 235 has also been used as the basis for the creation of new legal entities under Community law, such as the EEIGs; and in the establishment of the European Regional Development Fund in 1975 and its contribution to the European Monetary System. Even though the exact mechanics of the Monetary System were enacted through the European Council, the powers of the European Monetary Co-operation Fund (EMCF) were enacted using Article 235 as a basis. In order for the Community's objectives to be achieved (the 'gradual convergence of Member States' economic policies, the smooth functioning of the common market and the attainment of economic and monetary union') it was decided that the EMCF should be empowered to receive monetary reserves from the monetary authorities of the Member States and to issue Ecus against such assets.

As J Weiler put it in his 1991 book, *The Transformation of Europe*, Article 235 has been interpreted in such a wide and radical manner that 'it would become virtually impossible to find an activity which could not be brought within the objectives of the Treaty'.

Even if an amendment Treaty were deemed to be necessary (and it is certainly politically desirable), the precursor to an ESC could most probably be posted after the European Commission, pending the creation of a proper ESC.

Another way of efficiently setting up an ESC has been put forward by Jan Wouters, Professor of Law at the University of Leuven and Maastricht. Mr Wouters believes that three stages would be necessary for the setting up of an ESC. These stages would be as follows:

- 2001–2002 would be dedicated to the overall revision of EU securities law;
- 2002–2003 would see the setting up of a Provisional Securities Organ based on multilateral convention between EU Member States;
- 2004–2006 would see the signature of a treaty as a legal basis for the setting up of an ESC from 1 January 2006.

## PART IV

### 1   Conclusion

The analysis above reveals a need to bring regulation in line with contemporary market reality, as the information technology revolution and market integration continue to blur the boundaries of national jurisdictions. These effects place further pressure on the EU's slow and cumbersome legislative process – in reality, Member States take on average more than five years to adopt Directives. It has been argued in this chapter that the complacency demonstrated by the Americans in their pre-1934 fragmented regulatory system led to catastrophic financial consequences and as such, it should be a salutary lesson to Member States and the market participants involved in the European securities markets. Far from fearing the impact of a sole regulator one must understand that the ESC, like the SEC, would still resort to consultation from across the industry when it comes to proposing rules and amendments. With the ESC in charge of overall policy and surveillance, the exchanges and national regulators (or whatever pan-European entities may replace them) would still operate their own surveillance and compliance departments whilst also implementing ESC policies.

Critics, who warn against a hasty knee-jerk reaction to recent market developments, instead seek to sow the seeds of closer co-operation within the European Union.[79] Granted that a considered response is always preferable – after all, Rome was not built in a day – but a dialogue between Member States as to the creation of

---

[79] James W. F. Watson, *op. cit.*, note 47.

an ESC must commence urgently. It has to a large extent started with the Lamfalussy Committee of 'Wise Men'. The author has cited the ECB as a working and pragmatic institutional model within the EU institutional framework which may be usefully transposed into the context of European securities regulation. It has also been suggested that the process to an ESC may be facilitated by putting FESCO on a more formal footing, thereby endorsing an organisation that is both able to draft harmonised rules which are more flexible than the Directives, and to co-ordinate the implementation of these policies on a day-to-day level.[80] To a large extent the Lamfalussy Report by suggesting the creation of an EU Securities Committee together with an EU Securities Regulators Committee (which will consult with market professionals) is putting in place the precursor to a 'pan-European' Regulator.

It might be practically difficult to establish a Securities Commission for the euro-zone with political and national sensitivities to contend with, but what role a regulator like the ESC should have in underpinning investor confidence in the unified, stable European and global financial markets is of pertinent concern. The world is progressing towards a global securities market which will offer 24-hour trading and a debate on the virtues of a global financial regulator is not far off the horizon.[81] One can continue to hypothesise but in any case, Europe must now demonstrate the political will and urgency to succeed in seeing her ambition of a single financial services market come to fruition. In any event, the author believes that the consolidation of exchanges and clearing systems in Europe[82] will lead to an acute political question to which the ESC is the only answer and solution. Once Europe is left with one or two exchanges and one or two clearing securities systems, these massive organisations will have to be monitored and regulated by someone. It would be naïve, and ignorant of European history, to entertain the idea that the Member States whose regulatory authorities will not have jurisdiction over such 'mega' European exchanges and clearing systems will accept that a foreign regulatory authority, only accountable to one sovereign, will be responsible for the sanctity of the euro-zone capital markets, which is the by-product of EMU, built upon the condition of a sharing of powers – and the related transfers of sovereignty – at the ECB level. It would have been inconceivable for one particular NCB, say the Bundesbank, to be solely in charge of the euro, the single currency of 11 other sovereign nations. Equally, believing that we are about to see the UK FSA, the French Commission des Opérations de Bourse or the Luxembourg Government solely in charge of the central elements of a modern economy, that the securities markets are, without any power sharing arrangements with other Member States is an illusion. As happened in the case

---

[80] Fabrice Demarigny, 'Disentangling the Single Market' (2000) FR 4(4), 32.

[81] *See*, for example, the proposal of a World Financial Authority (WFA) in John Eatwell and Lance Taylor, *Global Finance at Risk: The Case for International Regulation* (Polity Press, 2000). Messrs Eatwell and Taylor contend that the significance of the WFA will be in its role of harmonising standards and procedures and defining the global scope and relevance of decision-making. Its functions in the dissemination of information, authorisation, surveillance, guidance and enforcement will inevitably be carried out by national authorities acting in conjunction with and as agents of the WFA.

[82] *See* Part II above.

of the ECB, a supranational political will and momentum is required if a single regulator is to become a reality. Market participants must make the case to governments; and governments must recognise the need for an ESC. Only then can national reservations (of a purely domestic character) be overridden.

For those who are disappointed by the conclusions of the Lamfalussy Report as being too timid, should remember that the Committee of Wise Men terms of reference were not to give alternatives to the FSAP, but rather to put forward practical steps to achieve the FSAP goals. Those of us who wish to see an ESC set up should take comfort that the Committee of Wise Men are calling for three important and immediate actions:

(1) the creation of an EU Securities Regulators Committee, an ideal precursor to a proper ESC (as was the EMI prior to the ECB);
(2) the creation of an EU Securities Regulators Committee (an ideal forum to pave the way to the equivalent of an ESCB); and
(3) the allocation of proper and sufficient resources to monitor progress (a potential basis for reliable and expert resources for a real ESC).

One should then remember the Initial Lamfalussy Report which states:

The functioning of this approach (summarised in Part III above) should be fully reviewed around 2004, though if, in the light of the half-yearly reports, it were manifestly failing to secure sufficient progress, there would be a case for a full review earlier.

It is clearly impossible to foresee the substance of a review of developments that have yet to take place. Various scenarios are conceivable however. At one extreme, the approach sketched out above might be succeeding in developing the single market in securities. In that case, its essentials could be maintained or strengthened if that seemed necessary. *At the other extreme, if the approach did not appear to have any prospect of success, it might be appropriate to consider a Treaty change, including the creation of a single EU regulatory authority for financial services generally in the Community.*

It will therefore be up to those who are hostile to the creation of a single European regulatory authority to ensure that a system that has so far failed us – harmonisation of national regulations and co-operation of national regulators – has delivered the necessary level of integration required by the markets. In the meantime, the creation of the Committees mentioned above, with appropriate resourcing, allows valuable time not to be wasted should the single regulator be eventually retained. 2004 coincides with the date of the next Inter-Governmental Conference, an ideal time to amend the Treaty if necessary or desirable.

*Chapter 8*

# Regulating European Securities Markets: Beyond the *Lamfalussy* Report

*Rosa M. Lastra*[1]

## INTRODUCTION

Since the launch of the euro in January 1999, it has become increasingly apparent that Europe lacks the integrated financial markets needed to exploit the full potential of European Monetary Union (EMU). Progress towards a single market in financial services is hindered by the existence of fifteen different national systems of financial legislation and regulation and by slow and rigid European Community (EC) procedures. Though the principles of home country control, mutual recognition and minimum harmonisation have proven successful in advancing the EC's goal of creating a single market in financial services, they are not without limitations. These limitations have become apparent in the process of integrating securities markets in Europe.

In this chapter, I shall survey some of the strategies that have been proposed to overcome these problems, in particular the proposals of the Lamfalussy Report,[2] that is, of the Final Report of the Committee of Wise Men on the Regulation of European Securities Markets, which was published on 15 February 2001 and adopted by the European Council in Stockholm on 23–24 March. The Lamfalussy Report (the 'Report') focuses on the question of *how* to speed up reform, that is on the processes and legal procedures needed to reform securities markets regulation, rather than on the question of *what* needs to be reformed. The mandate given to the Wise Men was confined to the workings of the law-making process concerning securities markets regulation in Europe. The Wise Men were asked to identify the imperfections of this process and to come up with recommendations for change. The mandate of the Wise Men was not to identify what should be regulated, nor to look at other relevant issues such as international implications or prudential considerations.

---

[1] I would like to thank Niels Thygessen for drawing important institutional issues to my attention and for making original suggestions and comments to various drafts of this paper. I would also like to thank the other members of the European Shadow Financial Regulatory Committee (ESFRC) for helpful discussions on this subject. The ESFRC published its statement No. 10 on 'The Regulation of European Securities Markets: the Lamfalussy Report' on 26 March 2001 in Madrid (available at <http://www.ceps.be>). However, some of the views presented in this article go beyond our proposals as a Committee and are not shared by some of its members. This article also benefited from a talk given by Alexandre Lamfalussy in London on 3 May 2001 (VIIIth SUERF Lecture) on the Report which bears his name.

[2] *See* <http://europa.eu.int/comm/internal_market/en/finances/general/lamfalussy.htm>.

*Mads Andenas and Yannis Avgerinos (eds), Financial Markets in Europe: Towards a Single Regulator?* 211–222.
© 2003 *Kluwer Law International. Printed in Great Britain.*

From a shorter-term perspective, it is no doubt rational for the European institutions and governments to focus on these procedures. The need for speeding up the legislative process is rather obvious as capital markets change fast and, on past experience, the adoption of directives in the field of financial regulation takes 2–3 years, followed by a 1–2-year period for national transposition. By definition directives are always running behind events in the markets.

From a longer-term perspective the two major issues at stake are, in my opinion, the creation of a single securities European regulator and the adoption of basic standards of securities regulation (or a basic code of European securities regulation). The Report stops short of proposing the former (though leaves the door open through a fall back remark)[3] and calls for the reform of the Investment Services Directive (ISD) and the prompt adoption of other measures included in the Commission's Financial Services Action Plan (FSAP). A well functioning capital market is in the interest of the citizens of the European Union. However, because Europe (with the exception of the United Kingdom) has typically been a bank-based financial system and because the development of capital markets requires a careful balancing act between the many parties involved (lawmakers, supervisors, self-regulatory organisations, market intermediaries, issuers and investors) the challenges ahead are complex and will require a great deal of dialogue and co-operation.[4]

The discussions in Stockholm in March 2001 and the preparatory discussion of the central features of the Report illustrate the mutual suspicions among national and European institutions (and between the latter) and the struggle of competencies between the European Parliament (EP), the Commission and the Council. The discussions also reveal that national governments remain very reluctant to cede power to the EP and the Commission with a transnational mandate.

In the ensuing Sections I analyse first the four-level regulatory approach proposed in the Report. Then, I discuss the longer-term issue of the conceivable creation of an agency for the supervision of capital markets, examining some issues of possible institutional design: structure, functions and status (features of independence, accountability and technical competence). I briefly consider the example of other experiences of European integration and the benchmark set by best practices in the United States. I finish this article with some concluding remarks.

## THE FOUR-LEVEL REGULATORY APPROACH

The major novelty of the Report is a proposed four-level regulatory approach, whose aim is to speed up the legislative process for the regulation of securities markets. Of these four levels, the main innovation is the distinction between 'core principles' in

---

[3] [I]f the full review were to confirm in 2004 (or earlier as the case may be) that the approach did not appear to have any prospect of success, it might be appropriate to consider a Treaty change, including the creation of a single EU regulatory authority for financial services generally in the Community'. Lamfalussy Report (*supra* note 2) at p. 41.

[4] See *EU Securities Market Regulation. Adapting to the Needs of a Single Capital Market*, Report of a CEPS Task Force, March 2001; Chairman: Alfred Steinherr, Rapporteur: Karel Lannoo.

Level 1 and 'technical implementing matters' in Level 2, which mirrors at the EU level what happens at the national level with the distinction between primary legislation and secondary regulation. According to Baron Lamfalussy, the Report brings about a 'governance change', a bottom-up approach (rather than top-down), which could also be applied to other areas of European integration.[5]

Level 1 refers to EU framework legislation and involves the EU Commission, Council and Parliament. This is the regular EU legislative process, albeit with a 'fast track' feature, according to the wording of the Stockholm Resolution of the European Council on More Effective Securities Markets Regulation of 23 March 2001.

The Stockholm Resolution invites the Commission to use regulations instead of directives, whenever this is 'legally possible'. The latter recommendation may prove to be problematic, because directives have been the preferred instrument in the pursuit of an internal market in financial services. Indeed, the Single European Act in its Declaration on Article 100a of the EEC Treaty[6] stated that: the Commission shall give precedence to the use of the instrument of a directive if harmonisation involves the amendment of legislative provisions in one or more Member States'. The Amsterdam protocol also states in its point 6: directives should be preferred to regulations'. Though the Wise Men's recommendation to use regulations is sensible, because differences in national transposition have often hindered the integration of financial markets, the new approach needs to be reconciled with the status quo in banking and insurance, where directives have been the norm.

As acknowledged, the reason why directives have been preferred is because their use is consistent with the principles of minimum harmonisation and mutual recognition, which have been the driving force of the Community's strategy to create a single market in financial services since 1985.[7] Regulations, as opposed to directives, are consistent with the principle of full or detailed harmonisation. And regulations leave no freedom to Member States with regard to their national transposition.

Level 2 refers to EU implementation and involves in addition to the EU Commission, a yet-to-be-created European Securities Committee (ESC) and a European Securities Regulators Committee (ESRC).

---

[5] VIIIth Suerf Lecture, *supra* note 1.

[6] This article has become Art. 95 (ex Art. 100a) of the EC Treaty following the Amsterdam Treaty renumbering.

[7] As I have explained elsewhere (*See* 'Central Banking and Banking Regulation', 1996, at p. 217 *et seq.*), the approximation of legislations in the field of banking and finance as required in Art. 100 of the original EEC Treaty had been difficult before 1985. Indeed while the Commission had succeeded in the approximation of laws (mainly through regulations) in the fields of quality, composition, labelling and control of goods, industrial property rights, public procurement, technical or administrative barriers to trade, industrial safety and hygiene, etc., the Commission had failed to approximate laws in other fields such as banking and financial services, transport, energy, telecommunications, etc., due to stark differences across Member States in the structure of their services industry and due to the political implications of the liberalisation of some 'key' services. A new strategy was needed, with new political initiatives and more flexible techniques for integration. The new strategy first envisaged in the 1985 White Paper on the Internal Market and legally enshrined in the 1986 Single European Act was rooted in the generalisation of the concept of mutual recognition on the basis of prior minimum harmonisation (rather than full or detailed harmonisation).

The Report suggests that the proposed ESC would be set up following the regulatory comitology procedure[8] suggested for implementing powers conferred on the Commission.[9] It would be composed of high-ranking officials – State Secretaries in the Finance Ministries of the Member States or their personal representatives – and would be chaired by the European Commissioner responsible for the Internal Market in Financial Services. The ESRC would be set up as an independent advisory group to the Commission (outside the comitology process) and would be composed of national securities regulators, building on the structure established by the Forum of European Securities Commissions (FESCO).

However, as opposed to FESCO, the ESRC will be entrusted with a real mandate, that of making proposals to the Commission on technical implementing matters. The Commission, on receiving these proposals will adjust them when it comes to areas where it has a comparative advantage, for instance with regard to competition law, or in issues which have an international dimension, such as relations with the USA.[10] The Commission will then transmit these proposals to the ESC, which will vote on the proposal. (The ESC can only turn down a proposal when there is a qualified majority vote against it.) The EP will then examine the final draft and within one month it will have to consider whether or not the draft measures exceed the scope of the implementing matters (Level 2). If Parliament passes a resolution stating that the [Commission's] proposal exceeds the implementing powers, the Commission, taking the 'utmost account of the Parliament's resolution' might then 'submit new draft measures to the Committee (ESC), continue with the procedure, or submit a proposal under co-decision procedure'.[11]

The role of the EP in Level 2 is rather limited (as opposed to its major role in the co-decision procedure in Level 1). Though the EP has been promised it will be kept fully informed of proposals developed at level 2, and though the Commission will 'take the utmost account of the Parliament's position', the EP remains concerned about the lack of transparency and democratic procedures in Level 2.[12] In particular the EP is concerned that it will be unable to exercise influence over the compromises struck between the Commission and the national authorities represented in the ESC and the ESRC.[13]

---

[8] This 'comitology' procedure is recognised under Arts 202 and 211 of the Treaty. Council Decision 1999/469/EC lays down the procedures for the exercise of implementing powers conferred on the Commission.

[9] The Report also states (*supra* note 2, at p. 31) that 'in order to permit the ESC to begin work as soon as possible – pending any formal conferment of implementing powers – the Commission could formally set it up as an Advisory Committee by a Commission Decision'.

[10] These two examples were mentioned by Alexandre Lamfalussy, VIIIth SUERF lecture, *supra* note 1.

[11] Lamfalussy Report (*supra* note 2) at p. 30. *See* also the Report at pp. 6 and 36.

[12] *See* Press Releases of the EP of 23 March 2001 and of 2 May 2001. In this latter Press Release the Chair of the EP's Committee on Economic and Monetary Affairs, Mrs. Randzio-Plath, expresses her extreme disappointment at the Commission's rejection of the offer the EP had made to have 'an exchange of letters' between the Commission, the Council and the EP.

[13] I thank Niels Thygessen for drawing this important point to my attention.

On 14 March 2001, the EP voted by 410 to 25 voted in favour of an appeals procedure or 'call back' that would have enabled the EP to review and halt legislation proposed at level two beyond the scope in the Lamfalussy Report which accords the EP such a right only if the proposal legislation goes beyond the implementing powers ('ultra vires') of the Commission and the ESC. To extend the EP's power to call back a proposal on substantive grounds was seen by the Council as setting a dangerous precedent for parliamentary involvement and as a recipe for slowing down the adoption of new proposals. On 2 May 2001 Commissioner Frits Bolkestein sent a letter to the Chair of the EP's Economic and Monetary Affairs Committee, stating that 'the Commission considers that a 'call back' provision is not compatible with the Treaty as it stands'.[14]

The concerns of the EP appear to be shared by a number of market participants who foresee a lack of transparency in the final stages of preparing legislation at level two.[15] While the national regulators in the ESRC will prepare their advice to the Commission in consultation with market participants, end-users and consumers, outside scrutiny will be cut off in the final stages of negotiation between the Commission and the national governments represented in the ESC. Keeping also this final stage transparent through monitoring by the EP may slow down an already cumbersome process, but could also improve the quality of the legislative output. In the absence of willingness of the European Council to give the EP – and through it the expertise of market participants – monitoring powers over implementation of legislation at level two, the co-operation of the EP in the full co-decision procedures at level one could prove difficult to ensure. That would imply a greater potential for delay and certainly an end to the ambition to have the new framework operational soon.

Following the adoption of the Stockholm Resolution, Christa Randzio-Plath, chair of the EP's Economic and Monetary Committee, wrote a letter to Commissioner Bolkestein, dated 19 April 2001, in which she proposed a three way agreement with the EP, the Council and the Commission on the Lamfalussy Report. However the EP's offer was rejected by the Commission.[16] According to the EP's offer, a formal exchange of letters between the three institutions on the Lamfalussy Report would have helped clarify the Stockholm European Council resolution, in particular as regards the distinction between political and technical measures, transparency and democratic control.

The struggle of competencies between EU institutions and Member States was evidenced throughout the preparatory discussions ahead of the Stockholm summit. Some Member States questioned the right of initiative of the Commission in proposing legislation. Apparently Germany, supported by Denmark and Greece, insisted in the ECOFIN discussion that the Commission in formulating its proposals should

---

[14] The letter is available as an attachment to the Press Release of the EP's Economic and Monetary Affairs Committee of 2 May 2001.

[15] See *Reaction to the Wise Men's Final Report by Working Party of the Federal Trust*, London, 13 March 2001.

[16] See Press Release of the EP's Committee on Economic and Monetary Affairs, 2 May 2001.

be bound by a majority in the advisory bodies of high officials and national regulators. Understandably the Commission was unwilling to see its right of initiative constrained; in the end the conflict was solved through skilful drafting.

However, one of the 'concessions' that the Stockholm Resolution introduced – in its point 5, para. 3 – was strongly criticised by the very author of the Report which the Resolution endorsed, Alexandre Lamfalussy.[17] This 'concession' appears to give the Council the right to intervene in the comitology process:

> [T]he Commission has committed itself, in order to find a balanced solution for those cases of implementing measures in the field of securities markets acknowledged in the light of the discussions to be particularly sensitive, to avoid going against predominant views which might emerge within the Council, as to the appropriateness of such measures. This commitment shall not constitute a precedent.[18]

The discussions have certainly revealed that national governments remain very reluctant to cede power to either of the two institutions with a transnational mandate – the EP and the Commission.

In one respect, the reluctance in the Council to see the influence of the EP and the Commission enhanced is understandable. Most of the expertise in the area of financial regulation is today found in national regulatory agencies and, of course, in the financial institutions affected by the legislation. There is a need for allocating much greater human resources in the staffing of both the Commission and the EP for them to become fully accepted for their professional capabilities in this complex area.[19]

Level 2 is particularly complicated and cumbersome. Why create two committees? Why so many steps back and forth? Instead of speeding up financial regulation, it appears that level 2 – in its current formulation – may actually slow it down. This is the reason why the ESFRC in its statement of March 2001 proposes that only one committee be established, and that such committee be composed of national securities regulators, to provide a degree of expertise and technical competence.

My reading of level 2 is that the Commission, which initiated the FSAP and which so far has been in charge (working together with the Council and the EP) of harmonising financial legislation in Europe, felt overburdened by the quantity and technical character of some financial legislative proposals with regard to securities markets and that therefore, thought it prudent to ask the Council to delegate the more technical aspects of this task to a technical committee, which would nevertheless function under the Commission's auspices. What the Commission did not foresee is the backlash which would come from the Member States, because of the perceived need to protect their vested interests and safeguard their own competencies in this field, and from the European Parliamant, because of its concerns about democratic legitimacy and transparency in level 2.

---

[17] VIIIth Suerf Lecture, London, 3 May 2001, *supra* note 1.

[18] Para. 3, point 5 of the Stockholm Resolution.

[19] I thank Niels Thygessen for drawing this issue to my attention.

Level 3 refers to national implementation and co-operation and involves the ESRC and the Member States. As stated in the Report (page 31) the ESRC is conceived as a committee 'with two hats'. On the one hand, in Level 2 'it would act as an advisory committee to the European Commission' and, on the other hand, in Level 3 'it would act alone as a fully independent committee of national regulators to ensure more consistent implementation of Community Law'. That is why the Report proposes (page 6) that the ESRC would work (in Level 3) on 'joint interpretation, recommendations, consistent guidelines and common standards (in areas not covered by EU legislation), peer review, and compare regulatory practice to ensure consistent implementation and application'.

Level 4 refers to enforcement and involves the Commission and the Member States. The Commission checks Member State compliance with EU legislation and may bring legal action against a Member State if a breach of Community Law is suspected.[20]

Echoing the words of Edward Kane in a poignant title for an article on credit allocation:[21]

Good intentions and unintended evil.... I suggest that the goal of speeding up financial legislation may be hindered rather than facilitated by the unnecessarily cumbersome four-level regulatory approach proposed in the Report. A simplified legislative procedure involving one rather than two securities committees is needed, as recommended by the ESFRC (March 2001).

THE FUTURE OF SECURITIES REGULATION IN EUROPE

The focus on procedures (the 'how' to reform) should not obscure the importance of the substance of the reform (the 'what' to reform). In this respect, as the ESFRC already called for in September 2000, it is important to close loopholes in the ISD that allow national authorities to discriminate against foreign exchanges. Increased emphasis should also be placed on common accounting standards and disclosure rules (ESFRC, March 2001). Progress in this area is essential. As Arthur Levitt pointed out in an article on the need for uniform, comparable and high-quality financial reporting: 'The history of capital markets shows that more information is good and that quality and timely information is better'.[22] Indeed, as Howell Jackson and Eric Pan point out,[23] because the market itself requires a high degree of transparency, a 'race to the top' takes place in terms of disclosure requirements.

---

[20] The problem, as Ian Wouters has rightly indicated, is that even with sufficient resources, Commission enforcement procedures are limited due to the nature and cumbersome procedure of infringement proceedings. See Ian Wouters, 'Towards a European Securities Commission? Reflections in an International and Transatlantic Perspective', in Mads Andenas and Yannis Avreginos (eds), *Financial Market Supervision in Europe: Towards a Single Regulator?* (Kluwer Law International, 2001) (forthcoming).

[21] See Edward Kane, 'Good Intentions and Unintended Evil, the Case Against Selective Credit Allocation'(February 1977) *Journal of Money, Credit and Banking* 1.

[22] See Financial Times, 2 May 2001, 'The World According to GAAP', by Arthur Levitt, former chairman of the US Securities and Exchange Commission.

[23] See Howell Jackson and Eric Pan, 'Regulatory Competition in International Securities Markets: Evidence from Europe in 1999 – Part I' (February 2001) *The Business Lawyer*, 56, 664 and 686.

It is possible that the apparent weakness of the approach adopted in Stockholm will be remedied over time, but it seems doubtful that it can deliver the results inhered within the short time horizon envisaged (2004). It is therefore appropriate to recall the longer-term ambition for creating a regulatory framework for Europe's financial markets, which incorporates both the best experience made in other areas of European integration, and the benchmark set by practices in the United States.

There are two contrasting views on financial supervision in Europe. The first, supported, in particular, by the United Kingdom, thinks that greater co-operation between national regulators and increased harmonisation through competitive pressures and self-regulation would best pave the road to a more efficient and integrated capital market. The second view, which finds support in France and some other continental countries, deems that supervision in Europe would be performed better by a centralised agency than by a large number of national authorities. Whether or not a new institution will be created will, however, depend on the political will of the Member States.

The main author of the Report himself contributed to the subject of the appropriate regulatory framework for Europe's financial markets in an article published in the Financial Times on 8 February 2000 on 'Regulation under Strain'. Professor Lamfalussy wrote then that a 'loose co-operative framework may be appropriate for navigating in fair weather, but not when a storm is blowing'. Furthermore, he added:

> 'We must avoid becoming trapped in a sterile debate of what is better: supranational institutions or improved co-operation. There might be a need for supranational institutions in some areas, but not in others. Centralised decision-making might go hand-in-hand with monitoring and implementation by national authorities'.

He proposed a pragmatic approach, that ought to include in his own words: 'a clear mandate, active participation of the parties, professional staff support and, last but not least, binding dates for the completion of the mandate', referring to 'the procedures that led to the ESCB' as a source of inspiration.

Indeed, the very structure of the ESCB with the European Central Bank at the centre and National Central Banks in the Member States could be replicated if a European System of Securities Committees were ever to be created: with a ESC at the centre and National Securities Commissions in the Member States. However, the analogy with the ESCB, though helpful from an structural/geographic point of view, cannot be stretched further to the functional/operational arena, as the powers that have been transferred with regard to the conduct of monetary policy are very different from the responsibilities that might be entrusted to a single securities regulator in Europe.

In my opinion, the real conundrum is precisely the scope of powers, the functions, that an European agency for the supervision of capital markets should have if ever created. Should it be modelled as a super Financial Services Authority (FSA) or as a European version of the US Securities and Exchange Commission (SEC)? The creation of the FSA in the United Kingdom and the proposed establishment of such an agency in Germany suggest a supervisory trend towards consolidation. But if the FSA has often been criticised as a 'regulatory Leviathan' and accountability remains a major concern, a European FSA would be far too powerful to be acceptable to politicians across Europe. Thus, if a centralised agency is to be created, it is more likely to be a European SEC rather than a European FSA.[24]

Nonetheless, the Lamfalussy Report suggests that:

> If the full review were to confirm in 2004 (or earlier as the case may be) that the approach did not appear to have any prospect of success, it might be appropriate to consider a Treaty change, including the creation of a single EU regulatory authority for financial services generally in the Community'. (Lamfalussy Report at p. 41.)

I had the opportunity of asking Baron Lamfalussy whether the wording of this statement was intentional when he spoke in London on 3 May 2001[25] and his answer was positive: the choice of words, 'single EU regulatory authority for financial services in the Community', was intentional. This means that the Report seems to indicate a preference for the conceivable creation of an European FSA rather than for the creation of a European SEC.

In its March 2001 statement, the ESFRC clearly stated that a European SEC 'for financial services generally' cannot be introduced as a default measure in response to the failure of the proposed new procedures. If such an authority were ever to be created, its design would require careful consideration and analysis. (Of course, such consideration and analysis were beyond the mandate given to the Wise Men.)

From a legal point of view the most relevant question is whether or not the creation of a new authority would require a Treaty amendment. Though the answer to this question is not readily apparent as it would, of course, depend on the range of powers entrusted to such an authority, I think that, in principle, a Treaty amendment might not be needed if what we aim to create is a single European securities regulator (though a Treaty amendment would be needed to create a mighty European FSA). Gilles Thieffry[26] has proposed – and I agree with him – that a European securities commission could be set up according to Art. 308 of the EC Treaty (ex Art. 235), which reads as follows:

> If action by the Community should prove necessary to attain, in the course of the operation of the common market, one of the objectives of the Community and this Treaty has not provided the necessary powers, the Council shall, acting unanimously on a proposal from the Commission and after consulting the European Parliament, take the appropriate measures.

Having briefly outlined the main challenges facing European securities regulation in the long-term, namely the adoption of common standards or rules and the issue of the possible creation of a single regulator, in the ensuing paragraphs I will ponder some of the lessons that the institutional design of the SEC in the USA may offer to the possible creation of a European SEC, particularly with regard to its functions

---

[24] The creation of such an agency may also prompt the transfer of prudential supervisory responsibilities – over credit institutions – from the national level to the European Central Bank level (Art. 105.6 of the EC Treaty).

[25] *Supra* note 1.

[26] *See* G.Thieffry, 'After the Lamfalussy Report: the First Steps towards a European Securities Commission?', *supra* Chapter 9 of this book.

and status. (The lessons of the US model are, of course, limited by the fact that the United States is a federal state while the European Union is a loose confederation of fifteen Member States, with various degrees of integration.)

THE SEC AS A POSSIBLE FUNCTIONAL MODEL

The history, status and powers of the US SEC offer some interesting features with regard to the possible creation of a single securities regulator in Europe.[27] As acknowledged, the structure of US securities markets is a product of the Securities Act of 1933, which established a federal system for the registration of new issues of securities, and the Securities Exchange Act of 1934,[28] which created a new federal agency, the SEC. Following the stock market crash of 1929, these pieces of legislation were enacted to promote stability and confidence in capital markets and to protect investors in view of the shortcomings and inadequacies of the state 'blue sky' laws. (The reason why state securities statutes were known as 'blue sky' laws is because some lawmakers believed that 'if securities legislation was not passed, *financial pirates would sell citizens everything in the state but the blue sky'*.)[29] The 1934 Act adopted a two-tiered regulatory structure. In addition to the general regulatory oversight of the SEC, the exchanges were to operate under the supervision of the self-regulatory organizations or SROs (such as the New York Stock Exchange), which are responsible for the daily operation of the exchanges and promulgate the operating rules for each exchange. The SROs themselves are subject to the oversight by SEC.[30] With this two-tiered structure the US Congress tries to strike a balance between protection of the integrity of the markets and the flexibility necessary to maintain an economically vigorous capital market.

The US SEC was established as an independent regulatory commission, endowed with three types of functions or powers: executive, rule making (quasi-legislative) and enforcement (quasi-judicial powers) in the field of securities regulation. This model of independent agencies or independent regulatory commissions has been applied in the US to many other areas of economic activity: money, energy, transport, telecommunications and so on. The choice made by the US Congress to create independent administrative agencies contrasts with the administrative design adopted in civil law countries, such as France, which have typically favoured centralisation and a hierarchical structure of the central government (with executive departments

---

[27] *See* for example, Jan Wouters, 'Towards a European Securities Commission? Reflections in an International and Transatlantic Perspective', *supra* Chapter 7; and Eric Pan, 'The Case for a Single European Securities Regulator', *supra* Chapter 12 of this book. For a discussion of the SEC *see* also Federal Trust, *ibid.* Annex II.

[28] *See* for example, Howell E. Jackson and Edward L. Symons, *Regulation of Financial Institutions* (1999), pp. 660 and 753.

[29] Blue sky laws were mainly antifraud laws and licensing laws. *Ibid.* at pp. 655–656.

[30] *Ibid.* at p. 662, the National Association of Securities Dealers (NASD) was set up in 1948, through an amendment to the 1934 Act. The NASD under the supervision of the SEC has the power to promulgate rules governing voluntary membership of non-exchange broker-dealers.

headed by a cabinet officer). Though in recent years, the advent of central bank independence on the one hand and the establishment of agencies to regulate privatised utilities on the other hand have signified a change in the administrative law tradition of civil law countries, important elements of that tradition remain deeply embedded in the legal framework of those countries.

With regard to its status, the features of relative independence and accountability of the SEC are valuable traits of the institution.[31] The reputation that the SEC has acquired over the years in its functions, as watchdog of capital markets is a testimony to the crucial role it has played in developing confidence in US capital markets.[32]

A European SEC could have regulatory or rule-making functions, but the broad legislative guidelines and standards would be still be set according to the regular EC legislative process. The idea is that given the need for expertise, flexibility, technical competence and de-politicisation in capital markets, a specialised and depoliticised agency – accountable to the EU Parliament, Commission and Council – would be better suited to issue rules than slow and bureaucratic procedures. A European SEC might also be entrusted with enforcement powers.[33]

If an European SEC were to be created, it would be imperative to design *ex ante* an appropriate framework of accountability and transparency. In a democratic community, the delegation of a mandate to a specialised agency or independent regulatory commission always needs to be counterbalanced by adequate mechanisms of accountability.[34]

## CONCLUDING REMARKS

The ambitions to 'support the Lisbon vision of a dynamic knowledge-driven economy, with good access to capital in order for business to invest, grow and create jobs' (terms of reference given by the ECOFIN Council to the Lamfalussy Group on

---

[31] However, independent regulatory commissions have also been the subject of extensive debate and criticism in the United States. For instance, the 1971 Ash Council Report (the Report of the President's Advisory Council on Executive Organization) on Selected Independent Regulatory Agencies, recommended that functions of six agencies, including the SEC, should be transferred to single administrators under the President. In particular the agencies were criticised for their alleged lack of accountability and their excess of independence. The Report is quoted in Kenneth Culp Davis, *Administrative Law and Government* (West Publishing Co., 1975), pp. 20–22.

[32] *Supra* note 27, at p. 754. 'Congress asked the SEC in its original mandate to wear two different hats. Under the first, known as the 'sunlight' hat, the SEC was to encourage the disclosure of truthful and complete information by corporations so investors could more accurately assess the value of the security. The second was as a 'market regulator', a hat which envisioned the SEC monitoring the structure and functioning of the markets themselves'.

[33] This is a very important issue, which exceeds the scope of this article. Effective enforcement might perhaps be facilitated by a dual institutional structure, akin to that of the ESCB.

[34] For a thorough discussion of accountability and transparency in the financial sector, *see* Rosa M. Lastra and Heba Shams, 'Public Accountability in the Financial Sector' in Eilis Ferran and Charles Goodhart, (eds), *The Challenges Facing Financial Regulation*, (Hart Publishing, 2002).

17 July 2000) may not be fully realized with the approach proposed in Stockholm for Securities market regulation.

Given the need to create a framework that fosters efficient capital markets, progress in the 'what' (what to reform) should not be hindered by political gridlock in the 'how' (how to reform). In this respect, it is worth noticing that though considerable progress in reforming trading systems and internal governance of European Exchanges has taken place over the last decade as a result of cross-border competition and the partial implementation of the ISD of 1992, important points of concern remain, as identified for instance in the statement by the ESFRC in June 2000.[35]

It is also important to bear in mind that the regulation of securities firms is not based on mandatory rules ('intrusive' regulation) but on disclosure obligations and fiduciary rules ('market friendly' regulation), which protect investors and enhance confidence in the market.

Whether or not an European SEC (or an European FSA) is ever created, it is necessary for academics and practitioners to commence a thorough discussion on its possible institutional design. Such a debate ought to focus on the structure, functions and accountability of such a new institution. Just to say that such an agency should not be created would tempt those who most fervently favour its creation to 'capture' the debate and to advance their cause in their own terms, which could appear 'too centralising' or 'bureaucratic' to those who oppose its creation. Such an approach, in the absence of adequate opposition, may lead to an inadequate institutional design. For instance, I think that the alleged democratic deficit of the European Central Bank might have been remedied or alleviated through a more thorough *ex ante* debate on accountability. Had such a debate taken place (akin to the debate that preceded the enacting of legislation in the United Kingdom granting operational independence to the Bank of England[36]) those who opposed the creation of such a new institution, could have 'minimised' its perceived damage by suggesting features of greater democratic participation and transparency.

Europe does need a well functioning capital market. If the current structure does not work efficiently enough – and there seems to be broad consensus that this is the case – then, such structure needs to be reformed. Greater efficiency, however, cannot be achieved at the expense of compromising democratic legitimacy and accountability.

---

[35] This statement – as well as other ESFRC statements – is available at <www.ceps.be>.

[36] *See* enquiry into 'The Accountability of the Bank of England', Treasury Select Committee, ordered by the House of Commons, 23 October 1997, Session 1997–98, HC 282.

Chapter 9


# Towards a European Securities Commission: A View from the Securities Markets Industry[1]

*Gregor Pozniak*


## 1 INTRODUCTION – THE CHANGED LANDSCAPE

There have been three major developments that characterise the changes in the European Exchange landscape over the past 20 years: the globalisation of financial markets, the revolutionary developments of technology, and European regulation. European Exchanges have reacted to the changes in their environment with, in several cases, drastic steps.


### 1.1 Globalisation of Markets

Supported by the developments in communication and information technology, financial markets have become truly global. Following the trend in the foreign exchange and international bonds sectors, the equities markets themselves have also moved from fairly national affairs to global cross-border operations. It is interesting to note in this context that the market mechanisms of those markets are now starting to follow in turn the equity markets, concentrating more than before on quality aspects such as centrality, transparency etc.


### 1.2 Technology

After delivering valuable support in the areas of order routing, settlement and clearing, information distribution, and other auxiliary activities of securities trading, information technology started to offer solutions for the Exchanges' core activity, the matching of supply and demand including the finding of a 'best' price for the trades. Electronic trading systems replaced the traditional trading activity on the floors of Exchanges where

---

[1] Sections 1 through 3 of this chapter reflect (and expand) the contents of the address given by the author at the British Institute of International and Comparative Law on 26 January 2001. Section 4 was added after the publication of the Lamfalussy Report of which the main recommendations were approved by the European Council in Stockholm on 23 March 2001.

The chapter is based on two reports by the Federation of European Securities Exchanges (FESE) on European regulatory structures, available at <http://www.fese.be/initiatives/european_representation/index.htm>. It has been updated in autumn 2002, mainly through the addition of footnotes.

*Mads Andenas and Yannis Avgerinos (eds), Financial Markets in Europe: Towards a Single Regulator?* 223–233.
© 2003 *Kluwer Law International. Printed in Great Britain.*

for centuries traders and brokers had struck their deals under the stringent requirement of physical presence. Communication technology made it possible to link traders in remote places to the trading mechanisms and to carry out (and settle and clear) large numbers of trades between participants that never saw each other.

Soon Exchanges, intermediaries, and regulators realised that any barriers for foreign investment firms to access to national Exchanges were neither timely nor wanted anymore nor could they be realistically upheld. And the single market for financial services had, moreover, become a prime target also for European politicians.

### *1.3    Regulation*

Following the opening of the single market for banks in the 1980s, it was the European Union's (EU's) Investment Services Directive (ISD) of 1993[2] that introduced the single passport principle, most notably for investment firms. At the same time – and much less noticed – 'regulated markets', that is, the European Exchanges, also received the right to 'place their screens' in other Member States, to link up remote Members to their trading platforms. From the very moment of the implementation of the ISD in their respective countries, European Exchanges have actively widened their Membership, thus offering their issuers access to the international investment community.

### *1.4    European Exchanges Today*

The European Exchanges of today rightly present themselves as modern, high-tech enterprises. They all operate fully electronic securities trading systems and have (with the exception of the German Exchanges) closed down their floors. They have invited foreign intermediaries to join the ranks of their clientele and many of them do a considerable share of their business with such remote Members.

Almost all European Exchanges are today demutualised. They have realised that their traditional mutual and non-profit structures (which had served them extremely well over many centuries and which had had their clear merits in earlier times) had become outdated and burdensome. Consequently, these Exchanges gave themselves a corporate outfit with modern and efficient decision structures and a clear profit orientation. Some have already offered their stock to other groups of their clients (investors and issuers), others have gone public or intend to do so.

In several European countries, whole securities market services groups have grown around the 'traditional' Exchanges, that is, the cash markets. With very few exceptions, the national derivatives markets are generally found today under the same roof as the national cash markets. Some of these groups went further and integrated also their national clearing and/or settlement institutions, their IT provider, information distribution services and others.

---

[2] Council Directive 93/22/EC on Investment Services in the Securities Field, as amended.

### *1.5   Alliances and mergers*

But opening up to foreign (remote) Membership and internal restructuring were clearly not enough, particularly not in the eyes of those global intermediaries that were the clients and became the shareholders of European markets. Through their new, corporate channels of influence, these global financial players expected and demanded from their Exchanges to develop solutions for a further reduction of costs Driven by their new for-profit business concepts, Exchanges themselves sought methods to curb their expenses. And they arrived at solutions that have indeed been very common in other sectors of the economy for many decades: co-operation, alliances, and mergers.

Following the internal concentration process in almost all European countries (today, only Germany and Spain count more than one 'traditional' Exchange), the European Exchanges started different forms of international co-operation: selling trading technology to other Exchanges, agreements for cross-membership and cross-listing, and first harmonisation efforts in the areas of membership and listing rules.

The first cross-border merger of Exchanges in Europe happened across the borders of the European Union when the future markets of Germany and Switzerland created Eurex. In 2000/2001, the next big merger project became reality: Euronext, the full merger of the Exchanges of Amsterdam, Paris, and Brussels. A new, joint corporate structure was established by its three participants; the 'amalgamation' of trading, clearing, and settlement systems is in the process of realisation. Euronext was from the beginning open for other European Exchanges; in the meanwhile, the Lisbon and Oporto Exchange (Portugal) has been incorporated. Moreover, Euronext has acquired LIFFE, the London-based Derivatives Exchange. The merger efforts of Deutsche Boerse and the London Stock Exchange (LSE) were aborted – but on the other end of Europe, Helsinki Exchanges bought majority stakes in the Exchanges in Tallinn (Estonia) and Riga (Latvia).

Norex, the alliance project between the Nordic Exchanges (Stockholm, Copenhagen, Oslo, and Iceland) relies on the use of one trading system and a common regulatory framework by several Exchanges that remain separate legal entities. The co-operation between SWX and Virt-X includes joint technology as well as close corporate links. Sharing technology was the way chosen by two smaller European Exchanges (Vienna and Dublin) who operate their equities markets on the German XETRA system.

### 2   CONSEQUENCES IN THE REGULATORY SPHERE

All of the above cannot miss its influence on legislation, regulation, supervision, compliance and enforcement.

In many jurisdictions, fairly little formal financial markets legislation existed until even the late 1980s. But at that time, many countries within the European Union and beyond introduced and modernised new financial markets legislation. On the European level, securities markets legislation started practically with the Listings Directive of 1979,[3] and the ISD – the European 'constitution' for securities markets – entered into force only on 1 January 1996.

The ISD introduced among others the single passport principle for investment firms, allowing intermediaries remote membership of financial markets and the placing of trading screens in other jurisdictions without further conditions or barriers. In this context, nearly all EU governments set up new or reinforced existing Securities Commissions. A certain shift of regulatory and enforcement powers away from self-regulatory organisations (Exchanges and others) to government and statutory legislation could be witnessed in several countries.

However, this did not happen across the board as it was widely recognised that self-regulatory organisations – if adequately equipped and supervised – do indeed offer a number of advantages, including low cost, flexibility, open norm or standard setting, process efficiency and expert sector knowledge. Against this, formal legislation allows far greater prosecution powers towards in principle all subjects, persons and corporations, and may bring harsher punishment. The formalities linked to official judicial action have however severely limited its application in practice.

In the area of supervision, most remained unchanged in the sense that supervision is very much limited to and focused on the national jurisdiction and to a large extent remains with national securities commissions and/or the market authorities. It is generally recognised that supervision has got to be very close to the trading markets to be effective. Where markets grow and link across borders or integrate, the exchange of information between supervisors and mutual recognition of each other's practices, become crucial. The intensified co-operation by national regulators in the cases of Eurex, of Euronext, and of Norex, indicate the flexibility that is required to maintain effectiveness of co-operation and thereby of supervision.

In the area of compliance and enforcement, the Exchanges and other self-regulatory organisations largely remain empowered to take action *vis-à-vis* their own Members and/or institutions that have accepted their authority via civil law contract. At the same time, formal crimes and misdemeanours as defined by law may be prosecuted by Securities Commissions via administrative measures, and through the Courts by official prosecution.

It is difficult to underestimate the impact for the organisation of society of the massive employment of modern technology including PCs, cellular phones and the Internet. All European Exchanges without fail have implemented Internet strategies and are constantly upgrading their systems.

It is of the greatest possible importance for the functioning of Europe's economy and its competitive situation *vis-à-vis* financial markets elsewhere that the regulatory arrangements in the EU and in the wider Europe continue to enable service providers

---

[3] Council Directive 79/279/EEC co-ordinating the Conditions for the Admission of Securities to Official Stock Exchange Listing, as amended. This Directive has been 'codified' into Directive 2001/34/EC of the European Parliament and the Council on the admission of securities to official stock exchange listing and on information to be published on those securities.

(including Exchanges) to build, enhance and strengthen fair and quality-conscious financial markets, assisted by the application of the latest technologies. 'Traditional' Exchanges have spent many millions of Euros to attain the status of supervised regulated quality markets that they have reached today. Highly sophisticated trading mechanisms and up-to-date clearing and settlement organisations, fine-tuned procedures, guarantee funds and informal redress processes for private investors all are aimed at insuring efficient and fair markets in which the smaller private investors are treated fairly.

New technology, as a matter of course, offers new chances for fraud and deceit. It is crucial for the confidence in Europe's financial markets that legislation, regulation, supervision and enforcement are not as inflexible as to prevent new developments and new products. At the same time, one should not allow new types of fraud and abuse to occur. This is a major challenge for Europe's legislators from the European Parliament down to self-regulatory organisations. It is important that approaches taken for legislation, supervision, compliance and enforcement are, in the first place, effective. It is equally important that legislation and supervisors are ready to co-operate to create and develop innovative structures to cope with the changing scene of Exchanges merging across borders and the use of the latest technological opportunities.

## 3   CONCLUSIONS AND RECOMMENDATIONS

### 3.1   In the Area of Regulatory Structures

Although in a number of important areas, a considerable degree of European legislative and regulatory harmonisation has been reached, Europe will continue to consist of separate and often rather differently organised jurisdictions with different legal context and traditions. The EU concept of subsidiarity also applies in principle to securities markets. Local and national connections do and will continue to count, even for large investors and major companies.

At the same time, it is necessary to invent, to arrange and to organise cross-border co-operation and structures in the areas of legislation, regulation, supervision, compliance and enforcement for financial markets. Such structuration however has to follow but cannot nor should try to lead developments in the markets.

Realising the need for such cross-border co-operation, the Securities Commissions from the European Economic Area (EEA) undertook in 1999 to establish the Forum of European Securities Commissions (FESCO). The Federation of European Stock Exchanges (FESE) existed until recently as a loose, private organisation discussing common problems and challenges, but started to publish consultative documents, standards papers (relating to areas where existing national or EU legislation did not provide sufficient guidance for the markets nor for the Securities Commissions themselves), and analyses and recommendations to the European Commission. At that time, the implementation of FESCO standards by Securities Commissions and other bodies had to be run along national lines and on the basis of powers given to those Commissions in their national legislation.

At an early moment, FESE published suggestions as to the possible structure, role, and working areas of FESCO:[4]

- FESCO should be given some of the functions of the Securities Committee as originally predicated in the ISD to help implement and adjust EU legislation. A similar idea has in the meanwhile been proposed by the Lamfalussy Group (see below).
- The competitiveness within Europe's markets is a crucial factor for its further rationalisation. This also determines its position *vis-à-vis* the markets in other time zones, in particular the US market. For this reason, too, FESCO should develop structures to effectively create a counterpart and single European voice in global securities bodies like the International Organisation of Securities Commission (IOSCO).
- The European Parliament is today the co-legislator for European financial markets legislation. Europe's Exchanges hope that the EP will find ways to minimise legislative imposition of structures on a European level where those would not (yet) be in the interests of overall market structure and function.
- They urge the Commission to enhance and deepen its monitoring role, together with national regulators, of the implementation and compliance processes of EU legislation in national contexts. Peer pressure and greater transparency will have to play a role here as well.
- For the years to come, the focus of legislators, regulators and markets should be on an organic (but not necessarily slow) development and intensification of current structures, instead of making efforts to impose a superstructure on market's participants and on existing national structures.
- FESE and its members therefore speak strongly against efforts leading to impose a body or institution along American lines at the EU level (The European Securities Exchange Commission (the 'European SEC') to regulate and supervise Europe's securities markets. While recognising that for the long term, a European Securities Commission (ESC) is a leading vision, such a body can only function effectively in a far more harmonised regulatory and legislative framework. Effectiveness of regulation, implementation, and supervision/compliance should take precedence and the addition of a new layer should certainly be avoided.

### 3.2  In the Area of Legislation

Instead of creating new bodies, current efforts in EU legislation for securities business should receive far higher priority with a focus on those areas where a sufficient degree of harmonisation or unification of existing national legislation seems feasible and within reach. Such EU legislation should support the creation of a cross-border level playing field.

---

[4] As explained in footnote 1, this chapter was basically written at the end of the year 2000. The author is aware – and FESE is not unhappy to witness – that many of its ideas and suggestions have become reality since then.

The 'Financial Services Action Plan' (FSAP)[5] was published in 1999 as an ambitious project, essential for the competitiveness of Europe's financial markets in the global competition. The Federation demanded early that European legislators should focus on a review of existing EU financial markets legislation, followed by modernisation where necessary, but only rarely by additions of new directives (or other legal instruments or policies to impose further harmonisation) where efficient and effective. Other instruments than directives (regulations on one hand; but also recommendations, interpretative communications, or other forms of 'secondary' legislation) should be actively considered (see also below). Combinations of formal legislation and informal self-regulation under appropriate supervision have often provided substantive results, for example, in the field of private investor redress.

European governments themselves should pay more attention to the cross-border aspects of their national financial market legislation and should be encouraged to self-impose a European discipline to ensure compatibility if not outright harmonisation with other jurisdictions. This, FESE urged, could apply to areas such as taxation, company law, takeover, and the statutes of the European Company.

FESE also underlined that national Security Commissions are close enough to their national markets to be able to steadfastly help harmonise implementing EU legislation and regulation and to take initiatives within their current legislation to harmonise standards and quality criteria: for markets, market participants, listed companies and the protection of the private investor.

Finally, long before the discussion about industry consultation heated up, FESE emphasised that inclusion into the legislative process of regulators and of market practitioners and their organisations in the form of meaningful and substantive consultation procedures is key to further integration of Europe's financial markets.

### 3.3 In the Area of Supervision

It is important that a high degree of intimate market knowledge remains part of all supervision efforts and mechanisms. This applies both to supervision of business conduct and market abuse as well as to supervision of the quality ('fit and proper test') and capital adequacy of market participants.

As a consequence of this observation, FESE emphasised that market supervision needed to remain at the level of or close to the markets, of course maintaining and where appropriate strengthening current procedures and forms of cooperation and information exchanges between market operators and supervisory Commissions.

The creation of FESCOPOL was seen as an important step. With FESCOPOL, FESCO established a mechanism for its Members for substantive exchanges of information between their agencies relating to cross-border aspects of the securities business as a special and dedicated part of their overall anti-abuse policies.

---

[5] Financial Services, 'Implementing the Framework for Financial Markets – Action Plan', (1999) COM232; *see* <website http://europa.eu.int/comm/internal_market/en/finances/general/action.htm>.

In general the FESE would see a benefit in greater efforts by both, FESCO's Members as well as Exchanges to increase the visibility and transparency of their market quality control powers and procedures.

### 3.4    In the Area of Compliance and Enforcement

As noted above, compliance and enforcement of quality criteria and standards, set by law, regulation or by self-regulatory organisations are closely and intrinsically linked to national legal systems and approaches in administrative law, in criminal law and in self-regulatory practices. Compliance and enforcement flow substantially from supervision and inspection practices.

Therefore, in the area of compliance and enforcement, no major changes are required or feasible in the short run. Market participants – intermediaries, market organisers, listed companies and investors – are all part of their national domestic jurisdiction. They know its mechanisms and traditions. The proximity of compliance and enforcement institutions is an important part in the effective prevention of market abuse, fraud and deceit and in the maintenance of fair markets.

In this context, FESE called for efforts to compare current systems and approaches, to ensure that in all jurisdictions effective anti-abuse legislation, regulation or self-regulation is in place and complete and that punishment of infractions is effectively and without fail enforced so as to prevent any market participant from escaping his dues for instance by changing jurisdiction. This work might also include comparison of available and practised punishment and corrective measures.[6]

### 4    The Report by the Committee of Wise Men on the Regulation of European Securities Markets (Lamfalussy Report)[7]

The FESE welcomed the Report by the Lamfalussy Committee as a valuable contribution with a view to streamline European legislative and regulatory procedures. In our view, the Wise Men identified correctly the key reasons why action was required: the economic benefits that can be expected from the realisation of the single market in financial services; the necessity to make and maintain Europe's financial markets competitive in the global context; the trends on Europe's financial markets and the increasing speed of change; the existing barriers in substantive matters, and the insufficiencies of the current regulatory system.

From the viewpoint of the Federation, we regarded it indispensable to make several comments, both to the Lamfalussy Committee and the European Commission on one hand and in public on the other:

- In view of the accelerating pace of change and innovation, the participation by the securities industry in any future structure of European legislation and

---

[6] At the time of the update of this article, the new Market Abuse Directive is about to be finalised.

[7] *See* website <http://europa.eu.int/comm/internal_market/en/finances/general/lamfalussy.htm>.

regulation needed and needs to be ensured. The Securities Committee and the Regulators' Committee as proposed by the Lamfalussy Committee should therefore be structured (and/or their procedures designed) in such a way that allows the industry to participate in an observer role and/or that market experts be allowed to accompany delegations of officials of Member States.[8] Many European Exchanges are also regulators in various forms and bring practical experience; they should be involved in the work of the Regulators' Committee, at least for issues that are wholly or partially within their remit.

- FESE recognised that the Wise Men's proposals were to raise institutional and political concerns. The Federation therefore urged all European institutions to overcome inter-institutional barriers in order to facilitate the implementation of the Lamfalussy proposals as soon as possible. A high degree of transparency of the consultation and discussion process would be of paramount importance, both for the build-up of confidence in the process and for the quality of the resulting legislation.

- On matters of substance, FESE argued for a thorough review of the ISD within a tight framework with the intention to repair the major flaws as identified and to provide more uniform interpretation and implementation. FESE suggested splitting the Directive in two parts, one aiming at market operators and the other one at market intermediaries.

- FESE urged the European Union to introduce a greater degree of functional regulation, among others to ensure a level playing field between all types of market operators, be they so-called traditional Exchanges, electronic communication networks (ECNs) Alternate Trading Systems (ATSs) or intermediaries that apply internalisation processes.

- FESE strongly supported and supports practical steps towards effective mutual recognition and implementation of the European Passport without limitations or additional national requirements for intermediaries, for issuers and also for market operators.

- FESE recommends the appropriate use of self-regulatory practices as a necessary and effective complement to governmental and regulatory approaches. This should specifically apply also in the area of regulation against market abuse where criminal law (being the ultimate remedy) ought to be assisted by regulatory and self-disciplinary powers.

- On the issue of Trans-Atlantic relations, FESE pointed out that modernisation of legislation and regulation in Europe had to be accompanied by rapid agreement with the US authorities aiming at full and immediate reciprocity of securities market access. FESE Members have always welcomed the penetration of and competition by American market organisers and intermediaries in the securities business in Europe. At the same time, however, some US authorities have taken a rather restrictive if not outright protectionist position in a number of areas relating to financial services and markets. The Federation advocated to

---

[8] No observer status of any kind was granted to industry. The secretive procedures of the ESC are one of the major areas of criticism *vis-à-vis* the Lamfalussy process at the end of 2002.

open soonest a dialogue with those most directly involved (FESCO, US SEC and Exchanges) now that the new US administration has taken up its responsibilities and encourages the Commission to maintain this issue on the World Trade Organisation (WTO) agenda.[9]

- On the issue of clearing and settlement, FESE Members underlined that the organisation of markets including of clearing, settlement and depository service provision is not an area susceptible for imposition of a structure by legislation or regulation and should be left to the interplay of competitive market forces. Suggestions for public or private monopolies should be resisted.

FESE Members welcome appropriate supervision of the provision of trading, clearing and settlement services and themselves have actively contributed to safe, fast and reliable mechanisms. They stand ready to support further efforts especially in the area of cross-border clearing and settlement within the European Union. They are desirous to establish mutual linkages with non-discriminatory access wherever demanded by market participants. A European Passport should be considered in this area as well.[10]

## 5   PERSONAL NOTE BY THE AUTHOR, NOVEMBER 2002

And now, almost two years later, where do we stand? Does the Federation have to eat humble pie? Were its proposals illusionary, too radical, too one-sided on behalf of its Members and Europe's regulated markets? Certainly not! FESE is proud to see many of its concerns addressed and of its proposals followed. Just to name a few:

- FESCO has grown into a Committee of European Regulators Committee (CESR), a Committee with far-reaching responsibilities on levels II and III of the legislative process under the Lamfalussy approach.
- Monitoring of implementation of EU financial markets legislation has become a key charge for Commission and CESR.
- Operators of Regulated Markets will continue to be involved in the supervision of market integrity, in the detection of market abuse, in the admission of participants and of securities.
- The role of self-regulatory structures is expressly recognised in new legislation, although not everywhere to the desirable extent.
- In the draft ISD, the issue of internalisation receives focal attention; ATSs (now MTFs) are subjected to functional regulation widely in line with that of Regulated Markets.

---

[9] In October 2002, the SEC Chairman confirmed publicly the intention on the side of the SEC to move forward on this issue. For the time being, the issue has been spared out from WTO negotiations on services.

[10] The area of clearing and settlement is being addressed in certain passages of the proposed new ISD and notably in the Communication from the Commission.

- After initial flaws, the European Commission has embarked on extensive consultation procedures with market practitioners; this has already led to acceleration in the completion of legislative projects and will continue to do so.
- The European Council proposes to extend the Lamfalussy approach to other areas of financial services, such as banking, insurance, and conglomerates.

At the same time, however, the Federation would also want to express some serious concerns:

- The ESC continues to act behind closed doors, in the secretive tradition of Council meetings. This stands in the way of serious consultation on all levels and in all phases of the legislative process.
- CESR takes its task very seriously indeed but seems to be in danger of overshooting. It has recently produced hundreds of pages of consultative documents on the level II recommendations in the areas of Market Abuse and Prospectuses. In its (over-)activity, CESR hereby ventures into areas where it should and need not go and arrives at a level of unnecessary and over-prescriptive detail. A complete elimination of any flexibility for national regulators or Regulated Markets threatens to eliminate likewise any incentive for quality and deprives Regulated Markets of their chance to brand their products (i.e. their market segments) in their competitive environment.
- The Lamfalussy process as employed now in the area of securities markets is a fragile construction. Europe needs streamlined and flexible legislative regulatory structures and procedures in many areas. The forthcoming Intergovernmental Conference will have to create the basis for modern, dynamic legislation by discussing and reshaping Article 202 of the Treaty.

# Chapter 10

# The Case for a Single European Securities Regulator*

*Eric J. Pan*

## INTRODUCTION

The US Securities and Exchange Commission (SEC), with its federal jurisdiction and rulemaking and enforcement powers, is the oft-cited model for a single European securities regulator – a European Securities Commission (ESC). At first glance, the choice appears obvious. For about seventy years, the SEC has overseen the development of the largest, most sophisticated securities market in the world.

The SEC model, however, deserves closer inspection as the conditions for a SEC-like legal authority in the European Union (EU) do not appear to be present. The European Union is not the United States. When it was created in 1934, the SEC enjoyed the backing of a strong federal government and supremacy over states' securities regulation. The United States was a unified country, with a strong, core political and economic ideology. And, most importantly, the United States was already a fully-functioning single market. A ESC today would have none of these advantages. In addition, a ESC would have a more difficult time exerting its authority over the European securities market because it would be competing against a powerful offshore regulator, the SEC in the United States.

This chapter agrees with those who believe that the EU needs a single securities regulator, but does not seek to portray the establishment of a single securities regulator as a *fait accompli*. Rather, this chapter proposes that the European Union is at a crossroads where it must choose how to achieve the benefits of financial integration. One path leads to a single securities regulator, promulgating mandatory rules. The alternative path leads to a system of regulatory competition between Member States.

In order to evaluate the merits of both paths, this chapter identifies the basic characteristics of the European securities market today. Most striking is the degree to which issuers opt out of European securities regulation in favor of US securities regulation and US market practice. In addition, this chapter evaluates the SEC's success as a single regulator and explores whether these factors behind the SEC's success are transferable to the European context.

---

* This paper was prepared in connection with a presentation to the British Institute of International and Comparative Law in January 2001. The views expressed in this paper reflect only those of Mr. Pan and not those of Covington and Burling. Mr Pan received support for his research from the Butterworths European Fund, Lauterpacht Research Centre for International Law at the University of Cambridge and University of Warwick.

*Mads Andenas and Yannis Avgerinos (eds), Financial Markets in Europe: Towards a Single Regulator?* 235–260.
© 2003 *Kluwer Law International. Printed in Great Britain.*

The goal of a single European securities regulator should not be to create a European twin of the SEC. Europe already has a dominant securities regulator – the SEC. Instead, the EU's goal should be to bring into existence a European regulator that can act as a counterweight to the SEC, representing Europe's interests in multilateral organizations, coordinating with the SEC in regulating the international markets, and working to remove the barriers that prevent the development of a true pan-European securities market. Ultimately, this is the most compelling reason why the EU should establish a ESC.[1]

### EUROPE AT A CROSSROADS: WHITHER A SINGLE SECURITIES REGULATOR?

Europeanists have long dreamt of a single European securities market. As early as 1960, the European Economic Community called on Member States to ease the movement of capital for, inter alia, the trading of securities quoted on stock exchanges.[2] The European Commission's 1985 White Paper reconfirmed the importance of a single securities market, stating:

> Work currently in hand to create a European securities market system, based on Community stock exchanges, is also relevant to the creation of an internal market. This work is designed to break down barriers between stock exchanges and to create a Community-wide trading system for securities of international interest.[3]

The Commission, the Forum of European Securities Commissions (FESCO) and the Committee of Wise Men each have made the case for an integrated securities market.[4]

---

[1] In making the case for a single European securities regulator, this paper focuses primarily on disclosure standards for equity offerings. Disclosure standards are those rules that pertain to what information an issuer must provide to investors, to exchanges and to governmental bodies before making an offering of its securities. In most cases, such information is provided in a prospectus and registration statement. Continuous, updated information is provided in periodic filings to the regulator and public. In addition, disclosure standards include liability provisions that lay out the civil and criminal penalties for issuers that do not provide adequate information in a complete, accurate or timely manner. Discussion of other types of securities regulation is beyond the scope of this chapter.

[2] *See* Tommaso Padoa-Schioppa, *The Road to Monetary Union in Europe* (1994) 50 (citing the First Council Directive implementing Art. 67 of the Treaty of Rome, 11 May 1960, and the Second Council Directive, 18 December 1962).

[3] *Completing the Internal Market*, White Paper from the Commission to the European Council, COM(85) 310 final at 29 (hereinafter White Paper).

[4] The consensus of these three groups is significant given the differences between them. The Commission is the only body with actual governmental authority. The creation of a single securities market would naturally enhance its power as decision-making responsibility moves from the states to the EU. FESCO was an intergovernmental organization composed of regulators from the Member States, but can only make recommendations. The members of FESCO now compose the Committee of European Securities Regulators (CESR). FESCO/CESR Members have the incentive to work through local authority. The Committee of Wise Men is a panel of independent experts appointed by the EU Economic and Finance Ministers to report on the regulation of the European securities market. The Wise Men have the

The need for a single securities market remains urgent.[5] Better and cheaper telecommunications technology makes cross-border investing and offering easier and less expensive. Furthermore, equity markets are rivaling the debt markets as a source of capital for European companies. As a result, investors and issuers are demanding larger, more liquid and more efficient equity markets. This demand is reflected in the tremendous growth of the European equity markets in the past two decades. Between 1979 and 1999, the value of European stock markets increased from $200 billion to $7.4 trillion.[6] In 2000, the value of European stock markets was about $9.3 trillion.[7] In order to continue this growth, Europe needs a single securities market permitting pan-European offerings and trading.

The European Union is at a crossroads. In deciding how it wishes to bring about a single securities market, the European Union faces two alternative paths. First, the EU can pursue a program of regulatory harmonization. This is a strategy universally recommended by the Commission, FESCO and the Wise Men. The program of harmonization seeks to make securities regulation uniform across Member States, facilitating cross-border securities offerings. Work on harmonizing regulations has been ongoing for over twenty years beginning with the implementation of the Admissions Directive,[8] Listing Particulars Directive (LPD)[9] and Public Offers Directive (POD),[10] but always with mixed success.[11]

Harmonization requires a single regulator because harmonization is a top-down process. There needs to be a chief regulatory body to decide which regulations to harmonize. There needs to be a body to coordinate the harmonization process. And, there needs to be a body to enforce harmonization. These are functions that should

---

least stake in any institutional model. *See* Final Report of the Committee of Wise Men on the Regulation of European Securities Markets, 15 February 2001 available at <http://europa.eu.int/comm/internal_market/en/finances/general/lamfalussyen.pdf> (hereinafter Final Report of the Wise Men).

[5] *See*, for example, Robert C. Pozen, 'Continental Shift: The Securitization of Europe' (May/June 2001) FOREIGN AFFAIRS, 9.

[6] *See id.* at 11.

[7] *See* Federation of European Securities Exchanges, *FESE 2000* Online Annual Review, available at <http://www.fese.be/annual_review/2000/index.htm>.

[8] Council Directive 79/279/EEC, 1979 OJ (L 66), amended Council Directive 82/148/EEC, 1982 OJ (L 62). The Admissions Directive sets the conditions for the admission of debt and equity securities to the official listing of a stock exchange.

[9] Council Directive 80/390/EEC, 1980 OJ (L 100), amended Council Directive 82/148/EEC, 1982 OJ (L 62), Council Directive 87/345/EEC, 1987 OJ (L 185), Council Directive 90/211/EEC, 1990 OJ (L 112) and Council Directive 94/18/EC, 1994 OJ (L 135). The LPD sets the conditions for listing on an official exchange.

[10] Council Directive 89/298/EEC, 1989 OJ (L 124). The POD sets the conditions for making a public offering.

[11] Consider the smug statement of a former Director-General of DG XV: 'I have to confess that I find myself cheerfully unrepentant in the face of the criticism that the Commission has not made any serious attempt to develop a theory of harmonization' quoted in Benn Steil, *Regional Financial Market Integration* (1998) fn. 6.

The Admissions Directive and the LPD have been amended and restated in Directive 2001/34/EC of the European Parliament and of the Council, 2001 OJ (L 184).

not be separated. Unfortunately, the Commission, at this time, is ill-equipped to fulfill the role of a central regulator. The well-documented problems with implementation of the directives demonstrates the difficulty of the Commission's task.[12]

The second path is regulatory competition. According to the theory of regulatory competition, optimal regulation can be achieved by offering market participants a choice of legal regimes. In short, market participants are 'consumers' of regulation. By providing them a choice, they will select the legal regime that best fits their needs. Mandatory regulation does not make available such a choice, ensuring that many market participants are forced to comply with a legal regime that produces suboptimal benefit relative to cost.

Under regulatory competition, legal regimes 'compete' for constituencies. Regulators who impose burdensome regulatory requirements would lose entities complying with their regulations, whereas regulators with more beneficial regulatory requirements would become more popular. From a market efficiency standpoint, regulatory competition will lead to 'better' regulation since regulators will try to adopt their regulations to fit the needs of investors while at the same point attracting more issuers.

Another advantage of regulatory competition is that regulatory competition permits the creation of a single market without requiring Member States to forfeit their power to regulate. This advantage is particularly important in the European context where Member States have so far proven very reluctant to give up control over their securities markets. The only difference between a regulatory competition system and the status quo would be that regulated entities can choose which Member States' regulations they wish comply with in making an offering.

Regulatory competition relies on the existence of three elements.[13] First, there must exist a diversity of legal regimes. Regulatory competition assumes that regulated entities will have a choice between various types of legal regimes. If there does not exist a choice (e.g., all regulators choose to adopt the same regulations), then there is no opportunity for regulated entities to seek a better regulatory regime and, therefore, to encourage regulators to make changes in their regulations.

Second, entity mobility must exist. Regulated entities must be able to shift between regimes. In the European context, entity mobility represents the existence of a true single market. Currently, in the case of securities regulation, issuers must always comply with their home country regulations. Short of reincorporating in another Member State, issuers do not have the ability to move between legal regimes. Thus, home country control is a barrier to regulatory competition. In addition, full faith and credit must exist between Member States. When an entity chooses its

---

[12] *See*, for example, Final Report of the Wise Men, *supra* note 3, at 14. Leaving actual regulation of the securities market to the Member States really meant that the securities markets in Europe were left unregulated. It has been observed that securities regulation has been virtually non-existent in Europe until the 1990s. Statement by Professor L C B Gower cited in Manning Gilbert Warren III, 'The European Union's Investment Services Directive' (1994) 15 U. Pa. J. Int'l Bus L 181, 185.

[13] *See* Howell E Jackson, 'Centralization, Competition, and Privatization in Financial Regulation' (2001) 2 *Theoretical Inquiries in Law* 649.

regulatory home, all other jurisdictions must honor this choice and cannot impose additional regulations.

Finally, there must be governmental responsiveness. Governments must care that entities are choosing other regulatory regimes. They must be willing to compete for these entities and reconfigure their regulations to make their legal regimes more attractive. Governments may desire to attract more issuers to their regulatory regime because it generates filing and registration fees, tax revenue and other benefits of being an attractive financial center.[14]

Regulatory competition is not a new idea in Europe,[15] especially in the context of financial regulation.[16] A limited form of regulatory competition has been operating in the EU since the late 1980s. The EU's main tool of regulatory competition has been the mutual recognition provisions in the LPD and POD. If an issuer meets the offering requirements of one Member State, it can conduct its offering in all Member States because the approval to conduct the offering provided by the first Member State satisfies the requirements of all of the other Member States.

Mutual recognition results in regulatory competition because it provides the two basic conditions for regulatory competition: diversity of legal regimes and entity mobility. In theory, mutual recognition allows entities to move to the Member State that has the most favorable regulations and then use the mutual recognition 'passport' to conduct business in all of the other Member States.

The mutual recognition provisions included in the directives were designed, however, to bring about harmonization, not generate diversity. As explained in the Commission's 1985 White Paper, mutual recognition, or 'competition among rules', was seen as a way to lead to harmonization by encouraging Member States to coalesce their regulations around a harmonized centre.[17]

The EU's version of mutual recognition does not produce real regulatory competition. Established entities are tied down to their home country regulations, lacking complete freedom of movement.[18] Furthermore, there is a limitation on the diversity of legal regimes. Directives provide for mutual recognition, but also provide for minimum standards. Minimum standards prevent competition below a prescribed regulatory floor which may be undesirable if the floor is set too high. Thus, the EU has not provided the conditions for true regulatory competition.

---

[14] *See*, for example, Howell E Jackson, 'Selective Incorporation of Foreign Legal Systems to Promote Nepal as an International Financial Services Center' in Christopher McCrudden (ed.) (1999) *Regulation and Deregulation: Policy and Practice in the Utilities and Financial Services Industry*.

[15] *See*, for example, A McGee and S Weatherhill, 'The Evolution of the Single Market: Harmonisation or Liberalisation' (1990) 53 Mod L Rev 575; J.M. Sun and J. Pelkmans, 'Regulatory Competition in the Single Market' (1990) 33 J Common Market Studies 67.

[16] *See*, for example, Gérard Hertig, 'Regulatory Competition for EU Financial Services' (2000) 3 J Int'l Econ L 349.

[17] *See id.* at 27–28.

[18] *See* White Paper, *supra* note 3, at 28. *See* also, for example, the papers in this volume that discuss the problems associated with home country control. New firms that are homeless or are willing to forgo access to their home market can strategically select a country that minimizes their regulatory burden.

As the European Union continues its quest for a single securities market, it needs to consider both the paths of harmonization and regulatory competition.

LESSONS FROM ACROSS THE ATLANTIC

The experience of the United States in establishing its own securities regulatory regime is very relevant to the European Union's current task and deserves close inspection.

Before the establishment of the SEC in 1934, US securities regulation shared many of the characteristics of current European securities regulation.[19] Every state in the union had its own set of securities laws known as 'blue sky laws'.[20] The most powerful regulatory authorities at that time were the two dozen regional stock exchanges, such as the exchanges located in New York, Boston and Pittsburgh. These exchanges set and enforced rules of admission and trading much like the major European exchanges do today. Also like the European exchanges, the regional exchanges were undergoing consolidation and fierce competition for new listings. It is important to note for sake of historical comparison that in the early 1930s it was not yet foreseen that the United States would be dominated by only two major stock exchanges, the New York Stock Exchange and the Nasdaq Stock Market; just as it is difficult to predict which exchanges will dominate Europe in seventy years time.

Also, like in Europe today, the growing need of US industry for more capital and the growing interest of retail investors in the stock market led to the tremendous growth of the equity markets. Between 1899 and 1930, retail investment increased by a multiple of 20 to 10 million Americans, laying the groundwork for the robust retail market that the United States has today.

As part of President Franklin Roosevelt's New Deal, the US federal government chose the path of harmonization. The twin pillars of US securities regulation are the Securities Act of 1933, which governs the public offering of securities, and the Securities Exchange Act of 1934, which governs the continuing obligations of the issuer following a public offering and establishes the SEC. The two statutes, and the regulations thereunder, articulate (i) the responsibilities and powers of the federal securities regulator, (ii) the mandatory disclosure rules that must be met by all issuers of securities in the United States, (iii) the investor protection rules, (iv) the registration and regulation of broker-dealers, (v) the regulation of exchanges and other self-regulatory organizations and (vi) the liability of issuers, executives and directors, broker-dealers and other market participants for misstatements, insider trading and other violations of the federal securities laws.

By all accounts, the SEC has been a success. The US securities markets are among the world's most efficient and liquid in the world, traditionally enjoying a high level

---

[19] For an excellent description of the US securities market in the early twentieth century and the creation of the SEC, *see* Thomas K McCraw, *Prophets of Regulation* (1984) 160 *et seq.*

[20] The term, 'blue sky' has its origins in the fact that these laws were originally enacted to prevent the offering and sale of worthless securities, securities that were, in the opinion of some legislators, worth no more than a piece of the 'blue sky'.

of investor confidence. As an agency, the SEC has been repeatedly praised throughout its almost seventy year history as a 'model agency'.

Despite its success, however, there exists a growing academic literature questioning the value of the SEC and its system of mandatory disclosure. In a series of papers, Roberta Romano of Yale Law School and Stephen Choi and Andrew Guzman of University of California Berkeley separately have proposed that the US permit issuers to choose their own securities regulatory regime as opposed to making all issuers abide by the federal regulatory regime.[21] Romano and Choi–Guzman believe that shifting the United States away from a single set of mandatory disclosure rules to a system of regulatory competition will produce more optimal levels of regulation and lead to more efficient markets.[22]

---

[21] Professor Romano's treatment of the subject can be found in Roberta Romano, 'Empowering Investors: A Market Approach to Securities Regulation' (1998) 107 Yale L J 2359. While Romano is principally concerned with fostering competition in securities regulation within the United States, her analysis extends to international transactions: 'Foreign issuers selling shares in the United States could opt out of the federal securities laws and choose those of another nation, such as their country of incorporation, or those of a US state, to govern transactions in their securities in the United States.' *Id.* at 4–5. The Choi–Guzman treatment appears in Stephen Choi & Andrew Guzman, 'Portable Reciprocity: Rethinking the International Reach of Securities Regulation' (1998) 71 Southern California Law Review 903, but is further developed in Stephen Choi, 'Regulating Investors not Issuers: A Market-Based Proposal' (2000) 88 California Law Review 280 and Andrew T. Guzman, 'Developing Capital Markets in a Global Economy' (draft of 11/1/98). Over the past few years a number of similarly motivated reform proposals have appeared. *See* Paul G. Mahoney, 'The Exchange as Regulator' (1997) 83 Virginia Law Review 1453 (advocating the delegation of securities regulation to exchanges); Alan R. Palmiter, 'Toward Disclosure Choice in Securities Offerings' (1999) Columbia Business Law Review 1 (proposing a system of greater issuer choice in securities regulation, albeit with minimal mandatory anti-fraud rules). A less radical but related reform proposal can be found in Merritt Fox, 'Securities Disclosure in a Globalizing Market: Who Should Regulate Whom?' (1997) 97 Michigan Law Review 696 (recommending securities regulation based on an issuer nationality rule – a proposal which eliminates the problem of overlapping regulatory structures but, does not permit the degree of issuer choice embraced in the Romano and Choi–Guzman proposals). *See* also Howell E Jackson and Eric J Pan, 'Regulatory Competition in International Securities Markets: Evidence from Europe in 1999 – Part I' (2001) 56 Business Law 653 (hereinafter Jackson and Pan Part I).

[22] *See* Romano, *supra* note 21, at 4–5. ('As a competitive legal market supplants a monopolist federal agency in the fashioning of regulation, it would produce rules more aligned with the preference of investors, whose decisions drive the capital market.') Choi and Guzman, *supra* note 21, at 923. ('The increase regulatory mobility that [regulatory competition] grants issuers and investors ... affects the incentives of domestic lawmakers to fashion regimes designed to maximize the welfare of securities market participants.')

Romano and Choi–Guzman have slightly different perspectives as to how regulatory competition is likely to play out. Structuring her proposals as an extension of US state competition over corporate charters, Romano seems to assume the emergence of a Delaware-style dominant and optimal jurisdiction. *See*, for example, Romano, *supra* note 21, at 3 ('The market approach to securities regulation advocated in this Article takes as its paradigm the successful experience of US states in corporate law ...'). Choi–Guzman, on the other hand, envision the emergence of a heterogeneous set of regimes, from which investors and issuers will select the system that best suits their needs.

[22] *See* Choi and Guzman, *supra* note 21, at 949. ('[A] diverse set of national regulations will arise and issuers will choose from this set of possible regimes.') For a discussion of this difference in perspective, *see* Romano, *supra* note 21, at fn. 216.

The basic problem with a mandatory disclosure regime is that all issuers must reveal the same information about themselves, without consideration of their individual characteristics or the needs of their target investors.[23] Given that preparing a disclosure statement, particularly for an initial public offering, is quite costly, these mandatory disclosure rules may price out some issuers from making offerings that are desirable by the market. For a standard US public offering (i.e. a registered offering of securities to retail investors) in 1999 legal fees averaged between $685,000–$850,000.[24] Accounting fees added another $660,000 if there needed to be reconciliation of the company's financial statements with United States generally accepted accounting principles (US GAAP).[25] In addition, the company needs to consider underwriting fees, printing fees, marketing fees, listing fees and the cost of management time.

From the investors' standpoint, disclosure is desirable. Certain companies may need to provide less information than others because investors may already understand a great deal of the company's business or certain types of information are more vital than others. For example, in the case of a new company trying to bring to market a new technology, the most important types of information are the composition of management, its business plan, description of technology and ownership of relevant patents. There may to be less urgency for updated financial statements or US GAAP reconciliation. In short, a mandatory disclosure regime is inefficient because it assumes what information investors need.

Under a regulatory competition regime, the amount of information provided by the issuer would be reflected in its price. Issuers that do not disclose much information about themselves would naturally receive a discounted price for their securities than other issuers that are more forthright. This discount would reflect the higher risk incurred by investors in investing in a company where there is less publicly available information. But this is market efficient. An issuer has an incentive to provide enough information to the marketplace to achieve the optimal price for its securities. In addition, the issuer's decision to disclose information is a function of the cost to the issuer for disclosing such information. Therefore, an issuer may accept a discounted price for its shares if the marginal cost of disclosing more information is higher than the discount. In a mandatory disclosure regime, the SEC imposes requirements that may cost too much to comply with compared to the benefit the issuer receives in providing such information.

The major criticism of regulatory competition is that there would be a 'race-to-the-bottom' by regulators in attempting to attract more issuers. Romano, Choi–Guzman and other proponents of regulatory competition deny this would happen. Whereas issuers have an incentive to withhold information from the marketplace; investors have an incentive to demand greater information from issuers. As a result, issuers that provide more information to investors than their competitors will

---

[23] There are special disclosure rules for companies in specific industries, such as utilities and insurance, but usually these rules require more information disclosure.

[24] *See* Howell E Jackson and Eric J Pan, *Regulatory Competition in International Securities Markets: Evidence from Europe in 1999 – Part II* (on file with the author) (hereinafter Jackson and Pan Part II).

[25] *See id.*

benefit from higher prices for their securities. Romano and Choi–Guzman believe that the sensitivity of the investor to the amount of available information is strong enough to prevent a race-to-the-bottom.

Romano argues that issuers and investors will naturally congregate at the regime that requires the optimal level of disclosure. This regime would become the favorite place for companies to issue securities just as Delaware has become the favorite jurisdiction of incorporation for US companies.[26] More importantly, regulatory competition is a dynamic system. Therefore, no regulator can maintain its attractiveness to issuers without staying attuned to the needs of the market and modifying its regulations accordingly. In comparison, the SEC operates like a monopolist – without competition it is immune from the needs of the market and, as a result, is not responsive to new developments in the securities field.

Choi–Guzman argue that the primary advantage of regulatory competition is that the market is able to incorporate multiple market equilibriums. Every issuer is different. Companies that cannot or do not choose to follow the full disclosure regime still will be able to issue securities in the marketplace. Likewise, investors that do not need as much information about certain companies (perhaps they are institutional investors or individuals with a great deal of knowledge of the issuer's industry) will be able to purchase securities from companies that only abide by less demanding regulations.

The Romano and Choi–Guzman recommendations are not generating fear at the SEC. The SEC is very secure in its position as the chief regulator of the US securities market. Their theoretical arguments, however, do raise valid questions about the superiority of the SEC model of mandatory disclosure. More importantly, in the case of the European Union, the Romano and Choi–Guzman arguments are appealing as it may be easier for the European Union to implement a system of regulatory competition than that of a single regulator.

### THE JACKSON–PAN STUDY

In 1999, Howell Jackson of Harvard Law School and I conducted a study of cross-border securities offerings.[27] Though the Romano and Choi–Guzman papers were at the time generating a vigorous theoretical debate there was little empirical work being done in this area. Through a survey of market participants, we set out to test

---

[26] The Romano proposal represents an extension of a familiar debate in US corporate law scholarship: whether corporations in the United states should be allowed to choose the state law under which to organize themselves. For a more review of the debate over regulatory competition in the context of corporate governance, see Jackson, 'Centralization, Competition, and Privatization in Financial Regulation', *supra* note 13. For a similar effort to locate the Romano and Choi–Guzman proposals in the corporate governance literature, *see* Merritt B. Fox, 'Retaining Mandatory Securities Disclosure: Why Issuer Choice is Not Investor Empowerment' (1999) 85 Va L Rev 1335.

[27] The results of this study is being published in two issues of *The Business Lawyer. See* Jackson and Pan Part I, *supra* note 21; Jackson and Pan Part II, *supra* note 24.

many of the assumptions being made by Romano and Choi–Guzman:

1. There does not exist issuer choice in the US securities regime;
2. The SEC is not responsive; and
3. The market would take advantage of the differences in regulatory regimes from the demand side (i.e. investors would differentiate between regimes effectively) and the supply side (i.e. issuers would take advantage of the diversity of regimes available).

During a three-week period in July 1999 and an additional ten days in November and December 1999, we conducted interviews with about fifty professionals in London, Brussels, Paris and Frankfurt. The average length of each interview was between an hour and an hour-and-a-half. The largest group of interviewees (28) were lawyers practicing in Europe (mostly in London), seventeen of these interviewees were practicing US law, seven were practicing English law, and the remaining four were practicing law of other European jurisdictions. The second largest group (13) consisted of regulatory officials, and the balance of the interviewees were investment bankers (9).

In selecting our list of interviewees, we attempted to reach a range of individuals who would have direct personal knowledge of the European capital markets and trans-Atlantic securities offerings. In terms of law firm interviewees, we were able to interview representatives of many of the largest law firms in Europe and the US with offices in London and Frankfurt.[28] Our regulatory contacts covered most of the principal regulatory agencies in the relevant jurisdictions, and our investment banking interviews included meetings with representatives from approximately half of the major firms doing business in London, measured by the volume of capital raised for issuers over the past few years.

### State of the European Securities Market

The Jackson–Pan study revealed several characteristics of the European securities market that are relevant to the regulatory competition-harmonization debate. First, issuer choice does exist in Europe. A European company can offer equity securities in six different transactions. The most limited transaction is a 'home offering'. This

---

[28] In approaching a number of prospective interviewees, a disproportionate number of our initial contacts were alumni of Harvard Law School. Our actual interviewees, however, received their legal training at a much wider range of US law schools.

According to one independent survey of the top law firms in Europe, the firms we visited represented eight of the ten leading advisers to issuers by deal value, eight of the thirteen leading advisers to issuers by deal number, nine out of ten of the leading advisers to issuers by deal value, and nine of the ten leading advisers to lead underwriters by deal number. *See* Rob Mannix, 'European Equity Clients Favour One-Stop Shops' (October 1999) International Financial Law Review 10. In the year prior to October 1999, these law firms acted as advisers to issuers in 66 equity deals worth $70.78 billion and acted as advisers to underwriters in 110 equity deals worth $85.98 billion. *See id.*

means that the European company only offers its securities to retail and institutional investors in its home country. In a home offering, the company only needs to comply with its home country's securities laws. These transactions are extremely rare today because the relative size of the investor market is so small.

The next transaction, which is more common, is a 'Euro-offering.' In a Euro-offering, the company registers its securities with its home regulator (enabling the company to sell its securities to retail investors at home), but prepares its offering documents to satisfy the POD professionals' exemption (enabling the company the sell to institutional investors across Europe).[29] In a Euro-offering, the company can reach a larger number of investors. As much of Europe's investment money is still controlled by institutional investors, structuring the transaction to take advantage of the professionals exemption allows the company to sell to a significant share of the European investment market.[30] As direct retail market in Europe increases, the Euro-offering may become less attractive.

The next three types of transactions are offerings directed at institutional investors located in both Europe and the United States. These transactions have been dubbed by practitioners as 'International-Style Offerings' given their global reach.

What make International-style Offerings distinctive are that issuers prepare disclosure documents not in line with any particular provision of European securities regulation, but rather in line with US securities regulation. International-style Offerings are offerings that can also be made to US Qualified Institutional Buyers (QIBs) under the Rule 144A private placement exemption.[31] As a result, the offering

---

[29] The Public Offers Directive exempts four types of issuing transactions from the prospectus requirement: transferable securities (i) offered to persons in the context of their trades, professions or occupations, (ii) offered to a restricted circle of persons, (iii) sold at a price not exceeding €40,000 or (iv) can only be acquired if the consideration is at least €40,000 per investor. *See* Art. 2, Council Directive 89/298/EEC, 1989 OJ (L 124). These exemptions are rightfully included because these are offerings are not really to the 'public'. The investor protection rationale does not apply because these transactions are limited offers to individuals who should have available a substantial understanding of the issuer. The first two types of transactions are very similar to the private placement exemptions recognized in US securities law. *See* Sec. 4(2) of the Securities Act of 1933. Issuers selling to a limited number of individuals and accredited investors do not have to produce a prospectus. The directive, however, does not use the term 'accredited investors,' but rather calls them persons in the context of their trades, professions or occupations. In this regard, the EU exemptions are broader than the Regulation D private placement exemptions because the broadly defined 'Professionals Exemption' allows offerings to be made to institutional investors (or what US securities law calls QIBs) without requiring a prospectus in addition to accredited investors. The closest US equivalent to such a transaction is a Rule 144A offering. Finally, the Public Offers Directive excludes certain types of securities from its coverage such as transferable securities offered in individual denominations of at least €40,000, sovereign issuances, transferable securities offered in connection with a merger or acquisition, units issued by certain collective investment undertakings and eurosecurities. Where the directives are silent, national regulations still apply.

[30] Currently, most European individuals invest through mutual funds. As a result, mutual funds have become the fastest growing investment vehicle in Europe, tripling in size from €1.2 trillion in 1995 to €3.6 trillion in 2000. *See* Pozen, *supra* note 5, at 12.

[31] Under Rule 144A, the purchaser may offer and resell those securities to any QIB if (i) the securities are not of the same class as securities of the issuer listed on a US stock exchange or the Nasdaq, (ii) the buyer is advised that the seller is relying on Rule 144A and (iii) unless the issuer is a reporting company

documents prepared for International-style Offerings are those which would otherwise be prepared for Rule 144A offerings. Issuers disclose more information about themselves in International-style Offerings than they do in Euro-offerings.

Because International-style Offerings are directed at US investors, European issuers are exposed to civil and criminal liability under Rule 10b-5 of the US securities laws. Rule 10b-5 makes it unlawful for any person, in connection with the purchase or sale of a security: (i) to employ any device, scheme or artifice to defraud; (ii) to make any untrue statement of a material fact or to omit to state a material fact necessary to make any statement made not misleading; or (iii) to engage in any act, practice or course of business that would operate as a fraud or deceit upon any person. Rule 10b-5 requires the demonstration of scienter or recklessness on the part of the defendant. Therefore, the defendant can limit its exposure to Rule 10b-5 liability by showing that it had performed appropriate due diligence. In a US offering, lawyers commonly prepare what is known as a Rule 10b-5 letter to confirm that the disclosure documents for the transaction satisfy the Rule 10b-5 requirements. Rule 10b-5 letters are not inexpensive. In 1999, each Rule 10b-5 letter had cost between \$235,000–\$300,000 in additional legal fees.

Therefore within the realm of International-style Offerings, European issuers choose between three options: (i) Rule 144A documentation with no Rule 10b-5 letter; (ii) Rule 144A documentation with one Rule 10b-5 letter prepared by counsel for the issuer; and (iii) Rule 144A documentation with two Rule 10b-5 letters prepared by counsel for the issuer and counsel for the underwriter. From the perspective of the European issuer, the need for Rule 10b-5 letters is correlated with the portion of the offering that will be sold to US investors. US companies, advised by US investment banks, that offer their securities exclusively to US QIBs under Rule 144A most always request two Rule 10b-5 letters since their exposure to liability is high. On the other hand, a European company that plans on offering its securities predominantly to European investors will not worry as much about Rule 10b-5 liability and thus may not even have one Rule 10b-5 letter prepared.

The final type of transaction that European issuers can choose is a US registered public offering. By registering its securities with the SEC, a European company will be able to sell its securities to US retail investors and to seek a listing on a US stock exchange.

These six types of transactions show the choice that European issuers have when they offer securities to European and US investors. This fact undermines a core assumption of advocates of regulatory competition that the current regulatory regime deprives issuers of choice.

---

or is exempt from the Securities and Exchange Act of 1934 the holder and a prospective purchaser from the holder, have the continuing right to receive from the issuer at or prior to the time of sale by the holder, upon request, specified financial statements of the issuer and information as to its business. A QIB is an institution which owns and invests on a discretionary basis at least \$100 million in qualifying securities or be a person with a net worth of at least \$25 million.

[32] *See* Marco Pagano *et al.*, *The Geography of Equity Listing : Why Do Companies List Abroad?* Centre for Studies in Economic and Finance, Working Paper No. 28 (December 2000), available at <http://www.dise.unisa.it/WP/wp28.pdf>.

*Table 1.* Cost estimates for international offerings by a leading US law firm

|  | International-style Offering with one rule 10b-5 letter | International-style Offering with two rule 10b-5 letters | US Registered Public Offering |
|---|---|---|---|
| Lawyer for issuer | $350,000–$400,000 | $350,000–$400,000 | $400,000–$500,000 |
| Lawyer for underwriter | Nothing | $235,000–$300,000 | $285,000–$350,000 |
| Total | $350,000–$400,000 | $585,000–$750,000 | $685,000–$850,000 |

*Table 2.* Cost estimates for international offering by a leading UK law firm

|  | Euro Offering | International-style Offering with no rule 10b-5 letter | International-style Offering with one rule 10b-5 letter | US Registered Public Offering |
|---|---|---|---|---|
| Lawyer for issuer | $75,000–$100,000 | $175,000–$250,000 | $200,000–$275,000 | $400,000–$500,000 |
| Lawyer for underwriter | Nothing | Nothing | Nothing | $300,000–$375,000 |
| Total | $75,000–$100,000 | $175,000–$250,000 | $200,000–$275,000 | $700,000–$875,000 |

The Jackson–Pan study confirms that the cost of doing an offering increases with the level of disclosure provided to the market. Particularly in the case of legal fees, the cost of each type of transaction in 1999 rose progressively from as low as $75,000 to almost $1 million. Tables 1 and 2 show the average cost of each type of transaction as charged by a US law firm and UK law firm respectively.

While these fee figures show a correlation between cost and disclosure, they also reveal how important legal fees are to an issuer's decision as to the type of transaction to undertake. One of the assumptions of proponents of regulatory competition is that the cost of mandatory disclosure outweighs the benefit of the mandatory disclosure regime which ends up pricing out some issuers from the market. When evaluated against the cost figures collected by the Jackson–Pan study, this assumption seems less valid. The approximate marginal cost of each type of transaction is between $100,000 and $150,000. In relation to a multi-million dollar offering, this cost differential is quite small. For a large corporation, such fees are practically *de minimis*. Therefore, if there is a reason why issuers would want to look for alternative disclosure regimes, we have to look beyond the factor of cost.

By far the most popular transactions were the variants of International-style Offerings. At least in 1999, about 60% of the transactions worked on by the lawyers we interviewed were International-style Offerings and 35% were US registered public offerings. Only the remaining 5% of the deals were Euro-offerings or home offerings.

The popularity of International-style Offerings is due to the fact that it serves two purposes. First, International-style Offerings are viewed as a superior way of offering securities across Europe. Interviewees described International-style Offerings as 'the best way to do a pan-European offering.' The main advantage of International-style Offerings is that they consist of a standard disclosure document that can be used for a variety of purposes. In the case of Euro-offerings, disclosure documents are prepared primarily in accordance with home country regulations. The professionals exemption does not in itself establish a particular model for a Euro-offering disclosure statement. International-style Offerings, however, follow the standard disclosure document developed for the Rule 144A exemption.

Second, International-style Offerings are versatile. In addition to Europe, International-style Offerings can be used to target to institutional investors in the United States. There are many reasons why European issuers seek to offer securities to US QIBs: the opportunity to tap a larger pool of investment capital, to sell to a more knowledgeable group of investors (particularly in the case of high-tech industries) and to increase price tension.

The data also undermines the regulatory competition proponents' assumption that the US mandatory disclosure regime poses an insurmountable barrier to foreign issuers. The popularity of International-style Offerings shows that European issuers are selling frequently to the United States. What is even more significant is that a further one-third of all European offerings are registered with the SEC. This data supports the view that despite the stringency of US securities regulation, more listings and offerings by European companies are directed at the United States than at other Member States in Europe.[32] Therefore, based upon the responses of the lawyers interviewed as high as 95% of all offerings made by European companies in 1999 were sold or could be sold to investors in the United States.

The data also confirms that the mutual recognition passport is underutilized. In 1999, there were almost no pan-European retail offerings. A pan-European retail offering means that shares are sold to all investors in Europe – both institutional and retail. In theory, pan-European retail offerings should be easy to complete because of the LPD and POD mutual recognition passport. In reality, the passport does not exist because the directives permit Member States to impose additional requirements on issuers seeking to offer securities in their jurisdictions.[33] For example, the directives condition the recognition of prospectuses on acceptable translation, which is a burden on issuers in terms of time and expense. The directives also permit Member States to require additional disclosure concerning information specific to the host country, such as the income tax system, paying agents located in the host country

---

[33] *See* FESCO, *A 'European Passport' for Issuers: A Report for the EU Commission*, FESCO/00-138b (20 December 2000) at 3. ('The day to day functioning of the mutual recognition of prospectuses shows that there is a need for modernization and enhanced flexibility. The extension of an offer or a listing to various [European Economic Area (EEA)] States proves to be complex and some times is an obstacle to real pan-European strategies. The obligations for an issuer to comply with various specific requirements in each EEA State, like the translation of the full prospectus, does not encourage mutual recognition of information documents.')

and investor notice procedures. Furthermore, the directives only require Member States to recognize outside prospectuses if they meet all of the requirements set forth by the directives. If the applying issuer received either a partial exemption or derogation from the reporting requirements of its home authority, the host authority can reject the approved prospectus if it does not recognize and grant the same exemption or derogation. This provision stifles innovations like shelf registration and other types of abbreviated securities registration schemes.[34] The barriers to a pan-European retail offering are so high that only a few transactions of this nature have been attempted, and no transaction has used the passport to access all of the European markets.[35] As a result, there remains no effective way for European issuers to make an offering to retail investors across the European Union.

The barriers to a working mutual recognition passport are well-known, and the removal of these barriers is the goal of many of the EU initiatives currently under consideration.[36] Such regulatory reform programs assume that the best way to develop a pan-European securities market is to encourage greater cross-listing of securities in Europe. Data from the Jackson–Pan study question the validity of this strategy. According to interviewees, issuers are not eager for multiple listings. One explanation is that issuers are able to reach retail investors already under the professionals exemption. For example, retail investors can subscribe to institutional investor offerings through mutual funds and other investment vehicles. In addition, retail investors can also buy securities through a 'loophole' in the professionals exemption resulting from the absence of resale restrictions on institutional investors. Unlike in the United States, many Member States do not restrict institutional investors

---

[34] The amendment to the Listing Particulars Directive, dubbed the 'Eurolist directive,' was meant to make it easier for established companies to seek additional listing on other European exchanges. *See* Giovanni Nardulli and Antonio Segni, 'EU Cross-border Securities Offerings: An Overview' (1996) 19 Fordham International Law Journal 887–891 (referring to Council Directive 94/18/EC, 1994 OJ (L 135)). According to the Eurolist directive, issuers who have had securities listed on an official exchange for at least three years and satisfactorily complied with all disclosure and admission requirements can prepare a special document that will still fulfill the obligations required by the Listing Particulars Directive. In short, established companies do not have to prepare a full listing prospectus, but rather a shorter prospectus that allows the issuer to incorporate and refer to other documents such as its latest annual report and previous prospectuses. The concept of Eurolist was originally proposed by the Federation of European Stock Exchanges (FESE) which proposed a system by which issuers could pay one single fee to its home exchange and be listed immediately on all other participating exchanges. The Eurolist directive helps this goal along by making it easier for currently listed companies to meet the disclosure requirements required to apply for the mutual recognition passport and gain access to the other European stock exchanges. *See* Marco Pagano and Benn Steil, (ed.), 'Equity Trading I: The Evolution of European Trading Systems' *in The European Equity Markets* 40 (1996); Eddy Wymeersch, 'The EU Directives on Financial Disclosure' (1996) 3 European Financial Services Law Review 40.

[35] One of the few pan-European retail offerings to succeed was the 1999 Deutsche Telekom offering. On 7 June 1999, Deutsche Telekom began offering 286 million new shares priced at €11 billion to retail investors in all eleven euro-zone countries. *See* David I. Oyama, 'Deutsche Telekom Adds to Incentives for Share Offering' Wall Street Journal (7 June 1999) A14; Silvia Ascarelli, 'Deutsche Telekom's Offering Makes a Strong Showing' Wall Street Journal (8 June 1999), A12. But even the Deutsche Telekom offering did not use the mutual recognition passport in all countries, but had to comply with local securities regulations.

[36] *See*, for example, *Final Report of the Wise Men*, *supra* note 3; FESCO, *A European Passport*, *supra* note 33.

from reselling to retail investors securities purchased through the professionals exemption.[37] Therefore, the barrier between retail and professional investors is porous.

Forcing issuers to list their securities in multiple markets does not make much sense from an economic standpoint. Splitting the trading of an issuer's securities into multiple markets is inefficient. Even with a well-working mutual recognition passport, the cost of issuing securities is higher due to the additional filing fees, associated legal fees, marketing fees and other costs associated with duplicated selling efforts in different markets. In addition, issuers will not receive the best possible price for their securities. Investors will not see all available buy and sell orders, trading volume per market will be lower and liquidity will be less than if trading was concentrated in a single market. The only ones who would benefit from such a system would be those market participants capable of exploiting arbitrage opportunities between markets.[38]

The European Union needs centralized markets that are openly accessible to institutional and retail investors alike. One way that the European Union can achieve this goal is by improving the Investment Services Directive (ISD).[39] The ISD creates a single license for investment services providers to do business in all EU Member States. So long as the service provider is authorized and supervised by a competent authority of one Member State, it is qualified to provide investment services in all of the other Member States. These activities are listed in the annexes to the directive.

The ISD accomplishes four things. First, the directive extends the investment services passport to specialized investment firms, permitting the communication and execution of transactions in financial instruments and the management of investments. Second, the directive establishes procedures for rights of access by investment firms and credit institutions to stock exchanges.[40] Third, the directive ensures that no resident of a Member State is denied access to the services provided by an investment firm based in another Member State. Finally, the directive creates a passport for exchanges to extend remote membership and access privileges.[41]

The ISD will encourage the creation of a single European securities market by enabling the development of pan-European stock exchanges.[42] Instead of forcing an

---

[37] The absence of resale restrictions on securities sold under the professionals exemption is addressed in greater detail in Jackson and Pan Part I, *supra* note 21, at 688–689.

[38] The adverse effects of market fragmentation has been concern of the SEC. *See* Notice of Filing of Proposed Rule Change to Rescind Exchange Rule 390; Commission Request for Comment on Issues Relating to Market Fragmentation, Release No. 34-42450 (23 February 2000) available at <http://www.sec.gov/rules/sro/ny9948n.htm>.

[39] Council Directive 93/22/EEC, 1993 OJ (L 141) (hereinafter ISD). *See* Jackson and Pan Part I, *supra* note 21, at 677–680.

[40] Without prejudice to the conditions for the admission of securities to official stock exchange listing as established by the Admissions Directive.

[41] *See* ISD Art. 15, *supra* note 39.

[42] One of the first stock exchanges to seize upon the opportunity of pan-European trading made possible by the ISD was EASDAQ, now known as Nasdaq Europe. *See* Dana T. Ackerly II *et al.*, 'EASDAQ – the European Stock Market for the Next Hundred Years?' (1997) 12 J Int'l Banking L 86. Since then Nasdaq Europe has been joined by an alphabet soup of competing exchanges such as Jiway (Morgan Stanley and OM Gruppen), Euronext (Belgian, Dutch and French stock exchanges), Virt-X (Swiss Stock Exchange and Tradepoint) and the ill-fated iX (Deutsche Börse and London Stock Exchange).

issuer to make its shares available across Europe through multiple listings, the issuer can instead list its securities on a single stock exchange that offers remote membership. The issuer can then expect investors from across Europe to purchase its shares on that exchange. This possibility will lead to greater competition among exchanges and ultimately consolidation, perhaps to the point of where Europe, like the United States, has two dominant stock exchanges and a handful of specialist exchanges.[43] More importantly, the development of pan-European stock exchanges will remedy the problems associated with market fragmentation, resulting in better pricing, greater volume, higher liquidity and other benefits of a more efficient stock exchange.[44]

The consolidation of stock exchanges in Europe will lead to some form of regulatory competition. In a more competitive environment, stock exchanges will compete against one another on the basis of pricing, volume, efficiency of trading

---

[43] Consider the statement made by the London Stock Exchange and Deutsche Börse when they initially announced their memorandum of understanding: 'Today, we start the process of harmonising the rules, conventions and technology for accessing the respective markets. Through this plan ... we aim to create the nucleus of a single European stock market ...'

[44] There is room for much improvement of the ISD. The ISD is still quite weak and vague. In many areas, the ISD has left the interpretation of terms to Member States which has led to uneven implementation and the maintenance of regulatory barriers to cross-border investment services. *See*, for example, Draft Communication 95/C 291/06, 1995 OJ (C 291/7). For instance, the ISD did not make clear the distinction between freedom of establishment and freedom of service. In addition, the ISD allows Member States to place additional burdens on foreign investment firms and credit institutions. In a pure mutual recognition system, investment firms should only have to meet the requirements of their home country. So long as they have the approval of the home authority, they can provide services in all other Member States. Instead, the ISD permits host Member States to require that investment firms meet local regulations such as prudential rules, rules of conduct and other rules necessary for the 'general good'.

The general good exception is particularly problematic because there is not a commonly understood definition of what constitutes the general good. The main questions usually revolve around intent and effect. Is a regulation being put into place for the intent of protecting the general good or is its true intent a protectionist one? And even if there is such an intent, should this regulation be allowed if it has the effect of preventing foreign firms from entering?

Another major weakness in the ISD is the limitation of trading to 'regulated markets'. With investment firms now permitted to provide services across borders and exchanges allowed to set up remote membership, there would be tremendous opportunity for alternative trading networks, electronic communications networks (ECNs) and new pan-European exchanges to siphon off trading volume from the traditional stock exchanges. Instead, the ISD gives Member States the authority to restrict trading of domestic securities to only 'regulated' markets. If a Member State chooses to do so, exchanges that are not deemed regulated would be prohibited from listing and trading these domestic securities. As a result, trading of a particular security would be concentrated in the regulated markets. The definition of a regulated market is ambiguous. The ISD defines a regulated market as a market that (i) is authorized to be a regulated market by the Member State, (ii) functions regularly and (iii) meets the transparency and reporting requirements described by the directive. In short, the criteria by which a market is deemed a regulated market is left to the whims of the Member State. The definition also offers no assurance that ECNs and other new exchanges can qualify to become regulated markets, and even if one Member State includes such alternative exchanges on their list of regulated markets the exchanges cannot handle securities from other Member States. The regulated markets limitation poses a strong obstacle to the development of pan-European trading systems by allowing Member States to withhold trading privileges to certain exchanges on the basis of criteria determined not at the EU level but at the Member State level.

platforms and prestige.[45] Stock exchanges will also compete against each other in terms of regulations. Not only will stock exchanges be able to modify their own market rules, but most likely Member States will modify their own securities regulation in order to protect their local exchange. The long term result will be that the market will eventually settle in a few widely-accepted regulatory regimes (i.e. the Delaware effect). Once a dominant exchange emerges, it will be less likely that issuers will switch to a competing exchange. As a result, the regulations of the dominant market will become the dominant regulatory regime in Europe. One can conceive, however, of an alternative. An enterprising stock exchange could dispense with securities regulation altogether and adopt an open regulatory structure where each issuer can select the regulatory regime it wishes to follow. In such a system, hundreds of companies may trade on the same exchange, but each company prepares disclosure documents according to different regulations.[46] Given that there is no precedent for such a system, it is unlikely that one will be actually implemented in Europe.

The most important observation made by the Jackson–Pan study is that there currently exists a *de facto* international standard of disclosure created by market practice. International-style Offerings are the most common types of offerings in Europe today. Not only are International-style Offerings considered the best way to make a pan-European offering, they are also the most popular choice for European issuers seeking to sell their shares in the United States.

There are several characteristics of International-style Offerings that are noteworthy. First, International-style Offerings use a standard that has not been set by a government or self-regulatory organization, but rather use a standard that has been selected by the market. Second, International-style Offerings provide a level of disclosure higher than that required by the minimum standard set in the LPD and POD or any single EU Member State. Third, International-style Offerings use a US standard originating from US practice with the Rule 144A private placement exemption. Fourth, the popularity of International-style Offerings in Europe is partially explained by the dominance of US investment banks in Europe and the importance of US law expertise in international securities transactions. Fifth, the adoption of the Rule 144A standard and the success of US investment banks and US law firms in Europe has given the SEC supreme influence over the EU securities market.

All of these characteristics are interrelated. International-style Offerings are products of market practice because they originated from market practice. Rule 144A is an exemption from SEC registration, but the offering documents for a Rule 144A offering incorporate many of the components of a US registration statement such as risk factors and management's discussion and analysis (MD&A). As US requirements are considered the most stringent in the world, European issuers that adopt the Rule 144A standard increase their level of disclosure when they adopt US market practice. The reason why European issuers do not adopt a different standard, such as

---

[45] One official of a major European stock exchange reported of entering into 'beauty contests' with other exchanges to woo the business of new companies. *See* Jackson and Pan Part I, *supra* note 21, at fn. 71.

[46] This system has been proposed separately in Choi–Guzman, *supra* note 21 and Jackson, *Selective Incorporation of Foreign Legal Systems to Promote Nepal as an International Financial Services Center*, *supra* note 14.

one centered around United Kingdom or German disclosure standards, can also be attributed to the role of US investment banks in Europe. In the past ten years, US investment banks have dominated the top ranks of leading securities underwriters.[47] As advisers to the largest European offerings, US investment banks have reacted to the absence of any real European standard by insisting on US-style disclosure documents – documents that they are used to preparing and marketing. Brought in to advise these investment banks, US law firms have ensured that US-style documentation has become a European standard as well.

The preparation of Rule 10b-5 letters demonstrate most clearly the 'gravitational pull' generated by US securities regulation and US investment banks and law firms on European practice. As stated earlier, though Rule 144A exempts the issuer from the liability rules associated with a registered offering, it does not exempt the issuer from Rule 10b-5 liability. As a defense against Rule 10b-5 liability, the issuer and the underwriter prepare due diligence letters known as Rule 10b-5 letters. Since Rule 10b-5 letters only have a function in the context of US securities regulation and are relatively expensive to prepare, one would not expect such letters to be prepared in an offering which is not directed at the US or where the size of the US offering is quite small. Full US market practice demands that two Rule 10b-5 letters be prepared, one by issuer's counsel and one by underwriter's counsel. Full market practice is quite common in Europe because US investment banks require the additional letters. In contrast, one interviewee noted that at least one European investment bank, as predicted, is less demanding in requiring the preparation of additional Rule 10b-5 letters.

Based upon the data collected by Professor Jackson and myself, there is some variation between International-style Offerings as a result of how many Rule 10b-5 letters are prepared. But we also found that two Rule 10b-5 letters are being prepared in cases where it is less important to provide such letters. In addition, Rule 10b-5 letters have become more common in Europe not only because US investment banks demand them but also because investors expect to see them. One German lawyer in Frankfurt noted that he often prepares due diligence letters for Europe-only deals. He does not call these letters 'Rule 10b-5 letters' since he and his colleagues are not US lawyers, but the preparation and due diligence done to prepare the letters is similar to that done to prepare a Rule 10b-5 letter. Thus, the Rule 10b-5 letter has become an integral part of International-style Offerings despite the fact that its reason for existence stems entirely from US securities regulation and US market practice.

### EVALUATING THE US SEC

Proponents of regulatory competition depict the SEC as monopolistic and unresponsive to the needs of the market.

---

[47] *See*, for example, Charles Pretzlik, *Survey – Europe Reinvented: US Banks Take Europe By Storm*, Financial Times (9 February 2001) available at <http://globalarchive.ft.com/globalarchive/articles.html? print = true&id = 010209007679>. In 2000, the top four out of five investment banks in European equities issues were US-based. US investment banks also dominated the top five spots for advising European mergers and acquisitions and bond offerings.

This description is too simplistic. The SEC is neither monopolistic, nor unresponsive. Though the SEC has a regulatory monopoly over the US securities market, the SEC does not behave like a monopoly. Despite views to the contrary, the SEC does not dictate a single regulatory standard that all issuers must follow. In particular, the SEC affords foreign issuers a number of exemptions from full compliance with US securities regulation.[48] As noted above, for example, Rule 144A has opened up the US markets to foreign issuers. In 1991, the SEC adopted the multijurisdictional disclosure system (MJDS) with Canada.[49] Under MJDS, Canadian issuers can use Canadian disclosure documents for public offerings to the US. In September 2000, the SEC adopted the disclosure standards for foreign private issuers recommended by the International Organization of Securities Commissions (IOSCO).[50] These exemptions and modifications to the US disclosure system, in particular Rule 144A, have been integral in permitting foreign companies to access the US markets.

Nor has the SEC been unresponsive. As part of our study, Professor Jackson and I asked lawyers at several law firms about their opinion of the SEC. Overwhelmingly, our interviewees were positive about the SEC though with some difference of enthusiasm between US law firms and UK law firms.

Our interviewees tended to evaluate the SEC in two respects. On the one hand, they looked at the SEC in its role as a rulemaker. Several lawyers brought up the Plain English requirement,[51] the proposed Aircraft Carrier Release[52] and the adoption of IOSCO disclosure standards. With regards to this aspect of the SEC's work, the lawyers were less enthusiastic. For example, several lawyers complained that the Plain English requirement was poorly implemented and generated confusion. Others

*Table 3.* Law firms' perception of the US SEC

|  | Very effective | Somewhat effective | Not very effective | Ineffective |
|---|---|---|---|---|
| US law firms | 6 | 1 | 1 | 0 |
| UK law firms | 1 | 3 | 0 | 0 |

---

[48] For a review of a number of the ways in which foreign issuers are treated more liberally than domestic US issuers, *see* Jackson and Pan Part I, *supra* note 21, at pp. 666–667; Daniel A. Braverman, 'US Legal Considerations Affecting Global Offerings in Foreign companies' (1996) 17 Nw J Int'l L & Bus 30; Marc I Steinberg and Lee E Michaels, 'Disclosure in Global Securities Offerings: Analysis of Jurisdictional Approaches, Commonality and Reciprocity' (1999) 20 Mich J Int'l L 246–251.

[49] *See* Multijurisdictional Disclosure and Modifications to the Current Registration and Reporting System for Canadian Issuers, Securities Act Release No. 6902, Exchange Act Release No. 29,354, 56 Fed. Reg. 30,006 (1 July 1991).

[50] *See* International Disclosure Standards Securities Act Release No. 7745, Exchange Act Release No. 41936, 17 CFR Parts 210, 228, 229, 230, 239, 240, 249 and 260 (28 September 1999).

[51] *See* Plain English Disclosure, Securities Act Release No. 7497, Exchange Act Release No. 39593, Investment Company Act Release No. 23011, 17 CFR Parts 228, 229, 230, 239 and 274 (28 January 1998).

[52] *See* Regulation of Securities Offerings Securities Act Release 7606A; Exchange Act Release No. 40632A, Investment Company Act Release No. 23519A (13 November 1998) (Proposed Rule). The release is called the 'Aircraft Carrier' because of its size and complexity.

criticised the Aircraft Carrier Release which would make substantial changes to disclosure requirements contained in the registration statement forms, rules governing pre-offering communications, rules governing the integration of private and public offerings and periodic disclosure requirements. One lawyer commented positively on the adoption of IOSCO disclosure standards, but noted that the IOSCO standards were effectively identical to the old Form 20-F and that the SEC has not budged its position on US GAAP reconciliation.

On the other hand, the interviewees positively commented on their experience dealing directly with the SEC staff when conducting public offerings in the US. For most interviewees, the SEC's presence is felt most strongly during the review of new filings before registration. In this context, interviewees found the SEC to be quite flexible and eager to work with foreign issuers. The SEC staff is considered to be very professional, extremely knowledgeable and willing to work within the schedules proposed by the issuer. This willingness to provide comments in a timely manner and to speak directly with counsel is essential in transactions which must be timed carefully.[53] The interviewees offered special praise for Paul Dudek, chief of the Office of International Corporate Finance at the SEC. Dudek is known for always being accessible to foreign issuers, to the point of giving out his home telephone number so that issuers can continue to contact him as they are approaching a filing or approval deadline. In addition, the SEC has traditionally provided special advantages to foreign issuers. Most important of these advantages has been confidentiality during the review process. Confidentiality makes the process of seeking SEC approval less risky since the issuer has more control over the timing of the public announcement of its offering and is able to avoid embarrassment if there is a failure to meet a certain deadline.

There are several reasons why the legal community rates the SEC and the SEC disclosure regime so highly. First, the SEC has a competent, professional staff. Though some interviewees commented that the SEC is taking longer to respond to drafts, no one questioned the ability of the SEC staff or the quality of their work. The SEC consistently attracts the best lawyers in the United States. Most of the lawyers who work in the corporate finance division, the division responsible for reviewing disclosure documents, are experienced securities lawyers.

Second, the SEC has many formal and informal avenues of communication with the securities industry, which ensures that the SEC acts with the support or at least with the consideration of market participants. As a federal agency, the SEC must follow notice-and-comment procedures prior to rulemaking. General notice of any proposed rulemaking must be first published in the Federal Register.[54] The public is

---

[53] Although the SEC does its best to meet the deadlines of the issuer, the SEC process remains unpredictable enough that many issuers find it difficult to conduct dual-listing transactions in both the US and Europe. Several interviewees cited deals where the US piece had to be downgraded from a public offering to a Rule 144A offering because SEC approval could not be obtained at the same time the offering was going to be made public in Europe.

[54] Proposed rules, comments and final rules are also made available on the SEC website at <www.sec.gov>.

then permitted to comment on the proposed rule. After receiving comments, the SEC issues a final rule, accompanied by a detailed explanation of the rule and references to comments received. Through the formal notice-and-comment process, the securities industry has strong input in new SEC rules. For example, in the case of the Aircraft Carrier Release, numerous business interest groups, law firms and investment banks vigorously criticized different provisions in the release. In response to the volume of negative comments received from the securities industry, the SEC has indefinitely delayed final rulemaking on the Aircraft Carrier Release. The experience of the Aircraft Carrier Release shows the value of industry participation in the SEC rulemaking process.

Beyond rulemaking, the SEC also interacts with the securities industry during the implementation of rules. When members of the securities industry have questions about the applicability of certain rules, the SEC issues 'no-action' letters which represent the unofficial view of the SEC on certain transactions or cases. As these no-action letters are made public, they serve as a valuable resource for lawyers to advise clients on how to comply with SEC rules. The SEC also works closely with issuers before registration statements become effective. It is common for lawyers representing new issuers to call the SEC for advice and negotiate exemptions from the registration statement. In the past, the Office of International Corporate Finance, for example, has had an unofficial policy to return all phone calls within two hours.

The SEC also keeps in close contact with the securities industry on an informal level. SEC staff members frequently meet with securities lawyers and investment bankers at conferences and other public settings. The closeness of the SEC to the private sector is also maintained by the 'revolving door' of lawyers and regulators who come in and out of the SEC, law firms, investment banks, industry interest groups and universities.

This combination of a dedicated and well-qualified staff and formal and informal communication with the securities markets makes the SEC a highly effective regulator.

## GETTING THE STORY STRAIGHT

One can make four general observations about the current state of the European securities market – observations that have great implications for the EU's plan to establish a single securities market.

First, international listings and offerings will not be decided by a race-to-the-bottom. Despite opportunities in the current securities regulation regime for a race-to-the-bottom, there is no indication that issuers seek only to provide the lowest possible levels of disclosure. Instead, current market practice in the European Union is to adopt the more burdensome US standard. US disclosure practice dominates the European securities market, even though the amount of disclosure required by the US standard is greater than the EU minimum standard and greater than any Member State standard. Given that many of these offerings are directed primarily at European investors, it is even more striking that European issuers are voluntarily providing more information than they are legally obligated to provide.

Second, the transatlantic securities market has not shown itself interested in dealing with multiple disclosure regimes. Market practice indicates that offerings tend to congregate around specific types of offerings with the majority either being International-style Offerings or US-registered offerings.

Issuers' lack of enthusiasm for multiple disclosure regimes is revealed in the failure of the EU's mutual recognition passport and the reliance on the professionals exemption. The biggest flaw in the passport is that issuers still have to comply with a variety of Member State securities rules. The benefit of being able to do a pan-European retail offering is outweighed by the cost of having to research and to comply with the law of every single Member State. On the other hand, the professionals exemption is extremely popular because issuers can prepare a single offering document and use it across the continent. Nonetheless, even with the professionals exemption, European issuers demand greater standardization. The definition of 'professional' differs between Member States. As a result, issuers must be careful to sell their securities to only those institutions and individuals that meet the various definitions. Again, the need to be aware of and satisfy different rules makes offerings more burdensome.

The market's desire for standardization, as opposed to diversity, stems from a desire for convenience and certainty. It is no coincidence that most disclosure documents look almost identical. They are similarly written, formatted and organized. Over time, these standardized documents have become familiar to both investors and issuers and, as a result, are an effective way to communicate information.

Third, securities offerings are relatively inexpensive. It is not the case that the cost of legal compliance with stringent disclosure standards prices out many companies from the equity markets. As described above, there are several offering options available to companies seeking to make pan-European or trans Atlantic offerings for less than $500,000 in legal fees.

Fourth, the current regulatory system in Europe is woefully inadequate. The fact that most offerings are done using the professionals exemption and following US disclosure standards (including the practice of providing due diligence letters) shows that European issuers are opting-out of the EU's securities regulation system. The problems with the EU's regulation system are well-documented. Both FESCO and the Wise Men Committee described the European Passport as seriously flawed and noted that the Commission has not ensured that Member States properly implement all of the directives related to securities offerings. Furthermore, the Commission has focused incorrectly on encouraging issuers to make multiple listings in Europe. Instead, the Commission needs to tear down the regulatory barriers that prevent exchanges and quotation systems from operating across Europe and being accessed by investors across Europe and elsewhere. In this respect, the European system suffers from both institutional and legislative weakness.

## EUROPE'S SINGLE REGULATOR

The European securities market is not in want of a securities regulator. In fact, the EU today has an effective single securities regulator – the SEC in the United States.

The influence of the SEC on the European market is extremely strong. In terms of market practice, SEC rules on disclosure and market conduct are followed in Europe, even when contact with the United States is incidental. At an institutional level, the SEC wields tremendous influence in intergovernmental organizations which has enabled it to win concessions from its counterparts in each of the EU Member States.

There are several reasons why the SEC has become such an effective regulator of the European securities market. First, the size and importance of the US capital markets makes compliance or future compliance with SEC rules always a serious consideration for European issuers. Such issuers appreciate the need eventually, if not immediately, to raise capital or to conduct business activities in the United States.[55] As a result, there is an incentive for European issuers to follow US regulations.[56]

The importance of the US market has in turn caused several European exchanges and regulators to recognize or adopt US disclosure standards. For example, the UK Listing Authority permits companies listing their securities on a UK exchange to prepare financial statements according to US GAAP. This courtesy is not reciprocated by the SEC. With respect to the more established exchanges, like the London Stock Exchange, acceptance of US disclosure standards is a way to attract listings from US companies. Other exchanges and markets accept US disclosure standards for a different reason. They are targeting new companies about to make an initial public offering in Europe and seek immediately or eventually to offer shares in the United States.[57] The US market is attractive to these companies because of higher valuations, greater investor interest in certain industries and the possibility of having acquisition currency. As a result, these companies place a premium on having the flexibility to do an offering in the United States without the need to revise their corporate reports or reconcile their financial records with US GAAP. Nasdaq Europe, formerly known as EASDAQ, exemplifies this strategy. The Nasdaq Europe Rule Book borrows extensively from the rules of the Nasdaq Stock Market in the United States.[58] Nasdaq rules are in turn derived from SEC rules and regulations. The reason Nasdaq Europe models its regulations on those of Nasdaq is to minimize the regulatory barriers to companies wishing to conduct a dual-listing on Nasdaq Europe and a US exchange. More importantly, it represents the growing acceptance of US standards in Europe as a way of accessing the US markets.

Second, the dominance of US investment banks and US law firms in the international securities markets ensures that US-style disclosure practices are used widely in Europe. These practices are now deeply engrained in Europe. The importance of US legal expertise in capital markets work is demonstrated by the tremendous push

---

[55] For a discussion of how a European company can list securities in both Europe and the United States, *see* Dana T. Ackerly II and Eric J. Pan, *Dual-Listing Securities in Europe and the United States in The Complete Guide to Listing on the London Stock Exchange* (2001).

[56] It has been estimated that US institutions own about 12% of European equities. *See* Pretzlik, *supra* note 47. *See* also Pagano *et al., supra* note 31 (finding that between 1986 and 1997 most cross-listing activity by European companies was directed at the US).

[57] *See* Ackerly and Pan, *supra* note 55.

[58] *See* Ackerly *et al.,* supra note 42, at 88.

by European law firms, particularly the large UK law firms, to build up their US legal expertise in the major European financial centers.

Third, the SEC has been active in expanding its regulatory powers abroad. As the sole regulator of the US market, it can exert strong pressure on market practice outside of the US. As a result, it has tremendous influence in intergovernmental forums like IOSCO. For example, in 1998 when IOSCO endorsed a core set of disclosure standards for the non-financial portions of a disclosure document, the recommended standards were effectively based on the SEC's 20-F disclosure requirements. The SEC conceded very little. Furthermore, IOSCO did not recommend common financial disclosure standards because the SEC refused to relent on its insistence of US GAAP.

The main reason, however, why the SEC is so influential in Europe is that the EU lacks a viable counter-weight to the SEC. At a Member State level there are many powerful regulators. The UK's Listing Authority, France's *Commission des Opérations de Bourse* and Spain's *Comision Nacionel del Mercado de Valores* and the various national exchanges, such as Deutsche Börse, all do excellent work promulgating listing and offering rules for the national markets, but there is little coordination at the EU level. Therefore, there exists a regulatory vacuum for cross-border offerings.

The EU needs a single regulator to create a single securities market. It needs a single regulator to coordinate and impose the necessary regulatory reforms to develop a well-working, cross-border securities market. And it needs a single regulator to represent the interests of European issuers and investors in international forums.

A single European regulator should not be viewed either as a rival or subordinate to the SEC, but rather as a partner to the SEC. It is ultimately in the best interests of European issuers and investors to have a regulatory regime that will enable them to access the broadest and deepest securities market possible. A single European regulator should therefore look beyond the parochial goal of enabling companies to list in two or more different markets at the same time to the goal of encouraging companies to make global offerings and allowing investors to make global investments. This goal would mean working with the SEC, building links with market professionals and asserting control over European securities regulation.

Under the current system, this cannot happen. Regulatory authority is dispersed. Interests remain local. Regulations are uncoordinated. The famous quote from former US Secretary of State Henry Kissinger succinctly describes the problem: 'When I want to talk to Europe, who do I call?'

THE CHALLENGE FOR EUROPE

The challenge for Europe is to create a single European regulator that has the authority and resources to drive the formation of a single European securities market. The single European securities regulator needs powers similar to those of the SEC. The single regulator needs rulemaking powers. It cannot rely on Member States to implement its rules, but must have direct rulemaking authority over the entire European market. The single regulator must also have enforcement powers. Without enforcement powers, the regulator will not be able to ensure that its regulations are carried out effectively. In addition, the single regulator must have formal and informal links with market professionals. The SEC notice-and-comment model should be adopted. It would be a mistake only to allow national governments or EU officials to evaluate and to debate the merits of new regulation. There has to be direct input from market participants in order to make sure that new regulations will be accepted and will be helpful to the market. The regulator must be a monopolist. Only by having absolute authority over the European securities market will it be able to force harmonization. Finally, the regulator must be able to recruit a dedicated and professional staff. It must consist of individuals who are experienced and understand the needs of the market.

The barriers to establishing a ESC are numerous. Support for subsidiarity remains strong in Europe. Very few countries are willing to give up control of their capital markets, even though the evidence shows they already have. The EU institutions lack the legislative and regulatory tools they need to act as or to create a successful securities regulator. Even if the political and institutional hurdles are surmounted, a regulator must develop common regulations and policies for all 18 countries in the EEA, countries that are divided by culture and legal tradition. Member States must be willing to give up their need for documents translated in their local language and agree on common definitions of professionals and retail investors. At the same time, new regulations must be understandable and effective in both the common law and civil law traditions, particularly with regard to legal issues such as fiduciary duty, enforceability of contract and corporate control.

By no means will these barriers be easy to overcome. But the benefits of creating a single securities market are tremendously high. A strong single regulator is essential to a well-working securities market, and a well-working securities market is essential to the economic health of the European Union. As the need for capital grows, European market participants will look increasingly toward the SEC to guide them for lack of any other relevant regulatory authority. It is not in the best interest of the European Union to let this happen.

# Horizontal Consolidation of Financial Supervision: The National, EU and International Perspectives

*Chapter 11*

# International Capital Markets and the Future of Economic Policy: A Proposal for the Creation of a World Financial Authority

*John Eatwell and Lance Taylor*

We must develop policies so that countries can reap the benefits of free-flowing capital in a way that is safe and sustainable. (President Clinton, September 14, 1998)

A global financial system, of course, is not an end in itself. It is the institutional structure that has been developed over the centuries to facilitate the production of goods and services. (Alan Greenspan, October 14, 1997)

### INTRODUCTION

This report[1] reviews the current behaviour and structure of international capital markets and suggests institutional and policy changes to improve their impact on the performance of real economies, or the production of useful goods and services.

The fundamental objective of all financial policy is to ensure the best possible outcome in the real economy. In this respect the simplistic complaint that the financial sector produces nothing by itself contains an element of truth. But it is only a small element. In a complex economy, with widespread division of labour through products, space, and time, a sophisticated financial sector is necessary for the organisation of production and distribution. An international financial system is necessary to sustain world trade and investment.

An economy without money markets would not work at all. The mobilization of large quantities of capital, and the allocation of that capital to profitable investments is the device that has transformed standards of living throughout the world in the past 200 years. Financial institutions must therefore be judged by the contribution they make to that process and hence to growth and employment. There is no point in having a financial sector that is in some sense 'efficient' in its own terms if the result is a less efficient real economy.

---

[1] What follows is the text of a report that was delivered to the Ford Foundation in August 1998, shortly before the Russian financial crisis. A postscript contains some reflections on the reactions to the analysis and the proposal. This report is funded by the Ford Foundation.

*Mads Andenas and Yannis Avgerinos (eds), Financial Markets in Europe: Towards a Single Regulator?* 263–282.
© 2003 *Kluwer Law International. Printed in Great Britain.*

Over the past year the persistent economic crisis in Asia has called into question much of the received wisdom that confidently asserted that liberalization has enhanced the economic contribution of international capital markets. The Asian crisis is but the most recent example of other similar episodes: the financial crises in Latin America in the early 1980s, the European exchange rate crises of 1992, and the Mexican bond crisis of 1994. The explanations offered for these severe disruptions are various; indeed each crisis has a set of local explanatory factors. But they also have a common element – the impact of highly liquid international capital markets. These recurring episodes, most of which involve severe costs in terms of unemployment, loss of real income, and even stagnation, pose important questions for policy-makers:

1. Given that every crisis has its own specific characteristics, what do their common factors suggest about particular strategies in international financial policy?
2. Should the ubiquitous policy stance of the past three decades in favour of inter national financial liberalization be qualified in the light of experience? If so, how?
3. Is any consistent policy toward financial markets, other than liberalisation, practically possible? Or can the genie never be put back into the bottle?

The succession of financial crises in the past 20 years, the scale of what is happening now in Asia, and the reverberations of the Asian problems throughout the world, suggest that there is an urgent demand for answers to these questions. Increasingly, financial crises are not 'local'. They have worldwide systemic implications. Satisfactory answers will require a clear *and convincing* theoretical and empirical characterisation of the relationship between financial liberalisation and economic performance. For without such a widely shared characterisation it will be almost impossible to formulate an internationally acceptable policy stance, even at the most general level. It is the objective of this report to present the skeleton of such a characterisation, and to draw from the argument a number of specific policy recommendations. These are necessarily tentative. If there is anything economists should have learned from the experience of the past two years, it is humility! Nonetheless, in distinctly un-humble manner, we believe the arguments presented in this report do provide an intellectual framework that might guide practical and successful reform.

The analysis in this report draws heavily on papers written by participants in a project on International Capital Markets and the Future of Economic Policy, organised by the Center for Economic Policy Analysis (CEPA) at the New School for Social Research and supported by the Ford Foundation.[2]

## THE ARGUMENT IN BRIEF

International capital market liberalisation began in the late 1950s when American and British banking authorities permitted external Eurocurrency credit markets to

---

[2] The papers are available at the CEPA website: <www.newschool.edu/cepa>.

emerge, beyond their regulatory control. However, the crucial change came in the early 1970s with the collapse of the Bretton Woods system of fixed exchange rates buttressed by capital controls of varying effectiveness. With that collapse, foreign exchange risk, previously borne by the public sector, was privatized.

The assumption of forex risk by the private sector required the dismantling of exchange controls to permit the hedging of risk, and so precipitated the development of the plethora of new financial instruments and the explosion of trading which characterize present day financial markets. Together with increased private sector risk went increased opportunity for profit: from the provision of risk-bearing services, from the potential for speculative profit inherent in fluctuating exchange rates, and, of course, from the extensive new opportunities for profitable arbitrage. Combined with domestic pressures for the removal of financial controls, the collapse of Bretton Woods was a significant factor driving the worldwide deregulation of financial systems. Exchange controls were abolished. Domestic restrictions on cross-market access for financial institutions were scrapped. Quantitative controls on the growth of credit were eliminated, and monetary policy was now conducted predominantly through the management of short-term interest rates. A highly geared global market in monetary instruments was created. Today the scale of activity in this market dwarfs payments associated with foreign trade and long-term investment. Daily flows approach 10% of the world's annual GDP. In stark contrast to most domestic financial markets, the global market is largely unregulated.

Financial liberalization and the massive increase in financial flows have undoubtedly brought some benefits to some countries at some times. Flows of investment toward emerging markets were seen, in the early 1990s, as a welcome replacement for official development financing. The relaxation of external capital constraints led to increases in growth and reductions in inflation. However, the overall economic record of the post-liberalization period, 1970 to the present, is less satisfactory. There has been the series of severe financial crises. But as well as these shocks and the associated losses in real income, trend growth rates have slowed throughout the world. In every G7 economy trend growth in the 1980s and 1990s has slowed to around two-thirds of the rate in the 1960s. In developing countries taken as a whole the average rate of growth has also slowed, to roughly the same extent. Even prior to the current crisis in East and Southeast Asia, trend growth per capita slowed in four out of seven of the region's major economies.

### Deteriorating performance of the real economy

The fundamental point at issue is what might be the connection between international financial liberalization and this widespread deterioration in performance.

It has become the conventional wisdom that trend performance is determined by 'the structure of the real economy'. From this perspective, financial factors may result in severe shocks and significant deviations from trend, but will not alter the underlying performance of the economy. Financial factors will not change the fundamentals. The only qualification of this separation of real and monetary phenomena is that liberalization, by removing financial imperfections, should improve trend performance.

An alternative view is that financial institutions do indeed affect the medium- to long-term trend performance of the economy. Liberalization not only increases the likelihood of shocks, it also alters the fundamentals. Hence financial factors can affect the medium-term characteristics of the economy. They could be the factors behind the poor trend performance observed in many economies, as well as periodic crises.

Three factors have forged a link between liberalization and low growth: volatility, contagion, and changes in public and private sector behaviour.

## Volatility

Liberalization has undoubtedly resulted in financial markets becoming more volatile, whether measured by short-term swings in exchange rates and interest rates, or the longer swings such as that in the real value of the dollar from an index of 100 in 1980, to 135 in 1985, down to 94 in 1990, and up again to 134 in 1998. Volatile financial markets generate economic inefficiencies. Volatility creates financial risk, and even if facilities exist for hedging that risk, the cost of capital formation is raised. The impact of financial market volatility is felt also in Latin America and East Asia. In the face of higher and more volatile real interest rates, US corporate defaults have increased enormously since the early 1970s.

## Contagion

And the damage done by financial volatility is not confined to countries with real economic imbalances – volatility is contagious. The Mexican bond crisis of 1994 propagated the 'tequila effect' throughout Latin America. The Asia financial crisis has spread throughout emerging markets, including Eastern Europe, Latin America, and South Africa. The stock market crash of 1987 spread rapidly from New York to all financial markets. A recent study of the 1992 ERM crisis (Buiter *et al.*, 1998) has concluded that systemic contagion makes the link between domestic macroeconomic conditions and the size of currency devaluations, let alone the likelihood of a crisis, 'tenuous'. Indeed, the link may even have the 'wrong' sign, with the financially virtuous suffering the greater punishment!

## Changed Behaviour in Both Public and Private Sectors

It will be argued in this report that the volatility, contagion, and hence uncertainty associated with liberal financial markets have not only imposed short-term shocks on the real economy of affected countries and regions, but have in fact led to changes in trend performance by inducing changes in behaviour in both public and private sectors.

*Public Sector*

That there has been a significant change in public sector behaviour is incontestable, and that change is typically attributed to the 'discipline' imposed on governments by the international financial markets. In contrast to the 1950s and 1960s when public sector objectives were typically expressed in terms of employment and growth, objectives are now defined in terms of financial and monetary targets, typically summarized as 'macroeconomic discipline'. It is clearly true that lack of macroeconomic discipline is no way to secure sustainable growth. But what is most striking about the superior economic performance of the 1960s, when objectives were customarily defined in terms of growth and employment, is that fiscal balances typically displayed lower deficits than has been the case since liberalization, and, indeed, fiscal surpluses were not uncommon (Matthews, 1968). The reason for this outcome was, of course, the interdependence between public sector and private sector balances: High levels of investment by the private sector, encouraged by a public sector commitment to growth and employment, in turn resulted in healthy fiscal balances, a result reinforced by relatively small current account deficits.

Macroeconomic discipline is a necessary component of sustained economic growth. Burgeoning fiscal deficits and high and rising inflation will undermine any growth strategy. But discipline needs to be associated with a public sector commitment to high levels of investment and employment. Small fiscal deficits, or even fiscal surpluses, may be more readily achieved when private sector investment is encouraged both by the financial environment and by public sector commitment to employment. If private sector investment is discouraged by an absence of public sector commitment to the high levels of employment and growth, fiscal prudence may be combined with recession.

Three elements link international financial liberalization to this change in public sector behaviour: the potential threat posed to financial stability and the real economy by large capital flows, the belief that those flows are motivated by a particular view of 'sound finance', and the fear that contagious financial crises may strike without warning. As the Bank for International Settlements (1995) has argued:

> In the financial landscape which has been emerging over the past two decades, the likelihood of extreme price movements may well be greater and their consequences in all probability further reaching.... At the macro level, the new landscape puts a premium on policies conducive to financial discipline. Strategically, a firm longer-term focus on price stability is the best safeguard, one which can only be achieved with the support of fiscal discipline.

However, the BIS then warns, 'yet such a safeguard is by no means always effective'.

*Private Sector*

The identification of changed behaviour in the private sector is more problematic. Ratios of investment to GDP have typically been lower in all countries since liberalization, suggesting a fall in private sector confidence. More specifically, defaults on US corporate bonds, which were at an all time low in the 1950s and 1960s, have increased significantly since the early 1970s. This finding may be explained by higher and more volatile real interest rates post-1970. Unsurprisingly, US business failures, which were also low in the 1950s and 1960s have been much higher since, and are correlated with high real interest rates and high debt-equity ratios. These patterns suggest, at very least, a less propitious climate for investment.

A decline in confidence in the private sector would also produce an increased desire for the opportunity of exit, further reinforcing the possibility of extreme swings in market sentiment which inflict both short- and long-term damage.

These negative effects are reinforced by the emergence of pro-cyclical forces associated with liberalization. The ability of governments to moderate cyclical forces by monetary policy has been severely diminished both by international liberalization and by the shift in corporate finance from the banks to the securities market. The result is that all monetary policy is now focused on manipulating the demand for money via major swings in increasingly high short-term real interest rates, damaging private sector investment.

### Developing Countries

In developing countries, the recent round of crises has been associated with clearly destabilizing behaviour by the private sector. The telltale signs included rapidly rising ratios of foreign and domestic debt to GDP as a consequence of external deficits readily financed by capital inflows (at least for a time), together with maturity and currency imbalances in national balance sheets. Standard market practices pushed local financial sectors toward taking long positions in domestic assets and short positions in foreign holdings. A private sector build-up of foreign currency borrowing (without proper hedging, despite the alleged ability of international capital markets to provide such services) was an immediate precursor of both the Mexican and East Asian crises. It was abetted by pro-cyclical financial regulation.

### Global Instability

Finally, the macroeconomic effects of liberalization can generate instability on a global scale. Industrialized economies can be destabilized by imbalances between flows and stocks induced by capital movements, although the time spans are likely to be longer and institutional responses more robust than those recently observed in Latin America, Eastern Europe, and Asia. In the case of the major economies there can be important feedbacks from national developments to the global system: Does the major borrower or lender, for example, behave in stabilizing or destabilizing fashion? What are its own weak points in terms of changes in stocks and flows? Such situations evolve over time. It seems likely that when imbalances emerge they are lagging indicators of the more fundamental processes which international financial liberalization has set in train. It follows that the global system can be at substantial 'systemic risk', in the phrase that regulators use for dangers transcending mere price fluctuations.

If international financial liberalization has indeed led to a change both in the environment for investment and in public and private sector attitudes toward investment, and has resulted in the mutually reinforcing hurt of severe swings in market sentiment and a general deterioration in medium-term confidence, then a deterioration in rates of growth and levels of employment is to be expected.

## THE POLICY CHALLENGE

The policy challenge is clear:

> Is it possible to secure the benefits of a flexible financial system, capable of mobilizing capital on a large scale, whilst at the same time ensuring that national economies and the wider world economy are protected from the systemic risks which financial liberalization brings in its wake?

The basic components of a new international financial order may be gleaned from the above analytical sketch:

(1) Since international financial liberalization results in a major increase in risk to both the national and the international real economy, an effective policy toward capital markets must be international in character. That is in the best interests of all.

(2) The performance of international financial institutions should be assessed in terms of their contribution to growth and stability of the real economy.

(3) Financial stability requires an effective lender of last resort.

(4) Efficient regulation is a necessary condition for there to be an effective lender of last resort.

(5) In the face of the sheer scale of capital movements today an international financial policy will only be possible if there is a high degree of mutually reinforcing cooperation between national monetary and financial authorities.

(6) The international economy is made up of national economies at widely differing levels of development in both real and financial sectors. It is most improbable that one simple policy prescription will be appropriate to all. National policies must be respected and supported within the context of an overall international financial framework. A blanket commitment to liberalization, openness and transparency will end in failure, and will endanger the development of the international market economy.

(7) It is a commonplace, accepted by virtually all, that national financial markets should be regulated. But once financial markets are open there is no meaningful distinction between the operations of national markets and the international market. Thus the regulatory principles which apply to the former also apply to the latter. The objectives of national regulator are consumer protection, the

maintenance of the highest possible standards of integrity, market conduct and professional skills in the financial services industry, and the minimization of systemic risk. These should be the objectives of international financial regulation.

(8) The predominant task of international financial regulation is to minimize systemic risk arising from the operations of securities and futures markets. At the same time, the regulator must avoid the creation of moral hazard. It is vital to guard against the failure of firms endangering the effective operation of the market as a whole. Yet securities firms that make bad judgements must be allowed to fail.

(9) The demands of international financial regulation cannot be coped with by purely co-operative structures. A new international regulatory entity with appropriate powers is required. An agreed framework should link that entity and national regulatory structures which will play a vital component part.

The history of the modern world economy teaches us that the disadvantages of the spread of liberal financial markets can be offset by sensible public intervention. After all, the 25 years after World War II were characterised by strategic liberalization within a controlled international environment, and by the enjoyment of the highest rates of growth and employment in modern times. But in recent years indiscriminate deregulation has dominated domestic and international economic policy, and re-regulation has been in political disfavour.

The Asian crisis should have changed all that. Some commentators continue to seek explanations of the crisis in the peculiar characteristics of the Asian economies – the same characteristics which a year or two ago were typically lauded for their contribution to the Asian miracle. But increasingly, economic policy-makers are recognizing the global risks inherent in international liberalization. The political equation will certainly change if western markets crash or global macro performance deteriorates significantly. It would be better to revise the system to avoid such misfortunes before they happen. This report is a contribution to that necessary revision.

## PROPOSED REFORMS

The reforms proposed in this report are not supposed to be definitive. Rather they are proposed in order to illustrate the practical argument of the report, and provide a starting point for subsequent debate and development. These reforms would, we believe, substantially improve real economic performance, reduce systemic risk, and significantly diminish the likelihood of collapse.

The overall objective of these proposals is to arrive at a pragmatic consideration of the relationship between capital market liberalization and economic performance, and to create an institutional framework that can put such a pragmatic consideration into effect. If liberal financial markets are not to be perceived as imposing unacceptable costs on national economic performance, then markets must be regulated. If necessary restrictions must be placed on capital flows, national governments must have the opportunity to exercise control over the opening of their own capital markets. Nothing brings liberal financial structures into disrepute so much as the spectacle of national economies being forced into recession by 'contagion' effects that bear no relation to their real economic circumstances. The success of Chilean and Chinese restrictions on short-term capital movements in limiting the damaging impact of contagion has been a salutary lesson.

The creation of an international body within which national policies on market openness can be debated and coordinated provides a route, perhaps the best route, to maintaining the benefits of liberal financial markets whilst minimizing the costs. The international body would also have the responsibility, in co-operation with national authorities, for directing and maintaining international regulatory structures.

It was the G10 'club' of central bankers that pioneered international financial regulation with the formation of the Committee on Bank Supervision and Regulation (based at the Bank for International Settlements, the BIS) in 1975. It was that Committee which formulated the capital adequacy requirements for banks in the 1980s. The then members of the club agreed to adhere to the requirements and to keep foreign banks that did not adhere out of their markets. The result was that countries voluntarily signed on to BIS requirements in order to achieve market credibility. The BIS has also sponsored a tripartite committee of banking, securities and insurance regulators to propose regulatory standards for financial conglomerates.

The International Organization of Securities Commissions (IOSCO) is the forum within which national regulators are developing common standards, and developing techniques of cross-border regulation. But IOSCO is essentially a cooperative organization. This is not enough. An executive authority with surveillance capabilities is required. The World Trade Organization (WTO) illustrates that it is possible to establish an international executive authority with enforcement powers. The key task will be to devise a set of arrangements geared to the maintenance of national and international financial stability, and supportive of high levels of growth and employment.

*A World Financial Authority*

It is proposed that a World Financial Authority (WFA) be established. This organization would be complementary to the WTO. A central task of the WFA is the development of international policies to manage systemic risk. The objectives of the WFA should include the requirement to pursue policies that assist in the maintenance of high rates of growth and employment.

It would be the task of the WFA both to develop rules which would ensure the adoption of best regulatory practice and effective risk management procedures (international *and* nationally), and to oversee the development of a credible guarantor and lender of last resort function. It will therefore need to build on the achievements of the G10 committees at the BIS, and IOSCO, to develop a framework for international financial regulation (including risk management procedures) and to ensure, via the powers ceded to it, that those rules are implemented.

But the WFA should not simply be a body that develops and imposes regulatory procedures. It should also be a forum within which the rules of international financial co-operation are developed and implemented. Most of the goals of an efficient international financial policy can be achieved by effective co-ordination of the activities of national monetary authorities. The problem is that the means of achieving that co-ordination are, at the moment, very limited. The WFA will fill that gap. It will also be the responsibility of the WFA to ensure that once national policies have been agreed by the WFA, states support each other's national policies. It is that mutual support which is the key to success.

The WFA should also be given the responsibility of ensuring transparency and accountability on the part of international financial institutions such as the IMF and the World Bank. There is at present no systematic evaluation of the activities of the Bretton Woods institutions, and this lacuna may well have contributed to the damaging criticism that the IMF in particular is imposing an essentially political program in the guise of technical conditionality. Martin Feldstein, for example, has argued that the IMF 'should not use the opportunity to impose other economic changes that, however helpful they may be, are not necessary to deal with the balance of payments problem and are the proper responsibility of the country's own political system'. Making the Bretton Woods institutions accountable to the WFA would introduce a 'safety valve' of evaluation and accountability that would make the IMF more effective.

Finally, the WFA should provide the necessary regulatory framework within which the IMF can develop as an effective lender of last resort. In many countries the WFA would simply certify that domestic regulatory procedures are effective. In those countries in which financial regulation is unsatisfactory, and which would therefore not have access to the IMF in a financial crisis, the WFA would assist with regulatory reform.

It is clear that there is no appetite today (especially in Washington) for the creation of a new international bureaucracy. Fortunately, the infrastructure for the WFA already exists in the form of the BIS committees and the co-operative cross-border regulatory framework already developed by IOSCO. With the backing of international agreement, adequate resources, and surveillance 'teeth', these institutions could be developed into the needed world authority.

## A Reorganized IMF

The IMF should be reorganized to take responsibility on behalf of the WFA for co-ordinating and partially funding international rescue operations when the need arises and when WFA-approved regulatory procedures are in place. There should be explicit consideration of how the IMF procedures should be developed to deal with problems of liquidity, and the development of a lender-of-last resort function. For example, the IMF could develop procedures to ensure that in the case of liquidity crises creditors should be 'bailed-in' to support the rescue rather than have their own positions 'bailed-out'. Whilst reducing systemic risk, care should be taken to minimize moral hazard. To the extent that creditors are protected, this should be at not insignificant cost. Most importantly, rescues should be based on prompt injections of liquidity instead of the current disastrous policy of prolonged attempts to restructure national economic systems using conditionality-laden credit disbursements as bait.

## A Refocused World Bank

The World Bank should direct its lending activities toward poorer countries unlikely to get access to open credit markets, subject to oversight from the WFA. It should also act as a co-ordinator and guarantor for a new global closed-end investment fund for emerging markets, a task completely in accord with the powers and functions incorporated in the Bank's charter. The fund could be capitalized by purchasing and holding government securities of the industrial countries in proportion to its shares held by residents of these countries. It would concentrate on long-term investments in the production of goods and services in developing countries, rather than short-term portfolio placements. The fund's shares could be bought and sold freely in many markets and many currencies. Although its share values would fluctuate, the fund would not be forced to sell off its underlying portfolio in the event of a downswing. This would protect emerging markets from abrupt fluctuations in capital movements of the sort observed in Mexico, East Asia, and elsewhere, reducing the need for capital controls. The creation of such a fund should improve the efficiency of investment by significantly reducing the cost of information needed by investors to put together balanced and diversified portfolios.

## The Role of National Authorities

Governments should be required by the WFA to improve control of national financial systems by imposing risk-weighted capital and/or reserve requirements on *all* major institutions, banks, mutual funds, insurance and pension funds, for all on-shore and off-shore and on-balance sheet and off-balance sheet operations (recognizing how difficult the identification of some of these operations may be). It should be recognized that traditional notions of capital adequacy monitoring are seriously inadequate in today's capital markets. Capital is no substitute for effective management. Risk management should be central to regulatory activity, internalizing, as far as may be possible, risk externalities, though the authorities will need to be aware of the pro-cyclical nature of risk assessment by firms. Particular attention should be paid to the management of foreign exchange risk.

The goals of the development of a new financial framework are to give the authorities leverage over both the supply and demand sides of credit markets, and to prevent imbalances in which national financial systems have long internal and short external net positions or blatant stock-flow disequilibrium positions. The former task will take some of the pressure off short-term interest rates and limit the pro-cyclical consequences of a monetary policy that is directed only at the demand side. The latter task will reduce systemic risk by focusing more attention than at present to system-wide implications of individual agents' attempts to take profits as well as hedge and insure their portfolios.

## The Management of Capital Movements

National governments, after appropriate consultations with the WFA, should be empowered to impose restrictions on external capital movements as they see fit. Effective controls, particularly on short-term capital inflows may well be necessary if free trade in goods and services is to be sustained. Yet there is a significant difference between limiting short-capital flows into a country, and closing markets to foreign goods. In the latter case a country may attempt to acquire a beggar-my-neighbour advantage. The same argument does not apply to the former case. So the usual requirement of regulatory capital and reserve ratios imposed on firms may be supplemented with quantitative or tax-based obstacles to cross-border flows of funds. Whilst there should be a presumption in favour of national policies, the form, scale and duration of such restrictions (which may, if necessary, be deemed permanent) should, however, be determined in consultations with the WFA. Once particular conditions for the management of capital movement have been agreed then Member States of the WFA should be required to provide assistance to fellow members in their operation.

## Financial Insurance

To diminish the damaging effects of moral hazard on institutional decision making, national compulsory deposit insurance and similar financial guarantee insurance systems should be associated with individuals and households rather than institutions.

## Complete Liberalization is Inefficient and Should be Abandoned

The experience of the past 20 years has demonstrated that complete liberalization is inefficient. Unmanaged financial markets are too prone to volatility and contagion to provide the stable financial framework necessary for high rates of growth and employment. Instead, a regulated international system, operating through a WFA will create the possibility of securing the benefits of capital mobility, whilst diminishing the costs. Indeed, such management is necessary if there is not to be a swing back to widespread protectionism. Campaigns to rewrite the IMF articles to require full capital market liberalization by all nations, and OECD proposal to write full capital liberalization requirements into a multilateral agreement on investment, are without sound intellectual foundation and should be abandoned.

### SUMMING-UP

The Asian crisis, the most severe of a regular series of financial crises since 1970, has demonstrated beyond all reasonable doubt that the international financial system as currently constituted is not working. It is not playing its historical role of stimulating real activity, funding real investment, and underpinning growth and employment. Instead, market volatility and contagion have resulted not only in huge negative shocks to the real economy, but also have been accompanied by a general slowdown in growth and employment throughout the world. Governments are often constrained to deflationary policies and companies are deterred by the additional costs and risk of committing resources to investment.

Historical experience has confirmed the necessity of regulation and of the lender of last resort in domestic markets. The same sort of measures are now required internationally. These measures are required if a broadly liberal world order is to survive.

## POSTSCRIPT (JULY 2001)

The financial crisis in the Fall of 1998 was the first post-World War II crisis in which events in emerging market economies seriously threatened the financial stability of the West, and where the origins of the crisis was clearly to be found in the workings of liberalized markets and private sector institutions. The spark was the financial crisis that overwhelmed many of the Asian economies in 1997, and spread to Russia in 1998, but the centre of the conflagration was the near failure of the hedge fund Long Term Capital Management. More than any of the other problems in the Fall of 1998, the threats that LTCM's difficulties posed to financial stability throughout the world illustrated beyond all reasonable doubt that the international financial system had entered a new era.[3] This was not a problem of sovereign debt, or macroeconomic imbalance, or a foreign exchange crisis. Instead it was the manifestation of the systemic risk created by the market driven decisions of a private firm, and of the behaviour of free financial markets. The potential economy-wide inefficiency of liberalized financial markets was indisputable.

In August 1998, in one of those remarkable coincidences that in retrospect look like good judgement, we had delivered the above Report to the Ford Foundation, dealing directly with the problem of systemic risk in liberal international financial markets. We had been drawn to this particular topic because of a shared irritation with the overblown claims for the efficiency of financial liberalization – claims that do not stand up to empirical scrutiny. For example, liberalization of international financial markets has coincided not only with increased financial instability, but also with a worldwide slowdown in the rate of growth. Whether there is a causal link between liberalization and that slowdown is, of course, a complex question. But the argument that liberalization has resulted in a higher growth rate than might otherwise be the case is very difficult to sustain (see Eatwell, 1996).

A key recommendation was the establishment of a WFA. We argued that for efficient regulation the domain of the regulator should be the same as the domain of the market that is regulated. None of the standard tasks of a financial regulator – authorization, the provision of information, surveillance, enforcement, and the development

---

[3] Alan Greenspan commented that he had never seen anything in his lifetime that compared with the panic of August–September 1998.

of policy – are currently performed in a coherent manner in international markets. Indeed, in many cases they are not performed at all. In the absence of a WFA the liberalization of international markets has resulted in a significant increase in systemic risk, that is, it has been inefficient.

Our prime objective in proposing the creation of a WFA was to test the regulatory needs of today's liberal financial markets. Whether a single regulator is created or not, the tasks that the model WFA should perform must be performed by someone if international financial markets are to operate efficiently. The WFA is a template against which existing international regulatory structures can be measured.

### What Tasks Should be Performed by a WFA?

A national financial regulator performs five main tasks: authorization of market participants; the provision of information to enhance market transparency; surveillance to ensure that the regulatory code is obeyed; enforcement of the code and disciplining of transgressors; and the development of policy that keeps the regulatory code up to date (or at least not more than 10 m behind the market in a 100 m race). These are the tasks that now need to be performed at international level, ideally as if performed by a unitary WFA.

For example, it is clear that criteria for authorization should be at the same high level throughout the international market: ensuring that a business is financially viable, that it has suitable regulatory compliance procedures in place, and that the staff of the firm are fit and proper persons to conduct a financial services business. If, in a liberal international financial environment, high standards are not uniformly maintained then firms authorized in a less demanding jurisdiction can impose unwarranted risks on others, undermining high standards of authorization elsewhere.

Similarly, as far as the information function is concerned, the failure to attain not only transparency but also common standards of information undermines the efficient operation of international financial markets, and creates risk. The persistent inability to agree international accounting standards is a prime example of just such a failure.

Surveillance and enforcement are the operational heart of any effective regulatory system. Without effective, thorough policing of regulatory codes, and uniform enforcement of standards by appropriate disciplinary measures (including exclusion from the market place) the international financial system is persistently exposed to unwarranted risks.

Finally, the policy function is the essential driving force of effective regulation. Regulatory codes must be adapted to a continuously changing marketplace. An important component of that change is international. As national financial boundaries dissolve, and as new products are developed that transcend international boundaries by firms with a worldwide perspective, the policy function must ensure that the regulator is alert to the new structure of the marketplace, the new systemic risks created, and to the new possibilities of contagion.[4] This requires a unified policy function,

---

[4] An important recent example was the use of credit derivatives in Indonesia that ultimately spread financial losses to South Korea.

capable of taking a view as to the risks encountered by particular markets and by the international market place as a whole.

### What Should be the Legal Foundation of WFA Action?

All these activities are necessary for the efficient operation of the new international financial order. All point to the need for a single authority determining common rules and exercising common procedures. But there are clear, in some cases overwhelming difficulties to attaining that goal, of which the problem of achieving common accounting standards are but a foretaste. All five core activities involve the exercise of authority, and hence trespass into very sensitive political areas. Nation states are naturally reluctant to cede powers to an international body, even if this might mean the acquisition of (collective) sovereignty over activities otherwise beyond their control. When powers are ceded, this is done typically by treaty, confirming collective rights and responsibilities, and, at least in principle, accountability. But it can also be done by the consensus and by the mutual recognition of self-interest that produces 'soft law'.

Art. IV of the Articles of Association of the IMF empowers the organization to 'oversee the international monetary system in order to ensure its effective operation'. To this end the provision that 'the Fund shall exercise firm surveillance over the exchange rate policies of members' has been interpreted as covering general macroeconomic surveillance, and, in the new Financial Sector Appraisal Program, *micro*economic surveillance of the operations of the financial sectors of member states.[5] The new FSAP surveillance concentrates on the adherence of national regulation and practices to core principles developed by the Basel committees of the G10, the International Organization of Securities Commissions (IOSCO) and the International Association of Insurance Supervisors (IAIS).[6] It is an activity of considerable sensitivity. Not only will comprehensive surveillance require large resources, but also the IMF could easily be drawn into the position of 'grading' national financial systems,

---

[5] Many characteristics of domestic financial systems may be only indirectly connected to 'the exchange rate' as such. Nonetheless, it is not unreasonable to link *domestic* regulation to *international* financial stability.

[6] For example, the June 2000 IMF 'experimental' Report on the Observation of Standards and Codes (ROSC) for Canada, prepared by a staff team from the International Monetary Fund in the context of a Financial Sector Assessment Program (FSAP), on the basis of information provided by the Canadian authorities, produced 'an assessment of Canada's observance of and consistency with relevant international standards and core principles in the financial sector, as part of a broader assessment of the stability of the financial system.... The assessment covered (i) the Basel Core Principles for Effective Banking Supervision; (ii) the International Organization of Securities Commissions' (IOSCO) Objectives and Principles of Securities Regulation; (iii) the International Association of Insurance Supervisors' (IAIS) Supervisory Principles; (iv) the Committee on Payment and Settlement Systems (CPSS) Core Principles for Systemically Important Payment Systems; and (v) the IMF's Code of Good Practices on Transparency in Monetary and Financial Policies. Such a comprehensive coverage of standards was needed as part of the financial system stability assessment for Canada in view of the increasing convergence in the activities of banking, insurance, and securities firms, and the integrated nature of the markets in which they operate' (IMF, 2000A).

with any downward revision of grades having the potential to produce dramatic financial consequences (IMF, 2000B). Nonetheless, the IMF, as an accountable body the powers of which are defined by treaty, can legitimately perform a surveillance function. Moreover, in due course the IMF will require countries seeking its assistance to conform to international regulatory codes and standards. In other words, it will be able to enforce conformity to those standards, with severe financial penalties (withdrawal of offers of assistance) for those who do not comply. It is to be doubted, however, whether it could, other than by persuasion, effectively enforce regulatory codes when they are infringed by the more powerful countries that do not requires the Fund's assistance (Eatwell and Taylor, 2000, chap. 7).

But the IMF is using a treaty-sanctioned surveillance function to examine adherence to codes and principles that are not themselves developed by accountable treaty bodies. The rules that the IMF is seeking (experimentally) to embody in its surveillance programme are predominantly formulated within non-treaty, 'soft-law' environments.

The adoption by the IMF of such rules as a criterion of surveillance suggests a process of transition from soft law to mandatory regulation, at least for those countries that are beholden to the IMF. Observation of Basel and other codes will become an IMF imposed obligation. If this happens, new questions will be raised about the accountability of the Basel rule-makers and their counterparts at IOSCO and the IAIS.

Even with this potential 'legalization' of international policy-making and of surveillance (which includes some standardization of the information function in the drive for 'transparency'), authorization and, for the richer countries, enforcement remain national activities – though even here agreements on home-host division of responsibilities inject an international dimension.

There is, in effect, a creeping internationalization of the regulatory function in international financial markets. That internationalisation is essentially confederalist in character, with national jurisdictions being the predominant legal actors guided by international soft law. So some of the functions of a WFA are being performed. But they are being performed imperfectly. Authorization is still essentially national, the information function is highly imperfect, surveillance (by the IMF) is as yet 'experimental', enforcement is national, and the policy function is predominantly driven by an exclusively G10 consensus. As measured against the template of a proper WFA there is a long way to go.

However, the difficulty of creating an effective framework of international regulation does not derive solely from international legal practice and from politics. An important element of disjuncture derives from history – from differences in national legal systems, in financial custom and practice and in structures of corporate governance. Even within the European Union, for example, there are major differences in national legal systems and in corporate governance that make the introduction of a common regulatory code not only difficult, but potentially damaging (see ECOFIN 2000 for an analysis of these difficulties within the European Union). Regulatory codes that enhance efficiency in one jurisdiction may have exactly the opposite effect in another.

However, whilst financial markets are 'seamless', they are not homogeneous. In consequence uniform financial regulations often have quite different practical effects. The result is that uniform codes will expose the financial system to different systemic risks in the light of their differential impact in different jurisdictions (Alexander and Dhumale, 2000).

This is the central weakness of the fixed regulatory requirements and ratios emanating from the Basel committees, and, the strength of the Basel system of codes. What is ideally required is that there should be an assessment of the relationship between the financial structure of national jurisdictions and the systemic risk emanating from each jurisdiction. That ideal is probably unattainable, since it would require detailed consideration and negotiation of each hypothetical national case – an overwhelming task. A more pragmatic approach would involve:

(a) the construction of specific rules in those cases which refer to basic institutional tenets that are universal, and are necessary for the success of any regulatory environment;
(b) in those circumstances where national legal and governance structures predominate the development of national codes derived from common internationally agreed general principles.

In case (b) regulation is developed at two levels: first, a set of general principles, second, from these principles should be derived codes that are both flexible as circumstances change and reflect the peculiar legal and governance structures of individual countries. This is, of course, the defining characteristic of the current soft law regime. But at present many of the principles are 'ideal types', to be desired rather than enforced. If principles are to be the foundation of an effective regulatory system they must be expressed through clearly articulated codes, which are regularly tested against the principles they are supposed to embody, and against the systemic risks they are supposed to manage. There will undoubtedly be differences of opinion as to whether a particular set of national codes accurately reflects shared principles, and it will be necessary to put in place powerful procedures for adjudicating disputes (another role for a WFA).

The cause of uniform adherence to principles will be reinforced by market competition, in rather the same manner as competition has led to the widespread adoption of Basel capital adequacy standards. Moreover increasingly open markets are likely to produce competitive convergence in standards and procedures of corporate governance that will in turn permit a movement toward uniform regulatory codes, that is, an increasing role for the universal rules referred to in (a) above.

### How Are these Tasks to Be Performed?

Whilst the template of a WFA clarifies the tasks that must be performed if international financial markets are to be regulated efficiently, it does not provide much guidance as to how the tasks are actually to be performed in the more likely absence of a unitary authority. In practical terms many tasks can and must be delegated to national authorities. But it is important that national authorities should operate within common guidelines. That is the importance of the WFA – not to tell national authorities what to do, but to ensure that in a single world financial market they behave in a coherent and complementary manner to manage the systemic risk to which, in a seamless market, they are all exposed. Effective international regulation will necessarily be confederal, with different responsibilities at appropriate levels of the system. But there must be a coherent confederation with common principles and common values, resulting in (converging) national codes enforced by national authorities to attain common goals.

Today an institutional structure of international financial supervision is emerging which embodies, albeit imperfectly, a few of the features of an idealized WFA. The authorization function is the responsibility of national regulators, with access to markets being determined by the presence or absence of agreements specifying the terms of mutual recognition. The information function is performed partly by the international financial institutions, particularly the BIS, partly by the International Accounting Standards Committee, and partly by national regulators, stock market rules, and so on. The surveillance function is performed by the World Bank–IMF financial sector programme, and by national regulators. The enforcement function is being developed as an implicit outcome of the World Bank–IMF financial sector programme, and is otherwise the responsibility of national authorities. The policy function is in the hands of the BIS committees, IOSCO and the IAIS, the Financial Stability Forum, the IMF, and national authorities.

This list of international regulatory activities has four major features:

(1) If the same list were compiled 10 years ago most of the regulatory functions, with the exception of the policy function, would lack any international dimension. Today in all areas other than authorization, international bodies are taking up some of the regulatory tasks.

(2) There is an eclectic mix of national institutions, international agreements (soft and hard) and international institutions (with varying degrees of legitimacy). Some powers are developing almost accidentally, such as the emergence of an enforcement power at the IMF via the FSAP programme. Others are developing by design, such as the work of the International Accounting Standards Committee. All are developing under the pressures for effective policy exerted by the process of financial market liberalization, particularly at times of crisis.

(3) The list deals only with major international regulatory developments, and omits the growth of regional regulation, notably in the European Union. The case of the European Union is particularly interesting since it involves the attempt to develop a fully liberalized, single financial market, characterized by a wide range of different legal practices and structures of corporate governance amongst member states.

(4) Measured against the template of a WFA the list displays an international regulatory structure that is limited, even incoherent. It portrays a patchwork response to crises rather rational response to the international development of systemic risk.

This patchy, often incoherent structure embodies significant threats to financial stability. On the one hand the growth of international institutions, such as the FSF, induces the feeling that 'something has been done' to tackle systemic risk. On the other hand, the very limited powers of any of the international structures listed above suggest that such complacency is a delusion.

The developments of the past 30 years, and more especially, the innovations of the last three years point to the recognition by states and by market participants of the need for coherent international regulation. But the present conjuncture, in which the predominant rule making bodies are the Basel committees, IOSCO and the IAIS, whilst the predominant international surveillance body (in so far as there is any international surveillance at all) is the IMF, is an awkward hybrid. Moreover, it embodies the unfortunate impression that rules are made by the rich nations and enforced on the rest.

What is needed is recognition of the power of the WFA template, and the design of international institutions that can meet the demands identified by the template in an accountable, coherent, and flexible manner. A number of challenges must be met if this goal is to be attained: (1) the development and acceptance of a common theoretical framework within which to confront the tasks of international regulation; (2) the integration of macroeconomic and microeconomic aspects of international regulation; (3) the development of procedures that (at least) alleviate the tendency for risk management to be pro-cyclical and pro-contagion; (4) the harmonization of risk management in differing corporate governance structures to obtain a common international regulatory outcome; (5) solving the political challenge of accountability in a soft law régime; (6) devising an institutional structure that performs the tasks of the template WFA.

As practical politics, these are rather grandiose objectives. But in pragmatic terms this framework can be used to generate practical proposals for dealing with specific problems (e.g. the use of short-term capital controls as the macro component of a regulatory régime). These specific proposals are more likely to be agreed upon internationally – if at all – than 'common theoretical frameworks'. But if they derive from the coherent framework of a WFA they are likely to be more effective and ultimately more acceptable, even within a neo-liberal political and economic environment.

REFERENCES

*Papers prepared for the International Capital Markets and the future of economic policy project, funded by the Ford Foundation*

Robert Blecker, 'International Capital Mobility, Macroeconomic Imbalances, and the Risk of Global Contraction' (1998).
Block, Thorsten, 'Financial Market Liberalization and the Changing Character of Corporate Governance' (1998a).
Thorsten Block, 'The Gold Standard, Financial Markets, and the Great Depression' (1998b).
Jenny Corbett and David Vines, 'The Asian crisis: competing explanations' (1998).
Jane D'Arista, 'Financial Regulation in a Liberalized Global Environment' (1998).
John Eatwell and Lance Taylor, The Performance of International Capital Markets (1998).
Roberto Frenkel, 'Capital Market Liberalization and Economic Performance in Latin America' (1998).

James Galbraith, William Darity Jr., and Lu Jiaqing, 'Measuring the Evolution of Inequality in the Global Economy' (1998).

Salih Neftci, 'FX Short Positions, Balance Sheets, and Financial Turbulence: An Interpretation of the Asian Financial Crisis' (1998).

Ajit Singh, ' "Asian Capitalism" and the Financial Crisis' (1998).

Lance Taylor, 'Lax Public Sector, Destabilizing Private Sector: Origins of Capital Market Crises' (1998).

## *Other references*

K. Alexander and R. Dhumale (2000). Enhancing Corporate Governance for Banking Institutions. A paper prepared for the Ford Foundation project on 'A World Financial Authority' (Centre for Business Research, Judge Institute of Management Studies, Cambridge, 2000).

Bank for International Settlements (BIS), 65th Annual Report (Basle, 1995).

Willem Buiter, Giancarlo Corsetti, and Paolo Pesenti, *Interpreting the ERM Crisis: Country-Specific and Systemic Issues*, Princeton Studies in International Finance, No. 84, (Princeton University, Princeton, NJ, 1998).

William Clinton, *Remarks by the President to the Council on Foreign Relations*, New York (14 September 1998).

J. Eatwell, International financial liberalisation: the impact on world development, ODS Discussion Paper Series, No. 12 (UNDP, New York, 1996).

J. Eatwell and L. Taylor, *Global Finance at Risk: the Case for International Regulation* (Policy Press, New York, 2000).

ECOFIN (European Union Economic and Finance Ministers), Initial Report of the Committee of Wise Men on the Regulation of European Securities Markets (Lamfalussy Committee) (Brussels, 9 November 2000).

Greenspan, Alan (1997). Globalization of Finance, remarks delivered at the 15th Annual Monetary Conference of the Cato Institute, Washington, DC (14 October 1997).

IMF (International Monetary Fund), *Report on the Observance of Standards and Codes: Canada* (IMF, Washington, DC 2000A).

Matthews, Robin, 'Why has Britain had full employment since the War?' (1968) *Economic Journal*.

*Chapter 12*

# International Standards and Standards Implementation

*George A. Walker*

## I INTRODUCTION

The question as to whether a new central regulatory agency should be set up within Europe raises a number of more general issues at the national and international as well as regional levels in terms of modern financial market supervision and control. In considering financial market reform, a basic distinction can be drawn between institutional or agency structures and substantive or regulatory programme initiatives. The single agency discussion is clearly concerned with institutional rather than substantive reform.

The single agency debate that has taken place to date appears principally to have been concerned with two separate developments. Within Europe, the main issue that has arisen is whether a single agency should be established to regulate securities markets on a centralised basis.[1] This is then concerned with the cross-border supervision and control of a single financial sector within a regional system. The other aspect of the single agency discussion that has also become of importance in recent years is whether a single integrated national authority should be established to supervise and regulate all financial markets at the national level.[2] This involves the cross-sector supervision of all (or most) financial markets on a single or integrated basis. The distinction is then between cross-border or cross-sector integration and the most appropriate institutional structure to be set up in each case. Although some common issues arise with regard to these two discussions, it must be accepted that they are distinct and that a different set of conclusions may emerge in each case.

Within Europe, the emphasis at the present time is on the creation of a single capital market.[3] While it has been proposed that banking supervision would remain to be dealt with on the basis of the existing system of (national) home country control and mutual recognition, it is, of course, possible that a single a cross-sector agency may also be considered within Europe over time. It is, for example, possible that the

---

[1] *See* Part II of this book.

[2] *See* G.A. Walker, 'United Kingdom Financial Services Reform,' *Yearbook of International Banking and Development Law* (1999), *See* also W. Blair QC, A. Allen, K. Palmer, P. Richards-Carpenter and G.A. Walker, *Banking and Financial Services Regulation* (2nd edn, 1999); and M. Blair QC, L. Minghella, M. Taylor, M. Theipland and G.A. Walker, *Blackstones Guide to the Financial Services and Markets Act 2000* (2001).

[3] *See* Alexandre Lamfalussy, *Report on the Regulation of European Securities Markets* (2001) [The Committee of Wise Men].

*Mads Andenas and Yannis Avgerinos (eds), Financial Markets, in Europe: Towards a Single Regulator?* 283–322.
© 2003 *Kluwer Law International. Printed in Great Britain.*

most recent initiative within Germany to follow the United Kingdom example in creating a single national authority may be in anticipation of such a wider European development.[4]

In contrast with these various single agency initiatives, the emphasis at the international level has been on substantive rather than institutional reform. This is necessary in light of the traditional doctrines of the sovereign autonomy of the nation state and the jurisdictional of exclusivity which this creates as well as the immense political difficulties that would arise in attempting to agree any necessary international treaty or convention to support such an initiative. It has to be accepted that it is (almost) impossible that any single international agency may be set up to regulate any specific financial sector, let alone all financial areas within the foreseeable. It is accordingly generally recognised that financial markets must continue to be regulated primarily at the national level with efforts focusing on inter-agency co-operation and information exchange rather than with the construction of any single international agency.[5]

There has been some more modest institutional reform following the Asian crisis in the late 1990s such with the establishment of the new G20[6] and the reconstitution of the Interim Committee of the IMF as the International Monetary and Financial Committee (IMFC).[7] These have, however, been essentially limited in both their

---

[4] *See* Chapter 17 of this book.

[5] *See* G.A. Walker, *International Banking Regulation Law Policy and Practice* (2001), Chaps 1 and 2.

[6] The G20 (originally the GX was set up to generate discussion and proposals for international financial reform and to build legitimacy for the process among development countries. The G7 had agreed at the Cologne Summit that an informal mechanism would be set up to promote dialogue between systemically important countries. Twenty countries including the G7 and other systemically important developing territories were to be invited to participate with the IMF and the World Bank also participating in the work of the new body. *See* 'G Force' (September 13), *Financial Times* 27 and 'G7 Prepares to give birth to its GX baby' (20 September 1999), *Financial Times* 4. For comment see, Walker, 'Not Another Country Club' (April 2000) *FRR* 1. The G20 replaces the earlier G22 or 'Willard Group' which was set up following a meeting of Financial Ministers and Central Bank Governors in Washington, D.C. in April 1998 to examine the stability of the international financial system and the effective functioning of global capital markets. *See* G22, Summary of Reports on International Financial Architecture (October 1998); Report of the Working Group on Transparency and Accountability (October 1998); Report of the Working Group on Strengthening Financial Systems (October 1998); and Report of the Working Group on International Financial Crises (October 1998). The original G22 had become unmanageable after its extension to include 26 and then 33 countries. The role of the G20 is now to extend the range of countries involved in the current efforts to construct a new international market framework and in so doing providing authority and legitimacy to the larger processes concerned and the essential work being undertaken. *See* Walker, *ibid.*

[7] The Interim Committee was renamed the International Monetary and Financial Committee in September 1999. The Interim Committee had originally been set up as an informal advisory ministerial body to the IMF during the early 1970s. Following the collapse of the Bretton Woods system of managed exchange rates, the Articles of Agreement of the IMF had been amended to allow a ministerial level council to be set to supervise the management and adaptation of the international monetary system. The Interim Committee was set up on a temporary basis until a formal agency system could be created. The anomalous position of the Interim Committee has now been corrected with its reconstitution as the formal IMFC. For comment, *see* Michel Camdessus, 'Global Financial Reform: The Evolving Agenda', Council of Foreign Relations, New York (4 June 1999); and Michel Camdessus, 'The IMF We Need', Georgetown (2 February 2000). *See* also Camdessus, 'The Role of the IMF: Past, Present and Future', Remarks at the Annual General Meeting of the Bretton Woods Committee, Washington, D.C. (13 February 1998), IMF Speech 98/4.

intent and effect. Of more importance from a regulatory perspective was the establishment of the Financial Stability Forum (FSF) by the G7 in February 1999.[8] The FSF was set up to provide a new policy discussion and development mechanism by having senior representatives from finance ministries, central banks, and supervisory agencies as well as the major financial institutions and sector committees meet together within a single body for the first time. It was hoped that FSF would then be able to take forward a number of aspects of supervisory and regulatory initiatives required in this area in a much more balanced and integrated manner. The objectives and mandate of the FSF are again, however, essentially limited in terms of any larger institutional reform.

While some more limited institutional initiatives have accordingly been taken forward at the international level, the focus of attention has been on substantive programme reform and, in particular, with international standards development and the consequent implementation of those measures. The most significant single development which has possibly taken place in this area has been the agreement of a single financial market rule book through the work of the FSF and, in particular, with the creation of its Compendium of Standards.[9]

Having agreed this single global rulebook, attention has then focused on securing its proper implementation. This has, in particular, been taken forward through the work of a Task Force on Standards Implementation, which was set up by the FSF under Mr. Andrew Sheng, Chairman of the Hong Kong Securities and Futures Commission. The Task Force has since produced a formal issues paper on standards implementation in March 2000[10] and a follow-up paper in August 2000.[11] It is now generally accepted that although a range of relevant standards can be agreed at either regional or international levels, these are meaningless without proper and consistent adoption and implementation. It is for this reason, that many of the most important recent initiatives at the international and regional levels have then been concerned with securing proper implementation of agreed measures.

The issue of institutional reform is still relevant at the international level although it is unlikely that any further major initiatives will be taken forward within the near

---

[8] *See* G.A. Walker, 'A New Beginning' (June 1999), *FT FRR* 1; Walker, 'Working Groups and Global Standards' (October 1999) *FRR*; Walker, 'The New Global Rule Book' (November 1999) *FRR* 1 and Walker, 'Financial Stability Standards' (November 1999) *FRR* 3. *See* also Walker, 'Standards Implementation' (April 2000) *FRR* 1; and Walker, 'Implementation Review' (November 2000) *FRR* 1.

[9] Rather than exist as a separate dedicated piece of written work, this takes the form of a virtual collection of all of the core standards in each of the principal subject areas and sub-areas within a single domain or uniform resource location (URL) on the internet which is then linked using hyper-text mark-up language (HTML) to all of the individual source sites concerned. *See* Walker, 'The New Global Rule Book', *op. cit.*, note 8. The full text in each paper is then not produced separately by the FSF but hyper-linked from its website to the location where it is already stored and made available by the particular sponsoring agency concerned. Although over 40 documents were originally included within the Compendium, the FSFA has since been able to agree 12 core standards from within these. *See* <www.fsforum.org>.

[10] *See* FSF, *Standards Implementation* (March 2000). *See* also Walker, 'Standards Implementation', *op. cit.*, note 8.

[11] *See* FSF, Report of the Follow-Up Group on Incentives to Foster Implementation of Standards (31 August 2000). See also Walker, 'Implementation Review', *op. cit.*, note 8.

future for the reason explained. The earlier gaps that had been identified in the new post-Asia crisis global environment were corrected with the establishment of the new G20 and reconstitution of the IMFC and then with the creation of the FSF as a new contact and co-operation device. While FSF has carried out important work in various other areas,[12] its major contribution has been agreeing the structure and content of the Compendium and then to attempt to facilitate its proper implementation. Following an outline of the structure and operation of the FSF, the purpose of this chapter is to consider the content of the Compendium and the work produced by the Task Force on its implementation.

## II    FINANCIAL STABILITY FORUM

The FSF was created by the G7 Ministers and Governors at their meeting in Bonn on 22 February 1999. The FSF was set up following a report by Hans Teitmeyer, the former President of the Bundesbank, to consider possible new structures required to enhance co-operation between national and international supervisory bodies and international financial institutions. The final report was produced on 11 February 1990 and endorsed by the G7 at their meeting later that month.[13]

The Teitmeyer Report considered the current arrangements for the supervision and surveillance of the international financial system. It noted the work of the various international institutions presently in place including the IMF, the World Bank, the BIS and the OECD as well as such other sector specific international groupings as the Basel Committee on Banking Supervision, IOSCO,[14] the IAIS[15] and other central bank expert groupings including the CPSS[16] and the CGFS.[17] Areas in which improvements were required in the present control system were also considered. The Report recommended that a systematic approach had to be adopted to ensure that any remaining gaps in international standards or codes of conduct were properly identified and corrected through co-operation and co-ordination between all relevant bodies including emerging market participants. Effective implementation of, in particular, the various core standards that had already been adopted had to be secured at the national level in co-operation with the international financial institutions. It was accepted that no fundamental institutional changes were required although a new financial stability forum had to be set up that could meet regularly to assess issues and vulnerabilities effecting the global financial system and to identify and oversee action needed to address the problems identified. The forum should report

---

[12] *See* Section 11 *infra*.

[13] *See* Hans Teitmeyer, *International Co-operation and Co-ordination in the Area of Financial Market Supervision and Surveillance* (11 February 1999).

[14] The International Organization of Securities Commissions. *See* <http://www.iosco.org>.

[15] The International Association of Insurance Supervisors. *See* <http://www.isisforum.org>.

[16] The Committee on Payment and Settlement Systems. *See* <http://www.bis.org>.

[17] The Committee on the Global Financial System (formerly the Euro-Standing Currency Committee). *See* <http://www.bis.org>.

directly to the G7 and replace the series of earlier ad hoc groups that had been convened by the G7 before then.[18]

Following the recommendations of the Teitmeyer Report, the composition of the FSF had to be limited to permit an effective exchange of views and ensure proper action within a reasonable time period. Each G7 country would accordingly have three members, one each from the Treasury or Finance Ministry, the central bank and supervisory agency (where this was conduct outside the central bank). The international financial institutions (including the IMF and the World Bank) and the main sector agencies (including the Basel Committee, IOSCO and the IAIS) would have two representatives each. The other bodies represented including the BIS, OECD, CPSS and CGFS would have one representative each.

The FSF would meet twice yearly although it would also operate through various working groups. Three working groups were initially set up at the first meeting which was held in Washington on 14 April 1999.[19] These were concerned with highly leveraged institutions (hedge funds),[20] offshore financial centres[21] (OFCs) and global capital flows.[22] A separate task force was set up to examine ways of promoting the implementation of international standards relevant to the strengthening of financial systems under Mr. Andrew Sheng.[23] A further study group was also asked to review recent experiences with deposit protection schemes and to consider the development of international best practices for these arrangements under Mons Jean Pierre Suboruin, President of the Canadian Deposit Insurance Co-operation.

The mandate of the FSF is to strengthen the surveillance and supervision of the international financial system. In connection with this, the FSF has been conducting work in the areas of disclosure, standards and training.[24] Although each of these initiatives is important, the FSF's most important contribution has been in the area of the standards.[25] The content of its Compendium of Standards is considered in the following Section

### III   COMPENDIUM OF STANDARDS

While the work of the FSF in respect of each of its key areas of activity of disclosure, standards and training is important, it is in the second area that the most substantial contribution has been made towards improving future financial stability.[26] The FSF recognises that the widespread adoption of high-quality internationally accepted

---

[18] *See* note 13 *supra.*

[19] *See* FSF, First Meeting of the Financial Stability Forum, Press Release (6 April 1999).

[20] For comment, *see* G.A. Walker, 'Hedge Fund Control' (May 1999) *FRR* 1.

[21] For comment, *see* G.A. Walker, 'Offshore Financial Centres' (Sept/Aug 200) *FRR* 1.

[22] For comment, *see* G.A. Walker, 'Global Capital Flows' (Oct 2000) *FRR* 1.

[23] *See* FSF, 'FSF Establishes Working Groups', Press Release (19 November 1999).

[24] *See* Walker, 'The New Global Rule Book', *op. cit.*, note 8; and Walker, 'Financial Stability Standards', *op. cit.*, note 8.

[25] *See* Walker, 'Financial Stability Standards', *op. cit.*, note 8.

[26] *See* Section II *supra. See* also Walker, 'The New Global Rule Book', *op. cit.*, note 8.

standards or codes of good practice can promote far more effective policy-making, well-functioning financial markets and a stronger international financial system.

Having this as its objective, the FSF has attempted to issue a series of guidelines in each of the core areas of policy transparency, (fiscal, monetary and financial), data dissemination (economic and financial), supervision and regulation (in each of the three core financial areas of banking, securities and insurance), information disclosure (including transparency, risk management and internal controls of individual institutions), corporate governance (with accounting, auditing and bankruptcy) and payment and settlement.

This initial list of relevant measures constitutes is an impressive catalogue. To secure the creation of an integrated rulebook dealing with all aspects of policy transparency and data dissemination, supervision including internal risk management, governance and payment and settlement would be an impressive achievement. The FSF considers that ensuring greater transparency in respect of the development of government policy in the areas of fiscal, monetary and financial matters as well as enhanced disclosure of economic and financial statistics will improve the accountability of policy-makers and allow markets to adjust more smoothly to economic developments, minimise contagion and reduce volatility.

The adoption of internationally accepted standards of financial market supervision and regulation will allow more effective policies to be implemented at the national level which promote sound and efficient markets as well as improved credibility and investor confidence. Better informed lending and investment decisions should be possible if market participants are provided with internationally recognised standards in respect of disclosure, transparency, risk management and internal control systems. The efficient operation of markets should also be improved through similar provisions in respect of accounting, auditing and insolvency provision (although progress has until now been slow in these areas) while improvements in corporate governance will promote confidence in the operation of the financial system. Technical improvements in the speed and stability of payment and settlement (which Gerald Corrigan liked to refer to as the plumbing) can further avoid unnecessary delays and protect national and international systems against larger systemic threats.

To secure these highly objectives, the FSF has created a virtual or electronic Compendium of Standards by linking all the existing core papers in each of these areas within its own new site or domain.[27] Rather than follow the full policy division or issue structure outlined above, however, the FSF has grouped policy transparency and data dissemination under a public sector heading. Each of the three core financial sectors of banking securities and insurance then have their own subject areas and sub-areas which include supervision and regulation as well as internal risk management and control. Governance, accounting and auditing as well as bankruptcy were grouped under corporate and payment and settlement given its own subject area.

The result of this restructuring was an even more basic public sector, banking, securities, insurance, corporate and payment and settlement division of core

---

[27] *See* note 9 *supra*.

standards. Each of these includes between one and five subsections which, in turn, contain between one to ten core policy papers representing the agreed best standards in the particular sub-areas concerned.[28]

The reason for the apparent revision or, at least, simplification, was unclear but presumably it was decided (or had always been assumed) that it would be necessary for each of the main sector committees and other agencies concerned to make their own initial selections as to relevant papers as well as to control the structure and content of their own area (and sub-areas) within the Compendium. No attempt had been made at that stage either to provide any coherent or consistent presentation of relevant papers across each area nor to consider how they may be further integrated over time. This early restructuring may then have been more apparent than real. The only problem, which arises, is that the FSF may not have, in fact, intended to be as ambitious and integrationist in its work as originally suggested or understood.

The provisional result of this work was nevertheless impressive. A virtual collection of all of the core standards in each of the principal subject areas and sub-areas has been created within a single domain which is then linked using HTML to all of the individual source sites concerned. The full text of each paper is then not held on the FSF site but hyper-linked to the location where it is already stored and available. This is a clever device in terms of information management and dissemination.[29]

A number of basic difficulties did arise with regard to definitions, structure and titling while the sections on accounting and auditing and insolvency did not contain any papers. There are still no core standards in each of these key areas. Certain other matters were also omitted (either deliberately or accidentally) such as in relation to financial conglomerates and securities clearance and settlement. These can, however, be corrected over time provided that there is a sufficient degree of co-operation and goodwill between the representatives from all of the various agencies and sector specific committees concerned.

The content of each of the main subject headings within the Compendium is considered in the following sub-sections.

### (1)   Transparency

Under the FSF's new regime, policy transparency is to be secured through the IMF's 1998 *Code of Good Practices on Fiscal Transparency*[30] (Table 1) and its 1999 *Code of Good Practices on Transparency in Monetary and Financial Policies*.[31]

While the Fiscal Code sets out a series of transparency requirements to provide assurances to the public and capital markets that a sufficiently complete picture of the structure and finances of government is available to allow its fiscal policy to be properly assessed, a series of further desirable transparency practices are set out in the

---

[28] *See* Tables 1–6.

[29] *See* note 9 *supra.*

[30] *See* IMF, *Code of Good Practices on Fiscal Transparency* (April 1998).

[31] *See* IMF, *Code of Good Practices on Transparency in Monetary and Financial Policies* (July 1999).

*Table 1.* Public sector

---

Policy Transparency
(1) IMF, *Code of Good Practices on Transparency in Monetary and Financial Policies* (July 1999)
(2) IMF, *Code of Good Practices on Fiscal Transparency* (April 1998)

Data Dissemination
(3) IMF, *Special Data Dissemination Standard (SDDS)* (March 1996)
(4) IMF, *General Data Dissemination Systems (GDDS)* (December 1997)

---

Monetary and Finance Code for central banks in relation to the conduct of monetary policy and for central banks and other agencies in respect of their financial policies.

Two sets of Good Transparency Practices are set out under the July 1999 Code which include provisions relating to the clarity of roles, responsibilities and objectives of central banks or financial agencies, open processes for formulating and reporting policies or policy decisions, public availability of information on relevant policies and accountability and assurances of integrity.

The 1999 Code does acknowledge that full transparency may not be appropriate in all circumstances and that limitations may have to be included where, for example, the effectiveness of specific policies could be damaged or market stability or the legitimate interests of supervised and other entities could be effected. The key objective, however, remains transparency although good policies are also promoted, for example, in the area of financial policy.

These are important measures, which have begun the process of establishing new global standards of openness and accountability in these three key policy areas. Of possibly more value than their substantive content has been their contribution to the development a new culture of disclosure and open discussion in connection with such matters.

The release of more specific data in the public sector is also to be promoted through the IMF's 1996 paper on Special Data Dissemination Standards (SDDS)[32] and its 1997 paper on General Data Dissemination System (GDDS).[33] While the SDDS was designed to provide guidance for countries, which might seek access to international capital markets in the dissemination of relevant economic and financial data, the GDDS assists in the provision of general economic, financial and socio-demographic data to the public in a comprehensive, timely, accessible and reliable manner.

By August 1999, there were 47 subscribers to the SDDS made up of industrial market countries, emerging market economies and transition economies. The GDDS was largely developed for countries, which were not able to satisfy all of the requirements set out in the SDDS. The GDDS is then aimed at promoting or supporting improvements over time rather than acting as an assessment mechanism as such.

These are again important papers in the promotion of full, timeous and accurate disclosure of relevant market data. With the transparency papers, most countries

---

[32] IMF, *Special Data Dissemination Standards* (March 1996).
[33] IMF, *General Data Dissemination System* (December 1997).

should now be able to adopt clearer specific policies as well as a more general operating culture of openness, responsibility and accountability in public affairs within which modern capital market based finance structures can develop.

## *(2) Banking*

With regard to banking, the main document is, of course, the Basel Committee's *Core Principles for Effective Banking Supervision* (Table 2).[34] This attempts for the first time to integrate all of the main aspects of supervisory and regulatory practice within a single paper and in so doing to provide a comprehensive model for national financial market control.

In addition to the 25 core rules established, a number of 'precepts' for effective banking supervision are developed with regard to such matters as (a) key objectives (the maintenance of stability and confidence in the financial system), (b) the importance of market discipline and good corporate governance, (c) need for operational independence, (d) the ability of supervisors to understand bank activity and risk management as well as (e) the value of bank risk profile assessments, (f) adequate supervisory resources, and (g) close co-operation between authorities.

*Table 2.* Banking

General
    (5) Basel Committee, *Core Principles for Effective Banking Supervision* (September 1997)

International Supervision
    (6) Basel Committee, *Principles for the Supervision of Banks' Foreign Establishments* (The Concordat) (May 1983)
    (7) Basel Committee, *Minimum Standards for the Supervision of International Banking Groups and their Cross-Border Establishments* (The Minimum Standards) (July 1992)
    (8) Basel Committee, *The Supervision of Cross-Border Banking* (October 1996)

Capital Adequacy
    (9) Basel Committee, *International Convergence of Capital Measurement and Capital Standards* (as amended, The Basel Accord) (July 1988)
    (10) Basel Committee, *Overview of the Amendment to the Capital Accord to Incorporate Market Risks* (January 1996)
    (11) Basel Committee, *Amendment to the Capital Accord to Incorporate Market Risks* (The Market Risk Amendment) (January 1996)
    (12) Basel Committee, *Supervisory Framework for the use of 'Backtesting' in Conjunction with the Internal Models Approach to Market Risk Capital Requirements* (January 1996)

Transparency and Disclosure
    (13) Basel Committee, *Enhancing Bank Transparency* (September 1998)
    (14) Basel Committee, *Sound Practices for Loan Accounting, Credit Risk Disclosure and Related Matters* (July 1999)

Risk Management and Internal Controls
    (15) Basel Committee, *Framework for Internal Control Systems in Banking Organisations* (September 1998)

---

[34] Basle Committee, *Core Principles for Effective Banking Supervision* (September 1997).

The Core Principles also set out five further preconditions for effective banking supervision which comprise (a) a sound and sustainable macro-economic policy, (b) a well-developed public infrastructure, (c) effective market discipline, (d) procedures for the efficient resolution of problems in banks, and (e) mechanisms for providing an appropriate level of systemic protection.

A number of principles are then set out dealing with all aspects of bank supervision and control. The most substantial of these is possibly Principle 1 which contains a number of preconditions for effective banking supervision. This then comprises eight separate conditions including (a) clear responsibilities and objectives for each super-visory agency, (b) operational independence and adequate resources, (c) a suitable legal framework which, in particular, secures (i) initial authorisation (or licensing) as well as effective on-going supervision of all relevant institutions, (ii) adequate powers to secure compliance with laws and safety and soundness concerns as well as (iii) legal protection for supervisors, (d) arrangements for sharing information between supervisors (where necessary), and (e) proper protections for the confiden-tiality of all information exchanged.

A number of further specific requirements are then set out with regard to licensing and structure (Core Principles 2–5), prudential regulation and requirements (Core Principles 6–15), methods of on-going banking supervision (Core Prin-ciples 16–20), information requirements (Core Principle 21), formal powers of supervisors (Core Principle 22) and cross-border banking (Core Principles 23–25).

The Core Principles have been criticised for their generality in many areas. The decision had, however, been taken at the beginning only to construct a general reference framework which could be used by all countries and not to try to create a detailed set of rules which may only be appropriate in a small number of jurisdic-tions. It would have been very difficult to balance these two competing considera-tions otherwise.

Most recently, the Committee has also issued a *Core Principles Methodology, which* is designed to assist in the conduct of compliance assessments in particular countries with regard to the implementation of the Core Principles.[35] This restates the objectives of the Core Principles and sets out certain considerations in conducting assessments. It then contains a large amount of detailed guidance on the assessment of compliance with each of the principles issued by the Committee. This is a very useful document especially for expert teams either preparing for or con-ducting on-site visits to determine material compliance with the Core Principles in any particular case. It accordingly adds further substance to the core rules and has to be strongly welcomed for that reason.

With regard to the supervision of international banks, the Committee's Compendium[36] contains the 1983 Revised Concordat[37] (which replaced the

---

[35] Basle Committee, *Core Principles Methodology* (October 1999).

[36] *See* Basle Committee, *Compendium of Documents* (April 1997).

[37] *See* Basle Committee, 'Principles for the supervision of banks' foreign establishments' (May 1983). *See* also Basle *Committee, Compendium of Documents,* Vol. 3 (April 1997), pp. 7–13.

Committee's original 1975 Concordat[38]), the 1992 Minimum Standards[39] and the October 1996 29 recommendations for the supervision of cross-border banking.[40] The 1983 Revised Concordat was partly issued in the response to the collapse of Banco Ambrosiano (a replacement paper to the 1975 Concordat was already being considered to deal with such matters as consolidated supervision) while the Minimum Standards were issued following the collapse of BCCI. Although there are nominally only four Minimum Standards, the supporting text extends this considerably. The October 1996 paper was originally prepared as an implementation report on the Minimum Standards which was conducted by a joint working group set up by the Basel Committee and the Offshore Banking Supervisory Group.

These papers contain the core supervisory framework for internationally active banks although strangely the 1990 Information Supplement[41] is not included (this represented the results of an earlier 1986 implementation report[42] into the operation of the 1983 Revised Concordat) nor are the later Core Principles (23–25) referred to separately which specifically deal with cross-border supervisory co-operation (although these may be considered only to reflect the rules set out in the other supervisory papers referred to).

Capital adequacy in respect of banks is to remain to be governed by the Committee's July 1998 Capital Accord[43] pending its future revision[44] as well as the January 1996 Market Risk Amendment.[45] As the separate January 1996 paper on

---

[38] *See* Basle Committee, 'Report to the Governors on the supervision of banks' foreign establishments' (September 1975). This also gave effect to the Committee's recommendations in relation to consolidated supervision. *See* Basle Committee, 'Consolidated Supervision of Bank's International Activities' (March 1979). This followed an earlier 1978 paper by the Committee. *See* Basle Committee, 'Consolidation of banks' balance sheets: aggregation of risk-bearing assets as a method of supervisory bank solvency' (October 1978). *See* also Basle Committee, *Compendium of Documents*, Vol. 1 (April 1997), pp. 83–84.

[39] *See* Basle Committee, 'Minimum Standards for the supervision of international banking groups and their cross-border establishments (July 1992). *See* also Basle Committee 'Report on International Developments in Banking Supervision' Report No. 8 (September 1992), Chap. III; and Basle Committee, *Compendium of Documents*, Vol. 3 (April 1997), pp. 23–27.

[40] *See* Basle Committee, 'The supervision of cross-border banking' (October 1996). *See* also Basle Committee 'Report on International Developments in Banking Supervision', Report No. 10 (June 1996), Chap. IV; and Basle Committee, *Compendium of Documents*, Vol. 3, (April 1997), pp. 28–53.

[41] *See* Basle Committee, 'Information flows between banking supervisory authorities' (April 1990). This had earlier been reproduced in Basle Committee, 'Report on International Developments in Banking Supervision' (September 1990), Report No. 7, Chap. VI, pp. 31–42, *infra. See* also Basle Committee, *Compendium of Documents*, Vol. 3 (April 1997), pp. 14–22.

[42] *See* Basle Committee, 'The Implementation of the Concordat', reproduced in Basle Committee, 'Report on International Developments in Banking Supervision' (September 1986), Report No 5, Chap. VII at 50.

[43] *See* Basle Committee, 'International convergence of capital measurement and capital standards' (July 1988) as amended.

[44] For comment, *see* Walker, 'So Close But So Far', *FT-FRR* (May 1999); Walker, 'Accord at Last', *FT-FRR* (June 1999); Walker, 'A New Capital Adequacy Framework' (August/September 1999) *FT-FRR*; Walker, 'The New Capital Accord' (April 2001) *FRI* 1.

[45] *See* Basle Committee, *Market Risk Amendment* (January 1996). *See* also, Basle Committee, *Overview of the Amendment to the Capital Accord to Incorporate Market Risks* (January 1996); and Basle Committee, *Supervisory Framework for the Use of 'Backtesting' in Conjunction with the Internal Models Approach to Market Risk Capital Requirements* (January 1996).

Back Testing is also to apply, the separate inclusion of the Market Risk Overview document is surprising although this does incorporate the April 1998 amendments.

Transparency and disclosure in the banking area are to be secured under the Committee's September 1998 paper on Enhancing Bank Transparency and its July 1999 paper on Sound Practices for Loan Accounting, Credit Risk Disclosure and Related Matters.[46] The first of these is directed at securing improved supervisory and public disclosure as a device to promote enhanced market discipline while the second assists banks and banking supervisors make better provision for loan losses and connected matters.

The subsequent reference to the Committee's September 1998 paper on Internal Control Systems[47] is somewhat confusing. This should follow Capital Adequacy and not Transparency and Disclosure although this may be a minor matter. In considering financial market control, the core objective should be full and proper risk identification and control, which begins with the internal risk management process of the individual bank. Transparency and disclosure and associated market discipline should be considered as supplements and not correctives to this.

The only unfortunate aspect of the Committee's work in this area has been the fact that it took it until September 1998 to issue any even outline guidance in respect of internal control systems (apart from the area of financial derivatives where a considerable amount of progress had been possible with IOSCO). The supposed reason for the failure of international authorities generally to attempt to deal with the specific problem of operational risk control and the quality of internal systems before was supposedly that it was too complex and firm dependent.

Proper internal risk management must remain the fundamental function of every financial institution in any market. Consequently, firms must be able correctly to identify and control the full range and volume of risk which their activities generate. Their ability, or inability, to do so should then be the primary focus of supervisory attention.

All of the debate over the last two decades which has focused on credit and market risk capital adequacy has, to a large extent, simply distracted attention from this core function of effective financial market supervision.

Supervisory authorities must examine the quality of the internal risk management and control systems of every financial institution. Only if something goes wrong at that level does capital even become relevant. Capital is designed to absorb loss which subsequently arises while the immediate focus of financial market activity and supervision should be on loss prevention.

### (3)    Securities

Securities firms are to be governed by IOSCO's 1998 core *Objectives and Principles of Securities Regulation* (Table 3).[48] This establishes the three fundamental objectives

---

[46] *See* Basle Committee, *Enhancing Bank Transparency* (September 1998). *See* also Basle Committee, *Sound Practices for Loan Accounting, Credit Risk Disclosure and Related Matters* (July 1999).

[47] *See* Basle Committee, *Framework for Internal Control Systems in Banking Organisations* (September 1998).

[48] *See* IOSCO, *Objectives and Principles of Securities Regulation* (September 1998).

*Table 3.* Securities

---

Regulation
(16) IOSCO, *Objectives and Principles of Securities Regulation* (September 1998)
(17) IOSCO, *Securities Activity on the Internet* (September 1998)
(18) IOSCO, *Guidance on Information Sharing* (November 1998)
(19) IOSCO, *Report on Co-operation Between Market Authorities and Default Procedures* (March 1996)
(20) IOSCO, *Co-ordination Between Cash and Derivative Markets: Contract Design of Derivative Products on Stock Indices and Measures to Minimise Market Disruption* (October 1992)
(21) IOSCO, *The Application of the Tokyo Communiqué to Exchange-Traded Financial Derivatives Contracts* (September 1998)
(22) IOSCO, *Principles for the Supervision of Operators of Collective Investments* (September 1997)
(23) IOSCO, *Principles of Memoranda of Understanding* (September 1991)
(24) IOSCO, *IOSCO Resolution: Principles for Record Keeping, Collection of Information, Enforcement Powers and Mutual Co-operation to Improve the Enforcement of Securities and Futures Laws*

Transparency and Disclosure
(25) IOSCO, *International Disclosure Standards for Cross-border Offerings and Initial Listings by Foreign Issuers* (September 1998)

Risk Management and Internal Controls
(26) IOSCO, *Methodologies for Determining Minimum Capital Standards for Internationally Active Securities Firms which Permit the Use of Models under Prescribed Conditions* (May 1998)
(27) IOSCO, *Operational and Financial Risk Management Control Mechanisms for Over-the-Counter Derivatives Activities of Regulated Securities Firms* (July 1994)
(28) IOSCO, *Risk Management and Control Guidance for Securities Firms and their Supervisors* (May 1998)
(29) IOSCO, *Client Asset Protection* (August 1996)

---

for securities regulation of (a) protecting investors, (b) ensuring that markets are fair, efficient and transparent and (c) reducing systemic risk.

IOSCO then develops 30 core principles dealing with the regulatory authorities (Principles 1–5), self-regulation (Principles 6–7), enforcement (Principles 8–10), co-operation (Principles 11–16), collective investment schemes (Principles 17–20), market intermediaries (Principles 21–24) and secondary markets (Principles 25–30).

These Core Objectives and Principles are then supplemented by IOSCO's other more specific papers on Internet Trading,[49] Information Sharing,[50] Financial Derivatives[51] and Collective Investment Schemes.[52] All of these are valuable measures which attempt to develop further certain key aspects of best standard and practice in each of the main sub-areas of activity within securities markets. The only obvious omissions appear to be in connection with investment advice and brokerage although they are included within the Core Objectives and Principles. The full range

---

[49] See IOSCO, *Securities Activity on the Internet* (September 1998).

[50] See IOSCO, *Guidance on Information Sharing* (November 1998).

[51] See IOSCO, *Co-ordination between Cash and Derivative Markets: Contract Design of Derivative Products on Stock Indices and Measures to Minimise Market Disruption* (October 1992); and IOSCO, *The Application of the Tokyo Communiqué to Exchange-Traded Financial Derivatives Contracts* (September 1998).

[52] See IOSCO, *Principles for the Supervision of the Operators of Collective Investment Schemes* (September 1997); and IOSCO, *Report on Investment Management Principles for the Regulation of Collective Investment Schemes and Explanatory Memorandum* (October 1994).

of papers produced by all of the IOSCO's working groups will also have to be reviewed again to ensure that all relevant core standards are included.

Of slightly more surprise is the inclusion of the papers on Default Procedures,[53] MoUs[54] and mutual cooperation[55] within IOSCO's general section. These may have been more appropriately, and consistently, included in a separate cooperation sub-heading although IOSCO appears to have adopted a completely different approach to Basel on this. The specific paper on stock index futures may also have been better placed in a separate product subcategory or heading which could then be developed further over time.

Transparency and disclosure in the securities area are to be achieved under IOSCO's September 1998 paper on International Disclosure Standards[56] while risk management and internal controls are to be secured under its four papers on capital models,[57] OTC derivatives,[58] more general control guidance[59] and client asset protection.[60] These are all valuable contributions to the development of more stable national and international securities markets although again the selection and ordering are somewhat questionable. Risk management is arguably of more importance than transparency and disclosure while the May 1998 control guidance paper is the most important key paper in respect of risk management. The omission of a separate capital sub-heading is also somewhat strange although IOSCO is possibly still sensitive to its inability to agree any common standards with Basel in the area of market risk. The absence of any reference to the joint IOSCO and Basel papers on financial derivatives is also strange. Further discussions are presumably continuing in this regard.

The inconsistencies which arise between the basic structure of the Basel and IOSCO sub-area headings confirm that initial paper selection and structuring was left to the separate sector authorities and not determined by the FSF (see Editorial). While each of the two major sector bodies will obviously adopt different approaches with regard to the discharge of their separate responsibilities and the development of appropriate rules and procedures for relevant risk control in their particular markets, it is unfortunate that more consistency has not been possible in this regard.

The ultimate objective of the FSF must, or, at least, should be the creation of a wholly integrated set of rules governing all aspects of market practice. To achieve this, each of the main papers selected should at some stage be reviewed to ensure their

---

[53] *See* IOSCO, *Report on Co-operation Between Market Authorities and Default Procedures* (March 1996).

[54] *See* IOSCO, *Principles of Memoranda of Understanding* (September 1991).

[55] *See* IOSCO, *Resolution: Principles for Record Keeping, Collection of Information, Enforcement Powers, and Mutual Co-operation to Improve the Enforcement of Securities and Futures Laws.*

[56] *See* IOSCO, *International Disclosure Standards for Cross-Border Offerings and Initial Listings by Foreign Issues* (September 1998).

[57] *See* IOSCO, *Methodologies for Determining Minimum Capital Standards for Internationally Active Securities Firms which Permit the Use of Models under Prescribed Conditions* (May 1998).

[58] *See* IOSCO, *Operational and Financial Risk Management Control Mechanisms for Over-the-Counter Derivatives Activities of Regulated Securities Firms* (July 1984).

[59] *See* IOSCO, *Risk Management and Control Guidance for Securities Firms and their Supervisors* (May 1998).

[60] *See* IOSCO, *Client Asset Protection* (August 1996).

operational consistency. Before that can even be considered, however, each of the main sector committees involved must begin to try to develop some common approach to the identification of the type and function of the main policy papers required.

### (4)  Insurance

Insurance undertakings are to be governed by the IAIS's September 1997 paper on *Insurance Supervisory Principles* (Table 4)[61] (IAIS's Core Principles) as well as supporting papers on cross-border supervision[62] (the Insurance Concordat) and the supervisory standards on licensing,[63] on-site inspections[64] and derivatives.[65] Despite its much more recent creation, the IAIS has been able to make a significant contribution to the development of parallel standards in the insurance area.

The lack of consistent treatment between the banking and insurance sub-site is, however, even more surprising as the IAIS has generally always adopted a very Basel-Committee type approach to market control. The IAIS and the Basel Committee have always tended to work closely together in relation to all key issues. The IAIS is, of course, also based at the BIS in Basel.

If a common three sector approach is to be constructed, it would have been of assistance if Basel and the IAIS, at least, could have provisionally agreed on some common format between themselves which they could then have discussed with IOSCO. The absence of any initial consideration of the need for some basic degree of consistency between the banking and insurance and banking, securities and insurance sub-sites is highly regrettable. As has already been stressed, the overall objective must be to create an integrated compendium of relevant rules. This has to begin with some common understanding of agreed definitions and standard's structure.

The absence of any separate sub-area in respect of conglomerates is also surprising. Presumably this may be added at a later stage. The inability for the three core sector fora to adopt a common approach with regard to the selection, identification and presentment of core documents makes this even more unfortunate. As the FSF

*Table 4.* Insurance

Supervision
(30) IAIS, *Insurance Supervisory Principles* (Core Principles) (September 1997)
(31) IAIS, *Principles Applicable to the Supervision of International Insurers and Insurance Groups and their Cross-border Establishments* (Insurance Concordat) (September 1997)
(32) IAIS, *Supervisory Standard on Licensing* (September 1998)
(33) IAIS, *Supervisory Standard on On-Site Inspections* (October 1998)
(34) IAIS, *Supervisory Standard on Derivatives* (October 1998)

---

[61] *See* IAIS, *Insurance Supervisory Principles* (September 1997).
[62] *See* IAIS, *Principles Applicable to the Supervision of International Insurers and Insurance Groups and their Cross-Border Establishments* (September 1997).
[63] *See* IAIS, *Supervisory Standards on Licensing* (September 1998).
[64] *See* IAIS, *Supervisory Standards on On-Site Inspections* (October 1998).
[65] *See* IAIS, *Supervisory Standards on Derivatives* (October 1998).

*Table 5.* Corporate Governance

| (35) OECD, *Principles of Corporate Governance* (May 1999) |
| --- |

freely admits (as had Hans Tietmeyer before it), it is essential that an integrated cross-sector approach is adopted. More consideration should accordingly be given to securing consistency (although not necessarily uniformity) and coherence across the specific sector rules developed.

### *(5)   Governance*

Corporate governance is initially to be secured solely under the OECD's May 1999 paper on *Principles of Corporate Governance* (Table 5).[66] Unfortunately no papers have yet been issued in the areas of accounting and auditing and bankruptcy.

The OECD's May 1999 paper attempts to improve the legal, institutional and regulatory framework for corporate governance in both OECD and non-OECD countries. A number of principles are developed under the headings of the rights of shareholders, the equitable treatment of shareholders, the role of stakeholders, disclosure and transparency and the responsibility of the board of directors.

Although some of the principles are still drafted in fairly general language, this is an important document insofar as it attempts to establish a minimum level of common standards in this area at the international level.

The absence of any papers in connection with accounting and auditing and bankruptcy is unfortunate although work has been proceeding in each of these areas for a considerable period of time. Some recent progress has been possible, for example, in connection with international audit standards although this work must continue.

While all discussion at the international level attempts to resolve differences between relevant national systems, the additional difficulty, which arises in these areas, is that various private law as well as other related company and insolvency law issues have also to be dealt with. This makes negotiations more complex as differences in national laws have to be resolved first (if at all) before more specific supervisory or regulatory issues can even be considered. It is always more difficult to secure agreement where such issues of substantive law as opposed to pure supervisory or regulatory practice are involved. It can only be hoped that more substantial progress may be possible in these areas in due course.

### *(6)   Payment and settlement*

The payment and settlement section has been divided into a general and securities sub-heading. The titling is again somewhat strange as the first sub-area is clearly concerned with payment and settlement in banking and financial markets and the second with clearance and settlement in securities markets. The first is accordingly

---

[66] *See* OECD, *Principles of Corporate Governance* (May 1999).

*Table 6.* Payment and settlement

---

General

(36) CPSS, *Core Principles for the Design and Operation of Payment Systems* (November 1999)

(37) CPSS, *Settlement Risk in Foreign Exchange Transactions* (March 1996)

(38) CPSS, *Real Time Gross Settlement Systems* (March 997)

(39) CPSS, *Report of the Committee on Interbank Netting Schemes of the Central Banks of the Group of Ten Countries* (The Lamafalussy Report) (November 1990)

Securities

(40) CPSS, *Delivery Versus Payment in Securities Settlement Systems* (September 1992)

(41) CPSS, *OECD Derivatives: Settlement Procedures and Counterparty Risk Management* (September 1998)

(42) CPSS, *Clearing Arrangement for Exchange-Traded Derivatives* (March 1997)

---

concerned with the completion of transfers of funds while the other with transfer and confirmation of title to security interests.

The main Committee on Payment and Settlement Systems (CPSS) has included its draft *Core Principles for the Design and Operation of Payment Systems* (Table 6),[67] its 1996 paper on Foreign Exchange Settlement Risk,[68] 1977 paper on Real Time Gross Settlement Systems (RTGSS)[69] and the 1990 Lamfalussy Report.[70] Insofar as the Lamfalussy Report provided the background to much of the subsequent work in this area, it may have been better to include this as the introductory paper and then the outline Core Principles and RTGSS paper.

The CPSS's separate paper on March 1996 on settlement risk and foreign exchange transactions is also included. It may have been better to have dealt with foreign exchange under a separate sub-heading within payment and settlement (which would then comprise banking, foreign exchange and securities). This may be reconsidered later.

With regard to securities, only the CPSS papers on Delivery Versus Payment (DVP),[71] OTC derivatives[72] and exchange-traded derivatives[73] papers are included. This suggests that there have been no attempts to integrate funds and securities transfers to date within a single section. This is unfortunate. Although distinct, the two core functions in both banking and securities markets are linked. One solution may have been to have a separate heading on *Payment and Clearance*. Alternatively, a separate clearance and settlement sub-heading could be included within securities. The failure to include any more specific securities papers within the existing *Payment and Settlement* area suggests that this sub-site was solely prepared by the CPSS without any wider initial discussion although hopefully again this can be corrected over time.

---

[67] *See* CPSS, *Core Principles for the Design and Operation of Payment Systems* (November 1999).

[68] *See* CPSS, *Settlement Risk in Foreign Exchange Transactions* (March 1997).

[69] *See* CPSS, *Real Time Gross Settlement* (March 1997).

[70] *See* CPSS, *Report of the Committee on Interbank Netting Schemes of the Central Banks of the Group of Ten Countries* (November 1990).

[71] *See* CPSS, *Delivery Versus Payment in Securities Settlement Systems* (September 1992).

[72] *See* CPSS, *OTC Derivatives: Settlement Procedures and Counterparty Risk Management* (September 1998).

[73] *See* CPSS, *Clearing Arrangements for Exchange-Traded Derivatives* (March 1997).

## IV   STANDARDS IMPLEMENTATION

Having considered the content of the FSF's Compendium, it now necessary to ensure that it is given full and proper effect in practice. This was accordingly the function assigned to Andrew Sheng and his Task Force on Standards Implementation.[74] A first issues paper was produced in March 20 with a follow up report in August 2000.[75]

The Task Force's remit was to explore key issues in, and to consider a strategy for promoting, the implementation of international standards relevant for sound financial systems. The terms of reference of the Task Force[76] were unusually detailed and included examining various implementation mechanics such as country commitments, technical assistance, compliance reports and incentive devices. The Task Force was also asked to identify relevant core standards, assist in the construction of suitable implementation strategies and develop possible incentive structures, self-assessment and external assessment programmes, progress information reporting requirements and resources management devices. The possible contribution to be made by the various international bodies concerned and, in particular, the IMF and the World Bank was also to be reviewed.

The issues paper was endorsed by the FSF at its third meeting in Singapore on 25–26 March 2000.[77] The various standard setting bodies (technical sector committees) in place were encouraged to continue to work with the IMF and the World Bank to increase leverage of resources for assessing observance of standards. Twelve core standards for sound financial systems control were issued (see Table 2) and further work was agreed in the area of market and official incentives to assist implementation.

Although the paper was considered and approved in March, it was only publicly released towards the end of May. The reasons for this are unclear although it would appear that the report was initially circulated among G7 and G20 finance ministries and central banks and other interested groupings or bodies. As there appears to have been no subsequent amendment, this was presumably not a consultation or revision exercise as such.

The reason for the delayed public release is then somewhat surprising although nevertheless welcome in light of the value and importance of the paper. Securing the proper implementation of all core and ancillary standards remains a fundamental problem at the international level. This arises from the traditional doctrines of sovereign autonomy and the absence of effective sovereign sanction, at least, in non-treaty or convention areas of activity. While a substantial body of increasingly detailed substantive regulatory provision has been constructed, operational adherence and compliance remains a sensitive and difficult issue (see FRR, June 1999).

### *(1)   International standards*

The issues paper proceeds by highlighting the importance of international standards and then examines various possible implementation mechanisms or devices. The

---

[74] *See* note 23 *supra.*
[75] *See* notes 10 and 11 *supra.*
[76] *See* Table 7.
[77] *See* Walker, 'Standards Implementation', *op. cit.,* note 8.

*Table 7.* Terms of reference

1. The Task Force should explore issues related to promoting the implementation of internationals standards relevant to strengthening financial systems.
2. The Task Force should consider a strategy for implementation of standards that may include:
    (a) countries announcing their commitment to implement standards and participate in credible assessments of compliance;
    (b) technical assistance in support of implementation efforts being prioritised;
    (c) relevant information on progress toward compliance of standards being made available; and
    (d) compliance with sound practices being rewarded by market participants and others to reinforce further efforts and implementation.
3. In support of the strategy, and taking into account country circumstances, the Task Force should:
    (a) identify the set of international standards most relevant to strengthening financial systems and ways of disseminating these standards such as through the FSF Compendium of Standards;
    (b) explore strategies for assisting countries in the practical implementation of standards;
    (c) explore official and market incentives that could encourage the process of implementation;[1]
    (d) outline options for generating credible self-assessments and independent assessments and for ensuring complimentarity between the two;
    (e) consider how, what kind of and to whom information on progress toward compliance with standards could be made available; and
    (f) consider how the resources required to support implementation and assessment of standards could best be mobilised.
4. The Task Force should consider how the various elements of the implementation strategy could best reinforce each other and what the rules and responsibilities of the various bodies in implementing it should be.
5. In all of the above, the Task Force should draw upon the work already carried out by the IMF, the World Bank, standard-setting bodies and others with respect to encouraging implementation of sound practices.

---

[1] Such incentives might include inter alia making access to certain types of official sources of financing conditional upon compliance (as in the case of the IMF CCL), preferential risk weights in the capital adequacy framework, consideration in market access decisions of key financial centres and more generous offers of technical assistance to enhance the capacity of countries to implement sound practices.

production of relevant standards is considered necessary to assist in the promotion of sound financial systems both domestically and financial stability more generally at the international level. Four immediate benefits arise from this: (a) financial regulation and supervision is strengthened, (b) transparency is enhanced, (c) institutional development facilitated and (d) vulnerability reduced. Standards may, of course, vary in scope, specificity and degree of international acceptance. They may also range from, at one extreme, broad principles to more complete and specific implementation or assessment methodologies at the other.

Many standards also increasingly overlap in function or effect and are consequently inherently interdependent in operation and function. Despite these advantages, however, the Task Force is also anxious to stress that standards are not 'ends in themselves but [only] a means of promoting sound financial fundamentals and sustained economic growth'. Implementation must also be sufficiently flexible to allow the standards to 'fit into a country's overall strategy for economic and financial sector development, taking account of its stage of development, level of institutional capacity and other domestic factors'.

## (2) Current Practice

Progress to date in developing and implementing standards is examined. A variety of standards have already been promulgated by the Basel Committee, the IAIS,

IOSCO, the IMF and the World Bank[78] and further more specific methodologies to assess observance with these standards prepared. Observance has also been facilitated through the IMF and World Bank experimental Reports on Observance of Standards and Codes (ROSCs) and Financial Sector Assessment Programme (FSAPs) as well ongoing IMF Article IV Consultation activity. Completion of current ROSCs and FSAPs has since been given further political impetus at the G20 meeting in Berlin on 16 December 1999.[79]

### *(3)   Implementation Processes*

Following this examination of the work conducted to date, the Task Force concludes that implementation of standards should be promoted through three key areas of focused activity; on ownership, incentives and resources. Efforts should accordingly be made to promote country involvement or ownership, to provide a judicious balance of market and official incentives as well as to mobilise sufficient resources at both the national and international levels.

### *(i)   Ownership*

The report recognises the general support, which exists in connection with standards implementation although this is intimately dependent upon local circumstances and conditions. Most countries recognise the benefits of adopting and implementing international standards but their success in doing so depends, in particular, upon local domestic policy priorities, their understanding of the implementation process itself and their capacity to deal with hidden economic losses which arise with standards adoption such with consequent more stringent accounting treatment or disclosure requirements. Countries are more willing to implement standards where they recognise their own national interests in doing so. The first key principle identified by the Task Force, then, is that implementation of standards is a sovereign decision which reflects national self-interests, especially in fostering a sound domestic financial system, enlightened self-interest in the promotion of a more general stable global financial system as well as recognition of responsibilities attached to participation in the new global economic and financial market place which has been created.

A number of devices are recommended to assist the development of ownership of relevant standards. These include aligning implementation to domestic policy priorities (such as through the FSAPs with involvement of all relevant official interest groups beyond the government and central bank (including banking, securities and insurance regulators, accounting authorities, statistical agencies, self-regulatory professional bodies and other domestic standards setting fora), exchange of experiences through international groupings and fora (such as the G20, IMFC, IMF, FSF and various regulatory committees), publication of implementation action plans and the

---

[78] *See* Annex C to the Report
[79] *See* note 6 *supra.*

conduct of periodic self-assessments. While each of these will assist the promotion of ownership from a national perspective, more general involvement must also be strengthened through the involvement of a wider range of economies in the larger policy development process itself. This can be effected either through extended committee memberships or, at least, full consultation on all key policy proposals (see FRR, April 2000).

*(ii) Incentive Structures*

Implementation can also be promoted through a range of market and official incentives. Market incentives will be relevant where market participants use information on a country's observance of standards in risk assessments which may then be incorporated, for example, in differentiated credit ratings, borrowing spreads, asset allocations or other lending and investment decisions. In practice, these will require participants to be familiar with the applicable standards concerned, accept their relevance to the specific risk assessments being undertaken, access to all necessary information on observance and use of these results in the final risk assessments. The effectiveness of market assessments may then be immediately enhanced through information disclosure and improved understanding of relevant standards. This must, however, also recognise the possible diversity of market activities (including bank lending, portfolio investment, foreign direct investment to credit ratings assessment) and market participants' different areas of interest, uses of information, risk assessment methodologies and the factors they affect or influence.

Official (as opposed to market) incentives are measures applied by the official sector to a particular economy or operating institutions within it conditional upon the market achieving a certain defined milestone or result in the implementation process. These may range from a commitment to implement standards to observance of standards as verified by an external assessment or assessor. Market and official incentives should be developed as complementary rather than alternative measures. The Task Force accepts that assessments of observance of standards are likely to be, at least, partly qualitative in nature which will require further work to assess if and how they can be effectively linked to official incentives in practice. These may then be more readily applied to encourage economies to adopt standards, announce credible implementation plans or participate in external assessments than for rewarding actual observance.

A range of possible official incentives is identified within the report (see Box 1, pp. 12–13). These include conducting surveillance of economic and financial sector vulnerabilities, providing technical and financial assistance, applying differentiated terms for official financing, linking membership in international groupings to implementation progress, restricting access to certain foreign institutions (access denial), variable risk weights, internal credit rating methodologies, enhanced supervision, regulatory enforcement and strengthened oversight especially in connection with payment systems providers. It is, however, accepted that more focused work is required to study the desirability and feasibility of the various possible official incentives and appropriate circumstances for their effective application by relevant international financial institutions and national jurisdictions.

### (iii)   Resources

The Task Force also accepts that standards implementation is resource intensive for both national authorities and international bodies. Substantial human and financial capabilities are required to support effective implementation. Resources must accordingly be effectively mobilised and managed through possible 'partnerships' between all of the various bodies involved in the implementation process.

Two specific areas of difficulty are identified with regard to capacity building and the conduct of progress assessments. Capacity building includes assisting in the formulation of effective implementation plans, providing technical assistance to improve institutional capacity and providing training opportunities for officials in relevant areas. Conducting assessments includes taking stock of countries' observance of standards and their on-going progress, identifying technical assistance needs and evaluating the effectiveness of such assistance.

Capacity building may, in particular, be strengthened through improving the co-ordination of international technical assistance resources, publishing training opportunities (such as through the new Directory of Training Opportunities in Financial Supervision on the FSF website which was set up jointly by the IMF, the World Bank and the BIS) and coordinating training schedules. The conduct of assessments may be further improved through the use of a modules-based approach which constructs a final assessment through a series of pre-agreed stages. Assessments could also be improved through ensuring that the most up-to-date expertise is always involved, maintaining the integrity of standards during the course of implementation, obtaining experience of the practical issues involved in national adoption and reviewing and further improving relevant standards.

Resource allocation may also be assisted through the use of such shared ownership structures as the IMF and World Bank ROSCs procedure. This provides a valuable mechanism for improving leverage of resources by allowing international financial institutions and regulatory committees to take primary responsibility for preparing assessments in their respective areas of expertise but within the context of a larger IMF/World Bank-based ROSC framework. FSAPs also have a joint ownership base with the IMF and the World Bank being responsible for the report but with assistance being provided by the other regulatory committees and national authorities involved.

### (4)   Implementation Strategy

In compliance with its mandate, the Task Force has developed an outline strategy to improve standards implementation. This is based on five key proposals: (a) identifying and developing international consensus on a number of key standards, (b) prioritizing standards for implementation purposes taking into account country circumstances, (c) designing and effecting an action plan to implement the relevant standards, (d) assessing progress in observance of standards on an ongoing basis and (e) disseminating information on subsequent progress in observance (see Table 9).

## (i) Core Standards

The Task Force accepts that a broad range of economic and financial standards are relevant to ensuring that financial systems operate in a sound and effective manner. It is, however, recommended that efforts be undertaken to identify a subset of core standards to make the greatest contribution to reducing vulnerabilities and strengthening the resilience of financial systems and to focus priority implementation on these standards at the national level. The Task Force has identified 12 key standards for this purpose (see Table 8). While the effectiveness of the FSF Compendium of Standards as a dissemination tool is recognised, recommendations are made with regard to the revision and extension of its content.

The Task Force notes, in particular, the difficulties which have arisen with regard to the multiplicity of standards in accounting and auditing and the lack of relevant international measures in the area of insolvency. Accurate, reliable and timely financial statements are clearly fundamental for economic efficiency and financial stability and the effective application of many standards depends critically on the quality of the underlying data and associated accounting practices involved.

The present quality of financial information provided on publicly listed companies is, however, considered to be short of user expectations which, in turn, leads to poor policies and weakened risk management. Efforts should accordingly be undertaken to promote further convergence between internationally recognised accounting standards. Countries should also then adopt the relevant standards, properly identify any of the relevant standard, or set of standards, they apply, ensure that its requirements are unambiguous, reliable, transparent and objective and apply and enforce them in a consistent manner.

*Table 8.* Proposed content and structure of the compendium. Part I: Key standards for sound financial systems

| | |
|---|---|
| 1. Macroeconomic fundamentals | |
| Monetary and financial policy transparency | *Code of good practices on transparency in monetary and financial policies,* IMF |
| Fiscal policy transparency | *Code of good practices in fiscal transparency,* IMF |
| Data dissemination | *Special data dissemination standard and General data dissemination system,* IMF |
| 2. Institutional and market infrastructure | |
| Insolvency | |
| Corporate governance | *Principles of corporate governance,* OECD. |
| Accounting | *International accounting standards (IAS),* IASC |
| Auditing | *International Standards on Auditing (ISA),* IASC |
| Payment and settlement | *Core principles for systemically important payment systems,* CPSS |
| Market integrity | *The forty recommendations of the Financial Action Task Force,* FATF |
| 3. Financial regulation and supervision | |
| Banking supervision | *Core principles for effective banking supervision,* Basel Committee |
| Securities regulation | *Objectives and principles of securities regulation,* IOSCO |
| Insurance supervision | *Insurance supervisory principles,* IAS |

*Table 9.* Outline strategy to promote implementation of standards

| | |
|---|---|
| 1. Identify and develop international consensus and key standards | |
| (a) Identify standards for sound financial systems and highlight gaps | International community |
| (b) Develop methodologies for assessment of observance of standards | Policy committees in co-operation with international financial institutions |
| (c) Disseminate information on and promote understanding of standards among national authorities | International community |
| (d) Secure international political commitment to implement standards | International community |
| (e) Engage market participants in dialogue on significance of standards | National authorities, international financial institutions and policy committees |
| 2. Prioritise standards for implementation taking into account country circumstances | |
| (a) Assess country's status in observance of standards, economic circumstances and financial sector vulnerabilities | National authorities in consultation with international financial institutions and policy committees |
| (b) Prioritise standards for implementation on the basis of assessment within framework of country's domestic policy agenda or reform programme | National authorities in consultation with international financial institutions and policy committees |
| 3. Design and effect action plan to implement standards | |
| (a) Publicly articulate adoption of standards | National authorities |
| (b) Announce action plan for implementation specifying intermediate targets, timetable, resource allocation and technical assistance needs | National authorities in consultation with international financial institutions and policy committees |
| (c) Provide technical assistance and other official incentives where necessary | International community |
| 4. Assess progress and observance of standards on ongoing basis | |
| (a) Conduct self- or assisted self-assessment of progress and observance of standards | National authorities in consultation with international financial institutions and policy committees |
| (b) Verify through external assessment (including peer reviews or IMF and World Bank led assessments) | |
| (c) Provide additional technical assistance where necessary | National authorities in consultation with international financial institutions and policy committees International community |
| 5. Disseminate information on progress and observance of standards Disseminate information on progress to market participants – national authorities. | |

## (ii)   Priority Implementation

Implementation priorities will clearly vary from country to country having regard to current observance of standards, economic circumstances, financial structures, legal and institutional frameworks and other related policy relationships. A balance will accordingly have to be struck in each case between relevant international and domestic considerations. This should, however, be developed through national authorities working closely with international financial institutions and standard setting committees.

*(iii)   Implementation Programmes*

National authorities should prepare and publicly release action plans for implementation, which should detail targets, timetables, resource allocations and technical assistance needs. Although this is a sovereign exercise, it should again be carried out in consultation with relevant international financial institutions and standard setting committees.

*(iv)   Progress Reports*

While country ownership is promoted through implementation self-assessments, this must be supported by effective external examinations to ensure credibility and accuracy. These should be conducted in co-operation with relevant financial institutions and standard setting committees developing, in particular, on current ROSC and FSAP procedures. These must also be undertaken in accordance with clear assessment methodologies which guide the assessment process, ensure complementarily between self and external assessments and facilitate comparability between country examinations.

*(v)   Published Results*

Market and official incentives can only operate where there is full dissemination of all relevant implementation data. While some delay in the release of summary assessments may be required in certain circumstances, for example, having regard to specific national concerns as to possible market responses or volatility, the general presumption should be in favour of full public release. If the assessments are not to be made publicly available, the reasons for failure to disclosure should be provided.

*(5)   Initial Policy Components*

The early work of the Task Force accordingly lead to the production of a considered and intelligent set of initial recommendations (see Table 9). Rather than be treated as a final report (which was stressed by the Task Force itself), the paper was better considered as an initial identification and provisional development of certain key issues in the area of standards adoption and compliance review. While much further work will clearly have to be undertaken, this was nevertheless a substantial and valuable first step in this regard.

The relatively detailed terms of reference are of interest although this should not be considered to undermine the quality of the original results produced by the Task Force itself. The three key implementation components identified (ownership, incentives and resources) will be of considerable operational value. While the latter two were highlighted in the FSF terms of reference, their emphasis and importance is restated. Although there is also some overlap between the ownership and incentives concepts and possibly some confusion with the specific addressees of incentive targets (the observing country or local market participants), this does provide a succinct and easy to use reference and rules framework for further development and application.

It has to be admitted that much of the detail contained in the paper is somewhat obvious, at least, in retrospect or on subsequent reflection. The structuring and articulation of the key ideas involved, however, is original and will be of considerable assistance in taking much of this work forward. Promoting country ownership as a first step is important to establish initial involvement in policy construction and the identification of areas of relevant self-interest in the subsequent implementation process. The use of a mixture of official and market incentives to promote further compliance will then be of value in practice while necessary operational steps can only be taken where proper resources are made available in all cases. The use of joint work programmes to strengthen capacity is insightful, especially having regard to the success of the IMF/World Bank ROSCs and FSAPs. Progress assessment may, however, have been better referred to in terms of disclosure which would have improved both self-interest (ownership) and peer group and market pressure (official incentives).

The report might also have more clearly stressed that each of the three core processes of ownership, incentives and resources are intimately connected. Their supportive and complementary roles might then have been highlighted, although this is arguably clear from their nature and operation. The mutually reinforcing and connected effects of these facilities could still have been more fully dealt with, for example, by representing them diagrammatically as three circular components or processes as with the United Kingdom RATE supervision by risk framework or the FSA's more recent ARROW proposal.

The two most important specific contributions made are the list of possible official incentives and the summary of core standards. The menu of official incentives included provides a valuable listing of mixed incentive and sanction-based devices to promote national adoption and compliance. The most severe of these will be access denial, failing which the threat of supervisory or regulatory action although it must be stressed that the general tone of the report as a whole is fundamentally non-aggressive and non-confrontational. The emphasis is then on the promotion of enlightened self-interest and voluntary adoption and compliance rather than with official sanction. Although somewhat dilute, this list of possible official action does provide a useful reference framework of compliance options.

The list of key standards for sound financial systems is also of particular value in clarifying the core elements within of the larger Compendium produced by the FSF.[80] While the Compendium already provides an excellent reference collection of all relevant market control rules, the identification of a limited number of key provisions for priority implementation is an enlightened and potentially valuable device. We have already seen how various standards such as in the banking area have moved from looser general rules of best practice to more effective absolute minimum standards. This was clearly demonstrated with the rewriting of the earlier supervisory papers in terms of minimum standards in 1992 (by Gerald Corrigan personally) following the model of the 1988 Basel Capital Accord. It can only be hoped that the same success may be achieved with this identification of a series of absolute key standards within the structure of the larger Compendium.[81]

---

[80] *See* Section III *supra.*

[81] It is possibly of interest that the first reference to this list of core standards in the report (at p. 19) is not internally subdivided although this was subsequently introduced (by Annex I at p. 45). The division

Apart from identifying this subset of absolute key provisions within the Compendium, the Task Force has also extended the general content of the Compendium to include a number of additional provisions in each of the main functional areas concerned. Data dissemination will, for example, be expanded to include the IMF Manual of Monetary and Financial Statistics (Fifth Edition) and its Balance of Payments Manual. Accounting and auditing will now include the International Accounting Standards and International Standards on Auditing.

A number of papers have also been added in connection with market integrity, money laundering and financial crime, market functioning, bank risk management and financial conglomerates. This is significant in confirming that the Compendium is not a fixed but a dynamic and evolving list of relevant control provisions and that the FSF itself is capable of development and adjustment without formal review or issuance procedures. It is of particular interest that this revision was conducted by an essentially ad hoc task force rather than the full forum itself although this was possibly partly, if not largely, due to the stature of Andrew Sheng himself. This may also mark the beginning of a larger process of internal revision, if not yet full integration, of relevant provisions within the Compendium.

Although the outline strategy or action plan for further work is possibly somewhat less revolutionary in content or effect, it will still be of value in taking this work forward. The strategy is clearly identification, priority, action plan, progress assessment and disclosure based. As such, this will provide a valuable outline checklist or reference tool for operational use in any particular case. Some more specific timetabling of possible action may have been provided and more clear integration of the strategy with existing assessment devices such as the ROSCs and FFAPs although the operation of the particular programmes adopted can obviously be reviewed and revised further over time.

The issues paper is then generally to be strongly welcomed. It contains an informed and considered examination of the main issues involved and provides a well-structured and modest but nevertheless workable implementation framework. While the specific relationships between the three core factors identified of ownership, incentives and resources may have not be fully developed at this stage, they nevertheless provide a valuable reference tool on which the rest of the framework can operate. The emphasis on the promotion of enlightened self-interest rather than sanction is also to be strongly commended. This possibly reflects a new level of maturity and enlightened indulgence in terms of general thought and policy in this area. The identification of a subset of core standards and larger revision of the content of the Compendium will also greatly assist in its confirmation as the new global rulebook for financial market stability.

With this latest set of recommendations, the FSF has made a further important contribution to the construction of a new integrated control framework in the financial area. Although possibly not revolutionary in terms of its immediate content or

---

of the key standards into macro-economic fundamentals, institutional and market infrastructure and financial regulation and supervision will further assist identify the principal objectives and underlying nature of each of the key standards selected.

effect, this will still assist in ensuring effective operational application of all of the core and other supporting standards adopted. We may also have then begun to close one of the most fundamental residual gaps left in the new control framework in a somewhat surprisingly modest and indulgent but still possibly more effective longer-term manner.


### V   IMPLEMENTATION REVIEW

The Financial Stability Forum (FSF) then issued a follow-up report on implementation mechanisms in August 2000.[82] The FSF set up the follow-up group to consider in further depth issues related to market and official incentives that could encourage national implementation (Table 10).[83] The group decided at an early stage to focus on issues related to market incentives and regulatory, supervisory and market access measures related to official incentives. The report does not consider the role of the IMF and the World Bank in light of the ongoing work being carried out in this area. This is unfortunate but understandable. The group also decided to focus on the twelve key standards issued by the FSF and rather than the Compendium as a whole at this stage.

The report recognises the considerable amount of work that has already been undertaken by the international financial institutions and standard setting bodies to promulgate and assess standards observance. This has, in particular, been taken


*Table 10.* Terms of reference

---

1. Building on the work of the FSF Task Force on Implementation of Standards, the group should explore how market and official incentives, including those referred to in the March 15 Issues Paper (Box 1), can be developed to encourage the implementation of international standards relevant for financial stability.
2. With regard to market incentives, the group should explore how to: enhance market participants' understanding of the role of standards in strengthening financial systems and their relevance to credit and investment decisions; encourage economies to disclose and markets to generate more, better and timely information on observance of standards; encourage the structuring and presentation of such information so that it can be more readily used in market pricing and allocation decisions; encourage market participants to use this information in their risk assessments.
3. With regard to official incentives, the group should: take stock of the experience with the existing incentives; explore the desirability of further incentives that could potentially be implied by international institutions and groups, and national authorities; evaluate options for the application of supervisory, regulatory and market access incentives by national authorities and consider how in practice they might be structured and activated.
4. The group should consider how the various elements of market and official incentives could best reinforce one another within the framework of the overall strategy to foster implementation of standards and outline possible next steps for the Forum's consideration in September 2000.
5. In undertaking its task, the group should informally engage in a dialogue with a cross-section of relevant participants drawing upon outreach programmes conducted by the IMF/WB in the context of work related to the implementation of standards, and solicit feedback from the FSF Task Force on Implementation of Standards.

---

[82] *See* note 11 *supra*.

[83] The terms of reference of the group are set out in Table 10.

forward through the joint IMF and the World Bank joint Financial Sector Assessment Programmes (FSAPs) and experimental Reports on the Observance of Standards and Codes (ROSCs). FSAPs are designed to assess financial sector vulnerabilities and to identify developmental priorities through an assessment of financial sector standards in any particular country. Although the work is coordinated through the IMF and the Bank, FSAPs also require collaboration between a number of national agencies and the international sector committees. The ROSCs are currently being used to assemble summary assessments of particular standards including financial sector compliance as part of the larger FSAPs. They also include data dissemination, physical transparency and it is understood that they may be developed to deal with corporate governance and accounting.

These are, of course, not the only assessment exercises conducted by the IMF and the Bank. The work of the IMF, in particular, includes its annual Art. IV surveillance assessments, safeguard assessments (SAs) and transparency code assessments (TCAs) which responsibility is now to be further extended to include OFCs. The Bank is also, of course, involved in a number of continuing parallel or joint assessment exercises with the Fund. This is crucial work and it has to be expected that this will increasingly become the focus of implementation initiatives.

The Follow-Up Report is divided into two parts. The report initially provides an assessment of market structures that was based on the conduct of a market outreach exercise. The report then develops a structured evaluation of the possible official incentives available.

### (1) Approach of the Follow-up Group

In developing its recommendations, the group recognised that the implementation of standards was not an end in itself but only a means to secure certain objectives including the promotion of sound financial systems, reducing vulnerabilities, improving transparency and providing a benchmark to assist domestic structural reform efforts.

The group also noted that market incentives can encourage national authorities and, where relevant, the private sector to give effect to certain standards. Separate official incentives may also have an important role in encouraging implementation and in reinforcing market discipline.

Relevant standards are, however, diverse and varied in scope and specificity which must be taken into account in designing appropriate incentives. Market and official incentives will also only work effectively where credible and timely information on standards compliance is available. Necessary data information collection and dissemination channels were accordingly essential.

### (2) Report Findings

The findings and recommendations contained in the Follow-Up Report are directed at promoting both market and official incentives.

*(i)    Market Incentives*

The working group accepts that market incentives will only have effect to the extent that market participants use information on an economy's observance of standards in their risk assessments and reflect this in their pricing or allocation of credit or investment decisions. Market incentives can therefore only work where participants are familiar with relevant standards and recognise their relevance, have access to (continuing) credible and timely information on observance and properly reflect this in pricing and allocation determinations.

To assist it understand to what extent these conditions may already be in place the working group conducted an outreach exercise involving one hundred financial institutions from 11 jurisdictions (Argentina, Australia, Canada, France, Germany, Hong Kong, Italy, Japan, Sweden, the United Kingdom and the United States). The institutions approached included commercial banks, investment banks and securities houses, institutional investors and asset managers as well as rating agencies. Part of the outreach exercise was conducted in co-operation with the IMF and the World Bank which were already involved with parallel exercises in Hong Kong and New York. The outreach was conducted through the collection of questionnaire surveys, bilateral meetings and certain focus group discussions (see Annexes D and E of the Follow-Up Report).

*(a)    Familiarity*
From the responses received, the working group concluded that standards awareness was limited in practice. Apart from with regard to sovereign risk analysts in the rating agencies and banks, familiarity was low with the relevant measures. Few knew of all twelve standards while knowledge about particular measures varied. (Somewhat surprisingly, the IMF's Special Data Dissemination Standard (SDDS) and the International Accounting Standards (IAS) and then the Basel Core Principles and the IMF Transparency Codes were the most familiar.)

To improve appreciation, the working group recommended that the national authorities represented on the FSF develop a sustained (educational) effort to raise awareness of standards in co-operation with the international financial institutions and sector committees. This could, for example, include organising or hosting conventions and seminars, further publications and websites as well as highlighting standards in relevant professional curricula.

Initial efforts had, however, to focus only on a few key financial centres, the standards of most interest and participants most likely to use the information provided. Information brochures and pamphlets, special website pages and other channels should also be considered to disseminate standards contents and supporting material in addition to passive websites. Business and finance schools as well as relevant professional bodies should also be encouraged to include standards and codes within their curricula (which is interestingly not expressly extended to law schools although it may fall within business law).

*(b)    Relevance*
Although standards compliance was not directly taken into account at the present time, observance with particular aspects of certain standards was clearly relevant in making pricing and investment decisions. The SDDS was considered to have been

particularly useful especially in light of its easy-to-follow (yes or no) response structure. A number of factors are referred to in order to explain why observance has not been considered to have been important to date. This includes the absence of any adequate legal framework, the overriding importance of political risk as well as of economic and financial fundamentals, the lack of any clear relationship between standards and risk or common use of international benchmark indices for portfolio investment decisions and the availability of alternative sources of information especially through direct data access at the national level.

For these reasons, the FSF should encourage the international financial institutions, sector committees and national authorities to demonstrate more clearly to market participants how information on observance may be valuable in assessing relevant risk factors. The role of standards should, in particular, be clarified by stressing their focus on weaknesses that precipitate or aggravate financial crisis, their ability to promote transparency and confidence and need for effective implementation. The international financial institutions and sector committees should undertake and publish new analytical work to explain why particular standards were adopted and the link between non-observance and financial sector vulnerability default and other risk. Feedback from the private sector should also be encouraged.

*(c) Access*
Observance information was currently mainly available through private sector rating agencies, industry groupings and local (market) representatives. Official sector assessments were available through the IMF and World Bank as well as certain national authority databases, reports and websites. While it was considered that the private sector could provide more and better quality relevant information over time, this had mainly to be provided through official channels initially. The working group accepted that some participants considered that there were insufficient market incentives for the conduct of private sector assessments, which was compounded by expertise limitations, data confidentiality problems and potential conflicts of interest. Against this, however, capture or relationship problems between countries and the international financial institutions meant that there was an increasingly important role for independent peer group, rating agency or consultancy firm reports.

The value of the ROSCs was specifically recognised although their recent introduction and restricted availability was accepted. The international financial institutions and sector committees should accordingly be encouraged to enhance the availability of observance information especially through enhanced disclosure and, in particular, extended use of the successful SDDS reports. To promote disclosure, national authorities should be encouraged to make self and external assessments more widely available and, where appropriate, disclose the reasons for non-compliance or qualified compliance. The possibility of extended SDDS disclosure through the IMF website, in particular, to include compliance with other standards should be considered especially through the use of hyperlinks to other sites.

*(d) Use*
With regard to operational adoption, compliance information was either currently not used directly or only used as a supplementary and not primary information source in the assessment of the quality and reliability of data. The use of qualitative as opposed

to quantitative assessments as well as lack of comparable or ranked information then constrained the use of observance reports. While some participants also wanted more substantial information and analysis, others would only use basic ratings or country scores. Only a limited number of countries were also involved with the current ROSC exercises. A number of observations were made by market participants with regard to improving ROSC report quality. This included trying to improve their availability, extend the assessments to include the definition and quality of data disclosed, provide concise executive summaries and improve report clarity and frequency. The international financial institutions were accordingly encouraged to review their current presentation of information through the ROSCs especially in connection with their clarity, relevance, presentation and ease of use as well as any other feedback received through the recent outreach exercises.

It has to be admitted that the recommendations with regard to improving market incentives are somewhat limited and arguably obvious. The main difficulties identified by the working group are concerned with observance report availability and its consequent use within the market. Information content and access had to be improved at the same time as awareness of its availability and value promoted. The working group does spend some time considering the problem of report relevance and use. It may, however, be that provided that sufficiently relevant, reliable and timely information is made available to the market it will be fully used in practice.

### (ii)   Official Incentives

The working group recognises the limitations of relying on market incentives by themselves and accordingly accepts the need to promote official incentives as a parallel control device. (see Table 11) Market incentives may, in particular, be inadequate by themselves to encourage implementation in light of the current low incorporation of country non-observance data in relevant assessments. Market discipline can also not deal with the significant negative externalities created through weak domestic financial systems at the international level. Official incentives may, by contrast, trigger and sustain ongoing national commitment, which would otherwise be ignored through market assessment devices. The official sector had anyway to lead by example and not just direction through the use of standards observance in connection with its own work.

In developing possible official incentives, the working group recommended that four principles were applied in developing further some of the main conclusions set out in the earlier Implementation Report. Incentives should initially foster country ownership or involvement. While adoption had to be voluntary, countries should nevertheless be strongly encouraged to participate through the use of self-assessments and external assessments. Second, incentives should be consistent with larger public policy objectives such as in connection with financial market supervision and regulation. Third, incentives should reinforce market discipline and minimise moral hazard. Fourth, incentives should be applied consistently through the adoption of clear and transparent criteria especially where qualitative rather than quantitative measures were concerned. Differing local country circumstances had, however, to be taken into account especially with regard to relative possible economic development and institutional capacity or resources.

In developing this further, the working group divides the possible official incentives into three general categories. These are based on the main objectives concerned within each group or categories (see Table 2). The three groups are considered to be mutually reinforcing (see Table 11):

(a) Group 1 is concerned with incentives designed to promote country ownership and build a necessary implementation infrastructure. The objective is to identify areas for improvement within the economic and financial system, adopt relevant standards, formulate, announce and execute effect action plans at the same time as build capacity.

(b) Group 2 is principally concerned with the promotion of market discipline and disclosure. This is designed to create market demand for information on assessments by encouraging economies to undertake external assessments and disclose information results and promote observance through market discipline.

(c) Group 3 is concerned with encouraging observance and disclosure. Economies are to be encouraged to enhance their observance and to undertake and disclose of assessments' results.

The three incentive groups would accordingly appear to be based on adoption, demand and observance (with disclosure being promoted under Groups 2 and 3 and parts of Group 1). Although the distinction between the three sets of incentives may not be completely clear (and may somewhat confusing in places), this is nevertheless useful in classifying and categorising the possible initiatives structures concerned.

*(a) Adoption*
The Group 1 incentives are considered to be relevant to all 12 key standards. These are generally to be applied by international institutions and groupings.

External assessments
Market and official incentives require external assessments of country compliance. This must, however, be based on clear methodologies to secure consistency and credibility, take proper account of the relevant economy's stage of development, institutional capacity and financial structure (to ensure relevance), and be voluntary directed to promote ownership and co-operation. Market discipline should also be improved through disclosure. If this may discourage initial participation in particular cases, assessment without supporting disclosure should nevertheless be promoted.

Policy dialogue
Technical and advisory dialogues should be encouraged to promote country ownership and peer group pressure in a positive rather than punitive manner. This would include policy advice through IMF Article IV consultations, World Bank economic and sector work and other IMF Bank executive board discussions as well as peer discussions through relevant international and regional groupings. Such dialogues should accordingly be enhanced and peer discussions of progress and experience promoted. Such a positive and non-penal or non-punitive approach may be essential to the longer-term success of many of the efforts in this area.

Membership
Membership of particular international groupings should be linked to implementation commitments. Appropriate concessions and exemptions should, however, be

*Table 11.* Official incentives

Group 1: Encourage adoption of standards and implementation plans
1. External assessment
   (a) Conduct external assessments of economies' observance of standards.
2. Policy Dialogue
   (a) Provide national authorities policy advice on implementing standards.
   (b) Encourage within relevant international and regional groupings commitment to implementing standards and peer discussion of progress and experiences in standards.
3. Membership
   Link economies' membership in international groupings to:
   (a) adoption of relevant standards (for aspiring members); and
   (b) progress in implementing standards (for existing members).
4. Technical assistance
   (a) Provide ongoing technical assistance and training.

Group 2: Promote market demand for disclosure of assessments and market discipline
5. Dissemination of information
   (a) Encourage the disclosure of external assessments of observance of standards.
   (b) Encourage the inclusion in bond prospectuses for international issues by sovereign jurisdictions material information on external assessments of their observance of relevant standards.
6. Incorporation in risk assessments
   (a) Encourage domestic financial institutions dealing with counterparties registered in foreign jurisdictions to consider in their risk assessments (such as internal credit ratings in the case of banks) information from external assessments of observance of relevant standards in these jurisdictions.
   (b) Issue informational advisories to domestic financial institutions urging caution in dealing with counterparties based in jurisdictions, or transactions involving jurisdictions, that have material gaps in observance of standards as highlighted by assessments, which need to reflect countries' specifics and vulnerabilities or have refused to undertake assessment.

Group 3: Urge observance of standards where material gaps are prevalent and disclosure of assessments
7. Market access measures
   Apply market access measures with regard to:
   (a) Host jurisdictions taking into account in deciding whether, and if so under what conditions, they will allow foreign institutions to operate in their markets, the degree to which those institutions' home jurisdictions observe relevant standards.
   (b) Where regulatory approval is required, home jurisdictions should place restrictions on their domestic financial institutions' in foreign jurisdictions with material gaps in observance of relevant standards.
8. Regulatory and supervisory actions
   Consider tightening supervision and regulation of:
   (a) Subsidiaries or branches of foreign financial institutions based in jurisdictions with material gaps in their observance of relevant standards; and
   (b) Domestic financial institutions dealing with counterparties based in foreign jurisdictions with material gaps in their observance of relevant standards by (i) conducting more extensive examinations, (ii) imposing higher public disclosure requirements (for unlisted entities), (iii) increasing regulatory reporting requirements, (iv) requiring more extensive external audits, (v) restricting inter-affiliate transactions, (vi) increasing scrutiny of customer identification and (vii) strengthening oversight of payment system providers.

considered to avoid unnecessary or inappropriate membership withdrawals or cancellations. Involvement should again be encouraged and not sanctioned.

Technical assistance
Country ownership (and buy-in) as well as institutional capacity can be promoted through technical assistance and training. Potential deficiencies identified through self and external assessments could often be dealt with increased through technical

assistance and country owned action plans. Necessary resources must, however, be made available either through individual institutional or group provision to ensure that all appropriate technical assistance needs are met. National authorities should accordingly be encouraged to support all necessary technical assistance initiatives either directly or through international financial institutions on an assessed needs basis.

*(b)   Discipline*
The Group 2 incentives are also relevant to all 12 key standards but are to be applied by relevant international groupings and national authorities.

Information dissemination
Market awareness of the significance of standards and consequent market discipline can be improved through information dissemination. National authorities should accordingly be encouraged to disclose assessment results either directly or through prospectus disclosures such as those attached to bond issues.

Assessment incorporation
Incorporation of information relevant to observance can also be promoted by encouraging institutions to consider relevant reports in their counterparty dealings. Domestic financial institutions should then be encouraged to exercise caution in dealing with counterparties in jurisdictions with material gaps in their observance reports. The objective of these measures should be to promote market discipline rather than direct supervisory or regulatory action to pressure market participants to take full account of all relevant risks (including country risk and other non-compliance).

*(c)   Observance and disclosure*
The Group 3 incentives are principally concerned with the various core principles produced to date and the FATF money laundering rules applied by national authorities.

Market access
Observance of relevant standards can be promoted through the taking of market access decisions having regard to considerations relevant to ensuring the safety and soundness of financial institutions. This could be achieved by requiring host jurisdictions to take into account the extent to which the parent territory observes relevant standards in allowing foreign institutions market access. Alternatively, the extent to which home authorities restrict domestic financial institutions' overseas operations where host country compliance is defective might be considered. This reflects the corrective action (dual key) provisions introduced into the Basel Committee's 1983 Revised Concordat and subsequently restated in the 1992 Minimum Standards (although it slightly amends the host based intervention rules set out at the end of the 1997 core principles).

Regulatory and supervisory action
A range of further regulatory and supervisory measures might also be considered by both home and host authorities to promote standards compliance. These may, for example, include imposing higher capital requirements in connection with activities undertaken in or connected with low compliance territories. Other measures might involve conducting enhanced examinations, imposing higher disclosure or reporting

requirements or more extensive external audits, restricting inter-affiliate transactions or increasing customer identification (know your customer) obligations. It has to be admitted that most national authorities have a range of devices available for punishing non-compliance although care may have to be taken to ensure their relevance (authority) and proportionality in all cases. Limited or defective larger country compliance may then not be sufficient to justify imposing additional prudential requirements on an individual institution of itself although this may still be relevant in taking into account the larger supervisory and regulatory environment within which the entity operates.

## VI   INCENTIVE STRUCTURES

A wide range of possible incentive devices or measures accordingly remains available to promote national standards adoption and compliance (see Table 12). The original Implementation Report produced by the FSF was important in providing an initial identification and listing of relevant incentive options. The Follow-Up Report is then of value in clarifying some of the particular considerations which apply with regard to the possible use of market and official incentive devices at the same time as more indirectly promote country ownership and again highlight the problem of necessary resource availability.[84]

With regard to the promotion of market incentives, it has to be admitted that the Follow-up Report is somewhat weak on substantive recommendation. It is nevertheless useful in identifying some of the reasons which account for the lack of use of compliance information in private pricing and risk allocation decisions until now. These would principally appear to be familiarity, relevance, access and use based. As noted, although a certain degree of residual concern may arise with regard to incorporation and application of relevant information by private sector agents, assuming that relevant, accurate and timely information is provided it has to be expected that it will be properly used in practice. Market discipline may then naturally follow from further improvements in data quality and provision.

Market discipline may, however, never be sufficient by itself. This is largely due to the fact that it is dependent upon the particular objectives and interests of the individual agent. Market discipline is clearly conditional upon relevant need and incentive. While every effort must be made to encourage and improve market discipline, unless there is any clear alignment of the market and public interest (which will rarely occur), it has to be accepted that it might never act as a perfect substitute for official supervision and control. It is for this reason that the further recommendations of the follow-up group with regard to official incentives are of use.

Of particular value in connection with the development of possible market devices was the outreach exercise conducted by the working group. In addition to a note the modus operandi followed,[85] the Report contains 11 pages, which summarise the

---

[84] *Ibid.*
[85] *See* Annex D.

*Table 12.* Principal recommandations

I.  Market Incentives
1.  National authorities represented on the FSF should develop a sustained education effort to help the raise the general level of awareness of standards among market participants in their respective financial centres drawing on resources and expertise from the international financial institutions and standard setting bodies.
2.  The FSF should encourage the international financial institutions and standard setting bodies to enhance further their ongoing educational efforts to help the level of awareness of relevant international standards especially with regard to conventions and seminars, publications and websites and professional curricula.
3.  The FSF should encourage the international financial institutions, standard setting bodies and national authorities to demonstrate better how information on observance of standards can help provide insights on the risk factors in which market participants are most interested and, in particular, through clarifying the role of standards, undertaking and publishing relevant analytical work and engaging the private sector in relevant activities.
4.  The FSF should encourage the international financial institutions and standard setting bodies to enhance the availability of information on observance of standards especially through encouraged information disclosure and the leveraging of the disclosure made available through the SDDS.
5.  The FSF should encourage the international financial institutions to enhance the presentation of information on observance of standards especially with regard to clarity, relevance, presentation and user-friendliness of the ROSCs taking into account, where relevant, the feedback obtained through recent outreach exercises.

II.  Official Incentives
    (a) Adoption of standards and implementation plans

    (i) External assessments

6.  The FSF should encourage the IMF, World Bank and standard setting bodies to continue enhancing the conduct of external assessments of observance of standards including those standards among the 12 key standards not currently included in the assessment programme.
7.  National authorities represented on the FSF should demonstrate leadership by undertaking assessments of their own observance of relevant standards.

    (ii) Policy dialogues

8.  The FSF should encourage the IMF and World Bank to consider how the mechanism for policy advice could be further enhanced such as through giving greater prominence to standards implementation issues within the Art. IV consultation process, with a view to helping economies identify an appropriate set of standards for priority implementation and develop effective action plans.

    (iii) Membership

9.  The FSF should encourage relevant international and regional groupings (G7, G20, APEC, ASEAN, CARICOM, CHFI, EFTA, , EU, IAIS, IOSCO, MFG, MERCOSUR, NAFTA, OECD and regional groupings of supervisors) to promote peer discussions of progress and experiences in implementing standards using ROSCs where appropriate. National authorities represented on the FSF should also encourage members in international or regional groupings that they are a part of to make a commitment to implement relevant standards.

    (iv) Technical assistance

10.  National authorities represented on the FSF should make a commitment, and encourage other economies as well, to provide technical assistance and training for standards assessments and implementation, co-ordinated either bilaterally or through the international financial institutions and relevant international groupings, on the basis of assessed needs.
    (b) Promote market discipline and disclosure

    (i) Information dissemination

11.  There should be a presumption that national authorities disclose assessments of observance of standards. National authorities represented on the FSF should demonstrate leadership by making a commitment to disseminate information on self and external assessments.

*Table 12. continued*

---

12. National authorities represented on the FSF should encourage the voluntary disclosure of material information on observance of relevant standards in bond prospectuses for international sovereign bond issues.

(ii) Risk assessment incorporation

13. National authorities represented on the FSF should encourage domestic financial institutions dealing with counterparties registered in foreign jurisdictions to consider in their risk assessments (such as internal credit ratings for banks) information from external assessments of observance of standards in these jurisdictions.

14. National authorities represented on the FSF should consider the desirability and feasibility of using informational advisories to encourage caution in dealing with counterparties based in jurisdictions or transactions involving jurisdictions with material gaps in their observance of standards.
(c) Encourage observance of standards and disclosure of assessments

(i) Market access measures

15. National authorities should be encouraged to give greater consideration to a foreign jurisdiction's observance of relevant standards as one of the factors in making market access decisions.

(ii) Regulatory and supervisory actions

16. National authorities should give greater consideration to a foreign jurisdiction's observance of relevant standards as one of the factors in supervision and regulation of:
(a) subsidiaries or branches of foreign institutions from that jurisdiction, or
(b) domestic institutions dealing with counterparties in that jurisdiction.

---

market's responses to the exercise.[86] To the extent that one of the core objectives is to encourage market involvement and assistance, this must be precursed on an understanding of what the market knows and expects. While only 10 (relatively simply drafted) questions were addressed, this is still of considerable use in beginning to develop a larger understanding and appreciation of how the market may become more involved in promoting better implementation over time. This is of essential value both in clarifying the arguably limited role performed by the market to date but possibly more importantly, in identifying and promoting its possible future responsibility in this area.[87]

The range of official incentives considered by the working group is based on adoption, demand and observance (see Table 11). While there may be some overlap between specific incentives and objectives (such as with market access and adoption or technical assistance and observance), this is useful in further developing country interest and involvement. Although the basic catalogue of possible official incentives is relatively simple, the working group has also provided a more substantial development.[88] As well as promote involvement and adoption, this is also of value in clarifying the responsibilities and roles of all of the separate agencies involved.

This is a necessarily limited report, which reflects a narrow mandate that the working group has itself further restricted. Having regard to its limited ambitions, this is nevertheless a useful paper in further clarifying the possible limitations and value of promoting and relying on market and official incentives to secure standards

---

[86] *See* Annex E.

[87] The only slight concern which may arise is that more information was not provided with regard to the list of invited institutions which participated to confirm its balance and representation.

[88] *See* Annex F of the Report.

observance and compliance. It is unfortunate (but understandable) that the working group has not commented on the success and possible future development of more of the official assessment programmes currently being developed by the IMF and the World Bank as well as all of the other supporting training and technical assistance initiatives already under way. More information would, in particular, have been welcomed with regard to the success (or otherwise) of the FSAPs and ROSCs and how the ROSCs may be further revised and refined over time. It has to be expected, at least, in the near future that most progress in this area may be secured through such official programmes rather than through these other (what can only be described as more ancillary or supporting) incentive devices. To that extent, the Follow-Up Report is fundamentally limited in its objectives and results.

It might also be argued that the report is based on an arguably unnecessarily strict division between market and official incentives and that these cannot be developed as primary or, at least, exclusive implementation devices. The working group, however, clearly recognises the importance of country support and incentive as well as the need for sufficient technical resources.

If the final objective of all of this work is to secure effective country adoption and observance, the focus of any continuing efforts should possibly be on the promotion of country as opposed to any other ancillary, supplementary or secondary incentive structures.

It has to be accepted, however, that the use of a combined or mixed approach (as originally recommended by the Implementation Group)[89] which involves the promotion of each of these core implementation options as significant but parallel devices may secure the best results over time. It for this reason that the further contribution made by the Follow-Up Report is to be welcome.


## VII  CLOSING COMMENT

The objectives of the FSF remain highly ambitious.[90] With the work conducted by the FSF to date, the international supervisory authorities are on the verge of creating a single set of core rules for the operation and proper control of all financial markets.

The significance of this is that work in this area has then progressed over three decades from initially only comprising limited initiatives to promote international supervisory cooperation (such as under the first Basel papers) to the production of common rules in a number of core regulatory or control areas such as capital adequacy (beginning with the 1988 Basel Committee Capital Accord).

Within the last decade, this has moved towards the establishment of a series of absolute core minimum standards in certain key areas, which have replaced the earlier more general rules of best practice. These were, in particular, adopted to secure more effective implementation and compliance. Although this work begins with the Basel 1992 Minimum Standards, the model for this was the 1988 Capital Accord.

---

[89] *See* Section IV *supra.*
[90] *See* Section II *supra.*

Most recently, it has been possible to produce full sets of core principles within each sector, which are designed to act as full systems models. These core principles do not just respond to one or more particular aspects of principally international supervisory or regulatory concern as before but create complete control frameworks for either national adoption or revision.

With each of these important initiatives, we have moved from limited supervisory co-operation to regulatory harmonisation, minimum standards and then core principles. The next stage in this development is the creation of a fully integrated rulebook for all financial markets and all aspects of market control.

Whether the FSF can succeed in producing this, however, will depend, first of all, on whether it can secure agreement on a basic structure for the new rulebook which is both clear and coherent. This has not yet been achieved in light of the obvious inconsistencies and gaps in the current Compendium. Of more importance than simple structural integrity, however, is whether the FSF can then also ensure that all of the separate measures selected can operate in a complete and consistent manner[91] and whether they can be given full effect in practice.[92]

While specific aspects of the new financial architecture are still changing and have yet to be confirmed, the shape of the new global rulebook is, at least, becoming clear. The FSF must accordingly continue to carry out its work in the area of standards development to ensure that a complete and coherent listing of all relevant measures is achieved. Of equal, if not more importance, however, it must also attempt to construct an effective policy to ensure that all agreed provisions are properly adopted and implemented in all national countries through the full range of incentive mechanisms already identified.

---

[91] *See* Section III *supra.*
[92] *See* Sections IV and V *supra.*

*Chapter 13*

# FSA Revisited, and Some Issues for European Securities Markets Regulation[1]

*Clive Briault*

## 1 INTRODUCTION

An earlier paper[2] put forward the case that a single national financial services regulator, covering a broad range of financial services activities and spanning both prudential and conduct of business regulation,[3] is likely to be well placed to deliver effective, efficient and properly differentiated regulation in the current financial environment. However, this does not mean that there is any universal ideal model for the institutional structure of financial services regulation, not least because financial markets have developed – and will continue to develop – differently in different countries.

In the United Kingdom and some other countries, the rationale for an integrated national financial services regulator reflects four primary considerations. First, market developments such as the increase in the number of financial conglomerates and the blurring of the boundaries between financial products. Second, the availability of economies of scale and scope and the importance of allocating scarce regulatory resources efficiently and effectively. Third, the benefits of setting a single regulator clear and consistent objectives and responsibilities, and resolving any trade-offs among these within a single agency. And fourth, the clarity of making a single regulator accountable for its performance against its statutory objectives, for the regulatory regime, for the costs of regulation and for regulatory failures.

These considerations, and the manner in which regulatory arrangements are being restructured in other countries, suggest that the balance of the argument is moving away from retaining or creating multiple financial services regulators differentiated by the types of firm they regulate, by the activities they regulate, or by the objectives of regulation. And, similarly, the arguments for creating a single, or at least more integrated, financial services regulator may be stronger in some countries than the arguments in favour of locating banking regulation within a country's central bank.

---

[1] An earlier version of this paper was presented at a conference on The Financial Supervision of Banks and Specialised Banks in the European University at the European University Institute on 15 December 2000. The views expressed are those of the author and not necessarily of the FSA.

[2] C.B. Briault, 'The Rationale for a Single National Financial Services Regulator'. Financial Services Authority, London, Occasional Paper 2 (May 1999).

[3] 'Regulation' is used in this chapter in its broadest sense to cover the full range of regulatory activities, including standard setting, authorisation, supervision and enforcement.

*Mads Andenas and Yannis Avgerinos (eds), Financial Markets, in Europe: Towards a Single Regulator?* 323–338.
© 2003 *Kluwer Law International. Printed in Great Britain.*

Finally, my earlier paper covered briefly the case for and against a transnational regulator. It concluded that, at least in present circumstances, the balance of the considerations remained against establishing such a regulator because it would have to operate across very different legal and cultural regimes, because it could be very distant (both literally in terms of geography and in terms of its approach) from most of the firms it regulates, and because the limited amount of cross-border business in financial services – especially in retail financial services – does not at present justify a shift to a transnational regulator.

The purpose of this chapter is not to repeat the arguments set out in the earlier paper, but to review developments over the last two years, particularly in the United Kingdom, in an attempt to measure the performance of a single national financial services regulator against the rationale for creating it in the first place. It is too early to draw firm conclusions, but the initial indications remain encouraging.

Following the publication of the Report of the Committee of Wise Men on the regulation of European securities markets,[4] this chapter also explores the advantages of incorporating some of the recently introduced features of UK financial services regulation into the proposed approach to the introduction, amendment and implementation of EU securities legislation.

The chapter is structured as follows. Sections 2–4 provide a brief update of recent developments in UK institutional arrangements, in other countries, and in markets. Sections 5 and 6 review progress to date in the United Kingdom in achieving economies of scale and scope, while Section 7 describes progress on risk-based regulation and resource allocation. Section 8 reviews some additional considerations relating to the links between regulators and central banks, while Section 9 discusses some aspects of European securities markets regulation from the UK perspective. Section 10 concludes.

## 2    INSTITUTIONAL ARRANGEMENTS IN THE UK

The Financial Services and Markets Act was passed by Parliament in June 2000, thereby providing a single modern and flexible legislative framework covering almost the entire financial services sector. The Act came into force at the end of November 2001.

The new legislation provides the framework within which the Financial Services Authority (FSA) operates, including four high-level statutory objectives, the powers that are available to the FSA, safeguards on the use of these powers, and a strong set of accountability mechanisms. But an important feature of the new legislation is that, apart from setting out in broad terms the 'threshold conditions' that a firm must meet in order to be granted permission by the FSA to undertake one or more regulated financial activities in the United Kingdom, it does not set out any detailed rules and regulations for these firms, leaving these to be set by the FSA itself.

---

[4] A. Lamfalussy, 'Final Report of the Committee of Wise Men on the Regulation of European Securities Markets' (European Commission, Brussels, February 2001).

The four statutory objectives of the FSA are to:

(a) maintain confidence in the financial system;
(b) promote public understanding of the financial system, including the awareness of the benefits and risks associated with different kinds of investment or other financial dealing;
(c) secure the appropriate degree of protection for consumers, having regard to the differing degrees of risk involved in different kinds of investment or other transaction, the differing degrees of experience and expertise that different consumers may have in relation to different kinds of regulated activity, the needs that consumers may have for advice and accurate information, and the general principle that consumers should take responsibility for their decisions;
(d) reduce the extent to which it is possible for a financial services firm to be used for a purpose connected with financial crime.

In an interim report as part of his review of competition and banking services in the United Kingdom, Don Cruickshank suggested that the FSA should be given a fifth statutory objective, 'to minimise the anti-competitive effects of requirements placed on authorised persons by the FSA'.[5] A competition objective was also proposed during parliamentary debate on the new legislation, but the outcome was to leave the four statutory objectives unchanged, whilst strengthening the emphasis on competition in the considerations set out in the Act to which the FSA must have regard in discharging its general functions.

The Act now includes two considerations relating to competition, namely the need to minimise the adverse effects on competition that may arise from anything done by the FSA in the discharge of its general functions; and the desirability of facilitating competition between firms regulated by the FSA. In addition, the Act provides for strong external scrutiny of the FSA with regard to the impact of its regulatory activities on competition. The Director General of Fair Trading, the Competition Commission and the Treasury each have a role to play in reviewing the impact of the FSA's rules and practices on competition, particularly if a rule or a combination of rules is considered to have a significantly adverse effect on competition.[6]

The other considerations to which the FSA must have regard in discharging its general functions are the need to use its resources in the most efficient and economic way; the responsibilities of those who manage the affairs of authorised persons; the principle that a burden or restriction imposed on a regulated firm should be proportionate to the benefits, in general terms, that are expected to result from the burden or restriction; the desirability of facilitating innovation in connection with regulated activities; and the international character of financial services and markets and the desirability of maintaining the competitive position of the United Kingdom.

---

[5] D. Cruickshank, 'Competition and Regulation: An Interim Report'. Review of UK Banking Services, London, (July 1999) p. 24.
[6] Financial Services Authority, 'Response by the Financial Services Authority to the Cruickshank Report on Competition in UK Banking' (Financial Services Authority, London, August 2000) p. 6.

The four statutory objectives and seven 'have regard to' considerations set out in the Act have provided a robust framework within which the FSA has developed both its Handbook of Rules and Guidance (see below) and its approach to risk-based regulation (as discussed in Section 7).

Meanwhile, the scope of the FSA has been widened further. In addition to the responsibilities of the nine regulatory bodies that the Chancellor of the Exchequer announced in May 1997 would be merged into a single regulatory authority[7] the FSA has also been given responsibility to be the UK Listing Authority, to regulate professional firms (solicitors, accountants and actuaries) that undertake a significant amount of regulated financial services activities, to regulate credit unions, and to introduce a regulatory regime for general insurance brokers and for mortgage advisers.

Consistent with both its statutory obligations and its stated intention to be open and transparent, the FSA has published more than 100 consultation papers since October 1997, covering all aspects of FSA policy and the entire text of the FSA's Handbook of Rules and Guidance (which came into force in its final form at the same time as the Act and contains in a single location the entire set of regulatory requirements placed by the FSA on regulated firms and approved persons). These consultation papers – and other related published papers – have, where appropriate, contained a cost benefit analysis of the proposed policy and a statement of why the proposed policy is consistent with the FSA's statutory objectives and 'having regard to' considerations (including competition) as set out in the Act. Consultation and accountability have also been enhanced through the active involvement of the Financial Services Consumer Panel and the Practitioner Forum, both of which are independent of the FSA and have been established on a statutory basis under the Act to make representations to the FSA in the interests of consumers and practitioners respectively.

Finally, the FSA continues to co-operate closely, and to exchange information, with the Bank of England and the Treasury, under the 1997 Memorandum of Understanding.[8] Discussions between the three institutions centre on a Standing Committee that has been meeting monthly since March 1998, and have covered a wide range of possible domestic and international threats to UK financial stability. The Memorandum of Understanding has helped to ensure timely and efficient co-ordination and allocation of work between the three institutions. The arrangements have not yet been put to the test in a period of financial instability, or of the 'failure' of a firm (or firms) posing a significant systemic risk. However, experience to date on co-operation and information-sharing between the three institutions suggests that the arrangements will work effectively in a crisis. Moreover, the FSA should, as a single financial services regulator, be able to provide better and more rapid access to information about the overall position of a financial conglomerate that ran into difficulties than might have been available in the past from the multiple regulators responsible for the conglomerate.

---

[7] C.B. Briault (1999) *op. cit.*, p. 6.

[8] Financial Services Authority 'Financial Services Authority: An Outline', Appendix 2 (Financial Services Authority, London, October 1997).

## 3 DEVELOPMENTS IN OTHER COUNTRIES

My earlier paper noted the existence of single national financial service regulators in Denmark, Iceland, Japan, Korea, Norway and Sweden, in addition to the United Kingdom. Hungary joined this list in April 2000, Latvia in 2001 and, more recently, Germany and Austria. The position remains under review in a number of other countries, including Finland, South Africa and Switzerland.[9]

## 4 MARKET DEVELOPMENTS

The trends identified in my earlier paper towards an increase in the number of financial conglomerates and a blurring of the boundaries between products has continued. Recent mergers and acquisitions, both in the United Kingdom and elsewhere, and both domestically and cross-border, have tended to involve existing financial conglomerates, or been confined to specific sectors. But financial services firms have also continued to expand through internal growth into new areas (in particular banks, insurance companies and fund managers extending the range of the services and products they offer). And new entrants to the financial services sector continue to widen the range of the financial services they offer to their customers (in particular, some of the new entrants that began by offering an internet-based deposit-taking service have since moved into investment business by offering their customers access to a range of managed funds).

## 5 ECONOMIES OF SCALE

In the United Kingdom, the Financial Services Authority (or rather the large number of regulated firms who meet its costs) has begun to benefit from the economies of scale arising from the move to a single set of central support services (information services, premises, financial control, etc.); a unified management structure; and a unified approach to standard-setting, authorisation, supervision, enforcement, consumer education and tackling financial crime. A single complaints handling regime and a single compensation scheme have also been established.

This unification has been reflected in the FSA costing no more, in real terms, than the sum of the predecessor regulatory bodies that are being brought together,[10] despite the wider scope of the FSA beyond the responsibilities of these predecessor

---

[9] *See* also the survey of recent developments in industrial, emerging and transition economies in P.J.N. Sinclair, 'Central Banks and Financial Stability' (2000) November *Bank of England Quarterly Bulletin*.

[10] It is difficult to provide a precise comparison of costs because of the changes in scope, the impact of transitional costs in moving to a single regulator, and the difficulties in allocating costs in earlier years to the regulatory functions of institutions with other responsibilities (in particular the costs of banking and insurance regulation when these were undertaken by the Bank of England and the Department of Trade and Industry respectively).

bodies, and despite the FSA's staff costs having to reflect (albeit not to the full extent) the markedly higher rate of earnings increases in the UK financial sector over the last few years than the increase in average earnings across the economy as a whole. Moreover, the FSA's budget has fallen in real terms in each of the four years from 1998/99 to 2001/02.[11,12]

## 6    ECONOMIES OF SCOPE

A single financial services regulator should be able to tackle cross-sector issues more efficiently and effectively than might be possible across a multiplicity of separate specialist regulators. And this should apply not only to the regulation of individual financial conglomerates, but also to other regulatory functions that have cross-sector implications. In this context the FSA has been able to adopt a consistent, coherent and clearly focused approach across various sectors of the financial services industry to cross-sector issues such as assessing the preparedness of regulated firms for the Year 2000; assessing the impact on regulated firms of actual and potential turbulence in the domestic and international economy; considering the risks and opportunities arising from the development of e-commerce in the financial services industry; considering the impact of low inflation on the providers of financial services and on their customers;[13] and maximising the effectiveness of the resources devoted by the FSA to consumer education and to enhancing the awareness of consumers of financial services (including, for example, proposals for the provision of comparative information to consumers on a range of financial products).

Similarly, the development of policy in the FSA – and in particular the construction of the FSA's single Handbook of Rules and Guidance – has been based in part on achieving an integrated approach, as reflected in the development of a single set of Principles for Businesses; a single set of Principles and a single Code of Practice for Approved Persons; a single statement of requirements for high-level systems and controls in regulated firms; and a single set of regulatory manuals setting out the FSA's approach to authorisation, supervision and enforcement. An integrated approach has also been adopted for the development of conduct of business and prudential requirements based more on the types of risk that may arise across a range of regulated activities (e.g. the failure to disclose information to customers, or the impact of credit, market and operational risks) than on organising these requirements by types of firm. However, this is not a 'one size fits all' approach, and appropriate differentiation will be achieved by taking into account the different degrees of

---

[11] Financial Services Authority 'Plan and Budget 2001/2' (Financial Services Authority, London, January 2001) p. 45.

[12] The Australian Prudential Regulation Authority achieved administrative economies equivalent to 10% of its operating costs as a result of integration between 1997/1998 and 2000/2001. *See* APRA, 'Annual Report' (Australian Prudential Regulation Authority, Sydney, July 2000) p. 45.

[13] E. Harley and S. Davies, 'Low Inflation: Implications for the FSA' (Financial Services Authority, London, Occasional Paper 14, April 2001).

protection required by different types of consumer and the different ways in which the FSA's requirements can be met according to the nature and size of a firm's business.

## 7  RISK-BASED REGULATION AND RESOURCE ALLOCATION

Any regulatory authority has to consider how it will allocate its limited resources in order to achieve, as far as possible, its high-level objectives. So the FSA has to consider the risks posed by individual regulated firms and by industry-wide developments to the achievement of its four statutory objectives, and to determine its own risk appetite within this context.[14,15] This is at the core of any risk-based approach to regulation and to resource allocation. And, in doing so, the FSA must have regard to the additional considerations set out in the Act (see Section 2). In the following text the four objectives will be considered in turn.

Market confidence is fundamental to any successful financial system; only if it is maintained will participants and users be willing to trade in financial markets and use the services of financial institutions. Maintaining this confidence involves preserving both actual stability in the financial system and the reasonable expectation that it will remain stable. This can be achieved through preventing material damage to the soundness of the UK financial system caused by the conduct of, or collapse of, firms, markets or financial infrastructure; and through explaining to consumers, firms and politicians the basis on which confidence in the UK financial system is justified – this includes stating explicitly what the regulator can and cannot achieve.

The FSA aims to maintain a regime that delivers as low an incidence of failure of regulated firms and markets (especially failures that would have a material impact on public confidence and market soundness) as is consistent with the maintenance of competition and innovation in the markets. This in turn requires careful evaluation of the probability of any collapse, and its likely impact on the financial system.

Maintaining market confidence does not imply that the FSA should aim to prevent all collapses, or lapses in conduct, in the financial system. Given the nature of financial markets, which are inherently volatile, achieving a 'zero failure' regime is impossible and would in any case be undesirable. Any such regime would be excessively burdensome for regulated firms and would not accord with the statutory objectives and principles set out in the Act. It would be likely to damage the economy as a whole and would be uneconomic from a cost–benefit point of view; it would stifle innovation and competition; and it would be inconsistent with the respective responsibilities of firms' management and of consumers for their own actions. Considerable dangers would arise if consumers or market participants believed that no firm would ever be allowed to collapse; this would reduce the incentive for individuals or firms to take due care in assessing the risk attaching to their financial decisions.

---

[14] Financial Services Authority 'A New Regulator for the New Millennium' (Financial Services Authority, London, January 2000).

[15] Financial Services Authority 'Building the New Regulator: Progress Report 1' (Financial Services Authority, London, December 2000).

Turning next to the public awareness objective, many consumers do not understand the financial system, the products and services offered and how they relate to their financial needs. Such consumers may not secure suitable products at fair prices; they may misunderstand the terms on which products are offered or may not realise the costs, risks and benefits of different product offerings. The FSA is pursuing two main aims under this objective, namely to improve general financial literacy and to improve the information and advice available to consumers, both from regulated firms and from the FSA itself. General financial literacy can be improved through programmes to help individuals acquire the knowledge and skills they need to be better informed consumers of financial services. And the availability and quality of generic information and advice to consumers can be improved through the efforts of both the financial services industry and the FSA.

On the objective to protect consumers, the principal risks which consumers may face in their financial affairs are the prudential risk that a firm collapses, for example, because of weak or incompetent management or lack of capital; the bad faith risk from fraud, misrepresentation, deliberate mis-selling or failure to disclose relevant information on the part of firms selling or advising on financial products; the complexity/unsuitability risk that consumers contract for a financial product or service they do not understand or which is unsuitable for their needs and circumstances; and the performance risk that investments do not deliver hoped-for returns.

The FSA has a clear role to play in identifying and reducing prudential risk, bad faith risk and some aspects of complexity/unsuitability risk. But it does not have a responsibility to protect consumers from performance risk, which is inherent in investment markets, providing the firm recommending the product has explained to the consumer the risks involved and has not made excessive and unrealistic claims. However, under the public awareness objective the FSA aims to ensure that consumers have a better understanding of the risks and opportunities involved in investment markets, so that consumers are better able to assume responsibility for their own decisions. And the level of protection provided by the FSA's regulation is tailored to depend on the sophistication of the consumer. Professional counterparties need (and want) much less protection than retail consumers.

Finally, confidence in the financial system and consumer protection will be seriously undermined if the financial system and individual institutions are abused for criminal purposes. The FSA is therefore charged with reducing the extent to which it is possible for the firms it regulates to be used in connection with financial crime. This includes money laundering; fraud or dishonesty, including financial e-crime and fraudulent marketing of investments; and criminal market misconduct, including insider dealing. The Act gives the FSA new powers in this area.

These objective-based considerations translate into a risk-based approach to regulation and to resource allocation in three main ways.

The first is the regulation of individual firms. The FSA assesses the risks posed by firms under two broad headings. One is the probability of an adverse event occurring, while the other is the impact that such an event might have. In considering the *probability* of a problem occurring, particular attention is paid to business risk, including a firm's strategy, capital, liquidity, the volatility and growth of earnings, and credit, market, underwriting and operational risks; control risk, including a firm's internal systems and controls, board and senior management, and compliance culture; and consumer relationship risk, including the nature of a firm's customers and products, and its marketing, selling and advice practices.

Meanwhile, *impact* is assessed in terms of the damage that a problem within a firm could cause to the FSA's statutory objectives. This depends on the degree of systemic significance of the firm (what impact would a problem at the firm have on the industry as a whole?); the perceived importance of the firm (the possible impact on market confidence); the size and nature of the firm's customer base; and, as a partial mitigating factor, the availability of compensation or redress for any losses suffered by consumers. The inclusion of the 'impact' factors, based on the FSA's four statutory objectives, means that the FSA does not look at risk in quite the same way as market participants.

A combination of these probability and impact factors then determines the nature and intensity of the supervision of individual regulated firms by the FSA. This supervisory relationship is along a broad spectrum. At one end of the spectrum is an intensive and continuous close relationship with a high-risk and high-impact regulated firm, in order to develop and maintain a detailed and timely understanding of current and potential areas of risk in a firm. At the other end of the spectrum, the supervision of firms with a low impact and probability grading relies primarily on the remote monitoring of a firm's business through information reported to the FSA electronically, supplemented by the sampling of particular lines of business undertaken by particular types of firm, and by thematic work (as described below).

So the allocation of the FSA's resources is determined by the result of the analysis of the risks posed by individual firms. And the need for such risk-based resource allocation is highlighted by the observation that the 1% of regulated firms in the highest impact category have a 64% share of the financial services markets in which they are active.

Experience of financial regulation suggests that it is also useful to take a broader perspective if a regulator is to be effective in identifying and heading off risks to its objectives. So the second major element in the risk-based approach is to look at industry-wide risks to the FSA's statutory objectives arising from developments in the economy and in products and markets, using sources of information such as the supervision of individual regulated firms, close contact with consumers and practitioners, the availability of data on complaints against firms, and developments in the Government's social policy.

At the broadest level the FSA considers the possible implications for the achievement of its statutory objectives of developments in the macro-economy (e.g. the implications of low inflation, the possible nature of the next recession, or the possibility of a stock market correction); of demographic trends (in particular the ageing population); and the agenda set by related Government policies.[16] And in terms of

---

[16] *See* P. Johnson, 'CAT Standards and Stakeholders' (Financial Services Authority, London, Occasional Paper 11, September 2000) for a discussion of the interface between regulation and some aspects of Government social policy.

specific products and markets, the FSA has recently undertaken special studies into the selling of mortgage endowments; the relaxation of standards in mortgage lending; the introduction of stakeholder pensions; the growth of unsecured credit; and the extent and distribution of lending to telecommunications firms.

The FSA is also paying particular attention to broader market developments such as the opportunities and risks arising from the rapid growth of e-commerce, and the concerns being expressed about a possible reduction in market liquidity. And in the international arena the FSA has contributed to work on enhanced disclosure and transparency by regulated firms; on the exposures of regulated firms to highly leveraged institutions; and on efforts to close gaps in the international regulatory system (including the absence of a complete set of identified lead regulators for major international firms; an inconsistent approach internationally to the regulation of re-insurance firms; and inconsistencies in insolvency and winding-up procedures across different countries).

As with the risks posed by individual firms, the main focus in prioritisation and resource allocation in this broad context is to assess the extent to which any of these industry-wide risks poses a threat to the FSA's statutory objectives. And as with individual firms, it should be possible to consider this in terms of both probability and impact.

The third major element of the risk-based approach is to assess which of the tools available to the FSA are the most appropriate – singly or in combination – to mitigate each of the risks posed to the statutory objectives either by individual firms or by industry-wide developments. These tools include disclosure (of product information, of trades undertaken, and of the financial soundness of firms); consumer education; the Ombudsman Scheme; the Compensation Scheme; standard setting; co-operation with overseas regulators (in authorisation, supervision, enforcement and standard-setting); authorisation (of firms and approved persons); supervision (on the risk-based approach described above); investigation; intervention; discipline; and restitution.

## 8    REGULATION AND CENTRAL BANKING

Two broad conclusions on regulation and central banking were set out in my earlier paper. The first was that although there need to be close links and a proper two-way flow of information between the relevant regulator(s) and the monetary authorities, this does not imply that the two functions need to be combined within the same institution. This applies to all of the 'core' roles of a monetary authority, including the setting of monetary policy to achieve monetary stability, the responsibility for financial stability and in particular the robustness of payment systems, and the lender of last resort function.

The second conclusion was that although 'systemic risk' provides a rationale for regulatory intervention, if the failure of some financial institutions could impose negative externalities on others, it does not require the creation of a separate regulator with a specific 'systemic risk' mandate. Indeed, the creation of such a regulator could increase the moral hazard problem arising from the perception that some financial institutions are more likely than others to be protected and supported in the event of problems arising. Also, it is not clear what, in practice, a 'systemic risk' regulator would do differently from a 'deposit protection' regulator, or why – where differences can be identified (e.g. to take account of the potential externalities arising from the systemic impact of the failure of some regulated firms) – they cannot be applied by a single regulator through appropriate differentiation (as, e.g. through the assessment and application of the 'impact' factor described in Section 7 above in the context of risk-based regulation, in particular reflecting the FSA's market confidence objective, and through taking account of systemic risk in the intensity of supervision and in the setting of minimum regulatory capital requirements for individual firms). And if the existence of multiple specialist regulators led to the emergence of inappropriately differentiated approaches then the market place could be seriously distorted.

There are, however, two issues that were not addressed in my earlier paper. The first – which is set out very clearly by Charles Goodhart,[17] and which has also arisen in discussions between the FSA and regulators from some other countries – is that in some developing and transition countries the central bank stands (almost) alone as an institution with independence from political interference, with high status and reputation, and with the resources to recruit and retain high calibre staff. In these circumstances the effectiveness of financial services regulation (at least of banks) could be compromised if this function was removed from the central bank. This could have a significant impact on the balance of considerations relevant to the creation of a single financial services regulator.

Second, a combination of the arguments for a 'systemic risk' regulator and for a pan-European regulator has generated the idea of a pan-European regulator of systemically significant (sometimes misleadingly termed 'too big to fail') financial institutions. This is usually combined with various assertions about the supposed inability of the regulatory, monetary and fiscal authorities in the 'home' (head office) country of these financial institutions to perform adequately one or more of the roles of lead supervising the institution (undertaking consolidated supervision, and collecting from and exchanging information with the 'host' country regulators in which the institution operates); of understanding the potential impact of the failure of the institution on the financial system in other countries in which the institution operates; and of providing liquidity support or even an injection of capital if the institution was to run into difficulties. But these assertions underestimate – or sometimes ignore completely – the extent to which national regulators (and national monetary and fiscal authorities) already co-operate among themselves in order to address the international aspects of the operation of financial institutions. And, as with the financial institutions themselves, these co-operative arrangements are global in reach, not confined to the European Union.

There would be a number of problems with establishing a pan-European regulator of systemically significant financial institutions. In particular, it would face all of the

---

[17] C.A.E. Goodhart, 'The Organisational Structure of Banking Supervision' (2000), mimeo.

problems that would arise in the context of a national 'systemic risk' regulator (see earlier in this section), and with any pan-European financial services regulator (as outlined in Section 1). In this latter context, a particularly important problem for a pan-European regulator is that it would not be feasible without more extensive harmonisation of the legal and judicial systems across the European Union. There is little point in a pan-European regulator that could not enforce its rules, or at least could not do so on a consistent and coherent basis. It is also not clear why a pan-European regulator would be better able to supervise a financial institution with operations in more than one member state (and indeed, in many cases, in countries outside the European Union) than the relevant home country regulator for each financial institution, working through the various bilateral and multilateral contacts, the information-sharing procedures and the methods of calculating a consolidated picture of the entire group, that together underpin the role of the lead supervisor of a financial institution.

Indeed, the EU Economic and Financial Committee concluded last year that 'the existing institutional arrangements provide a coherent and flexible basis for safeguarding financial stability in Europe. No institutional changes are deemed necessary.'[18] The Brouwer report did, however, recommend that cross-sector and cross-border co-operation should be strengthened yet further, both among regulators and between regulators, central banks and ministries of finance.[19]

There may nevertheless be an important question here about whether systemic risks are properly identified and assessed internationally, either at the European Union level or indeed globally. There have, for example, been proposals for a 'Euro-observatory of systemic risk,'[20] in addition to the work on financial stability already being undertaken by the Banking Supervision Committee of the European Central Bank. And globally, one of the purposes of the new Financial Stability Forum is to identify and assess vulnerabilities of the financial system. But in both these cases the identification and assessment of systemic risk is intended to be undertaken collectively and then communicated to the relevant, mostly national, authorities. There is no reason why the bodies undertaking the identification and assessment of systemic risk should also have any regulatory responsibilities.

## 9   EUROPEAN SECURITIES MARKETS REGULATION

The Initial and Final Reports of the Committee of Wise Men on the Regulation of European Securities Markets[21,22] set out convincingly the potential benefits of more

---

[18] H. Brouwer, 'Report on Financial Stability' (EU Economic and Financial Committee, Brussels, April 2000).

[19] The Economic and Financial Committee has undertaken a second study (*see* H. Brouwer, 'Report on Financial Crisis Management' (EU Economic and Financial Committee, Brussels, April 2001) looking at the arrangements within the EU for crisis management, which reached similar conclusions on the need for co-operation between these institutions.

[20] *See*, for example, CEPS, 'Challenges to the Structure of Financial Supervision in the EU' (Centre for European Policy Studies, Brussels, July 2000), pp. 18–19.

[21] A. Lamfalussy, 'Initial Report of the Committee of Wise Men on the Regulation of European Securities Markets' (European Commission, Brussels, November 2000).

[22] A. Lamfalussy (2001), *op. cit.*

integrated European securities markets; highlighted some of the obstacles to further integration; endorsed and prioritised the relevant aspects of the European Commission's Financial Services Action Plan for new or updated European Union Directives relating to the securities markets[23]; rejected the establishment of a pan-European securities markets regulator; and suggested a possible approach to achieving more rapid and more flexible EU legislation. The Stockholm European Council endorsed the Reports' conclusions in March 2001.

The Reports recommended that this new approach to introducing, updating and implementing EU legislation should be based around four 'levels'. These are first, the introduction of broad and high-level framework legislation setting out key principles rather than detailed legislative requirements; second, the establishment of an EU Securities Committee, supported by an EU Securities Regulators Committee, to introduce and update the technical detail of the framework principles; third, enhanced co-operation and networking among EU regulators with a view to ensuring the consistent and equivalent transposition of legislation made under the first two 'levels' into national requirements and regulations; and fourth, strengthened enforcement of EU legislation through more vigorous action by the European Commission and through enhanced co-operation among member states and their regulatory authorities.

In its earlier submission to the Committee of Wise Men[24] and in its comments on the Committee's Initial Report,[25] the FSA highlighted a number of parallels with the approach to financial services regulation adopted recently in the United Kingdom. The recommendation by the Committee that securities markets regulation in Europe should be based on a number of framework directives that can be amplified and amended from time to time at a lower level is similar to the thinking behind the broad and flexible financial services legislation introduced recently in the United Kingdom. Similarly, the United Kingdom approach described in Section 1 is reflected in the emphasis in the Final Report on the importance of an open and transparent approach to regulation; wide-ranging consultation with all interested parties (which in the case of securities markets includes issuers of capital and end-investors, not just the major financial intermediaries); and strong lines of accountability in both the formulation of framework directives and the lower level amplification of the high-level objectives.

In addition, as described in Section 2, the cornerstone of the UK's Financial Services and Markets Act is the set of four statutory objectives that define at the highest level the purpose of financial sector regulation, supported by the seven 'having regard to' considerations. This approach is reflected to a large extent in the 'overarching principles' set out in the Final Report, and again endorsed by the Stockholm

---

[23] European Commission 'Financial Services: Implementing the Framework for Financial Markets. Action Plan' (European Commission, Brussels, May 1999).

[24] Financial Services Authority 'Response by the UK Financial Services Authority to the Committee of Wise Men on the regulation of European Securities Markets' (Financial Services Authority, London, September 2000).

[25] H. Davies, 'Securities Regulation in Europe', Speech to the European Banking Conference, Frankfurt, 17 November 2000.

European Council. These principles are:

- to maintain confidence in European securities markets;
- to maintain high levels of prudential supervision;
- to contribute to the efforts of macro and micro prudential supervisors to ensure systemic stability.
- to ensure appropriate levels of consumer protection proportionate to the different degrees of risk involved;
- to respect the subsidiarity and proportionality principles of the Treaty;
- to promote competition and ensure that the Community's competition rules are fully respected;
- to ensure that regulation is efficient as well as encouraging, not discouraging, innovation;
- to take account of the European, as well as the wider international dimension of securities markets.[26]

These 'overarching principles' should also be relevant to the determination of the optimal extent of harmonisation in the regulation of European securities markets. The creation of the European single market – in financial services as in other sectors – has been founded on mutual recognition based on common core standards. And the extent of the detail contained in these common standards has varied significantly from subject to subject. Some commentators appear to favour as much harmonisation as possible, either as an indicator of European unification as an end in itself, or as a pre-requisite for achieving a single market. But full harmonisation in all areas would almost certainly create inflexibility and excessive bureaucracy, and would tend to stifle innovation and competition. The 'overarching principles' might therefore provide part of a broader conceptual framework that could be applied when deciding on the appropriate degree of harmonisation in any particular area.

For example, greater harmonisation in the regulation of securities markets might be most appropriate in areas closest to providing the equivalent of 'weights and measures' standards, such as accounting standards and continuing disclosure requirements for issuers of securities. There could be considerable benefits to end-investors if a reasonably high degree of consistency and comparability could be achieved in such areas. Equally, however, the regulation of exchanges and of alternative trading platforms might best be undertaken on the basis of a common set of higher-level core standards, or general principles, that could be met – or even exceeded – by the providers of these services in various ways. An approach based on a common set of higher-level core standards would facilitate competition and innovation in an area where rapid technological advances provide considerable scope for competition and innovation. These providers of exchange services might choose to compete by going well beyond the core standards, and thereby attracting both issuers and investors who feel more comfortable participating in 'super-equivalent' environments. Indeed, many exchanges and trading platforms already adopt such an approach. Meanwhile,

---

[26] A. Lamfalussy (2001) *op. cit.*, p. 16.

those providers wishing to offer a more basic, and possibly cheaper, service would still have to meet the higher-level core standards, thereby providing at least a minimum level of protection to investors.

Other areas that might best be served by a common set of higher-level core standards include those where the framework legislative requirements and the common regulatory standards have to operate in close conjunction with differing legal, institutional and cultural approaches across member states. The requirements and standards then need to set out the objectives of regulation, but the achievement of these objectives depends on the interface between regulation and other factors. The intention here must be to achieve reasonably consistent and coherent outcomes, but not necessarily through identical detailed standards.

A related consideration here is the concern that, in the absence of full harmonisation, national regulatory authorities will themselves 'compete' by setting the lowest possible standards in an attempt to attract business to their jurisdictions. Indeed, the United Kingdom is sometimes accused of succumbing to such temptations. In practice, however, it may be observed that the United Kingdom is super-equivalent in many respects in its implementation of EU legislation, including the standards and requirements set in the United Kingdom relating to the disclosure of the information by issuers; the transparency of trades undertaken on regulated markets and other standards set for regulated markets; authorisation requirements; product regulation; company law; and conduct of business requirements.

It is perhaps in part because of this super-equivalence, rather than despite it, that many of the major international financial services firms and service providers have chosen to locate in the United Kingdom. This may reflect market pressures for high standards and for capturing their potentially positive impact on market confidence among both issuers and investors. The presence in the United Kingdom of three competing equity exchanges and of more than fifteen alternative trading platforms may be one result of this. Market participants are attracted by regulatory regimes that are fair and that are capable of adapting in response to market developments, thereby delivering both investor protection and an environment in which securities markets can compete, innovate and prosper.

Finally, viewed from the perspective of a single financial services regulator, the recommendations in the Lamfalussy Committee Reports are equally of interest when considered in the context of EU legislation (and of its implementation at the national level) in other sectors of financial services, including banking and insurance. The need for EU legislation to be introduced, updated and implemented rapidly – and consistently with overarching principles – is just as important for banking and insurance regulation as it is for securities regulation. There would therefore be considerable merit in applying any revised procedures and processes on a reasonably consistent basis across each of the main sectors of the financial services industry, and in seeking greater cross-sector consistency in the substance of the EU legislation applying to different sectors of the financial services industry. Indeed, the 'overarching principles' and some of the key principles and high-level objectives to be set out in the proposed 'level one' framework legislation should be applicable to all financial services regulation.

## 10   Conclusions

It is too early to reach firm conclusions about the success of the UK Financial Services Authority in delivering the benefits expected from a single national financial services regulator. The FSA is only four years old, and the new legislation has only just come into force. However, a promising start has been made in responding to market developments; in achieving economies of scale and scope; in creating a unified approach to standard-setting, authorisation, supervision, enforcement and consumer education; in introducing risk-based regulation on a consistent basis across firms and markets; and in working collectively with the Bank of England and the Treasury to maintain financial stability.

In addition, the high-level statutory objectives, the considerations that the FSA must have regard to in carrying out its general functions, and the wide-ranging set of consultation and accountability mechanisms under which the FSA operates, may together provide a useful model for other regulatory regimes to follow, including the arrangements for the drafting and amendment of EU Directives.

*Chapter 14*

# Issues in Accountability[1] of a Single Financial Services Regulator: The UK's Financial Services Authority (FSA)

*Vasiliki An. Galanopoulou*

*'Quis Custodiet ipsos Custodes?'*[2] (D. Iuni Iuvenalis, Satura, VI, 346.)

## I  INTRODUCTION

The aim of the present chapter is to explore issues in accountability rather than responsibility of single regulatory agencies[3] (developed at national and/or regional levels) for the governance of financial institutions and markets. The main focus is on control and accountability[4] of the UK Financial Services Authority (FSA).[5] Having in

---

[1] Accountability is defined as 'the duty to give information or to interpret or justify actions and make amends, whereas responsibility may embrace having a "job" – actual control – and being liable to take the blame when things go wrong'. *See* D. Oliver, 'Ministerial Accountability: What and Where are the Parameters?' in D. Butler, V. Bogdanor and R. Summers (eds), *The Law, Politics and the Constitution, Essays in Honour of G. Marshall* (Oxford University Press, Oxford, 1999), 78 at 84 he defines ministerial accountability and distinguishes it from ministerial responsibility. An agency is accountable rather than responsible for its actions and functions.

[2] (Who Regulates the Regulators?) Is the truthful answer to this question that 'no-one' actually regulates the regulators in general and not only in the area of financial services regulation? *See* also C. Harlow and R. Rawlings, *Law and Administration* (Butterworths, London, 1997), at 329.

[3] Regulatory agencies are traditionally distinguished from service delivery agencies. Also regulatory agencies are distinguished between executive and non-executive agencies. In the UK service delivery agencies have emerged in the ambit of the Next Steps Program. The Next Step Agencies are mostly executive agencies that are based on framework agreements rather than a statute. The Cabinet Office oversees them. Contrary to that the FSA, which is an independent administrative authority or non-departmental public body is based on a statute, the Financial Services and Markets Act 2000 (hereinafter: FSMA 2000). The latter will become effective in November 2001. See HM Treasury, *Financial Services Regulation Implementation* (HM Treasury, Press Release, London, No 33/01, 15 March 2001). For the Next Steps Agencies *see* Craig, *Administrative Law, infra, op. cit.*, note 4, at pp. 94–106. See also T. Daintith and A. Page, *The Executive in the Constitution, Structure, Autonomy, and Internal Control*, (Oxford University Press, Oxford, 1999), at pp. 37–50.

[4] These two concepts are defined differently in the literature. *See* P.P. Craig, *Administrative Law*, (4th edn, Sweet & Maxwell, London, 1999), (Craig, *Administrative Law*), at 97; he gives the following definitions: 'Control means the way in which the parent department may influence or direct an agency', and 'Accountability means the answerability of the institution to the public, either through Parliament or through some more direct means of public participation'. Control is more extensively used in the area of departmental agencies whereas the concept of accountability is associated to independent regulatory authorities. In this chapter both terms are used interchangeably to refer to the FSA's regime of checks and balances.

[5] For comments on the development of one single national financial services regulator in the UK and some of the details about its new legal framework *see* C. Blair, *Financial Services and Markets Bill*

*Mads Andenas and Yannis Avgerinos (eds), Financial Markets in Europe: Towards a Single Regulator?* 339–357.
© 2003 *Kluwer Law International. Printed in Great Britain.*

mind the developments in the FSA's mechanisms of accountability the emergence of a single financial services regulator is explored. It is argued in the parts below that leaving aside any problem of practicality, the development of a single European financial services regulator to govern both financial institutions and markets should not be impeded by the lack of appropriate and effective mechanisms of accountability.[6]

In Part II, the institutional organisation of a single financial services regulator is examined. In general, rather than in excessive details, the issue of the reasons for the introduction of one single financial services regulator in a national and/or regional level is also examined. In Part III, the issues of controlling a single financial services regulator through its procedures to promulgate rules and require compliance with its rules are examined. In Part IV, the direct mechanisms of accountability of a single regulatory agency for financial institutions and markets are examined. In Part V, the issues of the extent and the intensity of judicial review of the decision-making function of the single regulatory agency are examined. Courts have extensively controlled administrative bodies and especially agencies.[7] Is the role of the Courts similarly important to control independent financial services regulators? In Part VI the conclusions of this chapter are summarised.

## II  The Institutional Organisation of a Single Financial Services Regulator

### A  Why a single financial services regulator[8]

The first question to ask is, why a single financial services regulator in a national or a regional and even international level? This is the first question answered in this

---

(House of Commons Library, London, Research Paper 99/68, 24 June 1999), C. Briault, *The Rationale for a Single National Financial Services Regulation* (FSA, London, OP No 2, May 1999) and published also in (1999) 1(6) *Journal of International Financial Markets* 249, E.Z. Lomnicka, 'Reforming the UK Financial Services Regulation: The Creation of A Single Regulator' (1999) *The Journal of Business Law* 480, and G. Walker, 'Banking and Financial Services in the United Kingdom: The New Regulatory Regime', in J.J. Norton (ed.), *1998 Yearbook of International Financial and Economic Law* (Kluwer Law International, The Hague, 1999), 507.

[6] The centralisation of regulatory and supervisory policies at EU level implies that the accountability of such an institutional structure will get a European dimension. This is one of the many arguments that currently are proposed against the introduction of a single European regulatory agency for the production and enforcement of standards of regulation for financial institutions and markets that conduct financial business having European dimension. The lack of European Demos has been associated with the problem of observing a centralised model of European Governance. *See*, for example: Commission of the European Communities, Commission Staff Working Document, Work Programme, White Paper on European Governance, *'Enhancing Democracy in the European Union'* (SEC (2000) 1547/7 final, Brussels, 11 October 2000). The introduction of the concept of European Citizen may change this attitude.

[7] The role of judicial control of independent administrative authorities has been rather extensive in the US. *See* for the role of independent agencies and their means of control and among others the role of judicial review as a means of control of independent agencies in 'Symposium: The Independence of Independent Agencies' (1988) 2&3 *Duke Law Journal* at pp. 215–328.

[8] A single financial services regulator is one of the elements of a new regulatory paradigm that is in search for the effective supervision of globalised consolidated financial institutions and organised

sub-part. In the following sub-part the organisational structure of a single financial services regulator is examined in more detail.

The transformation of the institutional organisation of financial institutions and markets and the products that are circulated in these markets due to the phenomena of globalisation and technological innovation[9] have questioned the transformation of state organisations and agencies that should be granted the responsibility for regulating such financial activity. During the last two decades of the twentieth century a new model of state[10] arose. Many industrialised countries faced the challenge of reforming their institutional and regulatory frameworks that governed their respective financial intermediaries and organised markets. Financial markets are a very important part of states' economic structure since huge amounts of state and private money are circulated through these organised markets. Financial intermediaries are the major players in these organised markets.

The transformation of national states (some speak of the model of a non-welfare state, in Great Britain the Labour government used the term Third Way)[11] should lead to the transformation of means of co-operation of national states at EU level.[12] The means of co-operation of EU Member States are going to, or at least should, change after the circulation of the Euro. The circulation of the single currency in a single market is expected to bring further changes to the structure and organisation of financial markets. Formalised means of co-operation that are based on bilateral or multilateral co-operation agreements[13] and other Memoranda of Understanding should be replaced by other more informal means of co-operation at the centre. Thus regulatory co-operation at a more centralised level should be enhanced. National interests and the lack of democratic legitimacy are to be overcome because of the changing role of national states.

---

markets. *See* about the elements of a new regulatory paradigm in M. Taylor, 'The Search for New Regulatory Paradigm' (1998) 49 *Mercer Law Review* 793 at pp. 794–797.

[9] Technological developments have created products that cannot be easily accommodated within traditional contractual forms such as debt, equity and insurance; an example is the recent emergence of credit derivatives.

[10] For an overview *see* I.F.I. Shihata, 'The Changing Role of the State and Some Related Governance Issues' (1999) 11(4) *European Review of Public Law* 1459 at pp. 1461–1464.

[11] In the academia it was Prof Giddens who introduced the concept. See Prof A. Giddens, *The Third Way: The Renewal of Social Democracy* (Polity Press, Oxford, 1998), at 7, where he has described the values central to the third way as being 'equality, protection of the vulnerable, freedom as autonomy, no rights without responsibilities, no authority without democracy, cosmopolitan pluralism and philosophic conservatism.' And *idem, The Third Way and its Critics* (Polity Press, Cambridge, 2000).

[12] Not only in the area of regulation of financial activity, but also in other areas, such as competition policy that is very much related to the regulation of financial markets. *See* also B.J. Rodger, 'Competition Policy, Liberalism and Globalisation: A European Perspective' (2000) 6 (3) *The Columbia Journal Of European Law* 289 at pp. 291–292.

[13] *See*, for example, Secs 194 and 195 of FSMA 2000 that provide an obligation to the FSA to intervene on a host State basis and at the request of or for the purpose of assisting the home State regulator. And Art. 19 of the ISD and Arts 22 and 28 of the Directive 2000/12/EC of the European Parliament and of the Council of 20 March 2000 *Relating to the Taking Up and Pursuit of the Business of Credit Institutions*, OJ 2000, L 126/1, 26/5/2000 (hereinafter Credit Institutions Directive) that provide for the co-operation obligations between the competent authorities of different national member states.

Academics and EU policy makers are discussing extensively the possibilities of the establishment of one centralized regulator. The latter can regulate European securities markets. The emergence of one single regulatory agency for all types of financial activities has been discussed less by both academics and EU policy makers than the introduction of a European securities regulator.[14] It can be argued that the establishment of a centralised regulatory agency for all financial institutions and markets is important because financial institutions and markets operate across-borders and across-sectors.[15] Centralisation in the administration and requirement of compliance with both prudential and conduct of business rules will solve a lot of problems that are associated with efficient and effective oversight of cross-border and cross-sectorial provision of financial services.[16] Internet developments also influence the way that financial services are provided. Cross-border and cross-sector provision of

---

[14] Although in these discussions the introduction of a single European financial services regulator is not precluded completely. It is rather suggested as a 'last resort solution or institutional alternative' to a centralised European securities regulator. See J.-V. Louis, 'Economic and Monetary Union (European Central Bank)', in J.A. Winter, D.M. Curtin, A.E. Kellermann, B. de Witte (eds), *Reforming the Treaty on European Union-The Legal Debate* (Kluwer Law International, The Hague, 1996), L.B. Smaghi and D. Gros, *Open Issues in European Central Banking* (MacMillan Press Ltd. in association with the Centre for European Policy Studies, London, 2000), E. Gualandri, 'European Monetary Union: Issues in Supervision' in E.P.M. Gardener and J. Falzon (eds), *Strategic Challenges in European Banking*, (MacMillan Press Ltd, London, 2000), 248 at 270, H. Evans, 'An International Financial Regulator?' in R. M. Lastra (ed.), *The Reform of the International Financial Architecture* (Kluwer Law International, The Hague, 2001), 107 at 115, P. Clarotti, 'European Financial Regulation', in R. M. Lastra (ed.), *The Reform of the International Financial Architecture* (Kluwer Law International, The Hague, 2001), 303 at 312, and more recently *see* also Initial Report of the Committee of Wise Men on the *Regulation of European Securities Markets* (Brussels, 9/11/2000) and also Final Report of the Committee of Wise Men on the Regulation of European Securities Markets (Brussels, 15/2/2001), also available at <http://europa.eu.int/comm/internal_market/en/finances/general/lamfalussyen.pdf>, at 8 (a single European regulatory authority is at present 'impractical' according to the Report).

[15] For the developments of the organisation of EU financial institutions across-borders and across-sectors, *see* Brouwer Report on the *Arrangements for Preserving Financial Stability in Europe*, (EFC/ECFIN/240/00-Final, Brussels, 8 April 2000, available at <http://ue.eu.int/newsroom/loaddoc.cfm>). In the literature they speak about the 'end of geography' because of the cross-border and cross-sector provision of financial services. The use of the cyberspace for the provision of financial services endangers the effective surveillance of production and distribution of these services in the future. *See* R. O'Brien, *Global Financial Integration: The End of Geography* (Royal Institute of International Affairs, Pinter Publishers, London, 1992).

[16] It has been observed that 'the EU's single financial market goes hand in hand with prudential soundness and financial stability. Steady EU-led convergence in regulatory requirements, underpinned by common ground-rules and pragmatic means of implementing and applying the EU Directives for a single market for financial services has already contributed greatly to achieving this goal. However, the heightened tempo of consolidation in the industry, and the intensification of links between financial markets call for careful consideration of structures for containing and supervising institutional and systemic risk, in particular where they arise in cross-sector groups combining insurance companies, banks and investment firms ('financial conglomerates'). *See* explanatory memorandum of the proposal for a *Directive of the European Parliament and of the Council on the Supplementary supervision of credit institutions, insurance undertakings and investment firms in a financial conglomerate and amending Council Directives 73/239/EEC, 79/267/EEC, 92/49/EEC, 93/6/EEC and 93/22/EEC, and Directives 98/78/EC and 2000/12/EC of the European Parliament and the Council* (Brussels, COM (2001) 213 final, 24/4/2001), at 2.

financial services is to be replaced by on-line and off-line provision of financial services.[17] The new EU regulatory framework should take into consideration all these technological developments and the use of the internet.[18] But these regulatory developments need to be supported by parallel institutional changes[19] that are going to design and enforce effectively the context of the regulatory framework. It can be argued that the changes in the regulatory framework should include harmonisation of both prudential and conduct of business regulation of financial services laws.[20] It can further be argued that effective application of both harmonised prudential and conduct of business regulation requires centralisation of its institutional structure.

In theoretical terms centralisation of Community financial regulation and the centralisation of the institutional arrangements for the administration and enforcement of the regulatory arrangements may be required because the spillover effects[21] of market integration are more evident in the centre of the EU rather than in the periphery and thus within the territories of national member states. The centralisation of the spillover

---

[17] *See* the recently adopted Communication from the Commission to the Council and the European Parliament, *E-Commerce and Financial Services*, Brussels 7/2/2001, COM (2001) 66 final (also available at <http://europa.eu.int/eur-lex/en/com/cnc/2001/com2001_0066en01.pdf>), at 6.

[18] The Europe initiative includes the following directives most of which lay the foundation on which further policy developments, including those for financial services, will be based. Thus, (a) Directive 97/5/EC of the European Parliament and the Council of 27 January 1997 *On Cross-Border Credit Transfers* OJ 1997, L 043/25, 14/2/1997, (b) Directive 98/26/EC of the European Parliament and the Council of 19 May 1998 *on Settlement Finality in Payment and Securities Settlement Systems*, OJ 1998, L 166/45, 11/6/98, (c) Directive 1999/93/EC of the European Parliament and of the Council of 13 December 1999 *on a Community Framework for Electronic Signatures*, OJ 1999, L 13/12 of 19/1/2000, (d) Directive 2000/31/EC of the European Parliament and of the Council of 8 June 2000, *on Certain Legal Aspects of Information Society Services, in Particular Electronic Commerce, in the Internal Market (Directive on Electronic Commerce)*, OJ 2000, L 178/1, 17/7/2000, (e) Directive 2000/46/EC of the European Parliament and of the Council of 18 September 2000 *on the Taking Up, Pursuit of and Prudential Supervision of the Business of Electronic Money Institutions*, OJ 2000, L 275/39, 27/10/2000.

[19] More recently this harmonisation has been defined as 'reflexive' harmonisation or 'dynamic regulatory competition'. The purpose of this type of harmonisation would 'not be to substitute for state-level regulation; hence, the transnational standard would not operate to "occupy the field" in the manner of a 'monopoly regulator' as, it is suggested, is often the case with US federal regulation. Rather, transnational standards would seek to promote diverse, local-level approaches to regulatory problems by creating a space for autonomous solutions to emerge when, because of market failures, they would not otherwise do so'. *See* S. Deakin, 'Two Types of Regulatory Competition: Competitive Federalism versus Reflexive Harmonisation. A Law and Economics Perspective on Centros', in A. Dashwood and A. Ward (eds), *The Cambridge Yearbook of European Legal Studies 1999*, Vol. 2 (Hart Publishing, Oxford, 2000), 231 at pp. 245–246. In the US the case of a monopolistic regulator that enhances competitive federalism that is the opposite of reflexive harmonisation has been discussed in the area of securities regulation by Prof Roberta Romano. *See* R. Romano, 'Empowering Investors: A Market Approach to Securities Regulation' (1998) 107(8) *The Yale Law Journal* 2359 at pp. 2392–2395.

[20] It has been observed that 'In Europe, ongoing work is about improving and modernising the framework of EU Directives, on making a reality of the single market in financial services, and on improving the information exchange between regulators. In a very real sense, there is already a single system of European regulation, which operates on the basis of a single home state regulator for financial institutions and the passport to other states'. *See* H. Evans, *supra, op. cit.*, note 14, at 115.

[21] That means that greater Community activity in one area suggests a fundamental shift of powers from the National to Community level. *See* also Vos, *infra, op. cit.*, note 72, at 1113.

effects might be greater after the development of e-commerce and the provision of financial products through the use of the latest technological means, like the Internet (e-finance). Similarly this centralisation of institutional arrangements is required because policy considerations for the adoption of specific economic measures, like for example the main monetary issues in the union, are decided in the center rather than in the periphery of the European Union. When considerations about issues of economic policy are taken at the centre it is rather important that issues that are related to the welfare of European citizens and the protection of their investing interests are decided in the centre.[22] Similarly compliance should be checked from the centre. The protection of consumers of financial products' interests, for example, might need to be arranged in a more centralised manner because of all these technological developments[23] and for reasons of reducing information and other transaction costs for consumers.[24] That does not mean that only policy making in relation to the protection of consumers' interests should be organised at a centralised level.[25] It also means that design, application and compliance of regulatory standards should be arranged in a more centralised manner. But the responsibility for enforcement of the rules that are introduced from the centre can be imposed on the decentralised financial services authorities.

The necessity to centralise policy design, rule design and compliance of issues concerning the structure and operation of financial institutions and markets in the United Kingdom, because of the structure of the markets and the consolidation of financial services, has been the main reason for the establishment of the FSA in a national territory.[26] Issues of the organisational structure of the FSA are discussed below. Some observations and suggestions about the development of a similar organisational structure at European level for the governance of financial institutions and markets are discussed at the end of the part below.

### B   The institutional arrangements for one single financial services regulator: the FSA's case

The UK's single financial regulator has been structured as a private company limited by guarantee formed under the Companies Act 1985 as the Securities and Investment

---

[22] Consistency of both macro-prudential and micro-prudential policies in the integrated financial markets seems important.

[23] It has been observed that 'Centralisation is required for reasons of consumer protection in the e-commerce area'. See G. Hertig, 'Regulatory Competition for EU Financial Services' (2000) 3(2) *Journal of International Economic Law* 349 at 351.

[24] See G.J. Benston, 'Consumer Protection as Justification for Regulating Financial-Services Firms and Products' (2000) 17(3) *Journal of Financial Services Research* 277 at 279.

[25] In a way policy making about the welfare of European citizens is taking place at the center. All the EU directives are designed at the center. It is up to individual member states to implement policy decisions of the center in their national territories. But the compliance with centralised rules relating to the structure and operation (thus supervision) of financial markets should be checked from the center.

[26] Gordon Brown, the Chancellor of the Exchequer, at the time of the introduction of the UK reforms, on the 20th of May 1997 commented: 'it is clear that the distinctions between different types of financial institution-banks, securities firms and insurance companies-are becoming increasingly blurred. Many of today's

Board for the purpose of carrying out functions under the Financial Services Act 1986.[27] It has not been structured as an executive agency of the government. Thus, it preserves its independence from direct political influences. FSA's independence allows the FSA to perform its functions more effectively.[28] The FSA is a single-headed agency[29] with legislative functions[30] and not a delegate organ of the government.[31] The FSA's private law organisation has also been adopted for reasons of flexibility and adaptability to the increased demands of the markets. The model of a multi-headed Commission was not accepted because multi-headed Commissions are usually associated with an incompetence to take quick and rational decisions.[32]

Even though the FSA has been structured as a private law body, it is not a private law organisation. It has been observed that 'if the organisation of a body is governed by typically public law clauses (for instance administrative regulations) and specially when the body has been authorised to exercise power functions, it is clear, from this fact, that it belongs to the public law category'.[33] Such private law organisations that are mainly public bodies for the promulgation of regulatory and other normative standards are clearly independent from direct political links of the executive branch of a state. They usually generate interesting issues of democratic legitimacy. Democratic legitimacy relates to issues of control and accountability. Democratic legitimacy of an independent administrative authority is enhanced when limits are imposed to the administrative authority's powers. At the same time, it is rather important that effective controls from the political organs of a nation state are in place.

Is it possible for a regulatory agency that ideally does not fit within the traditional three branches of government (the executive, the legislative and the judiciary) to be democratic because it satisfies the basic constitutional principles of separation of powers (inherent in this principle is the principle of parliamentary sovereignty) and the rule of law? In the US tradition, regulatory agencies' legitimacy has been established on the fact that these agencies are the fourth branch of government.[34] In the EU, independent regulatory agencies' legitimacy is based on the emergence of

---

financial institutions are regulated by a plethora of different supervisors. This increased the costs and reduces the effectiveness of supervision'. *See* Gordon Brown, *Statement to the House of Commons* (May 1997).

[27] See Sec. 1(1) of FSMA 2000. Even though the Authority is exempt from the 'requirement of the 1985 Act relating to the use of 'limited' as part of its name', *see* Schedule 1, para. 14 of FSMA 2000.

[28] For the advantages that are associated with independent regulatory authorities in the US tradition (since independent agencies are rather common in the US), *see* P.R. Verkuil, 'The Purposes and Limits of Independent Agencies' (1988) (2&3) *Duke Law Journal* 257 at pp. 259–267.

[29] *See* Schedule 1, para. 2(1) of FSMA 2000.

[30] *See* Schedule 1, para. 1(2) of FSMA 2000.

[31] This is important because such an agency must not always remain subordinate to the people's representatives, thus a national Parliament and the political constituencies in the Parliament or the Crown. *See* also Schedule 1, para. 13 of FSMA 2000, where we read that '(a) the Authority is not to be regarded as acting on behalf of the Crown; and (b) its members, officers and staff are not to be regarded as Crown servants'.

[32] In some instances though, multi-headed commissions were associated with the advantage of consensual, reflective and pluralistic decision-making. *See* Verkuil, *supra, op. cit.*, note 28, at 260.

[33] *See* T. Modeen, 'Study on Legal Systems and Procedures for the Delegation of Public Services' (1999) 11(3) *European Review of Public Law* 1115 at 1117.

[34] *See* G. Majone, *Controlling Regulatory Bureaucracies: Lessons from the American Experience*, (EUI Working Paper SPS No 93/3, Florence, May 1993) (Majone, *Controlling Regulatory Bureaucracies*).

the model of the regulatory[35] instead of the model of the parliamentary state.[36] For most of the regulatory agencies in the EU[37] a new model of democratic legitimacy and control has been proposed.[38] Most of the details are associated with this model are discussed in Parts II–IV.[39]

Based on the efficiency reasons that suggest that a single financial services regulator is an ideal institutional model for the regulation of the current consolidated financial institutions and markets it can be argued that the FSA is a pilot model for the emergence of a similar institutional structure at EU level. It is suggested that the latter can be allocated the same functions as the FSA. The institutional model of a single European financial services regulator should be an organisation with its own administrative functions. It should also be in some respects independent from national interests in order to administer effective application of rules and enhance compliance by national Member States with both EU prudential and conduct of business regulation. It should be different from an advisory or regulatory committee, it

---

[35] The introduction of the concept of 'regulatory state' in Europe has been appointed to Professor G. Majone. *See* G. Majone, *Regulating Europe* (Routledge, London, 1996), (Majone, *Regulating Europe*), and *idem*, 'The Rise of the Regulatory State in Europe', in R. Baldwin, C. Scott, and C. Hood (eds), *A Reader on Regulation* (Oxford University Press, Oxford, 1998), (Majone, *The Rise of the Regulatory State in Europe*), 192.

[36] Such a model 'assumes a considerable degree of separation of powers: legislature lays down the legislative framework within which agencies have to operate, and they check whether the objectives and guidelines that have been set for agency action have actually been respected, but they are not supposed to monitor agency's day-to-day activities, save in exceptional circumstances'. *See* R. Dehousse, 'European Institutional Architecture After Amsterdam: Parliamentary System or Regulatory Structure?' (1998) 35 *Common Market Law Review* 595 at 617.

[37] The agencies in the EU level can be distinguished into three categories. Thus, the independent agencies that are provided in the EC Treaty and they have the status of EU institutions (the European Central Bank and the European Investment Bank: *see* Arts 8 and 9 (ex Arts 4a and 4b) respectively of the Treaty of Amsterdam amending the Treaty on European Union, the Treaties establishing the European Communities and Certain Related Acts, signed at Amsterdam, 2 October 1997, OJ 1997, C 340/105 of 10th of November 1997 (hereinafter: EC Treaty)), the other independent agencies that have been established because of special framework agreements (the European Centre for the Development of Vocational Training, the European Foundation for the Improvement of Living and Working Conditions, the European Environmental Agency, the European Training Foundation, the European Centre for the Control of Drugs and Drug Addiction, the European Agency for the Evaluation of Medical Products, the Office for Harmonisation in the Internal Market (Trade Marks and Designs), the Agency for Safety and Health at Work), the Community Plant Variety Office, the Translation Centre for the Bodies of the European Union, the European Monitoring Centre on Racism and Xenophobia, the European Agency for Reconstruction: *see* <http://europa.eu.int/agencies/carte_en.htm>, and the EU advisory and regulatory committees in the ambit of European Comitology. The latter are agencies that are not very much independent because transparency is lacking. Their administrative structure is based on the EC Commission's administrative structure and details. The use of Committees in the area of EU financial services has been enhanced by the Commission's Financial Services Action Plan. *See* on this point Hertig, *supra, op. cit.*, note 23, at 362, where he further argues that this might lead to an increase in the EU regulatory burden.

[38] For the ECB, *see* Magnette, *infra, op. cit.*, note 71, at pp. 326–327.

[39] It has been observed that 'Parliamentary democracy tends, as a consequence, to be superseded by a de facto democracy of organised interests and parliamentary sovereignty makes way for expert sovereignty'. *See* Judge G.F. Mancini, *Democracy and Constitutionalism in the European Union, Collected Essays*, (Hart Publishing, Oxford-Portland Oregon, 2000), 68.

should be granted independence from national authorities but it should co-operate closely with national financial regulatory authorities. This co-operation framework is suggested to be similar to the European Central Bank (ECB) framework of co-operation with national central banks in the Eurosystem. The ECB co-operates closely with national central banks in the Eurosystem for reasons of enforcement in the periphery of the measures that have been decided at the centre by the ECB. The ECB certifies compliance of its measures. Many of the elements of how such a single European financial services regulator can be kept accountable to the public authorities of national Member States and other European policy making institutions are becoming clearer from the discussion that follows in the following parts of this chapter.

It is argued below that a single regulatory agency for financial institutions and markets at EU level should be based on the same principles of accountability that apply to the FSA's case. Issues in accountability of a single financial regulator are discussed below. The FSA is taken as an example. The FSA's mechanisms of accountability are also compared with the ECB's mechanisms of accountability.

### III   THE PROCEDURES AND FUNCTIONS OF A SINGLE FINANCIAL SERVICES REGULATOR AND THEIR LIMITS

#### A   The role of objectives of regulation for a single financial services regulator

A single financial services regulator has to follow special procedures. The details of these procedures are also the regulator's limits of its powers. This has been defined as procedural accountability of an agency.[40] Procedural accountability more precisely is the control over an agency that has followed in most of its functions well-defined procedures. The degree of answerability of an agency to well-defined procedures can be based on the use of some specific standards. Statutorial principles and objectives[41] are the standards that can be used to check the degree of answerability of a single financial services regulator to its procedures.[42] Regulatory objectives have been used as useful guidelines for legitimacy controls over Central Banks that are agencies.[43]

---

[40] *See* also T. Posser, 'Theorising Utility Regulation' (1999) *Modern Law Review* 196 at 200, he uses the same term for the accountability regime of utilities regulators.

[41] Or otherwise 'Distinct "Constitutional-Type" Normative Goals'. *See* M. Everson, 'Independent Agencies: Hierarchy Beaters?' (1995) 1(2) *European Law Journal* 180, (Everson, *Independent Agencies*), at 187.

[42] It has been observed that an instrument to exercise effective agency control is that of 'the focused statutory statement of agency tasks. Such a detailed legal mandate thus serves as the starting point for agency oversight; only where the accepted parameters of agency discretion are made explicit does there exist a yardstick for the evaluation of agency performance'. *See* Everson, *Independent Agencies, supra, op. cit.,* note 41, at 190. The regulatory objectives are the standards of conduct of the staff of the regulatory agency.

[43] *See* R.M. Lastra, *Central Banking and Banking Regulation* (LSE Financial Markets Group, London, 1996), at pp. 51–61, and F. Amtenbrink, *The Democratic Accountability of Central Banks, A Comparative Study of the European Central Bank* (Hart Publishing, Oxford, 1999), at 333. It has been also observed

Political scientists have observed that the credibility of community institutions is enhanced if these institutions are granted the responsibility of observing specific objectives.[44] In a similar manner, domestic regulators are credible in the national and international context if they are required by law to observe specific objectives. Accordingly, the FSA's credibility and thus efficiency are enhanced when the FSA closely observes its regulatory objectives.[45] The review of these objectives should be conducted on an objective basis.

Some risks may endanger the FSA's responsibility for implementing its regulatory objectives. They are usually risks that arise because of the FSA's regulatory and supervisory functions and responsibilities.[46] The FSA has studied and estimated these risks in close co-operation with the regulated industry.[47]

The FSA should estimate successfully the risks that influence the implementation of its objectives. It can thus preserve its internal and external credibility. The FSA's internal credibility means that the FSA legitimately conducts its functions (authorisation, supervision (in the narrow sense),[48] enforcement and adjudication powers) and designs its rules[49] if it follows its statutory objectives. The FSA is statutorily obliged to consult the regulated industry in performing its basic legislative functions and on 'the extent to which its general policies and practices are consistent with its general duties under Section 2'.[50] Further to that when the Authority (the FSA) proposes rules it must publish a draft of the proposed rules which among other things must include 'an explanation of the Authority's reasons for believing that making the proposed rules is compatible with its general duties, under Section 2'.[51]

---

that 'The theory of bureaucracy suggests that independence coupled with accountability for the achievement of a specified statutory objective could provide the correct incentives to decision-makers within the central bank. The achievement of its legal goals is the raison d'etre of every administrative agency, including a central bank'. *See* C. Hadjiemmanuil, *The Choice of Institutions for Monetary Stability in an Emerging Economy: Independent Central Bank or Currency Board?* (December 1997), at 5, with further references to the bibliography.

[44] *See* G. Majone, 'The Credibility Crisis of Community Regulation' (2000) 38(2) *Journal of Common Market Studies* 273.

[45] *See* Sec. 2 of the FSMA 2000.

[46] These risks are different from the traditional market risks. *See* H. Davies, '*A Radical New Approach to Regulation*' (Speech delivered on Monday 11/12/2000 at the Royal Lancaster Hotel), available at <http://www.fsa.gov.uk/pubs/speeches/sp67.html>.

[47] *See* Financial Services Authority, (FSA), *Building the New Regulator, Progress Report 1* (FSA, London, December 2000). The FSA according to this report intends to study the risks that arise in the implementation of its objectives. The FSA specifically intends to study the impact and probability of risks arising that may hinder the implementation of its objectives. The required data has been provided by the regulated industry itself.

[48] It is distinguished from supervision in general that traditionally includes all the functions of a financial services regulator.

[49] It has been observed that 'the detailed procedure for making rules is an important part of the accountability framework for the FSA, and goes well beyond what was required of any of the existing regulators'. *See* M. Blair, QC, L. Minghella, M. Taylor, M. Threipland, and G. Walker (eds), *Blackstone's Guide to the Financial Services and Markets Act 2000* (Blackstone Press Ltd., London, 2001), at 149.

[50] *See* Sec. 8 of FSMA 2000.

[51] *See* Sec. 155(2)(c) of FSMA 2000.

At the same time, the FSA's external credibility means that the FSA legitimately conducts its functions and designs its rules if it is under the horizontal control of the constitutional organs. The latter should control the FSA's functions based on the estimation of the degree to which the FSA has managed to observe its regulatory objectives.[52]

It can be argued that the close links between the regulatory agency and its regulatory objectives can put the right balance between market liberalisation and legitimate prudential regulation. If the regulatory agency performs duties that direct it to respect specific objectives then the problem of the liberalisation of tight controls over financial activity is resolved.[53] The obligation of the controllers to observe regulatory objectives is the substitute to the complete liberalisation of the structure of the markets. Not only is the regulatory agency under control, but also innovation and competition can prevail in a regime of regulation, the perimeter of which has been defined in a statute as in the FSA's case.[54]

At the same time, the problem of democratic control over the controllers still remains. Can we regard statutory objectives as efficient mechanisms to preserve adequate levels of democratic control of political independent regulatory agencies

---

[52] The FSA is indirectly controlled by the Parliament and the Government. Also the FSA's decisions are subject to judicial review. The FSA's indirect accountability to the Parliament is based on (a) the FSA's responsibility for laying its reports in front of the Two Houses of the Parliament (*see* Secs 12(5), 17(5) 163(12)(b) and Schedule 1 para. 10 (3), of the FSMA 2000), (b) the Parliament's responsibility for approving the about 80 statutory instruments and other types of secondary legislation that are required for the implementation in practice of the FSMA 2000 in November 2001 (*see* Sec. 429 of the FSMA 2000). The FSA's indirect accountability to the Government is based on (a) the Treasury's responsibility for appointing the Chairmen and the members of the FSA's Boards and other governing bodies (*see* Schedule 1 para. 2(1), (2), (3), and 3(2), (3), Secs 9(3), 10(3), and 212(3) of the FSMA 2000), (b) the FSA's responsibility for laying its Annual Report to the Treasury (*see* Schedule 10, para. 10(1), (2)(a) and (b) of the FSMA 2000, (c) the Treasury's right to inquire the conduct of inquiries in the public interest (*see* Sec. 14 of the FSMA 2000), (d) the Treasury's powers to issue statutory instruments (for example the regulated activities and the exemption Orders) (*see* Secs 22 and 38 of the FSMA 2000). The FSA decisions are subject to judicial review according to the general principles of administrative law. In addition to that, the FSA as an administrative body is liable in damages to the regulated industry on the basis of the tort of misfeasance in public office. For the administrative liability of public regulatory authorities, *see* M. Andenas and D. Fairgrieve, 'To Supervise or to Compensate? A Comparative Study of State Liability for Negligent Banking Supervision', in M. Andenas and D. Fairgrieve (eds), *Judicial Review in International Perspective* (Kluwer Law International, The Hague-London-Boston, 2000), 333 at pp. 334–335. All the constitutional organs according to the individual provisions mentioned above ought to control FSA's functions using as a guiding tool FSA's regulatory objectives.

[53] There is a tension between market liberalisation and prudential supervisory standards. A single regulatory agency can resolve this tension if it observes specific regulatory objectives. Market liberalisation is preserved and the regulators implement prudential standards. The regulators can implement these standards having in mind their regulatory objectives without impairing market liberalisation. *See* also J.J. Norton 'Pondering the Parameters of the "New International Financial Architecture": A Legal Perspective', in R.M. Lastra (ed.), *The Reform of the International Financial Architecture* (Kluwer Law International, The Hague, 2001), 3 at 37 he discusses this tension between financial markets liberalisation and the necessity to preserve adequate prudential standards.

[54] The Constitutionalisation of the FSA should be precluded though. Its legal framework, the FSMA 2000 is subject to be repealed by another Act of Parliament. The annulment of an Act is also associated to the lack of a formal written constitution in the UK.

and authorities? In the present times when states are organised neither on the model of welfare state nor on the model of regulatory state, but where a 'third way' is actually sought for the organisation of current states,[55] it is most appropriate to search for new more sophisticated mechanisms of democratic checks and balances of independent administrative and other regulatory authorities.[56]

### B   Other arrangements for the use of a single financial services regulator's procedures as a means of the agency's accountability: the FSA's case

A certain degree of transparency and other participation rights of the main actors that are part of the regulated industry, the so-called market participants,[57] are additional requirements to guarantee the effectiveness of the use of the FSA's performances as a means to exercise democratic controls and balances. The single regulator's compliance in its regulatory and other governance functions with its regulatory objectives is guaranteed by an increased transparency and other participation rights that are allocated to individual market participants and other end users of financial products. Market industry participation[58] can also resolve the tension between liberalisation of controls on the one hand, and the necessity to preserve some standards of prudential supervision on the other.

The accountability of a single financial services regulator that is based on the performances of the regulator relates to the characterisation that the regulation has become proceduralised. That means that the regulator is not actually imposing its rules, or is exercising other regulatory functions alone, but it produces its rules and exercises its other regulatory functions in close co-operation with the regulated industry. The proceduralisation of regulation has been criticised by the advocates of capture theory.[59] According to this theory, a single financial services regulator can be captured not only by the interests of financial institutions, but it can also be captured by the interests of well-organised markets.[60]

---

[55] They even going to suggest the integration of economic integration with social democratic values.

[56] Professor Craig describes three models of democracies. Thus, the model of traditional pluralism, the model of market-orientated pluralism and the third way. *See* Craig, *Administrative Law, supra, op. cit.,* note 4, at pp. 28–44.

[57] Market participants are specific categories of stakeholders whose interests should be taken into consideration by the regulator when the latter designs its rules. The literature has already spoken about a 'stakeholder approach to regulation'. *See* D. Souter, 'A Stakeholder Approach to Regulation', in D. Corry, D. Souter, and M. Waterson, *Regulating Our Utilities* (Institute for Public Policy Research, London, 1995). Is it time to accept a 'stakeholder approach to regulation' in the area of financial services regulation?

[58] This market industry participation is an expert rather than a representative or delegate participation. *See* also Harlow and Rawlings, *supra, op. cit.,* note 2, at 337.

[59] *See* about the public interest and public choice theories in the area of financial services in P.L. Kahn, 'The Politics of Unregulation: Public Choice and Limits on Government' (1990) 75 *Cornell Law Review* 280

[60] The argument against this thesis suggests that 'individual intermediaries' preferences may prove very volatile, due to constant changes in market structures and the development of internet-assisted distribution channels'. Accordingly these preferences cannot influence the single financial regulators' decisions. *See* Hertig, *supra, op. cit.,* note 23, at 365.

On the contrary it can be argued that these procedures guarantee the openness of the regulatory process itself. Openness, or in other words transparency, has replaced direct political influences. The latter are not so important for the current liberalised financial markets. On the contrary, it seems that liberalisation and transparency are much more preferable to the markets themselves rather than direct political influences. The latter have been criticised of hindering innovation and competition to develop. If one reads throughout the FSA's documents, one can estimate that a good job is done since the regulator now does not have to report in every stage to the minister or to the government in order to take appropriate regulatory measures.

This proceduralisation of financial services regulation[61] can be controlled by the imposition of detailed regulatory objectives on the one hand, and by the recognition of greater role for the Courts.[62] Open hearings and public debates may serve similar purposes. All these requirements are sufficiently provided in the UK's legal framework of regulating financial institutions and markets in the United Kingdom. The provisions of the Financial Services and Market Act 2000 stipulate regulatory objectives for the FSA.[63] At the same time, the FSA's descisions are subject to judicial review based on the application of the general principle of law that allows judicial review of decisions of administrative bodies.[64] The FSA's decisions are under consideration by an independent Tribunal.[65] The FSA is also liable for damages.[66]

The FSA is also statutorily obliged to co-operate closely with the regulated industry. More specifically the regulatory agency is statutorily obliged to give reasons and explain the context of its decision to grant or refuse to grant a specific permission in

---

[61] *See* also J. Black, 'Proceduralising Regulation: Part I' (2000) 20(4) *Oxford Journal of Legal Studies* 597.

[62] It has been observed that the 'industries that are being regulated are generally those which display features of natural monopoly, or the need for prudential supervision in the public interest (as with financial services) for example. These industries are also part of the global economy. It is part of the wider strategy of the firms involved to act increasingly as multinationals. As such issues of wider public and political concern are being handled by regulators, who are, in effect, the nationally-based of a wider transnational business system. It may be essential for good governance and public responsiveness for these bodies to be subjected to scrutiny not just by market players but by the wider public to ensure that proper regulation of markets is actually taking place. Judicial review may provide the only forum in which decisions could be formally challenged and the courts could play a role in overseeing the decision-making process from the perspective of rationality and legality, and ensuring that decisions are made which are not simply pandering to special interests at the expense of wider public policy goals'. *See* J. Black and P. Muchlinski, 'Introduction', in J. Black, P. Muchlinski, and P. Walker (eds), *Commercial Regulation and Judicial Review* (Hart Publishing, Oxford, 1998), 1 at 14.

[63] *See* Sec. 2(2) and (3) of FSMA 2000.

[64] More recently they proposed the codification of the grounds that allow judicial review. *See* T.H. Jones, 'Judicial Review and Codification' (2000) 20(4) *Legal Studies* 517 at 518.

[65] See Secs 55, 57, 58, 62(4), 63(5), 67(7), 76(6), 77(5), 78(12), 88(7), 89(4), 92(7), 127(4), 184(3)(b)(iii), 186(5), 187(4), 197(4)(e), 200(5)(b), 208(4)(b), 245(2)(b), 252(4)(b), 255(2), 256(5), 259(4)(e) & (10), 260(2)(b), 265(5), 268, 269, 271(3)(b), 276(2)(b), 280(2)(b), 282(4)(e) & (8), 300, 320(4), 321(11), 331(9), 345(5), 350(4)(e), 386(3), 388(5), 393(9) & (11), Schedule 3, Paras 19(12)(b), 22(3)(b) of FSMA 2000, (reference of matters to the Tribunal whose decisions can be appealed in front of a Court of Law), and Sec. 137 of FSMA 2000, which states that a decision of the Tribunal is subject on appeal on a point of law in front of the Court of Appeal and the Court of Session in Scotland.

[66] In two specific instances the FSA is liable in damages. *See* Schedule 1, para. 19(3) of FSMA 2000.

the form of a warning or decision notices depending on the specific circumstances.[67] The regulatory agency is statutorily obliged to bring to the attention of the regulated industry the content of its rules.[68] The regulatory agency is also responsible for following a specific procedure in explaining the prerequisites for the enforcement of its decisions in cases of breach of a financial institution statutorial responsibility.[69] Another element that highlights this openness of the FSA's regulatory practices to the regulated industry is the provision of the FSMA 2000 that states the FSA's responsibility for holding an Annual Public Meeting.[70]

### C    The use of an agency's procedures as a means of the agency's accountability: the ECB's case

Similar procedures have been proposed or are currently practised for regulatory agencies at EU level.[71] Below the ECB is examined, because it is the most appropriate European Agency[72] to take into consideration for the emergence of a single European financial services regulator. The ECB and the arrangements that characterise the organisation of the European System of Central Banks should be taken into consideration in the design of a single regulatory agency for financial institutions and markets at EU level and its relationships with national financial regulatory authorities.[73]

Treaty provisions guarantee the ECB's legal and political independence.[74] The ECB's independence[75] and accountability have been discussed extensively in the literature.[76] The ECB's procedures are mechanisms of control of ECB's practices as in the FSA's case. The ECB is obliged according to the Protocol on the Statute of the

---

[67] *See* Sec. 52 of FSMA 2000. A warning notice is a formal notification to the person or the regulated firm concerned that the FSA proposed to take certain action. A decision notice contains the FSA' s decision to take certain action, subject to a person's right to refer a case to the independent Financial Services and Markets Tribunal.

[68] *See* Sec. 155 of the FSMA 2000.

[69] *See* Secs 207 and 208 of the FSMA 2000.

[70] *See* Schedule 1 para. 11 of the FSMA 2000.

[71] *See* P. Magnette, 'Towards "Accountable Independence"? Parliamentary Controls of the European Central Bank and the Rise of a New Democratic Model' (2000) 6(4) *European Law Journal* 326.

[72] For an account of the role of other European Agencies *see* E. Vos, 'Reforming the European Commission: What Role to Play for EU Agencies?' (2000) 37(5) *Common Market Law Review* 1113.

[73] *See* also J. Wouters, *Towards a European Securities Commission? Reflections in International and Transatlantic Perspective*, in this volume, *supra*.

[74] *See* Art. 108 (ex Art. 107) of the EC Treaty and Art. 7 of the ESCB Statute. Nonetheless, the extent of Council's intervention has led some to question the ECB's real political independence. *See* Magnette, *supra, op. cit.*, note 71, at 329.

[75] More recently CBI has been defined as independence that 'is beyond independence from political, executive and legislative power. It equates with independence from private or collective economic interests, autonomy versus the short term, frequently imposed by capital markets and, finally, freedom of action vis-à-vis the monetary policy of other central banks.' *See* L. Jospin, 'A Prime Ministerial View of Central Banks' (2000) 11(1) *Central Banking* 52 at 52.

[76] *See* P. Brentford, 'Constitutional Aspects of the Independence of the European Central Bank' (1998) 47 *International and Comparative Law Quarterly* 75 and L. Gormley and J. De Haan, 'The Democratic Deficit of the European Central Bank' (1996) 21 *European Law Review* 95.

European System of Central Banks and of the European Central Bank (hereinafter ESCB Statute) to observe specific objectives.[77] The acts or omissions of the ECB are open to review or interpretation by the ECJ.[78] Thus, judicial review guarantees that the ECB and the other organs of the Eurosystem follow the procedures that they are statutorily obliged to follow.

The degree of openness and transparency of the ECB's regulatory process is less than the degree of openness and transparency of the FSA's regulatory process. It is up to the ECB's discretion to publish its decisions, recommendations and opinions.[79] Openness and transparency in regulatory processes come from the British tradition. They cannot easily be accepted at European level, where the political bargaining is the most decisive factor for issues like which is the most appropriate legal and institutional regulatory framework for the regulation of economic activities.[80] The ECB's procedures are not an effective means to control the ECB's functions. The special arrangements (basically transparency and participation rights) are rather mis-used in the ECB's case.

Based on the above, and if the FSA's institutional model is accepted for the regulation and supervision of the markets, a centralised European regulatory agency for the governance of financial institutions and markets at EU level should be able to design and implement its regulatory process in a more open and transparent way than is currently established for the ECB and the ESCB. That means that such an agency should be independent not only from other Community institutions, but also from national authorities responsible for tackling regulatory matters over national financial institutions and markets. It also means that its procedures should be more open and transparent and it should also be guaranteed that such an agency closely co-operates with institutionalised market participants and especially end users.[81]

Such a type of an agency's vertical accountability should not be seen more as responsibility than as a type of the regulatory agency's responsiveness to the increased demands of liberalised financial markets (or market economy). The new democratic model[82] that academics are trying to build for the ECB and the ESCB might be very helpful in these respects.[83]

---

[77] It is the ESCB that is required to observe these objectives. *See* Art. 105 (ex Art. 105) of the EC Treaty and Arts 2 and 3 of the ESCB Statute.

[78] *See* Art. 35 of the ESCB Statute.

[79] *See* Art. 110 (2) (ex Art. 108a(2)) of the EC Treaty and Art. 34.2 of the ESCB Statute.

[80] *See* F. Hayek, *Law, Legislation and Liberty* (Routledge, London, 1963).

[81] That of course does not mean that such an agency will gain in powers and would be subject to capture by the interests of the regulated industry which it is going to be responsible for consulting. See a footnote number 12 in the essay by H.E. Jackson and E.J. Pan, 'Regulatory Competition in International Securities Markets: Evidence from Europe in 1999 – Part I' (2001) 56(2) *The Business Lawyer* 653 at 660 where they note that such a possibility has been observed as credible by two eminent academics (their argument is limited to securities markets though). It can be argued that the special arrangements that have been established in the FSA's case – like the objectives of regulation, greater openness and public participation – should get established and adopted first.

[82] *See* Magnette, *supra, op. cit.*, note 71, at pp. 337–339.

[83] In more theoretical terms it has been observed that 'an agency could develop as a focal point for policy-making, producing policy documents to which national agencies, citizens and NGOs could

Apart from the ECB, more recently the Committee of Wise Men on the Regulation of European Securities Markets stated the importance of special arrangements for the centralisation of the design, implementation, application and enforcement of regulatory standards for the governance of financial institutions and consolidated European exchanges. These procedural arrangements are the substitutes of traditional means of an agency's accountability. Some of the measures that have been developed in the FSA's legal framework are also observed in the Final Report of the Wise Men. Accordingly, the Committee suggested the importance of consultation[84] of a European Securities Committee with market participants[85] and end users for any measure of regulation that are due to adopt. Such an element is evidently an element that enhances the democratic legitimacy and accountability of the proposed Securities Committee.

## IV   ACCOUNTABILITY OF A SINGLE FINANCIAL SERVICES REGULATOR TO THE POLITICAL ORGANS OF A NATION STATE

Horizontal checks and balances are exercised over an agency by the political organs of a nation state. Thus, a national single financial services regulator is controlled directly by the main constitutional organs; the organs of the executive, the parliamentary and the judiciary branches of a national state. The organ of each respective branch of government is entitled to exercise powers of control over a regulatory agency. This control can be more effective if and when a specific procedure is followed. In reality this control is an institutional rather than procedural control over the agency. Specific procedures to exercise control should be followed by each individual branch of government.

In the FSA's case the institutional control is exercised by the government, especially through the checks and balances that are performed by the Treasury.[86] A Standing Committee of both of the Houses of the Parliament controls FSA's functions. The judiciary has the powers to subject FSA's decisions to judicial review.[87]

The institutional accountability of an agency is an important way of controlling regulatory practices. These mechanisms of horizontal accountability are mechanisms

---

contribute; in other words, its primary role would not be that of policing but to stimulate a policy network whose work could be fed into the formal policy-making process through the comitology.' *See* C. Harlow, 'The European Union', in R. Blackburn and R. Plant (eds), *Constitutional Reform- The Labour Government's Constitutional Reform Agenda* (Longman, London, 1999), 231 at 245.

[84] *See* Final Report of the Committee of Wise Men on *The Regulation of European Securities Markets* (Brussels, 15/2/2001), *supra, op. cit.*, note 14, at 25.

[85] Early and institutionalised involvement of market participants and consumers in the legislative process is strongly recommended. See Final Report of the Committee of Wise Men, *supra, op. cit.*, note 14, at 21.

[86] Most importantly the FSA has to submit its Annual Report to the Treasury. *See* Schedule 1, para. 10 of FSMA 2000.

[87] *See* above, note 55.

of influence that are exercised over a single regulatory agency more than constraint mechanisms. Institutional accountability guarantees that the FSA rules and processes are legitimate. The mechanisms of institutional accountability though are not sufficient to constraint political influences. As it is mentioned above influence rather than constraint is the main characteristic of the mechanisms of horizontal accountability.

The FSA's legal framework provides regulatory objectives for the constitutional organs to check and balance FSA's legislative functions. In many respects these regulatory objectives should be seen as means of diminishing the possibility of political influences. The FSA is also responsible for observing these objectives. But it must be accountable to the constitutional organs of the state to the extent that it manages to conform to its regulatory objectives.[88]

At European level the ECB's horizontal accountability is enhanced through the various means that have been developed to link it with other EU institutions. These institutions are the Parliament, the European Council and the Commission and other national authorities responsible for designing main policy guidelines and implementing measures that have been accepted at the centre. Monetary policy is performed at the centre of the European Union. Institutional balances of the European institutions are important safeguards for the implementation and democratisation of the centralised EU monetary policies. Thus, ECB's policies and principles are under scrutiny by European Parliamentary Committees.[89] Its budget is subject to Annual Review by the European Parliament and the Court of Auditors. All these measures enhance co-ordination of the Bank's policies with National Member States' policies without jeopardizing the former's political independence.[90]

Again the Committee of Wise Men suggested for the proposed European Securities Committee, a democratic and flexible environment that can be enhanced by the preservation of the appropriate institutional balance.[91]

V    THE ROLE OF JUDICIAL REVIEW OF THE DECISIONS OF A SINGLE FINANCIAL
SERVICES REGULATOR

The role of the courts in reviewing decisions of administrative bodies should be re-examined. Both at UK and EU level some credit should be given to the role of Courts in reviewing administrative decisions. This is related to the model of democracy that is currently accepted by modern states.

---

[88] It is the issue of the extent that the FSA is accountable to constitutional organs.

[89] *See* Art. 113 (ex Art. 109b) of the EC Treaty.

[90] *See* M. Everson, 'The Constitutional Law of the Euro? Disciplining European Governance', in P. Beaumont and N. Walker (eds), *Legal Framework of the Single European Currency* (Hart Publishing, Oxford-Portland, 1999), 119 at pp. 136–137.

[91] See Final Report of the Committee of Wise Men, *supra, op. cit.*, note 14, at 24, where they observe that the process 'would be democratic and flexible with the range and scope of implementing powers being defined by the Council of Ministers and the European Parliament by co-decision on a case by case basis for each level 1 proposal'.

It has been observed that 'the concept of governmental accountability to Parliament should not preclude the exercise of independent political authority by Courts, Tribunals or other bodies not accountable to democratic control'.[92] It has also been observed that 'a special governmental function for Courts is founded on their ability to determine whether the decisions of agencies of government have been made within the terms of those agencies' legal authority or whether necessary principles of natural justice have been complied with in decision-making'.[93]

The right balance between judicial review and effective administration should be of major concern. The possibilities of un-elected judges to intervene and judge policy considerations should be limited. In the FSA's case when judges intervene to evaluate the FSA's responsibility to observe its statutory objectives are not going to intervene in policy making decisions. And thus in the merits of the agency's decision. They are just going to apply the statute.[94]

It has been observed that the 'prime responsibility for exercising power and deciding what ought to be done lies with the administrative decision-maker. The Courts are concerned with ensuring that a decision-maker properly interprets the law, does not infringe one of the recognised public law principles governing the exercise of discretionary power (such as not having regard to irrelevant matters or not rigidly fettering the exercise of discretion) and follows a fair procedure in reaching a decision'.[95]

At European level, it has been observed that the ECB's democratic deficit can be alleviated through judicial review.[96] Professor Craig has described very clearly the substance of judicial review. He has observed that 'judicial propriety has been secured, ostensibly at least, by making sure that the Court' intervention is framed in terms of the *ultra vires* doctrine, the content of which is itself legitimated by invocation of legislative intent, thereby ensuring that there is, in formal terms, no clash with sovereignty. The Wednesbury test is the outgrowth of this pattern of thought, seeking to ensure that substantive judicial review does not transgress the cherished boundary between review and judgement on the merits'.[97]

---

[92] *See* A. Boyle, 'Sovereignty, Accountability and the Reform of Administrative Law' in G. Richardson and H. Genn (eds), *Administrative Law and Government Action, The Courts and Alternative Mechanisms of Review* (Clarendon Press, Oxford, 1994), 81 at 101.

[93] *See* R. Cotterrell 'Judicial Review and Legal Theory', in G. Richardson and H. Genn, *Administrative Law and Government Action, The Courts and Alternative Mechanisms of Review* (Clarendon Press, Oxford, 1994), 13 at 16.

[94] Even earlier the literature was concerned to what extent judges can intervene in the policy making part of an administrative agency's decisions. *See* R. Cranston, 'Reviewing Judicial Review', in G. Richardson and H. Genn (eds), *Administrative Law and Government Action, The Courts and Alternative Mechanisms of Review* (Clarendon Press, Oxford, 1994), 47 at 79 (he refers to the special problem of judicial deference).

[95] *See* C. Lewis, 'Judicial Review and the Role of the English Court in European Community Disputes', in M. Andenas and F. Jacobs (eds), *European Community Law in the English Courts*, (Clarendon Press, Oxford, 1998), 101 at 101.

[96] *See* P.P. Craig, 'EMU, the European Central Bank and Judicial Review', in P. Beaumont and N. Walker (eds), *Legal Framework of the Single European Currency* (Hart Publishing, Oxford, 1999), 95, (Craig, *EMU, the European Central Bank and Judicial Review*), at 95.

[97] *See* P. Craig, 'Substantive Legitimate Expectations and the Principles of Judicial Review', in M. Andenas (ed.), *English Public Law and the Common Law Of Europe* (Key Heaven Publications Plc, London, 1998), 23 (Craig, *Substantive Legitimate Expectations and the Principles of Judicial Review*), at 50.

The terms and procedures that apply for judicial review of decisions of EU policy making institutions apply in the ECB's case. Thus specific reasons should exist in order for an ECB's act to be subject to judicial review.[98] The specific applicant should show that he has a standing. Lastly, the applicant has to establish that the ECB has infringed one of the grounds of review that are set out in Art. 230 (2) (ex Art. 173 (2)) of the EC Treaty.[99]

## VI  CONCLUSIONS

The above discussion highlighted the transformation of basic legal concepts for the control of the controllers of financial activity. Apparently these transformations relate to the transformation of the role of national states at a regional and international level.[100]

Public and private law practices are intermingled to control the controllers of financial activity. In such an environment the control of the controllers is more effective if both the constitutional doctrines of the rule of law and the separation of power are preserved. On the other hand, the role of judicial review and remedies are re-valued and re-examined under a different perspective. It can be argued further to the above analysis that the traditional values of court interventions (either in the format of judicial review or in the form of remedies) should be restated in the current regimes of technocratic-executive governance and functional rather than representative democracies.

---

[98]  *See* Art. 230 (ex Art. 173 (1)) of the EC Treaty.
[99]  For more details *see* Craig, *EMU, the European Central Bank and Judicial Review, supra, op. cit.,* note 96, at pp. 100–112.
[100]  In political sciences this is associated to the 'hollowing out' thesis.

*Chapter 15*

# Financial Market Regulation in Germany: The New Institutional Framework

*Mads Andenas and Jens-Hinrich Binder*

## I  INTRODUCTION

The decision on the future organisation of German financial market regulation was made by the German Federal Parliament (the *Bundestag*) on 1 March 2002.[1] A new single financial regulator, the *Bundesanstalt für Finanzdienstleistungsaufsicht*, was established from 1 May 2002. The new body is responsible for the supervision of banking activities, the licensing of both credit institutions and securities firms, and the ongoing supervision of prudential standards firms formerly within the ambit of the Federal Banking Supervisory Office, the *Bundesaufsichtsamt für das Kreditwesen*, under the *Kreditwesengesetz* of 1961 (as amended, hereafter: the Banking Act).[2] Furthermore, the *Anstalt* will conduct the surveillance of the provision of investment services, which used to be performed by the Securities Supervisory Office (*Bundesaufsichtsamt für den Wertpapierhandel*) under the *Wertpapierhandelsgesetz* of 1998 ('the Securities Trading Act').[3] Finally, the agency licenses and supervises insurance firms and incorporates the functions of the Federal Insurance Supervisory Office (*Bundesaufsichtsamt für das Versicherungswesen*) under the *Versicherungsaufsichtsgesetz* of 1901 (as amended, 'the Insurance Supervision Act').[4]

The new agency, the result of a merger of the existing three federal agencies, marks the end of the predominantly functions-based structure at federal

---

[1]  And by the Second Chamber ('Bundesrat'), comprising of representatives of the 15 federal states, or 'Länder', on 22 March 2002. The Act has been published officially in the *Bundesgesetzblatt* (Federal Law Gazette) 2002-I, 1310. An English translation should soon become available at the new agency's website, <http://www.bafin.de>.

[2]  Now in force in the version of 9.9.1998, *Bundesgesetzblatt* 1998-I, p. 2776, as amended.

[3]  *Bundesgesetzblatt* 1998-I, p. 2708. An official translation, in addition to other relevant legal documents, is available at the Bundesaufsichtsamt's website at <http://www.bawe.de>.

[4]  For an in-depth comparison of the regulatory bodies and their functions, *see* R. Schmidt, in: Prölss and Schmidt (eds), *Versicherungsaufsichtsgesetz mit Europäischem Gemeinschaftsrecht und Recht der Bundesländer*, 11th edn, Munich (1997), Introduction, notes 136–149, with numerous further references. An English translation of the Act is available at <http://www.bav.bund.de/en/gesetze-und-verordnungen/vag/vag.pdf>.

*Mads Andenas and Yannis Avgerinos (eds), Financial Markets in Europe: Towards a Single Regulator?* 359–379.
© 2003 *Kluwer Law International. Printed in Great Britain.*

level. It continues to operate broadly within the existing statutory framework. The reform is confined to institutional aspects, and there will be no major amendments to the substantive regulatory laws. The new supervisory agency may eventually assume responsibilities for the monitoring of electronic trading platforms set up by foreign exchanges within Germany, under proposals for a reform of exchange supervision, released by the Federal Ministry for Finance in November 2001.[5] In principle, however, the reform will leave untouched the local Exchange Supervisory Bodies (*Börsenaufsichtsämter*) at *Länder* level, which are the listing authorities and supervise the trading process.[6] Similarly, local bodies at *Länder* level will remain responsible for the supervision of minor insurance firms of only regional relevance.

This chapter seeks to examine the changes to the regulatory structures in light of the perceived shortcomings of the existing regimes, as well as changes in the market environment that may have driven the reform process. The current institutional arrangements will be addressed first, as they form the setting within which the reform will be implemented. The ongoing reform discussion and the contents of the reform Bill will then be analysed. Although the final outcome of the legislative process is far from settled, this chapter will attempt to evaluate its merits and to discuss some specific problems that may arise in its implementation.

## II   THE REGULATORY LANDSCAPE UNTIL 2002

### A   Overview

As noted above, responsibility for financial markets regulation in Germany has been divided between three different agencies at federal level and Börsenaufsichtsbehörden (Exchange Supervision Bodies) in those of the Länder which host stock or commodities exchanges.[7] All three federal agencies are similar in terms of their legal character and organisation. All are separate 'Bundesoberbehörden' within the ambit of the Federal Ministry for Finance, that is, part of the federal administration.[8] They are accountable to and subject to directions issued by the Ministry, but enjoy a considerable degree of independence. The budget

---

[5] *See* the proposals for a 'Fourth Law for the Promotion of the Financial Markets in Germany': Federal Ministry for Finance, *Regierungsentwurf. Entwurf eines Gesetzes zur weiteren Fortentwicklung des Finanzplatzes Deutschland* (*Viertes Finanzmarktfördergesetz*), Art. 2 (amending the Securities Trading Act), Part 10. This issue appears to be highly contentious, and may become exposed to major amendments throughout the legislative process. Implementation of these proposals is, however, independent from the creation of a single regulatory agency as such.

[6] *See* H.-D. Assmann, in: Assmann and Schneider, *Wertpapierhandelsgesetz* 2nd edn (Kommentar, Cologne, 1999), Sec. 4 Securities Trading Act, notes 3–7.

[7] *See infra*, Sec. II C.

[8] *Cf.* Secs 5(1) Banking Act, 3(1) Securities Trading Act, 1 Gesetz über die Errichtung eines Bundesaufsichtsamtes für das Versicherungswesen (Law Establishing a Federal Insurance Supervisory Office).

of all three bodies respectively has been funded mostly by the industry and, to a minor extent, by the state.[9]

The decentralised structure reflects the diversified markets in which financial activities are still conducted in a number of federal states, even though Frankfurt emerged as the country's most important financial centre after World War II. Both exchanges and some important banking and insurance groups are located in cities such as Hamburg, Düsseldorf, and Munich. In this environment, German regulators have always had to cover a much wider range of places if they wanted to ensure supervision 'on site'. This is most obvious in the areas of banking supervision, which is in part conducted through the local branches of the *Bundesbank*, the *Landeszentralbanken*, and of exchange supervision, which lies traditionally with numerous authorities at *Länder* level.[10]

Historically, the regulatory focus at the federal level was exclusively on the prudential supervision of banks and insurance firms and, in addition, the monitoring of the trading process at the various exchanges. Consumer-related market conduct issues have only recently become subject to federal legislation, and have been heavily influenced by European directives and emerging international best practice. Traditionally, the relationship between customer and service providers would have been dealt with exclusively under general provisions in the relevant Private Law codifications, such as the Civil Code (*Bürgerliches Gesetzbuch*), the Commercial Code (*Handelsgesetzbuch*), and, more recently, the Unfair Standard Contract Terms Act (*Gesetz zur Regelung des Rechts der Allgemeinen Geschäftsbedingungen*), with no administrative interference.[11] In consequence, financial markets supervision has traditionally been more public law-oriented, and directed towards regulation in the public interest rather than the protection of individuals. In this system, the relationship between a provider of financial services and its clients or other providers would be determined by a set of refined principles of contract law as set out by the relevant statutes and case law. The enactment, in 1998, of a unified law on securities regulation and the creation of a federal agency responsible for the monitoring of the trading activities of investment firms are thus a new development which has led to a realignment of regulatory turf between federal institutions and the traditional Länder-based exchange supervisors.[12]

The regulatory landscape also reflects the traditional universal banking system within the country, in which the major banking institutions conduct retail, wholesale, and investment banking activities, and would also often engage in securities

---

[9] *Cf.* Secs 51(1) Banking Act: 90% of all costs to be financed by the industry; 11 Securities Trading Act, 101 Insurance Supervision Act.

[10] *See infra*, Sec. II B for further details.

[11] For a good introduction to the legal framework for banking activities generally, see K.J. Hopt, in A. Baumbach and Hopt (eds), *Handelsgesetzbuch, mit GmbH & Co., Handelsklauseln, Bank- und Börsenrecht, Transportrecht (ohne Seerecht)*, 30th edn, Munich (2000), Appendices 7 and 8.

[12] *Cf.*, for example, the provisions of the Securities Trading Act dealing with insider trading, disclosure requirements, and rules of conduct, *see* further *infra*, Sec. IIC. And *see* Schmidt, *loc. cit.*, notes 4 and 167 with regards to similar developments in the regulation of insurance businesses.

trading.[13] The Banking Supervisory Office is traditionally at the very centre of the regulatory framework, a position which is reflected by its extended competencies which include the prudential supervision of investment firms.[14]

## B   Banking regulation

Rigorous banking supervision through a separate government body, a *Bundesaufsichtsamt für das Kreditwesen*, has been a common feature in Germany since 1934, when the first Banking Act was enacted. The current legal and institutional framework dates back to 1961. From the war until then, banking supervision had been conducted by various authorities at Länder level, but within a framework that ensured inter-agency cooperation.

The adoption of rules-based regulatory arrangements replaced the principle of *Bankenfreiheit* (freedom of banking) that had prevailed ever since the Prussian *Gewerbeordnung* (the Commercial Code containing administrative and private law rules for the pursuit of commercial businesses which did not even mention credit institutions as a specific category). Almost 'modern' insofar as the regulatory objectives and administrative competencies were concerned, the adoption of the new model in 1934 marked a significant change in policy. It was driven by the experiences with the catastrophic banking crisis of the 1930s[15] which had brought further distress to the already severely shaken post-war and post-depression country and, in the public perception, necessitated a radical change in the attitude towards the conduct of banking activities.

Consequently, the *Reichskreditwesengesetz* [the 1934 Banking Act[16]] provided, *inter alia*, for the establishment of an *Aufsichtsamt für das Kreditwesen*,[17] introduced licensing requirements in connection with a minimum capital requirement for the

---

[13] For an introduction, *see* T. Baums and M. Gruson, 'The German Banking System – System of the Future?' (1993) 19 *Brooklyn Journal of International Law* 101; B. Mössinger-Vent, 'The German Banking System' (1991) *Journal of International Banking Law* 180 and 222.

[14] In addition to the banking and investments institutions named above, the Bundesaufsichtsamt's scope includes the supervision of the German equivalents to UK building societies (Bausparkassen, *see* the Bausparkassengesetz, BGBl 1991-I, 454, as amended), Mortgage Lenders (Hypothekenbanken, *see* the Hypothekenbankengesetz, BGBl 1998-I, 2674, as amended), as well as specialised Merchant Banks financing maritime activities (Schiffsbanken, *see* the Schiffsbankengesetz, BGBl 1963-I, 302, as amended). *See* further *infra*, text and note 23.

[15] As to an analysis of which *see*, for example, K.E. Born, *Die deutsche Bankenkrise 1931. Finanzen und Politik* (1967); K. Pleyer, 'Bankkrisen und die Vorgeschichte der Bankenaufsicht', in: *Festschrift der Rechtswissenschaftlichen Fakultät zur 600-Jahr-Feier der Universität zu Köln*, 1988, p. 115. The crisis was triggered by the crash of one of Germany's then six biggest banks, the *Darmstädter und Nationalbank* which failed, at least partly, due to a totally insufficient capital-to-assets ratio and consequential illiquidity after the realisation of large exposure lending risk.

[16] For a contemporary account of the 1934 Act and its origins from an English point of view *see* Allen, in: A.M. Allen, S.R. Cope, L.H. Dark and H.J. Witheridge (eds), *Commercial Banking Legislation and Control* (1938), p. 185.

[17] Note the conformity of the terminology with the modern Banking Act.

setting up of banking businesses, obliged banks to provide information about current business, including their respective liquidity ratio, and restricted large exposures.[18] Most of the new provisions had their roots in a series of emergency decrees by the *Reichspräsident*. These decrees, together with irregular bank holidays, had been issued in an attempt to restrain the effect of some 357 bank insolvencies between 1931 and 1932.[19]

The Banking Act of 1961 which, with several amendments, is still in force, is in many respects a direct successor of the 1934 Act and incorporates many of its provisions. Criticism of the 1934 Act and of the legislative and administrative approach to bank crises as a whole has been rare and the basic principles of regulation have remained virtually unchallenged ever since. This seems remarkable, considering that its 'model' (the 1934 Act) had passed parliament only after the National Socialists came into power in 1933.[20]

The 1961 Act has been subsequently changed on a number of occasions. These changes were partly triggered by internal developments, most notably by the the 1974 crash of the Cologne *Bankhaus Herstatt* which led to a substantial reinforcement of the Supervisory Authority's emergency powers.[21] The major part of the amendments, however, were initiated in view of incoming EC directives.[22]

Initially responsible only for the banking sector as such, or 'credit institutions' in the terminology of the Banking Act, the Federal Banking Supervisory Office has subsequently been entrusted also with the licensing and prudential supervision of investment firms.[23] This, again, reflects the close ties between the two sectors in the

---

[18] Similar to Secs 10, 11 of the modern Act, the Banking Act 1934 only formulated abstract criteria and empowered the supervisory body to develop more detailed conditions on the basis of which the banks' respective businesses would be evaluated, *see* Secs 11 and 16–7 of the 1934 Act and, for further discussion *infra*, Sec. III A 2.

[19] *Cf.* Born, *op. cit.*, note 15, p. 174.

[20] But *see* H. Linhardt, 'Kreditinstitute im Wettbewerb. Das Verhältnis von Landesaufsicht und Bundesaufsicht', (1957) *Wirtschaft und Wettbewerb* 3, p. 13, who argued that the Banking Act and the introduction of the new Supervisory Body reflected the regime's political motive to gain control over the credit sector as a key to the nation's industry as a whole. Criticism on that ground, however, has never been accepted by the majority of both legal scholars and practitioners. A contemporary English study of the 1934 Act describes its character 'as a compromise between a completely nationalised banking system and an entirely free one' (Allen, *loc. cit.*, note 16, p. 199) as well as an 'ingenious measure whereby the state is able both to safeguard the interests of the community and to use the banking system in the furtherance of its economic policy' (*ibid.*, pp. 223–224).

[21] *See* Secs 46a, 46b Banking Act and, for further details, E. Hüpkes, *The Legal Aspects of Bank Insolvency: A Comparative Analysis of Western Europe, the United States, and Canada* (2000), p. 57. The new provisions effectively introduced a system of controlled management as a means for crisis management, which is reinforced by a moratorium on the institution's liabilities and, to some extent, replaces insolvency proceedings.

[22] *See*, for example, the overview in V. Szagunn, U. Haug and W. Ergenzinger, *Gesetz über das Kreditwesen. Kommentar* (6th edn, Berlin and Cologne, 1997), Introduction Secs II, III; and, more recently, R. Meixner, 'Neuerungen im Bankenaufsichts- und Kapitalmarktrecht' (1998) *Neue Juristische Wochenschrift* 862.

[23] With the 6th amendment to the Banking Act in 1997, the Federal Banking Supervisory Office was formally entrusted with the prudential supervision of non-banking securities firms and thus became

traditional universal banking system in which both activities are to a large extent conducted by the same type of firms. Its formal role is to 'counteract undesirable developments in the banking and financial services sector which may endanger the safety of the assets entrusted to institutions, adversely affect the proper conduct of banking business or financial services or involve serious disadvantages for the national economy'.[24] Located first in Berlin and from the year 2000 in Bonn, the Banking Supervisory Office used to be a rather small administrative body directly responsible to the Ministry of Finance.[25] It had a staff of 520,[26] mostly civil servants and thus bound by the strict rules of public salaries in Germany.

Under the Banking Act, the Banking Supervisory Office was required to maintain close co-operation with the *Bundesbank*. Section 7 provides for an extensive exchange of information and makes broad derogations from different duties of confidentiality for this purpose. The Office's President could attend meetings of the *Bundesbank* Council 'whenever matters within his field of responsibility are discussed'.[27] Furthermore, the *Bundesbank* is closely involved in the development of prudential standards.[28] It is also the 'channel' through which the supervised institutions pass their statistical returns to the supervisory authority which ensures permanent information about market developments.[29]

## C   Securities regulation

### 1   Overview

Prior to 1994, capital markets regulation was seen as synonymous with legal rules governing the emission of stocks, and dealing in the same. These rules were contained in statutes such as the *Aktiengesetz* (Stock Companies Act), the *Börsengesetz* (Exchange Act), and, in part, in the Banking Act; responsibility for the supervision was exclusively with exchange supervisors at *Länder*-level without any federal interference.

---

responsible for the monitoring of all providers of financial services providers except insurance firms. The new law implemented the EC Directive on investment services in the securities field (Council Directive 1993/22/EEC of 10.5.1993, OJ L 141/27 of 11 June 1993, the Capital Adequacy Directive (Council Directive 93/6/EEC of 15.3.1993, OJ L 141/1 of 11.6.1993, on the capital adequacy of investment firms and credit institutions), as well as the so-called Post-BCCI-Directive (Council Directive 1995/26/EC of 29.6.1995, OJ L 168/7 of 18.7.1995, on the reinforcement of prudential supervision).

[24] Sec. 6 Banking Act.
[25] A Bundesoberbehörde, *see* Sec. 5(1) Banking Act.
[26] *See* <http://www.bakred.de/bakred/aboutus.htm>.
[27] Sec. 7(3) Banking Act.
[28] *See*, for example, Sec. 10(1) Banking Act for the capital adequacy 'Principles', Sec. 11 Banking Act for liquidity 'Principles' (as to the functions of such 'principles' *see supra*, note 18, and further *infra*, Sec. III A 2). Under these provisions, the Bundesbank has to be consulted in the drafting process, which results in close cooperation.
[29] *See*, for example, Deutsche Bundesbank, 'Die Mitwirkung der Deutschen Bundesbank an der Bankenaufsicht', in: *Bundesbank, Monatsbericht September 2000* (Monthly Report September 2000), 33, p. 37.

The role of regulation in this area was limited to ensure compliance with legal provisions concerning the listing procedure, admission of traders, and trading activities generally. Insider trading and investor protection were not regulated by statute, but left to self-regulation by the various German exchanges.[30] The first Exchange Act was enacted in 1896, in the aftermath of a major banking crisis in 1891 which had been triggered by highly speculative trading activities.[31] The system in place until 1994 emerged through a series of subsequent amendments to the Exchange Act, which did not, however, affect the general scope of regulation. Börsenaufsicht remained 'Rechtsaufsicht' (supervision with a view to compliance with institutional and trading requirements) rather than 'Marktaufsicht' (market supervision with a view to market conduct, including the prohibition of insider trading, and consumer protection).

The current system of securities regulation was then established in 1994, by the *Zweites Finanzmarktförderungsgesetz*.[32] In addition to the network of Länder-level exchange supervisors, the Federal Securities Supervisory Office was created, to 'counteract undesirable developments in securities trading which may adversely affect the orderly conduct of securities trading or provision of investment services or non-core investment services or which may result in serious disadvantages for the securities market'.[33] Under the new system, the federal agency became responsible for insider surveillance (including *ad hoc* disclosure of price-sensitive information),[34] compliance with notification and disclosure requirements in the event of changes in the percentage of voting rights in listed companies,[35] and compliance with the rules of conduct as set out by Sections 31 and 32 of the Act.[36] Supervisory competencies with regard to listing and trading, as well as other more technical aspects of the operation of exchanges remain with the respective authorities at Länder level.[37]

The move for a new concept of 'market supervision' independent from the operation of individual exchanges was motivated by external, notably EC-triggered influences. Germany faced the need to implement the Transparency Directive,[38] the

---

[30] For an overview in this respect, *see* the Exchange Supervisory Bodies' website at <http://www.boersenaufsicht.de>. From 1961 onwards, however, the Exchange Act contained certain disclosure requirements, *see* E. Schwark, *Börsengesetz. Kommentar zum Börsengesetz und zu den börsenrechtlichen Nebenbestimmungen*, Munich (1994), Introduction, note 11.

[31] *See*, generally, *id.* notes 1 *et seq.* For a more detailed account of the historic development of German exchanges generally, *see* H. Merkt, 'Zur Entwicklung des deutschen Börsenrechts von den Anfängen bis zum Zweiten Finanzmarktförderungsgesetz', in K.J. Hopt, B. Rudolph and H. Baum (eds): *Börsenreform. Eine ökonomische, rechtsvergleichende und rechtspolitische Untersuchung* (Stuttgart, 1997).

[32] Zweites Finanzmarktförderungsgesetz (Second Financial Market Promotion Act) 1994, *BGBl* 1994-I, 1749. For an account of subsequent amendments to the Securities Trading Act (in English) see the federal authority's website, <http://www.bawe.de/english/chron_e.htm>, and *see* Assmann, *loc. cit.*, note 6, Introduction, notes 29 *et seq.*

[33] Sec. 4(1) Securities Trading Act.

[34] Part 3 Securities Trading Act.

[35] Part 4 Securities Trading Act.

[36] Part 5 Securities Trading Act.

[37] *See*, generally, Assmann, *loc. cit.*, notes 6, 1 *et seq.*; Schwark, *loc. cit.*. notes 30, 32–52.

[38] Council Directive 88/627/EEC of 12.12.1988 on the information to be published when a major holding in a listed company is acquired or disposed of, OJ L 348/62 of 17.12.1988.

Insider Dealing Directive,[39] and the Securities Services Directive,[40] and it was felt that the complex new requirements and the consequential reduction of the existing self-regulatory mechanisms could not properly be dealt with at Länder level. Furthermore, a federal body was considered necessary in view of the increasing cross-border relations of German exchanges, which implied a need for a unified representation in international organisations such as IOSCO.[41]

## 2   *Exchange supervision*

Exchanges currently operate in nine of the 15 German Länder.[42] The responsible authorities vary from state to state, pursuant to Länder law, but are generally part of a Ministry.[43] Their activities under the Exchange Act 'shall extend to the compliance with exchange law provisions and orders and to the orderly conduct of exchange trading and the settlement of exchange transactions'.[44] In addition, each exchange is required under the Exchange Act to establish a Trading Supervisory Office (Handelsüberwachungsstelle), which bears part of the supervisory burden.[45] In particular, the Office 'shall systematically and completely record and evaluate data regarding exchange trading and the settlement of exchange transactions and shall conduct necessary investigations'.[46] It is an independent organ of the exchange itself, but cooperates closely with the Supervisory Authority on Länder level and has its own regulatory competencies.[47] A 'Wertpapierrat' (Securities Council) is to be established at each exchange. Its duties are defined by section 3 Exchange Act. They include '(1) the adoption of the Exchange Rules ('Börsenordnung'), (2) the appointment and removal of the members of the Board of Management in consultation with [the Länder-level authorities], and (3) the supervision of the Board of Management (...)'.[48] Neither of these bodies is responsible for the listing of securities, which is conducted by a Board of Admissions ('Zulassungsstelle') provided for by the Börsenordnung.[49]

---

[39] Council Directive 89/592/EEC of 13.11.1989 coordinating regulations on insider dealing, OJ L 334/30 of 18.11.1989.

[40] Council Directive 93/22/EEC of 10.5.1993 on investment service in the securities field (as amended), OJ L 141/27 of 11.6.1993.

[41] *See*, for further details, Federal Ministry of Finance, Discussion Paper *Konzept Finanzplatz Deutschland*, 6 January 1992 (reprint in [1992] *Wertpapiermitteilungen* 420).

[42] Hamburg, Bremen, Lower Saxony, Berlin, Saxony, Northrhine-Westphalia, Hesse, Bade-Wurttemberg, Bavaria.

[43] Under Sec. 1(1) Exchange Act, this has to be an Oberste Landesbehörde (an administrative body at Ministry level).

[44] Sec. 1(3) Exchange Act.

[45] Sec. 1b Exchange Act.

[46] Sec. 1b(1) Exchange Act.

[47] *See* Schwark, *op. cit.*, note 30, Introduction, note 23.

[48] Sec. 3(2) Exchange Act.

[49] Sec. 4(3) No. 2 Exchange Act. The admission procedure is set out in Secs 36–39 (Admission of Securities to Trading on an Exchange with Official Quotation), 50 (Admission to Options and Futures Trading), 71–74 (Admission of Securities to Exchange Trading with Non-Official Quotation).

In sum, unlike the area of banking supervision, the regulation of exchanges in the country still relies to a considerable extent on self-regulatory institutions. These are recognised by public law as integral parts of the regulatory structure and command considerable competencies. It should be noted, in this respect, that throughout all historic development to date, the German exchanges have retained their legal status as public law entities so that even decisions made by the self-regulatory organs of an exchange have a somewhat formal status and can rely on enforcement under public law.[50]

## 3   Federal securities regulation

By contrast, the surveillance of insider dealing and market conduct issues in its current structure has from its beginning been entrusted entirely to a public law body, the newly created Federal Securities Supervisory Office. It was established as an independent federal body pursuant to the Securities Trading Act. The authority used to be located in Frankfurt and employed some 140 staff.[51] Its functions are set out in Section 4(1) Securities Trading Act.[52] Within the agency, a Securities Council (*Wertpapierrat*) which comprises representatives of the *Länder*, the *Bundesbank*, and the Banking Supervisory Office has been created.[53] This premium 'assist(s) with supervision. It shall advise the Federal Securities Supervisory Office, in particular – (1) on issuing regulations and establishing guidelines for the supervisory activity of the Federal Securities Supervisory Office; (2) on the effects of supervisory issues on stock exchanges and market structures, and on competition in securities trading; and (3) on the demarcation of responsibilities between the Federal Securities Supervisory Office and [the *Länder*-level authorities]'.[54] The council has to report to the *Bundesaufsichtsamt* at least once a year.[55]

Under Section 6 Securities Trading Act, the Securities Supervisory Office had to maintain close co-operation with the relevant authorities at Länder-level, the Federal Banking Supervisory Office and the *Bundesbank*.[56] Upon request, the *Länder* authorities are required to act on behalf of the Federal Securities Supervisory Office, now the single Federal Regulator, 'in implementing urgent measures for monitoring the ban on insider dealing (...)'.[57] Furthermore, the federal agency is responsible for the coordination of supervisory policy and on-going supervision with the competent foreign authorities.[58]

---

[50] *Cf.*, for further discussion, Schwark, *op. cit.*, note 30, Sec. 1 Exchange Act, notes 14–19.

[51] *See*, for further details, <http://www.bawe.de>.

[52] *See supra*, text and note 33.

[53] Sec. 5(1) Securities Trading Act.

[54] Sec. 5(2) Securities Trading Act.

[55] *Ibid.*

[56] Sec. 6(5) Securities Trading Act provides for an automatic exchange of data between the Bundesbank and the Bundesaufsichtsamt.

[57] Sec. 6(2) Securities Trading Act.

[58] Sec. 7 Securities Trading Act.

## D   Insurance regulation

The primary competence for the supervision of insurance companies has been with the *Bundesaufsichtsamt für das Versicherungswesen*, which was created as an independent federal body under the Act Establishing a Federal Insurance Supervisory Office 1951.[59] It was located in Bonn, and had some 275 staff.[60] Minor insurance firms or associations with only regional operations are regulated by a number of *Versicherungsaufsichtsbehörden* at *Länder* level.[61]

The functions of the *Bundesaufsichtsamt* are set out in Section 81(1) Insurance Supervision Act. Its role is to ensure, inter alia, the 'orderly conduct of insurance businesses, including compliance with regulatory rules, rules governing the insurance contract, all other rules concerning the insured person (...)'. In short, the functions encompass both prudential supervision and monitoring of the market conduct.

## E   Interagency co-operation

As noted above, the regulatory bodies at the federal level were under a statutory obligation to cooperate with each other. However, the respective provisions do not generally provide detailed guidelines for such co-operation, the development of which was consequently left to agreements between the different bodies themselves. Traditionally, inter-agency co-operation had never been conducted on an institutionalised basis. The respective competencies were exercised separately, and communication took place *ad hoc* wherever and whenever it was deemed necessary. This changed on 3 November 2000, when the three Federal Aufsichtsämter, the Bundesbank and a representative of the Federal Ministry of Finance signed an agreement establishing a new *Forum für Finanzmarktaufsicht* [Forum for Financial Markets Supervision], a type of non-institutional, yet formal union of administrative institutions unknown in German public law.[62]

It was envisaged that meetings of the Forum would be conducted on a regular basis (at least twice a year) so as to allow on-going discussion of regulatory policy, concrete measures in cases where more than one regulator was involved, and suggestions for amendments to the legislative framework.[63] The Preamble to the agreement

---

[59] Gesetz über die Errichtung eines Bundesaufsichtsamtes für das Versicherungswesen of 31.7.1951 (*BGBl* 1951-I, 480), as amended on 16.11.1972 (*BGBl* 1972-I, 2097).

[60] *See*, for further details, <http://www.bav.bund.de/en/wir-ueber-uns/versicherungsaufsicht.html#2>.

[61] As to the legal and institutional frameworks respectively see Schmidt, *loc. cit.*, notes 4, 70–72, 76–93. According to the Federal Insurance Supervisory Office (*ibid.*), regional insurance businesses account for just 1.5 percent of the gross premia collected by the country's insurance sector. The competent authorities at *Länder* level are required to cooperate closely with the federal agency, *see* Sec. 152 Insurance Supervision Act.

[62] *See* 'Vereinbarung zur Zusammenarbeit zwischen dem Bundesaufsichtsamt für das Kreditwesen, dem Bundesaufsichtsamt für das Versicherungswesen, dem Bundesaufsichtsamt für den Wertpapierhandel und der Deutschen Bundesbank', available at <http://www.uni-leipzig.de/bankinstitut/dokumente/2000-11-03-01.pdf>.

[63] *Ibid.*, Sec. 4.

expressly refers to the changing circumstances in the financial markets. Closer and more formal inter-agency co-operation was seen as increasingly important, given the trend towards cross-sector conglomerates, closer links between market participants generally, and the consequential risks.[64]

## III INCOMING CHANGES: THE 2002 REFORM ACT

The new Act[65] consists of 22 articles, the first of which includes the draft Act Establishing an Integrated Financial Markets Supervisory Institution,[66] while the rest specifies the necessary amendments to the existing legislative framework. The Act itself will not be the relevant source of law for the on-going supervisory activities, which can be found in the new Act as set out by Art. 1 and the relevant statutes as amended by Arts 2–19.

### A Organisational issues

#### 1 Creation of a Bundesanstalt

The new regulatory body, the *Bundesanstalt*, is to be established under Art. 1, Sec. 1, from 1 May 2002. As a public law *Anstalt*, it will have an independent legal personality, but will be responsible to the Federal Ministry of Finance in respect of both legal and substantive issues.[67] The Anstalt will be located in both Frankfurt and Bonn; a reflection of the current situation, and partly due to arrangements made with respect to the transfer of the German Capital from Bonn to Berlin, in return for which Bonn was guaranteed certain administrative functions.[68]

The *Bundesanstalt* will be headed by a President, a Vice-President and three deputies (for Banking, Insurance and Securities Trading).[69] An Administrative Council (Verwaltungsrat) will be established, whose task will be to monitor and support the *Bundesanstalt*'s administration.[70] The Council will be chaired by representatives of the Ministry of Finance and will consist of representatives of other ministries, Parliamentarians, and representatives of the market participants.[71] The Bundesbank has the right to participate in its meetings, albeit without voting rights.[72]

---

[64] *Ibid.*, Preamble.

[65] *See supra*, note 1.

[66] The official short title is 'Finanzdienstleistungsaufsichtsgesetz'; as a matter of convenience, this part of the Act will hereafter be referred to by the German acronym 'FinDAG'.

[67] Sec. 2 FinDAG.

[68] *See* the explanatory notes to the Bill, which refer expressly to the 'Berlin/Bonn-Gesetz' of 26 April 1994, *BGBl* 1994-I, p. 918.

[69] Sec. 6 FinDAG.

[70] Sec. 7 FinDAG.

[71] In total 21 members, of which ten will be nominated by credit institutions, insurance firms and other providers of financial services, *see* Sec. 7(3) FinDAG.

[72] *Ibid.*

In addition, the *Bundesanstalt* will establish a Consulting Council (*Fachbeirat*) of 24 members, consisting of academic scholars, representatives of market participants, consumer organisations, and the Bundesbank.[73]

One major difference between the new and existing institutions will be the Bundesanstalt's staff structure. While most permanent personnel employed by the existing regulatory bodies are civil servants whose salaries are thus governed by restrictive public law rules, the new Act will allow more flexibility. The *Bundesanstalt* will be given the right to employ such civil servants,[74] but it can also have other employees who may receive salaries in excess of the restrictive civil service standards.[75]

Initially, it was envisaged that the administrative costs not only of the *Bundesanstalt* but also of the *Bundesbank* would be recovered in full by way of levies on the supervised institutions.[76] In order to avoid significant additional costs for the market participants, the relevant provisions were then amended so as to exclude administrative costs of the *Bundesbank*, while the *Bundesbank*'s costs will be recoverable in full.[77] This again will distinguish it from the existing mechanisms, whereby the institutions contribute only part of the overall cost incurred.

## 2    *Methods of supervision*

In principle, the reform as currently anticipated will leave untouched the armoury of regulatory competencies exercised by the three federal authorities under the respective legal framework. These include wide discretionary powers – generally in the form of the authorisation to issue 'directions' or 'orders'[78] to regulated institutions – which are then complemented by a range of more specific competencies, *inter alia* to gather information[79] and, if deemed necessary, to revoke the license of regulated institutions.[80] In addition, the Banking Act and the Insurance Supervision Act provide for detailed competencies with regard to financial crises in regulated institutions, in effect allowing gradual administrative interference with the affairs of troubled institutions and, to a considerable extent, substituting general insolvency law for that purpose.[81] However, the reform Bill does provide for the harmonisation of the current set of administrative sanctions available under the different laws,[82]

---

[73]  Sec. 8 FinDAG

[74]  Sec. 9 FinDAG.

[75]  *See* Sec. 10 FinDAG.

[76]  Secs 13–17 FinDAG (Bill, 1st version, as to which *see infra*, note 97). And *see supra*, text and note 9 for the present arrangements.

[77]  *See* Secs 13–16 FinDAG.

[78]  *See* Secs 6(2) Banking Act, 4(1) Securities Trading Act, 81(2) Insurance Supervision Act.

[79]  *See* Secs 24 (notification of specific events), 25 (monthly returns) and 26 (annual reports), 44 (request for further information and on-site inspections) Banking Act; 16 (insider dealing), 29(1) (general disclosure requirements), 35(1) (compliance with rules of conduct) Securities Trading Act; 83 Insurance Supervision Act. For the relationship between the Banking Supervisory Office and the Bundesbank concerning the processing of statistical information *see supra*, text and note 29.

[80]  Secs 35(2) Banking Act, 87 Insurance Supervision Act.

[81]  *See* Secs 45–46b Banking Act; 88, 89 Insurance Supervision Act. And *see supra*, text and note 22.

[82]  *See* Sec. 17 FinDAG.

while the criminal sanctions for contraventions of the regulatory requirements will continue to be determined by the relevant statutes.[83]

The new *Bundesanstalt* will also continue to enjoy the various rule-making competencies in place under the respective statures. Under a number of provisions in the Banking Act, the Insurance Supervision Act and the Exchange Act, the supervisory bodies are empowered to issue sub-delegated secondary legislation in the form of 'Rechtsverordnungen' (comparable to statutory instruments in UK law).[84]

Furthermore, the agency will retain the right to issue 'soft law' instruments, such as 'guidances' or 'principles'. An important example for these can be found in Secs 10 and 11 Banking Act, which provide for the issuance of 'principles' interpreting the provisions' abstract criteria for capital adequacy and liquidity standards.[85] While these so-called 'principles' are not legally binding stricto sensu, particularly not in relation to courts, they indicate how the Supervisory Office will exercise its discretion under the Act, for example, with respect to corrective action under Sec. 45 Banking Act.[86] However, under the *Gleichheitsgrundsatz* [the Principle of Equality], which is founded in Art. 3 of the *Grundgesetz* (the German Constitution), the Supervisory Office is bound to apply these principles to all credit institutions in the same way so that, in effect, they might be characterised as 'quasi binding'.[87]

### 3 Future role of the Bundesbank and the Forum für Finanzmarktaufsicht

In principle, the new law does not affect the mechanisms for the coordination of supervisory activities with the *Bundesbank*. Indeed, the current *Forum für Finanzmarktaufsicht*[88] will be given a formal status,[89] and the Bundesbank's competencies in particular under the Banking Act will be more refined.[90] In response to a suggestion submitted by the European Central Bank (ECB),[91] the Forum will be assigned advisory functions also with regard to the stability of the financial markets generally.[92] The Bundesbank will remain an integral part of the conduct of banking supervision in Germany. It will be closely involved in the collection of information about market participants, and its local branches, the *Landeszentralbanken*, will

---

[83] *See*, for example, Secs 56 Banking Act, 38, 39 Securities Trading Act.

[84] *See*, for example, Secs 22, 24, 31 Banking Act; 9, 11, 34, 34a, 35 Securities Trading Act.

[85] For further examples see the powers of the Federal Securities Supervisory Office to issue guidances and guidelines under the Securities Trading Act, for example, Secs 29(1), 35(6) Securities Trading Act. *See*, for further discussion in this respect, Assmann, *loc.cit.*, note 6, notes 22–28.

[86] *See*, for example, F. Reischauer and J. Kleinhans, *KWG. Loseblattkommentar für die Praxis*, Berlin (1995), Sec. 45 Banking Act note 1; Lindemann, in: Boos *et al.* (eds), *Kreditwesengesetz. Kommentar zu KWG und Ausführungsvorschriften*, Munich (2000), Sec. 45 Banking Act note 6.

[87] *See* Lindemann, *ibid.*

[88] As to which *see supra*, Sec. II E.

[89] *See* Sec. 3 FinDAG.

[90] *Cf.*, for example, Art. 2, nos. 9 (amendments to Sec. 7 Banking Act), 46 (amendments to Sec. 44 Banking Act) FinDAG.

[91] ECB, Opinion of 8 November 2001 (*infra*, text note 101), in particular paras 5–10.

[92] *See* Sec. 3, sentence 5 FinDAG.

remain the supervisory 'watchdog' in the regions. When it decides to order on-site inspections, the *Bundesanstalt* will be empowered to do this through the *Bundesbank* and its local branches.[93]

Unlike, for example, the United Kingdom, Germany has never had a tradition of 'lender of last resort' operations on the part of the central bank, other than in respect of ordinary liquidity support to the banking sector on a day-to-day basis. However, following the crash of Bankhaus Herstatt in 1974, the *Bundesbank* (as a majority shareholder) and major market participants set up the so-called *Liquiditäts–Konsortialbank* as an institutionalised lender of last resort.[94] This institution is partly financed by the banking sector, so that in the case of a banking failure where support is granted, the financial burden does not lie only with the taxpayer.[95] One of the rare occasions on which this mechanisms was applied was the successful reorganisation of the SMH-Bank in 1983.[96] This arrangement will persist, so that the *Bundesbank* – in its capacity as part of the European System of Central Banks – will continue to play an important role not only with regards to day-to-day supervision but also in the set-up of measures in extraordinary crises.

## B   History and rationale

The legislative process has been long and burdensome. First announced by the Federal Minister for Finance on 25 January 2001, the proposals and the first draft of the reform Bill[97] faced criticism in particular because of its close ties with a structural overhaul of the country's central bank, the *Bundesbank*. Motivated largely by the need to redefine the *Bundesbank*'s structure following the transfer of most of its monetary competencies to the ECB in 1998, the Government's plans for a structural reform of the *Bundesbank* have proved extremely controversial both within the *Bundesbank* and throughout the political discussion. For constitutional reasons, the

---

[93] *Ibid.*

[94] *See* Carl Theodor Samm, '*Zur Novellierung des Kreditwesengesetzes*', in: [1976] *Österreichisches Bankenarchiv* 308, p. 312.

[95] *Cf.* the statement of the President of the *Bundesbank*, Ernst Welteke, in H. Engler and J. Essinger (eds), *The Future of Banking* (London, 2000), p. 304.

[96] SMH (an acronym for the merged private banks of Schroeder, Münchmeyer, Hengst & Co.) went into deep waters in 1983. Following informal meetings of the Supervisory Body, the *Bundesbank* and the major German banks, the main creditors agreed to provide further liquidity. Formal insolvency proceedings were prevented and the bank was taken over by a foreign institution. For an account of the case, *see* T. Kramer, *Der SMH-Fall. Eine Fallstudie an Hand von Presseveröffentlichungen* (1985).

[97] Released on 25 January 2001, *see*: *Bundesministerium der Finanzen* (Federal Ministry of Finance), *Gesetzentwurf der Bundesregierung: Gesetz zur Schaffung einer integrierten Finanzmarktaufsicht (Finanzdienstleistungs- und Finanzmarktaufsichtsgesetz*. The Bill, including a detailed set of explanatory notes, is available at <http://www.bundesfinanzministerium.de/fach/abteilungen/geldkred/fdag.pdf>. The draft Bill for the reform of the *Bundesbank* was released on the same day (<http://www.bundesfinanzministerium.de/fachveroeff/AbtVII/BBkGdoc.zip>). A more recent version has been published as *Bundestags-Drucksache* 14/7033, available (in German only) at <http://www.bundestag.de>. The explanatory notes will hereafter be quoted in the first version; the second version has not brought any relevant amendments in this respect.

consent of the Federal States was necessary,[98] which was granted only following major concessions with regard to the decentralised decision-making arrangements within the *Bundesbank*.

As both legislative projects are closely linked, not only technically but certainly in scope, and as both are treated by the Government as two pillars of a single reform project, the ensuing delays also affected the creation of a single financial regulator.[99] With the on-going participation of the *Bundesbank* in the supervisory process secured, the Bank's governing council, the *Zentralbankrat* eventually declared its support for the reform proposals, albeit by a narrow majority and under a number of conditions.[100] Despite its declared preference for the combination of monetary and banking supervisory functions, the reform plans have also been endorsed in principle by the European Central Bank.[101]

The project of regulatory reform within Germany has a long history. Earlier efforts had been made to reform the institutional arrangement for the supervision of the German exchanges, when, in 1996, the Federal Ministry of Finance commissioned an extensive report on the structure and regulation of the German exchanges. Following a major analysis and based on extensive comparative studies, two scholars, Professors Hopt and Rudolph recommend the streamlining and centralisation of the supervision of exchange trading, as well as the creation of unified *Handelsüberwachungsstellen* for the conduct of on-site supervision of day-to-day trading. After an extensive debate, however, these suggestions were not pursued any further,[102] although a number of important suggestions submitted in their report may now be introduced with the Fourth Law on the Promotion of Financial Markets in Germany.[103]

More influential proved to be the recommendations submitted by an expert committee (the Pöhl Committee) chaired by Karl Otto Pöhl, a former President of the *Bundesbank*.[104] Among other proposals for a more streamlined structure of the

---

[98] On the Constitutional implications of the reform project *see* further Binder and Andenas, *supra*, note

[99] For an account of the debate following the announcement of the reform proposals see Binder and Andenas, supra, note, text and notes. 2–4.

[100] *See* Bundesbank, 'Pressenotiz: Stellungnahme des Zentralbankrats der Deutschen Bundesbank zur Reform der Bundesbankstruktur und der Finanzaufsicht' (available in German only), press release dated 23 March 2001 <http://www.bundesbank.de/de/presse/pressenotizen/archiv01/pdf/pr230301.pdf>.

[101] *Cf.*, with regard to the alignment of supervisory functions generally, ECB, *The Role of Central Banks in Prudential Supervision* (ECB 2001; <http://www.ecb.int/pub/pdf/prudentialsupcbrole_en.pdf>) and, specifically with respect to the proposed creation of a single regulator, ECB, 'Opinion of the European Central Bank of 8 November 2001 at the request of the German Ministry of Finance on a draft law establishing an integrated financial services supervision' (ECB 2001, <http://www.ecb.int/pub/legal/con200135_en.pdf>). See further, on the German reform proposals ECB, 'Opinion of the European Central Bank of 2 August 2001 at the request of the German Ministry of Finance on draft Seventh Law amending the Deutsche Bundesbank Act' (ECB 2001, <http://www.ecb.int/pub/legal/op0117en.pdf>).

[102] *See*, with further references, Andenas and Binder, *supra*, note 3.

[103] *Supra*, note 5. As these amendments will deal primarily with the legal framework for exchange supervision, they are of no interest in this context.

[104] *See* K.O. Pöhl *et al.*, 'Bericht zur Strukturreform der Deutschen Bundesbank' (4 July 2000), <http://www.uni-leipzig.de/bankinstitut/dokumente/2000-07-04-01.pdf>.

Bundesbank and the network of its *Länder* branches, the *Landeszentralbanken*, the Committee recommended the transfer of all banking supervisory powers to the *Bundesbank* and the subsequent dissolution of the *Bundesaufsichtsamt für das Kreditwesen*. With regard to the area of banking supervision, the Committee argued that the changing structure of capital markets and their increasing macroeconomic importance generally rendered a combination of monetary and supervisory competencies desirable. The conduct of monetary operations in which the Bank participated would benefit from more comprehensive information about the banking sector. On the other hand, the growing influence of capital markets on the overall economic structure necessitated careful liquidity precautions, which would be facilitated by the concentration of functions.[105] In addition, the report referred to the Bank's existing supervisory functions, which – in addition to its function as 'lender of last resort' – [106] further illustrated the close link between regulatory and monetary functions.[107] The findings of the Pöhl Committee were later adopted by the *Bundesbank*.[108]

Though challenged by some authors, the Pöhl Committee's recommendations became the basis for much of the subsequent discussion. Consequently, the general expectation prior to the announcement of the creation of a single financial regulator was that the forthcoming reform would result in the transfer of banking supervisory functions to a newly structured *Bundesbank*, while the regulatory arrangements for other sectors of the financial industry would remain largely unchanged. Throughout the better part of the consultations, a complete overhaul of markets supervision seems to have been totally out of question. Similarly, the creation of a single regulator which would comprise all existing federal regulatory bodies was not even mentioned in a study commissioned by the Federal Ministry for Finance on the Constitutional implications of a number of alternative institutional models.[109] Until the Government decided otherwise, it appeared, therefore, that the transfer of banking supervisory powers to the *Bundesbank* would almost certainly become reality.[110]

Why precisely the change of policy occurred cannot be ascertained from the available public statements. From both the timing and a number of parallels in the official explanations it would appear, however, that the reform may well represent, at least to some extent, an attempt to replicate the creation of the Financial Services Authority in the United Kingdom, albeit in a rather restricted and far less ambitious way. Instead of pursuing further the concept of a combination of monetary and supervisory

---

[105] *Ibid.*, Sec. 4.5.

[106] As to which *see supra*, Sec. III A 3.

[107] Pöhl Committee Report, *loc. cit.*, note 104, Sec. 5.6.

[108] *See Bundesbank, loc. cit.*, note 29, pp. 43–45.

[109] *See* W. Heun, 'Rechtsgutachten zur verfassungsrechtlichen Zulässigkeit verschiedener Organisationsmodelle zur Umgestaltung der Bankenaufsicht' (5 September 2000), <http://www.uni-leipzig.de/bankinstitut/dokumente/2000-09-05-01.pdf>.

[110] *See*, for example, U. Häde, 'Bankenaufsicht und Grundgesetz. Zur Übertragung von Aufgaben auf bestehende Bundesbehörden nach Art. 87 Abs. 3 GG' (2001) *Juristenzeitung* 105, pp. 108 *et seq.* The paper, which discussed the constitutional impacts of what was commonly regarded as the most probable solution, was published only a week after the Government's announcement, which is therefore not yet taken into account.

functions, the official explanations focussed on the need for structural reform in view of a changing market environment, which was to be reflected in the structure of the regulatory framework.

As the lines between the various sectors of financial services became increasingly blurred, an integrated supervisory body was the appropriate legislative answer to this problem. In recent years, financial service providers other than banks had increasingly provided services traditionally reserved for banks, while banks had expanded in the areas formerly occupied by insurance and securities firms. In consequence, all sectors were competing with each other, offering similar or even identical financial products through comparable sales structures.[111] New forms of pension funding would lead to further convergence across the sectors.[112] Moreover, there were close ties between the different sectors already in place. In this context, the explanatory notes to the Bill refer expressly to the merger, in 2001, of *Dresdner Bank* and the *Allianz* insurance group, which has created the first 'bancassurance' group in Germany.[113] All these developments also necessitated convergence on the part of the regulatory bodies.

Apart from structural policy considerations, the notes reflect the Government's desire for operational improvements and increased efficiency, particularly in view of the incoming challenges effected by the new Basle capital adequacy requirements. Evidently, the amendments to the structure of salaries payable to highly qualified banking experts within the new regulatory body have played an important part in the reform discussions in this respect. At the same time, however, the overall cost for the regulatees is expected to decrease, given the possible synergies effected by the merger.[114]

IV  EVALUATION

The explanatory notes accompanying the Bill advocate the application of equal rules to all providers of financial services regardless of traditional boundaries between the various sectors.[115] This would appear to be in contrast to the proposed maintenance of the existing legislative framework for the actual administrative performance of supervisory functions. Like the British Financial Services Authority before the implementation of the Financial Services and Markets Act 2000, the new *Bundesanstalt* will continue to operate under the current statutes which, as noted above, are largely structured along traditional sectorial lines but that also have a functions-based division of supervisory responsibilities. It remains to be seen whether this arrangement will remain effective, or whether a more substantial reform similar to the one implemented within the United Kingdom will follow. It seems that a more

---

[111] *See* Explanatory Notes, *supra*, note 97, pp. 76–77.
[112] *Ibid.*, p. 77.
[113] *Ibid.*, p. 78.
[114] *Ibid.*, p. 79.
[115] *Ibid.*, p.78.

substantial UK-style harmonisation is not too likely to occur in the present situation. The discussion has always revolved around *institutional* deficiencies of the current supervisory structure and potential remedies in this respect, rather than focussing on the actual administrative competencies of the three existing supervisory agencies. Unlike the United Kingdom, the German system has not recently met any challenges similar to those caused by major failures such as *BCCI* or *Barings*. Those events not only highlighted institutional defects but also led to a complete redesign in the supervisory competencies. No such need was felt in Germany where regulatory failures in recent history have been perceived to be due to a lack of resources rather than to an insufficient legislative basis for action.[116] In short, and judged only from past supervisory experience, there appears to be little pressure for a fundamental reform similar to that brought about by the FSMA 2000.

It may be asked if the maintenance of the diverse legislative framework for the conduct of day-to-day supervision may still compromise a real integration of regulatory functions and defeat the fundamental objective of the proposed reform. It certainly will prevent the application of really equal rules (however defined) to all regulated but, as has been noted with regard to the regulatory reform within the United Kingdom,[117] that objective may well prove illusory anyway. Prudential supervision – with regard to systemic stability as in the case of banks or just to the safety and soundness of individual institutions as in the case of insurance firms – will continue to be different from consumer- and market conduct-related regulation both in scope and supervisory techniques. Even the UK Financial Services and Markets Act, as an example for truly integrated legislative arrangements, contains specific provisions with regard to certain types of financial services while other provisions, although not expressly reserved for specific firms, are unlikely to be applied to others.[118] Differences between different types of service providers continue to be effective despite growing convergence on the financial markets. Whether or not these differences would advocate a more objective-based institutional approach rather than an integrated structure of regulatory authorities,[119] remains an open question. Yet they would not actually *preclude*

---

[116] The administrative armoury for prudential supervision of banks and securities houses under the Banking Act, for example, had been upgraded in the 1970s and 1980s, following the *Herstatt* crisis in 1974 and also influenced by incoming EC legislation, *see supra*, text and notes 21, 22. It is widely believed to provide a satisfactory basis for both early remedial action and crisis management on the part of the regulatory body. Similarly, the competencies provided for under the Securities Trading Act have not been found wanting. As for the prudential supervision of insurance firms, no failure has occurred in recent years, *Cf.* Peter Henning, *Die Zwangsliquidation von Versicherungsunternehmen…*, Karlsruhe (1998), pp.7–8.

[117] *Cf.*, David Llewellyn, 'The Economic Rationale for Financial Regulation', *FSA Occasional Paper* No. 1 (Financial Services Authority, London, April 1999), pp. 9–10.

[118] *Cf.*, for example, Sec. 48 of the Act with regard to 'Assets requirements', including the appointment of a trustee in case the respective institution holds assets on behalf of consumers.

[119] *Cf.*, Michael Taylor, *'Twin Peaks': A Regulatory Structure for the New Century* (Centre for the Study of Financial Innovation, London, December 1995); idem, *Peak Practice: How to Reform the UK's Regulatory System*, (Centre for the Study of Financial Innovation, London, October 1996). In view of the fundamental differences between systemic prudential protection and consumer protection objectives, Taylor proposes

integration of regulatory functions *to the extent possible*, as demonstrated by the Financial Services Authority in the United Kingdom. If the existing arrangements merely reflect the inherent differences between the respective requirements for the supervision of various types of financial services and their providers, an integrated agency may still prove workable although it operates under different statutory frameworks. In the German context, the existing delineation of supervisory competencies is indeed to a considerable extent functions-based rather than purely structured along the boundaries of traditional sectors. The regulatory functions performed under this legislation as it has evolved over the years may appear to be inherently less duplicative than a purely sector-based model – and thus generally suited for application by an integrated supervisory body.

The question appears to be whether, in view of the proposals outlined in the Bill, the forthcoming reform is indeed likely to generate the expected increase in regulatory efficiency and effectiveness by facilitating the conduct of intrinsically distinct functions by a single agency. If not, an objective-based separation of competencies may represent a preferable alternative. The potential benefits which a single regulatory body may yield have repeatedly been discussed in the academic literature, both from an economic and a legal point of view,[120] and it would not appear necessary to add to that theoretical debate. However, the German model will certainly have to be tested in this respect, and, although much will depend on the actual implementation of the changes by the staff involved, it would seem appropriate to ask whether the proposed legislative framework really allows for the expected benefits.

First, the new integrated structure will only to some extent really 'mirror' the market. Although the explanatory notes stress the emergence of a more and more integrated market for financial products and, in consequence, the blurring of boundaries between traditional sectors,[121] institutional 'bancassurance' is not a common phenomenon in the German financial system.[122] Although the links between banks and insurance companies have traditionally been close, they never really went beyond mere cross-ownership and the provision of certain combined bank-insurance services.[123]

---

the adoption of a two-tier regulatory structure responsible for both aspects respectively. *See*, for further discussion, Christos Hadjiemmanuil, 'Institutional Structure of Financial Regulation: A Trend Towards "Megaregulators?"', also published in this volume.

[120] *See*, for example, Charles Goodhart *et al.*, *Financial Regulation: Why, how and where now?* (London/New York, 1998), p. 152; Joseph J. Norton, *Financial Sector Law Reform in Emerging Economies* (London, 2000), pp. 112 *et seq.*; Clive Briault, 'The Rationale for a Single Financial Services Regulator', *FSA Occasional Paper* No. 1 (Financial Services Authority, London, May 1999), pp. 18–26; Karel Lannoo, 'Financial Supervision in EMU' [1998] *Yearbook of International Financial and Economic Law* 145, Sec. II.B, and, for a more recent discussion, Hadjiemmanuil, *ibid*, note 119. The analysis presented here follows the latter text insofar as the list of the perceived advantages of an integrated model is concerned.

[121] Explanatory notes, *loc. cit.*, note 97, p. 77.

[122] For an account of recent tendencies in this area and the supervisory consequences, *see* Schmidt, *loc. cit.*, notes 4, at 137, 144 *et seq.*

[123] *See*, for further details, Schmidt, *loc. cit.*, notes 4, 137–8.

The merger between *Allianz* and *Dresdner Bank*, and a closer tie between *Munich Re* and *HypoVereinsbank*,[124] have created the only entities of that kind within the country, and the prospects for further moves to that direction are far from settled. It may indeed be the case that further convergence may come from the recent reform of the pensions system within the country, which increases the trend towards more integrated financial products combining elements of traditional banking, investment and insurance activities. An integrated supervisory agency may then indeed prove beneficial in scope – even though licensing and the on-going supervisory assessment of the provider's conduct will continue to be based on different regulatory criteria.

Second, the question is whether integration may also yield benefits in terms of achieving a more coherent regulatory net and avoiding jurisdictional gaps as well as regulatory overlap. In this respect, the result seems more doubtful, not least because under the present system the elements of *prudential* supervision are rather clearly allocated to only two[125] rather than a sector-based multitude of regulatory agencies which already prevents overlapping jurisdictions to a significant extent. Similarly, it is unclear whether the new arrangement will lead to improved coherence with regard to the criteria for licensing and ongoing supervision – again because different types of enterprises will continue to exist and have to be evaluated under different criteria. On the other hand, an integrated authority may prove particularly advantageous to the emerging bankassurance groups which fall within the ambit of both banking and insurance supervision.

The most probable effect could be a combination of beneficial economies of scale and scope in the pursuit of the different supervisory functions from under a 'common roof', involving, not least, an improved flux of information between the responsible departments of the agency. The need for such improvement could be seen as illustrated by the establishment of the *Forum für Finanzaufsicht* mentioned above,[126] which already served the purpose of furthering inter-agency co-operation. In principle, this objective may well be served even better through a full-scale merger. However, while the UK Financial Services Authority has meanwhile moved from a sector-based to a more functions-oriented internal organisation,[127] a similar move within the new German *Bundesanstalt* will certainly face obstacles caused by the maintenance of the existing locations in Bonn and Frankfurt. This political compromise effectively means that the agency will not really be operating under 'one roof', and the relevant staff will continue to be resident and operating in different locations which could severely hamper internal integration and thus compromise the legislative objectives.

---

[124] *See*, for example, Anonymous, 'Let the revolution begin', *The Economist* (7 April 2001), p. 101. There have been attempted mergers between banks and insurance groups before, but thus far this model has been unsuccessful.

[125] Namely the banking and the insurance supervisory authorities.

[126] *See supra*, Sec. II E.

[127] *Cf.*, Financial Services Authority, *Plan & Budget 2001/2*, <http://www.fsa.gov.uk/pubs/management/PB2001_02.pdf>, p. 56.

One clear advantage, however, will be that the *Bundesanstalt* will be free from the restrictive employment regulations applicable to the existing three bodies. The new framework will allow for far more attractive working conditions which may well attract more qualified personnel and thus improve performance. This effect is independent from the concept of integration as such and could also have been achieved equally as well either through the transformation of the existing bodies into separate *Anstalten* or through the transfer of supervisory functions to the *Bundesbank*, which also operates under a less restrictive regime.

At any rate, Germany will probably continue to have a diversified regulatory structure, partly due to its Federal traditions and economic structure, as the *Länder* will maintain their competencies with regard to the supervision of trading at the various exchanges. With regard to the substantive rules for financial regulation within the country, the Government does not yet appear to anticipate any major changes to the existing statutory framework.[128] Given that the current statutory competencies have not proven to be insufficient in any major crisis in recent years, remedies for the unsatisfactory split of locations and, in consequence, a more flexible framework for the internal integration of regulatory functions may indeed be far more urgent than harmonisation of the administrative armoury for the supervision of the financial markets as such. Yet practitioners have criticised the existing laws of being far too complex and unsystematic,[129] so that a reform of more substantive issues may follow in due course. The ECB, at any rate, has expressly encouraged such a move.[130]

---

[128] *Cf.*, Explanatory Notes (*loc. cit.*, note 97), p. 79.

[129] *See*, for example, J. Marwede, 'Die sechs goldenen Regeln der Bankenaufsicht', in M. Lutter, M. Scholz and W. Sigle (eds), *Festschrift für Martin Peltzer zum 70. Geburtstag* (2001), 301.

[130] *See* ECB, Opinion of 8 November 2001, *supra*, note 101, para. 4.

*Chapter 16*

# Twin Peaks *à la francaise*: Reforming Financial Services Regulation in France[1]

*Duncan Fairgrieve*

## 1 INTRODUCTION

Traditionally, financial supervision has been organised along sectoral lines with specialist agencies responsible for supervising the banking, securities, and insurance sectors. Over the last few years, there has been a growing tendency for countries to move towards a more integrated approach. Debate has been heightened in Europe in recent times with the move in the United Kingdom towards an entirely unified model.

Although the UK's Financial Services Authority (FSA) is not the first single authority,[2] it is the first such development in a major international financial centre. It is for this reason perhaps that the FSA has become the most prominent example of an integrated financial sector supervisory agency. It seems also to have been something of a trend-setter. Amongst the trend-followers one can name Austria,[3] and Finland, with Germany as a heavy-weight partial adherent to the *mode*.[4] The single regulator would seem to be the institution of choice for the new era of supervision and regulation.[5]

The worldwide zest for reform has not gone unnoticed in France. Indeed, plans are afoot to streamline the current regulatory system. It is instructive to examine the present architecture of financial regulation in France, the weaknesses that this presents, and the reforms which have been proposed. Such an analysis illustrates the complexities of this area of the law, and highlights the fact that in designing a regulatory system a number of competing concerns and objectives are at work. The need to find an appropriate architecture has challenged traditional legal concepts.

---

[1] I am very grateful for comments on an earlier draft of this chapter by Professor Martine Lombard, Professeur à l'Université de Paris II Panthéon-Assas, and Monsieur Pierre-Henri Conac, Maître de Conférences, L'Université de Paris I, Panthéon-Sorbonne.

[2] *See* Gorton, 'The Swedish Financial Market in a Legal Perspective' and Lau Hansen, 'Developing a Single Financial Regulator: the Experience of Denmark', in Andenas and Avgerinos (eds), *Financial Market Supervision In Europe: Towards A Single Regulator?* (forthcoming).

[3] 'Auch Österreich plant Allfinanzaufsicht', in *Frankfurter Allgemeine Zeitung* (23 March 2001), p. 14.

[4] *See* Andenas and Binder, 'German Financial Reform: the Single Regulator and the European Dimension', in Andenas and Avgerinos (eds), *Financial Market Supervision In Europe: Towards A Single Regulator?* (forthcoming).

[5] Transition countries have also warmed to this model. Estonia has just established a Financial Supervisory Authority (legislation passed by Parliament on 9 May 2001) which will unify banking, insurance and securities regulation within one authority.

*Mads Andenas and Yannis Avgerinos (eds), Financial Markets in Europe: Towards a Single Regulator?* 381–396.
© 2003 *Kluwer Law International. Printed in Great Britain.*

## 2   The Present System: Multiplicity of Regulators

### *Overview of the present system*

*Banking supervision*

In France, after World War II, prudential supervision of commercial banks took place by means of a system known as direct governmental involvement in banking supervision.[6] Under this regime, all large commercial banks were subject to the control of a commissioner appointed by the Minister of Finance. This commissioner took part in all sessions of the Board of Directors of the commercial banks under his control, as well as the bank's general meetings. He had broad rights of control of the banks, and in particular could veto any decision of the Board of Directors which he considered to be against the national interest. This highly interventionist approach to prudential supervision created a very close relationship between the Ministry of Finance and the banks in question.

A new system of bank control was set up by the Banking Law of 24 January 1984.[7] This Banking Law provided for a number of separate supervisory bodies, a situation criticised by one commentator as a fragmented approach.[8] The day-to-day technical side of supervision is carried out by the *Commission Bancaire* (or 'Banking Commission').[9] However, some other supervisory work is undertaken by the *Comité de Réglementation Bancaire et Financière*,[10] the *Comité des Etablissements de Crédit et des Entreprises d'Investissements*.[11] Since the reform of 1984, the *Conseil National du Crédit et du Titre*, created in 1945,[12] which originally had important supervisory functions, is now merely an advisory body.[13] The powers of the *Commission Bancaire* were recently reinforced by the law of 25 June 1999.[14]

In France, the *Commission Bancaire* plays the predominant role in ensuring that credit institutions comply with the relevant laws and regulations. It is thus charged with investigating the operating conditions of credit institutions, the soundness of their finances, and that they adhere to principles of good business practice.

---

[6] *See* excellent comparative study of Wernhard Möschel, 'Public Law of Banking' in *International Encyclopedia of Comparative Law*, Vol. IX, (1991) Chap III at paras 3–56 *et seq.*

[7] Loi Numéro 84-46 of 24 January 1984, *Journal Officiel*, 25 January 1984, p. 390. This law has been amended on several occasions.

[8] *See* excellent study, Léguevaques, *La Prévention et le Traitement des 'Faillites' Bancaires*, (Thesis, University of Toulouse, 2000).

[9] Arts 37–50, Title III of the Banking Law. Until 1984, this body was known as the *Commission de Contrôle des Banques*.

[10] This body establishes prudential regulations and ratios – Arts 33–36 of the Banking Law.

[11] Issues authorisations to commence banking operations to credit and banking institutions – Art. 15 of the Banking Law.

[12] It was originally known as the *Conseil National du Crédit*.

[13] Art. 24 of the Banking Law.

[14] Law No 99-532 of 25 June 1999, *Journal Officiel* 29 June 1999, p. 9487. For an evaluation of the effect of this law on banking supervision, see Decoopman, 'Renforcement des Pouvoirs et Coordination des Autorités de Contrôle du Secteur Financier' [1999] *Revue de Droit Bancaire et de la Bourse* 148.

Different types of intervention are available to the *Commission Bancaire* in its supervisory role.[15] It increasingly conducts investigations *in situ* in the head office of the Bank itself, its parent company, or subsidiaries.[16] The *Commission Bancaire* has a number of powers which may be used if banks fail to adhere to the rules, such as the delivery of a warning or reprimand,[17] the issuing of an injunction,[18] or the more draconian powers of appointing a temporary director[19] or nominating of an official receiver.[20] The *Commission Bancaire* also has an armoury of disciplinary measures which include the prohibition of the exercise of certain banking activities; temporary suspension of one or more persons in charge of the management of the bank; withdrawal of the banking licence,[21] or a variety of pecuniary sanctions.[22]

## Commission des Opérations de Bourse

The *Commission des Opérations de Bourse* (universally known by its acronym 'COB') was set up by Executive Order of 28 September 1967, and its powers have been increased by recent legislative intervention.[23] It is an independent administrative authority (*autorité administrative indépendante*), which means that although it is a governmental organisation it has a good deal of independent management and decision-making powers. The COB has three main objectives: to promote the protection of investors' savings; to ensure that adequate information is provided to investors; to supervise the proper operation of the financial markets.

The COB is composed of a Chairman and nine members. Their work is prepared by a number of departments under the authority of a Director-General, assisted by a Secretary-General. The Chairman is appointed by the French government for a period of 6 years. Amongst the nine members who are appointed for a period of 4 years, three are designated by the principal judicial institutions (*Conseil d'Etat, Cour de Cassation, Cour des Comptes*), one is designated by the Governor of the *Banque de France*, another by the *Conseil des Marchés Financiers* (CMF), another by the *Conseil National de la Comptabilité* (CNC), and three are distinguished personalities designated on the grounds of their financial and legal expertise by the Speakers of the

---

[15] For example, the ability to request a wide range of documents relating to the running of the bank: *see* further Arts 39 and 40 of the Banking Law.

[16] Arts 39 and 41 of the Banking Law. *See Annual Report of the Commission Bancaire 1995*, page 5 'reinforcing on-site supervision.'

[17] Art. 42 of the Banking Law.

[18] Art. 43 of the Banking Law.

[19] If it is considered that the directors of a banking institution cannot fulfil their functions normally anymore or that the management of an institution cannot be reasonably maintained: Art. 44 of the Banking Law.

[20] Art. 46 of the Banking Law.

[21] Art. 45 of the Banking Law.

[22] *Ibid. See Conseil d'Etat*, 30 November 1994, *Ministre de l'Economie*, [1994] *Recueil des Décisions du Conseil d'Etat* 521.

[23] Namely by the Laws of 2 August 1989 (providing for the levy of administrative sanctions, such as fines) and 2 July 1996. *See* generally N. Decoopman, 'Commission des Opérations de Bourse' Fascicule 1510 in *Juris-Classeur Banque-Crédit-Bourse* (Paris, 1998).

Senate and National Assembly and the Chairman of the *Conseil économique et social*. The COB is financed by fees levied on persons whose market activities come within its ambit of intervention (chiefly issuers of financial instruments, unit trusts, mutual funds).

The COB is empowered to issue regulations concerning the operation of the markets under its supervision, prescribing the rules of business practice incumbent upon persons making public offerings.[24] The COB also adopts 'instructions' and 'recommendations' in order to clarify the interpretation and application of its regulations. Any person, whether French or foreign, who carries out a public offering is obliged to draw up a prospectus for the purpose of informing investors, which must be approved by the COB. The COB also supervises the information disclosed prior to other financial operations, such as mergers and acquisitions. The COB exercises prudential control over, and supervises the conduct of, asset management companies,[25] unit trusts and mutual funds.[26]

The COB also exercises important enforcement powers. It can conduct investigations and may impose fines on a person or company which acts in breach of its regulations, for instance, in respect of insider dealing, the provision of false information or price manipulation. This enforcement role has been under intense scrutiny in recent times, and the COB's procedures have had to be overhauled. This will be examined further below.

Another important organisation, which is closely linked to the COB,[27] is the *Conseil de discipline de la gestion financière*.[28] This body is composed of nine members who are predominantly drawn from the financial services industry,[29] and exercises a disciplinary power in respect of institutions offering unit trusts and the management of securities portfolios.[30]

## Conseil des Marchés Financiers

The *Conseil des Marchés Financiers* ('CMF') was created by the Law on the Modernisation of Financial Activities of 2 July 1996,[31] which transposed into French law the EU directive on investment services of 10 May 1993.

The CMF is a professional body and its board is made up of sixteen members appointed by the Ministry of Finance for a four-year term, many of whom hail from the world of finance. Different members are chosen to represent the interests of financial intermediaries, the commodity markets, and investors. In addition, a *Commissaire*

---

[24] *See*, for example, new rules which impose restrictions on the acquisition or divestiture of stock in relation to an initial public offerings: 'Paris lawyers refuse to panic over new IPO rules' *International Financial Law Review*, April 2001.

[25] *See* Law of 2 July 1996.

[26] *See* Law of 23 December 1988.

[27] The offices of the *Conseil de discipline de la gestion financière* are located at the COB.

[28] Created by the Arts 37 and 38 of the Law No 89-531 of 2 August 1989.

[29] Art. L. 623-1 Code Monétaire et Financier.

[30] Art. L. 623-2 Code Monétaire et Financier.

[31] The CMF resulted from a merger of the *Conseil des Bourses de Valeurs* and the *Conseil du Marché à Terme*.

*du Gouvernement* and a representative of the *Banque de France* attend CMF meetings but do not vote. The CMF is subject to private law.

The CMF exercises regulatory and supervisory powers over a broad range of financial services,[32] with the exception of asset management for third parties, which is supervised by the COB. It defines the general principles governing the organization and operation of regulated markets in financial instruments, and monitors the regularity of transactions carried out on regulated markets.

The CMF has a role in the authorisation of investment service providers. It approves the program of operations of new credit institutions and investment firms before they can be authorized by the *Comité des Etablissements de Crédit et des Entreprises d'Investissement.* The CMF regulates investment services provided by investment firms and credit institutions on regulated or non-regulated markets, covering rules of conduct, issuance of professional licenses to persons working on the markets, and the establishment of a guarantee fund to protect the clientele of an investment service provider against the possibility that the firm will default.

The CMF also plays an important role in the regulation and approval of tender offers. Any public tender offer for a French company quoted on a regulated market in France is subject to the CMF's prior approval. Further, the CMF may examine offers for the securities of foreign companies quoted on a regulated market in France.

The CMF has powers of supervision and sanction that enable it to enforce compliance with the rules for which it is responsible. These sanctions are exercised by specially formed disciplinary committees.

### La commission de contrôle des assurances

The *Commission de contrôle des assurances* (CCA) is responsible for the supervision of insurers and reinsurers.[33] It ensures that these institutions have an adequate financial structure to undertake the provision of insurance, and that they abide by the relevant primary and secondary legislation.[34] The CCA is an *autorité administrative indépendante*, though it has close links with the Ministry of Finance. Its five members are nominated by the Minister of Finance for a period of five years.[35]

In order to undertake its supervisory and regulatory role, the CCA has a wide range of powers,[36] such as on-site investigations of regulatees,[37] and official requests for information.[38] In order to ensure that its regulations are respected, the CCA also has the power to issue injunctions to force the regulatees to take certain measures.[39] It may also impose disciplinary measures upon offending institutions or persons,[40]

---

[32] Generally see the Law on the Modernisation of Financial Activities of 2 July 1996.

[33] Created by Law No 89-1014 du 31 décembre 1989. For more information, see the CCA's website <http://www.finances.gouv.fr/guide/CCA>.

[34] Art. L. 310-12 of the *Code des assurances.*

[35] Art. L. 310-12-1 of the *Code des assurances.*

[36] *See* Art. L. 310-13 *et seq.* of the *Code des assurances.*

[37] Art. L. 310-13 of the *Code des assurances.*

[38] Art. L. 310-14 of the *Code des assurances.*

[39] Art. L. 310-17 of the *Code des assurances.*

[40] As laid down in *Code des assurances* (Arts L 310-18 and L 310-18-1).

which run from mere warnings or reprimands to more draconian measures such as fines, the prohibition on undertaking certain business activities or the withdrawal of licences.

### Critique of the present system

*Agency fragmentation*

From this description of the regulatory system in France, it is self-evident that there is a plethora of different bodies charged with undertaking the supervisory role. Multiple agencies need not necessarily be problematic: combined action can be effective. If the ambit of intervention of each agency is clearly defined, and there are sufficient means of co-ordination and co-operation, then an effective and cost-efficient system may be devised. Indeed, some French commentators have seen a virtue in diversity, arguing that competition between twin regulators with similar remits can have beneficial effects, encouraging a healthy climate of competitiveness and thus providing ever better standards of supervision.[41]

On the other hand, agency fragmentation can create inefficiency. Overlapping jurisdictions may result in confusion over which institution should take the lead, and can also create unhelpful turf wars. Where several agencies are responsible for functionally similar markets and products, this inevitable increases the danger of regulatees not being properly supervised by either authority. Indeed, in the United Kingdom, prior to the FSA, the chairman of one of the most important supervisors, the Securities and Investments Board, recognised that a fragmented system lead to 'below par regulatory performance'.[42]

The present French system, like the now-abandoned English system, does seem to suffer chronically from multiple-agency syndrome. There is a bewildering fragmentation of responsibility. The COB, the CMF, and the *Conseil de discipline de la gestion financière* all potentially have an interest in dealing with market misconduct.[43] Not only is there confusion created by a number of bodies undertaking a functionally similar role, but there is often a total overlap. A good example of this is the case of disciplinary matters concerning investment companies. Both the COB and the *Conseil de discipline de la gestion financière* have a similar jurisdiction in this respect, which potentially could have led to chaos. This has been avoided by an agreement between these bodies that the *Conseil de discipline de la gestion financière* should take a lead role.[44]

---

[41] Pierre-Henri Conac, 'La fusion de la COB et du CMF' in *Mélanges AEDBF-France III* (Paris, 2001); M.-A. Frison-Roche, 'Vers une Nouvelle Autorité de Régulation Boursière' interview published in *Les Petites Affiches*, 11 December 2000.

[42] Andrew Large, delivering the Chancery Bar Association and Combar Spring Lecture in 1994, as cited by Howard Davies, delivery the same lecture, 'Financial Regulation and the Law' (3 March 1999) available at <www.fsa.gov.uk>.

[43] And if the behaviour constitutes a criminal offence, then many other institutions of the criminal justice may also be involved. *See* N. Decoopman, 'Conseil des Marchés Financiers' Fascicule 1520 in *Juris-Classeur Banque-Crédit-Bourse* (Paris, 1998) para. 74.

[44] Confirmed by the *Conseil de discipline de la gestion financière*.

Overlap is by no means limited to enforcement activities. Another example is found in the regulation of public offerings. All public offerings are regulated by the general rules found in Title V of the *Règlement general du CMF*, and each individual offering is closely supervised by both the CMF and the COB.[45] In sum, the division of labour and responsibility between the CMF and the COB can be seen as uncertain and unjustified.[46]

There is no doubt that a good deal of these problems have stemmed from the plethora of speedily-drafted legal texts regulating financial services in France, many of which have failed to take sufficient account of the overall architecture of financial regulation.[47] If there is confusion for professionals, there is likely to be even more lack of certainty for investors.

*Inadequate status of the regulatory authorities*

Difficulties have also been encountered in ensuring that regulatory bodies have the appropriate attributes to undertake their supervisory role. The present regulatory bodies are of a very heterogeneous nature. The COB is an *autorité administrative indépendante* which means that it acts with a good deal of autonomy from the state,[48] but is nonetheless characterised as a public body. The *Commission Bancaire* is similarly considered to be an *autorité administrative indépendante*, though it has very close links with the French Central Bank. On the other hand, the *Conseil des Marchés Financiers* is a very different type of creature both in architecture and approach. It is a private law legal entity,[49] not an *autorité administrative indépendante*; it is dominated by professionals rather than civil servants.

The CMF's more 'supple' architecture has been favourably compared with the less adaptable and less market-orientated model of the COB.[50] Indeed, the COB's status as an *autorité administrative indépendante* has presented certain disadvantages. The fact that it did not originally have a *personnalité morale* meant that the COB could not be party to legal actions. Thus, if an action for damages was brought for regulatory failure, it lay against the State rather than the COB itself.[51] Moreover, the COB could not initiate legal proceedings itself. In order to remedy the latter

---

[45] *See* discussion in M.-A. Frison-Roche, 'How should the powers of regulatory authorities be established in terms of law?' official translation of 'Comment fonder juridiquement le pouvoir des autorités de régulation ?' in *Sécurité et régulation financières*, Revue d'économie financière, 2001, pp. 85–100.

[46] *See* summary of reasons for merging the COB and CMF as articulated by (an unconvinced) M.-A. Frison-Roche, 'Vers une Nouvelle Autorité de Régulation Boursière' interview published in *Les Petites Affiches*, 11 December 2000.

[47] *See* view of Pierre-Henri Conac, 'La fusion de la COB et du CMF' in *Mélanges AEDBF-France III* (Paris, 2001).

[48] For an in-depth discussion of *autorités administratives indépendantes*, *see Rapport Public 2001: Les Autorités Administratives Indépendantes, Etudes et Documents du Conseil d'Etat* (La Documentation Francaise, 2001).

[49] Art. 27, Law on the Modernisation of Financial Activities of 2 July 1996.

[50] E. Benhamou, 'L'Annus Horribilis des Autorités Boursières' in *La Tribune*, 28 December 2000.

[51] Conseil d'Etat 22 June 1984, *Société 'Pierre et Cristal'* [1984] Recueil des Décisions du Conseil d'Etat 506.

defect,[52] a legislative amendment in 1996 provided that the President of the COB could initiate legal proceedings in its name.[53] Another potential problem arose from the fact that permanent staff of public bodies must be civil servants, the nomination of which entails a specific recruitment procedure. Legislative provisions were passed in order to allow bodies like the COB to recruit more freely from the open market in order to ensure that they gained staff with the necessary skills.[54]

French law is thus struggling to come to terms with a hybrid type of legal body, the role, status and legal basis of which are not easily articulated within the classical public–private law model.

### Human rights influence

European Human Rights law has also had a significant impact on French financial regulation. Art. 6 of the European Convention for the Protection of Human Rights and Fundamental Freedoms (ECHR) is not only the least favourite provision of certain English judges,[55] it has also ruffled the well-groomed feathers of French regulators.

The focus of the problems has been the disciplinary and enforcement role of the COB. Various judicial decisions since 1996 have forced the COB to refine its procedure.[56] The most radical change has occurred recently. In a judgment of 7 March 2000, the *Cour d'Appel de Paris* quashed a decision of the COB of 18 June 1999 imposing a sanction upon the accountancy firm KPMG.[57] The Court considered that the procedure followed by the COB in this particular instance was not in accordance with Art. 6(1) ECHR (guaranteeing a fair trial). The same members of the board (*collège*) of the COB were involved in the investigation of the case, the decision to start the actual disciplinary procedure, the notification of the 'charges', as well as the ultimate decision on whether the rules had been breached and the disciplinary measures to be imposed. These persons could not be considered to be 'objectively impartial.'

This decision had drastic effects. The disciplinary mechanism of the COB was suspended for many months whilst the procedures were modified. The authority and

---

[52] N. Decoopman, 'Commission des Opérations de Bourse' Fascicule 1510 in *Juris-Classeur Banque-Crédit-Bourse* (Paris, 1998), para. 6.

[53] Art. 1 of Law of 2 July 1996, *la loi de modernisation des activités financières*.

[54] Law No 84-16 of 11 January 1984 *relative au statut de la fonction publique*. *See* N. Decoopman, 'Commission des Opérations de Bourse' Fascicule 1510 in *Juris-Classeur Banque-Crédit-Bourse* (Paris, 1998), para. 14.

[55] *See* Lord Hoffmann, 'Human Rights and the House of Lords' (1999) 62 MLR 159.

[56] In 1996, the *Cour de Cassation* declared that the COB's disciplinary procedure had to conform with Art. 6 ECHR: Cass. com. 9 April 1996, Dalloz 1998. *Sommaires-Commentés* 65. *See* for earlier modification of the decision-making process: Cass. Ass. Plen. 5 February 1999, *Oury*, JCP *Edition Entreprise* 1999.957.

[57] CA Paris 7 March 2000, *Société KPMG Fiduciaire de France*, JCP *Edition Entreprise* 2000.538. *See* analysis of A. Couret, 'Incompatibilité de la procédure de sanction pécuniaire de la COB avec l'article 6 de la CEDH', JCP *Edition Entreprise* 2000.992; E. Garaud, 'Droits des Affaires et Droits de l'Homme' JCP *Edition Entreprise* 2000.986.

reputation of the COB was greatly damaged.[58] Commentators observed in vivid language that the 'worms had entered the fruit'.[59]

The sanctions procedure was reformed in August 2000,[60] in order to ensure compatibility with the requirements of the European Convention. There is now a greater degree of separation between the operational function of investigation and the decision-making determining the disciplinary measure. The Director-General of the COB investigates the prima facie case and may ask the board to commence disciplinary proceedings, by means of the nomination of an investigatory *rapporteur* (one of the nine members of the board of the COB) who will decide whether to issue the 'warning notices' or charges which begin the proceedings. The report which is established by the *rapporteur* after extensive investigation is presented to the Board of the COB (which does not include the Director-General) who will make a decision (without the *rapporteur*) as to whether a disciplinary measure should be imposed, and if so, which sanction.

However, the newly reformulated procedure of the COB has not escaped criticism. Some commentators have taken issue with details,[61] others have seen more fundamental problems. Professeur Frison-Roche has argued that problems will always remain whilst the status of regulators in French law are seen through the lenses of the public–private law dichotomy.[62]

### Recourse to the courts

Uncertainty also derives from the way in which judicial supervision is organised. Different courts have jurisdiction over similar cases. This position has only recently been clarified for the current regulatory institutions. For those who might tempted to advocate a separate administrative jurisdiction in the United Kingdom, the French litigation in this sphere is a salutary tale. After the 1989 reforms attributed jurisdiction for a large part of the litigation deriving from this area to the civil courts, namely the *Cour d'Appel de Paris*,[63] the hapless Monsieur Delcourt was patiently awaiting judgment in an action he had brought to quash the decision of the COB which have effectively shut down his investment business.[64] The *Conseil d'Etat*, which had been

---

[58] A process which been exacerbated by the allegations of insider dealing concerning an important member of the COB: Pierre-Henri Conac, 'La fusion de la COB et du CMF' in *Mélanges AEDBF-France III* (Paris, 2001).

[59] E. Benhamou, 'L'Annus Horribilis des Autorités Boursières' in *La Tribune*, 28 December 2000.

[60] By two Government Decrees: No 2000-720 and 2000-721 of 1 August 2000, *Journal Officiel*, 2 August 2000, pp. 11938 and 11939. For commentary on this see R. Salomon, 'La Réforme de la Procédure de Sanction de la COB par les décrets du 1 Aout 2000' (2000) Revue de Droit Bancaire et Financier 312; J. Daigre, 'La Nouvelle Procédure de Sanction de la COB: Une Réforme en Clair-Obscur' JCP *Edition Entreprise* 2000.1602.

[61] J. Daigre, 'La Nouvelle Procédure de Sanction de la COB: Une Réforme en Clair-Obscur' JCP *Edition Entreprise* 2000.1602.

[62] *See* the wide-ranging essay on French regulatory law: M.-A. Frison-Roche, 'Le Droit de la Régulation', Dalloz 2001.*Doctrine*.610.

[63] Law No 89-531 of 2 August 1989.

[64] This is known as the *affaire Compagnie diamantaire d'Anvers*: *see* N. Decoopman, 'Commission des Opérations de Bourse' Fascicule 1510 in *Juris-Classeur Banque-Crédit-Bourse* (Paris, 1998), para. 158.

on the brink of giving a decision on the substantive issue, held that the legislative reforms entailed that the reform was to be heard by the Civil courts.[65] This could have been resolved fairly quickly, except that the civil courts were not sure that they had jurisdiction either,[66] and so the *Tribunal des Conflits* had to decide which of the reluctant judges was to decide the issue. The civil courts were subsequently given jurisdiction,[67] but the long delays in the French judicial systems and the complexity of the issues meant that the final decision on the substantive decision was not reached until 1999: 14 years after the start of the litigation.[68]

The decision over the appropriate supervisory authority – civil or administrative – is an extremely technical issue, with arguments on both sides. On the basis of principle, there are arguments in favour of the administrative courts having jurisdiction: their familiarity with the system of judicial review and applying the rules of state liability. The contrary view in favour of the civil courts' jurisdiction rests upon the commercial nature of many of these disputes, lying in the area of financial law. There is also the practical consideration that if the *Conseil d'Etat* is competent then, due to a specific rule in France, only one of a limited number of senior lawyers may act as advocate, whereas if the civil courts have jurisdiction then, in the first instance, the *Cour d'Appel de Paris* will be the competent and no such restrictions on rights of audience apply.


## 3    THE PROPOSED SYSTEM: TWIN PEAKS

The process of competitive reforming has caught on in France. Reforms are currently been undertaken, with an important Parliamentary Bill, known as the *Project de loi portant réforme des autorités financières*, currently winding its way through the legislative process.

The *project de loi portant réforme des autorités financières* will involve an overhaul of the existing architecture of financial supervision in France. The proposals reflect a dual track approach to financial supervision, which has become known as the 'twin peaks' approach. The characteristic of this approach is that regulation is split between agencies specializing on prudential supervision on the one hand and conduct of financial market regulation on the other.

In the proposed French system, the supervision of the markets will be the responsibility of a newly created body known as the *Autorité des Marchés Financiers*, which has already gained the acronym AMF.[69] This new entity will be created by a merger of the *Commission des Opérations de Bourse*, the *Conseil des Marchés Financiers* and the *Conseil de discipline de la gestion financière*. The AMF will be

---

[65] Conseil d'Etat 6 July 1990, JCP *Edition Entreprise* 1990.I.20126.

[66] *Cour d'Appel de Paris*, 29 May 1991.

[67] *Tribunal des Conflits* 22 June 1992, JCP 1993.II.22035.

[68] Cass. com. 30 November 1999.

[69] For an excellent in-depth critique of the AMF, *see* Pierre-Henri Conac, 'La fusion de la COB et du CMF' in *Mélanges AEDBF-France III* (Paris, 2001).

an *autorité administrative indépendante*,[70] and will have financial independence and will be able to initiate judicial proceedings. The AMF will have a 15-person governing body and two sub-committees one specialised in public offers of securities and another focused on disciplinary matters and sanctions.[71] The latter body will decide upon the punishments for violation of the financial regulation except for insider dealing which will now be a matter solely for the French criminal courts.

Prudential supervision will be subject to less radical reform. Despite initial flirtation with the idea of a merger, the twin bodies of the *Commission Bancaire* and the CCA will remain separate, and instead there will be a certain *rapprochement* by means of enhanced communication and co-operation. There will be a certain amount of cross-board participation: five people will sit on the boards of both bodies. The *Commission Bancaire* and the CCA will meet twice a year in order to discuss subjects of mutual interest.[72] In order to ensure greater co-ordination, the law aligns the requirements for the licensing of insurance companies with the model applied to banks.[73] Whether this *rapprochement* metamorphoses into a creeping merger will be revealed in the future, but for the moment the two bodies will remain separate.

### 4 AN EVALUATION: TWIN PEAKS À LA FRANCAISE AND THE SINGLE REGULATOR

The arguments for a single regulator have been well-rehearsed. This is not the place to examine these arguments in detail: this has been covered admirably in other papers in this collection.[74] As a backdrop to the discussion of the French structure, it is nonetheless worth sketching the basic perceived advantages. A single regulator is designed to reduce the cost of compliance *and* the cost of ensuring compliance. From the regulator's perspective, the single authority allows for economies of scale and size leading to greater cost efficiency and a higher quality of regulatory activity. In terms of the regulated institutions, the one-stop shop allows for a reduction in possible conflicting requirements set by different institutions. The merging of the various sectoral supervisory bodies within one super-regulator is also said to mirror market developments in which there has been a gradual blurring of the traditional boundaries between institutions and products. As retail investment increases there has been a commensurate heightening in the need for consumer protection, as well as consumer awareness, which may be most effectively provided within a single regulatory institution rather than a fragmented structure.

At present, however, these are theoretical arguments. It remains to be seen how the single regulator concept fares in a major financial centre like London. Time only will tell whether this is an effective manner to ensure efficient regulation.

---

[70] Art. 2 of the *project de loi portant réforme des autorités financiers*.

[71] Art. 3 of the *project de loi portant réforme des autorités financiers*.

[72] Art. 20 of the *project de loi portant réforme des autorités financiers*.

[73] *See* Paris Europlace: Journal, April 2001, p. 10.

[74] *See* the earlier chapter in this collection by Mads Andenas, 'Is the Case for a Single Regulator Made Out?'

## Evaluation of the French approach

The new French approach will bring a certain amount of benefits to financial regulation. The creation of one institution to supervise financial markets should mean a more simple and predictable system for professionals and consumers alike.[75] The overlapping jurisdictions will thereby be removed. A single system for financial market regulation should also entail a reduction in the cost of running the system, and should also be accompanied by a reduction in the cost of compliance. This ultimately should increase the competitiveness of the French financial marketplace. Moreover, this development has taken place in the context of an increasing integration of the European capital markets, and particularly the creation of Euronext. The merging of the French authorities will no doubt facilitate the co-operation between the European regulators. Indeed, the Lamfalussy report of 2001 highlighted the plethora of public bodies in the European Union which deal with securities markets regulation and supervision,[76] and concluded that this caused fragmentation and confusion at a European level and recommended that more convergent regulatory and supervisory structures were necessary. The French reforms would appear to be moving in this direction, by rationalising the number of financial markets regulators.

Despite the advantages which have been created by the recent reform, there are still some potential weaknesses.

### The financial markets supervisory body: the AMF

The architecture of the new AMF represents an attempt to reconcile the orthodox format of regulatory bodies with the exigencies of modern regulation. During the legislative process, there were important developments concerning this point. It was thought desirable for the new regulator to be a recognised legal entity,[77] a *personnalité morale*, and thus this was reflected in the initial drafts of the Bill. However, this existence of a *personnalité morale* is, in orthodox public law terms, incompatible with the status as an *autorité administrative indépendante*, and so after the Bill's passage through the *Conseil d'Etat*, the reference to *personnalité morale* was dropped.[78] In order to endow the AMF with the powers and personnel to undertake its provide functions properly, express provisions are found in the Bill. It has been given a broad right to initiate and defend legal proceedings. It has a good deal of flexibility in recruitment; indeed more than the COB.[79]

---

[75] See 'Orientations Générales' in the *project de loi portant réforme des autorités financiers*.

[76] *Final Report of the Committee of Wise men on the Regulation of European Securities Markets* (15 February 2001).

[77] Which would afford the AMF a greater flexibility and adaptability, such as in concluding employment contracts.

[78] See discussion of P.-A. Gailly, *Vers la Création d'une Autorité des Marchés Financiers* (Chambre de Commerce et d'Industrie de Paris, 15 March 2001).

[79] The AMF can recruit staff on the basis of private law contracts: Art. 7 of the *project de loi portant réforme des autorités financiers*.

A compromise has thus been reached on the shape and form of the AMF. It retains its links to the state through its status as an *autorité administrative indépendante*, whilst being given the tools for its regulatory role. It has also been endowed with the financial independence with which to recruit employees from the financial services industry.

The reforms have also looked particularly carefully at the disciplinary procedure, unsurprisingly given the role which this played in undermining the COB's credibility.[80] In the context of the AMF, the sub-committee on disciplinary matters and sanctions is designed to create a distinction between the operational function of investigation and the decision-making as to the disciplinary measure. However, this procedure is not completed. The Bill states that the enforcement procedure will be regulated by a future Decree.[81]

The reform is also intended to have addressed another of the perceived weaknesses of the present structure, that of double jeopardy, double sanction for one offence.[82] So, the AMF will no longer be able to impose an administrative sanction for insider dealing: this will now be solely for the criminal justice system.[83] However, commentators have expressed some concern about this provision. Although many perceive the objective of the reform as commendable, doubts have been expressed about whether the criminal justice system is the right forum in which to bring these cases, especially those of a less-than-severe nature.[84] The French criminal justice system is slow and it is uncertain whether the necessary resources will be provided in order to absorb the increase in cases.[85]

## Rapprochement between the Commission Bancaire and the CCA

The recent reforms aim to enhance the co-operation between these bodies. The Government's initial desire to merge these two organisations has failed. Prudential supervision will therefore be exercised by the *Commission Bancaire*, with its close links to the *Banque de France*. This approach to prudential supervision has the approval of the European Central Bank. In a recent paper, the ECB indicated its preference for national central banks to retain a fundamental role in prudential supervision in euro area countries.[86] From a Eurosystem perspective, the attribution of macro- and micro-prudential responsibilities to the central banks is thought to be beneficial. Indeed, the German government has revealed that in the recent reforms prudential responsibility will lie with the central bank.

---

[80] *See* text by note 58.

[81] Art. 4 of the *project de loi portant réforme des autorités financiers*.

[82] 'Orientations Générales' in the *project de loi portant réforme des autorités financiers*.

[83] Art. 10 of the *project de loi portant réforme des autorités financiers*.

[84] Pierre-Henri Conac, 'La fusion de la COB et du CMF' in *Mélanges AEDBF-France III* (Paris, 2001).

[85] Pierre-Henri Conac, 'La fusion de la COB et du CMF' in *Mélanges AEDBF-France III* (Paris, 2001); P.-A. Gailly, *Vers la Création d'une Autorité des Marchés Financiers* (Chambre de Commerce et d'Industrie de Paris, 15 March 2001) p. 34; M.-A. Frison-Roche, 'Vers une Nouvelle Autorité de Régulation Boursière' interview published in *Les Petites Affiches*, 11 December 2000.

[86] *The Role of Central Banks in Prudential Supervision* (European Central Bank, 22 March 2001).

However, the architecture of financial regulation is not simply determined by an objective cost–benefit analysis. It is often shaped by the political imperatives. The French proposals are no exception. To understand the resulting compromise position, the complex rivalries must be explained.

The *Commission Bancaire* has traditionally been very close to the French Central Bank, *la Banque de France*. The President of the *Commission Bancaire* is the Governor of the Central Bank,[87] and the *Commission Bancaire's* staff are generally on secondment from the *Banque de France*.[88] On the other hand, the *Commission de contrôle des assurances* is under the organisational control of the Ministry of Finance.

There has traditionally been lively competition between the French Treasury and the French Central Bank for influence and power.[89] The Treasury has tried, but has so far failed, to gain greater influence over the *Commission Bancaire* to the detriment of the *Banque de France*. The latter body, which is in the process of re-defining its role after the institutional changes consequent upon European Financial and Monetary Union, was resistant to any change which might reduce their influence. The present reform, which leaves banking supervision with the *Commission Bancaire*, separate from the *Commission de contrôle des assurances*, favours the Central Bank's approach.

There is also another political – and admittedly unpublicised – explanation for the proposed architecture of the new body. The career civil servants of the *Banque de France*, who ensure the day-to-day operation of the *Commission Bancaire*, were resistant to any move which might draw them away from the *Banque de France*, which provides prestige as well as advantageous working conditions.[90]

*Evaluation: a conclusion*

French legislative reforms in this area have often been characterised by impetuosity and haste. These current reforms are no exception to this trend,[91] and some of the features referred to above underline this point. It may well be that the French reform is just an evolutionary step towards the unitary approach. If the UK system is successful, then there will no doubt be an irresistible momentum towards that model given the likely economic benefits for financial services operators.

## CONCLUSION: TAKING A BROADER VIEW

The regulation of financial services necessitates the combination of a wide sphere of functions within the hands of one institution. Financial markets are extremely

---

[87] Art. 38 of the Banking Law.

[88] Art. 39 of the Banking Law.

[89] *See* Léguevaques, *La Prévention et le Traitement des 'Faillites' Bancaires* (Thesis, University of Toulouse, 2000), para. 283ff.

[90] *See* 'La Réorganisation voulue par Bercy inquiète la Banque de France' *La Tribune*, 17 August 2000.

[91] Pierre-Henri Conac, 'La fusion de la COB et du CMF' in *Mélanges AEDBF-France III* (Paris, 2001).

complex and fast-evolving. It is unsurprisingly then that the law governing regulation is also a complex and intricate area, which is not always easily accommodated within orthodox legal conceptions. In English law, the challenge posed to traditional judicial review by commercial regulation has been well documented.[92] In the French system, the regime of *autorités financières* has also challenged ordinary legal concepts in a number of ways.

First, the notion of financial regulation has posed a challenge to orthodox public law concepts in French law.[93] Regulators play a very complex role in a sphere overlapping both administrative and commercial law. Conceptual difficulties have arisen in a number of ways. We have seen the difficulty in French law of actually finding an acceptable status for these bodies which allows for both flexibility in composition and powers within the archetype classification of administrative bodies. Jurisdictional problems have also arisen in respect of the appropriate supervisory judicial authority. Tradition demands that bodies acting in the public interest should solely be within the ambit of the administrative courts. However, there are reasons why the civil courts have also a role to play. These underlying tensions explain, though by no means justify, the fudged compromise of a dual jurisdictional compromise.

Second, another element which has been challenged is the operation and procedure of administrative bodies. These are bodies which are charged with a delicate role spanning both administration, policy making, and a quasi-judicial role (disciplinary powers). This is a common feature of regulators in many countries, of which France is just an example. It is this duality of policy-making and rights-determining functions which has potentially caused a problem. The full force of this problem has been felt through the influence of Human Rights Law. Art. 6 ECHR has been a constant force for reform in France, and no doubt will come to play that role in the United Kingdom now that the Human Rights Act 1998 is in force.

Finally, another point to note is the way in which foreign law concepts and influences have challenged the orthodox approach to regulation. This area affords a tremendous scope for comparative reflection across national boundaries. It goes without saying that the influence of European Community Law is vast. But this area also allows for a more direct transfer of concepts between states.[94] The nature of the subject matter and the need to organise co-operation at a nation state level also makes this an ideal sphere for comparative reflection. It is noteworthy that the debate concerning the next generation of financial regulators and the appropriate architecture has been made by constant reference to other countries' institutions. This makes it a fertile area for cross-fertilisation of ideas and institutional solutions, again challenging the orthodox domestic legal interpretation and characterisation of the regulators.

---

[92] J. Black, P. Muchlinski and P. Walker, *Commercial Regulation and Judicial Review* (Hart Publishing, Oxford 1998).

[93] P.-A. Gailly, *Vers la Création d'une Autorité des Marchés Financiers* (Chambre de Commerce et d'Industrie de Paris, 15 March 2001), p. 16.

[94] For the influence of American Law on the French system, *see* M.-A. Frison-Roche, 'Exemples de régulation et de contrôle étrangers' in *Droit, finance, autorité. Sociologie comparée des autorités de marchés financiers* (Laboratoire de sociologie juridique de l'Université Panthéon-Assas Paris II, 1999).

These overlapping and intertwining challenges have thrown up real problems for the French state. These regulatory bodies – of uncertain legal pedigree – wield broad powers in the sphere of vital economic importance. And yet, the concepts of regulation and regulatory agencies are not unified into a specific legal category. These bodies do not fit neatly within the orthodox interpretation of the traditional administrative structure of the French State. There has been a questioning of the legitimacy of the powers of regulation. Professeur Frison-Roche has argued that these problems will always remain whilst the status of regulators in French law are seen through the lenses of the public–private law dichotomy. The new era of regulation demands a fresh approach to the law of regulation and the legal status of regulators:[95] '[T]he concepts of regulation and regulatory agencies are not unified into a specific legal category. Paradoxically, the legal system fails to account for the existence of such bodies, while at the same time the law is becoming a growing element of the regulation system. The legal analysis of regulatory authorities thus seems to be going astray, on the one hand because it is torn between traditional, administrative structures and private, commercial mechanisms, on the other hand because as of today it has failed to produce both a satisfactory link between the different kinds of authorities and a clearly identified legal source of their powers'.[96]

---

[95] *See* the wide-ranging essay on French regulatory law: M.-A. Frison-Roche, 'Le Droit de la Régulation', Dalloz 2001.*Doctrine*.610. *See* also P.-A. Gailly, *Vers la Création d'une Autorité des Marchés Financiers* (Chambre de Commerce et d'Industrie de Paris, 15 March 2001), p. 16.

[96] *See* excellent Art. of M.-A. Frison-Roche, 'How should the powers of regulatory authorities be established in terms of law?' official translation of 'Comment fonder juridiquement le pouvoir des autorités de régulation?' in *Sécurité et régulation financières* (Revue d'économie financière, 2001), pp. 85–100.

Chapter 17

# Financial Market Regulation: The Case of Italy and a Proposal for the Euro Area*

*Giorgio di Giorgio, Carmine di Noia and Laura Piatti*

## I INTRODUCTION

The evolution of financial markets has been particularly significant in the last decades with regard to intermediaries, capital markets and financial instruments. Structural changes have mainly involved the more traditional financial operators in banking, but have also involved investment firms and insurance companies.

Regulatory arrangements have also been the object of significant change. Such dynamics are at the centre of attention at international venues. A number of countries (the United Kingdom, Australia, Germany and Japan) have recently undertaken important changes in their regulatory systems.[1] In other European countries, evolutionary trends are moving in the same direction. Moreover, with the start of Phase III of the EMU, the responsibility for monetary policy in the euro zone has been assigned to the European Central Bank, while banking and financial supervision tasks have been left to domestic agencies. A relevant novelty in Europe is then 'the abandonment of the coincidence between the area of jurisdiction of monetary policy and the area of jurisdiction of banking supervision'.[2] The 'double separation' (geographical and functional) between central banking and banking supervision, and the absence of any explicit reference to 'who takes care of financial stability' in Europe, did cast some doubts about the efficacy of the current regulatory arrangements in preventing and managing financial crisis and are currently at the centre of a lively debate.

The objective of the present work is to set up a proposal for the reorganisation of regulatory arrangements and supervisory agencies in financial markets both in Italy and the European Union.

---

* This chapter was presented at the 22nd SUERF Colloquium, co-organized by the Oesterreichische Nationalbank and the University of Vienna, and held in Vienna in April 2000. We thank Karel Lannoo, Andy Mullineux and Michael Taylor for useful discussion and comments. A revised version focusing only on the Italian case was published in the *Rivista Italiana degli Economisti (1,2001)*, while Di Giorgio and Di Noia have considerably expanded the part dealing with the Euro Area in a new work which was circulated as a working paper (2/2001) of the Wharton Financial Institutions Center, and is about to come out in the *Brooklin Journal of International Business Law*. The opinions here expressed are only those of the authors and do not necessarily coincide with those of the Institutions they are affiliated with.

[1] Concerning these issues *see* Coffee (1995), Dale (1997) and Taylor (1997).
[2] Padoa Schioppa, 1999.

*Mads Andenas and Yannis Avgerinos (eds), Financial Markets in Europe: Towards a Single Regulator?* 397–420.
© 2003 *Kluwer Law International. Printed in Great Britain.*

The essay opens with a section investigating objectives and theoretical models for the regulation of the financial system.[3]

We then describe recent evolutionary dynamics in financial markets, intermediaries and instruments. We focus first on the Italian situation. Here, we highlight some 'anomalies' proper to the current regulatory system. Hence, we present a proposal for a new configuration for supervising the domestic financial market through the assignment of different objectives or 'finalities' to different authorities.[4] This perspective would thus entrust the attainment of the three objectives of supervision on the entire financial market – stability, transparency and investor protection, competition – to three distinct authorities regardless of the subjective nature of the intermediaries, whether they be in banking, finance or insurance.[5] This scheme would innovate current arrangements by delegating to a sole authority the objective of transparency in banking and the suppression of misleading advertising of financial products. In addition, it would highlight the objective of competition (especially in banking) as a distinct finality explicitly monitored by the regulator. Moreover, for the sake of consistency, the existing rules applying to other forms of financial intermediation would be extended to include the life insurance sector.

We then extend our proposal for a regulatory reform in Italy to the euro area. This requires explicitly addressing the problem of who takes care of financial stability in the euro area. We re-examine the issue of the need for a lender of last resort and of the proper relationship of the European Central Bank (ECB) with other financial market regulators. We propose to establish a European System of Financial Supervisors, with three distinct independent authorities (plus the ECB) at the European level. These agencies ought to be characterised by homogeneous procedures in terms of their creation, functioning and funding. They will push and co-ordinate the work of the three corresponding national authorities in each member country.

The chapter is organised as follows. In Section II we describe the objectives and the motivations for financial markets regulation and we identify four models of regulatory structure. In Section III we deal with the regulatory framework currently in place in Italy. We first highlight what we think are its problematic features and anomalies. We then present an hypothesis of reform based on a fully coherent application of the supervisory model by objectives (or by finality). In Section IV we argue that such a reform could be extended to the euro area. Finally, we summarize our conclusions.

## II    MODELS FOR FINANCIAL MARKET REGULATION AND SUPERVISION

### II.1    Financial market regulation

The theoretical underpinning for public intervention in economic matters is traditionally based on the need to correct market imperfections and unfair distribution of the

---

[3] *See* also Goodhart and Shoenmaker (1992); Dewatripont and Tirole (1994); Merton and Bodie (1995) and White (1997).

[4] *See* also Di Noia and Piatti (1998).

[5] The reference is, in the following, to life-insurance, whose behaviour is very close to the other financial intermediaries.

resources. Three more general objectives of public intervention derive: the pursuit of stability, equity in the distribution of resources and the efficient use of those resources.

The regulation of the financial system can be viewed as a particularly important case of public control over the economy. The accumulation of capital and the allocation of financial resources constitute an essential aspect in the process of the economic development of a nation. The peculiarities of financial intermediation and of the operators who perform this function justify the existence of a broader system of controls with respect to other forms of economic activity. Various theoretical motivations have been advanced to support the opportunity of a particularly stringent regulation for banks and other financial intermediaries. Such motivations are based on the existence of particular forms of market failure in the credit and financial sectors.[6]

*The objectives of financial market regulation*

The definition of the term 'financial market' has traditionally included the banking, financial and insurance segments. The bounds dividing institutions, instruments and markets were clear-cut, so that further distinctions were drawn within the different classes of intermediaries (with banks specialised in short or medium/long term maturities, functional/commercial operations, deposits and investments; with financial intermediaries handling broker-dealer negotiations, asset management and advisory functions, and with insurance companies dealing in life and other insurance policies). In this essay, as the bounds dividing the various types of financial institutions are becoming increasingly blurred (Corrigan, 1987), we shall refer to the financial market as an economic space wherein operators of various kinds – banks, financial intermediaries, mutual funds, insurance companies, pension funds – offer financial instruments and services.

A primary objective of financial market regulation is the pursuit of macro- and microeconomic stability. Safeguarding of the stability of the system translates into macro-controls over the financial exchanges, clearing houses and securities settlement systems. Measures pertaining to the micro-stability of the intermediaries can be subdivided into two categories: general rules on the stability of all business enterprises and entrepreneurial activities, such as the legally required amount of capital, borrowing limits and integrity requirements; and more specific rules due to the special nature of financial intermediation, such as risk based capital ratios, limits to portfolio investments and the regulation of off-balance activities.

---

[6] White (1996) identifies certain categories of 'market failure', describing them with special regard for the financial markets: (i) situations of market power brought about because of collusion, concentration, technological conditions or public regulatory conditions; (ii) economies of scale, as in the case of capital markets where an inverse relation exists between the volume of transactions and the costs of transaction; (iii) externality (spill-over) effects, as in the case of a bank failure generally affecting the confidence of savers in the entire banking system; (iv) public good problems, as in the case of the property of prices formed on the exchanges; (v) information asymmetries, typically found among buyers and sellers of financial products; (vi) individuals who are unable to know their own best interest, as in the case of forms of savings they are 'unacquainted with' present in financial markets.

A second objective of financial regulation is transparency in the market and in intermediaries and investor protection. This is linked to the more general objective of equity in the distribution of the available resources and may be mapped into the search for 'equity in the distribution of information as a precious good' among operators.[7] At the macro level, transparency rules impose equal treatment (e.g. rules regarding takeovers and public offers) and the correct dissemination of information (insider trading, manipulation and, more generally, the rules dealing with exchanges microstructure and price-discovery mechanisms). At the micro level, such rules aim at non-discrimination in relationships among intermediaries and different customers (conduct of business rules).

A third objective of financial market regulation, linked with the general objective of efficiency, is the safeguarding and promotion of competition in the financial intermediation sector. This requires rules for control over the structure of competition in the markets and, at the micro level, regulations in the matter of concentrations, cartels and abuse of dominant positions.

Specific controls over financial intermediation are justified by the forms that competition can assume in that field. They are related to the promotion of competition as well as to limiting possible destabilising excesses generated by competition itself.[8]

## II.2   *Financial market supervisory models*

There is neither a unique theoretical model nor just one practical approach to the regulation and supervision of financial markets. Significant differences are found in the literature in terms of both definition and classification of regulatory models and techniques.

We identify four approaches for financial market supervision and regulation: 'institutional supervision', 'supervision by objectives', 'functional supervision' and 'single-regulator supervision'.

### Institutional supervision

In the more traditional 'institutional approach' (also known as 'sectional' or 'by subjects' or 'by markets'), supervision is performed over each single category of financial

---

[7] One of the classic instances of market failure is relative to the presence of information asymmetries. However, some recent theories of financial intermediation (Allen and Santomero, 1997) seem to go beyond theories based on information: a look at reality in fact shows that while transaction costs and asymmetric information have greatly decreased, the activity of intermediation has considerably increased. Financial markets seem to be more and more markets for intermediaries than for investors or firms. The nature of all financial intermediaries (not only banks, but also mutual funds, financial intermediaries, financial firms, pension funds) seems to be that of operators who perform risk management activities on behalf of third parties and decrease the 'costs of participation' in the financial market: these two aspects have not yet been the object of in-depth analysis by intermediation theorists. These same two motivations are thought to contribute to the building of long-term relationships between intermediaries and customers in such a way that the latter avoid *ex ante* research costs by simply buying the implicit insurance supplied by the intermediaries (Allen and Gale, 1998).

[8] On more than one occasion the European Commission has reaffirmed the applicability to financial markets of the general regulation on competition. The Court of Justice has also upheld such orientation.

operator (or over each single segment of the financial market) and is assigned to a distinct agency for the entire complex of activities. In this regulatory model, which follows the traditional segmentation of the financial system into three markets, we thus have three supervisory authorities acting as watchdogs over, respectively, banks, financial intermediaries and mutual funds, and insurance companies (and the corresponding markets). The authorities control intermediaries and markets through entry selection processes (e.g. authorisations and enrolling procedures in special registers), constant monitoring of the business activities (controls, inspections and sanctions) and eventual exits from the market (suspensions or removal).[9]

'Institutional' regulation facilitates the effective realisation of controls, being performed with regards to subjects that are regulated as to every aspect of their activity and as to all the objectives of regulation. Each intermediary and market has only one supervisory authority as a counterpart. The latter, in turn, is highly specialised. As a result, duplication of controls is avoided and the costs of regulation can be considerably reduced.

The institutional approach seems to be particularly effective in cases of intermediaries of a very similar type and that do operate in just one of the three traditional segments of financial intermediation. *Vice versa*, the institutional model may give rise, in the presence of more subjects entitled to perform the same financial intermediation activities,[10] to distortions in the supervisory activity caused by the enforcement of different dispositions for operations of the same nature that are executed by different entities. The disadvantages of this approach are represented by the previously mentioned trend toward multiple-sector activities and by the progressive de-specialisation of the intermediaries. In turn, these phenomena are connected to the growing integration of both markets and instruments, that frequently leads to the building of large financial conglomerates. In a context where the boundaries separating the various institutions are progressively being erased, it is no longer possible to establish whether a particular subject is a bank, a non-banking intermediary or an insurance company; or whether a group is involved more in one or another of such activities. Therefore, there is the risk that 'parallel' systems of intermediaries may be created, reflecting the diversity of the respective control authorities. In this case, the way the controls are set up may become a destabilising rather than stabilising factor. Moreover, the intermediaries might be induced to choose their juridical status in a way, which is contingent on the different rules that discipline different subjects.

A further possible element of weakness in the model lies in the fact that when a single authority supervises a category of subjects and pursues more than one objective, the result of the control activity might not be effective in the event that different objectives are in conflict.[11]

---

[9] As an example of the institutional approach, one can consider the regulatory system provided for the insurance market and intermediaries in Italy by the Isvap (*see* below – Section III).

[10] Consider the negotiating activity in the stock exchange performed by both banks and financial intermediaries, or else the gathering of savings realized by life insurance companies, similar to that undertaken by mutual funds.

[11] The classic example is the trade-off between the objective of stability and that of competition (*see* below – Section III).

## Supervision by objectives

The supervisory model by objectives (or by finalities) postulates that all intermediaries and markets be subjected to the control of more than one authority, each single authority being responsible for one objective of regulation regardless of both the legal form of the intermediaries and of the functions or activities they perform. According to this scheme, an authority is to watch over both market stability and the solvency of each intermediary, whether in banking, finance or insurance; another authority will be responsible for the transparency of financial markets and will control the behaviour of banks, financial intermediaries and insurance companies toward customers; a third authority will guarantee and safeguard competition over the entire financial market and among intermediaries.[12]

The basic advantage of this regulatory model lies in the fact that it is particularly effective in a highly integrated market context and in the presence of polyfunctional operators, conglomerates and groups operating in a variety of different business sectors. At the same time, it does not require an excessive proliferation of control units.

The most attractive feature of this scheme is that it provides uniform regulation for the different subjects engaged in the same activities.

Compared to the 'institutional' model, a regulatory framework organised by objectives may produce a certain degree of multiplication of the controls. And sometimes it could lead to a lack of certain controls. Indeed, the specific assignment of competencies with respect to the objectives of regulation is not necessarily univocal and all-inclusive in practice. In such a model, each intermediary is subject to the control of more than one authority, and this may be more costly. The intermediaries might in fact be required to produce several reports relating to supervision, often containing identical or similar information. At the same time, the intermediaries may have to justify the same action to a whole set of authorities contemporaneously, even though for different reasons. *Vice versa*, a deficit of controls might occur whenever the exact areas of responsibility are not clearly identifiable in specific cases.

## Functional supervision

The third regulatory model is the so-called 'functional supervision', or supervision 'by activity'. It considers as 'given' the economic functions performed in the financial system; unlike other lines of thought regarding supervisory activities, this approach does not postulate that existing institutions, whether operative[13] or regulatory,[14] must necessarily continue to exist as such, in terms of both their structure and role.

---

[12] In the Italian system, the supervisory model by objectives has found application, at least nominally, in the Finance Law "Testo Unico delle disposizioni in materia di intermediazione finanziaria" (DL 58/1998) where it is established, with reference to intermediaries, that the competent authority in the matter of risk containment and financial stability is the Banca d'Italia, while the Consob is responsible for transparency and proper behaviour.

[13] Banks, mutual funds, intermediation firms, insurance companies and other financial intermediaries.

[14] Bodies for controlling stability, supervisory organs to guarantee transparency, antitrust authorities and other supervisory agencies.

The 'functions' or activities undertaken are considered to be more stable than the institutions that perform them. Competition among financial systems is thought to drive existing institutions to evolve in a dynamic perspective in the direction of new and more efficient forms.

According to Merton and Bodie (1995), the financial system is considered to perform six basic functions:

- to provide ways of clearing and settling payments in order to facilitate trade;
- to provide a mechanism for the pooling of resources and for portfolio diversification;
- to provide ways of transferring economic resources through time, across borders, and among industries;
- to provide ways of managing risks;
- to provide price information to help coordinate decentralised decision making in the various sectors of the economy;
- to provide ways of dealing with the incentive problems created when one party in a transaction has information that the other party does not have or when one party acts as agent for another.

In the functional supervisory model, each type of such financial services should be regulated by a given authority independently of the operator who offers it. Hence, also this approach has the important advantage that it calls for the same rules to be applied to intermediaries who perform the same activity of financial intermediation even though such operators may fall into different categories from a legal standpoint. For example, activities including investment management, the gathering of deposits, lending, and savings invested in insurance/retirement funds are each subject to homogeneous rules established by individual authorities, which independently supervise such activities regardless of the institutions engaged. This approach fosters economies of specialisation within the supervisory authorities and might represent a rather attractive solution for the regulation of integrated, advanced financial markets. However, it is not without drawbacks. This model envisions an overlapping of bodies controlling the same subject: there is the risk of an excessive division of competencies among the regulatory agencies.[15]

---

[15] Oldfield and Santomero (1997) view financial institutions as a set including banks, insurance companies, investment companies (open and closed funds, other forms of collective investment, pension funds), origination firms (investment firms, credit institutions, insurance brokers and financial promoters), market-makers (specialists, dealers and reinsurance companies), stock exchanges (cash and derivatives), clearing houses and other financial operators. The services provided by these financial institutions can be classified in six different activities: origination (identification, evaluation and creation of financial activities originating with the customers of an institution), distribution (the collection of funds through the sale of new financial products), servicing (the management of payments flow from financial activities issuers to holders), packaging (pooling and tailoring of financial activities to fit the specific needs of customers through greater personalization of goods and services offered), intermediating (setting up of financial activities and contemporaneous buy-back of different financial activities on the part of the same intermediary), market making (purchase or sale of financial activities). In a regulatory perspective this taxonomy might lead to an arrangement wherein every activity would correspond to a different supervisory activity.

A further disadvantage of the functional approach is that finally what is subject to failure is not the activity performed, but the institution. In case of serious problems of stability, it would be essential to guarantee protection and oversight with regard to the institutions rather than to individual operations (Padoa-Schioppa, 1988).

### Single-regulator supervision

The single-regulator supervisory model is based on just one control authority, separated from the central bank, and with responsibility over all markets and intermediaries regardless of whether in the banking, financial or insurance sector. This authority would be concerned with all the objectives of regulation (stability, transparency and investor protection, maybe competition).

In the regulatory practice, the centralised supervisory model has typically characterised early stages of financial system development, often in periods when the central bank was the only institution that supervised the activity of financial intermediaries. Faced in recent times with the globalisation and integration of the markets, the English brought this model back into being with the creation of the Financial Services Authority (FSA) (see Briault, 1999).[16] The British executive's decision to merge the pre-existent supervisory authorities – part of the Central Bank staff, the Securities Investment Board, the directorship of the Department of Trade and Industry competent in the insurance field and the Security Regulatory Organisations (SROs) – in the FSA is based on the search for a more efficient organisation of regulatory activities including a reduction in the costs of regulation itself. Also, it was considered useful to have just one agency accountable to the Parliament and to the market.[17]

The advantages of this approach lie in the economies of scale that it produces. Fixed costs and logistical expenses, the costs of administrative personnel and the compensation for the top management are all considerably reduced. Moreover, this scheme calls for a unified view, which is particularly useful and effective with respect to polyfunctional groups and conglomerates. By the same token, the costs of supervision charged to the subjects regulated and/or to the taxpayer decrease.

However, the validity of this model depends to a high degree on its internal organisation: if the numerous areas of competence and specialisation are not well-structured and coordinated, the risk is to slow the decision-making process. As underlined by Wilson (1989), what counts is a clear definition of the agency's 'mission'. Also, the presence of a sole regulator might render collusive relations more immediate and direct ('regulatory capture'). Finally, it might exacerbate problems of self-contradiction in the event that the authority should find itself forced to pursue conflicting supervisory objectives. This sort of problem might in part be overcome thanks to an internal organisation divided 'by objectives', but the fact that there is only one top management would end

---

[16] The single-regulator model was first developed in Scandinavia (Denmark, Norway and Sweden) more than a decade ago. *See* Taylor and Fleming (1999).

[17] The costs of the FSA are funded directly by the market through a system of contributions and taxes charged to the supervised institutions.

up in the prevalence of a single objective as final consequence of the decision-making process.

### II.3    Is there an optimal model for supervision?

Our presentation of the main regulatory models of the financial system should have made clear how hard it is to establish which alternative offers a decisively superior arrangement. In real life we find a prevalence of 'mixed' approaches, which borrow in heterogeneous fashion elements that are proper to more than just one model.

The institutional model could be considered a good candidate only in a context with rigidly separated financial segments, and where no global players are at stake. Nowadays, we think that this picture does not apply to the major advanced countries, where we do observe high integration in financial markets and intermediaries and a strong presence of polyfunctional groups and conglomerates.

The most evident problems with regard to the functional supervisory model are the following: (i) it might call for too many regulators, corresponding to the numerous functions and activities that the intermediaries perform; (ii) it does not explicitly address questions regarding the stability (possible failures) of the single institutions.

Hence, we think that modern financial systems should rely on either a single regulator or independent agencies, each one responsible for one of the three objectives of regulation.

However, we are particularly concerned with the possible conflict of interest in pursuing different objectives when these are assigned to the same agency. Clearly, the 'single-regulator' model is truly affected by the possible incompatibility among the supervisory objectives.[18] In the credit sector, for instance, we find a clear trade-off between competition and stability (at least in the short run). The need to safeguard stability led, particularly in moments of economic and financial tension, to the use of instruments designed to limit competition, such as institutional barriers to entry in the market, or to the legal imposition of limits to operative activities. In financial systems where banks are prevalent but not efficient enough to compete cross-border, the objective of competition is usually sacrificed more easily than that of macroeconomic stability. The consequence is a 'stable' environment in terms of the number and identity of the intermediaries. But this is obtained by altering the free play of competition through measures that prevent exit of inefficient actors from the market.

Another case is that of the possible conflict between the objectives of stability and transparency. Again with regard to the banking sector, scarce transparency in fund gathering activities (e.g. in the issue of securities) might allow the application of interest rates below market rates. Such behaviour could be considered functional to the strengthening of the stability of banks, but it would result in direct injury to investors.

The most immediate response to this important problem might be to attribute to different authorities different objectives of supervision, that is to adopt the regulatory

---

[18] Moreover, the single-regulator model could also lead to excessive concentration of regulatory powers.

model by objectives as the benchmark for advanced financial systems. This solution could be designed so as to avoid an excessive proliferation of authorities and thus limit the increase in both direct and indirect costs of regulation.[19] In what follows, we will present a proposal of reform of the regulatory framework currently in place in Italy which is inspired by this model. We will also argue that such model could be usefully adopted at the euro level.

## III   REGULATORY ARRANGEMENTS IN IHE ITALIAN FINANCIAL SYSTEM

### III.1   *Integration among intermediaries, markets and instruments*

As already mentioned, banking, securities and insurance segments are becoming increasingly integrated in terms of markets, intermediaries and financial instruments. The boundaries separating banking, securities and insurance activities are in fact on their way out in most developed financial systems because of the strong process of technological, geographical and functional integration among these three sectors; and as a consequence of the de-specialisation of the intermediaries. The 'reserved activities' that characterised financial operators by type are constantly decreasing at both the normative and operative level. As a matter of fact the traditional tripartite division of the financial market failed to take into consideration that the creation and allocation of savings among sectors with a cash surplus and sectors with a cash deficit were basically unitary phenomena: hence, a unitary view of financial inter-mediation and its regulation should be adopted.

In the case of Italy, the processes of integration within the financial market have come about in a rather articulated fashion.

As regards the intermediaries, ownership integration has been accentuated, coming about mainly through the transfer of capital shares among institutions, or among controlling and controlled firms.[20] Another form of integration among intermediaries may be detected in the transformation of their legal status, even when continuing to perform basically the same intermediation activities as before. This occurred in particular with investment firms (SIM – società di intermediazione mobiliare), which have been legally transformed into banks, even though they have not as their primary objective the issue of deposits or the provision of loans. The reasons for this 'arbitrage' among legally diverse forms are multiple: access to credit of last resort and to the interbank liquidity market; possibility of directly managing customers' liquidity; concerns about a sounder image ('too bank to fail'); differing modalities for crisis management; different regulatory costs; different supervisory authorities to have to deal with.

---

[19] The literature available to date on both fronts is not vast. An important contribution is Goodhart (1988). Attention is also called to a recent empirical work by Franks, Schaefer and Staunton (1997) on the direct and indirect costs of the regulation of financial markets, which among other things evidences the absence of research on the benefits of regulation.

[20] For a detailed and analytical description of the issues in Secs III1 e III2, *see* Di Noia e Piatti (1998).

As regards the markets, considerable integration has taken place between the banking/insurance markets and the securities markets. This occurred by virtue of the issue and quotation on either the Stock Exchange or other markets of securities (equities and bonds) of both banks and insurance companies. The Italian financial market is thus experiencing a progressive coincidence between issuers and financial intermediaries.[21] This feature is likely to develop even further. These intermediaries have in fact become, with the 'privatisation' process of the Stock Exchange and of the MTS (the Wholesale Government Bonds Market), owners and managers in the same regulated financial markets, which have been transformed into corporations. Recently, some banks have also started to manage directly alternative trading systems (as the TLX, by Unicredito Italiano).

As regards the integration among financial instruments, we observe that many of these, while keeping their legal status, have rapidly changed their economic function. This is due to both exogenous factors – such as fiscal considerations, or different regulations applied to similar financial tools – and to endogenous factors – such as the different behaviour of sellers and buyers (here we refer in particular to certificates of deposit and bonds issued by banks, and to certain types of life insurance policies).

The role of insurance companies as financial intermediaries is also constantly increasing, thanks to contracts involving life insurance and capitalisation, whose services are directly tied to investment funds or to stock exchange or other financial indices (so-called unit-linked or index-linked contracts).[22] Nowadays, the inclusion of the life insurance segment among those activities subject to financial regulation is something accepted in the major financial systems. Over the last few years, market changes have actually lessened the distinctiveness of some schemes of life insurance compared to other financial products. In the English system, for instance, long-term life insurance contracts are included in the notion of investment (financial instruments) as provided by the Financial Services Act of 1986. This law and its implementing rules regulate the selling of long-term business (life and pensions, see also Boléat, 1998). Insurance companies have the same treatment of unit trusts in terms of their selling activity. The recent establishment of the FSA will further reduce the distinctiveness of insurance companies by applying a common regulation to all financial institutions. In the US system, variable annuities and variable life insurance contracts whose yield is tied to 'separate accounts'[23] fall under the Investment Company Act of 1940, which provides the general guidelines relative to investment activities, reinvestment, and the buying and selling of financial securities. Besides,

---

[21] This phenomenon seems to be peculiar to Italy. Data on stock exchange capitalization indicate that the weight of the financial sectors in the Italian stock market is much higher in 1998 (42.4% of market capitalization) than in other advanced countries (18.2% in the US, 26.4% in France, 33.7% in Germany, 26.9% in the UK, 18.2% in Japan). *See* IRS, Rapporto sul Mercato Azionario 1999.

[22] Whenever an insurance company offers these kinds of financial products, it unquestionably falls into the category of subjects engaged in the activity of financial intermediation, as it is linking economic sectors in surplus with those in deficit.

[23] In such contracts, the value of what the owner may receive during the pay-in (and sometimes the pay-out) period depends upon the investment performance of the separate account into which his or her payments have been invested.

as contract owners assume certain investment risks under variable contracts, the contracts are securities under the Securities Act of 1933. In Italy, on the contrary, insurance companies are excluded from the set of rules that apply to banks and to other financial intermediaries. The exemption from such rules derives from the fact that life insurance policies are not considered financial instruments (see Art. 1 of the Finance Law) and that insurance companies are not authorised to perform investment services. Although there is an increasing tendency to recognize the high degree of contiguity between certain insurance products and typical financial products, the regulatory differences in the Italian system remain significant. Italian insurance companies are supervised and controlled by only one supervisory authority, the Isvap (Istituto di Vigilanza sulle Assicurazioni Private).

## III.2  The regulatory model

Financial markets regulation in Italy has been obviously affected by the structure and the evolution of the financial system. It was traditionally focused on banking inter-mediaries. The major changes in the past three decades have come about under the pressure of both the European directives and of increasing cross-border financial market integration. Such changes have been grafted onto a regulatory system whose basic approach was to carve a three-way division of the financial market into bank-ing, securities and insurance sectors. This division was reflected in a three-way division of the intermediaries and a corresponding division of the regulatory author-ities: Banca d'Italia, Consob (Commissione Nazionale per le Società e la Borsa) and Isvap. New regulations were frequently introduced and in a rather uncoordinated fashion. The final outcome is a structure of controls, which is difficult to classify into any one of the theoretical models previously illustrated. The distribution of compe-tencies among the different supervisory authorities is in fact characterised by a 'mixed' approach (see Table 1).

As for insurance companies, the institutional model is followed (with Isvap super-vising them for stability and transparency). The institutional model is partly used also for banks. They are supervised by Banca d'Italia for stability and transparency in all typical banking activities (deposits and loans), as well as for those aspects regarding competition (Law 287/1990 excludes the Antitrust Authority from having primary control over banks).

Then, there is the case of pension funds where a mixed institutional-functional approach is used. Here an activity, the payout of private pensions, is reserved to well-specified financial intermediaries while at the same time being an exclusive object coming under the control of Commissione di Vigilanza sui Fondi Pensione (Covip). Nevertheless, the Ministry of Labour issues general directives in the matter of the supervision of pension funds (with the Ministry of the Treasury), and supervises the Covip. The Ministry of Labour does also authorise the exercise of this activity, while the Ministry of the Treasury, after hearing the Commission's opinion, issues regula-tions setting limits and criteria in the matter of investments, and the rules to be observed in the case of conflicts of interest.

*Table 1.* Competent authorities for the supervision of financial intermediaries in Italy

| Intermediaries ↓ | Objective → | Stability | Transparency and proper behaviour | Competition |
|---|---|---|---|---|
| Banks | | BankItalia, Cicr, Min.Tesoro | BankItalia, Cicr, Consob, Min.Tesoro (Antitrust) | BankItalia (Antitrust) |
| Investment firms | | BankItalia, Min.Tesoro | Consob, (Antitrust) | Antitrust |
| Life insurance | | Isvap, Cipe, Min. Industria | Isvap, (Antitrust), Cipe | Antitrust, (Isvap), Cipe |
| Investment funds | | BankItalia, Min. Tesoro | Consob, (Antitrust) | Antitrust |
| Pension funds | | Commissione Fondi Pensione, Min.Lavoro, Min.Tesoro | Commissione Fondi Pensione, Min.Tesoro (Antitrust) | Antitrust |

The model by objectives formally characterises the regulation of entities officially authorised to perform investment services, with regard to such activities: banks, investment firms, investment management firms, mutual funds and Società di Investimento a Capitale Variabile (Sicav). These intermediaries are supervised by Consob insofar as transparency and investor protection and by Banca d'Italia insofar as 'limitation of risk and financial stability' (Art. 5, Paras 2–3, Finance Law). Moreover, the Antitrust Authority has exclusive competence for the rules on competition for all authorised subjects with the exception of banks.

A supervisory model by objectives seems to emerge with respect to the entire securities market, and not just to the intermediaries. The recent evolution of the normative framework assigns to the Consob all the powers in the field of transparency in the market (secondary regulation of the solicitation of public saving, of insider trading, of takeovers and public offers, etc.). Similarly, Banca d'Italia might be considered responsible in the matter of stability (regulation – not necessarily exclusive – of compensation, liquidation, clearing houses, wholesale securities markets, central depository, settlement systems, etc.). The Antitrust Authority might be considered responsible for guaranteeing competition among different exchanges.

### III.3   Current regulatory problems

Our previous description of the regulatory framework adopted in the Italian financial system should have already indicated the presence of some rather peculiar features. In this section we want to underline those peculiarities that we view as regulatory problems.

Many of these problems derive from the dominant role traditionally performed by banks in the Italian financial system, and hence from their regulator, the central bank.

A premise is necessary: for a long time the Bank of Italy has been representing a relevant and positive exception in the Italian public administration sector. However, a logically incoherent assignment to the same institution of mutually conflicting tasks might still be dangerous and lead to an inefficient functioning of the financial system. This is true with regard to the regulatory objectives as well as to the policy instruments that can be activated in order to reach the former.

A first problem is that of having banking supervision conducted in a regime of monopoly by the central bank.[24] This feature is unique among G7 countries. Even though we will not discuss it here, we want to underline that the problem has only partially been solved with the start of the EMU and the assignment to the ECB of full responsibility for monetary policy in the euro area. As a matter of fact the national central-bank governors participate to formulate the monetary policy strategies and decisions and are responsible for their implementation in the domestic economy. Hence, so far there is no complete separation of tasks.

A striking anomaly, which is unique in the euro area, is represented by the assignment to the Bank of Italy of the task of preserving competition in the banking sector. We do not think that there is any motivation nowadays to give such a responsibility to an Institution different from the one (the Antitrust Authority) that supervises this feature in all other economic sectors. The rationale of this regulation is to be found in the fact that the Antitrust Authority was established only recently in Italy (1990). In absence of such an Institution, the possibility that dominant coalitions and excessive market power could arise in the banking sector was considered too dangerous and justified the assignment of the task of preserving competition in the market to the already existing Institution controlling the banking system for prudential supervision. Today, however, no reason remains to assign the same objective of regulation to different Institutions in different sectors.

Moreover, it is logically incoherent to assign responsibility for competition in one sector to the same Institution that is responsible for the stability of the same sector. As already stressed, at least in the short run, an obvious conflict emerges between the two objectives of stability and competition. And, as a matter of fact, in many of the M&A operations in the Italian banking sector, the opinions of the Antitrust Authority (which are not compelling) and those of the Bank of Italy have been opposite (Cafagna and Sciolli, 1996). A competitive market is by nature unsteady, in the sense that allows for the entry of new firms and the exit of the inefficient ones. In recent periods there were examples of this peculiar role of the Bank which stopped some takeovers of some banks over other banks because they were hostile. Beside, the Bank stated that it is necessary for the Bank to know in advance any intention to launch a takeover: but in the event of listed banks, reasons of investor protection would make necessary that any price-sensitive news should be disclosed to the market, or at least to the market authority.

---

[24] *See* Di Noia and Di Giorgio (1999) for an updated discussion of the pros and cons of separating monetary policy responsibilities from the ones for banking supervision and regulation. *See* also Goodhart and Shoenmaker (1992).

The Authority, which is responsible for the stability of the system, could indeed have a regulatory bias for the protection of firms that should be left to exit the market. The usual motivation of the risk of contagion and of investor protection would be advocated. However, we think that the risk of contagion is not necessarily and inevitably linked to all single bank crisis. Moreover, this risk could be countered with other instruments, including more transparency and information diffusion in the market.

We also think that there is no clear argument to protect the interest of investors other than bank depositors. Why should the bond and equity holders of a bank be more protected than those of a non-financial firm? In addition, we should also notice that the 'small and naive' depositors are already protected by an explicit deposit insurance system.

Another anomaly in the Italian financial system is that the Bank of Italy owns relevant shares and equities of either banks or other financial institutions controlling banks. The Bank of Italy invests in equities both part of its ordinary reserves and part of the contributions of the employees' pension fund.[25] Quite obviously, monetary policy decisions in terms of interest rates (previous to the start of the EMU) and the supervisory and regulatory decisions have such a relevant effect on the profitability conditions of the supervised entities that the Central Bank should be not allowed to be a shareholder of the same entities. At least, its equity investments should be decided and managed by one or more totally independent and autonomous financial manager.

Another problem stems from the different regulation given to life insurance firms, particularly when they act purely as financial intermediaries. The life insurance industry, throughout contracts such as unit and index-linked schemes, has been gradually losing its distinctiveness. We think it should no longer be regulated as a different function from banking and financial investment, nor having its own regulator. A step in this direction may be represented by a recent decree approved by the Italian Parliament (February 2000) on the fiscal treatments of pension funds, which establishes equivalent fiscal regimes for mutual funds and unit and index-linked short-term contracts.

### III.4 Prospects for regulatory reform of the Italian financial system

In this section, we shall present the basic lines of our operative proposal for a regulatory reform of the Italian financial system. With the Finance Law, Italian legislators have already begun to reorder competencies among the various supervisory authorities. We think that it would be wise to go further. Regulatory arrangements

---

[25] Some data: by the end of 1999, the Bank of Italy owned shares higher than 2% of the company capital in 10 listed firms, including a bank (Italfondiario, 8%), a financial holding company (IFI) and many insurance companies (Alleanza, Generali, INA, La Fondiaria), that in turn were either involved in the control of, or controlled by, other Italian banks, whose supervisor is Bank of Italy itself.

in the Italian financial system should be organised according to a clear division of competencies strictly in line with the 'by objective' model. The object of such a regulatory change should be the entire securities, banking and life insurance market.[26]

The authority responsible for (micro) stability should supervise the stability of the entire financial market and of single financial intermediaries whether in banking, securities or insurance (authorisations; professional registers; supervision in the area of information, regulations and inspections of intermediaries and conglomerates; other matters regarding stability; crises management). We think that this authority should also manage deposit insurance and the investor compensation scheme. In fact, the current agencies (the Fondo interbancario di Tutela dei Depositi (FITD), and the Fondo Nazionale di Garanzia) have no regulatory and supervisory powers at all. These agencies simply act as the cash management department of other regulating institutions when reimbursing depositors and investors. There are clearly cost reductions that could be achieved by their elimination. As regards macroeconomic stability, this authority should only cooperate with the central bank in supervising security settlement and payment systems and clearing houses; but it could be charged with supervision over financial instruments in wholesale markets, with particular regard to government bonds and derivatives.

The authority responsible for transparency and investor protection should supervise disclosure requirements and the proper behaviour of intermediaries and the orderly conduct of trading in all financial intermediation activities performed by banking, securities, and life insurance intermediaries (including discipline and control in the area of transparency in contracts). Moreover, this authority would be assigned powers in the area of misleading advertising by financial intermediaries. Finally, it should control macro-transparency in financial markets (including the discipline of insider trading, takeovers and public offers).

The authority for competition should guarantee fair competition, and should avoid abuses of dominant position and limit dangerous concentrations in banking, security and insurance sectors. A non-binding opinion of the authority for stability might be contemplated in certain instances.

As we have previously mentioned, the major problem of supervision by objectives is the possible duplication of supervisory activities. The necessary coordination and resolution of eventual controversies could be provided by a Commission for the Supervision of the Financial System (as in the Corrigan Report – Corrigan 1987) which would assist the Ministry of the Treasury, which in turn should be charged with oversight in the area of fund gathering, credit practices and other financial activities. The commission would be the natural place for activities involving proposals and consultation concerning measures regarding financial market regulation.

---

[26] In terms of international application, a regulatory structure embracing the whole financial market including the insurance market is to be found both in the previously-cited English and Scandinavian reforms and in the reform of the Australian system. The Australian reform establishes a clear division of competencies by objectives, excluding, as in the United Kingdom, the central bank from microstability controls over intermediaries.

In practice, we propose the following major reforms for the Italian financial regulatory framework:

(1) To create a new institution (Financial Supervision Authority) responsible for financial supervision by separating the Banking Supervision Department of the Bank of Italy (*Vigilanza*) and merging it with the deposit insurance fund (FITD).

(2) To assign to the Financial Supervision Authority responsibilities in terms of microeconomic stability of all financial intermediaries, including banks, investment firms, institutional investors, life insurance companies and pension funds. Macroeconomic stability and controls over security settlement and payment systems should be left under the responsibility of the Bank of Italy.

(3) To subtract any responsibility in terms of competition in the banking and insurance sectors to either the Bank of Italy or the ISVAP and assign them only to the Antitrust Authority.

(4) To assign to the CONSOB all powers and responsibilities in terms of transparency, disclosure requirements, investor protection and misleading advertising in all financial markets.

(5) Covip should be abolished; ISVAP would be responsible only for the activities of the insurance companies which are not alike those of other financial intermediaries (*ramo danni*).

Our three distinct independent authorities ought to be characterised by homogeneous procedures in terms of their creation, functioning and funding, as well as by similar attributions of powers.[27] A sketch of our proposal based on a 'four-peak' model of financial regulation follows (Figure 1).

## IV    FINANCIAL STABILITY AND REGULATION IN EUROPE

In the recently established euro-area, and given the increasing integration among European financial markets, it could seem quite useless to present proposals of institutional reforms for financial market regulation that are limited to single countries. In this section, we will argue that a natural extension to the financial system at the euro level of the regulatory model by objectives could be considered a good

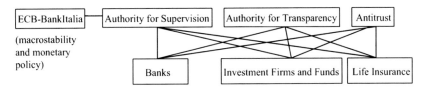

*Figure 1.* A 4-peak model for financial regulation.

---

[27] *See* Di Noia and Piatti (1998).

candidate to solve some problematic issues regarding financial stability and the need for more coordinated transparency and investor protection rules. These topics are currently at the centre of a lively debate (see Padoa Schioppa, 1999; Lannoo, 1999; Vives, 1999) and are discussed more in detail in a companion paper (Di Giorgio and Di Noia, 2001).

We start by observing that in the European Monetary Union (EMU), the principle of separating monetary policy and banking supervision responsibilities has been clearly established in the statute of the European Central Bank (ECB). The latter empowers the ECB to set out and conduct monetary policy in the euro area, but leaves the responsibility for banking supervision to the national authorities. It could be argued that a problem of institutional separation between monetary policy and banking supervision agencies does not exist any longer in the euro area,[28] even though in countries where the national central bank (NCB) is a monopolist in banking supervision, the separation is not complete as the NCB Governor does also participate to the definition of the general strategies of European monetary policy which are set out in the ECB Governing Council.

However, as argued above, the term banking supervision should be replaced by that of financial supervision. The stability of the financial system could not be so much at risk because of the loan/deposit activities performed by banks. Instead, financial instability could be induced by activities linked to portfolio management, which are typical of investment banks and securities firms.[29]

The real problem to tackle should then be that of who takes care of financial regulation and supervision in the EMU. At the moment there is no clear assignment of roles and responsibilities agreed upon at EU level. However, we think that there is no point in having a common monetary policy and aiming at an always more integrated financial system in the euro area while keeping different financial regulations and supervising rules in each member country. As a matter of fact, these institutional differences are an important barrier to further financial integration. In this field, the principle of minimum harmonisation and mutual recognition, that was originally thought to be able to naturally induce over time a convergence of regulatory behaviour and more uniform rules, clearly did not work. Moreover, there is a concrete risk that competition in this area will not even generate the more efficient outcome: on one side there exists an obvious incentive to promote less demanding domestic financial regulations and supervision in order to let the own country become more attractive for running financial business; while on the other side it is not clear who will pay the costs of potential insolvency following excessive risk taking behaviour and financial misconduct in a member country (see below). Finally, with increasing international banking activities and a European real time gross settlement system in place

---

[28] In fact, 'even in countries where the competent authority for banking supervision is the central bank, by definition this authority is, functionally speaking, no longer a central bank, as it lacks the key central banking task of autonomously controlling money creation' (Padoa Schioppa, 1999).

[29] A well known recent example of a serious threat to financial stability is the LTCM case. Here, a non-bank institution was rescued thanks to the moral suasion of the FED, that is not responsible for the supervision of hedge funds.

(Target), the argument that domestic regulators and supervisors have better knowledge and can exercise more efficient control becomes day by day less effective (see Prati and Schinasi, 1999).

Another important point is that no clear tool or any responsibility to counter and/or manage the risk of financial instability and crisis has been established in Europe. The Treaty is silent on this topic. It is not even evident that the role of lender of last resort will be performed by the ECB, as it would be desirable being an essential function of a central bank (see De Cecco, 1999). In fact, this solution will probably occur only in the case of a widely spread liquidity crisis affecting the whole euro area. But what will follow a liquidity crisis located in a single country? And what will follow a solvency crisis?

Suppose we face a situation in which a single financial institution located in a member country is in trouble. What kind of intervention, if any, is currently allowed? One of the typical forms of public intervention seems lost, and probably the most natural, that of central bank last resort loans. The ECB will not intervene in favour of a single institution, especially if its financial links are mostly domestic. Also because it could always assign some of the responsibility for the crisis to the domestic financial regulator–supervisor. The domestic central bank cannot intervene by providing funds without an explicit authorisation by the ECB. In this case, it will have to convince the latter that the institution is facing a liquidity and not a solvency crisis, according to the Bagehot's doctrine (1873), and/or that the risk of potential spread and contagion of the crisis is high.[30] This requires time and resources. The other two traditional instruments, bail out through a safety net provided by the banking system or through the government budget will ultimately shift the burden on the shoulders of domestic taxpayers, especially in the framework established in the Stability and Growth Pact. Given the current level of taxes in Europe, this is hardly an optimal solution.

We think that a much higher degree of co-ordination in the field of financial regulation and prudential supervision is both desirable and needed in the EMU. Our view is not limited to the banking system but embraces all financial intermediaries. A somehow good example of international co-operation can already be found in the banking supervision, with the Basle Committee working on a wide range of topics with no formal by-laws, but a very strong leadership. On the contrary, the securities supervision has not succeeded in establishing a similar long record of international rule making. In a world of complete mobility of capital and financial services, where institutions and markets operate without frontiers, supervision should operate at the same level, that is to say, it must be structured internationally.[31] Moreover, following the view we adopted on the national base, we think that the European supervisory system would gain both in consistency and effectiveness if all stability oriented rules, all transparency oriented rules and all competition oriented rules for all types of financial institutions were either issued or (may be better) coordinated by distinct independent agencies at the euro area.

---

[30] *See* Freixas *et al.* (1999), Bruni and de Boisseu (1999), and De Cecco (1999).

[31] This does not necessarily lead to the creation of a European SEC (*see* Lannoo, 1999a; Karmel, 1999), even though such hypothesis could become realistic in the medium run.

Of course, we are aware that it is not easy to structure and create such an integrated system of rules and institutions in the European Union, that it will require time, resources and a widespread collaborative attitude. Hence, we list not one but three possible paths of institutional changes that can reintroduce the function of lending of last resort in the euro zone and at the same time allow for a sounder scenario in case of a financial crisis. The last solution is the one we prefer, inspired by the same logic we used for our proposal of reform of the Italian financial system. However, we view also the other two following ways as better solutions with respect to the current situation.

(1) A first possibility is to assign supervisory powers and responsibilities in the banking sector to the ECB. However, even leaving aside the arguments against the solution of merging banking supervision and monetary policy, this arrangement would still be not satisfactory and would require other institutional changes, as it would be certainly desirable to have a common supervisor for all financial intermediaries. The Maastricht Treaty would then have to be amended, as it explicitly forbids that supervisory powers regarding insurance firms be assigned to the ECB.

(2) A new European System of Financial Regulation (ESFR), structured similarly to the ESCB, could be established. A European Financial Regulation Authority (EFRA) should be at the centre of the system. The EFRA should be formally separated by the ECB, both in order to avoid excessive concentration of powers as well as for other arguments.[32]

In a first stage, the EFRA would harmonize and coordinate financial regulation in member countries, design common principles and guidelines for prudential supervision and set out appropriate disclosure instruments and requirements. This central agency should sponsor the necessary institutional change at domestic level leading to merging and re-organisation of supervisory and regulatory powers in the financial sector of each member country. At the end of the process, in each country there will be just one national agency, similar in structure to the Financial Service Authority recently established in the United Kingdom. This national agency will participate to the definition of the general strategies and principles of financial regulation in the area, becoming a member of the ESFR. It will be responsible for the implementation in the domestic country of both the rules and the supervisory duties agreed upon at the euro level.[33] In each single country, this agency will be the sole responsible for financial stability and correct disclosure of all financial intermediaries – being in charge of banks, securities firms, mutual, pension and hedge funds, life insurances – and of all securities markets.

(3) Establish two new different European Agencies, one responsible for the microeconomic stability ('European Financial Supervision Authority') and one for the transparency, investor protection and disclosure requirements ('European

---

[32] *See* Di Noia and Di Giorgio (1999). Another relevant issue is 'who pays for financial supervision and how much it costs'. An attribution to the ECB of these functions could be less transparent given that they may be confused in the monetary policy ones (thus inducing lower accountability).

[33] Both the national and the central European levels of financial supervisors should exist, given the current level of harmonization in the financial market legislation, which is far from complete, in particular with respect to taxation, accounting rules and banking crises management.

Authority for Market Transparency') of all financial intermediaries. The two central agencies should co-ordinate the different domestic agencies in each member country. In this solution, we will then have two different European systems of financial regulators, according to the principles that suggest replacing 'institutional' regulation by 'functional regulation' (or by objective).

Under both (2) and (3), no antitrust power will be given to any member of the ESFS, so as to avoid the trade-off between competition on one side and stability and transparency on the other. Moreover, agencies responsible for supervising market competition do exist at both euro and domestic levels. We think that it would be wise to transform in a third separate and independent central agency the EU Antitrust DG. This will then coordinate and promote the harmonised activities of domestic Antitrust agencies. In each Member State, the national Antitrust agency will safeguard competition in all economic sectors.

A special Committee (and desk) for the lending of last resort function could be established at the ECB, with the participation (only for information and communication purposes) of members of the (one or two) ESFS. The ESFS (or the one responsible for 'supervision') will promote the participation of intermediaries, in each country, to a limited insurance fund that could provide good quality collateral to institutions facing liquidity problems in order to be able to qualify for central bank financing. The national agency will manage the fund and assess whether an institution is just illiquid or insolvent. In the latter case, provision of collateral should be denied. The domestic government could still decide whether to bail out the institution or not, being responsible and (politically) accountable for the decision.

Our suggested 4-peak model for financial regulation in Europe is sketched in Figure 2.

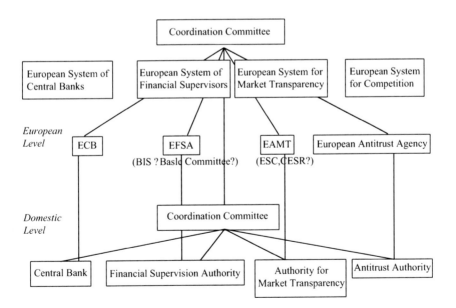

*Figure 2.* European system of financial regulation.

## V   CONCLUSIONS

In this chapter we argued that financial market regulation should be re-designed and harmonised in Europe according to a regulatory model by 'objectives' or finalities'. We have first analysed the case of Italy and sketched a comprehensive proposal for the reform of its financial system regulation. This would call for assigning to three distinct and independent agencies (separated by, but coordinated with the central bank) all supervisory powers and regulatory responsibilities in financial markets and on financial intermediaries, regardless of these being insurance companies, banks or investment firms. One agency should be responsible for financial microstability, another for transparency and disclosure requirements, and the third for protection of competitive features in the markets.

In view of the criticism addressed to the current assignment of financial regulatory and supervisory powers in the European Union, we think that the previous scheme could be extended and nested into a wider context as the euro area. In particular, we are in favour of the establishment of two new European financial regulation agencies, each formally separated by the ECB. These agencies should be responsible for the comprehensive co-ordination of both legislation and execution of regulation in financial markets: the first European agency should be responsible for the microeconomic stability of all intermediaries, while the second for transparency and disclosure requirements. The third objective of guaranteeing competition in financial (and non-financial) markets is already safeguarded by having the Antitrust General Direction of the European Commission plus the domestic agencies. It would be wise to transform in a central and independent European agency the EU Antitrust General Direction. The latter and the two newly created central agencies will be at the centre of three European Systems of Financial Regulators, each one structured similarly and working in connection to the ESCB, thereby requiring active participation of national agencies in member countries. A 4-peak regulatory model 'by objective' would be in place in the Euro Area as well as in each member country.

## REFERENCES

F. Allen and A. Santomero, 'The Theory of Financial Intermediation', (1997) *Journal of Banking and Finance*, n. 11.

F. Allen and D. Gale, 'Innovations in Financial Services, Relationships and Risk Sharing' (1998) *Journal of Political Economy*.

A. Blinder, *Central Banking in Theory and Practice*, (MIT Press, Cambridge, 1998).

M. Boléat, 'The Insurance Industry and the Financial Services Authorities' (1988) 6(1) *Journal of Financial Regulation and Compliance*, vol. 6. No. 1.

C. Briault, 'The Rationale for a Single National Financial Services Regulator' (1999) *FSA Occasional Papers*, n. 2.

F. Bruni and C. de Boissieu, 'Lending of Last Resort and Systemic Stability in the Eurozone,' Paper presented at the Conference on the Lender of Last Resort at LSE (1999).

L. Cafagna and S. Sciolli, 'Ruolo e responsabilità delle istituzioni: l'Autorità Antitrust' in AA.VV. *Quali banche in Italia? Mercati, assetti proprietari e controlli* (Edibank, Milano, 1996).

C. Calomiris and R. Litan, 'Financial Regulation in a Global Marketplace' (1999), mimeo.

J. Coffee, 'Competition versus Consolidation: the Organizational Structure in Financial and Securities Regulation' (1995) *Business Lawyer*, n. 2.

G. Corrigan, *Financial Market Structure: A Longer View* (Federal Reserve Bank of New York, 1987).

R. Dale, 'Reorganizing the regulation industry' (1997) *Financial Regulation Report*, n. 2.

H. Davies, 'European Central Banking – East and West: Where Next?', (1997) May *Bank of England Quarterly Bullettin*.

M. De Cecco, 'The Lender of Last Resort' (1999) *Economic Notes*, 1.

J. Dewatripont M. e Tirole, *The Prudential Regulation of Banks* (MIT Press, Cambridge, 1994).

G. Di Giorgio and C. Di Noia, 'Financial Regulation and Supervision in the Euro Area: a Four-Peak Proposal,' Wharton Financial Institutions Center (2001), w.p.n.2/2001.

C. Di Noia and G. Di Giorgio, 'Should Banking Supervision and Monetary Policy Tasks Be Given to Different Agencies?' (1999) *International Finance* 3.

C. Di Noia and L. Piatti, 'Regolamentazione e mercato finanziario: analisi e prospettive di riforma per il sistema italiano' (1998) *Quaderni di Finanza CONSOB*, n.30.

FSI, *Financial System Inquiry Final Report* (Australian Government Publishing Services, 1997).

J. Franks, S. Schaefer and M. Staunton, 'The Direct and Compliance Costs of Financial Regulation', (1997) *Journal of Banking and Finance*, n. 11.

X. Freixas, G. Giannini, G. Hoggarth and F. Sousa, 'Lender of Last Resort: a Review of the Literature' (1999) November *Financial Stability Review*.

C. Giannini, 'Enemy of None but a Common Friend of All? An International Perspective on the Lender of Last Resort Function' (1998) Banca d'Italia *Temi di Discussione* n. 341.

C. Goodhart, 'An Incentive Structure to Financial Regulation' (1996) *Special Paper*, LSE Financial Markets Group, n. 88.

C. Goodhart, 'Myths about the Lender of Last Resort' (1999) *International Finance* 3.

C. Goodhart and D. Shoenmaker 'Institutional Separation between Supervisory and Monetary Agencies' (1992) *Giornale degli Economisti e Annali di Economia*, n. 9–12.

R. Karmel, 'The Case for a European Securities Commission' (1999) 38 *Columbia Journal of Transnational Law*.

IOSCO, Objectives and Principles of Securities Regulation (1998).

K. Lannoo, 'Do We Need a European SEC? Securities Market Regulation in the EU' (1999a), mimeo.

K. Lannoo, 'Financial Supervision in EMU' (1999b), mimeo.

D. Llewellyn, 'The Economic Rationale for Financial Regulation'; FSA Occasional Paper (1999).

R. Merton and Z. Bodie, 'A Conceptual Framework for Analyzing the Financial Environment', in Crane D. *et al.* (eds), *The Global Financial System, A Functional Perspective* (Harvard Business School Press, Cambridge, 1995).

G. Oldfield and A. Santomero, 'Risk Management in Financial Institutions' (1997) 39(Fall) *Sloan Management Review*.

M. Onado, 'The Consequences of European Financial Integration for the Regulatory Authorities' (1999), mimeo.

T. Padoa-Schioppa, 'Sistema finanziario e regolamentazione' (1998) *Bollettino Economico*, n. 11.

T. Padoa-Schioppa, *Il governo dell'economia* (Il Mulino, Bologna, 1997).

T. Padoa-Schioppa, 'Global Supervision: a Term in Search of a Content' (1998) March *BNL Quarterly Review* (Special Issue).

T. Padoa Schioppa, 'EMU and Banking Supervision' (1999) *International Finance* 2.

J. Stiglitz, 'The Role of the State in Financial Markets', in Proceedings of the World Bank Annual Conference on Development Economics (1993).

M. Taylor, 'Redrawing the regulatory map: A proposal for reform' (1997) *Journal of Financial Regulation*, n. 1.

M. Taylor and A. Fleming, 'Integrated Financial Supervision: Lessons of Scandinavian Experience' (1999) *Finance and Development*.

X. Vives, 'Banking Supervision in the European Monetary Union' (1999), mimeo.

L. White, 'International Regulation of Securities Markets: Competition or Harmonization?', in A. Lo (ed.), *The Industrial Organization and Regulation of the Securities Industry*, (NBER, Cambridge, 1996).

L. White, *Technological Change, Financial Innovation, and Financial Regulation: the Challenges for Public Policy* (Wharton Financial Institutions Center, 1997), p. 33.

J. Wilson, *Bureaucracy* (Basic Books, 1989).

# Chapter 18

# The Swedish Financial Market in a
# Legal Perspective – Some Aspects

*Lars Gorton*

## 1 GENERALLY

### 1.1 Introductory remarks

During the last 15 years the financial sector in Sweden has been the object of much legislative and regulatory change covering public law aspects as well as private law aspects.[1] Gradually specific consumer protective legislation has been introduced, which derives from EU directives or has been introduced as Swedish national rules, particularly the Consumer Credit Act 1992:830.[2] Generally several rules emanate from EU directives, others have developed through the work of the Basle Committee, and others still have originated in developments primarily in the US financial markets. In the private law sphere there have been a number of court decisions related to in particular suretyships (financial guarantees) and to professional negligence. In such perspective the financial law area is a vast legal domain, where rules of different character are intertwined.

The financial sector is characterised by a number of different functions which have changed gradually but also by a number of changes related to the particular actors involved in the area.[3] New actors of various types have evolved beside the traditional banks and insurance companies, and the traditional, established actors have gradually altered their functions, sometimes adding new services in order to be able to offer more complete financial services, sometimes selling off certain parts of their activities and purchasing others in order to focus on and become more specialised in particular fields. Deregulation (or rather reregulation) of the financial markets, larger

---

[1] A further step has been taken through the thorough survey of the financial sector in SOU 1998:160. This is also a follow up of the financial crisis hitting Sweden in the early 1990s primarily due to bad debts. The survey also gives a proposal for new banking legislation.

[2] This act replaced a former act 1977:981 although more in form than in substance.

[3] In some countries banks are important also as owners of industrial and other companies, whereas in other countries banks are basically not allowed to invest in other business than financial business. Following the financial crisis in the United States in the 1930s particular legislation (the Glass-Stegal Act) was introduced in 1933 whereby banks had to make a choice between being commercial banks and investment banks (merchant banks). The rationale behind this was mainly transparency. The Glass-Stegal Act was repealed in 2000.

*Mads Andenas and Yannis Avgerinos (eds), Financial Markets in Europe: Towards a Single Regulator?* 421–445.
© 2003 *Kluwer Law International. Printed in Great Britain.*

entities, the use of new technology and the creation of new financial products have all contributed to the structural changes of the financial sector. All those changes have also had implications on the legal framework, whether of public, regulatory type or of private law type.

Swedish financial markets are no exception to the development that has taken place, and the rules have also developed in similar ways although in some respects lagging after the development in US and English law.[4]

During a period after the Second World War the financial sector, in particular the banking sector, was heavily regulated (more or less to various degrees in different countries), and in Sweden with Sveriges Riksbank (the Swedish Central Bank) as a strong regulatory body beside the two authorities supervising the banking sector and the insurance sector. At the time the Central Bank was close to the Department of Finance and was a strong arm of the Swedish political establishment in respect of economic and monetary matters.

The changes of the legal framework of the financial markets are thus at the same time the result of the changes in the market but also the prerequisite for such changes. We may thus in a European historical perspective follow the gradual changes in the financial practice and the financial law, where the public and the private law aspects in different periods sometimes converge and sometimes diverge. The financing of wars historically had an important impact on the development of financial devices. Apart from the banking system developed during the medieval times in Italy, later in Rotterdam and subsequently in London, the financing of business ventures was in periods mainly done through partnerships and later through companies. In this perspective we can see the development of financing and investment broadly, whether in the form of loan, investment in equities or other.

The development during the twentieth century has been hugely affected by economic-mathematical research, which has led to further possibilities for and also (but more slowly) to increased requirements for better financial information to share-holders and better control of particularly publicly listed companies as well as better information in various financial matters.[5] New financing devices were gradually introduced, sometimes rather more sophisticated improvements of already existing devices, sometimes new financial products (not the least options and derivatives). The growing demand of consumer protection has also played an important role. Although the technical economic development of new financial products has been more rapid in the United States as well as in England there has been a similar development in Sweden, and US and English regulations and conditions have had at least in certain ways an important impact on the Swedish financial markets and the legal framework around it. The development of the economic and the legal structures are thus closely intertwined in the financial area.

---

[4] In spite of the differences between the civil law and the common law systems the legal framework around the financial sector has been much influenced by US and English law. This is particularly true in respect of international loan agreements.

[5] In particular insider regulation and take over rules may serve as illustrations to this development.

## *1.2 Some basic features of the Swedish situation*

Looking at the Swedish financial markets from a legal point of view a number of features are apparent. During the 'regulatory period' several public duties were placed upon the banks in order to achieve the promotion of the economic policy of the government. Banks were obliged to purchase and hold government bonds, the interest rate was set by the Central Bank and used as *one* important measure in the Swedish economic and monetary policies. Banks and to a less extent insurance companies, although often privately owned, rather seemed like semipublic entities, where public rather than private rules mattered. Or one may say, because of the strict public regulation the need of legal protection of individual customers seemed to be less called for. On top of that there was also in Sweden considerable leftwing call for the nationalisation of banks during the 1970s, and legislation was carried through whereby the government appointed a certain number of directors on the boards of the banks.

Different official bodies had different regulatory functions: The Central Bank basically set interest rates, issued new coins and notes and was a lender of last resort. Companies and private persons had to apply to the Central Bank for permit to make international payments, and there was a far-reaching reporting system. The Central Bank, a body with relations to the Parliament was closely tied to the government. Today the Central Bank shall be and is independent from the government. In order to establish a bank an application has to be made to the government, which could decide to give a permit. This also applied to foreign banks wishing to have a Swedish affiliate. The Bank and the Insurance Supervisory Authorities respectively supervised their respective areas and issued rules and regulations in and for the different financial sectors. Banks and insurance companies were before the deregulation based on national ownership, and foreign ownership was basically shut out. Foreign directors were basically excluded from Swedish bank boards. The banking sector was thus very much a closed sector, regulated heavily by the government and with a rather inflexible structure.

Banks have since long time been described as entities borrowing money from the public at large and lending money to private persons to companies and for that matter also to the government. They are also involved in domestic and international payments. The definition has changed slightly due to various EU Directives.

With the development of new financial devices and instruments new entities appeared in the financial markets offering new services, such as for example leasing and factoring, which were in this particular form new devices, although not necessarily completely new when looking at them from a functional point of view. The new financial entities were not bound by the regulations applicable to the traditional banks, and so the new actors could offer new services or old services on terms and conditions not available to the traditional actors. New legislation later reduced the differences in regulation of banks and other financial institutes. Furthermore new finance instruments were developed, such as derivatives and securitisation etc.[6]

---

[6] *See* about this development broadly SOU 1998:160, p. 177.

Particularly in the field of corporate finance new solutions appeared, which required new rules related to the financial market. New technology also added to or was a prerequisite for the creation of new financial and payment methods.

The changes have been dramatic and fundamental covering the organisation side, the different functions involved as well as new instruments and other devices. The role of the banks have changed and banks are now, for example, much less involved in the financing of large corporations than earlier, and instead banks seem to be more involved in off balance sheet operations, such as the organisation and management of investment funds of different types. Special bank departments as well as independent financial institutions assist the large corporations in the issuance of bonds etc. in various financial markets. To all this the growing number of elderly people adds a steadily growing need for the financing of pensions also demanding new and more flexible solutions.

Some other features are the increasing consumer protective measures as well as the Europisation and the globalisation of the businesses. Reregulation and new types of competition patterns have evolved. With the technological and economical changes there has been a need of legal adaptation, and rules partly focusing on other questions and problems than earlier. This development is true with respect both to private law rules and to public/administrative rules. Another important aspect is the EC focus on antitrust questions. New rules have thus evolved gradually concerning the financial sector, covering the relation between the financial entities and the regulator (the public law/administrative side), the relation between different financial entities (where matters of contracts, agency, corporate law and antitrust law nature become particularly important) and the relation between financial entities and their customers (matters of general private law character).

## 2   BANKS AND SUPERVISING AUTHORITIES

### 2.1   Role of banks

A fundamental question concerns why banks by tradition have been regarded as conducting a business, which is considered unusually risky seen from the society's point of view. The reason seems to circle around the concept of *systemic risk*, which is the risk that would occur when bank customers in large numbers and at the same time gather to withdraw money from their bank accounts (so-called *runs*).[7]

One of the traditional functions of a bank is that of an intermediary of capital in the sense that it borrows money from the savers (the general public, whether private persons or companies) and lends money in its own name to other customers, likewise whether private persons or companies or for that matter the government. The length of and the conditions for the borrowing and the lending may vary, and there

---

[7] On the question of risk (different risks) and risk management in the financial sector *see*, i.a. SOU 1998:160, p. 178ff.

are risks connected with this difference. As a compensation to the savers for lending money to the bank (or for depositing the money with the bank as the banks may prefer to see it) the bank pays to the saver a certain interest, and it charges to its customers an interest rate which is normally higher when lending money. The difference between the interest paid and the interest received is known as the *margin*, which is one of the fundamental sources of income in traditional banking. Apart from this the banks may also charge its customers various fees and commissions. Presently banks are, however, also involved in several activities of off balance sheet character.

An important part of the banking business is to handle the payment system, so that payments could be made from one person to another, without them having to carry and deliver cash on all payment occasions. This is one of the items where technology has meant fundamental improvements, both from time and security point of view.[8]

## 2.2   Supervision and control

In Sweden, different supervising bodies are involved in the financial sector with various functions and within different areas. They have to a large extent their counterparts in other countries, which may, however, be clothed with somewhat different functions. In Sweden, those entities which are most involved are Riksbanken (the Central Bank), Finansinspektionen (the Financial Supervisory Authority – below referred to as FSA), Riksgäldskontoret (the National Debt Office), Exportkreditnämnden (the Export Credit Guarantee Department), Konkurrensverket (the Competition Authority) and Konsumentverket (the Consumer Protection Authority). Some few words should be mentioned about their different activities.

*Riksbanken.* In Sweden the Central Bank has today more limited and narrow functions than it used to have. As outlined above it was earlier more closely related to the government and to the Parliament. Through legislation during the late 1980s,[9] which is an effect of international negotiations and agreements in particular on European level the Central Bank is now by law independent from the government and the treasury. The Central Bank shall supervise and be responsible for the money market while the Treasury remains responsible for the financial markets. This distinction has been upheld and the Central Bank has therefore as its main target to check the rate of inflation, and it has to use as its main method the interest rate.

The Swedish Central Bank thus continuously supervises and controls the balance of payments and the state of foreign currencies held and owed. Banks have to report daily to the Central Bank on payments going out of the country and on payments being received from abroad into the country.

---

[8] In Swedish law, *see*, i.a. Arnesdotter, *Moderna betalningsmetoder – betalning och girering* (Stockholm, 1996) and Lehrberg, *Moderna betalningsformer* (2nd edn, Stockholm, 1999). A more thorough survey has been given by Brindle and Cox (eds), *Law of Bank Payments* (London, 1996). With respect to the European development *see* i.a. van Empel, 'Payment systems. Recent developments at EC level' (2000) 2 *Luiss International Journal* 154ff.

[9] Lag (1988:1385) om Sveriges Riksbank.

The primary task of the Central Bank is thus to be responsible for the monetary and currency policy (including the administration of the gold and currency reserve) and the issuance of coins and notes (until Sweden eventually becomes a member of the EMU and adopts the Euro).[10] The Central Bank also administers the clearing between commercial and other banks, borrows money from them and lends money to them. It is still the 'lender of last resort', which means that it could in exceptional cases financially support banks with liquidity problems, something that may today be regarded as doubtful taking into consideration EU rules on state aid.[11]

The Central Bank's primary function today is the money policy and it has set as its aim to maintain an inflation which does not exceed 2½% p.a. The bank mainly works with market operations in order to control the interest level, which means that it buys and sells state papers through repurchase agreements, and the banking system will thereby, hopefully, keep in check the level of liquidity in the economy.

The Swedish currency regulation which was a relic from the Second World War was abolished in 1990, and can again only be reinstated in a crisis situation.

*Finansinspektionen (The Financial Supervisory Authority – FSA).* The second main regulatory body is the FSA which is that authority, which acting for the government may decide on permits for banking activities and supervises the different actors in the financial markets, such as banks, insurance companies and other financial institutes and operations on the stock exchange. FSA was formed in 1991 after a merger between the previous Banking Supervisory Authority and the Insurance Supervisory Authority.

It is a government authority under the ministry of finance. FSA's main tasks is to supervise that there are useful financial rules and that the rules are followed, that the actors in the financial markets act in compliance with the 'soundness' requirement to maintain financial stability and to control and supervise the lending and lending terms and conditions, etc. Thus much regulatory power has been delegated to it through a number of enactments whereof the act on banking activities (referred to as BRL) and the act on financial activities (referred to as LFV).[12]

FSA furthermore issues, and supervises standards applied in the financial markets in accordance with the rules which have been introduced, but it also issues its own regulations in order to improve the services of the banks and other financial institutes. FSA is also the main supervising body in respect of certain stock exchange

---

[10] Sweden is not yet a member to the EMU and has not adopted the euro as its currency. This means that the Swedish Central Bank still has some responsibilities which in other countries have been transferred to the European Central Bank (ECB). Following European requirements the Swedish Central Bank is nowadays independent from the government in its role as supervisor. Although Sweden is not a member of the EMU consideration has to be taken to the development in Europé and decisions taken by the ECB and ESCB.

[11] The last time so far that financial support was required was during the financial crisis in 1992–94, when a particular body was set up to handle the problems in the financial sector, and when also a number of 'bad banks' were organized to take care of bad debts from some of the banks.

[12] The rules on supervision of the banks and other financial institutes appear in Chap. 7 of the act on Banking activities – Bankrörelselagen (1987:617) and in Chap. 5 of the Act on Financial Activities – lag (1992:1610) om Finansverksamhet.

matters, such as insider trading. FSA activities are financed through fees payable by banks, insurance companies and other financial institutes under FSA supervision.

*Riksgäldskontoret (The National Debt Office).* The National Debt Office has a completely different function being the entity for the government borrowing. It negotiates loan agreements but also issues government guarantees in order to facilitate the borrowing for large projects (such as, for example, the bridge between Malmoe and Copenhagen). This could be both in order to make it possible to borrow in the financial markets or to lower the rate of interest payable to the lender, since the government backing of a loan will normally mean that a lower interest rate has to be paid.

*Other important authorities in the financial sector.* Among the other agencies in the financial sector the Competition Authority deals with antitrust matters related to the financial markets. The Consumer Board shall support consumers and develop protective measures to the benefit of consumers. There is a particular department in the Consumer Board handling matters related to the financial sector, proposing new rules, negotiating with the banks on certain amendments to terms and conditions applied *vis-à-vis* consumer customers. There may still be some risk of conflict between FSA activities and those of the Consumer Board, but basically the FSA activities are geared at the financial markets, whereas the Consumer Board shall be more involved with the consumer perspective.

Apart from the regulatory aspects, disputes in the financial sector between banks and customers etc. are generally referred to the general courts, but disputes related to consumer customers are often handled through a simplified procedure. Such simplified procedure is normally less sophisticated and less costly and based on written documentation only. There is thus firstly a bureau of complaint related to banks where customers could address their claims. As a next step the Board of Complaints in a particular financing division deals with matters between financial entities and consumers.

## 3  SWEDISH LEGAL RULES IN THE FINANCIAL MARKET

### 3.1   Generally

Swedish law is part of the Nordic law family. There is thus a common basis with the 'civil code' tradition. The Nordic countries are, however, often regarded as forming a separate legal family. There is, however also, by tradition strong influence from common law. Furthermore, being a member of the EU, Sweden like the other Member States has to follow the legislative measures taken by EC. The growing EC legislation has had a huge impact on the general development of Swedish law. Not least during the last few decades much legislation has been brought about through EC in order to achieve a certain law harmonisation in the union. The area of financial law is one of those legal domains where the legislative efforts have become particularly significant during the relevant period.[13]

---

[13] About this development generally, *see*, for example, Mohamed, *European Community Law on the Free Movement of Capital and the EMU* (Stockholm, 1999).

As outlined above several different financial services exist in the financial markets and there are also several institutions providing these various services, such as banks and other similar institutions, insurance companies, brokers and different consultants.[14] The services include among other things the borrowing and lending, payments, sale and purchase of shares, bonds, different types of derivatives, investment advice, prospectus advice, etc.

Financial law is by no means a very precisely defined legal domain. For the purposes of this chapter I mean thereby the law related to financial markets and transactions in them as well as financial structures. I shall, however here only mirror two particular aspects of the financial law sphere, namely, on the one hand rules in Sweden introduced as a consequence of the changes of the EU banking directives and on the other hand rules related to hostile take over bids. They both form part of the financial law area, but they represent distinctly different areas. Furthermore the legislative methods used have been quite different in these particular legal fields, the one being based on rules of traditional legislative nature, the other being of more self-regulatory character.

Before delving into these particular matters in somewhat more detail I wish, however, to point rather broadly at some other legal features around the financial law.

### 3.2    Rules related to the public law/administrative law aspects

In spite of the deregulation which has taken place, Swedish law has an abundance of administrative rules related to banks and other financial institutions. The public law rules in this area are mainly the responsibility of the ministry of finance, whereas corresponding rules of private law character are basically dealt with by the department of justice. This may lead to certain differences in the legislative approach. Furthermore, as mentioned earlier, a portion of the public administrative rule making has been delegated to FSA within the legal frames given in the legislation.

The legal framework of the financial markets is probably one of the most expanding law areas for the time being. The main public administrative legislation relates to the Central Bank, acts on banking and other financial activities, on capital ratio etc. but also acts on the trading with financial instruments, on insiders, on equity funds, etc.

From a structural legal point mention could also be made of some differences of legislative approach. In Swedish law certain rules, such as those related to insider dealings and to take over practice are basically treated as part of stock exchange law, whereas they would in other countries rather be seen as part of the company law area. This does not, of course, play an important role from a practical point of view, but it serves as an illustration of differences in legal outlook.

---

[14] As mentioned BRL and LFV are the most prominent pieces of legislation in this field, but apart from those several other acts have been passed.

## 3.3   Corporate and antitrust law aspects

During the early decades of the twentieth century there were in Sweden like in many other countries a large number of banks and savings banks which were gradually merged or which went into bankruptcy. The attitude from the government was then to create control and supervision of banks to prevent unsound and illegal practices but new rules were also introduced aiming at generally better accounting and auditing principles. The main focus was thus on the regulation of the financial markets and actors.

Looking at the corporate as well as the competition angle there have during the last 20 year period been two separate developments. There was previously in Swedish law a particular Bank Company Act as well as a separate Act on Savings Banks. With respect to commercial banks the general Company Act now prevails with some specific rules on bank companies which are mainly found in BRL.

Antitrust law has not been a Swedish legislative stronghold until the impact of EC law greatly changed the situation. The previous attitude of strict regulation has been replaced by a stronger focus on deregulation (or rather European reregulation) and competition legislation which applies also to the financial sector. Thus EC competition rules and rules on state aid have come to play an ever increasing role in the financial area.

The European and for that matter the international deregulation coupled with the new EC regulatory measures have had a huge impact in the financial field, and similarly competition aspects (antitrust aspects) have come to play an important role, and the several European directives in the financial sector and the banking sector have been introduced in parallel with the growing antitrust interest, as well as rules on state aid.[15]

Basically banks thus follow the general corporate principles also in respect of mergers.

## 3.4   Private law aspects

On the private law side the situation is basically different.[16] Generally there seems to be little legislation of traditional private law type geared specifically at the financial area and different relations *vis-à-vis* banks and other actors.

---

[15] The Rome Treaty rules on state aid have been discussed in connection with e.g. the financial difficulties of Credit Lyonnais, and the financial support given by the French government. Barings bank, on the other hand, was not bailed out by the English government. Sweden was not a member of EU at the time when the government set up a fund to save some banks which fared economically very badly in the aftermath of the financial upheaval in the beginning of the 1990s. There has, however, been a discussion whether these measures would have been permissible in a EU perspective.

The national and international mergers within the financial sector during the last 10–15 years period have caused some work for the European Commission and for other competition agencies.

[16] To point at the legal structure there have in Swedish law been published two separate ssurveys on e-commerce, the first dealing with e-commerce in a general business perspective and the second one dealing with e-commerce in relation to private law matters.

There are on the other hand several rules of general nature (contract law of obligations) which apply broadly and which are also applicable in the financial sector and on banking relations. General contract law rules naturally have basic importance in this sphere as in other business relations and likewise do special contract rules, which may be important for analogy if not directly applicable. Furthermore, customs and practices of various character may have great importance. The law of torts likewise plays an important role, and particularly the intersection between rules of contract law and tort law nature.

Rules on ownership and financial security, such as pledge and lien (from a perspective of obligatory law guarantees (surety) have an equal practical importance), bankruptcy rules and priority rules play a paramount role for banks and other financial entities. In the traditional private law sphere rules related to promissory notes, cheques and bills of exchange as well as rules on suretyship (the latter is rudimentary in the Swedish code book[17]) appear to be of particular concern for the banking sector. Apart from the Consumer Credit Act (1992:830), which contains various types of rules related to bank loans and other credits (from a consumer point of view), there is no general Swedish legislation on credits. This being said the act on Promissory notes[18] has general application. There is also particular legislation on bills of exchange and on cheques.

The relations between bank and the customer (commercial customer or consumer customer) were not really considered by the Swedish legislator until the consumer law gradually developed leading to a set of consumer protective acts from the beginning of the 1970s. This is also a field where EC law has come to play a role and several directives have been adopted geared at the promotion of consumer protective legislation.[19]

Apart from bankruptcy and reorganisation matters and general questions related to pledge and other matters where a third party relation may be involved there are during the last decades two dispute areas in particular, which appear rather frequently in Swedish courts: namely the law related to suretyship and the law related to 'professional negligence'. Whether the insider regulation may in the future also lead to private law suits is an open question, and present Swedish tort rules hardly seem to open up for such law suits.

A number of Swedish cases related to suretyship have been reported, and there seems to be a growing trend for an increase in requirements on banks to inform sureties (guarantors) of the financial status of a debtor or at least to give information of particular risks involved in a guarantee. There seems thus to be an extended duty of information, particularly in connection with general guarantees (sureties given for the general present and future debts of the debtor up to a certain limit). Whether this

---

[17] It merits to be mentioned that new special rules have been introduced in Finland and in Norway dealing with among other things suretyship.

[18] Lag (1936:81) om skuldebrev.

[19] Apart from the Consumer Credit rules there is for example an amended proposal (12932/99) for a Dierctive concerning the distance marketing of consumer financial services amending Directives 97/7/EC and 98/27/EC.

development will also in a longer run lead to a more extended general lender liability is debatable, although there seems to be certain features of such liability in the development.[20] There are certainly trends whereby a bank may face liability due to its involvement in its business as selling shares in funds or in giving advice to the customer etc. This is thus an area where there may be room for further legal creativity. It also merits to be mentioned that a proposal for a new Company Act will contain rules on prospectus liability.

## 4 BANKING LAW RULES

### 4.1 Some short comments on the EC law frames

As mentioned above it is necessary to keep in mind the importance of the rules developed on the EC level as well as the interconnection between different rules in the Rome Treaty as amended as well as the relation between primary and secondary EC law.

First, there is an interconnection between the general principles of the introductory sections of the Rome Treaty and the rules in subsequent parts on freedom of capital movements. There is also a link between these latter rules and the economic and monetary rules. On top of this follow then also particular rules on the regulation of the banking sector and the freedom of establishment and various company law rules and stock exchange provisions.

The freedom of establishment is governed by Articles 52–58 in the Rome Treaty, the free movement of services by Articles 59–66 and the free movement of capital by Articles 67–73.[21] Following particular legislative steps through secondary legislation and the introductions of the Single European Act, the Maastricht Treaty and the Amsterdam Treaty the original rules have been amended. As we have seen the EC law has been quite expansive in the financial law area, and the development has run along two lines: one total harmonisation line and one (if I may call it) the mutual recognition line. According to the latter activities carried out within one country and in accordance with the standards of or with relevant permissions from that country should also be permissible in other member countries without separate permission from that country.

The legal framework around the financial area is characterised by the capital directives carried through in sequences[22] in order to achieve a liberalisation in the

---

[20] 'Lender liability' here involves the relation between the bank and the borrower. Did the bank not check the buyer's creditworthiness? 'Lender liability' could also mean the risk that a lender faces when financing a project where an environmental disaster follows, such as the financing of a tanker causing an oil spill, or financing a chemical company causing emissions, explosions etc. Now, of course, the lack of credit worthiness checking could possibly be one ingredient with respect to the bank's possible liability to a third party suffering damage due to an environmental disaster. As is well known the doctrine of the 'deepest pocket' plays an astonishing role in US court practice.

[21] The articles on capital were reformed fundamentally in the Maastricht Treaty.

[22] The first capital directive of 11 May 1960 for the implementation of Art. 67(1) EEC as amended through directive 63/21 EEC and the second directive 88/361/EEC.

financial field. The first one had limited scope, and was geared at the creation of a certain liberalisation with respect to foreign exchange, and also with respect to the trading of certain equities and financial documents its achievement was rather limited. The second capital directive has gradually opened up for an increased financial integration.[23]

As a consequence of this development also banking and ancillary directives have been introduced. The first banking directive set a basis for a common market with banking services over the borders, and the intention was to create harmonisation and with a host country control.[24] The second banking directive has a different feature and is based upon minimum harmonisation and mutual recognition.[25] It is founded on the three principles of one permit on minimum conditions, home country control and mutual recognition.

### 4.1.1   Soundness in financial activities

The mutual recognition presupposes that the supervision and control of financial activities are carried out in a sufficient way in the different member countries so that mutual trust will be upheld.

It is obvious that there is a need for some complementary rules to support the abstract parts of the principle due to the uncertainty that may arise in connection with a regulation of the mutual recognition. There should never be a duty of mutual recognition for financial institutes some through its activity is a risk for the functioning of the financial market. It is hereby evident that there is a need for a complementary functioning for the functioning of the principle, since the directive that makes possible the common banking market, is based on a system of home country control, which in its turn has been created through the mutual recognition.

Consequently it was realised already in the early phase of the common banking market that unless there was some support of the second banking directive the whole construction of the common banking market would be questioned, since the stability in such a market would point at weaknesses. Such situation of instability was. Of course, looked upon with great suspicion in connection with the launching and the beginning of the common banking market. Together with the forthcoming liberalisation of the movement of capital and the knowledge that the risk taking of banks is of importance not only for the finances of one financial institute, there was a direct incitement that further regulation would be necessary for the due functioning of the banking market.

The aim of the regulation giving the general framework for a sound activity and for a supervision and control of the activity is really to avoid risk which may give rise to disturbances in the market which may mean an undermining of the confidence in the market.

---

[23] *See* in particular Mohamed, in particlar pp. 67ff and 81ff. He has analyzed in depth the rules of the freedom of capital and their relation to financial services.

[24] 77/780/EEC, *see*, i.a. Mohamed, p. 189.

[25] 89/646/EEC, *see*, i.a. Mohamed, p. 190f.

The first step was to achieve and decide on a directive which could form a concrete basis in order to adapt the inner market in safe custody leading to the stability of the common banking market.

One important element in the European development is the gradual turn between an all over harmonisation and one standard within the European Union to home state control, where an acceptable basic standard shall be recognised by the other member states. The financial sector is characterised by the latter viewpoint, although there have been company directives which are not only minimum directives. This also means, however, that there may always be a discussion whether requirements are applied differently between home country actors and those coming from another country.

### 4.2   The second banking directive

There is one requirement running through the rules related to the financial markets, namely the effort to maintain trust in the market and in the financial institutions.

Some words should in this connection be said about the basic contents of the second banking directive. The ingress lays down the aim of the rules and the general ideas behind it, where, among other things it shall form part of the creation of a single European market. This also means that more of the fundamental goal is the promotion of freedom of movement of the capital.

There is reference to the principles mentioned above, and it is emphasised that the draftsmen acknowledge that the EC rules may not be sufficient but there may be need of additional domestic legislation.

There are in Arts 1–3 certain definitions, and i.a. credit institute is set out as an entity which receives money for deposit and lends money for its own account.

Technically the definition is based less on who is acting than on the function, but there are also some restrictions in Art. 2 with respect to certain institutions and what they are allowed to do. Art. 18(1) also points out that only affiliates of credit institutions could be established based on the home country control. Art. 3 underlines the monopoly character of the functions in the sense that only credit institutions are allowed to receive money for deposit from the general public.

Art. 4 sets a minimum capital requirement for a credit institution at 5 million euros at the establishment of the entity. An affiliate is thus covered under the capital requirement on the main company.

It goes almost without saying that a fundamental basis is, for the upholding of these principles, that there is in all member countries a supervising authority, which is in a position to exercise its control function, that it can and will take necessary steps when necessary and that it works on a good faith basis in relation to all institutions in the market without favouring national entities.

One important element is the creation of and maintaining of the freedom of establishment in the financial sector, and that all member states shall in accordance with Art. 18(1) see to it that a credit institution permitted to work in that particular country for one or more financial services shall also be allowed to perform such activities in the host country whether as affiliate or through the offering of the service. There are also certain duties of information from the affiliate to the host country financial supervisory authority in accordance with Arts 19–21.

### 4.3    Swedish rules

#### 4.3.1    In general

During the 1980s and 1990s there have been a fast technical and financial developments in the world markets and simultaneously a deregulation or rather reregulation of the financial markets, not the least within the European Union. The Swedish financial landscape has during the same period changed correspondingly through a gradual Swedish adaptation to the new conditions. These development lines have lead to fundamental changes in the Swedish banking and financial legislation during the 1980s and the 1990s,[26] and a revised banking legislation was introduced in 1987 and later amended as already outlined above.

The Swedish membership in EFTA had lead to a gradual adaptation to the EC financial rules through various directives. The EEA agreement in 1992 made an important step in the further development. When Sweden became a member of EC in 1995 much of the legislative work necessitated by the membership had already been carried through.[27]

#### 4.3.2    Soundness requirement in Swedish banking law

The rules on financial activities broadly set out the scope of the activities permitted, that is what the financial institutions are allowed to do and what they are required to do, but there is also a general requirement of soft law character, namely the requirement for 'soundness' in the financial business set out in LFV 1:4:

> The activities of a financial institution shall be conducted in such a manner that the trust of the general public in the credit market shall be maintained and elsewise elsewise that the activity could be regarded as sound.

This could be compared with Art. 2:1 in the proposal for a new act on banking activitites (SOU 1998:160):

> Banking activities shall be conducted in such a way that the ability of the bank to perform its services shall not be put at risk.

---

[26] An important step was taken when the Swedish foreign currency *regulations were abolished*. These rules had been introduced during the Second World War. *See*, i.a. *Afrell, Klahr & Samuelsson*, Lärobok i kapitalmarknadsrätt (Stockholm, 1998) pp. 33–34 and 116–117. This development is also illustrated in *Funered*, Bankernas risktagande. Stockholm 1994, pp. 29–33.

[27] *See* about this development prop. 1992/93:89, p. 102.

The proposal to this adds in 2:4 the following:

Banking activities shall also elsewise be conducted in accordance with good banking standard.

The rules on 'soundness' is based on the requirement in the second banking directive on the need of trust in the market and between the member countries, which requires of course the solvency of the financial institutions. The provision 1:4 of LFV mirrors the requirements of the directive, but the new rules quoted are, of course, not yet in force, but they reflect what could probably be regarded as requirements already upheld in practice in the supervision by the FSA.

Thus, apart from the principle of soundness a set of various rules have been introduced which could be regarded as a net for the promotion of confidence in the financial market, such as rules on capital adequacy, the supervision of large exposures etc.

### 4.3.3   Swedish banking rules

Already the EEA agreement had thus forced Sweden to adopt the first and the second bank directives, and the second banking directive meant that Sweden had to introduce amendments to its legislation with respect to banks and other credit (financial) institutes.[28] Sweden thus introduced amendments in respect of permits to conduct banking and financial activities as well as rules on home country control, but also on the concept of 'credit institute'. The previous authorities supervising the banking sector and the insurance sector respectively were merged into one new authority, the Financial Supervisory Agency (FSA). The FSA tasks were amended.[29] In order to harmonize the Swedish legislation to the EC law definition of credit institute there was need of a uniform legislation for the actors of the market. For this purpose a new act was introduced, the Financial Activities Act, now captioned 'lag (1992:1610) om finansieringsverksamhet',[30] below referred to as LFV.

LFV 1:1 sets out a number of definitions and item 5 defines 'credit institute', as far as I can see inconformity with the second banking directive. A credit institute is defined by its activities which consists in the borrowing from the general public and the lending of money for own account. Thus the cumulative requirement of the directive Art. 1, item 1, has been met.

LFV sets out in 3:1 activities which are allowed, and the activities there mentioned correspond to the list of activities in the annex of the Directive. Similarly banks are defined by their activities. BRL describes bank activities in 1:1 and 1:2 and sets out a list of banking activities in 2:1 stating, i.a. that a bank's activity embraces borrowing from the general public and the advance of credits. It also goes on to

---

[28] *See* Prop. 1992/93:89 p. 102, Bankrörelselag (1987:617) and Lag (1992:1610) om finansieringsverksamhet.

[29] SFS 1992:102 Sec. 1. This piece of legislation was later replaced by SFS 1996:596, the decree with instructions for the FSA.

[30] Law on financial activities, *see* SFS 1997:453, p. 771.

enumerate a number of other banking functions which correspond to Article 3 in the Directive. There is thus a focus on the borrowing and also on the lending.

7:15 ff spell out measures to be taken against banks which are not acting in accordance with the permit or the rules, and 7:21 requires FSA to prohibit somebody from acting as a bank who has no permit as such. As far as I can judge the Swedish rules are in conformity with Art. 3 of the Directive.

The LFV set out a requirement of permit for other Swedish credit institutes than. Here there is also mention of the situations when this main provision does not apply, mainly when foreign credit institute wishes to establish an affiliate in Sweden. Chapter 2, Secs 8–9 set out the principles of mutual recognition, since a foreign credit institute which has a permit according to its country's laws will not need to have a Swedish permit. Sweden thus follows the principles of the directive on home country control and supervision. Only a demand for a notification to FSA is maintained.

There are corresponding rules for banks in BRL 1:4–5. After amendments BRL now prescribes that a foreign bank operating with a permit from its home country will not have to seek a permit in Sweden for the activities of an affiliate.

The first minimum harmonising directive Art. 4 requires a capital of at least 5 million euros in order for a permit to be given, and the two Swedish legislations set out the same minimum amounts. Banks and other credit institutes shall, as a main rule at the time of the decision of a permit according to BRL 9:4 and LFV 2:4 have a capital of at least 5 million euros.

Similarly Swedish credit institutes and banks shall have the same right to establish an affiliate or offer its services in other member countries without having to apply for a separate permit. In accordance with BRL 1:6–8 Swedish banks may after having notified the FSA establish an affiliate or offer its services in another member country. A corresponding possibility shall also apply to other financial institutes in accordance with LFV 2:11–13.

FSA is the authority which gives the permit, and that means that FSA is also the authority which exercises the home country control for Swedish banks and other financial institutes that establish an affiliate or offer their services in other member countries. The supervision shall according to the directive Article 13 embrace the activities as well as *ingripanden*. The Swedish rules are found in BRL Chap 7 and in LFV Chap 5.

Thus Swedish legislation had to be amended in order to meet the transition from host country control to home country control. FSA has the authority and the duty to check and supervise that the requirements set out in the directive are fulfilled when it comes to the permit and that the conditions are upheld. For this purpose the FSA shall in conformity with the directive be in a positions to take meaures and apply sanctions if the conditions are not fulfilled and if a sound banking practice is not strived for.

According to Secs 15–16 in BRL and Secs 16–18 in FVL the FSA shall revoke the permit from the relevant bank or other financial institute in those cases where the agency takes the standpoint that applicable rules on permit and sound activities are not followed.

Sweden has thus chosen to tighten up the requirements with a basis in the minimum harmonisation. Even if Sweden through the regulation makes it clear that FSA will take necessary measures if a Swedish bank or other financial institute does not live up to the rules FSA may not always count on the same support from the other authorities concerned. National rules may not put on a requirement to take steps but only allows the authority to revoke the permit.

Such result may come up when regulation is carried out through minimum harmonisation but it may be partly balanced through the mutual recognition. As already pointed out the principle presupposes a credibility between the member countries. In other words the national agencies in the different member countries should not use the relatively discretionary judgment in the national legislation in such a manner that an affiliate of a bank in one country is favoured through a softer judgment than by other authorities in respect of sound banking and even disregard from certain neglect. Every agency has a duty to see to it that there is an efficient supervision. In order to make this possible or at least to faclititate such a confidential relationship in an individual casethere are in the directive also certain rules on an exchange of information between the authorities. A close cooperation may and should thus complete the minimum harmonisation.

With respect to the regulation of the exchange of information which is a mutual assistance between the different authorities Sweden has chosen to follow the formation of the directive and also sets out in BRL Chap 7, Secs 8–9, respectively, chap 5, Secs 9–10 and 20 in FSL that the FSA may in connection with the unsuitable conduct of the bank or the financial institute may hint at a duty of the credit institute's situation. If there is no rectification the FSA shall notify the agency of the country where the bank or the financial institute is situated. The FSA shall also see to it that all necessary information for an efficient supervision, shall be given to the relevant authorities of the home country.

Even if all national legislation would in a correct way make the rules of the directive part of the national law, there is always a risk of use of the regulation possibilities allowed by the directive. Certain space of interpretation in the directive may be wider or more narrow in the national rules and may be used to some extent in a positive or a negative way. The weak points of the regulation must, however, not lead to doubts, since there is then a risk that the efficiency of the regulation is undermined, which may affect the whole construction of the common bank and financial market, since this is based on confidence.

## 5 HOSTILE TAKE OVER BIDS

### 5.1 In general

Sweden like, for example, the United Kingdom has adopted a self-regulatory system for the regulation of 'take over bids'. There is order maintained in the financial market through a nexus of various rules laws including public statutes and self-regulatory rules.

A 'take over' of a company involves several different aspects of law, whether it is a hostile bid or not. Firstly, matters of general contract law nature are involved, but then also problems related to antitrust law, company law, stock exchange law, labour law, tax law, etc. will have to be taken into consideration. In Swedish law stock exchange rules have become separate from company law issues for reasons of tradition. The new set of various stock exchange rules have not been made a part of company law, but they are sometimes referred to as part of administrative law sometimes as part of financial law (in a broad perspective). Irrespective hereof it goes without saying that company law and stock exchange law are closely interrelated. I shall here disregard all aspects except for those related to company law or stock exchange law, although the others may be of equal importance from a practical point of view.

## 5.2   Swedish company law rules and stock exchange rules

### 5.2.1   Common aspects

Swedish company law is based on the division of powers and functions between the shareholders, the board of directors, the managing director and the auditors. These are all regarded as company bodies with various powers to act for and bind the company or to check the organisation and the managing of the company. The bodies are then seen as making up a balance of power.

In connection with a 'take over bid' there is no particular 'take over body' involved but basically a take over is an act where the owners of the company should be involved. It may, of course be questioned whether the bodies acting for the benefit of the company and the shareholders under normal business condition should also be the bodies involved in a hostile take over.

In a corporate governance perspective a great variety of situations may arise depending on the shareholders' power and/or the directors' power and the interrelation between them, that is, the balance power between them and their different interests. Where there is one large shareholder, a managing director close to that shareholder and an otherwise weak board of directors the situation is quite different from where shareholders balance out each other, and there is a strong managing director or as in situations where the board of directors consists of directors who have been appointed by different groups of interests. In many situations it will therefore not be easy to see and judge which is the better solution for the company, for the individual directors and for the shareholders, respectively. There is thus a built in conflict of risks in all hostile take overs where different persons or group may for different reasons favour one solution or another.

There are no particular requirements with respect to the bodies to be involved in connection with take over business, but the handling of such matter will depend on the power position of the owners, the board of directors and the management, respectively.

A strong managing director with little direct owner interest may turn out to be a strong person in connection with a take over transaction, although he should not from a principal point of view be involved except on a consultative basis to the shareholders. The managing director's power position will be stronger when there are only several small shareholders without one having a considerable stake in the company. In a company with one or some few large shareholders and several small holders the larger ones may tend to have a particular interest not shared by the many small ones.

This means, that there will often be a hidden or an open collision of interests in the case of a take over (a shareholder may wish to sell its shares at a high price, the managing director wishes to maintain his positions, the larger shareholders/directors may wish to maintain the company intact because of a wider strategy plan etc.). So far there is, however, no requirement that a take over bid should be handled by a separate body but the main principles on powers, functions and balances will be the same in day to day business as in case of a take over bid.

### 5.2.2 The Swedish Company Act (Aktiebolagslagen 1985:1385)

The company act contains a number of rules with respect to mergers. These rules are, however, of a rather technical nature setting out formalities in connection with a merger. There are no particular rules in the Company Act concerning the take over bid and how a bid should be treated. What can be found in the Company Act are certain provisions related to the target board's handling of its shareholders and provisions with respect to compulsory acquisitions. The rules are, however, basically of general nature: the board of directors and the managing director have a general duty in relation to the company but also in relation to the shareholders, who should be treated equally. There is also a general rule of good faith in the handling of matters in relation to the company and the shareholders.

I shall here only very briefly point at certain provisions which may have particular interest in this connection. Arts 8:15 and 9:15 in the Company Act spell out these two principles. It is thus stated that the board of directors as well as the managing director 'may not enter into legal transactions or undertake other measures which are likely to give an undue advantage to a shareholder or to a third party to the detriment of the company or a third party'. Those principles will have basic importance in connection with take over transactions where Swedish companies are involved.

Another matter which may have some importance in this connection is that Swedish companies, whose shares are listed on a stock exchange, on an authorised market place or some other regulated market, may now within a limited frame acquire and sell its own shares. The new provisions are mainly covered by rules in the Company Act and entered into force on 10 March 2000. Even though the possibilities of buying and selling own shares are limited in several respects, and even though it is important that such operations do not negatively impact on the confidence in the stock market, the amendments have created new possibilities to set up an arsenal of defences in a hostile take over situation. This new possibility has been used by a number of companies for various reasons, to increase the stock exchange value, to distribute capital etc. I am, however, not aware of to what extent this possibility has been used in individual hostile take over situations.

### 5.2.3 The Financial Instruments Trading Act (Lagen /1991:980/ om handel med finansiella instrument – FTA)

The other angle, thus the stock exchange rules, is found i.a. in the captioned legislation. In relation to these rules the FSA (Finansinspektionen) plays the main role as the supervising and controlling body, and in the present perspective particularly in relation to prospectuses and disclosures of share transfers.

FTA requires a purchaser to disclose a shareholding if it reaches or exceeds any of the following limits: 10%, 20%, 33⅓%, 50% or 66⅔%. Shares held by related parties, such as relatives and group companies are to be treated as the acquirer's own shares. Furthermore the disclosure has to be made to the target as well as the Stockholm Stock Exchange (SSE) and should cover the purchaser's shareholding after the acquisition, the number of shares acquired and the time of acquisition.[31]

A further set of rules of importance is the Listing Agreement for the Stockholm Stock Exchange (SSE), which is a private agreement which all public companies have to sign in order to be listed on the stock exchange. This agreement also contains, among other things, certain disclosure requirements to which listed companies are subject.[32]

Furthermore the Swedish Industry and Commerce Exchange Committee's (NBK) has issued a Recommendation for public offers for the acquisition of shares in 1999. This recommendation contains rules on structure, form and timetable for takeovers on the Stockholm Stock Exchange, which is the backbone of the major take over procedures currently applied in Sweden. The recommendations are included as an appendix to the Listing agreement of the SSE (which applies to companies listed on SSE as well as those quoted on the OTC market). The recommendations are thus of binding nature and apply to offers for all Swedish companies with widespread ownership.

There are also Recommendations issued by SSE concerning buyouts of businesses or shares from stock market companies, etc. (1991) contains rules on Management Buyouts (MBO).

### 5.2.4  NBK's public offer recommendation

In 1971 that the Stockholm Chamber of Commerce Stock Exchange Committee (NBK), drew up the first recommendations concerning public offers for the acquisition of shares in and mergers between companies.[33] The recommendations incorporated the basic features of the London City Code on Takeovers and Mergers and remained in use until 1988.

Equity capital is, however, increasingly of cross-border nature, and in view of the competition between the various capital markets there was a growing concern that Swedish market would appear less attractive if the regulatory system was considered to be less sophisticated than that of other countries. Thus, in 1988 and once more in 1999 the recommendations were amended in order to adapt the rules to the increased requirements of market information and the extensive developments of the stock markets.

---

[31] Jansson, Regelbildningen på värdepappersmarknaden (Stockholm, 1995), p. 153.
[32] *See*, i.a. Norberg and Alfrell, Samuelsson.
[33] Jansson, p. 245f.

The Industry and Commerce Stock Exchange Committee's recommendations do not aim at supplying the markets with more precise regulations concerning the contents, forms and structure of take over bids. Instead, just like the Williams Act in the United States and the City Code in the United Kingdom, they emphasize the importance of providing the shareholders with the time and space to make coercive free decisions concerning the opportunity to profit from potential competing bids. Thus, in a takeover context, the recommendation concerning Public Offers for the Acquisition of Shares (1999) primarily contains two important principles aimed at the protection of shareholders. First, Art. II.13 underlines the manager's duty to act in good faith to general benefit of the shareholders. Second, item II.5 underlines the principle of equal treatment of shareholders, reminding of the provisions in the Company Act 8:15 and 9:15.

Item II.13 prescribes:

If the board or senior managment of the target company has good reason to assume that a serious offer is imminent, due to information received from a person/entity who intends to make a public offer to the company's shareholders, or if an offer of this nature has already been made, the target company may not take any measure regarding the company which is designed to put the issue of the offer or adherence to the offer at risk, unless such measures are approved by a General Meeting of shareholders. However, the requirement of approvals by a General Meeting may be waived if it is clearly esential that action must be taken with the greatest possible speed, in view of the needs of the company and its owners.

Art. II.5. reads as follows:

All shareholders with identical terms are to be offered identical compensation per share. However, if special relationships, compensation may be offered to such shareholders in another form, but with the same value.

A publicly listed company which does not act in accordance with the NBK's recommendations will be in breach of the registration contract of the SSE, where reprisals such as penalty for non-compliance and de-listing are commonplace.[34]

It is also important to note that the amended version of the Recommendation concerning the acquisition of shares includes a material change in relation to the 1988 Recommendation. The 1999 edition contains certain rules in respect of mandatory offers and states, i.a. that:

... anyone who has less than 40 per cent of the total number of votes in a company, and who obtains 40 per cent or more of the total number of votes in the

---

[34] Fällman, Motåtgärder vid företagsförvärv. Särtryck ur betänkande från ägareutredningen (SOU 1990:1), p. 63.

company ... must make a public offer for the acquisition of all the remaining shares issued by the target company.[35]

If, however, the acquirer divests shares within 4 weeks so that its shareholding amounts to less than 40% of the votes, the obligation to make an offer no longer applies. Moreover, as the mandatory offer is a new item in Swedish law, a need for a supervisory authority in a position to provide unquestioned rulings on the application of provisions concerning public offers has been recognised. This particular role has been given to the Swedish Securities Council (Aktiemarknadsnämnden), '... which may grant exemptions from the provisions, and also interpret the Recommendations in other respects'.[36] The Security council is a self-regulatory body that has charged itself with issuing statements on what constitutes good market practice on the Swedish stock market. It has no power to impose sanctions for non-compliance except publicity. It is notable that the Council has rendered approximately 40 official statements relating to take overs since its establishment in 1986.[37]

In addition to shareholder protection, NBK recommendations also contain disclosure provisions which in certain ways collide with the disclosure laws of the Financial Instruments Trading Act.

Below is an effort to set out some of the main principles of the act and the Recommendations respectively:

| *The act* | *The recommendations* |
| --- | --- |
| Only requires the disclosure of a change in number of votes | Also require the disclosure in the proportion of the share capital |
| The disclosure is to take place when percentage threshold is passed | The disclosure is to take place when a large number of percentage threshold is passed |
| Calculation of percentage thresholds exclusively based on shares issued by the company | Shares which result from the conversion of convertible debt instruments are included in the basis of calculating percentage thresholds |
| Reporting is confined to shares; certain cases other shares which are equated with debt instruments | Apply – in addition to shares – to, however, other types of financial instruments which are also taken in to account |

The NBK recommendations are to be applied in parallel with statutory provisions, which may certainly call for mind-teasing complexity, and one may ask whether they are not far too complicated to be the basis for the regulation.

### 5.2.5   The making of a tender offer in Sweden

There is in all corporate bidding matters an element of contract law beside the corporate law and the stock exchange provisions. The latter thus set a limit to the former.

---

[35] Recommendations, Item III.1.
[36] Recommendations concerning public offers for the acquisition of shares, p. 52.
[37] Recommendations, p. 59ff.

That means that there are corporate rules with respect to the practical handling of bidding matters, but there are also matters of contractual nature, such as could an offer be revoked? If so under what circumstances? Could a bidder be liable for revoking an offer? The question has been raised in Sweden where an offer was revoked due to the bidder's recalculation of risks. From a stock exchange point of view the revocation was considered questionable, and it still remains to be seen whether some shareholders will pursue the matter in a contract law dispute.

Swedish law does not make a distinction, as such, between hostile and recommended bids when announcing an offer. According to the listing agreement the target company must immediately inform the SSE when it has been acknowledged that a third party has planned to make a public offer for its shares or other corresponding financial instruments issued. The bidder on the other hand has to issue a press statement as soon as it has decided to propose an offer to a general meeting or if it intends to make a public offer. The press announcement should include the main terms of the offer, including the details of any conditions or other important prerequisites, information as to the number of shares and voting rights that it already owns or controls as well as information concerning to what extent it already has target shareholders' approval.

The announcement should furthermore include a brief explanation of the reasons for the offer and for the presumed effects that the offer is believed to have in respect of the bidder's future financial results and market position. There is no obligation to notify the target of the offer before making the press announcement, although this is normally done.[38]

### 5.2.6   *Offer time table*

After the offer has been announced through the press statement the bidder has to prepare the formal contractual offer to the shareholders, that is, a prospectus. The period of acceptance stated in the prospectus has to be at least three weeks and may not commence before the filing of and the publication of the prospectus. There is, on the other hand, no stipulated maximum offer period, but it should not be excessively long (which is of course not very precise).

The typical, or rather standard timetable rules, apply to both contested and to friendly take overs, but the process may take longer time in case a competing bid is announced and the target may have to make a statement responding to the second bid. Otherwise the acceptance period is confirmed in the prospectus and may only be extended if the bidder has reserved the right to do so. Further, unless the offer is conditional, the bidder is basically obliged to implement the offer. Yet, if the target takes defensive action which makes the implementation irrational or if a more favourable bid comes forward, the bidder is always allowed either to withdraw its initial offer or improve it.

---

[38] Wikström and Ahlberg, Company law in Sweden (Stockholm 1998)

### 5.2.7   *Minimum levels of consideration*

As stated above an acquiring party may set out different conditions in its offer, and it may wish to include unilateral acceptance conditions in its offer, which also obliges it to state that the shareholders have a right to withdraw their acceptance. Offers could be made subject to obtaining 90% positive responses from the share-holders. Offers are also often made conditional upon obtaining EC and/or national competition authority approval.

In practice, however, an acceptance can be withdrawn at any time until the bidder proclaims that the conditions of the offer have been fulfilled, or, if such announce-ment is not made, until the final date of acceptances. Furthermore, the principle of equal treatment of shareholders in the Company act as well as the NBK recommen-dation should again be underlined. All shareholders holding the same type of shares should be offered identical conditions. The purchaser may exclude certain kinds of shares and securities, but a partial offer is only acceptable under certain circum-stances, and each category of shareholders shall have fair and reasonable treatment. The bidder may, for example, want to make open share purchases before, during or after the offer period of a public offering. The bidder is in principle free to do so, but the acquisitions thus made may not be more favourable than the offer itself, unless the offer is adjusted accordingly. This principle serves to protect the principle of equal treatment of the shareholders.[39]

### 5.2.8   *Outstanding minority shareholdings*

From a practical point of view there is a great variation between different Swedish companies with respect to the level of voting rights needed to have effective control of the company. In large companies with widespread ownership there is normally need of a smaller part of the total shareholding than in a company where a large fraction of the shares are held on a few hands. Therefore the mandatory bid rule benchmark of 40% is probably on the high side with respect to large companies with several shareholders. On the other hand, in a medium sized or small company, where one owner or a group of owners control more than 50% of the voting power, an acqusition of control of the company may thereby be facilitated (or blocked for that matter). Furthermore, the Swedish compulsory acquisition rules recognize that once an offer has been accepted by a substantial majority of the shareholders, the bidder should be able to purchase the outstanding minority interests and those interests should equally have a right to be purchased. The Swedish company Act sets the limit at 90% in order that such compulsory purchase shall be possible. This means that a shareholder having 90% of the shares in a company shall have a right to acquire the remaining 10% irrespective of when and how the shares have been acquired.[40]

---

[39] Wikström and Ahlberg, p. 411f.
[40] *Id.*, p. 803.

### 5.3    Target response

The target board thus has a duty to react in case of a bid. In accordance with the NBK's recommendation Item II.13, the target board shall not take any defensive actions intended or designed to put at risk the issue of the offer or unless a general meeting of the shareholders decides on or approves of such action. The Recommendation applies from the time when the Board or the senior management of the target has good reason to believe that a bona fide offer is imminent.

The Board may, however, act without the approval of a General Meeting of the shareholders if, in the opinion of the company and its owners, it is clearly essential that action be taken without delay. Thus, after a bid has been launched, the target board can take any defensive action sanctioned by the shareholders at a General Meeting of the shareholders, provided that they are in accordance with the Company Act. Obviously there is no room here to delve further into the practical legal/economic problems that may arise in such situations.

## 6    Concluding Remarks

It merits again to be underlined that there has for different reasons been a development of new rules in the financial, but that the courts have also been involved (in respect of certain legal domains) to an extent which is quite unusual for Swedish conditions. On the other hand the development is by no means unique for Sweden. The financial crisis in the beginning of the 1990s created a demand for new rules, for more liability on the part of the banks etc. The pattern is the same as always following disastrous events, whether they follow immediately, which is the most common or only at a later stage. Although there has already for a time been a lot of activity this development will continue, not unlikely in all the domains above referred to.

*Chapter 19*

# A Path-dependent Route towards a Single Financial Regulator: The Experience of Denmark

*Jesper Lau Hansen*

## INTRODUCTION

Undoubtedly because of its small size, it is a well-kept secret that Denmark is quite a pioneer in regulating financial markets. At the time when the Big Bang revitalised the financial Square Mile of London in 1986, a similar reform was undertaken in Denmark to scrap a trading system originating in the nineteenth century and introduce a high-technology replacement. This led to the dematerialization of securities trading at the Copenhagen Stock Exchange based on a central securities depository that could perform the necessary functions of registration, settlement and clearing, in contrast to the abandoned Taurus project of the same period, the London Stock Exchange's proposed electronic transfer system. The Copenhagen Stock Exchange got these functions to work well enough to inspire the systems introduced in Norway and Sweden.

Denmark had another head start within financial supervision, as a single financial supervisor was established in the late 1980s. The debate on creating a single regulator for the financial markets in the European Union may benefit from a closer look at Denmark's experience since it entails all the characteristics of path dependence, including the necessary compromises and the persistence of vested interests.

## GATHERING THE REGULATORY FUNCTIONS

The single financial regulator in Denmark, the Danish Financial Supervisory Authority (Finanstilsynet), covers practically all of Denmark's financial market, including stock exchanges and broker-dealers, central securities depositories, banking (commercial and savings), insurance and mortgage credit.

This gathering of regulatory functions has resulted from a development stretching back to the early twentieth century. In about 1900, the various functions performed by the financial players were subjected to public regulation by parliamentary acts designed to link special functions with specialised institutions, each under sector-specific supervision. As the functions carried out by the various institutions started to converge, the acts were replaced by new acts merging the regulation established by the previous acts, including the supervisory bodies. This, in turn, has led to the emergence of a single financial supervisor, the Financial Supervisory Authority.

*Mads Andenas and Yannis Avgerinos (eds), Financial Markets in Europe: Towards a Single Regulator? 447–456.*
© 2003 *Kluwer Law International. Printed in Great Britain.*

However, this is not a comprehensive supervisory body, as certain areas are left outside the jurisdiction of the Financial Supervisory Authority, nor are all the regulatory functions gathered at the Authority, as especially policy-making power seems to be prone to capture by vested interests, which have usurped this power at some time during the historical development. The development occurred as follows.[1]

## REGULATION OF BANKING

Banking was the first financial sector to be regulated by acts of Parliament. Savings banks were introduced in 1810 and accepted deposits from the public. They were organized as private foundations. Ordinary or commercial banks were introduced in 1846 and were organized as public limited-liability companies (*aktieselskaber*) primarily using their share capital for investment but also later accepted deposits. Commercial banks and savings banks competed fiercely, as did the savings banks among themselves. The international crisis of 1873 left a lingering depression in Denmark and, as a consequence, the savings banks were subjected to regulation by a special act on savings banks of 1880 introducing limited public supervision. A crisis in 1907–1908 among commercial banks led to the establishment of a parliamentary committee in 1910 to draft an act on banks. The legislative process was delayed by the outbreak of the First World War, which affected Denmark although it remained neutral. However, after the War, an act on banks was passed in 1919 including special banking supervision.[2] To differentiate between the forms of banking, it was decided that savings banks engage primarily in accepting and safeguarding deposits from the public, and considerably stricter rules were therefore imposed on how savings banks placed funds compared with commercial banks. As both forms of bank accepted deposits from the public and as the commercial banks further were able to attract share capital, the commercial banks soon dominated the banking industry. Inspired by Sweden, which abandoned the strict distinction between commercial and savings banks in 1968, Denmark's Parliament passed a common act covering both forms of banks in 1974, merging the two independent supervisory bodies in the process to form a unified banking supervision. An amendment in 1988 permitted savings banks to organise as public limited-liability companies, and most savings banks took advantage of this opportunity to reorganize. The banking sector concentrated substantially in the 1990s through mergers and acquisitions, and commercial banks have taken over most of the former savings banks.

---

[1] For accounts of this development in Danish, *see* P. Schaumburg-Müller, *Tilsynet med de finansielle institutioner* [The supervision of financial institutions] (Akademisk Forlag, 1992), Chap. 4, and J. Lau Hansen, *Fondsbørsen* [The Stock Exchange] (Greens Jura, 1999), pp. 69–74.

[2] At the time, a civil servant, the Banking Inspector, carried out public supervision. Only later was the Inspector authorized to employ assistants, which changed the character of the supervision to a supervisory body.

## SECURITIES TRADING

Stock exchange trading started in Copenhagen as a private organisation in the 1840s and was formally organised as a private association in 1871. The Copenhagen Stock Exchange was located in the Royal Exchange and was formally under the supervision of the Merchants' Society, which had overall responsibility for the affairs of the Royal Exchange. In reality, however, the Copenhagen Stock Exchange was only self-regulated, and the brokers and dealers that were members of the Exchange resisted all interference by outsiders. An attempt to subject the Copenhagen Stock Exchange to the regulation and supervision of the Merchants' Society through an act of Parliament in 1888 failed because of political deadlock. The widespread speculation experienced during the First World War finally led to an act of Parliament in 1919 introducing a dual system of supervision. The Minister of Trade was authorized to appoint the chair of the Board of Directors of the Copenhagen Stock Exchange as a civil servant. The Board would control the operations of the Exchange and the broker–dealers, in their new dual capacity, as members of the Exchange. As the act left the establishment of stock exchanges open and clearly envisaged more than one national stock exchange, the act also created a Stock Exchange Commissioner to supervise the entire industry. The act included provisions on how a stock exchange was to be organised; this was probably intended to safeguard the operation of the exchanges and maintain public confidence in these institutions. However, it was apparently overlooked that these provisions were too strict for the only other and little-known stock exchange, located in Denmark's second largest city, Aarhus. Thus, the act of 1919 unintentionally but directly closed the only competitor to the Copenhagen Stock Exchange, leaving it with a *de facto* monopoly that has lasted to this day. In 1921, the Chair of the Board of Directors of the Copenhagen Stock Exchange was appointed as the state county prefect in Ribe County. As Denmark had no other stock exchanges, the Stock Exchange Commissioner could become the Chair, performing a dual function as supervisor of the Exchange and of the industry, both being effectively the same. When he retired, the act of 1919 was amended in 1930 and the arrangement continued. However, the supervision was carried out by the Banking Inspector who served as chairman, and civil servants attached to the office of the Banking Inspector performed the function as stock exchange supervisor. When the act of 1930 was amended in 1972, the stock exchange supervision was effectively transferred to banking supervision. The act of 1972 granted the Copenhagen Stock Exchange the legal monopoly that the act of 1919 had unintentionally bestowed on it *de facto*. This left the Exchange as a public institution and the Board of Directors, still with some directors appointed directly by the relevant Minister, maintained its status as the most immediate regulator and supervisor of the Exchange.

## THE INSURANCE SECTOR

Insurance was first subjected to public regulation by an act of 1904 regulating life insurance. The act was the result of Nordic cooperation, and similar acts were passed in Sweden in 1903 and in Norway in 1911. The act introduced an Insurance Council as the supervisory body. Insurance against loss and damage was later regulated by an act of 1934, which assigned supervision to the Insurance Council. Pursuant to an act of 1959, the two forms of insurance were covered by a common act, whereby the Insurance Council could continue supervising the insurance industry.

## MORTGAGE–CREDIT INSTITUTIONS

*Mortgage credit* in its institutionalised form originated in Germany in the 1760s, and raising capital through mortgage in real estate has a long tradition. Organized mortgage credit was first introduced in Denmark by an act of Parliament in 1850. The Parliament maintained control of the industry in the following years through acts establishing new credit institutions. Public confidence was reassured by limiting the institutions to primary mortgages and by establishing limits on the estimated value of the property. As the mortgage–credit system caught on, institutions for secondary mortgages arose and were regulated by an act of Parliament in 1897. In 1936, the various acts on primary and secondary mortgage–credit institutions were harmonized, and in 1970 the Parliament passed a common act for all mortgage-credit institutions. Mortgage credit is immensely important in Denmark as the primary source of financing real estate and as a means of providing equity loans for real estate owners. Supervision was maintained with the Ministry of Industry until it was transferred to the newly established Ministry of Housing in 1949. A 1989 amendment to the act of 1970 implemented several European Community directives on credit institutions and allowed mortgage–credit institutions to be organised as public limited-liability companies. Many institutions were reorganised and took part in the concentration of the 1990s in mergers with banks and insurance companies.

## CREATING A SINGLE SUPERVISOR

In the 1980s, it became apparent that the functions performed by the players of the financial market were becoming entangled, a process that was expected to accelerate as the single European market by the end of 1992 approached. The Single European Act of 1986 had heralded an intensified effort to regulate transnational competition by issuing directives on the establishment and the provision of services applying the principles of home state control and mutual recognition.

In spring 1986, the Minister for Trade and Industry initiated an analysis of the structure of the Ministry. This led to substantial reform in the form of amendments to several acts introduced in Parliament in late 1987. At the presentation of the bills before Parliament, the Minister motivated the reform as follows:

> The present organization of the Ministry's affairs is the result of years of development and tradition characterized by the assumption of new tasks delegated to the Department or to existing or new agencies. This development has to some

extent been marked by an organic growth, in which the assumption of new tasks to a lesser degree has led to changes in the overall organization.[3]

The purpose of the reform was stated as follows:

> The principle of the division of labour between the Department and the agencies is that the Department shall assist the political leadership especially with questions of advice, planning, development, coordination and control, whereas the agencies shall, beside administering the regulations within their field, participate in the departmental assistance to the Minister based on their expertise in the various fields of administration. A general purpose is to ensure that the agencies are delegated greater responsibility for administration, whereby more of the Department's tasks can be assumed by the agencies.[4]

One result of the reform was a reduction in the number of agencies. Thus, the Banking Authority, which already performed stock exchange supervision, merged with the Insurance Authority as of 1 January 1988 under the new name of the Financial Supervisory Authority. In 1990, the supervision of mortgage–credit institutions was transferred to the Financial Supervisory Authority as well. Because of the importance of mortgage credit, the political responsibility was kept with the Ministry of Housing until 1994, when it was transferred to the Ministry of Economic Affairs. The Financial Supervisory Authority was an agency under the Ministry of Trade and Industry (formerly the Ministry of Industry) until it was transferred as well to the Ministry of Economic Affairs in 1996. Thus, nearly all of Denmark's financial market had a single financial supervisor.

THE ONES THAT GOT AWAY

*(a)    Insurance and other forms of financial business*

The gathering of regulatory functions to create a single financial regulator did not wholly succeed. In the merger between the supervisory bodies for banking and insurance, the Insurance Council managed to preserve its authority. A similar council did not exist within banking, and consequently no such council was found necessary when the two supervisory bodies merged in 1988. The Insurance Council represented, among others, policyholders, the insurance companies and the pension funds. According to the act, the Financial Supervisory Authority was to perform its duties 'together with' the Insurance Council with the Council as responsible for the overall administration of the acts covered by the Financial Supervisory Authority within insurance and with power to decide on matters of greater importance.

---

[3] Minister for Trade and Industry, Nils Wilhjelm, Parliamentary Reports 1987–1988 (1st session), the Debates (FF), column 2006 [translation by the author].

[4] *Ibid.*, column 2007 [translation by the author].

To strengthen the system of single supervision, the Financial Business Act was passed in 2001.[5] The act introduces a single framework for enterprises engaged in financial business, such as investment companies (including stockbroker companies), insurance companies and pension funds, the banking sector, mortgage–credit institutions and, finally, the holding companies of such financial players. The framework includes all the provisions on organisation, internal governance and supervision that used to be in the different acts addressing the various sectors, but often displayed various degrees of differences due to the fact that the provisions had been introduced in the acts at different times. The new act thus serves as a common basis and supplements the different sector acts such as the acts on banking, investment services, insurance and mortgage–credit, respectively.

During the session in Parliament, it was decided to amend the Financial Business Bill to arrange for the introduction of Financial Business Council that would comprise representatives of the covered financial sectors and replace the Insurance Council. The Financial Business Council is comprised of a chair and a vice-chair both appointed by the Minister, a representative of the Danish Central Bank, a representative of the Consumer Council, a representative of commercial interests jointly appointed by a string of organisations within trade, industry, shipping and agriculture; a representative of the mortgage–credit industry, a representative jointly appointed by a string of organisations within banking and investment service; and a representative jointly appointed by a string of organisations within the insurance and pension business.[6] The Financial Business Council is competent to make decisions regarding supervisory matters of general public importance and supervisory matters which entail significant consequences to financial undertakings and financial holding companies. It further provides advice to the Danish Financial Supervisory Authority on issuing regulations, and assists it in its information activities. The Financial Supervisory Authority acts as a secretariat for the Council and thus performs the day-to-day administration.

Not only did the Insurance Council survive, albeit in a new form, the concept was extended to other kinds of financial business, including those where this form of direct business involvement in policy making had hitherto been unknown. The powers of the Financial Business Council are, however, more limited in that it is only to advice the Danish Financial Supervisory Authority in performing its regulatory functions. Nonetheless, the Financial Business Council still enjoys the power to decide on cases involving high-profile policy issues.

### (b)   The securities market

As mentioned previously, the market players customarily influenced the regulation of the Copenhagen Stock Exchange through representation on the Board of Directors. The Board would decide on the operation of the Exchange and issue the

---

[5] *Cf.* Act No. 501 of 7 June 2001.
[6] *Ibid.*, Sec. 65(1).

necessary regulations, whereas the stockbroker companies that had replaced the broker–dealers in 1986 were supervised by the Banking Authority, and later the Financial Supervisory Authority. When the Exchange was privatised by the second stock exchange reform of 1995, this authority was transferred to the Securities Council. The Securities Council has a representation similar to that of the Exchange's Board before the reform. The Council has authority to regulate the securities market, including the organised stock exchanges. Further, the Council must consent to regulations issued by a stock exchange, that is the Copenhagen Stock Exchange, and a decision made by an exchange can be brought before the Council if it is deemed to be of special importance.[7] Similar to the Financial Business Council, the Financial Supervisory Authority acts as the secretariat of the Securities Council.

During the preparations for the first stock exchange reform of 1986, the working committee recommended that a council be established representing, among others, investors and consumers, that is, both large and small investors. This recommendation was not followed, and the Board of Directors of the Exchange continued to be the primary regulator, although the interests of large investors were taken into account by granting them representation on the Board. Nor were consumers included when the Securities Council was established after the second reform of 1995. Including consumer interests was difficult because of the delicate balance of powers achieved in the Securities Council. When the Copenhagen Stock Exchange was privatised, ownership was transferred to the securities traders (stockbroker companies and overwhelmingly the banks) and the issuers. The transfer of authority to the Council would give it powers to overrule the Exchange, and during the debate on the Stock Exchange Reform Bill the new owners of the Exchange fought vehemently to avoid potentially being outvoted in the Council. They comprised half the Council, and the other half consisted of representatives of public authorities and large investors such as insurance companies, pension funds and the two labour-market funds. However, the bill presented to Parliament suggested that the chair of the Council, who was to be appointed by the Minister, would command two votes in case of a tie, and could consequently decide the issue.

The lobbying effort by the exchange owners failed because of a lack of political support, and they had to accept an amendment to the bill, whereby the Minister would appoint a chair and a vice-chair, each having one vote. However, the owners succeeded in having written into the new bill that the Council would not be a 'senior-board' in relation to the Board of Directors of the Exchange.[8] Including consumer interests in the Council would further exacerbate the predicament of the owners of the Exchange.

The absence of consumer protection within the scheme of securities regulation resulted in the Consumer Ombudsman having independent authority within securities transactions according to the general Marketing Practices Act. Thus, regulation of

---

[7] *Cf.* the Securities Trading Act, Secs 83(6) + (7) and 88(2), respectively.

[8] The reference to a senior-board is in the commentary to the revised bill, *cf.* Parliamentary Reports 1995–1996, Part A, column 2004.

securities trading by the ordinary investor could arise from two equally competent sources: the Securities Council and the Consumer Ombudsman. The Securities Trading Act made no attempt to solve this problem of conflicting competences but alluded to co-operation as the way out. It did not last, in June 2001 the conflict came to a head when the Securities Council and the Consumer Ombudsman each issued their own set of rules on the best execution of securities transactions and the two sets of rules were mutually incompatible. With consumer interests represented on the Financial Business Council, the case for including them in the Securities Council was strong, and by an amendment of the Securities Trading Act in 2002 a representative jointly appointed by the Consumer Council and the Danish Shareholders Association was admitted to the Securities Council.[9]

This amendment to the Securities Trading Act furthermore transferred supervisory powers from the private stock exchanges and regulated markets to the public Securities Council. This shift of power was in response to the trend of EU law visible in the directive proposals of recent years that supervision should be performed by a public body rather than by a private market to avoid obvious conflicts of interests. However, the reform is, at least for now, just window dressing. The amendment made it possible for the Securities Council to authorise private enterprises, that is, the recognised markets, to carry out its powers of supervision, and that possibility was taken up immediately upon the act entering into force. For the time being, the Securities Council and the Danish Financial Supervisory Authority that serve as its secretariat have not the manpower or expertise needed to take on these powers themselves. However, when the call for independent bodies to carry out supervision is made by EU law, the regulatory framework is ready.

### (c)  Competition

The concentration experienced in the 1990s has given rise to competition problems that fall outside the jurisdiction of the Financial Supervisory Authority. This applies especially to the market for securities transactions, where trading is dominated by Danske Bank and Nordea. Small-scale securities transactions in Denmark traditionally take place outside the Copenhagen Stock Exchange as over-the-counter transactions carried out by banks. This is a hugely lucrative business for the banks but leaves the Exchange with a small and often illiquid market. When the banks became the main owners of the Exchange after the reform of 1995, they had a conflict of interest. The merger of Danske Bank and RealDanmark (a mortgage–credit institution) in October 2000 activated Denmark's new rules on merger control. The Danish Competition Authority only accepted the merger on the condition that Danske Bank, among other things, reduce its ownership of the Exchange and work for a larger share of securities transactions to be carried out on the Exchange. The Competition Authority pointed out that if the share of transactions carried out on the Exchange does not increase, the Authority would recommend introducing

---

[9]  Act No. 427 of 6 June 2002 amending the Securities Trading Act *et al.*

concentration rules mandating the use of the Exchange. Thus, the Competition Authority may also initiate regulation of the financial market.

## WHAT CAN BE LEARNED?

Denmark's experience shows that a clear division of functions, each connected to a special institution, has disintegrated. The financial players tend to spread out their business across a plethora of functions, often combining different institutions within huge financial conglomerates. This has rendered obsolete the supervision of the financial market based on institutional characteristics. Further, restricting an institution to only performing a certain traditional function may stifle it in competition and have drastic consequences. The fate of the savings banks in relation to the commercial banks in Denmark is a case in point. Such restriction is often justified by maintaining public confidence. Nevertheless, the development of the financial market would suggest that the public is better served by dynamic competition subject to prudent supervision rather than petrified preservation of existing business structures. The hypothesis that protective measures can stifle competition by serving as barriers to entry is also illustrated by the inadvertent creation of a monopoly for the Copenhagen Stock Exchange when the first Stock Exchange Act of 1919 destroyed the embryonic stock exchange in Aarhus and prevented the formation of other competing exchanges.

Another related point is the ubiquity of the public limited-liability company. The ability to separate ownership and management, despite its well-known corporate governance problems, and the potential to attract investment capital by issuing shares seem to be major competitive assets. Most financial players have reorganized as public limited-liability companies when given the chance. From a regulatory viewpoint, organizing financial players as commercial companies rather than as private foundations entails the further benefit of making it clear that these players are profit-seeking entities, and that regulation should be left with another commercially disinterested party. The recent shift of supervision from the private recognised markets to the Danish Financial Supervisory Authority is testament to this change that is evident in European Union law as well.

Further, events in Denmark demonstrate that regulatory developments are path dependent. Making a clean break with the past is difficult and may not even be advisable considering the upheaval. Vested interests tend to prevail and to be able to maintain their influence even after reform. Even though a single supervisory body had been formed by the late 1980s, the acts on the different financial sectors remained diverse and a common basis was not introduced until 2001. Events in Denmark also show that creating a single financial supervisor is far easier than creating a single financial regulator. The Financial Supervisory Authority is practically the sole financial supervisor and regulator within the technical fields of accounting, solvency, etc. Nevertheless, in policy-making, the various interest groups have maintained their influence, as demonstrated by the Financial Business Council and the Securities Council.

Finally, the question is whether developments in Denmark have been beneficial. Is a single financial regulator desirable? Although the Financial Supervisory Authority appears to be a single financial supervisor, its internal organisation reflects the various supervisory functions it has taken over, each represented by a division. Nevertheless, there is widespread satisfaction with the Financial Supervisory Authority within the financial industry because it offers a one-stop shop with the harmonisation and rationalisation that its organisation as a single public body allows. This reduces the cost of compliance, which increasingly is *the* key competitive factor in today's global economy. What is good for a diminutive financial market such as Denmark's must surely be good for the greater European market as well. If, as prophesied by developments in Denmark, a single European financial regulator is harder to achieve than a single supervisor, then the lack of a single regulator could be mitigated by insuring that the boundaries between each of the regulatory bodies is as clear as possible.

*Chapter 20*

# Horizontal Consolidation of Financial Supervision: Impact on the Operations of the European Investment Bank

*Roderick Dunnett*[1]

## Introduction

The aim of this chapter is to contribute some ideas, from the viewpoint of a multilateral development bank (or MDB) on this area of public policy. It focuses on the concept of a single organisation for the supervision of banks, capital markets, investments funds and insurance companies established within, or carrying on business in, the European Union. The chapter examines the effects of horizontal supervision and consolidated financial supervision. It draws on the report of the Lamfalussy Committee of Wise Men,[2] which discusses the feasibility of a horizontal European supervisory regime over security markets.

The underlying theme is that the European Investment Bank may reduce the risk borne by economic agents and that it may thereby strengthen the stability of the financial system and further one of the aims of a supervisory regime.

## The European Investment Bank

The European Investment Bank (EIB) is a legal entity limited by shares held by the Member States of the European Union. It is established by the Treaty on European Union. It has legal personality in the Member States and is recognised outside the Union as possessing international legal personality. It is subject to relevant European Community legislation and implements applicable EU directives. It is an instrument of common EU economic policy. The Governors of the Bank comprise the ministers, normally the finance ministers, designated by the Member States. In short, it is a public European body.

It is also a bank. It finances investments projects on market-based financial terms. It raises its funds on the world's capital markets. Its staff members are employed on contract, not as public officials.

The original, and still the main, mission of the Bank is to advance the economic development of the Member States, with emphasis on the financing of

---

[1] The views expressed in this paper are those of the author and not necessarily those of any institution.

[2] EU Commission, *Final Report of the Committee of Wise Men on the Regulation of European Securities Market* (Brussels, 15 February 2001).

*Mads Andenas and Yannis Avgerinos (eds), Financial Markets in Europe: Towards a Single Regulator?* 457–468.
© 2003 *Kluwer Law International. Printed in Great Britain.*

regional development, large public infrastructure projects and advanced technology. In practice, the Bank takes part in most sectors of economic activity and in particular supports 'human capital' or 'knowledge-based' projects, notably in education, health and cultural heritage.

The Bank has been for many years the largest non-sovereign borrower on the international capital markets, borrowing in the year 2002 some €38,000 million gross. In some national markets, for instance the UK domestic bond market, the Bank is the largest current issuer of debt. In that year, it committed credits amounting to €40,000 million and it held, at year-end, assets of €220,000 million. Through its affiliate, the European Investment Fund (EIF), it supports the funding of venture capital and various forms of specialised finance of which its portfolio, at year-end, stood at €700 million. This chapter examines the supervisory regime from all these angles.

## Basel II Capital Accord[3]

In January 2001, the Basel Committee on Banking Supervision, meeting under the aegis of the Bank for International Settlements (BIS), announced the New Basel Capital Accord. This accord was supplemented in December 2001 and July 2002 and, if adopted by the chief member banks of the BIS, will come into force in 2006. The pillars of this accord are the following:

- minimum capital adequacy requirement for regulated banks;
- supervisory review of banks' controls, their level of capital and their risk management;
- tighter market discipline through enhanced accounting disclosure.

### Foreseeable Impact of Single Regime

This chapter touches on these three pillars of the supervisory regime, but especially capital adequacy, and reflects how a horizontal consolidated (in short, *single*) supervisory body would manage them. The analysis is both theoretical and practical. In theory, the presence of a common supervisory system changes nothing. A single European Supervisor would not have authority over the EIB any more than would a national supervisor. Furthermore, the manner in which those principles affect the EIB does not depend on whether they are implemented by a single European authority or by a set of national authorities. In practice, however, there might be a difference. Consequently, the paper looks at how the rules might be interpreted or applied differently under the authority of a single supervisor.

The effect is both active and passive; active, in the sense that the Bank would tend to adapt to the rules that might evolve under the influence of a single supervisor; and passive, in the sense that the rules on capital reserves set against claims on the EIB could affect its funding techniques and its methods of risk protection.

The paper examines three propositions.

*The first proposition* is that, since the EIB operates in the financial markets, a single supervisory regime would, by changing the cost for regulated institutions to carry certain types of asset or liability, affect the EIB's mode of operation.

*The second proposition* is that a single financial supervisory regime would have a certain aim in common with the EIB, namely to reduce risks that financial market imperfections induce financial institutions to take.

*The third proposition* is that the EIB and the authorities of a horizontal supervisory system could usefully compare practices and policies on certain current issues.

*First proposition: impact on EIB operations*

*Supervisory regime and EIB assets*

The Basel II regime, once it is translated into EU legislation and is implemented at the national level, aims to be more flexible than the present regime. In being more flexible, it will be more complex and less predictable in its impact. Such a change of regime could have three particular effects on the EIB's lending activity. The new regime does not itself create a horizontal regulatory structure but creates common rules that are a pre-requisite to such a structure. It also provides the rudiments of a consolidated supervisory system, in that it takes more flexible account of banks' holdings in insurance companies, non-insurance financial entities and commercial entities for the purpose of defining capital adequacy.

*Credit derivatives or guarantees*

Over a third of the EIB's assets comprise claims on commercial banks. Many of those claims are contingent claims, such as guarantees and standby letters of credit. The costs to commercial banks of carrying the corresponding liabilities, and especially the associated prudential capital costs, are under constant scrutiny. The financial markets do not lack ideas for reducing those costs, and it is part of the EIB's task to help put the best of those ideas into practice. The rules of a single supervisory system could affect this task, by making it cheaper for a commercial bank to issue an instrument committing it buy risk assets from the EIB than to issue it a guarantee.[4]

The implementation of the New Basel Capital Accord will cause such an instrument to be used more for its inherent advantages, and less for its qualities as a means of regulatory arbitrage. In other words, the new rules may tend to narrow the regulatory component of the price differential. Thus the price will be affected more by perceived risk and less by technical factors. For a bank that is able to evaluate the operational risk in using this kind of instrument, the Basel II rules will tend to allow it to allocate less capital to that risk. Under a single supervisory regime, this process could lead to wider use of such instruments.

To take a theoretical example, the use of credit derivatives could be valuable where, for prudential reasons, the EIB seeks to reduce credit exposure on a corporate borrower to make room for new EIB credits to finance the borrower's new investment projects. Assuming that the EIB has a comparative advantage over other financial institutions in assessing the risks of industrial investments, and that the market price of the risk on old exposure is less than on new, on account of imperfect market assessment of new debt, the EIB may rationally buy credit support on mature debt to allow it to acquire new debt.

*Major public works projects*

A field of activity that could benefit from reform of supervisory practice is that of international infrastructure projects. Many such projects are financed with debt instruments carrying limited rights of recourse to promoters. The lack of a common legal regime for investments in such international projects is a handicap to financing them. The obstacles are legislative, such as unequal fiscal treatment and divergent accounting rules, and political, such as the state's power to evade its project commitments on grounds of public policy. If the Member States could work towards common standards on such matters, it would make it easier to finance these projects.[5] A common supervisor could be a spur to the common adoption of the needed reforms.

The need for governments to improve the conditions of project finance becomes more apparent since the publication of the Basel II rules. They may oblige a majority of banks to provide higher risk weightings for project finance assets and other 'specialised lending' assets.

The Basel II rules will permit regulators to differentiate between institutions which qualify as 'advanced' arrangers of project finance deals, on the one hand, and institutions which lack the scale, diversity, expertise and internal systems to graduate beyond the 'foundation' level, on the other. These rules will, it is expected,[6] compel regulated institutions to allocate more capital to specialised lending assets and thereby deter them from acquiring such assets. By contrast, large institutions, because they could qualify as advanced, could allocate less capital to assets in this sector than they are now obliged to do. This trend may allow them to undercut smaller, local institutions. If this forecast should be realised, the costs to promoters of arranging project finance transactions may rise. This may strengthen the relative position of the larger institutions. It may thereby affect the trend in the EIB's exposure to large banks, as well as the pricing of the transactions in which it participates. The EIB may thus be induced to consider shifting its balance of assets in this sector from claims on banks to claims on project assets and revenues. If this were to happen, the EIB would be demonstrating its potential to offset the price effects of the Basel II rules and to play a modest, countervailing role. This, in turn, may compel the Bank to extend its own range of analysis.

*Country risk weighting*

The third example relates to the supervision of banks' exposure to country risk. The instalment of a common system for regulating this risk may lead to greater flexibility. Such a change would have an impact on the Bank's programmes for external lending. Under these programmes the EIB finances projects located in countries outside the European Union. The first programme is for lending to central and Eastern European countries, the second is to support development of the Mediterranean non-member countries, and the third is to lend to European corporations, or their local subsidiaries, to fund investments in Asian and Latin American countries. The fourth programme, for lending to certain developing countries, as recently renewed by the agreement signed in Cotonou between the European Community and the African, Caribbean and Pacific states, will enter into force in the year 2003.

Many of the Bank's loans within these programmes are guaranteed by commercial banks. For three of the programmes, the EIB has negotiated with the European Commission, acting under the authority of the European Council, a community political risk guarantee. For the fourth programme, it obtained a similar guarantee from the Member States of the European Union. These guarantees cover the EIB against losses on loans arising from certain types of political action.[7] The guarantees allow the Bank to relieve commercial bank guarantors from corresponding political risks. In particular, the EIB may conditionally relieve a defaulting commercial bank, acting through a subsidiary or a branch in the country concerned, where the default is due to a change in a country's exchange controls. Since national banking supervisors currently tend to impose higher capital allocations on risks in non-OECD countries than risks in OECD countries,[8] this instrument, by reducing the country political risk, allows banks to reduce the capital allocated to their non-OECD risk exposure.

The use of this instrument would be affected in opposite ways by the new Basel II rules. On the one hand, the new regime, by being more flexible in the method of assessment of corporate risk, could diminish the pressure on the EIB to relieve borrowers and guarantors of other kinds of political risk.[9] On the other hand, the new emphasis on banks' internal credit ratings is likely to make the EIB's acceptance of political risk all the more valuable to promoter-borrowers.

### Supervisory regime and EIB liabilities

Having considered the assets side of the EIB, it is instructive to consider also the liabilities side. Here, also, three examples may be offered. The first is a horizontal issue. The second and third are issues of consolidated supervision.

---

[3] *See* Basel Committee on Banking Supervision, *The New Basel Capital Accord: an Consultative Document* (January 2001).

[4] Typically, such a commitment takes the form of the sale of an option to swap a loan asset for a prime governmental debt that has the same maturity profile as the loan.

[5] *See* Freshfields (now Freshfields Bruckhaus Deringer), *Project Finance* (3rd edn, 1995) and Mateu Turró, *Going trans-European: Planning and Financing Transport Networks for Europe* (Pergamon, 1999).

[6] *See*, for instance, *The Banker*, August 2002.

[7] EIB's use of its power to relieve guarantors of political risk parallels the actions of the IBRD affiliate, the Multilateral Investment Guarantee Association. MIGA, by insuring the political risk on a bank loan to a Brazilian company has, allegedly for the first time, caused the rating agencies to rate a Brazilian corporate loan more highly than Brazilian government debt.

[8] Thereby creating a distortion in market terms for debtor countries. See, for the case of Mexico, Heath Price Tarbert, *Rethinking Capital Adequacy: The Basle Accord and the New Framework* (The Business Lawyer, American Bar Association, February 2001).

[9] Certain MDBs adopt a different technique for relieving commercial banks of country political risk. It is known as the B-loan technique. The MDB sells participations in its loans. Since the political guarantees that the MDBs receive from countries hosting the projects extend to the commercial bank participants, the latter, as well as their supervisory authorities, consider that they are protected against country risk.

*Weighting of claims on MDBs*

The first is simple. It is linked more to a change of rule than to a change in supervisory regime. It concerns the risk weighting the supervisor may impose on regulated banks' claims on multilateral development banks, including the EIB. At present, under the EU directives regime, which derives from Basel I, regulated bank claims on the EIB must carry a minimum weighting of 20%.[10] That means that a commercial bank need allocate against its claims on the EIB only 20% of the capital that it must allocate to its ordinary banking claims. Claims on the EIB may likewise be conditionally excluded from the limits on large exposures of banks. Under the new accord, claims on the EIB will, on certain conditions, be zero weighted. The zero weighting of EIB bonds will make them more attractive assets for commercial banks, especially as collateral for derivative operations. Their attractiveness will be further enhanced, if the bonds are accepted as collateral for credit lines from the European Central Bank. This should tend to reduce the cost to the EIB of its borrowings.

Since an EU Directive only sets minimal prudential standards for national supervisors, the instalment of a horizontal supervisory regime would have the advantage for the EIB that this minimum weighting could become a uniform weighting in all EU countries.

*Index-linked debt issues*

The second example relates to inflation-linked debt. The EIB has sold such debt to UK life insurance funds. This example illustrates how a level playing field between economic agents depends on fair disclosure rules, which a single regime would tend to bring about.

UK life assurance companies wish to satisfy their clients' demand for consumer price-index-linked life policies. The UK's insurance regulations, as well as international accounting standards, induce the insurer to offset the business risks that it faces. The insurer gains a benefit in covering its inflation-indexed liability with a similarly indexed asset. Borrowers from the EIB may have clients ready to take a price-indexed loan. For example, a UK hospital operator or road operator may receive from its National Health hospital trust or, respectively, from 'shadow' road tolls an annual income linked to the retail price index. The borrower therefore has an interest to take exposure on the price index, if it may thereby reduce the fixed element of its financial cost. The EIB can bring added value as an intermediary, by assuming the credit risk on the hospital operator and passing the price index risk onto the life assurance fund. This particular product is, for the time being, mainly of interest in the United Kingdom, where certain private operators of public services are remunerated from public funds on index-linked terms. A common regulatory regime might apply stricter rules on pension funds and life assurance funds, in particular on the matching of assets and liabilities. Thus an index-linked asset would interest a wider range of investment funds. The challenge to the EIB would then be to find takers of index-linked loans.

---

[10] Directive 2000/12/EC of the European Parliament and the Council of 20 March 2000 relating to the taking up and pursuit of the business of credit institutions, OJ L 126 of 26.05.2000, Art. 43(7).

*E-securities*

The third example relates to the issuing of EIB bonds targeted to the retail investment market. This is done by the offering of bonds for subscription by electronic means. It becomes more interesting for the Bank, if it may access the entire European market at once, and if it may do so by electronic means falling under a single supervisory system. The Bank has arranged one such so-called e-bond issue, denominated in sterling. A single horizontal consolidated regime, taking account of common rules on electronic commerce, would facilitate the development of this type of issue.

*Conclusion*

In conclusion, these three examples illustrate the first proposition, namely that a change in the application of rules on capital adequacy and financial market regulation will tend to induce a corresponding shift in the pattern of the EIB's assets and liabilities.

The links between the supervisory regime and the EIB's lending and borrowing activity are thus evident. There are, however, other links between financial regulators and the activities of a multilateral development bank, such as the EIB. The paper will now examine these links.

*Second proposition: financial market imperfections*

The second proposition is that certain of the goals of public banks and supervisory systems, or at least the consequences of their actions, are the same, namely improving the efficiency of the capital markets.

*Asymmetric information*

The EIB's mission or niche could be expressed to be the redressing of capital market imperfections in the *common interest*.[11] The classical economic justification for state interference in a market is that the market fails to allocate resources efficiently. The capital market, in particular, may fail for one or more reasons. It may, for instance, fail because of *asymmetric information* or, to be more explicit, because the saver, that is, the offeror of capital funds, is not aware of the needs, identity, risk profile or competence of bidders for capital funds, such as the promoters of capital investment projects. There are two examples to mention, in which imperfect knowledge of participants creates a niche for a public institution like the EIB.

As a first example, a European credit institution, located in a financial capital, and lacking precise information on the market for credit in certain European regions or among certain classes of business, may be deterred from lending in such markets, although the common EU public policy encourages such lending. The EIB is an instrument of that policy. If commercial banks are deterred, by the strictness of a single supervisory regime, from conducting geographically widespread credit operations, the EIB's task of promoting development of the more backward regions of Europe may grow in importance.

---

[11] *See* P.L. Gilibert, The EIB as a Financial Intermediary, EIB Papers (February 1986).

The second example concerns investors' information on the demand for capital from promoters of investment projects. A multilateral development bank, widely recognised in the market, may use its reputation not only to raise funds on its own account but also to further the process of putting investors in touch with promoters. The EIB has certain means to do this but its subsidiary the EIF, which invests in venture capital funds on selective and rigorous principles, may have more scope to do so, in particular by building and sustaining confidence of investors in such funds.

The ability of a multilateral development bank to build confidence is well shown by the European Bank for Reconstruction and Development (EBRD). The EBRD's willingness to take equity in a commercial bank in a post-communist European country is widely taken as an endorsement of the management quality of that bank and as an encouragement to other investors. In such a case, the investor who has superior information may give a lead to investors who are less well informed.

The responsibility that may fall on an MDB is not a light one. Investors and regulated credit institutions may, despite all disclaimers, rely on an MDB at the various stages of an investment project, from appraisal to implementation. The MDB, especially where it operates in a riskier environment, may be at pains to ensure that other financiers do not rely on its superior information. Paradoxically, in order to avoid legal liability in case its information is defective, it does not make full use of its perceived information advantage.

*Maturity transformation*
Secondly, the market may also fail because it is unable to match the maturity requirements of the saver with those of the borrower: savers, and especially deposit holders, prefer short-term commitments, while users of financial capital require long-term commitments. There is, in other terms, a need for *maturity transformation*. In the case of the EIB, the maturity mismatch between assets and liabilities is less pronounced than the mismatch in the balance sheets of many commercial banks, but it still exists.[12] The EIB's ability to take loan assets of long maturity enables regulated banks, in many instances, to complement the EIB by taking assets of a shorter maturity. Together, the EIB and the banks may thus provide borrowers with financial packages adapted to their cash flow. Jointly, they thereby help stabilise the financial system.

*Financial innovation*
Thirdly, the market does not always allocate financial risk or credit risk optimally. Financial innovation can be profitable where it helps distribute risk efficiently. The greater transparency that would result from a large financial market, regulated by a single supervisor, could encourage financial innovation. New financial techniques are needed, for instance, to fund the especial requirements, and cover the especial risks, of high-tech ventures or of privately managed public works. EU policy favours giving support to such projects.[13] To fund such projects, a company may wish to raise

---

[12] *See* the notes to successive EIB annual reports and accounts.
[13] Council of Ministers, Conclusions of Lisbon summit meeting, 17–18 April 2000.

public capital in novel ways or to employ novel means of marketing.[14] While the EIB itself may rarely invent new financial instruments, it can help to develop capital markets in, for example, new financial products or in lesser-known currencies. Moreover, the EIF uses complex and novel financial techniques in the funding of venture capital.[15] In the past, regulators were reserved regarding financial innovation. They may have sometimes perceived it as a means to circumvent official regulatory action, a means of tax avoidance or a means of exchange control evasion.[16]

The value of financial innovation is nowadays more clearly understood.[17] A central regulatory authority may be better placed than a set of national authorities to monitor the effects of innovation, and may be better ready to take necessary or urgent regulatory action. Consequently, a central authority may be less averse to innovation and quicker to accommodate flexibility in the markets that it regulates. Such innovation may be especially important in the financing of new market sectors or new technologies. These fields of finance, like dynamic sectors in general, draw on techniques from various corners of the financial market. A single regime would strengthen this trend.

*Third-world investment*

Fourth, there may be a failure to seize profitable but risky investment opportunities. An example is in the sphere of development finance for third-world countries, especially in communication technology.[18] There may be a large market for telecommunications projects in those countries. Banks and the investing public of Western countries might share the investment burden of such projects and, more generally, might be readier to finance profitable technological advances in those countries. A consolidated framework for facilitating and monitoring such ventures might strengthen investors' and private donors' confidence and thereby encourage this

---

[14] *See* various articles in *EIB papers* for 1999 and 2000.

[15] These may include an EU financial participation, for instance in investment funds with a priority focus on providing risk capital for Trans-European network projects (see Regulation EC/2336/95, OJ L 228 of 23.09.1995, as amended by Regulation EC/1655/1999, OJ L 197 of 29.07.1999).

[16] Innovation was seen to be limited in importance because:

(1) it was exhaustible;

(2) it was a response to regulatory interference with the market, rather than the creation of a product responding to market needs;

(3) credit was essentially a simple concept, comprising capital, interest and maturity. *See* P.L. Gilibert and A. Steinherr, The Impact of Financial Market Integration on the European Banking Industry, EIB Papers (March 1989). The authors might today take a more liberal view of innovation.

[17] *See*, for instance, Eric Brieys and François de Varenne, *The Fisherman and the Rhinoceros: How International Finance Shapes Everyday Lives*, John Wiley & Sons, Inc, 2000.

[18] A report of the United Nations Development Programme, published in 2000, (item (9) in bibliography) showed that there are benefits to be gained by the poorest and most backward countries from installing a broad band telecommunications infrastructure. The private sector applies a heavy discount to future financial returns from those countries, and a regulator would expect the financier to apply a high-risk weighting to his investment in such infrastructure. The payback may come over many years, and may not translate into high-financial returns.

activity. A central, flexible regulatory system could help to remove obstacles in the way of the private funds focused on such countries. It could perhaps even encourage such funds, and thereby complement the work of development institutions.

*Third proposition: multilateral development banks and banking supervisors*

Evidence for the third proposition lies in the relationship between the activities of multilateral development banks and the banking supervisory regime and, in particular, in an analysis of how the EIB's activity would shape the context of a European banking supervisor's responsibilities.

There are many ways in which an MDB may impinge on a banking supervisory system. Among them are the following.

(1) *Common risk management methods*:  The development bank's methods of risk management may resemble those of the general banking sector. They may, therefore, usefully undergo comparison with peers. Risk management is increasingly an independent function within a bank. This function tends to develop its own principles and its own personal networks. It may become natural for risk controllers in MDBs to exchange views with their counterparts in regulated banks, especially on methods of internal risk management. This would take the peer review proposals of the Lamfalussy Committee a step further.[19]

The EIB aims to adopt the best current practice, for example in its loan grading methods, its capital allocation rules, its 'unexpected loss' adjustment technique and its management of risk. By these and other techniques, it strives to achieve for itself the standards that a regulatory regime induces commercial banks to accept, if not stricter standards.

(2) *Reliance on project risk appraisal*:  A factor specific to MDBs derives from their strength in the field of project finance. The EIB, in particular, has set itself a standard for the assessment of the technical and economic feasibility of projects.[20] The EIB's activity in this field is described above in the connection with the first proposition formulated in this chapter. The EIB's interest, like that of other MDBs, may influence commercial banks to take credit risk on a project, even though the EIB, in common with other MDBs, does not divulge its technical analysis. Nevertheless, if regulated banks rely on an MDB's analysis in making their credit assessments, the banking supervisory authority may wish to check that the reliance is well placed.

(3) *Common corporate governance issues*:  The Basel Committee has recommended that the same principles of corporate governance apply to government-owned banks as to banks in private ownership.[21] One might expect MDBs to follow similar

---

[19] *See* EU Commission, *Final Report of the Committee of Wise Men on the Regulation of European Securities Market* (Brussels, 15 February 2001).

[20] *See* the mission statement of the Bank on its website, <http://www.eib.org> and its annual report.

[21] *See* Basel Committee on Banking Supervision, *Principles of Governance of Banks* (January 2001).

principles of governance, adapted to their particular mission and ownership. MDBs might find relevance in the principles enunciated by the Basel Committee. A single regime could be better placed to raise standards of corporate banking governance. The EIB is working to adhere to such standards. The EIB differs from other MDBs in that, as a Community organism, it falls within the competence of EU bodies concerned to enforce principles of sound administration. In particular, it comes within the purview of the European Ombudsman. It is also accountable to the European Court of Auditors for its management of a part of European Community income and expenditure and it renders an account of its policies to the European Parliament. These bodies, as well as the EIB's own governing organs, exercise a considerable control.

(4) *State-owned banks and commercial banks*: In Europe in recent years the fairness of competition between state-owned banks and commercial banks has been widely debated. The subject of this debate may extend to the global plane. In Europe, there may exist a trend to separate the social from the commercial activities of governmental banks. The German Landesbanken and other independent credit institutions, which have notably benefited from public support, will, under agreements concluded between representatives of the European Commission and of Germany,[22] separate more clearly between their public policy operations and their market operations. A privileged regime could be acceptable for the former, while unacceptable for the latter. By parity of treatment, one could imagine a global dual supervisory system, by which, on the one hand, the developmental policies of MDBs would be regulated by their shareholders or by the organs to which shareholders would delegate the task, while, on the other hand, the capital-market operations of the MDBs could be observed, if not regulated, by financial market supervisors. In the case of the EIB, this kind of outcome might result from the creation of a European horizontal supervisory regime.

(5) *SMEs' cost of borrowing*: In April 2001, certain financial press observed that the implementation of the Basel accord rules in the EU, based on credit ratings or internal operational risk methodologies, would tend to increase the capital allocation required for loans to small and medium sized enterprises.[23] Thus the policy of building a stable banking system could conflict with the policy of reducing the cost of funds to small businesses. A horizontal supervisory system would sharpen this conflict. In July 2002, the Basel Committee relented and modified its proposed rules to allow banks that apply an adequate system of internal credit ratings to apply less capital against loans to SMEs than against other loans. It thus acknowledged the need to encourage the supply of capital to small enterprises. Whereas the Basel Committee did so by relaxing the prudential requirements, the EIB might contribute to the same objective, through the terms that it offers in its credits to commercial banks, even without a differentiating in its allocation of capital.

---

[22] Understanding on *Anstaltslast and Gewährträgerhaftung* of 17th July 2002 and understanding about the orientation of legally independent special credit institutions in Germany of 1st March 2002.

[23] *See*, for example, *The Economist*, 21 April 2001.

In summary, these points of contact indicate a joint interest both in pursuing the objectives of an effective banking supervisory system and in finding a balance between policy goals.

## CONCLUSION

The chapter has demonstrated the three propositions. The first proposition, on the effect upon the EIB of regime changes affecting the financial sector's assets and liabilities, has been demonstrated by several examples. The second proposition, on the parallelism of aims of banking supervisors and MDBs in addressing market imperfections, is provided by reference to certain imperfections that could be tackled in common. The third proposition, on the benefits of exchanges of views between MDBs and financial market supervisors, is illustrated by several examples.

In conclusion, under a single supervisory regime, the EIB, in dealing with financial institutions, would help them allocate risk efficiently and help them adapt to new capital adequacy rules. At the same time, its operations would serve to advance the common goal of financial stability, in parallel with the general goals of European economic policy.

Lightning Source UK Ltd.
Milton Keynes UK
UKOW041601050213

205863UK00001B/72/P